Anthropology

....

CONTEMPORARY PERSPECTIVES

THIRD EDITION

Anthropology

CONTEMPORARY PERSPECTIVES

THIRD EDITION

EDITED BY

David E. K. Hunter

AND

Phillip Whitten

BENTLEY COLLEGE

Little, Brown and Company

BOSTON   TORONTO

Library of Congress Catalog Card No. 81-83154

ISBN 0-316-38266-3

9 8 7 6 5 4

SEM

Published simultaneously in Canada
by Little, Brown & Company (Canada) Limited

Printed in the United States of America

This book is dedicated to Elaine, with respect and appreciation

Preface

....

Anthropology is an exciting discipline. And why not? It encompasses all of the human experience: from the evolutionary processes that have molded us; to the civilizations, both ancient and modern, that we have forged; to the ways we communicate with each other; to the kaleidoscopic variety of human culture.

Anthropology is also a fast-changing discipline—enlivened by new discoveries, theories, problems, and debates on issues of fundamental importance to the understanding of human nature, society, and behavior.

• In the area of human evolution, for example, important fossil finds have been unearthed in the badlands of East Africa with startling regularity since the mid-1970s. Each discovery has broadened our understanding of our evolutionary history while simultaneously raising new and intriguing problems. In fact, these finds have so altered our ideas about the evolution of our own species that in each edition of this anthology we have been compelled to rework the entire section on human evolution.

• The publication of Edward O. Wilson's blockbuster book, *Sociobiology*, in 1975, raised anew (and at a more sophisticated level than before) the question of the extent to which human behavior is governed by our genetic inheritance. Are we, indeed, captives of our own genes—or, to put it more scientifically, is there a human biogram? Are certain behaviors biologically, rather than culturally, determined? These are some of the questions anthropologists have tackled with gusto. And from the research and writing—not to mention the storm of controversy—they have engendered, no doubt will come a deeper understanding of just what kind of creature *Homo sapiens* is.

• Sex roles is another topic of intense and heated debate these days. And it is a debate to which anthropology can contribute a great deal. Are the sex roles we have grown up with "natural," that is, biologically ordained? Or are they cultural conventions, created in the past to solve challenges posed by the environment and hence subject to modification as the physical and social environment changes? If the latter, what are the benefits and costs—both to the individual and to society as a whole—of radically altering a society's traditional sex roles? Because anthropology, far more than any other social science, takes a cross-cultural perspective, it can bring a great deal of research and knowledge to bear on the question of the diversity in human sex roles and other related questions.

These are just a few of the many important and exciting issues with which anthropologists are grappling today. In this, the third edition of *Anthropology: Contemporary Perspectives*, we have attempted to convey the excitement and relevance of contemporary anthropology to beginning students. The needs and interests of these students were foremost in our minds when we selected the articles for this anthology. The selections had to strike a balance between academic quality and level of difficulty. They had to be intrinsically interesting to students, both in subject matter and in writing style. And they had to relate to the introductory course in anthropology as it is taught in most North American colleges and universities. The resulting collection thus reflects both the important ongoing work of modern anthropology and the ways introductory anthropology is taught, while providing interesting, enjoyable reading for the college undergraduate.

The articles come from a broad range of sources, including major books and such journals and semi-popular magazines as *American Anthropologist, Discovery, Harvard, Horizon, Human Nature, Mosaic, Natural History, Psychology Today, Science, Science Digest, Scientific American, Smithsonian,* and *The Sciences.* Some articles were written specifically for this volume. Most of the articles are recent (over 80 percent date from the 1970s and '80s, and more than one-third were first published in the last four years), and many reflect new discoveries and changes in the discipline of anthropology. But we also have included a number of the "classic" articles as well. The authors include such prominent anthropologists as Laura Bohannan, Robert Carneiro, Napoleon Chagnon, Yehudi Cohen, Ernestine Friedl, Edward T. Hall, Michael Harner, Marvin Harris, William Howells, Jane B. Lancaster, Richard B. Lee, Richard E. Leakey, David Maybury-Lewis, Margaret Mead, Horace Miner, Ashley Montagu, June Nash, David Pilbeam, Marshall Sahlins, Ralph Solecki, Melford E. Spiro, S.L. Washburn, and Peter M. Worsley, as well as leading individuals in other social sciences, journalists, and professional science writers.

This third edition of *Anthropology: Contemporary Perspectives* is actually a major revision of the book, both in subject matter and in organization. More than one-third of the articles are new to this edition, and they explore such subjects as human evolution; sociobiology; the origin of the first Americans; the incest taboo; marriage and kinship; politics and social control; economics; sex roles; the impact of modernization and industrialization on small, marginal societies; applied anthropology; and medical anthropology. Articles that were retained from the first and second editions of the book were those judged most successful in a poll of users.

We have reorganized the third edition of *Anthropology: Contemporary Perspectives* to increase its compatibility with the leading textbooks in both introductory anthropology and cultural anthropology, and to allow it to be used as the *only* book in either of these courses.

• There are six main sections of the book, with Sections II through V corresponding to the major subdisciplines within anthropology.

• Within the six sections there are fifteen Topics, corresponding to the subject matter common to virtually all texts and courses in introductory anthropology: human evolution; human diversity; archaeology; language, thought, and communication; fieldwork; family, kinship, and social organization; economy and society; sex roles; belief and rituals; and so on.

• In addition, we have significantly expanded both the section and topic introductions, explaining important basic concepts and providing students with a carefully detailed framework that will enhance their understanding and appreciation of the selections that follow.

• Also, we have added an extensive Glossary containing more than five hundred definitions of important terms used in the book.

• Finally, we have retained the popular facsimile format of the book in the third edition, keeping original photographs and artwork wherever possible.

In revising the book we were helped enormously by the assistance we received from our own students and from hundreds of instructors and students who used the second edition. We are also deeply indebted to the following instructors who provided in-depth critiques of the second edition and of our plans for its revision: Dean E. Arnold, Wheaton College; Peter J. Brown, Emory University; Ralph Detrick, Hibbing Community College (Minnesota); Penny Van Esterik, University of Notre Dame; Allen C. Fanger, Kutztown State College; William Fisher, Northeastern University; Charlotte Frisbie, Southern Illinois University, Edwardsville; J. Patrick Gray, North Texas State University; David Hakken, SUNY-Tech, Utica; Helen E. Hause, Wayne State University; Simon D. Messing, Southern Connecticut State College; R. A. Meyers, Davidson College; Roy A. Miller, Jr., North Texas State University; Weldon Park, Rhode Island Junior College; Robert E. Polley, Edinboro State College; Marion St. John, Diablo Valley College; Mary Jo Schneider, University of Arkansas; Helen H. Schuster, Iowa State University; David Scruton, Ball State Univesity; and Karl Steinen, West Georgia College.

We would also like to thank the college division staff at Little, Brown, with whom we worked so effectively: our original editor, Jane E. Aaron, who offered valuable suggestions in revising the book; Garrett White, the editor-in-chief, who took over for Jane; Lee Ripley, the developmental editor, whose helpfulness and encouragement made working with her a pleasure, and whose competence is unsurpassed; Wayne Ellis, the production editor; and Kathryn S. Daniel, the book editor, who returned to the book after having worked on its first edition. We also appreciate enormously the fine and competent work done by our administrative assistant, Iris Stein.

Finally, we owe a debt of gratitude to the original authors whose articles we selected. Without their work, and their permission and that of their publishers to reprint it, this book literally would not have been possible.

Contents

· ·

I
Introduction to Anthropology   1

TOPIC ONE   **The Study of Anthropology**   2

1. The Tree of Anthropology   3
DAVID E. K. HUNTER AND PHILLIP WHITTEN

Anthropology is the study of human beings. It is divided into four major branches: physical anthropology, archaeology, linguistics, and cultural anthropology. This article traces the historical roots of anthropology and discusses the five major themes that distinguish anthropology today. (Original Essay, 1982)

II
Physical Anthropology   10

TOPIC TWO   **Human Evolution**   13

2. The Emergence of *Homo sapiens*   15
BOYCE RENSBERGER

Where did modern humans—*Homo sapiens sapiens*—first evolve? And what became of the Neanderthal people: Were they absorbed, superseded, or bypassed by the wave that was ultimately to become us? Rensberger explores the current state of knowledge about the evolution of our own species. (*Mosaic*, November/December 1980)

3. Neanderthal Is Not an Epithet but a Worthy Ancestor   26
RALPH S. SOLECKI

Until recently it has generally been assumed that Neanderthals were not in the main line of evolution to *Homo sapiens sapiens*. However, recent evidence suggests that the opposite might well be the case. Evidence from Shanidar cave indicates that for some sixty thousand years, these hunter-gatherer-foragers lived in caves in groups of about twenty-five. They hunted large game successfully, cared for the crippled, and buried their dead with flowers. (Excerpted from *Shanidar: The First Flower People*, in *Smithsonian*, May 1971)

TOPIC THREE   **Primatology and Human Behavior**   30

4. The Origins of Human Social Behavior   32
EDWARD O. WILSON

Sociobiologists, the author tells us, are searching for the human biogram—the "set of inborn responses and behavioral tendencies that adapt human beings to social life." This will be accomplished, he hopes, through a careful study of human evolution. (*Harvard Magazine*, April 1975)

5. What We Can't Learn About People From Apes   38
S. L. WASHBURN

In a rejoinder to sociobiology, a distinguished anthropologist argues that human behavior is so varied and complex that little can be predicted from studying the biology we share with other primates. (*Human Nature*, November 1978)

Anthropology

···

CONTEMPORARY PERSPECTIVES

THIRD EDITION

Peoples and Sites Discussed in This Book

(Article numbers are in parentheses.)

Driftwood Creek (13)

Putu (13)

Old Crow (13)

Bering Land Bridge (13)

Girl's Hill (13)

The Eskimo (Inuit) (15, 35)

The Irish Tinkers (41)

Neander Valley (2)

Cro-Magnon (2)

La Chapelle-aux-saints (12)

La Ferrassie (2)

Anzick (13)

Calico Hills (13)

The "Nacirema" (19)

The Iroquois (35)

Cahokia (12)

Santa Rosa Island (13)

Del Mar (13)

The Hopi (15)

Folsom (13)

Jebel Irhoud (2)

The Navajo (15)

The Aztecs (32)

Teotihuacan (32)

Tenochtitlán (32)

Tikal (32)

The Tiv (20)

Valley of Mexico (11)

Tlapcoya (13)

The Yanomamö (18, 24, 35)

The Machiguenga (30)

Bolivian tin miners (37)

Pikimachay Cave (13)

Fell's Cave (13)

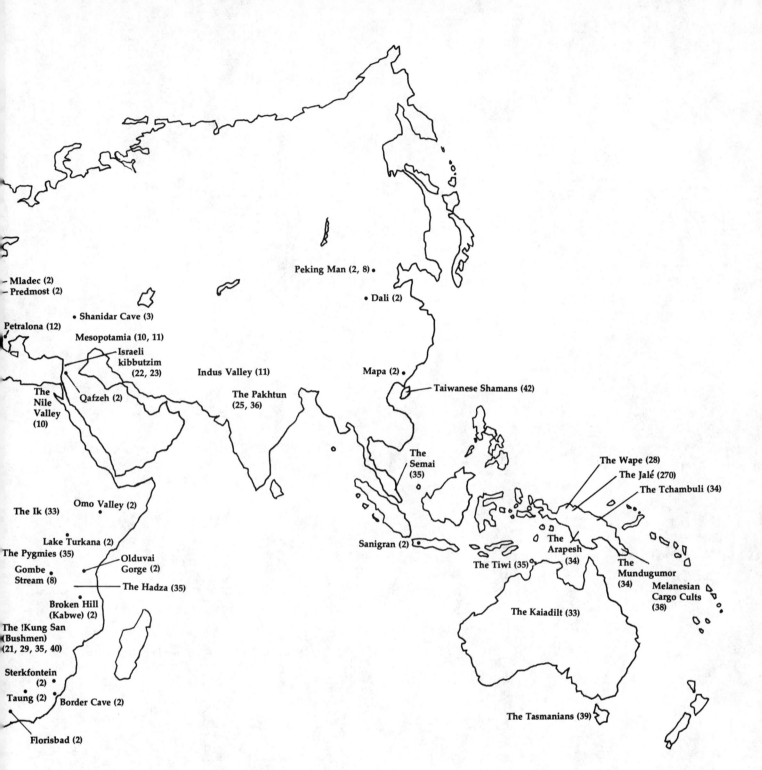

Mladec (2)
Predmost (2)
Petralona (12)
• Shanidar Cave (3)
Mesopotamia (10, 11)
Israeli
kibbutzim
(22, 23)
The
Nile
Valley
(10)
Qafzeh (2)
Indus Valley (11)
The Pakhtun
(25, 36)

Peking Man (2, 8) •
• Dali (2)

Mapa (2) •

Taiwanese Shamans (42)

The Ik (33)
Omo Valley (2)
Lake Turkana (2)
The Pygmies (35)
Gombe
Stream (8)
Olduvai
Gorge (2)
The Hadza (35)
Broken Hill
(Kabwe) (2)
The !Kung San
(Bushmen)
(21, 29, 35, 40)
Sterkfontein
(2)
Taung (2)
Border Cave (2)
Florisbad (2)

The
Semai
(35)

Sanigran (2)

The Wape (28)
The Jalé (270)
The Tchambuli (34)

The
Arapesh
(34)
The Tiwi (35)
The
Mundugumor
(34)
Melanesian
Cargo Cults
(38)

The Kaiadilt (33)

The Tasmanians (39)

I
Introduction to Anthropology

○ ○

This collection of articles will introduce you to some of the many facets of anthropology. In each section we provide a general framework and some historical comments to help you understand the significance of the readings within the general discipline of anthropology. The introductory notes are especially extensive in sections II (Physical Anthropology) and III (Issues in Archaeology), because these topics are more likely than others to lie outside of the realm of the daily world of discourse of most students.

We introduce you to anthropology in Topic 1, The Study of Anthropology. Here, we sketch both the historical roots and the modern subdisciplines of anthropology in order to provide you with an overall framework on which to organize your reading of the articles collected in this reader.

The Study of Anthropology

What is anthropology? For one thing, it is an academic discipline whose history, subdisciplines, and major theories we trace in the article that opens this anthology. But we believe deeply that anthropology is more than just an "academic" discipline, for its scope embraces all of humankind—past and present. Whether or not you go on to concentrate your studies in an anthropology major, we believe that taking an introductory course in anthropology will enrich your life and broaden your perspectives. It will expose you to foreign peoples, strange places, unexpected customs, new viewpoints, and—again and again—the universals at the heart of the human condition everywhere.

We leave it to you to discover these universals, to find yourself in the enormous diversities of peoples and cultures, life-styles and world views represented in the articles reprinted here.

In the article titled "The Tree of Anthropology," the editors of this volume provide you with a guide to sampling the fruit of a tree whose roots are deep and whose boughs spread wide.

1

The Tree of Anthropology

BY DAVID E. K. HUNTER AND PHILLIP WHITTEN

....

THE BRANCHES OF THE TREE

Anthropology is a way—or rather a collection of many different ways—of studying human beings and their closest primate relatives. The term *anthropology* comes from two Greek words: *anthropos*, meaning "man" (in the sense of human being), and *logos*, meaning "to reason" (or study).

If one thinks of the overall discipline of anthropology as a tree, then it is a tree consisting of four major branches and many smaller branches and twigs. The four major branches are physical anthropology, archaeology, linguistics, and cultural anthropology.

1. *Physical anthropology* is the study of human biology—but not just biology alone. Whether studying the fossil remains of our ancestors, the distribution of diverse genes among the world's contemporary populations, the mechanisms of genetic inheritance, the differing shapes and colors characterizing people in various regions, or even the behavior patterns of humans and their primate relatives, physical anthropologists are concerned with the manner in which all these things are related to the natural and social environments in which the subjects are living. So physical anthropology really is the study of the biological processes of humans and their primate relatives in their natural and social contexts or environments.

2. *Archaeology* is the retrieval and study of human remains. This includes not only their bodily remains (which certainly can tell us a great deal about how they lived and died), but also the remains of the things they built, produced, and made use of. In other words archaeologists attempt to find and study all the traces that human groups have left behind—of themselves and of all their activities—and they seek to understand the ways these remains are related to each other and the environments in which they occur.

3. *Linguistics* is the study and analysis of human communication systems, but most especially of language. Some linguists attempt to reconstruct the earlier language forms from which our present languages have evolved. Others study modern languages in order to learn how they encode the range of human experiences, what grammatical forms they feature, or what separates language from the communication systems of other species. Some linguists are concerned with what language usage can reveal about the different social groups within a society. Others are interested in what can be learned about the nature of the human mind from the study of language. So linguistics is *not* what many people take it to be—the mere learning of a lot of different languages—rather it embodies the use of research into languages in order to better understand the nature of human beings as a species.

4. *Cultural anthropology* is the study of culture and cultures. Culture consists of the shared patterns of behavior and associated meanings that people learn and participate in within the groups to which they belong. Every group, down to each individual family, has its own culture, and each culture is unique. Of course some cultures are quite similar to each other (say, the family cultures of a specific community); others are very different (nomadic Arab culture and Eskimo culture, for example). Some anthropologists study the nature of culture in general as an element of human existence; others are more interested in studying a specific culture (perhaps the culture of a Norwegian fishing village or a *barrio* in Mexico City). Culture, by providing "designs for living," enables humans to be extremely flexible and resourceful in solving problems posed by the natural environment, and our species is unique in that it inhabits virtually every niche that nature has wrought on our planet. The better we understand culture, the closer we shall come to understanding what it means to be a human being.

At this point it might be helpful to return to the image of the "tree of anthropology" with which we opened this essay. Until now we have concentrated on a description of its branches—its four main branches and even a number of its smaller branches and twigs. Some readers might even be tempted to ask whether, in all this diversity of interests encompassed by anthropology, there is in fact any trunk to the tree. Is there a central core that holds the whole thing together?

That is a reasonable question, and at times even anthropologists have had cause to ask it. In fact there is a trunk to be found. It is worth looking for because it is in the trunk of the tree that we find what makes anthropology different from all the other social sciences and also what makes it a worthwhile discipline to study and practice. We shall lead you to an appreciation of the trunk somewhat indirectly, however, by first describing some of the major roots of anthropology. We do this because we think that an understanding of the origins and development of the discipline will make its current practice more comprehensible and enticing.

THE ROOTS OF THE TREE

The origins of anthropology—as indeed of so much of our civilization—can be traced back to ancient Greece and the civilization of the Middle East. Historians claim as their father a Greek named Herodotus (484?–425? B.C.), and so might anthropologists as well. He traveled widely and recorded the life-styles of some fifty different peoples. He also formulated the idea that all peoples are *ethnocentric*—that is, they consider their own way of life superior to all others, and they judge other life-styles (for the most part negatively) in terms of the norms and values of their own.

With the fall of Rome in the fifth century A.D., much of the knowledge and thought of the classical civilizations were lost to Europeans for almost a thousand years. Medieval scholars were not so much interested in human beings or even in the nature of the world around them as they were in discovering as much as could be learned about God. Of course, they attempted to learn about God by studying the universe that God had created, and they did make many important discoveries about the world. But their concern to find "divine order" and "divine principles" underlying the manifest world blinded them to many of its most interesting features. It really was not until the Renaissance emerged in the fifteenth century, bringing with it a rediscovery of the treasures of classical learning, that European scholars began to investigate the natural environment as well as human societies with a view to understanding them on their own terms.

Already in medieval times, however, Europeans had been exposed to the existence—on distant shores accessible only to the hardiest of travelers—of many "strange and exotic" peoples. Throughout the Renaissance and Enlightenment periods, as Europe extended its economic interests ever farther abroad, exploration and colonization enabled scholars to visit these faraway places and make records (often fantastically misinformed and distorted) of the peoples they discovered and observed. By the eighteenth century, the vast riches to be made through control of the populations and resources of Africa, Asia, and the Americas induced governments and private enterprises to take more seriously the value of careful study of these so-called primitive peoples. After all, the better one understood them, the more efficiently one could set about exploiting them.

The Church too was quick to grasp the opportunity to extend its influence through missionary activities. Naturally, in order for their activities to be successful, these missionaries required information about the languages and customs of the people they would seek to convert to Christianity.

For many reasons, then, Europeans came to be interested in acquiring information about foreign peoples. Travelers, missionaries, sea captains, colonial administrators, adventurers, traders, and soldiers of fortune ranged across the world recording their impressions of the peoples they encountered. They brought these accounts back with them to European "armchair scholars," who attempted to study them by comparing them to each other—and to European society—in a more or less systematic manner. Inevitably, these efforts tended to "prove" the superiority of European society over all the "primitive" societies thus studied. These eighteenth- and nineteenth-century researches developed into what has come to be called the *comparative method* of social science research. Through the application of this method, a great many schemes of social and cultural evolution were put forward, all of which placed the institutions of European society securely at the top of the evolutionary pyramid.

Until the middle of the eighteenth century, there was no separate discipline that one might call social science. To the extent that society was studied, it was done within the all-purpose framework of history. But by around 1750, the study of society had become sufficiently specialized to deserve the label "social science"—a separate discipline having split off from historical studies and embarked on its own development. For about one hundred years, the study of human nature and society evolved along the lines we have already described, embodying loosely all the different approaches to the building of a science of humankind.

A century later Darwinian evolutionism arrived. The impact of Darwinism on human thought was profound, and its effects on social science were no less dramatic. The two outstanding changes in the study of human nature and society that resulted were (1) the application of evolutionary theory to virtually all aspects of the study of humankind, and (2) the split of such studies into increasingly specialized, separate disciplines.

The Emergence of Evolutionary Thought

The Christian doctrine that Creation had been a single event (pinpointed at 9:00 A.M. on September 23 in 4004 B.C. by Archbishop James Ussher in the early 1600s, who deduced that time from a careful study of Genesis) became more and more troublesome. Already in the sixteenth century Vasco Núñez de Balboa discovered that America was not an extension of Asia but, rather, a separate continent—and the origin of the "Indians" became a source of heated argument. This debate rapidly expanded into controversy about the degree of relatedness—and inherent levels of ability—of all the diverse peoples around the world.

To the *polygenists* the differences between human groups were so vast that they could not accept even a common origin for all people. Rebelling against a narrow acceptance of Genesis, they insisted that scientific inquiry must prevail over the Bible (a courageous position at the time). They argued that God must have created human beings a number of times in different places and that all people were not then descendants of Adam and Eve. Their numbers included many of the period's leading skeptics and intellectuals, such as Voltaire and David Hume. It is hardly surprising that these thinkers, attaching as they did such great significance to human physical variation, should have been racial determinists and indeed racists, ascribing to their own "stock" superior mental abilities. Voltaire, for instance, discussing the state of civilization among Africans, argued:

> If their understanding is not of a different nature from ours, it is at least greatly inferior. They are not capable of any great application or association of ideas, and seemed [*sic*] formed neither for the advantages nor the abuses of philosophy (quoted in Harris 1968:87).

Monogenicism defended the Scriptures' assertion of a single origin for all humans. Isolated groups, such as the "Indians," were accounted for by the claim that they had come from Atlantis (a mythical continent that was believed to have stretched from Spain to Africa before sinking beneath the waters of the Atlantic Ocean) or that they were the descendants of one of the lost tribes of Israel. Monogenists accounted for "racial" differences in terms of populations adapting to the problems posed by different environments—an idea that would become central to Darwin's principle of natural selection. But they also tended to believe, along with the French biologist Jean Baptiste de Lamarck (1744–1829), that physical characteristics acquired by an individual in the course of his or her lifelong development could be passed on biologically from one generation to the next (an idea rejected by Darwin and the mainstream of subsequent evolutionary thought).

Because monogenists tended to defend the validity of the Biblical version of human origins, they also accepted the very recent dates that Biblical scholars had established for human creation. Thus although they, like the polygenists, divided the human species into "races," they deduced that these "races" must be of very recent origin and that, although people exhibited differences in response to environmental pressures, these differences were of minimal importance with regard to basic human abilities. For instance, Johann Friedrich Blumenbach (1752–1840), a German physician who developed an interest in comparative human anatomy, published a study in 1775 in which he identified five "races": Caucasian, Mongolian, Ethiopian (including all sub-Saharan blacks), Malayan, and American. For this effort he is frequently called the "father" of physical anthropology. However, Blumenbach was far from convinced that these categories were anything more than artificial constructions of convenience in the service of science: "When the matter is thoroughly considered, you see that all [human groups] do so run into one another, and that one variety of mankind does so sensibly pass into the other, that you cannot mark out the limits between them." And he adds, with a tone of wryly modern wisdom, "Very arbitrary indeed both in number and definition have been the varieties of mankind accepted by eminent men" (cited in Montagu 1964:41).

(The debate between monogenists and polygenists raged on through the nineteenth century and continues to this day. Although most human biologists since Darwin have aligned themselves in the monogenist camp, the writings of Carleton S. Coon (1904–1981), a contemporary anthropologist, were firmly polygenist. He argued in *The Origin of Races* (1963)—a controversial work—that the human species evolved five different times into the five "races" that he believed constitute the population of the world today.)

Let us return, however, to our account of the emergence of the theory of evolution. By the late eighteenth and early nineteenth centuries, discoveries (especially in biology and geology) were gradually forcing scholars to reassess their acceptance of a date for the creation of the earth derived from scriptural study. More and more geological strata in the earth's crust were coming to light, and it became clear that the thickness of some strata, and the nature of the mineral contents of many, demanded a very long developmental process. In order to account for this process, these scientists faced the need to push back the date of Creation, as we will see shortly. In addition, the fossilized record of extinct life forms accumulated, obliging scientists to produce plausible explanations for the existence and subsequent disappearance of such creatures as the woolly mammoth and the saber-toothed tiger.

In 1833, Sir Charles Lyell (1797–1875) published the third and last volume of his *Principles of Geology*, a work that had a tremendous influence on Darwin. Lyell attacked such schools of thought as *diluvialism*, whose followers claimed that Noah's flood accounted for what was known of the earth's geological structure and history, and *catastrophism*, whose adherents proposed that localized catastrophes (of which the Biblical flood was merely the most recent) accounted for all the layers and cracks in the earth's crust. He argued that the processes shaping the earth are the same today as they always were—uniform and continuous in character—a position that has come to be called *uniformitarianism*. However, Lyell was unable to free himself entirely from a doctrinaire Christian framework. Although he could envision gradual transformations in the inanimate world of geology, when he discussed living creatures, he continued to believe in the divine creation of each (unchanging) species, and he accounted for the extinction of species in terms of small, localized natural catastrophes.

Some biologists did comprehend the implications of comparative anatomy and the fossil record. For instance, Lamarck advanced his "developmental hypothesis," in which he arranged all known animals into a sequence based on their increasing organic complexity. He clearly implied that human beings were the highest product of a process of organic transformation and had been created through the same processes that had created all other species. However, Lamarck's imagination was also bound by theological constraints, and he did not carry his research through to its logical conclusion. Rather than limiting himself to natural forces as the shapers of organic transformation, Lamarck assumed an underlying, divinely ordered patterning.

Before scholars could fully appreciate the antiquity of the earth and the processes that gave rise to all species—including the human species—they had to free themselves from the constraints of nineteenth-century Christian theology. A revolution of perspective was necessary, a change of viewpoint so convincing that it would overcome people's emotional and intellectual commitment to Christian dogma. The logic of the new position would have to be simple and straightforward and would have to rest on a unified, universally applicable principle.

As we shall see shortly, students of human *society* had been grappling with these issues for almost a century. Herbert Spencer (1820–1903) developed the theory of evolution as applied to societies and based it (in the now immortal phrase) on the "survival of the fittest." His writings and those of Thomas Malthus (1766–1834), the political economist who pessimistically forecast a "struggle for survival" among humankind for dwindling resources, profoundly influenced two naturalists working independently on the problem of the origins of species: Both Alfred Russel Wallace (1823–1913) and Charles Robert Darwin (1809–1882) arrived at the solution at the same time. They hit on the single, unifying (and natural) principle that would account for both the origin and the extinction of species—*natural selection*. In 1858, they presented joint papers on this topic, and the next year Darwin published *On the Origin of Species*, a book that captured scholars' imaginations and became the first influential work that popularized the concept of evolution as applied to the world of living organisms.

What is natural selection? It can be put simply and straightforwardly: *Natural selection is the process through which certain environmentally adaptive features are perpetuated at the expense of less adaptive features.*

Two very important points must be stressed with regard to natural selection: (1) *It is features—not individuals—that are favored*, and (2) *no features are inherently "superior."* Natural selection is entirely dependent on the environment. Change the environment, and the favored adaptive features change as well.

Evolutionism in Social Thought

As we have mentioned, since medieval times, Europeans had been exposed, through the reports of adventurous travelers, to the existence of many "strange" peoples living in "exotic" places on distant shores. Thus, European scholars accumulated a body of information (much of it quite unreliable) about foreign societies, and quite a few set about trying to compare societies in more or less systematic ways. By the late eighteenth century and throughout the nineteenth century, the *comparative method* of social science resulted in the elaboration of theories of social and intellectual progress that developed into full-blown evolutionary theories, frequently referred to as *classical* or *unilineal evolutionism*. The Marquis de Condorcet (1743–1794), for instance, identified ten stages of social evolution marked by the successive acquisition of technological and scientific knowledge: From the limited knowledge needed for hunting and gathering, humanity passes through the development of pastoralism, agriculture, writing, and the differentiation of the sciences, then through a temporary period of darkness and the decline of knowledge in the Middle Ages, leading to the invention of the printing press in 1453, the skeptical rationalism of René Descartes' philosophy, then to the founding of the French Republic of Condorcet's day, and eventually, through the application of scientific knowledge, to a world of peace and equality among the nations and the sexes. His *Outline of the Intellectual Progress of Mankind* (1795) is viewed by many as the outstanding work of social science produced in eighteenth-century Europe, even though its ethnocentric bias is blatant (Harris, 1968:35).

Auguste Comte (1798–1857), who is sometimes called one of the "fathers" of social science, followed Condorcet's approach to social evolution. For him, too, the progress of the human intellect moved social evolution forward. However, he identified only three stages of evolution, characterized respectively by "theological thought," in which people perceive the universe as animated by a will much like their own (evolving from animism through polytheism to monotheism); "metaphysical thought," in which abstract laws of nature are discovered; and finally "positive thought," represented by the scientific method (of which his own writings were the embodiment in the social sciences). By the way, it is interesting to note that Comte also believed that each person passes through these three stages in the course of his or her individual development.

The writings of Herbert Spencer on social evolution were preeminent during much of the middle and late nineteenth century. As mentioned earlier, it was he who first introduced the term *evolution* into the scientific literature. And in his classic *First Principles*, published in 1862,[1] he provides a definition of the term that has not significantly been improved upon to this day. *Evolution*, Spencer points out, *is not merely change*. It is "change from an indefinite, incoherent homogeneity to a definite, coherent heterogeneity; through continuous differentiations and integrations." In other words, to Spencer *evolution is the progress of life forms and social forms from the simple to the complex.*

Spencer's work is often neglected by contemporary anthropologists, who tend to trace their historical roots to two other major nineteenth-century evolutionists, Sir Edward Burnett Tylor (1832–1917) and Lewis Henry Morgan (1818–1881). Morgan's work in many ways is derived from that of Spencer. Like Spencer, he viewed social evolution as the result of societies adapting to the stresses of their environments. In his classic study, *Ancient Society* (1877), Morgan identified seven stages of social evolution:

   I. Lower Status of Savagery
       Marked by simple food gathering

  II. Middle Status of Savagery
       Marked by knowledge of fishing and the invention of fire

  III. Upper Status of Savagery
       Marked by the invention of the bow and arrow

  IV. Lower Status of Barbarism
       Marked by the invention of pottery

  V. Middle Status of Barbarism
       Marked by the domestication of plants and animals, irrigation, and stone and brick architecture

  VI. Upper Status of Barbarism
       Marked by the invention of iron working

  VII. Civilization
       Marked by the invention of the phonetic alphabet

Sir Edward Tylor lacked the concern with social systems of Spencer and Morgan. He was more concerned with *culture* than with society, defining culture all-inclusively as "that complex whole which includes knowledge, belief, art, morals, law, custom, and any other capabilities and habits acquired by man as a member of society" (1958:1; orig. 1871). Tylor attempted to demonstrate that culture had evolved from simple to complex and that it is possible to reconstruct the simple beginnings of culture by the study of its "survivals" in contemporary "primitive" cultures.

In spite of the fact that their individual evolutionary schemes differed from one another in important ways, these classical evolutionists shared one overriding conviction: Society had evolved from simple to complex through identifiable stages. Although it could not be claimed that every single society had passed through each of the stages they described, nevertheless they believed they had found sequences of developmental stages through which a "preponderant number" of societies had passed (Carneiro 1973:91) and that these sequences represented progress. At the turn of the century, this position came under furious assault by Franz Boas and his students and vanished from the American intellectual scene. It reemerged in the 1940s to become one of the major conceptual tools that prehistorians and archaeologists use to reconstruct the human past.

The Emergence of Specialized Disciplines

As we noted earlier, until the mid-eighteenth century, the social sciences had no separate identities—the study of history embodied them all. And it wasn't until the rise of evolutionary theory in the nineteenth century that the social sciences began to differentiate themselves, began to split off from each other through a specialization of interests and research methodologies.

Perhaps the major splitting of the social sciences in the mid-nineteenth century was the emergence of the separate disciplines of sociology and anthropology, which to this day have maintained their distinct and individual identities. Sociologists tended to follow the

---

1. The word *evolution* does not appear in Darwin's *On the Origin of Species* until the 1872 edition!

positivist approach of Auguste Comte described earlier and shared with Comte a preoccupying interest in European society. Anthropologists, on the other hand, remained interested in a far broader range of data: archaeological finds, the study of "races" and the distribution of diverse human physical traits, human evolution, the comparative study of cultures and cultural evolution—all more or less unified by evolutionary theory. And whereas sociologists focused on European society, anthropologists, in their worldwide search for data, tended to concentrate on the "primitive" or preindustrial societies (Voget 1975:114–116.) It is in this context that the four main branches—physical anthropology, archaeology, linguistics, and cultural anthropology—emerged as separate, but still interrelated, subdisciplines.

THE TRUNK OF THE TREE

As you have seen, the roots of anthropology go very deep and they spread wide across the world. Its branches, large and small, are numerous and diverse. Where then is its trunk? What holds anthropology together?

In order to work—to plan, execute, and evaluate their research—all scientists must be trained in the sets of beliefs and practices that characterize their disciplines in a fundamental way. This set of beliefs and practices—in essence the core and underpinning of a scientific discipline—is sometimes termed the *paradigm* of that science. Although no scientist will ever fully utilize all the elements of a paradigm in his or her research, nevertheless such research is planned, undertaken, and evaluated by other scientists in terms of the ways in which it contributes to and reflects the paradigm as a whole.

Anthropology has such a paradigm—which is the trunk of the tree. It consists of five themes that have developed gradually as anthropology has emerged as a distinct discipline. These are the *comparative*, the *holistic*, the *systems and process*, the *case study*, and the *"insider-outsider"* themes. Before we explain and elaborate on each of these, we wish to emphasize one important point: Not all anthropologists conduct their day-to-day work in terms of all five themes, but all anthropologists do appreciate their importance and understand their own and others' work within the context these themes provide.

The Comparative Theme

As we mentioned above, a major aspect of the split between anthropology and sociology in the nineteenth century was that whereas sociology focused on Western society, anthropology continued the tradition of comparing and contrasting peoples and cultures throughout the world. These comparisons are made in two ways: (1) by *synchronics*, which is the comparison of anthropological data across a wide geographical area (including many peoples and cultures) at one point in time (usually the present or recent past); and (2) by *diachronics*, which involves comparison of such data through a very extended period of time but limited to one geographical region (and only a few peoples and cultures), thus revealing patterns of evolution (be it biological, social, or cultural).

The Holistic Theme

Another feature of the sociology-anthropology split was that sociologists came to concentrate their attention on society and social systems, whereas anthropologists continued to attempt to tie together all aspects of human biology and behavior—that is, biology, society, culture, and even psychology. The concern with the *whole* picture of the human condition is termed *holism*, and it is a fundamental aspect of anthropology. That is one reason anthropologists find themselves at odds with so many contemporary scholars and popularizers who wish to account for human behavior by reducing it to one simple underlying determinant, such as "race," territoriality, sexual dimorphism, or the structure of the human brain.

The Systems and Process Theme

Herbert Spencer introduced the concept of the *social system* in the early nineteenth century. In the last few decades anthropologists have rediscovered the fact that it is not very productive to describe and analyze societies and cultures in terms of static lists of their traits. Rather societies and cultures are understood as open systems, each possessing many subsystems and all such systems containing their own patterned processes. For example, archaeologists are no longer satisfied merely to catalog the material remains that they retrieve from prehistoric societies. Rather, they attempt to understand what such remains can tell us about the ways these societies adapted to and utilized the elements of their natural environment, how they organized themselves into social groups, the ways such groups interacted among themselves and with each other, and so forth. Physical anthropologists have essentially abandoned the static concept of "race" as useless and have turned instead to investigating the ways in which genes express themselves changeably in different environments. This concern with systems, processes, and dynamics has greatly enriched the discipline of anthropology.

The Case Study Theme

You will recall that anthropology developed on the fringes of European society and continued with a preoccupation with distant and remote peoples and places. Those hardy souls who ventured forth to study such out-of-the-way societies found themselves cut off, for long periods of time, from contacts with their homes. They lost track of current events in European affairs and consequently immersed themselves in the detailed study and description of the daily happenings among the people they were studying. It was a challenge to keep their objectivity while at the same time working to gain people's trust and even their affection. This form of social research is called *participant observation*. It is characteristic of much of the research undertaken by anthropologists, who seem on the whole to be much less comfortable with grand abstractions than with the concrete world of stones and bones, phonemes and morphemes, rituals, economic transactions, and pottery sherds. For every grand (and grandiose!) theory of society or human behavior that is so lightly bandied about in the popular media, one is sure to hear a quiet but insistent anthropological gadfly asking, "But what about the case of the Tasaday?" or "But how does that fit with what we know about forest-dwelling baboons?" Sadly, the wider public remains for the most part uninformed of the objections anthropologists have raised to the widely proliferated, pseudoscientific writings claiming "proof" for such things as prehistoric extraterrestrial visitors.

The "Insider-Outsider" Theme

Because anthropologists, more than other social scientists, have concentrated so much of their research on studying remote peoples with life-styles, mores, values, subsistence systems, and languages very different from our own, it has fallen on anthropologists to grapple with the problem of translating the *perspective of the people being studied* (the "insider's" view) into the *perspective of Western social science* (the "outsider's" view). Neither view is inherently correct, of course, and both complement and supplement each other. But it is easy to get them mixed up both during the process of learning about the people one is studying, and again after having completed one's research when trying to make it meaningful to colleagues, students, and even the public at large. After all, anthropologists are just as vulnerable as anybody else to succumbing to the insidious distortions of ethnocentric thought. Guarding against this is an important element of anthropological research. Because anthropologists are sensitized to the many and subtle ways people look down upon one another, the study of anthropology can be a valuable contribution to an individual's maturation and education.

THE TREE OF ANTHROPOLOGY

In this brief introductory essay, we have presented you with the branches, roots, and trunk of the "tree of anthropology." The articles that follow are many of its fruits. Naturally, we have selected this offering to make the study of anthropology enticing. We think the articles are clear and informative, and not a few of them are warmed by a sense of humor. We have been careful, however, to allow as many as possible of the voices of our discipline to be heard in these pages. The differences of opinion, the disputes and controversies that currently enliven the lives of anthropologists, are offered to you for your own consideration.

We hope that you will pause a while at the tree of anthropology, that you will taste of its fruit and rest in its shade. We hope that some of you will be moved to climb up into its branches, to see the world from the unique vantage points they offer. But most of all, we hope that those of you who choose to wander on through the other niches of the garden of academia will have found your stay here refreshing, that you will have acquired a new set of perspectives, perhaps a new understanding or awareness. If that is the case, then this awareness will enrich all of your future travels.

References

Carneiro, Robert
　1973 "The Four Faces of Evolution," in John J. Honigmann (ed.), *Handbook of Social and Cultural Anthropology*, Chicago: Rand McNally, pp. 89–110.
Coon, Carleton S.
　1963 *The Origin of Races*, New York: Alfred A. Knopf.
Harris, Marvin
　1968 *The Rise of Anthropological Theory: A History of Culture*, New York: Thomas Y. Crowell.
Montagu, Ashley
　1964 *Man's Most Dangerous Myth: The Fallacy of Race* (4th ed., rev.), New York: Meridian Books.
Tylor, Sir Edward Burnett
　1958 (orig. 1871) *The Origins of Culture*, Part I of *Primitive Culture*, New York: Harper Torchbooks.
Voget, Fred W.
　1975 *A History of Ethnology*, New York: Holt, Rinehart and Winston.

II
Physical Anthropology

○ ○

Physical anthropology has broadened a great deal over the last three decades, and it now includes many subjects that overlap with other disciplines. In a loose way, we may define physical anthropology as the study of primate biology in its natural and social environments—with a special emphasis on the study of our own species. Yet it is useful to break apart this large and rather loosely connected branch of anthropology into two major subbranches: *paleontology*, the study of our extinct ancestors (through their fossilized remains); and *neontology*, the comparative study of living primate groups.

Many scholars trace the origins of modern physical anthropology to the work of Johann Blumenbach (1752–1840), who systematically undertook to collect and study human skulls from many populations around the world. He devised ways of making very precise measurements on these skulls and used these measurements to produce an encyclopedic work on what he called the "races" of the world.

One of Blumenbach's central ideas was that the "races" developed as biological responses to environmental stresses. This notion was elaborated upon in the nineteenth century by numerous scholars, such as Anders Retzius (1796–1860), who in 1842 devised a formula for computing long-headedness and narrow-headedness:

$$\frac{\text{head breadth}}{\text{head length}} \times 100 = \text{cephalic index}$$

A low cephalic index indicates a narrow head; a high index a broad head. Fourteen years later, Retzius published a survey of cranial indexes based on the measurement of skulls from private collections, in which he distinguished a vast number of "races" determined by virtue of their cephalic indexes.

Others followed the lead of Blumenbach and Retzius, and a wide number of techniques were developed through which the human body could be systematically measured. Such measuring is called *anthropometry* and remains to the present day an important aspect of physical anthropology. Anthropometry contributes to our understanding of fossil remains by providing scholars with precise methods for studying them. It also provides concrete data on variations in body shape among human populations, replacing what previously had been rather impressionistic descriptions. Thus body measuring became one of the major tools for determining "racial" classifications. However, by the end of the century, it was being attacked by scholars who pointed out that anthropometric traits of all ranges could be found represented among individuals within each of the so-called "races."

After the publication of Darwin's *On the Origin of Species* in 1859, natural selection became the core concept of physical anthropology, and evolution its primary concern. Thomas Huxley (1825–1895), a naturalist who enthusiastically took up Darwin's theories, added great impetus to the study of human evolution by showing that the human species was not qualitatively distinct from other primates but, rather, only the most complex in an evolutionary continuum from the primitive lower primates through monkeys, the great apes, and finally humankind.

The study of the fossil evidence for human evolution was slow in developing. By 1822, reports had come from Germany about findings of the fossilized remains of many extinct animals in limestone caves. These reports impelled William Buckland (1784–1856), reader of geology at Oxford University, to investigate the limestone Paviland Cave on the Welsh coast. There Buckland found the same kinds of extinct animals as had been reported in Germany—as well as flint tools and a human skeleton. This skeleton came to be called the Red Lady of Paviland, because it had become stained with red ochre. (Subsequently it was determined that the skeleton was that of a male.) As a Christian minister, Buckland was hard pressed to explain this human presence among extinct creatures. He resorted to the contorted conclusion that the animal remains had probably been swept into the cave by flooding and that the human skeleton had been buried there long after Noah's flood by local inhabitants.

Similar mental gymnastics kept scholars from acknowledging what, in fact, their eyes were seeing: ancient human remains among extinct animals, attesting to a vastly longer human existence than Christian doctrine permitted. Only after the Darwinian revolution could people permit themselves to make accurate interpretations of these fossil materials. In 1860, for example, Edouard Lartet (1801–1873), while investigating a cave near the village of Aurignac in southern France, found human remains associated with the charred bones of such extinct animals as the woolly mammoth, the woolly rhinoceros, the cave bear, and the bison. The evidence he reported finally convinced many people, including the prominent geologist Charles Lyell, of the antiquity of humankind. It is hardly coincidental that these events happened the year after the publication of Darwin's *On the Origin of Species*.

Eight years later, in 1868, Louis Lartet followed his father's lead and excavated an ancient rock shelter that had been exposed in the course of the construction of a railway in the Dordogne region of France. He found five human skeletons: three adult males, one adult female, and one unborn baby. These people were associated with the same kinds of extinct animals and cultural artifacts as those found by his father at Aurignac. They came to be viewed as representatives of the so-called Cro-Magnon population (fully modern humans) that produced the impressive Aurignacian Upper Paleolithic culture.

In 1857, fragments of a human skeleton were found in a limestone cave near Düsseldorf in Germany. The skull cap, however, displayed what at the time seemed to be shockingly ape-like features. It was extraordinarily thick, had massive ridges over the eyes, and had little in the way of a forehead. This specimen, which came to be called Neanderthal man (sometimes spelled Neandertal, in keeping with current German spelling), raised for scholars the possibility of finding fossil populations of primitive people who were ancestral to the Cro-Magnon types and, thus, to modern human beings. In 1889, Eugene Dubois (1859–1940) traveled to Southeast Asia with the deliberate intention of finding such fossilized evidence of human evolution. There, during 1891 and 1892, in a site on the bank of the Solo River on the island of Java, he found some molars, a skull cap, and a femur (thighbone) of so primitive a nature that he thought them at first to be the remains of an ancient chimpanzee. By 1892, he revised this assessment and decided that he had, indeed, found an evolutionary ancestor of the human species, a creature he eventually called *Pithecanthropus erectus* (erect apeman). Naturally, as with all such finds, a great debate about its evolutionary status ensued; but today we agree with Dubois that his Solo River find is indeed a human ancestor, one of many that have since been found and are now grouped together under the term *Homo erectus* (erect man).

Although physical anthropology emerged as a fully developed discipline only after the theory of evolution had established itself in the minds of Europe's leading thinkers, already in the 1700s, scholars were engaged in the serious study of human population biology—as in the researches of Blumenbach and Retzius. However, as we indicated in "The Tree of Anthropology" (Hunter and Whitten) with which we opened this reader, eighteenth-century research on human biology was marred by the polarizing effects of the Great Debate of the day: the bitter feud between the *polygenists* and the *monogenists*. The former saw the biological and behavioral differences between the world's populations as being so substantial in nature that they could not accept a common origin for all the world's peoples. They argued (contrary to the teachings of the Scriptures) that God must have created people a number of different times in a number of different places. Monogenists, on the other hand, argued for a single origin for all peoples. Whereas polygenists perceived "racial" characteristics as permanent and immutable, monogenists insisted that they were changeable and came about as a result of the influence of the natural environment upon local groups.

Blumenbach himself was a member of the monogenist camp and recognized that the five "races" he posited were as much a matter of classificatory convenience as they were a reflection of the real world. Nevertheless, this debate proved rather fruitless until a means could be found to resolve it. That means proved to be the revolutionary theory proposed jointly by Alfred Russel Wallace (1823–1913) and Charles Robert Darwin (1809–1882) in 1858, and popularized by the publication in the following year of Darwin's masterpiece, *On the Origin of Species*.

If there is any one concept that united the discipline of physical anthropology, it is the theory of evolution. Its assumptions, axioms, hypotheses, and premises are the foundation upon which virtually all work in this area rests. It is important that you grasp how all-pervasive evolutionary thought is—how it has been assimilated into virtually all the social and biological sciences. Many of the readings in this and other sections of this book make explicit and implicit reference to evolutionary theory. We shall let them speak for themselves; but first we wish to clarify one aspect of the theory that is widely misunderstood and yet is also its central principle—the principle of natural selection.

Simply, *natural selection* can be defined as *the process through which certain environmentally adaptive features are perpetuated in organisms at the expense of less adaptive features.* That really is it. But its simplicity is deceptive, and the concept frequently (perhaps generally) is misunderstood. Here we shall address two widely held misconceptions about natural selection:

1. There is no such thing as an evolutionary "favored" individual. *Features* are favored, not individual organisms.

2. There is no such thing as an inherently "superior" feature (let alone an individual organism). What is meant by the term *superior* is the degree to which a feature is adapted to its environment. Change the environment, and a "superior" feature may well become an "inferior" feature.

Natural selection, then, is relative—relative to the environment. And because the environment is always changing, natural selection is an ever-changing process. No group, individual organism, or specific feature will ever reside permanently on top of the evolutionary ladder. Here, as elsewhere, the one constant is change.

In the context of this general introduction, we now present the articles of this section. They are grouped into three topics: Human Evolution, Primatology and Human Behavior, and Human Diversity. We discuss each of these separately.

Human Evolution

....

When the editors of this reader were college undergraduates (in the early 1960s) taking their first anthropology courses, the academic world still was in uproar over the fossil skull and teeth found by Mary and Louis Leakey in 1959 at Olduvai Gorge in northern Tanzania (East Africa). These fossilized remains, named *Zinjanthropus boisei* by the Leakeys, were dated at 1.75 million years ago—almost a million years older than similar fossils which had been found in southern Africa. The possibility that the australopithecines—the direct ancestors of human beings (at least that is what they were thought to be then)—could be over a million years old was absolutely shocking.

The following two decades have seen the unearthing of previously undreamed of riches in fossil finds. And most of these finds have not been limited to specimens of Neanderthals and *Homo erectus,* our two most direct and recent ancestors. Rather, the bulk of the finds have been of much more ancient hominids and therefore shed light on the very beginnings of the human line.

You should not imagine for a moment that scholars have reacted calmly to these discoveries. Almost every significant new find produced a flurry of heated debate over (1) its taxonomic status (that is, its place in the evolutionary hierarchy) and (2) its significance (that is, the degree to which it confirmed or invalidated previous views of human evolution). At first, it was merely a matter of pushing back the emergence of human ancestors earlier and earlier: the australopithecines became "older" throughout the 1960s and 1970s—first one, then two, then three million years old. But then, as more and more fossils were found, the questions became more profound and subtle. For instance, what was the relationship between the emergence of erect bipedalism (walking on two legs) and the evolution of the large, complex human brain? Did large brains favor the invention of tools or, the other way around, did the invention of tools promote the enlarging of the brain?

The most recent and, in many ways, the most interesting debate concerns hominid finds from East Africa. There Mary Leakey and her son Richard Leakey, working respectively at Laetoli (thirty miles south of Olduvai Gorge) and at Lake Turkana (in Kenya), have found remarkable hominid specimens. They identify these specimens, some of which are as old as 3.35 to 3.75 million years, as belonging to our own genus *Homo.* Their main antagonist is Donald Johanson, whose fieldwork has been mainly in the Afar Triangle (in Ethiopia), west of the lower end of the Red Sea. Johanson's finds are the same age or slightly older than the Leakeys' and one of them, a skeleton he calls Lucy, is remarkably complete (over 40 percent of her bones were found). Johanson gives his finds the taxonomic label *Australopithecus afarensis.* He claims that the Leakey finds older than 2 million years are members of the *same* species and that this species is the earliest example of a true hominid ancestor to human beings.

One of the most puzzling problems confronting students of human evolution was the fact that the interpretations of early hominid fossil remains did not fit in with the studies comparing human and ape amino acid molecules. Scientists studying amino acid molecules had, for over a decade, shown that systematic comparisons of these molecules from related species could be used to compute how far back in the evolutionary past their ancestors had split apart. Using these methods, Allan Wilson and Vincent Sarich of Berkeley arrived at a date of 5 to 6 million years ago for the split between pongids (apes and their ancestors) and hominids (humans and their ancestors). On the other hand, fossil studies, which counted *Ramapithecus* as the first true hominid, set the date of that split some 9 million years earlier. There seemed to be no way out of this dilemma other than to favor one view or the other (and most anthropologists favored the latter). Some authors even went so far as to suggest that the amino acid time clock might be accurate for the whole animal kingdom—but not for human beings.

Two developments contributed to a solution to this puzzle: (1) the reinterpretation of ramapithecine remains and (2) the discovery of Lucy.

David Pilbeam of Yale has been one of the world's foremost students of ramapithecines, the small creatures who inhabited Africa and Asia 8 to 15 million years ago and whose jaws (the only remains ever actually found) seemed to show true hominid features. In the late 1970s, Pilbeam decided that he and others had been wrong to think of *Ramapithecus* as a true hominid—that their thinking had been "prejudiced" by the assumption that a specimen had to be either pongid or hominid (that is, reflecting current conditions). Pilbeam reinterpreted ramapithecines as an intermediate form— neither truly pongid nor truly hominid—which had evolved from earlier pongid populations (dryopithecines) and had eventually died out. That left a new possibility: namely, that a *later* fossil population would be found, one that might qualify as the first true hominid (replacing *Ramapithecus*). This would, therefore, make possible a meeting of the minds between those who studied fossils and those who studied amino acid time clocks. The first fully hominid fossils might indeed be only 5 million years old.

But was there such a fossil population? Richard Leakey thinks he and his associates have found one—a creature he has named *Homo habilis* ("handy man"). *Homo habilis,* which dates back over 2 million years, produced stone tools and had a brain one-third to one-half as large as our own. This population clearly was ancestral to *Homo erectus,* the immediate ancestors of *Homo sapiens.* But what was the origin of *H. habilis?*

Leakey believes that *H. habilis* evolved directly from a much earlier pongid ancestor, possibly the cat-sized pongid *Aegyptopithecus* (Egyptian ape) whose remains, found near Cairo, date back some 28 million years. Therefore Leakey views the other main fossil populations that are similar to, and precede or are contemporary with, *H. habilis* to be parallel side-branches of hominids—that is, evolutionary dead ends.

This is where Johanson's discovery of Lucy becomes important. She is the earliest, most complete, fully erect and bipedal hominid remain ever found. Johanson has coined the term *Australopithecus afarensis* for the population of fossils to which Lucy belongs, the earliest of which date back some 3.8 million years. *A. afarensis,* though walking on two legs, had a smaller brain than *H. habilis,* and Johanson believes that *A. afarensis* is the ancestor of the "handy man," the link between *H. habilis* and the pongid line. In this view, *H. habilis* joins *A. afarensis* and *A. africanus* (found in southern Africa) as one single, continuous evolutionary line. (In this view the more rugged, "robust" line of *australopithecines* remains an evolutionary *cul-de-sac.*)

At least one very important issue is at stake in the Leakey-Johanson debate. If Leakey's view is right, it would appear that bipedalism and large brains evolved more or less together and that they were associated with the manufacture and use of tools. If Johanson's view is right, then our ancestors first evolved an upright posture and tool use, and only afterwards did the brain become enlarged.

In "The Emergence of Homo Sapiens," Boyce Rensberger takes up the tale at a later but equally important time. He accepts the Johanson interpretation of early hominid origins and focuses on the evolution of *H. sapiens* from *H. erectus,* our direct ancestor. Here, too, there is debate, especially over the position of the large-headed, heavy-browed, stoop-shouldered Neanderthals. The "replacement hypothesis" portrays Neanderthals as evolutionary deadends, whereas the "unilinear hypothesis" views them as an early form of our own species who evolved into modern Europeans.

Rensberger lays out the arguments and data offered by both sides of this debate—and in the end suggests that it is too early to take sides. Regardless of which side ultimately is right, however, Ralph Solecki argues that it is important to recognize the cultural sophistication of Neanderthals. In "Neanderthal Is not an Epithet but a Worthy Ancestor," Solecki shows you the "human" side of Neanderthals: their caring for the aged, their sentimentality, perhaps even their religiosity. Although social and cultural evolution in the last 100,000 years has been vast, it appears that, by the time of the Neanderthals, the basic features of human society (and possibly even human personality) were already well developed.

2

The Emergence of *Homo sapiens*

BY BOYCE RENSBERGER

later modern

Neander Valley

Cro Magnon

La Chapelle-aux-saints

Mladec

Predmost

La Ferrassie

Petralona

Neanderthal

Jebel Irhoud

Qafzeh

Choukoutien
(Peking Man)

Dali

Mapa

modern

Neanderthal equivalent

Omo

Broken Hill
(Kabwe)

Sanigran

late erectus—early sapiens

Border Cave
Florisbad

archaic sapient

modern

On the line to Homo. *Skull fragments from sites around the world suggest at least two possible routes toward the emergence of* Homo sapiens sapiens.

Milford Wolpoff, by permission

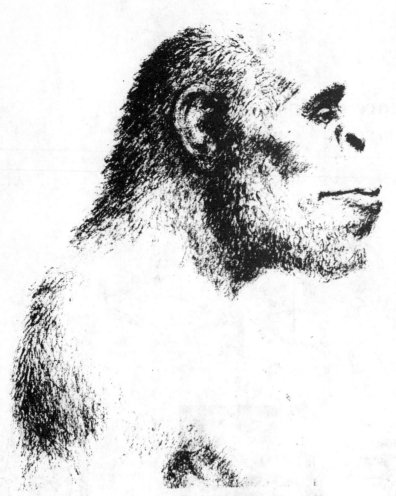

Australopithecus afarensis

According to one side of paleoanthropology's most enduring controversy, a confrontation that was to become humanity's most dramatic clash of two cultures took place in Europe's Upper Paleolithic period, some 35,000 years ago. On the one hand there were the Neanderthals, ostensibly beetle-browed hulks who trudged about Europe and the Middle East for more than 30 millennia, starting at least 70,000 years ago. Massively built people, they purportedly made up in brute strength what they lacked in wit and cunning.

At the same time, somewhere beyond Neanderthal's mostly European range—perhaps in Africa or Southwest Asia—a new breed of human being was on the rise, fully modern, anatomically and intellectually indistinguishable from ourselves. These people would soon produce magnificent cave paintings and sculpture. The most durable evidence of their culture is sophisticated weaponry indicative of a hunting prowess well beyond that of the Neanderthals.

In a geological moment, as some interpret the stratigraphy of excavations all over Europe, the Neanderthals disappeared. They were succeeded instantly by the moderns, sometimes called Cro-Magnon after the French site where several specimens were found. By 35,000 BP (before the present) the Neanderthals were gone. Fully modern people were the sole surviving form of human being on earth.

Where did the Cro-Magnons and their ilk come from? Did they exterminate the native Neanderthals? Did they simply outcompete them for food and other resources? Did they interbreed, producing genetic mixtures that survive as today's Europeans? Or was there no sharp division at all but rather a gentle evolutionary blurring as one form of creature developed naturally into another more suited to changing times?

The replacement hypothesis—the notion that a group from outside invaded the Neanderthals' range and superseded them through extermination, outcompeting or in-

terbreeding—is only the most popular guess as to what actually happened to the Neanderthal. As with so many other questions in paleoanthropology, the data that must be relied upon to answer this one have vexingly limited reliability. Many fossils are not securely dated, skeletons are often only fragmentary and it is frequently unclear whether a group of skeletons from the same site represents one or many populations. Honest but widely divergent opinions are common. The evidence supporting Neanderthal replacement, for example, can also be read to suggest a unilinear hypothesis: that fully modern human beings descended directly from the Neanderthals with relatively little contribution from outside of Europe or the Middle East.

Neanderthal's place

Since the original discovery of a Neanderthal skull in the Neander Valley of Germany in 1856—the first extinct form of human being ever found—scientific thinking about the emergence of fully modern humans has been in more or less continuous ferment. The evidence is, in some ways, more obscure than that for the earlier stages of human evolution. In recent years the effort to understand the final steps in human evolution—the steps that gave rise to our own kind, to people indistinguishable from us—has been overshadowed, at least in public perception. More attention, for example, has been drawn to the search for the earliest hominids, the first, still-apelike creatures considered to be on the direct evolutionary line to *Homo*, even though kinship to us might lie in hardly more than two-legged locomotion. (For a fuller discussion of human evolution up to the hominid divergence see the *Mosaic* special on human origins: Volume 10, Number 2.)

The earliest known creatures that are undisputedly hominids (members of the human family after it diverged from the pongid, or ape, family) date from 3.8 million years ago. They are of the species known as *Australopithecus afarensis*, a two-legged animal with a body of rather human proportions, but not much more than a meter tall and with a head only slightly different from an ape's. According to a newly emerging interpretation, *A. afarensis*, named in 1978, could have been the common ancestor of two lineages. One included the two previously known forms of *Australopithecus*: *A. africanus* and *A. robustus*. The other lineage was *Homo*. The oldest *Homo* known, usually called *Homo habilis*, is represented by the famous skull 1470 from Kenya, dated at about 1.8

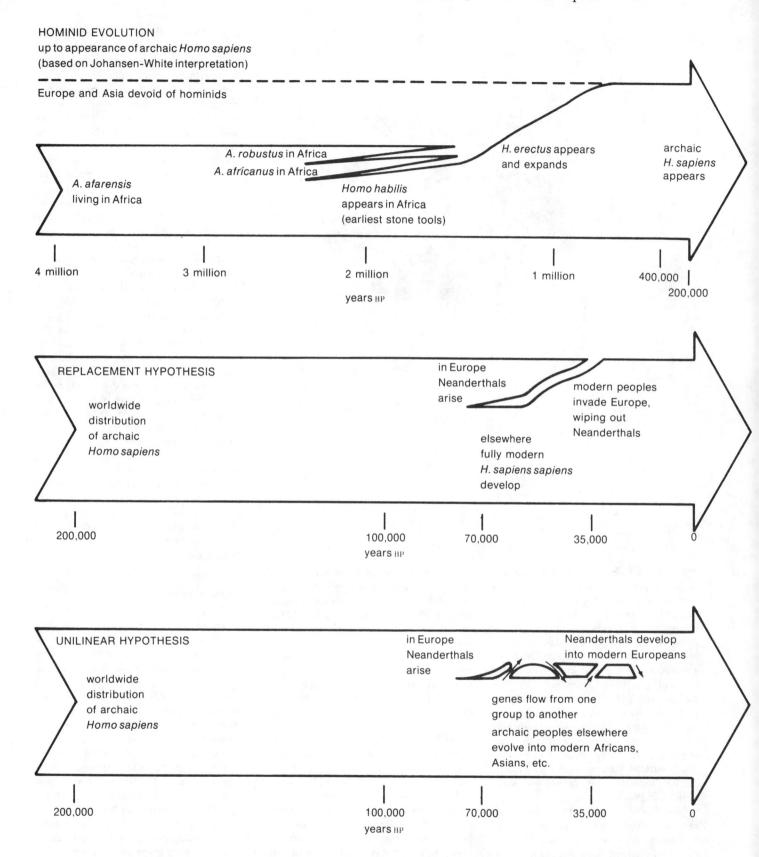

HOMINID EVOLUTION
up to appearance of archaic *Homo sapiens*
(based on Johansen-White interpretation)

Europe and Asia devoid of hominids

A. robustus in Africa
A. africanus in Africa

A. afarensis
living in Africa

Homo habilis
appears in Africa
(earliest stone tools)

H. erectus appears
and expands

archaic
H. sapiens
appears

4 million   3 million   2 million   1 million   400,000

years BP   200,000

REPLACEMENT HYPOTHESIS

worldwide
distribution
of archaic
Homo sapiens

in Europe
Neanderthals
arise

modern peoples
invade Europe,
wiping out
Neanderthals

elsewhere
fully modern
H. sapiens sapiens
develop

200,000   100,000   70,000   35,000   0

years BP

UNILINEAR HYPOTHESIS

worldwide
distribution
of archaic
Homo sapiens

in Europe
Neanderthals
arise

Neanderthals develop
into modern Europeans

genes flow from one
group to another

archaic peoples elsewhere
evolve into modern Africans,
Asians, etc.

200,000   100,000   70,000   35,000   0

years BP

The place of Neanderthals. Time line represents hominid evolution and two theories of Neanderthals' place in the line to modern Homo: *In the unilinear hypothesis, they are in the main stream; in the replacement hypothesis, they were bypassed.*

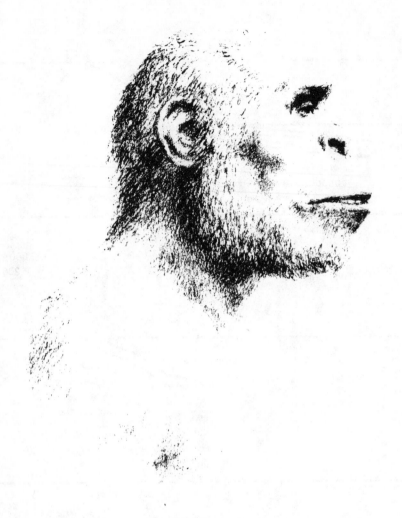

Australopithecus robustus

million years. Its brain was only half the size of that of people living today.

By about 1.5 million years ago, *H. habilis* had evolved into *H. erectus*. This appears to have been the first hominid to spread from Africa into Eurasia. Peking Man, who may have lived anywhere from 700,000 BP to 400,000 BP, is one well-known example. Not until the final 10 percent of the 3.8 million-year span—within the last 400,000 years—did the earliest examples of *Homo sapiens* emerge. These, however, were still not fully modern people. Their brains, for one thing, were only about 83 percent as big as ours on the average. Usually called "archaic sapiens," they ranged over most of the Old World.

Only in still more recent times—perhaps around 70,000 years ago—did they evolve, in Europe, into the classic Neanderthals, who are designated *Homo sapiens neanderthalensis*. The archaic sapiens also evolved into fully modern peoples, *Homo sapiens sapiens*.

There is evidence that the evolutionary growth of the brain—a trend that began early and slowly in hominid evolution—attained its present level something like 115,000 years ago—the last 3 percent of the 3.8 million years of the hominid career. Some say it was not until the last one percent. It remains one of the great challenges of anthropology to discover which of those figures is so: by what route—through, around or over Neanderthal—archaic sapiens became modern.

Another way

While the replacement hypothesis is perhaps the most widely held answer to the challenge, advocates of the unilinear hypothesis have not been overborne. They hold that the transition in Europe from Neanderthal to fully modern people may not have been as instantaneous as is often implied. Many thousands of years can disappear into a geological instant and, advocates note, the skeletons called Neanderthal show a high degree of variation that cannot be ignored.

Some Neanderthals are decidedly more modern looking than others; some specimens even appear transitional between classic Neanderthals and moderns.

After all, the differences between the Neanderthals and their modern successors are largely matters of degree. Brains are already at their maximum size. Nearly all the differences involve decreases in the robustness of bones. People become less heavily muscled and bones become correspondingly lighter and thinner. Skeletal buttressing diminishes. Once-massive brow ridges become smaller, and what is left of a snout continues to recede under the eyes and nose.

In the unilinear view there was no cultural clash, just a gradual evolution, largely confined to Europe in the case of the Neanderthals, though similar changes would have been taking place independently and perhaps, though not necessarily, coincidentally in Africa and Asia as well. Australia, like the New World, remained uninhabited until quite recently. People first reached Australia around 40,000 BP. They appear to have been fully modern. Entry into the New World is more controversial, with most estimates ranging from 12,000 to 30,000 BP. (See "Pre-Clovis Man: Sampling the Evidence," *Mosaic*, Volume 11, Number 5.)

For years the Neanderthal controversy rested at this point, with few new developments pointing either way. Adherents of neither side could point to reliably dated remains of fully modern people much older than about 35,000 years, and certainly not from anywhere outside of Europe and the Middle East.

Ancient moderns

Then a controversial new interpretation of ancient human bones—first found some 40 years ago in Border Cave in South Africa, 400 meters from the Swaziland border—suggested that modern people were living in southern Africa a startling 115,000 years ago. This was fully 45,000 years before the more primitive Neanderthals first appeared. As some view it, the replacement hypothesis received a major boost, and the unilinear hypothesis a major setback, at Border Cave.

Was Africa the real birthplace of *Homo sapiens sapiens*? Did descendants of those early Africans spread north through the Middle East to swamp the Neanderthals and become the ancestors of today's Europeans? Or did modern peoples evolve independently in Africa and Europe and, presumably, in Asia too? Those are among the questions that hang on the Border Cave dates. Unfortunately, the dates are far from secure;

again, vexingly, the evidence can be read several ways.

"There's no doubt that the Border Cave specimens are fully modern," says G. Philip Rightmire of the State University of New York at Binghamton. His detailed study of the single, adult partial skull found there (the other remains are an infant skull and an adult mandible) has established that fact. Using a statistical analysis of 11 measurements of the partial skull (including such things as the projection of the brow ridges and the distances between various bony landmarks), Rightmire has established that the Border Cave *Homo* falls within the range of variation exhibited by living peoples. Further, it comes closest to resembling today's so-called Hottentots, a South African ethnic group similar to the Bushmen (or San) but rather distinct from African Negroes. "The idea that fully modern humans appeared only 35,000 to 40,000 years ago is certainly subject to quite drastic change...."

"The problem is, though, that the dating isn't that solid. There's a good deal of assumption-making going on before one can arrive at the date of 115,000 years," Rightmire observes.

The scientist principally responsible for the date, Karl W. Butzer of the University of Chicago, is rather more confident. And he sees major implications not only in such an early emergence of modern humans but in that it may have taken place in Africa. Since most anthropologists are of European ancestry, he observes, it has been almost a foregone conclusion that Europe must be the homeland of modern human beings. "Border Cave completely explodes contemporary thinking about *Homo sapiens sapiens*," says Butzer.

Assumptions and inferences

Like many other fossils and artifacts from the crucial period in human evolution between 400,000 BP, when *Homo erectus* died out, and about 35,000 BP, when modern forms become well established, the Border Cave remains are not easily datable. They are too old for such reliable standbys as radiocarbon dating and not suitable for potassium/argon dating, which requires volcanic minerals. One new method, amino acid racemization, has yielded a date at Border Cave that supports the 115,000-year estimate. The technique, however, is controversial and not widely accepted. Another, molecular evolution, requires soft tissue. More sensitive methods of radiocarbon dating are in development and within a few years may be able to reach about 100,000

Australopithecus africanus

years or more. (For more on these subjects, see "Pre-Clovis Man; Sampling the Evidence," in *Mosaic*, Volume 11, Number 5; "Molecular Evolution; A Quantifiable Contribution," *Mosaic*, Volume 10, Number 2; "The Significance of Flightless Birds," *Mosaic*, Volume 11, Number 3; and "Extending Radiocarbon Dating," *Mosaic*, Volume 9, Number 6.)

The chain of assumptions and inferences necessary to reach any date at all for Border Cave is typical of the problems anthropologists face at many of the key sites that bear on this crucial stage of human evolution. Butzer's Border Cave date is based on a detailed analysis of sedimentary deposits in the cave. There are some 20 layers of dust, grit, rubble and the detritus of human occupation. Each layer has distinctive geological and chemical attributes. Some, for example, contain extensive amounts of rock particles that flaked off the cave roof because of frost weathering. These layers indicate a period of colder climate. Other layers show certain

mineral transformations that require protracted warm and humid periods.

The younger sediments in the cave, back to one laid down about 50,000 years ago, have been radiocarbon dated. Using intervals between the radiocarbon dates, Butzer has calculated rates of sediment accumulation and extrapolated the rates to older sediments. He has also correlated the cave's cold-phase sediments with climatological data from ocean cores. By these methods, Butzer calculates that the skeletal remains at issue came from sediments deposited 115,000 years ago during a period of cool and moderately wet climate. From the bones of animal species found at the same level, it has been deduced that the habitat was then a mosaic of woodland and savanna.

The assumptions necessary to calculate a finite date in Border Cave are enough to inspire skepticism among some anthropologists, although such methods are commonly relied upon after expression of certain caveats. At Border Cave, one additional caveat is

Homo habilis

that the critical adult skull did not come from a controlled excavation. It was found in a dump outside the cave, having been tossed there in 1940 by someone digging in the cave for guano.

An important link between the skull and the 115,000-year-old layer is that bits of sediment wedged into cracks in the bone match most closely the sediments of that layer. Even more important, in Butzer's view, was a 1941 excavation that *did* carefully document an infant skull in the same beds. And in 1974 a fully modern adult jaw was excavated from a layer estimated at 90,000 BP. It was well below the layer radiocarbon-dated to more than 50,000 years. "Dating of the key fossils to between 90,000 and 115,000 years is not proved beyond a reasonable doubt," Butzer concedes, "but

it's very probable. The probabilities of being mistaken are very small."

In Butzer's view, anatomically modern people probably originated in southern Africa some time before 115,000 BP. The area meets certain geographic criteria: that evolution is thought to take place chiefly on the periphery of a species' range and that in such locales environments are often different enough from those at the core of the range, so that different traits are favored by natural selection. Southern Africa, at one extreme of the hominid range, which included much of Africa and Eurasia, would seem an ideal site. It had the added advantage, Butzer suggests, of offering a wide variety of habitats within a small area. The range, from seacoast to plains to desert to mountains, should have favored the survival

of people with a high degree of intelligence and adaptability.

Archaic sapiens

Locality aside, there is general agreement among paleoanthropologists that *Homo erectus* was the ancestor of all later forms of human beings. From about 1.5 million years ago until perhaps 400,000 years ago *Homo erectus* was the sole human species on the planet. Specimens are known from many parts of Africa, Europe, China and Indonesia.

The transition from *Homo erectus* to *Homo sapiens* could have taken place anywhere in this vast range. Fossil skulls with features that seem intermediate between *Homo erectus* and modern people—those usually termed archaic sapiens—have been found in Europe, Asia and Africa.

The best known African specimen of archaic *Homo sapiens* was once called Rhodesian man. It is a remarkably complete skull that was found in 1921 near what was then Broken Hill in Northern Rhodesia and is today Kabwe, Zambia. It was once estimated to be 40,000 years old; newer evidence, putting it in line as a possible ancestor to the Border Cave people, suggests it is at least 125,000 years old and perhaps much older.

Butzer believes the case for a southern African origin of modern human beings is now strong. From there, the Chicago researcher suggests, this evolutionary trend toward more modern features gradually spread northward, reaching the Middle East by about 50,000 BP. This date is based on some fairly modern-looking human remains from Qafzeh, in Israel. The Qafzeh bones have proved difficult to date (various methods have yielded widely differing dates), but a reasonable compromise puts the bones at around 50,000 BP. From the Middle East, gateway from Africa to Eurasia, Butzer speculates, modern peoples spread out, to replace the Neanderthals and their ilk.

Strong dissent

While several American, British and South African anthropologists tend to agree with Rightmire and Butzer about the significance of the Border Cave, there are prominent dissenters. Among them is Richard G. Klein of the University of Chicago. He has specialized in interpreting the hunting skills of peoples living over the last 130,000 years, especially in southern Africa.

"Those Border Cave remains didn't come out of excavations. They came out of dumps," says Klein, recalling the guano diggers churning through the cave deposits. (They never did find any guano.) "To me that's not evidence. I remain to be convinced that the bones are as old as they say. We've all too often been misled by this kind of thing."

Like many paleoanthropologists dealing with what they consider to be equivocal or isolated pieces of evidence, Klein prefers to set this one aside. It is better, he feels, to try to make sense of unarguable data. In Klein's view this approach leaves the title of oldest anatomically modern *Homo sapiens* with the Qafzeh people in Israel, if one accepts an age for them of around 50,000 years. (Various methods have given dates from 33,000 to 56,000 BP.)

Klein believes there was a replacement of Neanderthals by modern people, but that the Middle East probably makes a better candidate place of origin than does Africa. His analysis of European sites suggests that, while the replacement in any one place may have been rapid, it took some 5,000 years (from 40,000 to 35,000 BP) for the wave of replacement to sweep from the Middle East westward to the Atlantic.

Among advocates of the replacement hypothesis there is debate about whether the invaders slaughtered the natives or interbred. Most suspect both and argue about the ratio. Klein, however, takes an extreme position, rejecting flatly the notion of interbreeding: "I would think that the behavioral gulf between these two very different kinds of people would have been so great that there would have been no desire at all to mate."

Klein remains unconvinced, for example, that the Neanderthals, along with other archaic *Homo sapiens*, had crossed the mental threshhold that makes modern peoples distinctive. He disputes the contentions of other scientists that Neanderthals, who produced no art, buried their dead with grave goods. (See "On the Emergence of Language," *Mosaic*, Volume 10, Number 2.) More important, Klein argues that the Neanderthals were unable to make superior weapons. They were "rotten hunters," he declares.

Additionally, from his studies of South African sites where the bones of prey animals were preserved, Klein has deduced that people of the African Middle Stone Age, who were culturally comparable to the European Neanderthal of the period called the Middle Paleolithic, were able to bring down only the weakest and least dangerous animals. Using fossil teeth to determine the maturity of the prey species, Klein has proposed that Middle Stone Age hunters generally killed animals under a year old. Very few animals in their prime are represented in the preserved garbage of those times. The

Homo sapiens (archaic)

prey-age distribution is comparable to that of lions. The two exceptions are the eland and the bastard hartebeest. Unlike other bovids, both can be driven in herds. Klein suspects that Middle Stone Age hunters learned this and drove entire herds off cliffs.

Fully modern people from the Later Stone Age, comparable to Europe's Upper Paleolithic, Klein has found, were able to kill any animal they chose. Bones from such sites reflect an age distribution closer to that of living groupings and also include remains of more dangerous animals such as wild pigs.

The difference, Klein suspects, was in the weaponry. Armed with little more than rocks and clubs, neither the Middle Stone Age *Homo* nor the Neanderthal could get close enough to an animal in its prime and they dared not approach dangerous prey. They

lacked the ability to invent such superior weapons as the spear thrower or the bow and arrow that make it possible to kill from a distance. The remains of such weapons have been found in sites of modern peoples in Africa and Eurasia, but not in sites occupied by their evolutionary predecessors. Later sites also show abundant remains of fish and flying birds, species absent from earlier sites. Since fishing and fowling require specialized tools and skills, Klein suspects these findings help differentiate the mental abilities of archaic and modern *Homo sapiens* on any continent.

New skills

Once the transition from Neanderthal to modern occurred, whether by competition, breeding or succession, there appears to have

Homo erectus

The unilinear view

Milford H. Wolpoff would take that bet. Wolpoff, at the University of Michigan, is one of the leading advocates of the unilinear hypothesis—the view that there was no sudden, single replacement of one kind by another. Rather, he suggests, the Neanderthals by and large evolved into today's Europeans. The anatomically modern population represented at Qafzeh did not invade Europe but, instead, having derived from an archaic *Homo sapiens* there, gave rise to today's Middle Easterners and North Africans. The Border Cave people, whatever their age, then would be the ancestors of today's southern Africans. Other fossil remains from Asia, such as the Neanderthal-like people represented at Mapa and Dali in China, are in the line that led to modern Asians.

"Any theory of human evolution," Wolpoff notes, "has got to account for the differences among modern populations. A modern European skull looks different from a modern African skull. And both of them look different from a modern Chinese or a modern Australian."

Indeed, while all living peoples unquestionably belong to the subspecies *Homo sapiens sapiens*, most members of each population—sometimes designated a race or ethnic group—share certain distinctive skeletal features. In fact, using the kind of statistical comparison of measurements that Rightmire applied to the Border Cave skulls, it is often possible to distinguish between rather closely related groups such as the Bushmen and the Hottentots.

"You look at what the distinctive features of modern Europeans are and then you look at the fossil populations to see where those features first appear, and you find them in the Neanderthals," Wolpoff says. One feature he likes to cite is the big nose. European anthropologists tend to euphemize the feature, including it in what they call the "midfacial prominence," but it is clear that people of other races find Europeans distinctive because, among other things, of their noses. Europeans have the most prominent noses of the living races. It begins jutting out at a fairly sharp angle just below the brow. In Africans and Asians, the nasal bone descends well below the browline before curving outward. The fleshy part of the nose may be broader in some groups but it rarely protrudes farther than or begins to protrude as high as the Europeans'.

Neanderthals had big noses. Only half jokingly, Wolpoff says their noses must have resembled that typified by Charles de Gaulle. In Neanderthals the feature is often

been a great population explosion. It has been estimated that the density of post-Neanderthal humans was anywhere from 10 to 100 times that of Neanderthals. Erik Trinkhaus of Harvard has suggested that one reason may have been the Neanderthals' greater need for food energy. He estimates that, on the basis of the massiveness of Neanderthal skeletons and the necessary corresponding musculature, they may have needed twice as many calories to stay active as their more slender successors. This, however, would account for only part of the population difference. Klein argues that, since the basic resources available to both groups were the same, modern people could have been so numerous only if they were more effective exploiters of their environment.

"I don't know what it was," Klein says, "but the people who appeared 35,000 years ago knew how to do an awful lot of things their predecessors didn't. Something quite extraordinary must have happened in the organization of the brain."

It could not have been an increase in brain size, for Neanderthal brains were already just as large as ours today. Much of the older literature, in fact, asserts that they were larger, though this is now thought to be the result of early Neanderthal samples that included mostly males. Even among people today male brains are, on the average, considerably larger than female brains with, obviously, no difference in intellectual power.

"I'm quite convinced," Klein says, "that in Europe it was a physical replacement of one kind by another. And I'm prepared to bet that that's what happened in Africa too and at about the same time."

considered an adaptation to a cold climate, because a larger nose is presumed better for warming inhaled air. Anatomically-modern fossil populations from outside Europe, such as the people of Qafzeh or of Border Cave, lack this feature.

Wolpoff cites a variety of other anatomical features that, in the same way, are characteristic of a modern race and that first appear in the archaic *Homo sapiens* fossils from the same area. These include various subtle contours of the skull bones: for example the more flattened face of Asian peoples and the slight bulge that bridges the brow ridges above the nasal root in the African skull.

"To me it makes the most sense to assume that those distinctive features were inherited from the people who were already living in the area and who already had the feature," Wolpoff says. For most other parts of the world, most anthropologists accept such parsimony, he declares, but not for Europe.

Neanderthal types

One of the chief reasons, in Wolpoff's unilinear view, that the Neanderthal controversy continues is too great a reliance on typological thinking. In other words, when people think of the Neanderthals, one particular skull—often beetle-browed—or a closely related group of skulls comes to mind. And when people think of more modern successors, they think of another set of distinctive skeletal traits, including less prominent, loftier brows. Between the two stereotypes there are great differences, and they lead to the view that the earlier could not have given rise to the later in so brief a time.

"People forget just how much variation there is in every population," Wolpoff observes, pulling, as he talks, various casts from cabinets in his laboratory and arranging them on a table. (He maintains what is considered to be the most complete collection of fossil hominid casts in the United States.) "Every feature that is considered to distinguish modern Europeans from Neanderthals can be found in [one or another] Neanderthal sample."

Modern features are rare among Neanderthals and certainly not typical, he concedes, but this is exactly what would be expected of evolution. Natural selection works by acting on traits that are already expressed. A trait may be represented at a very low frequency in a given population; if it becomes advantageous, after many generations it will come to predominate.

The Neanderthals, in Wolpoff's view, were far from homogeneous either at any one time or throughout the 35,000 or so

Homo sapiens neanderthalensis

years they existed. Modern traits—less massive bones or higher foreheads, for example—are present but rare in the earliest specimens. In the later Neanderthal populations, such traits become more common. There are even some skulls that appear to be a blend of Neanderthal and modern features, so much so that some authorities have guessed them to be hybrids. Unilinear advocates, on the other hand, see them as evidence of evolutionary transition.

Even *Homo erectus*, the immediate ancestor of *neanderthalensis* and other *Homo sapiens*, and often said to have been remarkably stable in its million-year career, actually changed with time. Brain size, for example, grew some 20 to 25 percent between the earliest and latest specimens.

And the transition from *H. erectus* to *H. sapiens* was gradual. There is no gen-

erally accepted way to define the boundary. There are specimens that look like hybrids of the two types and might have been taken for such if they were not dated to about 400,000 BP, when the transition was in progress. There are similarly gradual transitions elsewhere in human evolution. There are, for example, specimens that look intermediate between the archaic sapiens and classic Neanderthals. And there are, among the fossils called "anatomically modern," many examples that are considerably more archaic in appearance than are living people.

Again, because of the lack of reliable dates for many of the specimens, it is not always possible to arrange them in chronological order. But by using estimated dates and archaeological associations, it is possible to produce what amounts to a morphological continuum from *H. erectus* to *H. sapiens*

Homo sapiens sapiens (Cro Magnon)

sapiens into which *H. sapiens neaderthalensis* fits nicely.

Wolpoff holds that the Neanderthals were simply European representatives of a phase of human evolution through which people also evolved in Asia and Africa. This has sometimes been misunderstood as an assertion that archaic sapiens from Asia and Africa were Neanderthals. Rather simplified, Wolpoff's idea is this: Since· the parent stock of all modern peoples was *Homo erectus*, and since modern people today despite minor differences all differ from *Homo erectus* in the same way, people everywhere had to evolve through intermediate stages that exhibit similar intermediate features.

These intermediate features, along with the results of natural selection in the unique European environment, in Europe produced a classic Neanderthal. In Africa, the same gradation is represented by specimens found in Ethiopia's Omo Valley, at Florisbad in South Africa and at Jebel Irhoud in Morocco. They lack certain distinctive Neanderthal features; instead, they have uniquely African traits. Comparable Asian specimens would be the skulls from Mapa and Dali in China.

Mainstream Neanderthals

Wolpoff also asserts that the Neanderthals were not the dull-witted brutes that Klein envisions. In fact, he sees no reason to doubt that they were anything other than squarely on the intellectual continuum, almost if not already the equal of modern human beings.

One recent discovery in France lends new support to this view. Bernard Vandermeersch of the University of Paris has found a Neanderthal skeleton in clear and direct association with stone tools more sophisticated than the Mousterian tools that are typical of most Neanderthals. These advanced tools are of a type known as Chatelperronian. The kit includes such Mousterian examples as scrapers and irregularly shaped flakes for cutting. But it also includes some of the long, regularly shaped blades, struck from a flint core, that are typical of the tool kit of more modern people.

Until now the finer, Chatelperronian tools have always been considered early examples of the work of modern people. Now it appears that Neanderthals were capable of just that transition to more advanced technologies. Additionally, the modern people of Qafzeh, considered by replacement advocates as possible sources of the invasion, made and used the cruder Mousterian tools. "What is all comes down to," Wolpoff argues, "is that if you look at all the European evidence, there is no great jump. You don't need invasions."

But are there inconsistencies? Would the people of Border Cave, assuming they were fully modern 115,000 years ago, have bided their time in Africa while less advanced peoples occupied Eurasia? Wolpoff is reserving his opinion on the reliability of the Border Cave date. But, he argues, it makes little difference how old those people are. Citing Rightmire's conclusion that they most closely resemble modern Hottentots, Wolpoff suggests that they were simply the ancestors of today's southern Africans. The distinctively African features in the Border Cave skeletons do not appear in any European fossils. From this, Wolpoff concludes that the Border Cave people are unlikely to have contributed in any large part to modern European ancestry.

The unilinear hypothesis should not be understood to rule out mating between otherwise separated groups. Indeed, most authorities assume it must have been a common occurrence. It is the norm today in many traditional cultures for men and women to seek their mates from other bands or clans or villages. This practice, if extended indefinitely, means that genes are flowing more or less continuously over the entire inhabited range. One effect of this practice, well documented for living peoples, is that physical traits that are predominant in one area slowly diffuse to the surrounding areas. If a trait is advantageous in all environments, it will quickly spread. But if the environment of the surrounding area does not favor the trait, the introduced gene will remain at a low frequency. If bearers of this gene in the surrounding area chance to mate with someone from an area still more distant from the trait's center, the gene will be spread farther but still at a frequency related to its utility.

Shared traits

Many physical traits among modern peoples (skin color, height, head shape, etc.) are distributed in this way and will continue to exist in continua so long as there is outbreeding at the range margins. So long as the environment at the core of the area exhibiting the trait continues to favor that trait, it should remain common there. Like ripples on a pond, the trait should continue spreading so long as the force making the ripples remains active.

In this way, Wolpoff suggests, traits that are only locally advantageous will spread some distance away but will remain rare at that distance. On the other hand, traits that are advantageous in all environments, such as a larger brain, will spread throughout the inhabited region and reach high frequencies throughout.

The flow of universally advantageous genes, Wolpoff suggests, would be likely to spread them to neighboring peoples before the originating population progressed so far that it could use the advantage to invade or exterminate its neighbors.

Replacement advocates, of course, disagree. They envision early peoples as so widely dispersed that, from time to time, groups became cut off—perhaps isolated by a desert or a mountain range. These insular groups would not spread any of their newly evolved advantages until they had developed well beyond their contemporaries elsewhere and then breached the isolating constraints. Thus big-brained peoples, if isolated long enough, might eventually break out and replace their small-brained contemporaries.

There is no clear sign that the controversy over the emergence of anatomically modern peoples will be resolved soon. Undoubtedly more fossils will be found. But perhaps more important, existing discoveries must be reanalyzed with the aid of new techniques, new or extended dating methods and fresh eyes. One very serious handicap to any single investigator is the difficulty of access to most of the original fossils (which are housed in isolated collections around the world) or even to casts of the bones (which are either expensive or unavailable). Hominid fossils are often treated as the personal property of their discoverer and sometimes access is granted only to a favored few. A full description of the bones may be years or decades in coming, and until then convention dictates that no one else may analyze or interpret the material in detail.

Compared to the rich and active lives led by thousands or millions of members of now extinct hominid species in the many past environments of the planet, the bits of bone that have been found in the past century—in all only a few score—are a pitifully meager basis from which to develop a believable story of human evolution. Still the broad outline of a fairly coherent story has emerged. Indeed, the origin of human beings in apelike ancestors is among the best documented speciation events in paleontology. Only the details remain troublesome.

And as the details come closer to illuminating the differences and similarities among living peoples, we may rightly become more rigorous and, inevitably, more contentious in evaluating the evidence. Clues to many of the most important events or processes in human evolution may never amount to proof, at least in the eyes of other disciplines.

And yet it is nothing less than the heritage of our species that is at stake. We have, after all, come a long way from the view of the shocked lady who is alleged to have said, when Darwin's ideas of descent from the animals first burst forth, "Let us hope that it is not true, but if it is, let us pray it does not become generally known."

Like orphans searching for our parents, we want to know where we came from, how we got here, how we are really related to the rest of the living world. It can be argued, in fact, that providing this knowledge is paleoanthropology's highest use. In this light, even the smallest quibbles about how human evolution took place are matters of vital substance for us all.

3

Neanderthal Is Not an Epithet but a Worthy Ancestor

BY RALPH S. SOLECKI

The top of a skull was perched on the edge of the yawning excavation in the huge cavern. At first it was difficult to realize that we had before us an extreme rarity in human paleontology.

Except for its heavy brow ridge, the skullcap looked like a gigantic egg, soiled and broken. When fully exposed on the narrow excavation shelf, it was an awesome sight—obviously the head of a person who had suffered a sudden, violent end. The bashed-in skull, the displaced lower jaw and the unnatural twist of the head were mute evidence of a horrible death.

As we exposed the skeleton which lay under a heavy burden of stones, we had confirmation that this individual had been killed on the spot by a rockfall. His bones were broken, sheared and crushed on the underlying stones. A large number of rocks must have fallen on him within a split second, throwing his body backward, full-length down the slight slope while at the same time a block of stone severed his head and neck from his trunk.

Among his remains there were small concentrations of mammal bones, which might have been rodent nests. But it is equally possible these bones were dropped there as part of a funeral feast for the dead.

This was "Nandy," as we called him, a member of the species *Homo neanderthalensis* who had died about 48,000 years before. In the scientific literature he is referred to as Shanidar I, because his were the first adult human remains that we identified as Neanderthal from a cave near the village of Shanidar high in the mountains of Kurdistan in northern Iraq.

Large, airy, and conveniently near a water supply, Shanidar Cave is still a seasonal home for modern Kurdish tribesmen, as it has been for various groups of men for thousands upon thousands of years. I had led our expedition to Shanidar Cave in a search for cultural artifacts from the Old Stone Age in this part of Kurdistan, Iraq. Human remains, much less Neanderthal remains, were not the goal, yet altogether in four expeditions from 1951 to 1960 we uncovered nine Neanderthal skeletons.

Laboratory studies of these remains continue to this day and the results are bringing the Neanderthals closer to us in spirit and mind than we would ever have thought likely.

The Neanderthals have been a nettling problem ever since the first find was made more than 100 years ago. This was the famous faceless skull and other skeletal parts found during quarrying operations around a cave in the Neander Valley not far from Düsseldorf in Germany. Primarily through the writings of one man, Marcellin Boule, who was a greatly respected Frenchman in the field of human paleontology, the owner of the Neander skull was soon cast in the role of a brutish figure, slow, dull and bereft of sentiment.

Although we now know much more about Neanderthal man—there have been at least 155 individuals uncovered in 68 sites in Europe, the Near East and elsewhere—he still seems to hang in space on the tree of human evolution. Some anthropologists feel that he had reached a "dead-end" branch on this tree. In any case, his time span on Earth (about 80,000 years) was more than double that of modern man who replaced him, but roughly one-tenth of the time span of *Homo erectus* who preceded him.

An abundance of Neanderthals

The classical hypothesis, now abandoned, was that Neanderthal man was an ancestral stage through which *Homo sapiens* passed. A second theory is that Neanderthal man was a species apart from *Homo sapiens,* contemporary but reproductively isolated, as donkeys are from horses. The third is that Neanderthal man was a subspecies of early *sapiens,* forming a geographic race. On the whole, the evidence appears to indicate that the Neanderthal did not gradually change into *sapiens,* but was replaced by invading *sapiens.* The greatest difficulty for human paleontologists is that there is a real scarcity of skeletal finds to which they can point with confidence as *sapiens* of an age comparable to that of the Neanderthals.

There was, however, no scarcity of Neanderthals at Shanidar Cave. Prior to the discovery of Nandy, or Shanidar I, we had recovered the remains of an infant. It was later identified as Neanderthal by our Turkish colleague, Dr. Muzaffer Senyürek of the University of Ankara. When it was found, we had little reason to suspect that it was a Neanderthal child.

But not so with Nandy. "A Neanderthal if I ever saw one," is the comment in my field notes for the day of April 27, 1957, the day we found him. Although he was born into a savage and brutal environment, Nandy provides proof that his people were not lacking in compassion.

According to the findings of T. Dale Stewart, the Smithsonian Institution physical anthropologist who has studied all the remains of the Shanidar Neanderthals (except for the Shanidar child), Shanidar I lived for 40 years, a very old man for a Neanderthal—equivalent to a man of about 80 today. He was a prime example of rehabilitation. His right shoulder blade, collar bone and upper arm bone were undeveloped from birth. Stewart believes that his useless right arm was amputated early in life just above the elbow. Moreover, he must have been blind in his left eye since he had extensive bone scar tissue on the left side of his face. And as if this was not enough, the top right side of his head had received some damage which had healed before the time of his death.

In short, Shanidar I was at a distinct disadvantage in an environment where even men in the best condition had a hard time. That Nandy made himself useful around the hearth (two hearths were found close to him) is evidenced by his unusually worn front teeth. Presumably, in lieu of his right arm, he used his jaws for grasping. But he could barely forage and fend for himself, and we must assume that he was accepted and supported by his people up to the day he died. The stone heap we found over his skeleton and the nearby mammal food remains show that even in death he was an object of some esteem, if not respect, born of close association against a hostile environment.

The discovery of Shanidar I was for us a major, and unexpected, event. The discovery, about a month later on May 23, of Shanidar II was overwhelming.

The initial exposure was made by Phil Smith, then a Harvard University graduate student, who laid bare the great eye sockets and broken face of a new Neanderthal. My first impression was of the horror a rockfall could do to a man's face. The lower jaw was broken, the mouth agape. The eye sockets, crushed out of shape by the stones, stared hollowly from under a warped heavy brow ridge, behind which was the characteristic slanting brow of the Neanderthal.

From later reconstruction of the event, we determined that Shanidar II was killed by a relatively minor rockfall, followed closely by a major rockfall that missed the dead man. His demise did not go unnoticed by his companions. Sometime after the tumult, thunder and subsiding dust of the crashing rocks, they returned to see what had happened to their cave mate. It looks as though a small collection of stones was placed over the body and a large fire lit above it. In the hearth we found several stone points, and several split and broken mammal bones nearby that may have been the remains of a funeral feast. It appears that, when the ceremony was at an end, the hearth was covered over with soil while the fire was still burning.

As with the first two adults, Shanidar III was found in the course of cleaning and straightening the profile of an excavation. It was as if some Near Eastern genie was testing my alertness by tucking away the skeletons on the borders of the excavation proper.

Like the other two, Shanidar III had been accidentally caught under a rockfall and instantly killed. One of his ribs had a strange cut. X rays taken at Georgetown University Hospital revealed that he had been wounded by a rectangular-edged implement of wood and the wound had been in the process of healing for about a week when he died. Most likely, he had been disabled in a conflict with unfriendly neighbors and was recuperating when he was killed. Clearly, the dangers of the caveman's life were by no means shut out when he crossed the portal to his airy home.

On August 3, 1960, during our fourth and last season at Shanidar, we uncovered the fragile and rotted bones of Shanidar IV. While Stewart exposed these remains, I started to explore the stones and soil near the place where three years before we had found Shanidar III. Parts of his skeleton were missing and unaccounted for in our collection.

In my first trowelings, several animal bones turned up. One did not look like an animal bone; it looked human. Later I encountered a rib bone that Stewart authenticated as human, but it was not until I uncovered a human molar tooth that we confirmed the presence of Shanidar V. This was becoming too much.

Within four days we found several other bones of this fifth Neanderthal including the scattered fragments of the skull. It appeared that he too was killed by a rockfall, perhaps the same one that killed Nandy.

There was yet another discovery to be made. Stewart was clearing around the southern side of Shanidar IV when he encountered some crushed pieces of a humerus near the skull. "It doesn't make sense," said Stewart, "not in anatomical position." His immediate reaction was that he hated to think that there was yet another Neanderthal in the cave. Furthermore, there were already two humeri for Shanidar IV, the correct number, and now a third: Here was Shanidar VI.

In the space of only five days we had discovered three Neanderthal skeletal groups. Before us were the vast problems of preserving, recording and transporting the remains safely to the Iraq Museum in Baghdad. In the course of feverishly carrying out these activities, we discovered—in some loose material associated with Shanidar VI—more bones which later proved to be from yet another Neanderthal, Shanidar VII. These two, VI and VII, were females. We also retrieved some bones of a baby.

The skeleton remains of IV (a male), VI, VII and the baby (VIII) all appeared to lie in a niche bounded on two sides by large stone blocks. The nature of the soft soil and the position of the stone blocks leads me to believe that a crypt had been scooped out among the rocks and that the four individuals had been interred and covered over with earth. The child had been laid in first; the two females next, perhaps at a later time. The remains of these three were incomplete. Shanidar IV, the adult male, received the main attention of the burial. Probably, to make room for Shanidar IV, the bones of the others were disturbed.

As part of the archaeological routine, I had taken soil samples from around and within the area of Shanidar IV and Shanidar VI, as well as some samples from outside the area of the skeletal remains. These were sent for pollen analysis to Mme. Arlette Leroi-Gourhan, a paleobotanist in Paris.

Under the microscope, several of the prepared slides showed not only the usual kinds of pollen from trees and grasses, but also pollen from flowers. Mme. Leroi-Gourhan found clusters of flower pollen from at least eight species of flowers—mainly small, brightly colored varieties. They were probably woven into the branches of a pine-like shrub, evidence of which was also found in the soil. No accident of nature could have deposited such remains so deep in the cave. Shanidar IV had been buried with flowers.

Someone in the Last Ice Age must have ranged the mountainside in the mournful task of collecting flowers for the dead. Here were the first "Flower People," a discovery unprecedented in archaeology. It seems logical to us today that pretty things like flowers should be placed with the cherished dead, but to find

flowers in a Neanderthal burial that took place about 60,000 years ago is another matter and makes all the more piquant our curiosity about these people.

Regarding their livelihood, we can certainly say the Neanderthals of Shanidar were hunters/foragers/gatherers. They most likely made a seasonal round of their wilderness domain, returning to shelter in Shanidar Cave.

The animals they hunted are represented in the cave by the bones of wild goat, sheep, cattle, pig and land tortoise. More rare are bear, deer, fox, marten and gerbil. It should be noted that the most common animals represented are the more docile type, the gregarious herbivorous mammals. It is likely that the Neanderthals caught them by running them over cliffs in herds or, conceivably, by running them into blind canyons where they could be slaughtered. There are several such canyons within easy striking distance of Shanidar Cave.

Communal life in a cultural backwater

The picture of the lone stalker cannot be ruled out in the case of the Neanderthal but, since these people lived in a communal setting, it would be more natural for them to have engaged in communal hunting. And the fact that their lame and disabled (Shanidar I and Shanidar III) had been cared for in the cave is excellent testimony for communal living and cooperation.

By projecting carbon 14 dates that we have received for certain portions of the cave, I estimate that its first occupation was at most about 100,000 years ago. For perhaps 2,000 generations, over a period of some 60,000 years, we think that groups of Neanderthals—probably numbering 25 members at a time—made their seasonal home in Shanidar Cave. Preliminary findings from the analysis of pollen samples show that, through the long history of their occupation of the cave, the climate vacillated from cool to warm.

Yet throughout the period, the Neanderthals changed little in their means of adapting to these climatic changes. Their tool kit remained much the same throughout: It included their flaked stone tools identified as a "typical Mousterian" industry of points, knives, scoopers and some perforators, all struck off from locally derived flint pebbles. Only a few fragments of bone tools were found. With this meager tool kit Neanderthal man was able to survive and prosper in his own way.

Shanidar seems to have been a kind of cultural backwater, a "refuge" area bypassed by the stream of history because of the remoteness of the area—a condition still reflected in the Kurdish tribal compartmentalizations of today.

Then, around 40,000-35,000 B.C., the Neanderthals were gone from Shanidar Cave, replaced by a wave of *Homo sapiens* whom we have called Baradostians. We have no skeletal remains of these people but ample evidence that they possessed a brand new stone tool kit. Using the same raw materials available to their predecessors, the Baradostians used the Upper Paleolithic technique of flint-knapping, striking off blades which were used as blanks for tools. They had more stone tool types, a variety of bone tools and they also possessed a woodworking technology such as the Neanderthals never had. Probably they used elaborate wood-carving stone tools to fashion traps and more advanced kinds of hunting apparatus and with this equipment they pursued much the same kind of game animals (mainly goats) as their extinct Neanderthal predecessors had.

By 35,000 B.C., the Neanderthals seem to have disappeared from the world altogether and we may well ask, what did Upper Paleolithic *Homo sapiens* have that the Neanderthals did not have? To my way of thinking, there were probably two things that weighed heavily in the balance. One was language. Jacquetta Hawkes, the English student of language and prehistory, feels that although the Neanderthal was a skilled toolmaker, his tool kit shows a conspicuous lack of invention and adaptability. He was probably handicapped because he did not develop a fully articulate and precise language. This was the new weapon which we think his Upper Paleolithic replacement possessed and used to make a tool kit so diversified that in the graver category he had more working edges than master cabinetmakers are accustomed to working with today. With his greater articulateness, he was able to describe and demonstrate the details of the manufacture of these stone tools to his people, including the children who were to carry on the group's activities.

The second critical cultural achievement of Upper Paleolithic man, in my opinion, is his ability to keep track of events for the future. Alexander Marshack, a research fellow at Harvard, has provided us with this recent and powerful insight into prehistoric man. Thousands of notational sequences have been found on engraved bones and stones dating as far back as at least 30 millennia. These markings have been puzzled over or guessed about by archaeologists since the time they were first discovered more than 100 years ago. Marshack has determined that they served Upper Paleolithic man as a kind of farmer's almanac tied in with a lunar notational count. Some are illustrated with the natural history of the events, giving the possessor of the object a mnemonic device reminding him when to expect the change of seasons and the movements and dispersal of game.

An ancestor of sympathetic character

In short, this was of tremendous economic advantage to Upper Paleolithic man, and it gave him a control over his environment and destiny such as was evidently denied to his predecessor, the Neanderthal.

So, men with these remarkable abilities and all that flowed from them overtook and presumably eliminated the Neanderthals. We have long thought of the Neanderthals as ultimate examples of the Hobbesian dictum that the life of a primitive man is "nasty, brutish and short." They have been characterized as having a near-bestial appearance with an ape-like face in profile, a thick neck, stooped shoulders and a shuffling gait. But now it appears that they were actually very similar to *Homo sapiens* in skeletal structure. Stewart's study of the Shanidar Neanderthals led him to the conclusion that below the head there was not too much difference between these early men and modern man. Of course, one cannot deny the bulging prominent eyebrows and the heavy coarse-featured face of the Neanderthal in general, though Anthropologist Earnest Hooton once said: "You can, with equal facility, model on a Neanderthaloid skull the features of a chimpanzee or the lineaments of philosopher."

His own biological evolution is something man really does not have conscious control over. But his culture, his social and religious life, is something else. In the millions of years of evolution that began with the ape-like hominids of Africa it is among the Neanderthals that we have the first stirrings of social and religious sense and feelings: the obvious care with which the lame and crippled were treated, the burials —and the flowers. Flowers have never been found in prehistoric burials before, though this may simply be because no one has ever looked for them. And to be sure, only one of the burials in Shanidar Cave yielded such evidence. But the others buried there could have died during the wrong season for flowers, since death knows no season.

The Neanderthal has been ridiculed and rejected for a century but despite this he is still our ancestor. Of course we may still have the privilege of ridiculing him, but in the face of the growing evidence, especially in the light of the recent findings at Shanidar, we can not actually reject him. And what person will mind having as an ancestor one of such sympathetic character, one who laid his dead to rest with flowers?

Primatology and Human Behavior

....

Human beings are mammals, members of the order Primates. And they are very closely related to some living primates, most notably chimpanzees, gorillas, and orangutans. As primates, human beings have certain evolutionary traits in common with other primates (and other mammals as well); but our species is also distinctly different from all other animal species. At this moment, scholars are actively debating the degree to which it is possible to understand or explain human behavior in terms of the behavior patterns that seem to be innate in other species, particularly other primates.

Edward O. Wilson is, at this moment, a very controversial figure. In 1975, he published a book called *Sociobiology: The New Synthesis*, in which he gathered together all the information biologists had accumulated about genetically transmitted behavior among the world's animals. But he went one step further: he argued that, contrary to the cherished beliefs strongly held by many anthropologists, human behavior also has fundamentally, innate patterns. Three years later, in 1978, Wilson developed these views at length in his next book, *On Human Nature*.

Initially, Wilson's arguments stimulated heated debate which, at times, became ugly and personal. Several of his colleagues at Harvard organized the Sociobiology Study Group of Science, which became a forum for attacking Wilson and his followers. The study group argued that any attempt to account for human behavior genetically will inevitably cater to reactionary politicians seeking to protect the interests of groups with social, economic, and political power in society. In a letter to *The New York Review of Books*, they proclaimed that "Wilson joins the long parade of biological determinists whose work has served to buttress the institutions of their society by exonerating them from responsibility for social problems" (Dec. 11, 1975:60–61).

A careful reading of Wilson's books reveals, however, that he has made no direct, declarative statements tying human behavior to genes. Rather, he uses what to his critics is a maddening "suppositional" style; he

supposes there *might* be genes that would favor certain forms of social behavior, then proceeds to ponder how such genes might be expressed. His critics point out, with some justification, that many lay readers are apt to miss this reserve and read Wilson's speculations as definitive. (Indeed, subsequent works by others have done so, most egregiously in the area of the study of sex roles, where Wilson himself is apt to use language decidedly deterministic in flavor. See Topic Twelve for a fuller discussion of these materials.)

Both Wilson and his adversaries have recently toned down their public rhetoric. But the debate and its bitterness does show that science is not pursued in a vacuum. Its findings can be and often are appropriated for social, economic, and political purposes—regardless of scientists' intentions. Thus, in a society still organized to some degree along "racial" (and sexual) lines in its distribution of wealth and access to institutions of power, scientific theories and findings that even suggest the possibility that social institutions may, to whatever degree, be rooted in innate biological traits will be used to justify the status quo and undermine pressures for change. For example, if certain research suggests that intelligence is unevenly distributed among the "races" of our society, some pressure groups will use these findings to justify terminating programs like Head Start, which are designed to compensate for social inequalities. It was fear of such misuse of Wilson's work that fueled the bitterness of his critics' attacks.

All the articles in Topic Three address themselves to these issues. In the first, Wilson introduces the large question of "The Origins of Human Social Behavior." He argues that humans are not as completely under the control of their genes as Konrad Lorenz suggests, but are more so than pure learning theorists (behaviorists) like B. F. Skinner claim. In this article he focuses on interpreting the fossil record, but in other places he discusses our primate relatives at length, drawing comparisons between them and us.

S. L. Washburn objects to such comparisons in

"What We Can't Learn about People from Apes," in the article that follows Wilson's. Along the way, Washburn notes that in the twentieth century "biological explanations are considered more scientific than social ones," a telling point that partly accounts for sociobiology's widespread appeal. But his most subtle and important point—and one that is least well understood by lay persons—is that "It is impossible to infer that special genes account for human behavior simply because the behavior has a biological basis." You will find out why when you read this article.

In "Is It Our Culture, Not Our Genes, That Makes Us Killers?" Richard E. Leakey and Roger Lewin attack Konrad Lorenz's notion that innate aggression in human beings is so powerful that it will overwhelm all social structures designed to curb it. Rather, they argue, human life—though rooted in biology—is primarily determined by culture; that is, the behavior patterns and their meanings learned, taught, and shared by members of social groups. David Pilbeam, in "The Naked

Ape: An Idea We Could Live Without," argues that biological determinists use fallacious logic and faulty data in their formulations. And he, too, points out that (wittingly or not) they play into the hands of reactionary politicians.

The final article in this topic takes a different tack to criticize Lorenz and others who argue for the innate primacy of human aggression. In "Sharing in Human Evolution," Jane Lancaster and Phillip Whitten argue that, to the extent that there is a human "biogram" (as Wilson would put it), the evidence from both fossil remains and cross-cultural comparisons with still-surviving hunting and food-gathering groups argues that human beings are primarily characterized by a predisposition toward cooperation and sharing rather than toward violence and aggression. This article shows how looking for biological foundations for human behavior rooted in our evolutionary past need not reduce human beings to "naked apes" and also need not support right-wing political stereotyped views.

4

The Origins of Human Social Behavior

BY EDWARD O. WILSON

For the past twenty years biologists and anthropologists have been cooperating in an attempt to trace human social evolution. The task is one of the most difficult in science, because the human species has leaped forward in a way that all but denies self-analysis.

On anatomical grounds we are certainly primates, and our closest living relative is the chimpanzee. But the extraordinary mental evolution that characterizes *Homo sapiens* has distorted even the most basic primate social qualities into nearly unrecognizable forms. Individual species of monkeys and apes have plastic social organizations, easily modified by learning to adapt societies to particular environments; man has extended the trend into an endlessly varying ethnicity. Monkeys and apes are able to adjust their aggressive and sexual interactions somewhat to fit the needs of the moment; in man this adjustment has become multidimensional, culturally dependent, and almost endlessly subtle. The formation of close bonds and the reciprocation of favors among individuals are rudimentary behaviors in other primates; man has expanded them into great contractual networks in which individuals consciously alter roles from hour to hour as if changing masks.

The biologists and anthropologists are constructing a new discipline, comparative sociobiology, to trace these and other human qualities as closely as possible back through time. Besides adding perspective to our view of humankind and perhaps offering some philosophical ease, the exercise will help to identify the behavior and rules by which individual human beings increase their Darwinian fitness through the manipulation of society.

In a phrase, we are searching for the human biogram—the set of inborn responses and behavioral tendencies that adapt human beings to social life. One of the key questions is, to what extent is the biogram an adaptation to the more or less civilized existence of the past ten thousand years and to what extent is it a useless vestige of earlier social evolution? Our civilizations were jerry-built around the biogram. How have they been influenced by it? Conversely, how much flexibility is there in the biogram, and in what portions of it particularly? Experience with other animal species has shown that when an organ or a behavior pattern is as grossly changed as human behavior has been, evolutionary reconstruction is very difficult. This is the crux of the problem in the historical analysis of human behavior.

In pursuing this matter I believe that we can safely discard two extreme interpretations that have attracted a great deal of attention in recent years. Human beings are not thinly clothed instinct machines. For example, we are not in the grip of a basic aggressive instinct that must be relieved periodically by war or football games, as suggested by Konrad Lorenz. Our aggressive tendencies are real, and predictable to a large extent, but they are finely adjusted to circumstances and capable of remaining dormant for indefinite periods in the right environments. Nor are men stimulus-response machines molded by reward, punishment, and a few basic learning rules, as suggested by B. F. Skinner and the extreme behaviorists. The truth is much more complicated and interesting than either of these two alternatives. The human mind is something in between—a kind of palimpsest, from which the codes of several key periods in evolution will eventually be deciphered. This is why the study of human prehistory is so important to the understanding of modern psychology.

Modern man can be said to have been launched by a two-stage acceleration in mental evolution. The first occurred during the transition from a larger arboreal primate to the first man-apes (*Australopithecus*). If the primitive manlike creature *Ramapithecus* is in the direct line of ancestry, as current opinion holds, the change may have required as much as ten million years. *Austra-*

From *Harvard Magazine*, April 1975. Adapted from *Sociobiology: The New Synthesis* by Edward O. Wilson, Cambridge, Mass.: The Belknap Press of Harvard University Press, Copyright © 1975 by the President and Fellows of Harvard College. All accompanying figures from same source. Reprinted by permission of the publishers.

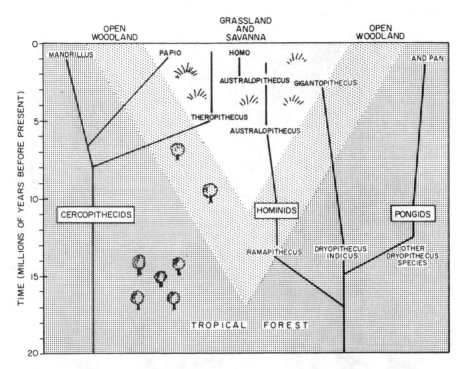

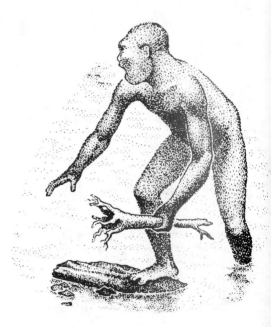

This simplified evolutionary diagram of the Old World primates shows that only three existing groups have shifted from the forest to the savanna. They are the baboons (Papio), the gelada monkey (Theropithecus gelada), and man.

lopithecus was present five million years ago, and by three million years ago it had divided into several forms, including probably the first primitive *Homo*, or "true" man. The evolution of these intermediate hominids was marked by an accelerating increase in brain capacity. Simultaneously, erect posture and a striding, bipedal locomotion were perfected, and the hands were molded to acquire the unique human precision grip. These early men undoubtedly used tools to a much greater extent than do modern chimpanzees. Crude stone implements were made by chipping, and rocks were pulled together to form what appear to be the foundations of shelters.

The second, much more rapid phase of acceleration began about 100,000 years ago. It consisted primarily of cultural evolution as opposed to a genetic evolution of brain capacity. The brain had reached a threshold, beyond which a wholly new, enormously more rapid form of mental evolution took over. This second phase was in no sense planned, and its potential is only now being revealed. The study of man's mental and social origins involves two questions that correspond to the dual stages of mental evolution.

What challenges in the environment caused the human ancestors to adapt differently from other primates and started them along their unique evolutionary path?

Once started, why did the human line go so far?

Scientists have concentrated on two indisputably important facts concerning the biology of *Australopithecus* and early *Homo*. First, the evidence is strong that the "gracile man-ape," *Australopithecus africanus*, the species closest to the direct ancestry of *Homo*, lived on the open savanna of Africa. The wear patterns of sand grains taken from the Sterkfontein fossils suggest a dry climate, while the pigs, antelopes, and other animals found in association with the fossils are of the kind usually specialized for existence in grasslands. The australopithecine way of life came as the result of a major habitat shift. The ancestral *Ramapithecus* or an even more antecedent form lived in forests and was adapted for progression through trees by arm swinging. Only a very few other large-bodied primates have been able to join man in leaving the forest to spend most of their lives on the ground in open habitats (see diagram below). This is not to say that bands of

Australopithecus africanus spent all of their lives running about in the open. Some of them might have carried their game into caves and even lived there in permanent residence, although the evidence pointing to this often-quoted trait is still far from conclusive. Other bands could have retreated at night to the protection of groves of trees, in the manner of modern baboons. The important point is that much or all of the foraging was conducted on the savanna.

The second peculiar feature of the ecology of early men was the degree of their dependence on animal food, evidently far greater than in any of the living monkeys and apes. The *Australopithecus* were catholic in their choice of small animals. Their sites contain the remains of tortoises, lizards, snakes, mice, rabbits, porcupines, and other small, vulnerable prey that must have abounded on the savanna. The man-apes also hunted baboons with clubs. From an analysis of 58 baboon skulls, Raymond Dart estimated that all had been brought down by blows to the head, fifty from the front and the remainder from behind. The *Australopithecus* also appear to have butchered larger animals, including the giant sivatheres, or horned giraffes, and dinotheres, elephantlike forms with tusks that curved downward from the lower jaws. In early Acheulian times, when true men of the genus *Homo* began employing stone axes, some of the species of large African mammals became extinct. It is reasonable to suppose that this impover-

ishment was due to excessive predation by the increasingly competent bands of men.

What can we deduce from these facts about the social life of early man? Before an answer is attempted, it should be noted that very little can be inferred directly from comparisons with other living primates. Geladas and baboons, the only open-country forms, are primarily vegetarian. They represent a sample of at most six species, which differ too much from one another in social organization to provide a baseline for comparison. The chimpanzees, the most intelligent and socially sophisticated of the nonhuman primates, are forest-dwelling and mostly vegetarian. Only on the infrequent occasions when they kill and eat baboons and other monkeys do they display behavior that can be directly connected with ecology in a way that has meaning for human evolution. Other notable features of chimpanzee social organization, including the rapidly shifting composition of subgroups, the exchange of females between groups, and the intricate and lengthy process of socialization, may or may not have been shared by primitive man. We cannot argue either way on the basis of our perception of ecological adaptation. It is often stated in the popular literature that the life of chimpanzees reveals a great deal about the origin of man. This is not necessarily true. The manlike traits of chimpanzees could be due to their having converged toward the human species in evolution, rather than sharing ancestral traits, in which case their use in evolutionary reconstructions would be misleading.

The best procedure to follow, and one that I believe is relied on implicitly by most students of the subject, is to extra-

At the threshold of autocatalytic social evolution two million years ago, a band of early men (Homo habilis) forages for food on the African savanna. In this speculative reconstruction the group is in the act of driving rival predators from a newly fallen dinothere. The great elephantlike creature had succumbed from exhaustion or disease, its end perhaps hastened by attacks from the animals closing in on it. The men have just entered the scene. Some drive away the predators by variously shouting, waving their arms, brandishing sticks, and throwing rocks, while a few stragglers, entering from the left, prepare to join the fray. To the right a female sabertoothed cat and her two grown cubs have been at least temporarily intimidated and are breaking away. As they threaten the men, they reveal the extraordinary gape of their jaws. In the left foreground, a pack of spotted hyenas has also retreated but is ready to rush back the moment an opening is provided. The men are quite small, less than five feet in height, and individually no match for the large carnivores. According to prevailing theory, a high degree of cooperation was therefore required to exploit such prey; and it evolved in conjunction with higher intelligence and the superior ability to use tools. In the background can be seen the environment of the Olduvai region of Tanzania as it may have looked at this time. The area was covered by rolling parkland and rimmed to the east by volcanic highlands. The herbivore populations were dense and varied, as they are today. In the left background are seen three-toed horses (Hipparion), while to the right are herds of wildebeest and giant horned giraffelike creatures called sivatheres.

The drawing is by Sarah Landry.

polate backward from living hunter-gatherer societies. In the table above this technique is made explicit. From the anthropological literature, I have listed the most general traits of hunter-gatherer peoples. Then I have evaluated the degree to which each behavioral category is subject to evolution by noting the amount of variation in the category that occurs among the nonhuman primate species. The less variable the category, the more likely that the trait displayed by the living hunter-gatherers was also displayed by early man.

What we can conclude with some degree of confidence is that primitive people lived in small territorial groups, within which males were dominant over females. The intensity of aggressive behavior and the ways in which its expression varied according to circumstances remain unknown. Maternal care was prolonged, and the relationships

were at least to some extent based on ties between mothers and their offspring. Speculation on the other aspects of social life is not supported either way by the variability data and is therefore more tenuous. It is likely that the early hominids foraged in groups. To judge from the behavior of baboons and geladas, such behavior would have conferred some protection from large predators. By the time *Australopithecus* and early *Homo* had begun to feed on large mammals, group hunting almost certainly had become advantageous and even necessary, as in the case of the African wild dog. But there is no compelling reason to conclude that men did the hunting while women stayed at home. This occurs today in hunter-gatherer societies, but comparisons with other primates offer no clue as to *when* the trait appeared. It is certainly not essential to conclude a priori that males must be a specialized

hunter class. Among chimpanzees males do the hunting, which may be suggestive. But among lions, the females are the providers, often working in groups and with cubs in tow, while the males usually hold back. In the case of the African wild dog both sexes participate. This is not to suggest that male group hunting was not an early trait of primitive man, but only that there is no strong independent evidence to support the hypothesis.

This brings us to the prevailing theory of the origin of human sociality. It consists of a series of interlocking hypotheses that have been fashioned from bits of fossil evidence, extrapolations back from extant hunter-gatherer societies, and comparisons with other living primate species. The core of the theory can be appropriately termed the "autocatalysis model." Autocatalysis is a word used in biology to denote a process in which the product of a reaction speeds

Social traits of living hunter-gatherer groups and the likelihood that they were also possessed by early man

Traits that occur generally in living hunter-gatherer societies	Variability of trait category among different species of monkeys and apes	Reliability of concluding early man had the same trait
Local group size: Mostly 100 or less	Highly variable but within range of 3-100	Very probably 100 or less but otherwise not reliable
Family as the nuclear unit	Highly variable	Not reliable
Sexual division of labor: Women gather, men hunt	Limited to man among living primates	Not reliable
Males dominant over females	Widespread although not universal	Reliable
Long-term sexual bonding (marriage) nearly universal; multiple wives general	Highly variable	Not reliable
Exogamy universal, abetted by marriage rules	Limited to man among living primates	Not reliable
The size and composition of subgroups change often	Highly variable	Not reliable
Territoriality general, especially marked in rich gathering areas	Occurs widely, but variable in pattern	Probably occurred; pattern unknown
Game playing, especially games that entail physical skill but not strategy	Occurs generally, at least in elementary form	Very reliable
Prolonged maternal care; pronounced socialization of young; extended relationships between mother and children, especially mothers and daughters	Occurs generally in advanced species of monkeys and apes	Very reliable

up the rate at which the reaction occurs, causing the reaction to accelerate. The theory holds that when the human ancestors became bipedal as part of their terrestrial adaptation, their hands were freed, the manufacture and handling of artifacts were made easier, and intelligence grew as part of the improvement of the tool-using habit. With mental capacity and the tendency to use artifacts increasing through mutual reinforcement, the entire materials-based culture expanded. Cooperation during hunting was perfected, providing a new impetus for the evolution of intelligence, which in turn permitted still more sophistication in tool using, and so on through cycles of causation. At some point, probably during the late *Australopithecus* period or the transition from *Australopithecus* to *Homo*, this autocatalysis carried the evolving populations to a certain threshold of competence, at which the hominids were able to exploit the antelopes, elephants, and other large herbivorous mammals teeming around them on the African plains. Quite possibly the process began when the hominids learned to drive big cats, hyenas, and other carnivores from their kills. In time they became the primary hunters themselves and were forced to protect their prey from other predators and scavengers. The autocatalysis model usually includes the proposition that the shift to big game accelerated the process of mental evolution. The shift could even have been the impetus that led to the origin of early *Homo* from their australopithecine ancestors two or more million years ago. Another proposition is that males became specialized for hunting. Child care was facilitated by close social bonding among the males, who left the domiciles to hunt, and the females, who kept the children and conducted most of the foraging for vegetable food. Many of the peculiar details of human sexual

behavior and domestic life flow easily from this basic division of labor. But these details are not essential to the autocatalysis model. They are added because they are displayed by modern hunter-gatherer societies.

Although internally consistent, the autocatalysis model contains a curious omission—the triggering device. Once the process started, it is easy to see how it could be self-sustaining. But what started it? Why did the earliest hominids become bipedal instead of running on all fours like baboons and geladas? Clifford Jolly has proposed that it happened in order to allow them to feed more efficiently on grass seeds. Because the early pre-men, perhaps as far back as *Ramapithecus*, were the largest primates depending on grain, a premium was set on the ability to manipulate objects of very small size relative to the hands. Man, in short, became bipedal in order to pick seeds. This hypothesis is by no means unsupported fantasy. Jolly points to a number of convergent features in skull and dental structure between man and the gelada, which feeds on seeds, insects, and other small objects. Moreover, the gelada is peculiar among the Old World monkeys and apes in sharing with man the following anatomical traits used in sexual display: growth of hair around the face and neck of the male and conspicuous fleshy adornments on the chest of the female. According to Jolly's model, the freeing of the hands of the early hominids was a preadaptation that permitted the increase in tool use and the autocatalytic concomitants of mental evolution and predatory behavior.

Autocatalytic reactions in living systems never expand to infinity. Biological processes normally change in a manner that slows growth and eventually brings it to a halt. But almost miraculously, this has not yet happened in human evolution. The increase in brain

size and the refinement of stone artifacts indicate a gradual improvement in mental capacity for at least five million years. With the appearance of the Mousterian tool culture of Neanderthal man some 75,000 years ago, the trend gathered momentum, giving way in Europe to the Upper Paleolithic culture of modern man about 40,000 years ago. Starting about 10,000 years ago, agriculture was invented and spread, populations increased enormously in density, and the primitive hunter-gatherer bands gave way locally to the relentless growth of tribes, chiefdoms, and states. Finally, after 1400 A.D., European-based civilization shifted gears again, and knowledge and technology grew at an accelerating pace.

There is no reason to believe that during this final sprint there has been a cessation in the evolution of either mental capacity or the predilection toward special social behaviors. The theory of population genetics and experiments on other organisms show that substantial changes can occur in the span of less than 100 generations, which for man reaches back only to the time of the Roman Empire. Two thousand generations, roughly the period since typical *Homo sapiens* invaded Europe, is enough time to create new species and to mold them in major ways. Although we do not know how much mental evolution has actually occurred, it would be false to assume that modern civilizations have been built entirely on capital accumulated during the long haul of the Pleistocene. The investigation of the genetic constraints on human behavior and their true meaning has just begun. As it proceeds we can hope to acquire a much deeper and more useful understanding of man's capacity to adapt to his relentlessly changing environment.

5

What We Can't Learn About People From Apes

BY S. L. WASHBURN

The past decade has witnessed an upsurge of interest, both popular and scholarly, in animal behavior, marked by an explosion of books and articles that stress the similarities between human beings and other animals. In the 1960s, researchers like Desmond Morris and Konrad Lorenz promoted the idea that by studying the behavior of other animals we could achieve greater understanding of human behavior. In the 1970s, sociobiologists like Edward O. Wilson have attempted to create a new science out of this approach.

The idea that human beings can learn more about themselves by studying animals that exhibit similar traits is deceptively captivating. After all, the study of animal behavior is fun as well as science. Most people find it fascinating to learn how bees communicate and the reasons fish and birds migrate; note the current popularity of animal behavior courses at universities. And it is easy to be charmed by a lovable chimpanzee that has been taught to brush its teeth, wash dishes, and speak in sign language (as indeed some have) so that we see it as being almost human—or, put another way, as a less-evolved form of human being.

But, of course, chimpanzees are not human beings, however endearing they may be, and although we can learn a great deal about chimpanzees by studying them, I question whether we can directly apply what we learn to interpreting the varieties of human social behavior. Because of my early research on the social organization of baboons, my work is often cited to support theories about the animal origins of human behavior. Obviously, we studied animal behavior to find both possible similarities and possible differences. As time has passed it is the differences that seem more important, especially when considering social behavior. Human evolution produced a unique kind of creature. The point I would like to stress is that a meaningful study of the complexities of human behavior must begin with human beings, *not* with other animals.

Theories about human behavior should proceed from an understanding of the relationship between nature (or biology) and nurture (or learning). In developing new theories of human behavior, emphasis has too often been placed on one to the relative exclusion of the other. Proponents of nurture commanded the field throughout the 1950s and most of the 1960s, as evidenced by the focus on environmental factors in human behavior. Now the pendulum seems to have swung back to nature, which is to say biology, as a means of explaining fundamental behavior patterns.

Sociobiology is part of this trend. The sociobiologists would have us believe that human beings are governed by a set of genetic universals. Their aim, in E. O. Wilson's words, is to develop "general laws of the evolution and biology of social behavior," which may then be applied to human beings. In their view, genes are responsible for a disparate mix of everyday human activities—from cheating and spite to creativity and altruism. As one means of supporting their theoretical contentions, sociobiologists select animals whose behavior matches certain preconceived notions of human contact. Based on observations of these animals—such as monkeys or apes—they will then draw conclusions about the behavior of human beings.

As an example of the ludicrous extreme to which this sort of reasoning can be taken, I can cite a recent textbook in which the author uses the behavior of nonprimates to make significant statements about primates. At one point a picture of a musk ox in a defensive posture is used to illustrate the possibility of atavistic behavior in human beings. By way of demonstrating the absurdity of this method of proof, let me reverse the situation. Try to imagine the reaction of the editor of a zoological magazine if I sent him an article on the musk ox in which the animal's defensive stance was illustrated by the British square formations at the Battle of Waterloo. The editor would surely think me a bit daft. Yet this type of reasoning is considered acceptable when animal behavior is compared with human behavior.

The claim that genes are responsible for different types of behavior in animals and in people is the most controversial part of sociobiological theory. More to the point, this way of thinking, in its application to human behavior, repeats the errors of past generations of evolutionists, social Darwinists, eugenicists, and racists. It is useful to recall that the eugenicists argued that genes were responsible for an assortment of human social ills, including crime, alcoholism, and other forms of behavior they regarded as undesirable. Zoologists Peter B. and J. S. Medawar aptly described this form of geneticism as "the enthusiastic misapplication of not fully understood genetic principles in situations to which they do not apply."

We have had more than a century of such misapplication of scientific theories, of people believing what they want to, often without any substantive data to support their claims. As a case in point, we might compare early studies of the behavior of the great apes with more recent investigations. Ape behavior received considerable attention in the late 19th Century as part of the general interest in human evolution. Literally hundreds of papers and monographs were written about these animals (R. M. and A. W. Yerkes compiled over 500 references in their 1929 work *The Great Apes*), many involving heated controversies over such aspects of ape behavior as promiscuity and monogamy.

However, none of these studies was based on scientific data collected through careful field studies. Instead, these early reports were essentially anecdotal, relying on

S. L. Washburn

accounts provided by travelers, hunters, and local people. One might reasonably ask how professional scientists could uncritically accept questionable information gathered in such a random manner. Part of the answer lies in the 19th Century view of animals as simple creatures of nature, whose behavior was largely instinctive. Given such a view, the reports of untrained observers gained an undeserved credibility. Besides, apes, with their human-like appearance and apparent similarities in behavior, fit nicely into evolutionary theory. Faith in the theory of evolution was so great that misinformation substantiating it was readily accepted without verification. Clearly, a theory should be seen as a license for serious research, not as a substitute for it. Yet the nature of ape behavior and its relation to human behavior was debated for more than a century before reliable studies were available.

During that period the image of the gorilla shifted from the 19th Century vision of a fearsome beast, who in romantic literature was seen confronting the brave hunter, to the more recent view of the peaceful gorilla and its cousin, the friendly chimpanzee. Neither perception is wholly accurate, but they are both examples of people in different times believing what they wanted to about these animals. It is only in the past 15 years, thanks to zoologist George Schaller's study of the gorilla and Jane Goodall's continuing investigations of the chimpanzee, that more reliable information has emerged. The evidence today is that chimpanzees, far from being docile, playful creatures, are by nature aggressive animals that jealously guard their territory even to the point of violence. Observers record situations in which chimpanzees from one group have killed and eaten an infant from another group. Similarly, gorillas are known to fight and sometimes kill other gorillas.

The current view of the violent apes does not sit well with those who would like to believe that apes (and therefore human beings) are inherently peaceful. Accounts of gorilla violence by Dian Fossey and last year's Leakey Foundation lecture by B. Galkidas-Brindamour describing the battle scars she found on Indonesian orang-utans were discomforting to listeners. Their distress points up the obvious conflict between behavioral fact and popular desire.

Although the information we now have on ape behavior is vastly superior to what was available before the Second World War, we still depend on the spadework of a small group of researchers operating in a limited number of geographical areas. Much more field work will have to be done before we have an adequate understanding of the social behavior of gorillas, chimpanzees, and other members of the ape family. Even with the aid of comparative anatomy, the fossil record, and studies of captive primates, it will likely be some years before meaningful comparisons between human behavior and that of our nearest animal relatives can be made. It is certainly premature to attempt to do so now.

Let me provide an example to clarify the issues I have raised. Sociobiologists, with their fundamentalist belief in a biological basis for all sorts of human behavior, have resurrected the old theory that the lack of regular mating cycles, or estrus, among human females is a primary reason for the rise of the human family unit. According to this hypothesis the loss of female estrous behavior during the evolutionary process led to monogamy—which, of course, is the bedrock of marital relationships in most human societies. Explaining the origin of the human family and of the social group in nonhuman primates in terms of sexual attraction has an obvious appeal. It combines 19th Century romantic notions about sex with the 20th Century need for a scientific rationale; and in our culture, biological explanations are considered more scientific than social ones.

But biological interpretations tend to be simplistic. When the available data are examined, the sexual-attraction theory does not hold up, whether we are dealing with human beings or our ape and monkey cousins. The most recent investigations of nonhuman primate behavior reveal that male-female relationships run the gamut from near-promiscuity, to consort relations of varying duration, and even to lifelong pair bonds. Furthermore, whether mating cycles are monthly or yearly, the social systems of these primates continue to function. Thus we learn from the studies of Ronald

Nadler, a psychologist at the Yerkes Primate Research Center, that the gorilla, the most continuously social of the great apes, has the shortest mating cycle. At the other extreme, the orang-utan, the most solitary of the great apes, will mate at any time, whether the female is in heat or not. Gibbons are the least sexually active of the apes and yet they form lasting pair bonds.

If even ape behavior is so complicated that it resists being categorized by a few labels like monogamy and promiscuity, then there ought to be caution about casually applying them to human beings. Yet sociobiologists attempt to reduce the extraordinary variety of human male-female customs to monogamy. But the word monogamy is not a label for any clearly defined behavior that could have a genetic base. It may mean a continuing relationship, such as marriage or the currently fashionable "living together," or a temporary one, and it may be modified by all sorts of variations in economic and social conditions as well as by diverse sexual practices.

The point I would emphasize about terms like monogamy or polygamy, when used to describe human behavior, is that they refer to systems of marriage, not to mating. Mating can and does occur outside of marriage in every known society; marriage is a social and legal contract involving rights and obligations and encompassing far more than sexual behavior. (Animal behaviorists seeking to draw conclusions about human behavior often ignore this fundamental difference.) In their use of words like monogamy, sociobiologists show a gross misunderstanding of social science. Insofar as they overlook different cultural interpretations of these terms, they also make the arrogant assumption that our culture is synonymous with human nature.

To my way of thinking, students of animal behavior are much too free in their use of the behavior of nonhuman species to make points about human behavior. They may cite evidence of aggression in insects, birds, lions, and a range of other creatures and then generalize about human aggression—as Konrad Lorenz did in his book *On Aggression.* Animal behavior is quite diversified—even within one species, as we saw in our discussion of the apes—and virtually any thesis can be defended if its proponent can randomly select any animal whose behavior supports his contention.

In promoting the idea that genes account for human behavior, sociobiologists are able to minimize the difference between what is learned and what is genetically determined—in other words, our biologically inherited behavior. But learning is the crucial factor in the two basic abilities that distinguish human beings from all other primates: the ability to walk on two legs (bipedalism) and human speech.

We now know from the fossil record that our ancestors were standing erect and using only their legs for walking at least three million years ago. The evolution of this new means of locomotion was the behavioral event that led to the separation of man from his ape relatives. And yet the brain of early man was no larger than that of apes, and both shared a similar anatomical structure. Therefore it was the uniqueness of the human brain that gave man the ability to *learn* how to do things that his fellow primates were unable to do.

Of course there is a biological basis for walking, and through the process of natural selection a complex anatomical restructuring of the human body—involving changes in bone structure and a reorganization of muscles—occurred that made bipedal locomotion possible. But the important point is that human beings do not instinctively walk; they must learn to walk, just as they must learn to speak. Interestingly, we make much of the fact that learning to speak takes years but tend to overlook the long period of time it takes for a child to learn to run and walk properly.

Since human walking is unique and far better understood than the ways other animals move about, it is more productive to start with what we know about human beings before we shift to comparisons with other animals. Observing chimpanzees knuckle walking will provide no information about the internal anatomical changes that led to fundamental differences between chimpanzees and human beings.

Further, the fact that all human beings share essentially the same biological base, with some minor anatomical variations, does not mean that they will all behave similarly. For example, a common biological base makes swimming theoretically possible for all human beings and other primates as well. But apes cannot swim and most human beings never learn how. Granted human intelligence, many of us may learn to use our arms and legs in a variety of ways that permit us to swim. But the structure of our arms (primarily the result of man's early life in the trees) and of our legs (which evolved for walking on land) did not evolve specifically to enable us to swim. Nor are special genes required. Swimming is a learned behavior that uses parts of our bodies that evolved for other purposes.

We can see from this example that even when a certain behavior has a particular biological basis, it is not possible to infer that special genes are involved. Human hands can be trained to do many different things, but although the behavior of the hands may be varied, the basic biology of bones, joints, and muscles is the same. Also, human beings elaborate on everything they do. People do not just walk and run; they hop, skip, and dance. They may also swim in many different ways, and there is no evidence that these elaborations are based on biological variations.

As in the case of walking, there is a biological basis for speech. The human brain makes it possible for us to learn languages, but there is nothing to suggest that the brain determines the language to be learned. Any normal human being is able to learn the language of his group, and even others if necessary or desired. The basic biology sets limits and possibly accounts for some linguistic universals, but there is an immense freedom of learning. The constraints are primarily in the difficulties human beings from one language group may encounter in learning to make the sounds that are peculiar to the languages of another group.

Human speech is based on a phonetic code, on a system in which short, meaningless sounds are combined into meaningful units, or words. Like all codes, the system is based on a relatively small number of units that may be combined in an almost infinite number of ways. Therefore the human system of communication is open; we can and do create new words to meet our needs, and no limit has yet been approached. The phonetic code is unique to our species; there is nothing comparable in any other animal, whether primate or nonprimate. In spite of great efforts by researchers, apes cannot be taught to speak in the human sense of the word.

Speech is the main form of human communication, and anyone who wishes to understand speech as distinguished from animal sounds must start with the human phonetic code. And the only way we know that such a code exists is by studying human beings. Comparisons between human and animal communication must begin with human behavior. If we start with monkey communication we learn that monkeys make roughly two to three dozen sounds, and we could speculate that adding more sounds could lead to speech. But closer examination reveals that when monkeys communicate they use a combination of gestures and sounds; and the gestures are nearly always the more important of the two. When the sounds are separated from the gestures and treated as an independent means of communication, the monkey system of "talking" falls apart.

The varieties of human languages, the ease with which they are learned, and the speed with which they change all combine to distinguish the behavior of *Homo sapiens* from that of the other primates. There may be minor regional differences in nonhuman primate communication—in the same way that there are dialects in the sounds birds make—but there is nothing comparable to the incredible diversity of human language. For instance, in one relatively small region of Africa—what is now Tanzania—over 100 tribal groups speak many languages. In that same area, all baboons use the same system of communication.

Language then is probably the best illustration of a common biological base facilitating the learning of an extraordinary variety of behavior. Viewed in this manner, biology actually validates two basic assumptions of the social sciences: first, that human populations, not individuals, have the same human potentials, and second, that human social systems are not determined by the basic biology of the species. Consequently, language gives the nature versus nurture (or genetic versus learning) controversy over human behavior an entirely new dimension. No comparable mechanism, nor any alternative biological system, allows virtually unlimited communication as well as the development of new symbols when needed.

Furthermore, human social groups can adapt to different situations because of knowledge and organization, both of which depend on speech. And it is this language-based knowledge and organization that lead, in turn, to technical progress. We might, in fact, define social science as the science that studies the nature, complexity, and effectiveness of human conduct that is made possible by language. Granted such a definition, it becomes clear that human behavior cannot usefully be reduced to that of other animals—even our closest primate relatives.

It has now been fairly well established on the basis of fossil records that, granting basic human biology, learning was the dominant factor in determining behavior even 30,000 to 40,000 years ago. Or, putting it somewhat differently, human cognitive abilities, speech, and social systems—which is to say, human nature as we know it today—had fully evolved more than 30,000 years ago. But in applying evolutionary theory to human conduct, sociobiologists generally make little effort to understand the complexity of human behavior. Instead they use the theory of evolution to make questionable comparisons between human and animal behavior without the neces-

sary research to validate their claims. Unsubstantiated opinions by researchers are too often presented as facts—or at least as worthy contributions to scholarship.

I would be the first to agree that the full understanding of the behavior patterns of any species must include biology. But the more that learning is involved, the less there will be of any simple relation between basic biology and behavior. The laws of genetics are not the laws of learning. As a result of intelligence and speech, human beings provide the extreme example of highly varied behavior that is learned and executed by the same fundamental biology. Biology determines the basic need for food, but not the innumerable ways in which this need may be met.

Out of the present controversy, which, on a positive level, has stimulated renewed interest in human and animal behavior, a new interdisciplinary biologically and socially based behavioral science may emerge. But in applying biological thinking we must take care not to ignore history, sociology, and comparative studies. For if we do, we will be condemned to repeat the scientific errors of the past.

For further information:

Bateson, P. P. G., and R. A. Hinde. *Growing Points in Ethology.* Cambridge University Press, 1976.

Dolhinow, P. J. *Primate Patterns.* Holt, Rinehart, and Winston, 1972.

Washburn, S. L., and Elizabeth R. McCown. *Human Evolution.* Benjamin/Cummings, 1978.

Wilson, E. O. *Sociobiology.* Harvard University Press, 1975.

6

Is It Our Culture, Not Our Genes, That Makes Us Killers?

BY RICHARD E. LEAKEY AND ROGER LEWIN

....

"The blood-bespattered, slaughter-gutted archives of human history from the earliest Egyptian and Sumerian records to the most recent atrocities of the Second World War accord with early universal cannibalism, with animal and human sacrificial practices or their substitutes in formalized religions, and with the worldwide scalping, head-hunting, body-mutilating and necrophilic practices of mankind in proclaiming this common bloodlust differentiator, this predaceous habit, this mark of Cain that separates man dietetically from his anthropoidal relatives and allies him rather with the deadliest of Carnivora." The message of these stirring words, written by Paleoanthropologist Raymond Dart, is clear: humans are unswervingly brutal, possessed of an innate drive to kill each other.

On the same subject, the Nobel Prize winner Konrad Lorenz, one of the founders of modern ethology, wrote with even more eloquence: "There is evidence that the first inventors of pebble tools—the African australopithecines—promptly used their weapons to kill not only game, but fellow members of their species as well. Peking Man, the Prometheus who learned to preserve fire, used it to roast his brothers: beside the first traces of the regular use of fire lie the . . . roasted bones of *Sinanthropus pekinensis* himself."

Lorenz sounded these dramatic phrases 14 years ago in his celebrated book *On Aggression,* the main burden of which is that the human species carries with it an inescapable legacy of territoriality and aggression, instincts which must be ventilated lest they spill over in ugly fashion. All these—archaeological evidence of cannibalism, the notion of territorial and aggressive instincts, of an evolutionary career as killer apes—were woven together to form one of the most dangerously persuasive myths of our time: mankind is incorrigibly belligerent; war and violence are in our genes.

This essentially pessimistic view of human nature was assimilated with unseemly haste into a popular conventional wisdom, an assimilation that was further enhanced by Desmond Morris (with *The Naked Ape*) and Robert Ardrey (with *African Genesis, The Territorial Imperative, Social Contract,* and more recently *The Hunting Hypothesis*). We emphatically reject this conventional wisdom for three reasons: first, on the very general premise that no theory of human nature can be so firmly proved as its proponents imply; second, that much of the evidence used to erect this aggression theory is simply not relevant to human behavior; and last, the clues that do impinge on the basic elements of human nature argue much more persuasively that we are a cooperative rather than an aggressive animal.

The rules for human behavior are simple, we believe, precisely because they offer such a wide scope for expression. By contrast, the proponents of innate aggression try to tie us down to narrow, well-defined paths of behavior: humans are aggressive, they propose, because there is a universal territorial instinct in biology; territories are established and maintained by displays of aggression; our ancestors acquired weapons, turning ritual displays into bloody combat, a development that was exacerbated through a lust for killing. And according to the Lorenzian school, aggression is such a crucial part of the territorial animal's survival kit that it is backed up by a steady rise in pressure for its expression. Aggression may be released by an appropriate cue, such as a threat by another animal, but in the protracted absence of such cues the pressure eventually reaches a critical point at which the behavior bursts out spontaneously. The difference between a piece of behavior that is elicited by a particular type of stimulus, and one that will be expressed whether or not cues occur is enormous, and that difference is central to understanding aggression in the human context.

There is no doubt that aggression and territoriality are part of modern life: vandalism is a distressingly familiar part of the urban scene, and there is war, an

As excerpted in *Smithsonian,* November 1977 from *Origins,* by Richard E. Leakey and Roger Lewin. Copyright © 1977 by Richard E. Leakey and Roger Lewin. Reprinted by permission of the publishers, E.P. Dutton. Photograph by Roger Lewin.

apparent display of territoriality and aggression on a grand scale. Are these unsavory aspects of modern living simply part of an inescapable legacy of our animal origins? Or are they phenomena which have entirely different causes?

To begin with, it is worth taking a broad view of territoriality and aggression in the animal world. Why are some animals territorial? Simply to protect resources, such as food, a nest or a similar reproductive area. Many birds defend one piece of real estate in which a male may attract and court a female, and then move off to another one, also to be defended, in which they build a nest and rear young. Intruders are soon met with territorial displays, the intention of which is quite clear. The clarity of the defender's response, and also of the intruder's prowess, is the secret of nature's success with these so-called aggressive encounters.

Such confrontations are strictly ritualized, so that on all but the rarest occasions the biologically fitter of the two wins without the infliction of physical damage on either one. This "aggression" is in fact an exercise in competitive display rather than physical violence. The biological common sense implicit in this simple behavioral device is reiterated again and again throughout the animal kingdom. For a species to transgress, there must be extremely unusual circumstances. We cannot deny that with the invention of tools, an impulse to employ them occasionally as weapons might have caused serious injury, there being no stereotyped behavior patterns to deflect their risk. And it is possible that our increasingly intelligent prehuman ancestors may have understood the implications of power over others through the delivery of one swift blow with a sharpened pebble tool. But is it likely?

The answer must be no. An animal that develops a proclivity for killing its fellows thrusts itself into an evolutionarily disadvantageous position. Because our ancestors almost always lived in small bands, in which individuals were closely related to one another, and had as neighbors similar bands which also contained blood relations, in most acts of murder the victim would more than likely have been kin to the murderer. As the evolutionary success is in the production and well-being of as many descendants as possible, an undifferentiated innate drive for killing individuals of one's own species would soon have wiped that species out. Humans, as we know, did not blunder up an evolutionary blind alley, a fate that innate, unrestrained aggressiveness would undoubtedly have produced.

To argue, as we do, that humans are innately nonaggressive toward one another is not to imply that we are of necessity innately good-natured toward our fellows. In the lower echelons of the animal kingdom the management of conflict is largely through genetically-seated mock battles. But farther along the evolutionary path, carrying out the appropriate avoidance behavior comes to depend more and more on learning, and in social animals, the channel of learning is social education. The capacity for that behavior is rooted in the animal's genes, it is true, but its elaboration depends also on learning.

For instance, among the Micronesian Ifaluk of the western Pacific, real violence is now so thoroughly condemned that "ritual" management of conflict is taught in childhood. The children play boisterously, as any normal children do; however a child who feels that he or she is being treated unfairly will set off in pursuit of the offender—but at a pace that will not permit catching up. As other children stand around, showing looks of disapproval, the chase may end with the plaintiff throwing pieces of coconut at the accused—once again with sufficient care so as to miss the target! This is ritual conflict, culturally based, not genetic.

Animal conflict occurs both between animals of different species and between individuals of the same species, and under differing environmental conditions. Anyone who argues for inbuilt aggression in Homo sapiens must see aggression as a universal instinct in the animal kingdom. It is no such thing. Much of the research on territoriality and aggression concerns birds. Because they usually must build nests, in which they will then spend a good deal of time incubating eggs, and still longer rearing their young, it is a biological necessity for them to protect their territory. It is therefore not surprising that most birds possess a strong territorial drive. But simply because greylag geese and mockingbirds, for instance, enthusiastically defend their territory, we should not infer that all animals do so. And it is not surprising that hummingbirds show considerably more territorial aggression than lions, even though the king of beasts is a lethal hunter. Our closest animal relatives, the chimpanzees and gorillas, are notably nonterritorial. Both of these species are relatively mobile and so they can forage for food over a wide area.

The animal kingdom therefore offers a broad spectrum of territoriality, whose basic determining factor is the mode of reproduction and style of daily life. Indeed, an animal may find it necessary to assert ownership of land in one situation and not in another.

That territoriality is flexible should not be surprising. If food resources and space are scarce, then there may well be conspicuous territorial behavior. Some individuals will fail to secure sufficient food or a place in which to rear a brood. These individuals are, of course, the weakest, and this is what survival of the fittest through natural selection really means.

Territorial behavior is therefore triggered when it

is required and remains dormant when it is not. The Lorenzians, however, take a different view: aggression, they say, builds up inexorably, to be released either by appropriate cues or spontaneously in the absence of appropriate cues. A safety valve suggested by Lorenzians for human societies is competitive sport. But such a suggestion neglects the high correlation between highly competitive encounters and associated vandalism and physical violence—as players, referees and crowds know to their cost through Europe and the Americas. More significantly, research now shows a close match between warlike behavior in countries and a devotion to sport. Far from defusing aggression, highly organized, emotionally charged sporting events generate even more aggression and reflect the degree to which humans' deep propensity to group identity and cohesion can be manipulated.

We can say therefore that territoriality and aggression are not universal instincts as such. Rather they are pieces of behavior that are tuned to particular lifestyles and to changes in the availability of important resources in the environment.

When the practice of hunting and gathering was becoming firmly rooted in the fertile soil of prehuman society, our ancestors would of course not have operated sophisticated kinship networks. But we do know that chimpanzees know who are their brothers and sisters and who are not. And we know too that chimpanzees and baboons do migrate between their various troops. The biological benefits of reducing tension and conflict between groups through exogamy almost certainly would have been achieved early in hominid evolution. The notion of hostile neighboring hordes is an image born of the mistaken belief in a belligerence written ineradicably into the human genetic blueprint.

Food shortage, either on the hoof or rooted in the ground, must nevertheless have been a cause of potential conflict between bands. Indeed, severe famine may well have forced hominids into belligerent confrontation with one another in open competition for the scarce food. And the band that lost out may even have ended as the victors' supper. But there is neither evidence nor any reason to suggest that hominid flesh, either roasted or raw, appeared on our ancestors' diet, specifically as a source of food, in any but the most extreme circumstances. A much more likely consequence of conflict over food resources, so far as can be judged from what we know of both animals and present-day hunter-gathers, would have been the dispersal of bands and even the temporary scattering of individuals, a practice that ensures the best use of the limited food that is available.

Along with lions, humans are one of the few mammals who on occasion deliberately eat each other.

Author Leakey painstakingly recovers more evidence of Man's past at the Lake Turkana site in Kenya.

When a male lion wins control of a pride, he will often consume the young cubs and set about producing offspring of his own. Ruthless and wasteful though it may appear, the biological reason for the dominant male's behavior is evident: the offspring produced by the pride will have been sired by a very powerful animal, providing a brutal but efficient method of natural selection. Cannibalism in humans, however, takes place for different reasons.

Two kinds of human cannibalism

Broadly, there are two sorts of cannibalism and the distinction between them is crucial. First, there is the eating of members of one tribe of individuals by another—usually as the end result of raids; such is the conventional version of the practice, and it is known as exocannibalism. In the second form, known as endocannibalism, people eat members of their own tribe.

Human cannibalism takes place primarily as part of some kind of ritual. Even among the infamous tribes in the highlands of New Guinea, the context is one of extensive tribal ritual. Months of preparation—weaving symbolic adornments and the carving of elaborate wooden images—precede a raid, and it is abundantly clear that the entire exercise has a powerful unifying effect on the tribe. The habits of the New Guinea tribes are, in any event, extremely rare, and as against cannibalism manifested in this extreme form we may set the other extreme, in which people swallow a small morsel of a dead relative as a mark of love and respect.

Altogether, then, the notion that humans are inherently aggressive is simply not tenable. We cannot deny that 20th-century humans display a good deal of aggression, but we cannot point to our evolutionary past either to explain its origins or to excuse it. There are many reasons why a youth may "spontaneously" smash a window or attack an old lady, but an inborn drive inherited from our animal origins is probably not one of them. Human behavior is extraordinarily sensitive to the nature of the environment, and so it should not be particularly surprising that a person reared in unpleasant surroundings, perhaps subjected to material insecurity and emotional deprivation, should later behave in a way that people blessed with a more fortunate life might regard as unpleasant. Urban problems will not be solved by pointing to supposed defects in our genes while ignoring real effects in social justice.

The fallacy of thus adducing our animal origins should be evident for wars as well. Wars are planned and organized by leaders intent on increasing their power. In war men are more like sheep than wolves: they may be led to manufacture munitions at home, to release bombs from 10,000 feet up, or to fire long-range guns and rockets—all as part of one great cooperative effort. It is not insignificant that those soldiers who engage in hand-to-hand fighting are subjected to an intense process of desensitization before they can do it.

With the growth of agriculture and of materially based societies, warfare has increased steadily in ferocity, culminating in our current capability to destroy even the planet. We should not look to our genes for the seeds of war; those seeds were planted when, 10,000 years ago, our ancestors for the first time planted crops and began to be farmers. The transition from the nomadic hunting way of life to the sedentary one of farmers and industrialists made war possible and potentially profitable.

Possible, but not inevitable. For what has transformed the possible into reality is the same factor that has made human beings special in the biological kingdom: culture. Because of our seemingly limitless inventiveness and our vast capacity for learning, there is an endless potential for difference among human cultures, as indeed may be witnessed throughout the world. An important element of culture, however, consists in those central values that make up an ideology. It is social and political ideologies, and the tolerance or lack of it between them, that brings human

nations to bloody conflict. Those who argue that war is in our genes not only are wrong, but in addition they commit the crime of diverting attention from the real cause of war.

One supreme biological irony underlies the entire issue of organized war in modern societies—the cooperative nature of human beings. Throughout our recent evolutionary history, particularly since the rise of a hunting way of life, there must have been extreme selective pressures in favor of our ability to cooperate as a group: organized food-gathering and hunts are successful only if each member of the band knows his task and joins in with the activity of his fellows. The degree of selective pressure toward cooperation, group awareness and identification was so strong, and the period over which it operated was so extended, that it can hardly have failed to have become embedded to some degree in our genetic makeup.

We are not suggesting that the human animal is a cooperative, group-oriented automaton. That would negate what is the prime evolutionary heritage of humans: their ability to acquire culture through education and learning. We are essentially cultural animals with the capacity to formulate many kinds of social structures; but a deep-seated urge toward cooperation, toward working as a group, provides a basic framework for those structures.

Unfortunately, it is our deeply rooted urge for group cooperation that makes large-scale wars not only possible, but unique in their destructiveness. Animals that are essentially self-centered and untutored in coordinated activity could neither hunt large prey nor make war. Equally, however, massive warfare would not be possible without the inventive intelligence that has produced the increasingly sophisticated hardware of human conflict. It is therefore as unhelpful to blame the scourge of war on our cooperativeness as it would be to blame it on our intelligence. To do either is to evade the real issue—those ideological values and behavioral habits on which nations are based, through which governments manipulate their people.

If we wish to, we can change our social structures without any fear of some primal urge welling to the surface and sucking us back into some atavistic pattern. We are, after all, the ultimate expression of a cultural animal; we have not totally broken free of our biological roots, but neither are we ruled by them.

7

The Naked Ape:
An Idea We Could Live Without

BY DAVID PILBEAM

. . . .

Last fall CBS Television broadcast a National Geographic Special, in prime time, called "Monkeys, Apes, and Man." This was an attempt to demonstrate how much studies of primates can tell us about our true biological selves. In a recent *Newsweek* magazine article, Stewart Alsop, while discussing problems of war, stated that nations often quarrel over geo-political real estate when national boundaries are poorly defined: his examples were culled from areas as diverse as the Middle East, Central Europe, and Asia. One of his introductory paragraphs included the following:

"The animal behaviorists—Konrad Lorenz, Robert Ardrey, Desmond Morris—have provided wonderful insights into human behavior. Animals that operate in groups, from fish up to our ancestors among the primates, instinctively establish and defend a territory, or turf. There are two main reasons why fighting erupts between turfs—when the turfs are ill-defined or overlapping; or when one group is so weakened by sickness or other cause as to be unable to defend its turf, thus inviting aggression."

Here Alsop is taking facts (some of them are actually untrue facts) from the field of ethology—which is the science of whole animal behavior as studied in naturalistic environments—and extrapolating directly to man from these ethological facts as though words such as *territoriality, aggression,* and so forth describe the same phenomena in all animal species, including man.

Both these examples from popular media demonstrate nicely what can be called "naked apery." When Charles Darwin first published *The Origin of Species* and *The Descent of Man,* over 100 years ago, few people believed in any kind of biological or evolutionary continuity between men and other primates. Gradually the idea of man's physical evolution from ape- or monkey-like ancestors came to be accepted; yet the concept of human behavioral evolution was always treated with scepticism, or even horror. But times have changed. No longer do we discriminate between rational man, whose behavior is almost wholly learned, and all other species, brutish automata governed solely by instincts.

One of the principal achievements of ethologists, particularly those who study primates, has been to demonstrate the extent to which the dichotomy between instinct and learning is totally inadequate in analyzing the behavior of higher vertebrate species—especially primates. Almost all behavior in monkeys and apes involves a mixture of the learned and the innate; almost all behavior is under some genetic control in that its development is channelled—although the amount of channelling varies. Thus, all baboons of one species will grow up producing much the same range of vocalizations; however, the same sound may have subtly different meanings for members of different troops of the same species. In one area, adult male baboons may defend the troop; those of the identical species in a different

environment may habitually run from danger. Monkeys in one part of their species range may be sternly territorial; one hundred miles away feeding ranges of adjacent groups may overlap considerably and amicably. These differences are due to learning. Man is the learning animal par excellence. We have more to learn, take longer to do it, learn it in a more complex and yet more efficient way (that is, culturally), and have a unique type of communication system (vocal language) to promote our learning. All this the ethologists have made clear.

Studies of human behavior, at least under naturalistic conditions, have been mostly the preserve of social anthropologists and sociologists. The anthropological achievement has been to document the extraordinary lengths to which human groups will go to behave differently from other groups. The term "culture," a special one for the anthropologist, describes the specifically human type of learned behavior in which arbitrary rules and norms are so important. Thus, whether we have one or two spouses, wear black or white to a funeral, live in societies that have kings or lack chiefs entirely, is a function not of our genes but of learning; the matter depends upon which learned behaviors we deem appropriate—again because of learning. Some behaviors make us feel comfortable, others do not; some behaviors may be correct in one situation and not in another—forming a line outside a cinema as opposed to the middle of the sidewalk, for example; singing rather than whistling in church; talking to domestic animals but not to wild ones. The appropriate or correct behavior varies from culture to culture; exactly which one is appropriate is arbitrary. This sort of behavior is known as "context dependent behavior" and is, in its learned form, pervasively and almost uniquely human. So pervasive is it, indeed, that we are unaware most of the time of the effects on our behavior of context dependence. It is important to realize here that although a great deal of ape and monkey behavior is learned, little of it is context dependent in a cultural, human sense.

In the past ten years there has been a spate of books—the first of the genre was Robert Ardrey's *African Genesis* published in 1961—that claim first to describe man's "real" or "natural" behavior in ethological style, then go on to explain how these behaviors have evolved. In order to do this, primate societies are used as models of earlier stages of human evolution: primates are ourselves, so to speak, unborn. *African Genesis, The Territorial Imperative, The Social Contract,* all by Ardrey, *The Naked Ape* and *The Human Zoo* by Desmond Morris, Konrad Lorenz's *On Aggression,* the exotic, *The Descent of Woman,* by Elaine Morgan, plus Antony Jay's *Corporate Man,* without exception, for some reason approach the bestseller level. All purport to document the supposedly surprising truth that man is an animal. The more extreme of them also argue that his behavior—particularly his aggressive, status-oriented,

Reprinted by permission from *Discovery* (Peabody Museum of Natural History, Yale University), Vol. 7, No. 2, 1972, pp. 63–70.

territorial and sexual behavior—is somehow out of tune with the needs of the modern world, that these behaviors are under genetic control and are largely determined by our animal heritage, and that there is little we can do but accept our grotesque natures; if we insist on trying to change ourselves, we must realize that we have almost no room for maneuver, for natural man is far more like other animals than he would care to admit. Actually, it is of some anthropological interest to inquire exactly why this naked apery should have caught on. Apart from our obsessive neophilia, and the fact that these ideas are somehow "new," they provide attractive excuses for our unpleasant behavior toward each other.

However, I believed these general arguments to be wrong; they are based upon misinterpretation of ethological studies and of the rich variety of human behavior documented by anthropologists. At a time when so many people wish to reject the past because it has no meaning and can contribute nothing, it is perhaps a little ironic that arguments about man's innate and atavistic depravity should have so much appeal. The world *is* in a mess; people *are* unpleasant to each other; that much is true. I can only suppose that argument about the inevitability of all the nastiness not only absolves people in some way of the responsibility for their actions, but allows us also to sit back and positively enjoy it all. Let me illustrate my argument a little.

Take, for example, one particular set of ethological studies—those on baboons. Baboons are large African monkeys that live today south of the Sahara in habitats ranging from tropical rain forest to desert. They are the animals that have been most frequently used as models of early human behavior; a lot of work has been done on them, and they are easy to study—at least those living in the savannah habitats thought to be typical of the hunting territories of early man. They are appealing to ethologists because of their habitat, because they live in discrete and structured social groups, and because they have satisfied so many previous hypotheses.

Earlier reports of baboon behavior emphasized the following. Baboons are intensely social creatures, living in discrete troops of 30 to 50 animals, their membership rarely changing; they are omnivorous, foraging alone and rarely sharing food. Males are twice as big as females; they are stronger and more aggressive. The functions of male aggression supposedly are for repelling predators, for maintaining group order, and (paradoxically) for fighting among themselves. The adult males are organized into a dominance hierarchy, the most dominant animal being the one that gets his own way as far as food, grooming partners, sex, when to stop and eat, and when and where the troop should move are concerned. He is the most aggressive, wins the most fights, and impregnates the most desirable females. Females, by the way, do little that is exciting in baboondom, but sit around having babies, bickering, and tending to their lords. Adult males are clearly the most important animals—although they cannot have the babies—and they are highly status conscious. On the basis of fighting abilities they form themselves into a dominance hierarchy, the function of which is to reduce aggression by the controlling means of each animal knowing its own place in the hierarchy. When groups meet up, fighting may well ensue. When the troop moves, males walk in front and at the rear; when the group is attacked, adult males remain to fight a rearguard action as females and young animals flee to safety in the trees.

Here then we have in microcosm one view of the way our early ancestors may well have behaved. How better to account for the destructiveness of so much human male aggression, to justify sex differences in behavior, status seeking, and so forth. I exaggerate, of course, but not too much. But what comments can be made?

First, the baboons studied—and these are the groups that are described, reported, and extrapolated from in magazine articles, books, and in CBS TV specials—are probably abnormal. They live in game parks—open country where predators, especially human ones, are present in abundance—and are under a great deal of tension. The same species has been studied elsewhere—in the open country and in forest too, away from human contact—with different results.

Forest groups of baboons are fluid, changing composition regularly (rather than being tightly closed); only adult females and their offspring remain to form the core of a stable group. Food and cover are dispersed, and there is little fighting over either. Aggression in general is very infrequent, and male dominance hierarchies are difficult to discern. Intertroop encounters are rare, and friendly. When the troop is startled (almost invariably by humans, for baboons are probably too smart, too fast, and too powerful to be seriously troubled by other predators), it flees, and, far from forming a rearguard, the males—being biggest and strongest—are frequently up the trees long before the females (encumbered as they are with their infants).

When the troop moves it is the adult females that determine when and where to; and as it moves adult males are not invariably to be found in front and at the rear. As for sexual differences, in terms of functionally important behaviors, the significant dichotomy seems to be not between males and females but between adults and young. This makes good sense for animals that learn and live a long time.

The English primatologist Thelma Rowell, who studied some of these forest baboons in Uganda, removed a troop of them and placed them in cages where food had to be given a few times a day in competition-inducing clumps. Their population density went up and cover was reduced. The result? More aggression, more fighting, and the emergence of marked dominance hierarchies. So, those first baboons probably were under stress, in a relatively impoverished environment, pestered by humans of various sorts. The high degree of aggression, the hierarchies, the rigid sex-role differences, were in a sense abnormalities. In one respect, troop defense, there is accumulating evidence that male threats directed toward human interlopers occur only after troops become habituated to the observers, and must therefore be treated as learned behavior too.

Studies on undisturbed baboons elsewhere have shown other interesting patterns of adult male behaviors. Thus in one troop an old male baboon with broken canines was the animal that most frequently completed successful matings, that influenced troop movements, and served as a focus for females and infants, even though he was far less aggressive than, and frequently lost fights with, a younger and more vigorous adult male. Here, classical dominance criteria simply do not tie together as they are supposed to.

The concept of dominance is what psychologists call a unitary motivational theory: there are two such theories purporting to explain primate social behavior. These are that the sexual bond ties the group together, and that social dominance structures and orders the troop. The first of these theories has been shown to be wrong. The second we are beginning to realize is too simplistic. In undisturbed species in the wild, dominance hierarchies are hard to discern, if they are present at all; yet workers still persist in trying to find them. For example, Japanese primatologists describe using the "peanut test" to determine "dominance" in wild chimpanzees by seeing which chimp gets the goodies. Yet what relevance does such a test have for real chimp behavior in the wild where the animals have far more important things to do—in an evolutionary or truly biological sense—than fight over peanuts? Such an experimental design implies too the belief that "dominance" is something lurking just beneath the surface, waiting for the appropriate releaser.

Steven Gartlan, an English primatologist working in the Cameroons, has recently suggested a different way of analyzing behavior, in terms of function. Each troop has to survive and reproduce, and in order to do so it must find food, nurture its mothers, protect and give its young the opportunity to learn adult skills. There are certain tasks that have to be completed if successful survival is to result. For example, the troop must be led, fights might be stopped, lookouts kept, infants fed and protected; some animals must serve as social foci, others might be needed to chase away intruders, and so on. Such an attribute list can be extended indefinitely.

If troop behavior is analyzed in a functional way like this, it immediately becomes clear that different classes of animals perform different functions. Thus, in undisturbed baboons, adults, particularly males, police the troop; males, especially the subadults and young adults, maintain vigilance; adult females determine the time and direction of movement; younger animals, especially infants, act as centers of attention.

Thus a particular age-sex class performs a certain set of behaviors that go together and that fulfill definite adaptive needs. Such a constellation of behavioral attributes is termed a role. Roles, even in nonhuman primates, are quite variable. (Witness the great differences between male behaviors in normal baboon troops and those under stress.) If dominance can come and go with varying intensities of certain environmental pressures, then it is clearly not innately inevitable, even in baboons. Rigid dominance hierarchies, then, seem to be largely artifacts of abnormal environments.

What is particularly interesting in the newer animal studies is the extent to which aggression, priority of access, and leadership are divorced from each other. Although a baboon may be highly aggressive, what matters most is how other animals react to him; if they ignore him as far as functionally important behaviors such as grooming, mating and feeding are concerned, then his aggression is, in a social or evolutionary sense, irrelevant.

I want to look a little more closely at aggression, again from the functional point of view. What does it do? What is the point of a behavior that can cause so much trouble socially?

The developmental course of aggressive behavior has been traced in a number of species: among primates it is perhaps best documented in rhesus macaques, animals very similar to baboons. There are genetical and hormonal bases to aggressive behavior in macaques; in young animals males are more aggressive, on the average, than females, and this characteristic is apparently related to hormonal influences. If animals are inadequately or abnormally socialized, aggressive behaviors become distorted and exaggerated. Animals that are correctly socialized in normal habitats, or richly stimulating artificial ones, show moderate amounts of aggression, and only in certain circumstances. These would be, for example, when an infant is threatened, when a choice item is disputed, when fights have to be interrupted, under certain circumstances when the troop is threatened, and occasionally when other species are killed for food.

Under normal conditions, aggression plays little part in other aspects of primate social life. The idea that the function of maleness is to be overbearingly aggressive, to fight constantly, and to be dominant, makes little evolutionary sense.

How about extrapolations from primates to man that the "naked-apers" are so fond of? Take, for example, dominance. Everything that I have said about its shortcomings as a concept in analyzing baboon social organization applies to man, only more so. Behaviors affecting status-seeking in man are strongly influenced by learning, as we can see by the wide variation in human behavior from one society to another. In certain cultures, status is important, clear-cut, and valued; the emphasis placed on caste in Hindu society is an obvious example. At the opposite extreme, though—among the Bushmen of the Kalahari Desert, for example—it is hard to discern; equality and cooperativeness are highly valued qualities in Bushman society, and hence learned by each new generation.

I've used the term "status-seeking" rather than "dominance" for humans, because it describes much better the kind of hierarchical ordering one finds within human groups. And that points to a general problem in extrapolating from monkey to man, for "status" is a word that one can't easily apply to baboon or chimp society; status involves prestige, and prestige presupposes values—arbitrary rules or norms. That sort of behavior is cultural, human, and practically unique.

As we turn to man, let's consider for a while human groups as they were before the switch to a settled way of life began a mere—in evolutionary terms—10,000 years ago. Before that our ancestors were hunters and gatherers. Evidence for this in the form of stone tool making, living areas with butchered game, camp sites, and so on, begins to turn up almost 3 million years ago, at a time when our ancestors were very different physically from us. For at least 2½ to 3 million years, man and his ancestors have lived as hunters and gatherers. The change from hunting to agricultural-based economies began, as I said, just over 10,000 years ago, a fractional moment on the geological time scale. That famous (and overworked) hypothetical visiting Martian geologist of the 21st century would find remains of hunters represented in hundreds of feet of sediments; the first evidence for agriculture, like the remains of the thermonuclear holocaust, would be jammed, together, in the last few inches. Hunting and gathering has been a highly significant event in human history; indeed, it is believed by most of us interested in human evolution to have been an absolutely vital determinant, molding many aspects of human behavior.

There are a number of societies surviving today that still live as hunters and gatherers; Congo pygmies, Kalahari Bushmen, and Australian Aborigines, are three well-known examples. When comparisons are made of these hunting societies, we can see that certain features are typical of most or all of them, and these features are likely to have been typical of earlier hunters.

In hunting societies, families—frequently monogamous nuclear families—are often grouped together in bands of 20 to 40 individuals; members of these hunting bands are kinsmen, either by blood or marriage. The band hunts and gathers over wide areas, and its foraging range often overlaps those of adjacent groups. Bands are flexible and variable in composition—splitting and reforming with changes in the seasons, game and water availability, and whim.

Far from life being "nasty, brutish, and short" for these peoples, recent studies show that hunters work on the average only 3 or 4 days each week; the rest of their time is leisure. Further, at least 10% of Bushmen, for example, are over 60 years of age, valued and nurtured by their children. Although they lack large numbers of material possessions, one can never describe such peoples as savages, degenerates, or failures.

The men in these societies hunt animals while the women gather plant food. However, women often scout for game, and in some groups may also hunt smaller animals, while a man returning empty-handed from a day's hunting will almost always gather vegetable food on his way. Thus the division of labor between sexes is not distinct and immutable; it seems to be functional, related to mobility: the women with infants to protect and carry simply cannot move far and fast enough to hunt efficiently.

Relations between bands are amicable; that makes economic sense as the most efficient way of utilizing potentially scarce resources, and also because of exogamy—marrying out—for adjacent groups will contain kinsmen and kinsmen will not fight. Within the group, individual relations between adults are cooperative and based upon reciprocity; status disputes are avoided. These behaviors are formalized, part of cultural behavior, in that such actions are positively valued and rewarded. Aggression between individuals is generally maintained at the level of bickering; in cases where violence flares, hunters generally solve the problem by fission: the band divides.

Data on child-rearing practices in hunters are well known only in Bushmen, and we don't yet know to what extent Bushmen are typical of hunters. (This work on Bushman child-rearing, as yet unpublished, has been done by Patricia Draper, an anthropologist at the University of New Mexico, and I am grateful to her for permitting me to use her data.) Bushman children are almost always in the company of adults; because of the small size of Bushman societies, children rarely play in large groups with others of their own age. Aggression is minimal in the growing child for two principal reasons. First, arguments between youngsters almost inevitably take place in the presence of adults and adults always break these up before fights erupt; so the socialization process gives little opportunity for practicing aggressive behavior. Second, because of the reciprocity and cooperativeness of adults, children have few adult models on which to base the learning of aggressiveness.

Thus, the closest we can come to a concept of "natural man" would indicate that our ancestors were, like other primates, capable of being aggressive, but they would have been socialized culturally in such a way as to reduce as far as possible the manifestation of aggression. This control through learning is much more efficient in man than in other primates, because we are cultural creatures—with the ability to attach positive values to aggression-controlling behaviors. Thus Bushmen value and thereby encourage peaceful cooperation. Their culture provides the young with non-violent models.

Other cultures promote the very opposite. Take, for example, the Yanomamö Indians of Venezuela and Brazil; their culture completely reverses our ideals of "good" and "desirable." To quote a student of Yanomamö society: "A high capacity for rage, a quick flash point, and a willingness to use violence to obtain one's ends are considered desirable traits." In order to produce the appropriate adult behaviors, the Yanomamö encourage their children, especially young boys, to argue, fight, and be generally belligerent. These behaviors, I should emphasize, are learned, and depend for their encouragement upon specific cultural values.

Our own culture certainly provides the young with violent, though perhaps less obtrusive, models. These I should emphasize again, are to a great extent learned and arbitrary, and we *could* change them should we choose to do so.

So far we have seen that fierce aggression and status-seeking are no more "natural" attributes of man than they are of most monkey and ape societies. The degree to which such behaviors are developed depends very considerably indeed upon cultural values and learning.

Territoriality likewise is not a "natural" feature of human group living; nor is it among most other primates.

As a parting shot, let me mention one more topic that is of great interest to everyone at the moment—sex roles. Too many of us have in the past treated the male and female stereotypes of our particular culture as fixed and "natural": in our genes so to speak. It may well be true that human male infants play a little more vigorously than females, or that they learn aggressive behaviors somewhat more easily, because of hormonal differences. But simply look around the world at other cultures. In some, "masculinity" and "femininity" are much more marked than they are in our own culture; in others the roles are blurred. As I said earlier, among Bushmen that are still hunters, sex roles are far from rigid, and in childhood the two sexes have a very similar upbringing. However, among those Bushmen that have adopted a sedentary life devoted to herding or agriculture, sex roles are much more rigid. Men devote their energies to one set of tasks, women to another, mutually exclusive set. Little boys learn only "male" tasks, little girls exclusively "female" ones. Maybe the switch to the sedentary life started man on the road toward marked sex role differences. These differences are almost entirely learned, and heavily affected by economic factors.

So much of human role behavior is learned that we could imagine narrowing or widening the differences almost as much or as little as we wish.

So, what conclusions can be drawn from all this? It is overly simplistic in the extreme to believe that man behaves in strongly genetically deterministic ways, when we know that apes and monkeys do not. Careful ethological work shows us that the primates closely related to us—chimps and baboons are the best known—get on quite amicably together under natural and undisturbed conditions. Learning plays a very significant part in the acquisition of their behavior. They are not for the most part highly aggressive, obsessively dominance-oriented, territorial creatures.

There is no evidence to support the view that early man was a violent status-seeking creature; ethological and anthropological evidence indicates rather that pre-urban men would have used their evolving cultural capacities to channel and control aggression. To be sure, we are not born empty slates upon which anything can be written; but to believe in the "inevitability of beastliness" is to deny our humanity as well as our primate heritage—and, incidentally, does a grave injustice to the "beasts."

8

Sharing in Human Evolution

BY JANE B. LANCASTER AND PHILLIP WHITTEN

. . . .

"There is evidence," wrote famed ethologist Konrad Lorenz in 1963, "that the first inventors of pebble tools—the African australopithecines—promptly used their weapons to kill not only game, but fellow members of their species as well. Peking Man, the Prometheus who learned to preserve fire, used it to roast his brothers: beside the first traces of the regular use of fire lie the . . . roasted bones of *Sinanthropus pekinensis* himself."

Thus was promulgated the view of humans as clothes-wearing "killer apes." Despite the fact that this concept ignores a vast array of cultural anthropological data and relies on misinterpretations and erroneous extrapolations of ethological observations, it undoubtedly has caught on. Books by Lorenz (*On Aggression, Behind the Mirror*), Robert Ardrey (*African Genesis, The Territorial Imperative, The Social Contract*), Desmond Morris (*The Naked Ape, The Human Zoo*), Lionel Tiger and Robin Fox (*Men in Groups*), and others all have sold remarkably well—some even making the best-seller charts. According to this view, humans, unlike their primate relatives, are innately territorial and warlike. Indeed, it is argued, this unique propensity for killing and violence is the one most responsible for our evolutionary success.

Proponents of the killer-ape theory make what appears at first glance to be a strong case. One does not need to look far to find evidence of human violence and destruction. In fact, however, the theory is wrong on both counts: aggression is *not* the characteristic that distinguished our early ancestors from the apes; and humans are *not* the only primates who kill their fellows.

Jane Goodall and her colleagues in Tanzania's Gombe Stream Reserve have observed a community of chimpanzees that split in two in 1970. By 1972 the observers noted a cooling of relations between the two groups. In 1974 several males from the original group attacked a single male from the splinter group, beating him savagely for about twenty minutes until he died. Since that time, a series of brutal gang attacks—including one in which a rock was thrown at a prostrate victim—has completely wiped out the second chimp community (*Science News*, 1978).

If aggression is not the trait that distinguished our forebears from other primates, what is? The answer lies in a distinctively human characteristic—sharing—and the evolutionary mechanism that made it possible.

BIPEDALISM

Sometime between five and ten million years ago our ancestors began to spend much of their time on the ground, walking on two legs. Long before we had developed large brains, before we had language with which to communicate, and before we could manipulate the environment to our own ends, we were bipedal.

Bipedalism was one of the earliest evolutionary changes that distinguished the human way of life from that of the ape. Some experts claim that hominids (the family of primates that includes human beings and our earlier fossil ancestors) first stood in order to run, or to fight, or to free their hands for using tools. But these scenarios are unlikely. The first adventurers on two legs, like toddlers learning to walk, were probably very clumsy and inefficient. Such awkwardness would be of little value in combat or in flight. Similarly, tool using by itself cannot explain the significance of bipedalism, since tools can be used as easily while sitting down as standing up. More likely the adaptive value of bipedalism lay in the social behavior that it helped bring about—cooperation and sharing.

Walking on the hindlimbs while clutching food to be shared with others in the forelimbs would have been an advantage to a primate group utilizing a large home range. In this context, bipedalism could evolve slowly over hundreds of thousands of years—as it undoubtedly did. Thus, rather than being violent killer apes, our ancestors—and we—can more accurately be described as *sharing* apes.

Unfortunately, we know very little about the original differentiation and emergence of the human family. The period between five and ten million years ago is virtually an archaeological blank. The fossil record picks up about four and a half million years ago with scraps of hominid bone and teeth, and later with simple stone tools. By about three to one-and-a-half million years ago, a new way of life had been firmly established—a way of life fundamentally different from that of the apes and distinctly human in its broadest features. This original adaptive system of the hominids was very successful, lasting several million years—most of the history of the human line.

There are only a limited number of ways we can use to reconstruct this stage in human evolution. The archaeological record, though reasonably full, is limited to accidents of preservation. However, we can expand our interpretation of the record by making judicious comparisons between the behavior of humans and of our closest living relatives, monkeys and apes. Other evidence can be gleaned from studies of the world's few remaining hunting-and-gathering societies.

THE BASIC PRIMATE PATTERN

There are few generalizations that can be made about all the higher primates. But some patterns seem to be so widespread among the Old World monkeys and apes that we can cautiously assume they must be very ancient and fundamental to the higher primate adaptation of life in social groups. The most significant of these patterns is the relationship between young animals and adults.

In all higher primate species, young animals spend years in physical and social dependence upon adults. This long dependence begins at birth, when the newborn first establishes a close one-to-one relationship with its mother. Unlike many other mammals, higher primates are not born into litters and hidden away in dens or nests. Instead, a single offspring is born, which for the first months of its life stays continuously in contact with its mother, clinging to her while she is moving, and resting in her arms to sleep. As Blurton-Jones (1972)

has pointed out, adaptations for continuous contact with mother involve many different anatomical, physiological and behavioral systems. These range from the anatomy of the hands and feet, distribution of body fat, composition of breast milk, sleep and sucking patterns, ease of satiation, tendency to vocalize, to the need for body contact for feeling secure.

Although this basic pattern holds true for all the higher primates (Old World monkeys, apes, and humans), there is a striking contrast in how this continuous contact relationship between mother and infant is maintained. Among all the Old World monkeys the responsibility of maintaining the relationship rests heavily with the infant. From the moment of birth, an infant monkey must be able to cling to its mother for long periods of time while she feeds, travels, grooms, or even leaps to safety. Infants unable to maintain body contact are likely to be eliminated through accident or predation from the gene pool. Monkeys need all four limbs for locomotion; clutching a weak or sick infant to the chest while trying to hobble on three legs is difficult and leaves the pair vulnerable to predators.

The same basic pattern is true for the great apes—though newborn apes are less developed than monkeys and are poor at clinging for the first few weeks of life. Mother apes help their poorly coordinated infants by walking on three legs and by restricting their movements and social interactions for several weeks after giving birth.

The close, continuous relationship between mother and infant gradually loosens as the infant is weaned and gains independence in locomotion. Once a young monkey or ape is weaned, it has sole responsibility for feeding and drinking. If it is too weak from illness or injury to do so, it will die before the concerned eyes of its mother. The mother will defend her youngster, groom it, sleep with it cradled in her arms, but feeding it solid foods is beyond her comprehension. Although isolated instances of food sharing among chimpanzees have been observed, basically the nonhuman primates are individual foragers.

In contrast with their early independence in feeding behavior, young monkeys and apes are dependent upon adults for protection for many years. Young primates remain at least until puberty in the safety of the group in which they were born; many never leave it. The prolonged period of juvenile development occurs in all the higher primates. During the years of development, the young primate has plenty of time to play, as well as to learn and practice the social and physical skills needed in adulthood.

CHIMPANZEE AND HUMAN BEHAVIOR

The general cleverness of chimpanzees has long been known. But it was not until the long-term field studies in Central Africa that particularly humanlike aspects of chimpanzee behavior were observed (Goodall, 1976; van Lawick-Goodall, 1971; Teleki, 1974, 1975). One of the most striking of these was the wide variety of tool use by chimpanzees in everyday life. These tools include the now-famous grass blades, vines or sticks used to "fish" for ants and termites in their nests; leaf sponges used to collect water, honey or wipe dirt off the body; twigs and sticks used to investigate and probe unfamiliar objects; rough hammer stones used to break open nuts; leafy twigs used as fly whisks; and finally sticks, stones and vegetation used as missiles in aggressive display. Chimpanzee tool use is similar to human in the sense that tools are an adaptive means to meet a wide variety of problems posed by the environment.

One of the marked differences between the use of tools by humans and chimpanzees is in the casualness and impermanence of the ape's tools. Although chimpanzees make their own tools in the sense that they strip a stick of leaves and side branches or chew up a mass of leaves for a sponge, they do not try to keep a particularly well-made tool for future use. Chimpanzees discard their tools because it is difficult for them to carry anything for long distances. When Goodall and her colleagues established a central feeding station at the Gombe Stream Reserve that provided bananas for the wild chimpanzees in the area, many came to load up a supply of bananas. They tried to carry bananas in every possible way: held in their mouths, hands and feet, tucked under armpits and chins, even slipped between flexed thighs and groins. Loaded up in this way, they retreated to climb nearby trees, dropping bananas every step of the way.

Another aspect of chimpanzee behavior that has excited students of human evolution is their sporadic attempts at the collective killing of small game. Sometimes these hunts involve several adult and subadult males who coordinate their movements to encircle the prey, some acting as diversions while others slip close enough to dash in for the capture. Prey (usually small gazelles) are killed and eaten immediately, the participants in the hunt dividing the prey simply by tearing it to pieces. Latecomers may get a mouthful by persistent attempts to pull off a piece or by begging.

The killing and eating of meat is clearly a special event in chimpanzee life. Witnesses of a kill show great interest and excitement and a clear desire for even a taste. The highly social, as opposed to nutritional, nature of chimpanzee cooperative killing and eating of prey has been noted by Geza Teleki (1975), who observed that a dozen or more chimpanzees may take a whole day to consume an animal weighing less than 10 kg (22 lbs). The small size of game killed by primates (baboons have also been reported to hunt small mammals on occasion) is very striking. The largest prey is under 10 kg—well under the body weight of an individual hunter. Shared foods are most often minuscule scraps, more social tokens than major sources of protein.

In spite of their tool use and hunting, the behavior of modern chimpanzees still fits squarely into the pattern described earlier for other primates. They are in no way quasi human. Like other monkeys and apes, they are basically individual foragers who live in long-term social groups. The infant is dependent on the mother for many years, but this relationship is based on a physical and psychological need for the mother's protection. Once weaned, young chimpanzees feed themselves. The basic diet is typical of many primates living in the tropics: vegetables, fruits and nuts, with some animal protein in the form of insects, small vertebrates and occasional small mammals. The important contrast between the feeding habits of human and nonhuman primates is not so much in what is eaten; rather it lies in whether each individual must forage for itself or whether there is a collective responsibility for gathering and sharing food between adults and young.

MODERN HUNTER-GATHERERS

In recent years the ways of life of hunter-gatherers have attracted renewed interest (Lee and Devore, 1968, 1976). Although only a few hunting-gathering groups remain in the modern world, they take on special significance when it is recalled that fully ninety-nine percent of human history was spent in the hunting-gathering stage. The peculiar demands of this life-style may well have left imprints on modern human biology and behavior.

There are certain ecological relationships and social behaviors found in all known tropical hunter-gatherers, which stand out in sharp relief when contrasted with the behavior of monkeys and apes. The first of these is a diet based on a balance of plant and animal foods. This balance is highly flexible and varies according to season, geographic location and long-term cycles in food availability. Our understanding of sex roles and the ecological basis of early human societies has shifted away from an emphasis on females as camp and infant tenders and males as food providers (Isaac, 1976; Tanner and Zihlman, 1976). In the process, our concept of "man, the hunter" has been modified to "humans, the hunter-gatherers."

Data from modern hunter-gatherers in the tropics indicate that meat is an important part of the diet, but always comprises well under fifty percent of the total. The basic day-to-day diet is provided by the collecting efforts of adult women, and consists mainly of vegetable foods and animal protein in the form of insects and nestling birds or eggs. Animal protein in large "packages"—that is, animals weighing over 20 kg—is provided by the efforts of adult males. Hunting, even in the tropics, is a risky occupation. It not only is potentially dangerous, but it is often unpredictable. Richard Lee (quoted in Hassan, 1975:35) found that among the San of the Kalahari, most hunters kill only one or two large animals a year. Among the Hazda of East Africa, as many as half the adult males fail to kill even one large animal a year, and some men kill only one or two in a lifetime. The question of whether or not a growing child eats or starves does not depend on the uncertain hunting success of a few adult males. As Isaac (1971:279) noted some time ago, the evolution of human behavior from a primate pattern involved not simply an increasing intensity of predation, but the unusual development of "a flexible system of joint dependence on plant and animal foods."

It is informative to look at the basic material possessions of a hunting-gathering woman who lives in the tropics. She must be able to carry all her possessions herself when she moves, because men are responsible for their own hunting equipment and for protecting the group. The most important items a woman possesses include a digging stick, a sling or net bag for carrying her infant, and a variety of bark and skin trays and containers for carrying and preparing food. This is all she needs to provide for her family. Significantly, none of these materials leaves a trace in the archaeological record.

The importance of carrying infants in a sling should be underscored because it is a major factor in human evolutionary history. Unlike Old World monkeys and apes, human infants are unable to cling to their mothers. In fact, they are dependent on their mothers to hold them for many months. Hunting-gathering women keep their infants with them continuously during their daily foraging. They use a sling, which suspends the infant from the mother's shoulder while leaving her hands and arms free. It appears that one of the costs our species paid for evolving larger brains was a prolonged period of infant helplessness. The invention of such a simple tool as a skin sling to carry an infant may have been a crucial turning point in human history because it permitted the survival of infants born with small, immature brains and the potential for major growth after birth.

The lives of hunter-gatherers differ sharply from those of other primates in the tropics by virtue of one very important behavior pattern: carrying and sharing. The carrying of infants, tools, or food to be shared allowed our ancestors to shift away from individual foraging to a pattern emphasizing the sharing of gathered and hunted foods within the social group. Among the Kalahari hunter-gatherers plant foods collected by women are shared among close family members. Meat—food which comes in much larger packages—is shared in a larger network.

The success of a system of sharing foods depends on one other behavioral innovation which sets humans off from other primates. This is the evolution of the home base, or camp. A home base need not be permanent. It can be nothing more than an agreed-upon location where members of the group can meet in order to share foods. Many monkeys and apes have favorite clumps of sleeping trees, where they often return for the night. A home base, however, is not just a location for sleeping. Rather it serves a much more important function as the site for the sharing of food among members of the social group. Like the shift from individual foraging to sharing, this represents a way novel among primates of utilizing a niche.

THE ARCHAEOLOGICAL RECORD

Glynn Isaac (1976), an archaeologist at the University of California at Berkeley, suggests that these behavioral elements—a flexible diet of plant and animal foods, food sharing, the carrying of food and equipment, and a home base—form a behavioral platform upon which the distinctly human way of life was established. The evidence for the early building of this behavioral platform comes from the fossil record, although not all elements of the pattern are equally clear. Accidents of preservation, and the bias against perishable plant foods and materials in favor of stone and bone, give a skewed view of the past.

Some of the earliest evidence of the shift in diet from foraging to hunting-gathering can be found at Olduvai Gorge and Koobi Fora in East Africa—sites dating from around three million to one-and-a-half million years ago. Here early stone tools are found in association with broken up mammal bones. These animals range in size from small

rodents to elephants, but it is clear that many are far larger than the 10 kg mentioned by Teleki as the largest prey taken today by nonhuman primates. The dismembering of a large mammal like an elephant or a hippopotamus suggests strongly that meat was not only killed cooperatively, but shared as well.

Evidence about the equipment of early hominids is very limited. Both at Olduvai and Koobi Fora, the two basic classes of stone tools—core tools and flakes—can be found. The rest of the probable technology and equipment of the early hominids—sharpened sticks for digging and stabbing, and slings and nets for carrying and gathering—will probably never be found in the archaeological record. At Olduvai a semi-circular stone windbreak has been discovered, perhaps the oldest structure built by our hominid ancestors. Concentrations of stone tools and broken bones here and at other sites attest to an essential element of the adaptive platform: a home base. The artifacts and bones tend to be located in particular ecological settings: patches about five to twenty meters in diameter, a size similar to the campsites of modern hunter-gatherers. They are usually located next to sandy streams, the kind which today provide strips of shade and are bounded by fruit trees. These bases were home for our remote ancestors. They were places where the hominids gathered together at night for warmth and protection against the great carnivores, and to share food.

The creatures living in these camps were fully bipedal, with brains somewhat larger than might be expected if they were apes. Although their molar teeth were massive by modern standards, there were no protruding canines like those used by other primates in aggression. The relatively small size of their crania clearly shows that the human adaptation of bipedalism, tool use, and home base long preceded the expansion of the brain and elaboration of culture so obvious later in the archaeological record. It is doubtful that these early hominids had language in any modern sense of the word. The small size of the brain argues against it, and their hunting and gathering activities and manufacture of simple tools did not demand language. Their life in small, face-to-face social groups suggests a communication system like that of modern chimpanzees.

SHARING AND SOCIAL ORGANIZATION

The elementary human adaptation, the one upon which all else is built, depends on a simple but unique change in ecological and social relations. This change was the shift from the individual foraging and feeding pattern of other primates to a system of sharing and cooperation, in which adults feed infants and juveniles. Associated with this assumption of responsibility to feed the young was a new economic interdependence between the sexes, one in which females gathered and males hunted. This ancient division of labor, permitting the flexible, joint dependence on plant and animal food, probably accounts for the early success of the first hominids. After all, they were small-sized, small-brained primates moving into a niche already crowded with highly successful group hunters such as lions, hyenas and wild dogs.

It is interesting to speculate on the effect of the economic division of labor on the social organization of early hominids. Comparative studies of Old World monkeys and apes indicate that attachment based on descent is one of the prime organizers of monkey and ape societies (Lancaster, 1975). This ancient principle is based on the attachment of an infant to its mother. In multigenerational primate societies, the early attachment is expanded to include other close relatives and descendents of the mother. It is reasonable to assume that the first social network through which hominids shared food was joined by female links. Much of the food was probably gathered by females. Male hunting must have added a new element to the equation. For the first time in primate evolution, males and females shared responsibility for feeding their offspring. Eventually this mutual economic interest probably led to the formation of a second set of emotional attachments, ones that linked specific males to specific females. It is unlikely that the early hominids had anything like the institution of marriage. But it is not unreasonable to speculate that couples formed special, more-or-less-enduring attachments that facilitated the feeding of offspring.

HUMANS: THE SHARING APES

What distinguishes our own species from our primate relatives is not any innate proclivity toward violence and aggression. Rather we can accurately be described as cultural animals whose outstanding characteristics are cooperation and sharing. What separated our family from the apes was a reorganization of the relationships between the sexes and between adults and young. This shift, which favored cooperative activities, permitted early hominids to exploit a niche new to primates. The ability to exploit this new niche rested on a few, rather simple behavioral patterns. These included bipedalism, the use of tools, the division of labor between male hunters and female gatherers, a home base, and most important—cooperation and sharing.

The archaeological record, the study of modern primates, and the behavior of present-day hunter-gatherers all attest to the significance of sharing in human evolution. It is the rock upon which all human culture is built; it is what makes us human.

REFERENCES

Blurton-Jones, N. 1972. Comparative aspects of mother-child contacts. In N. Blurton-Jones (ed.), *Ethological Studies of Child Behaviour.* London: Cambridge University Press.

Goodall, Jane. 1976. Continuities between chimpanzee and human behaviour. In Isaac and McGown (eds.), *Human Origins.* Menlo Park, CA: Staples Press, pp. 81–96.

Hassan, F.A. 1975. Determination of the size, density, and growth rate of hunting-gathering populations. In S. Polgar (ed.), *Population, Ecology, and Evolution.* The Hague: Mouton, pp. 27–52.

Isaac, Glynn. 1971. The diet of early man: aspects of archaeological evidence from lower and middle Pleistocene sites in Africa. *World Archaeology* 2:278–298.

Isaac, Glynn. 1975. The activities of early African hominids: A review of archaeological evidence from the time span two and a half to one million years ago. In Isaac and McGown (eds.), *op. cit.,* pp. 483–514.

Lancaster, Jane B. 1975. *Primate Behavior and the Emergence of Human Culture.* New York: Holt, Rinehart and Winston.

Van Lawick-Goodall, Jane. 1971. *In the Shadow of Man.* Boston: Houghton Mifflin.

Lee, Richard B. and I. DeVore (eds). 1968. *Man the Hunter.* Chicago: Aldine.

Lee, Richard B. and I. DeVore (eds). 1975. *Kalahari Hunter-Gatherers.* Cambridge, MA: Harvard University Press.

Science News. 1978. Chimp killings: Is it the 'man' in them? *Science News* 113:276.

Tanner, N. and A. Zihlman. 1976. Women in evolution. Part 1: Innovation and selection in human origins. *Signs* 1:385–602.

Teleki, Geza. 1975. Primate subsistence patterns: collector-predators and gatherer-hunters. *Journal of Human Evolution* 4:125–184.

TOPIC FOUR

Human Diversity

....

Since the beginnings of recorded history, the physical differences characterizing human populations have been of interest to both scholars and lay persons. Neontology, the study of the distribution of human biological traits, is a major area of interest of physical anthropologists.

In the eighteenth century, Johann Blumenbach, you will recall from the essay introducing this section, developed rigorous standards for measuring physical traits and used clusters of these measurements to identify "races." The concept of "race" quickly became incorporated into the scientific literature, and much of the research on human diversity has been undertaken using this concept. The term generally means a population that is distinguished from all other groups by virtue of manifesting an aggregate or cluster of innate biological traits. Indeed, the concept of "race" has won general (not just scientific) acceptance—so much so that, if you were to tell your neighbor that human "races" don't exist, you would be dismissed as a fool.

Yet in "The Concept of Race," Ashley Montagu demonstrates the ambiguities of the term "race." He points out that experts on the subject cannot agree either on a definition of the term or on the number of so-called races into which the human species is divided. Further, use of the term tends to distort biological research, and with its static connotations, it is rather incompatible with evolutionary theory (a cornerstone of physical anthropology).

In 1969, Arthur Jensen, an educational psychologist at the University of California at Berkeley, published an article in the *Harvard Educational Review* purporting to show that black people are innately less intelligent than whites. Jensen's conclusions were based in large part on studies by the late British psychologist Sir Cyril Burt—studies that have since been shown to be fraudulent. Nevertheless, Jensen and others have persisted in their attempts to demonstrate a relationship between "race" and intelligence, with devastating social consequences.

In recent years, numerous scientific books and articles have been written in an attempt to answer such questions as: What is "race"? What is the connection between skin color and intelligence? In 1978, biologist Paul R. Ehrlich and psychologist S. Shirley Feldman published a book called *The Race Bomb*, the first book addressed to the educated layperson to tackle these subjects.

Like most scientists, Ehrlich and Feldman see human races as artificial groupings based on skin color and a few other characteristics arbitrarily chosen by the classifier. This reduces the whole question of racial intelligence to one of skin color and IQ, which is as trivial—and as valid—as considering the relationship between eye color (or height or shoe size) and mental ability. It is true, of course, that people vary greatly in numerous characteristics. Some are taller, run farther, swim faster, are darker skinned, or more intelligent than others. Part of these differences can no doubt be explained by the different genetic inheritances of the individuals. But the fact that one individual may be taller or darker-hued than another tells us absolutely nothing about his or her mental ability.

From an anthropological and biological point of view, there is no such thing as "race." Scientists who study human diversity focus not on the characteristics of artificial "races," but rather on the worldwide distribution of specific genes. *Why*, for example, do people from colder climates tend to have lighter colored skin than people from tropical climates? *Why* do people from certain regions of Africa, Asia and southern Europe have a greater likelihood than others to be born with sickle-cell anemia? By studying such questions, physical anthropologists attempt to show the adaptive function a specific gene plays in relationship to specific environmental stresses.

But races have a *social* reality, of course. And this reality can be very powerful indeed. It was the social reality of race that allowed Adolph Hitler to murder six million Jews; it is the social reality of race that permits discrimination against blacks, Orientals, Native Americans, and other groups in our society.

In the United States, a person is socially—and even legally—defined as "black," regardless of personal color-coding, if any known ancestor was black. Thus, former U.S. Senator Edward Brooke invariably is described as "black" despite his light skin color.

Other societies, however, define racial groups differently, as Ehrlich and Feldman point out. Brazil, for example, has a much more flexible system of classification, based on wealth as well as skin color. In Brazil, a "Negro" is any of the following: a poverty-stricken white, a poverty-stricken or poor mulatto, a poverty-stricken black, a poor black, or a black of average wealth. In contrast, a "White" is defined as: a wealthy white, a white of average wealth, a poor white, a wealthy mulatto, a mulatto of average wealth, or a wealthy black. (See the table below.)

Montagu proposes substituting the term "ethnic group" for "race"—an idea with which we agree. However, because the concept of "race" still captures the popular imagination, because people still treat "races" as significant social groupings, and because in our society at least the political economy is "racially" stratified—"races" therefore are socially real entities whose existence must be acknowledged, even if their biological validity is questionable. For this reason, we continue to use the term "race," but we enclose it in quotation marks.

The Social Reality of Race in Brazil

Skin Color	Economic Status			
	Poverty-stricken	Poor	Average Wealth	Wealthy
White	N	W	W	W
Mulatto	N	N	W	W
Black	N	N	N	W

In Brazil, both skin color and economic status are used to determine "race." The groups marked N *in the table are considered Negroes, whereas the groups labeled* W *are considered whites.*

9

The Concept of Race

BY ASHLEY MONTAGU

. . . .

In this paper I desire to examine the concepts of a race as they are used with reference to man. I shall first deal with the use of this term by biologists and anthropologists, and then with its use by the man-on-the-street, the so-called layman—so-called, no doubt, from the lines in Sir Philip Sidney's sonnet:

> I never drank of Aganippe well
> Nor ever did in shade of Tempe sit,
> And Muses scorn with vulgar brains to dwell;
> Poor layman I, for sacred rites unfit.

I shall endeavor to show that all those who continue to use the term "race" with reference to man, whether they be laymen or scientists, are "for sacred rites unfit." Once more, I shall, as irritatingly as the sound of a clanging door heard in the distance in a wind that will not be shut out, raise the question as to whether, with reference to man, it would not be better if the term "race" were altogether abandoned.

At the outset it should, perhaps, be made clear that I believe, with most biologists, that evolutionary factors, similar to those that have been operative in producing raciation in other animal species, have also been operative in the human species—but with a significant added difference, namely, the consequences which have resulted from man's entry into that unique zone of adaptation in which he excels beyond all other creatures, namely *culture*, that is to say, the man-made part of the environment.

On the evidence it would seem clear that man's cultural activities have introduced elements into the processes of human evolution which have so substantially modified the end-products that one can no longer equate the processes of raciation in lower animals with the related processes which have occurred in the evolution of man. The factors of mutation, natural selection, drift, isolation, have all been operative in the evolution of man. But so have such factors as ever-increasing degrees of mobility, hybridization, and social selection, and it is the effects of these and similar factors which, at least so it has always seemed to me, makes the employment of the term "race" inapplicable to most human populations as we find them today.

Of course there exist differences, but we want a term by which to describe the existence of these differences. We do not want a prejudiced term which injects meanings which are not there into the differences. We want a term which as nearly mirrors the conditions as a term can, not one which falsifies and obfuscates the issue.

Terminology is extremely important, and I think it will be generally agreed that it is rather more desirable to allow the conditions or facts to determine the meaning of the terms by which we shall refer to them, than to have pre-existing terms determine the manner in which they shall be perceived and ordered, for pre-existing terms constitute pre-existing meanings, and such meanings have a way of conditioning the manner in which what we look at shall be perceived. Each time the term "race" is used with reference to man, this is what, I think, is done.

The term "race" has a long and tortured history. We cannot enter upon that here. The present-day usage of the term in biological circles is pretty much the sense in which it was used in similar circles in the 19th century, namely, as a subdivision of a species the members of which resemble each other and differ from other members of the species in certain traits. In our own time valiant attempts have been made to pour new wine into the old bottles. The shape of the bottle, however, remains the same. The man-on-the-street uses the term in much the same way as it was used by his 19th century compeer. Here physical type, heredity, blood, culture, nation, personality, intelligence, and achievement are all stirred together to make the omelet which is the popular conception of "race." This is a particularly virulent term, the epidemiology of which is far better understood by the social scientist than by the biologist—who should, therefore, exercise somewhat more restraint and rather more caution than he usually does when he delivers himself on the subject.

The difficulty with taking over old terms in working with problems to which they are thought to apply is that when this is done we may also take over some of the old limitations of the term, and this may affect our approach to the solution of these problems. For what the investigator calls "the problem of human races" is immediately circumscribed and delimited the moment he uses the word "races." For "race" implies something very definite to him, something which in itself constitutes a solution, and the point I would like to make is that far from the problem meaning something like a solution to him, it should, on the contrary, constitute itself in his mind as something more closely resembling what it is, namely, a problem requiring investigation.

Instead of saying to himself, as the true believer in "race" does, "Here is a population, let me see how it fits my criteria of 'race,'" I think it would be much more fruitful of results if he said to himself, instead, "Here is a population, let me go ahead and find out what it is like. What its internal likenesses and differences are, and how it resembles and how it differs from other populations. And then let me operationally describe what I have found," that is, in terms of the data themselves, and not with reference to the conditions demanded by any pre-existing term.

The chief objection to the term "race" with reference to man is that it takes for granted as solved problems which are far from being so and tends to close the mind to problems to which it should always remain open. If, with ritual fidelity, one goes on repeating long enough that "the Nordics" are a race, or that "the Armenoids" are, or that "the Jews" are, or that races may be determined by their blood group gene frequencies, we have already determined what a "race" is, and it is not going to make the slightest difference whether one uses the old or the new wine, for we are back at the same old stand pouring it into the old bottles covered with the same patina of moss-like green.

It is the avoidance of this difficulty that T. H. Huxley had in mind when in 1865, he wrote, "I speak of 'persistent modifications' or 'stocks' rather than of 'varieties,' or 'races,' or 'species,' because each of these last well-known terms implies, on the part of its employer, a preconceived opinion touching one of those problems, the solution of which is the ultimate object of the science; and in regard to which, therefore, ethnologists are especially bound to keep their minds open and their judgements freely balanced" (1895:209–10).

It is something to reflect upon that, a century later, this point of view has still to be urged.

In the year 1900, the French anthropologist Joseph Deniker published his great book, simultaneously in French and in English, *The Races of Man*. But though the title has the word in it, he objected to the term "race" on much the same grounds as Huxley. The whole of his introduction is devoted to showing the difficulties involved in applying to man the terms of zoological nomenclature. He writes, "We have presented to us Arabs, Swiss, Australians, Bushmen, English, Siouan Indians, Negroes, etc., without knowing if each of these groups is on an equal footing from the point of view of classification."

Do these real and palpable groupings represent unions of individuals which, in spite of some slight dissimilarities, are capable of forming what zoologists call "species," "subspecies," "varieties," in the case of wild animals, or "races" in the case of domestic animals? One need not be a professional anthropologist to reply negatively to this question. They are *ethnic groups* formed by virtue of community of language, religion, social institutions, etc., which have the power of uniting human beings of one or several species, races, or varieties, and are by no means zoological species; they may include human beings of one or of many species, races, or varieties. They are [he goes on to say] theoretic types (1900:2–3).

Writing in 1936 Franz Boas remarked "We talk all the time glibly of races and nobody can give us a definite answer to the question what constitutes a race." And recollecting his early days as a physical anthropologist Boas comments, "When I turned to the consideration of racial problems I was shocked by the formalism of the work. Nobody had tried

to answer the questions why certain measurements were taken, why they were considered significant, whether they were subject to other influences." (1936:140).

When, in the same year, 1936, Julian Huxley and A. C. Haddon published their valuable book on "race," *We Europeans*, they took pains to underscore the fact that "the existence of . . . human sub-species is purely hypothetical. Nowhere does a human group now exist which corresponds closely to a systematic sub-species in animals, since various original sub-species have crossed repeatedly and constantly. For the existing populations, the non-committal term *ethnic group* should be used. . . . All that exists today is a number of arbitrary ethnic groups, intergrading into each other" (1936:106). And finally, "The essential reality of the existing situation . . . is not the hypothetical sub-species or races, but the *mixed ethnic groups*, which can never be genetically purified into their original components, or purged of the variability which they owe to past crossing. Most anthropological writings of the past, and many of the present fail to take account of this fundamental fact" (1936:108). "If *race* is a scientific term," these authors point out, "it must have a genetic meaning" (1936:114).

Haddon, as an anthropologist, was familiar with Deniker's book, and it is possible that the noncommittal term "ethnic group" was remembered by him as one more appropriately meeting the requirements of the situation and thus came to be adopted by both authors in their book. It was from this source, that is from Huxley and Haddon, that I, in turn, adopted the term "ethnic group" in 1936 and have consistently continued to use it since that time. The claim is that the noncommittal general term "ethnic group" meets the realities of the situation head on, whereas the term "race" does not. Furthermore, it is claimed that "ethnic group" is a term of heuristic value. It raises questions, and doubts, leading to clarification and discovery. The term "race," since it takes for granted what requires to be demonstrated within its own limits, closes the mind on all that.

It is of interest to find that quite a number of biologists have, in recent years, independently raised objections to the continuing use of the term "race," even, in some cases, when it is applied to populations of lower animals. Thus, for example, W. T. Calman writes, "Terms such as 'geographical race,' 'form,' 'phase,' and so forth, may be useful in particular instances but are better not used until some measure of agreement is reached as to their precise meaning" (1949:14). Hans Kalmus writes, "A very important term which was originally used in systematics is 'race.' Nowadays, however, its use is avoided as far as possible in genetics" (1948:45). In a later work Kalmus writes, "It is customary to discuss the local varieties of humanity in terms of 'race.' However, it is unnecessary to use this greatly debased word, since it is easy to describe populations without it" (1958:30). G. S. Carter writes that the terms "'race,' 'variety,' and 'form' are used so loosely and in so many senses that it is advisable to avoid using them as infraspecific categories (1951:163). Ernst Hanhart objects to the use of the term "race" with reference to man since he holds that there are no "true races" among men (1953:545). Abercrombie, Hickman, and Johnson, in their *A Dictionary of Biology* (1951), while defining species and subspecies consistently, decline even a mention of the word "race" anywhere in their book. L. S. Penrose in an otherwise highly favorable review of Dunn and Dobzhansky's excellent *Heredity, Race and Society*, writes that he is unable "to see the necessity for the rather apologetic retention of the obsolete term 'race,' when what is meant is simply a given population differentiated by some social, geographical or genetical character, or . . . merely by a gene frequency peculiarity. The use of the almost mystical concept of race makes the presentation of the facts about the geographical and linguistic groups . . . unnecessarily complicated" (1952:252).

To see what Penrose means, and at the same time to make our criticism of their conception of "race," let us turn to Dunn and Dobzhansky's definition of race. They write, in the aforementioned work, "Races can be defined as populations which differ in the frequencies of some gene or genes" (1952:118). This definition at once leads to the question: Why use the word "race" here when what is being done is precisely what should be done, namely, to describe populations in terms of their gene frequency differences? What, in point of fact, has the antiquated, mystical conception of "race" to do with this? The answer is: Nothing. Indeed, the very notion of "race" is antithetical to the study of population genetics, for the former traditionally deals with fixed clear-cut differences, and the latter with fluid or fluctuating differences. It seems to me an unrealistic procedure to maintain this late in the day that we can readapt the term "race" to mean something utterly different from what it has always most obfuscatingly and ambiguously meant.

We may congratulate ourselves and in fact often do, that the chemists of the late 18th and early 19th centuries had the good sense to throw out the term "phlogiston" when they discovered that it corresponded to nothing in reality, instead of attempting to adapt it to fit the facts which it was not designed to describe, and of which, indeed, it impeded the discovery for a hundred years. The psychologists of the second decade of this century had the good sense to do likewise with the term "instinct" when they discovered how, like a bunion upon the foot, it impeded the pilgrim's progress toward a sounder understanding of human drives (Bernard 1924).

It is a hopeless task to attempt to redefine words with so longstanding a history of misuse as "race," and for this, among other cogent reasons, it is ill-advised. As Simpson has said, "There . . . is a sort of Gresham's Law for words; redefine them as we will, their worst or most extreme meaning is almost certain to remain current and to tend to drive out the meaning we prefer" (1953:268).

For this reason alone it would appear to me unwise to afford scientific sanction to a term which is so embarrassed by false meanings as is the term "race." There is the added objection that it is wholly redundant, and confusingly so, to distinguish as a "race" a population which happens to differ from other populations in the frequency of one or more genes. Why call such populations "races" when the operational definition of what they *are* is sharply and clearly stated in the words used to convey what we mean, namely, populations which differ from one another in particular frequencies of certain specified genes? Surely, to continue the use of the word "race" under such circumstances is to exemplify what A. E. Housman so aptly described as "calling in ambiguity of language to promote confusion of thought" (1933:31).

When populations differ from each other in the frequency of sickle-cell gene or any other gene or genes, all that is necessary is to state the facts with reference to those populations. That is what those populations are in terms of gene frequencies. And those are the operative criteria which we can use as tools or concepts in giving an account of the realities of the situation—the actual operations.

I have thus far said nothing about the anthropological conception of "race" because this is to some extent yielding to genetic pressure, and because the future of what used to be called the study of "race" lies, in my view, largely in the direction of population genetics. The older anthropological conception of "race" still lingers on, suggesting that it is perhaps beyond the reach both of scientific judgment and mortal malice. Insofar as the genetic approach to the subject is concerned, many anthropologists are, as it were, self-made men and only too obviously represent cases of unskilled labor. However, my feeling is that they should be praised for trying rather than blamed for failing. The new anthropology is on the right track.

Recently Garn and Coon (1955) have attempted to adapt the terms "geographic race," "local race," and "microgeographical race," for use in the human species. They define, for example, "A geographical race" as, "in its simplest terms, a collection of (race) populations having features in common, such as a high gene frequency for blood group B, and extending over a geographically definable area" (1955:997).

In this definition I think we can see, in high relief as it were, what is wrong with the continuing use of the term "race." The term "geographical race" immediately delimits the group of populations embraced by it from others, as if the so-called "geographical race" were a biological entity "racially" distinct from others. Such a group of populations is not "racially" distinct, but differs from others in the frequencies of certain of its genes. It was suggested by the UNESCO group of geneticists and physical anthropologists that such a group of populations be called a "major group" (Montagu 1951:173–82). This suggestion was made precisely in order to avoid such difficulties as are inherent in the term "geographical race." Since Garn and Coon themselves admit that "geographical races are to a large extent collections of convenience, useful more for pedagogic purposes than as units for empirical investigation" (1955:1000), it seems to me difficult to understand why they should have preferred this term to the one more closely fitting the situation, namely, "major groups." It is a real question whether spurious precision, even for pedagogic purposes, or as an "as if" fiction, is to be preferred to a frank acknowledgment, in the terms we use, of the difficulties involved. Garn and Coon are quite alive to the problem, but it may be questioned whether it contributes to the student's clearer understanding of that problem to use terms which not only do not fit the conditions, but which serve to contribute to making the student's mind a dependable instrument of imprecision, especially in view of the fact that a more appropriate term is available.

The principle of "squatter's rights" apparently applies to words as well as to property. When men make a heavy investment in words they are inclined to treat them as property, and even to become enslaved by them, the prisoners of their own vocabularies. High walls may not a prison make, but technical terms sometimes do. This, I would suggest, is another good reason for self-examination with regard to the use of the term "race."

Commenting of Garn's views on race, Dr. J. P. Garlick has remarked,

The use of "race" as a taxonomic unit for man seems out of date, if not irrational. A hierarchy of geographical, local and micro-races is proposed, with acknowledgments to Rensch and Dobzhansky. But the criteria for their definition are nowhere made clear, and in any case such a scheme could not do justice to the many independent fluctuations and frequency gradients shown by human polymorphic characters. Surely physical anthropology has outgrown such abstractions as "Large Local Race. . . . Alpine: the rounder-bodied, rounder-headed, predominantly darker peoples of the French mountains, across Switzerland, Austria, and to the shores of the Black Sea" (1961:169–70).

Garn and Coon do not define "local races" but say of them that they "can be identified, not so much by average differences, but by their nearly complete isolation" (1955:997). In that case, as Dahlberg (1942) long ago suggested, why not call such populations "isolates"?

"Microgeographical races" also fail to receive definition, but are described as differing "only qualitatively from local races." In that case, why not use some term which suggests the difference?

In short, it is our opinion that taxonomies and terms should be designed to fit the facts, and not the facts forced into the procrustean rack of pre-determined categories. If we are to have references, whether terminological or taxonomical, to existing or extinct populations of man, let the conditions as we find them determine the character of our terms or taxonomies, and not the other way round.

Since what we are actually dealing with in human breeding populations are differences in the frequencies of certain genes, why not use a term which states just this, such as *genogroup*, and the various appropriate variants of this?[1] If necessary, we could then speak of "geographic genogroups," "local genogroups," and "microgenogroups." A genogroup being defined as a breeding population which differs from other breeding populations of the species in the frequency of one or more genes. The term "genogroup" gets as near to a statement of the facts as a term can. The term "race" goes far beyond the facts and only serves to obscure them. A *geographic genogroup* would then be defined as a group of breeding populations characterized by a marked similarity of the frequencies of one or more genes.

A *local genogroup* would be one of the member populations of a geographic genogroup, and a *microgenogroup* a partially isolated population with one or more gene frequency differences serving to distinguish it from adjacent or non-adjacent local genogroups.

It is to be noted that nothing is said of a common heredity for similarity in gene frequencies in a geographic genogroup. The common heredity is usually implied, but I do not think it should be taken for granted, except within the local genogroups and the microgenogroups. One or more of the genogroups in a geographic genogroup may have acquired their frequencies for a given gene quite independently of the other local populations comprising the geographic genogroup. This is a possibility which is, perhaps, too often overlooked when comparisons are being made on the basis of gene frequencies between populations, whether geographic or not.

But this must suffice for my criticism of the usage of the term "race" by biologists and anthropologists. I wish now to discuss, briefly, the disadvantages of the use of this term in popular usage, and the advantages of the general term "ethnic group."

The layman's conception of "race" is so confused and emotionally muddled that any attempt to modify it would seem to be met by the greatest obstacle of all, the term "race" itself. It is a trigger word. Utter it, and a whole series of emotionally conditioned responses follow. If we are to succeed in clarifying the minds of those who think in terms of "race" we must cease using the word, because by continuing to use it we sanction whatever meaning anyone chooses to bestow upon it, and because in the layman's mind the term refers to conditions which do not apply. There is no such thing as the kind of "race" in which the layman believes, namely, that there exists an indissoluble association between mental and physical characters which make individual members of certain "races" either inferior or superior to the members of certain other "races." The layman requires to have his thinking challenged on this subject. The term "ethnic group" serves as such a challenge to thought and as a stimulus to rethink the foundations of one's beliefs. The term "race" takes for granted what should be a matter for inquiry. And this is precisely the point that is raised when one uses the noncommittal "ethnic group." It encourages the passage from ignorant or confused certainty to thoughtful uncertainty. For the layman, as for others, the term "race" closes the door on understanding. The phrase "ethnic group" opens it, or at the very least, leaves it ajar.

In opposition to these views a number of objections have been expressed. Here are some of them. One does not change anything by changing names. It is an artful dodge. It is a subterfuge. Why not meet the problem head-on? If the term has been badly defined in the past, why not redefine it? Re-education should be attempted by establishing the true meaning of "race," not by denying its existence. It suggests a certain blindness to the facts to deny that "races" exist in man. One cannot combat racism by enclosing the word in quotes. It is not the word that requires changing but people's ideas about it. It is a common failing to argue from the abuse of an idea to its total exclusion. It is quite as possible to feel "ethnic group prejudice" as it is to feel "race prejudice." One is not going to solve the race problem this way.

Such objections indicate that there has been a failure of communication, that the main point has been missed. The term "ethnic group" is not offered as a substitute for "race." On the contrary, the term "ethnic group" implies a fundamental difference in viewpoint from that which is implied in the term "race." It is not a question of changing names or of substitution, or an artful dodge, or the abandonment of a good term which has been abused. It is first and foremost an attempt to clarify the fact that the old term is unsound when applied to man, and should therefore not be used with reference to man. At the same time "ethnic group," being an intentionally vague and general term, is designed to make it clear that there is a problem to be solved, rather than to maintain the fiction that the problem has been solved. As a general term it leaves all

---

1. The term "genogroup" was suggested to me by Sir Julian Huxley during a conversation on September 29, 1959.

question of definition open, referring specifically to human breeding populations, the members of which are believed to exhibit certain physical or genetic likenesses. For all general purposes, an "ethnic group" may be defined as one of a number of breeding populations, which populations together comprise the species *Homo sapiens*, and which individually maintain their differences, physical or genetic and cultural, by means of isolating mechanisms such as geographic and social barriers.

The re-education of the layman should be taken seriously. For this reason I would suggest that those who advocate the redefinition of the term "race," rather than its replacement by a general term which more properly asks questions before it attempts definitions, would do well to acquaint themselves with the nature of the laymen as well as with the meaning of the phenomena to which they would apply a term which cannot possibly be redefined. If one desires to remove a prevailing erroneous conception and introduce a more correct one, one is more likely to be successful by introducing the new conception with a distinctively new term rather than by attempting redefinition of a term embarrassed by longstanding unsound usage. Professor Henry Sigerist has well said that "it is never sound to continue the use of terminology with which the minds of millions of people have been poisoned even when the old terms are given new meanings" (1951:101).

There is, apparently, a failure on the part of some students to understand that one of the greatest obstacles to the process of re-education would be the retention of the old term "race," a term which enshrines the errors it is designed to remove. The deep implicit meanings this term possesses for the majority of its users are such that they require immediate challenge whenever and by whomsoever the term "race" is used.

Whenever the term "race" is used, most people believe that something like an eternal verity has been uttered when, in fact, nothing more than evidence has been given that there are many echoes, but few voices. "Race" is a word so familiar that in using it the uncritical thinker is likely to take his own private meaning for it completely for granted, never thinking at any time to question so basic an instrument of the language as the word "race." On the other hand, when one uses the term "ethnic group," the question is immediately raised, "What does it mean? What does the user have in mind?" And this at once affords an opportunity to discuss the facts and explore the meaning and the falsities enshrined in the word "race," and to explain the problems involved and the facts of the genetic situation as we know them.

The term "ethnic group" is concerned with questions; the term "race" is concerned with answers, unsound answers, where for the most part there are only problems that require to be solved before any sound answers can be given.

It may be difficult for those who believe in what I. A. Richards has called "The Divine Right of Words" to accept the suggestion that a word such as "race," which has exercised so evil a tyranny over the minds of men, should be permanently dethroned from the vocabulary, but that constitutes all the more reason for trying, remembering that the meaning of a word is the action it produces.

References

Abercrombie, M., C. J. Hickman, and M. L. Johnson. 1951. *A Dictionary of Biology*. Harmondsworth, Penguin Books.
Bernard, L. L., 1924. *Instinct*. New York, Henry Holt and Co.
Boas, F. 1936. History and science in anthropology. *American Anthropologist* 38:140.
Calman, W. T. 1949. *The Classification of Animals*. New York, John Wiley and Sons.
Carter, G. S. 1951. *Animal Evolution*. New York, Columbia University Press.
Dahlberg, G. 1942. *Race, Reason and Rubbish*. New York, Columbia University Press.
Deniker, J. 1900. *The Races of Man*. London, Walter Scott Ltd.
Dunn, L. C. and Th. Dobzhansky. 1952. *Heredity, Race and Society*. Rev. ed. New York, New American Library.
Garlick, J. P. 1961. Review of *Human Races and Readings on Race*, by S. M. Garn. *Annals of Human Genetics* 25:169–70.
Garn, S. M., and C. S. Coon. 1955. On the number of races of mankind. *American Anthropologist* 57:996–1001.
Hanhart, E. 1953. Infectious diseases. In *Clinical Genetics*, Arnold Sorsby, ed. St. Louis, Mosby.
Housman, A. E. 1933. *The Name and Nature of Poetry*. New York, Cambridge University Press.
Huxley, J. S. and A. C. Haddon. 1936. *We Europeans: a survey of "racial" problems*. New York. Harper and Bros.
Huxley, T. H. 1865. On the methods and results of ethnology. *Fortnightly Review*. Reprinted in *Man's Place in Nature and Other Anthropological Essays*. London, Macmillan Co., 1894.
Kalmus, H. 1948. *Genetics*. Harmondsworth, Pelican Books.
———1958. *Heredity and Variation*. London, Routledge and K. Paul.
Montagu, M. F. Ashley. 1951. *Statement on Race*. Rev. ed. New York, Henry Schuman.
Penrose, L. S. 1952. Review of *Heredity, Race and Society*, by Dunn and Dobzhansky. *Annals of Human Eugenics* 17:252.
Sigerist, H. 1951. *A History of Medicine*. Vol. 1. New York, Oxford University Press.
Simpson, G. G. 1953. *The Major Features of Evolution*. New York, Columbia University Press.

III
Issues
In Archaeology

o o o o o o o o o o o o o o o o o o o o o o o o o o o o o o o o o o o o o o o o o o o o o o o o o o o o o o o o o o o o o o o o o o o o o

Archaeology is the systematic retrieval and study of the remains (both of people and their activities) that human beings (and their ancestors) have left behind on and below the surface of the earth. Like physical anthropology, archaeology gradually emerged as a separate discipline in the course of the nineteenth century. It split off from the generalized study of ancient history as scholars—mostly geologists, initially—began to focus on finding material remains of ancient precivilized populations in Europe.

Actually, it was a geological debate that helped lay the groundwork for the emergence of archaeology. The prevailing view among geologists until well into the nineteenth century was that the various strata that compose the earth's crust were the result of either Noah's flood (diluvialism) or a series of catastrophes of which the flood was the most recent (catastrophism). One of the first geologists to dispute these notions was William Smith (1769–1839). Dubbed "Strata" Smith by his detractors, he assembled a detailed table of all the known strata and their fossil contents and argued a uniformitarian position: that the eternally ongoing processes of erosion, weathering, accumulation, and the movement of the continents accounted for their large number. He was supported by James Hutton (1726–1797) in his influential work *Theory of the Earth*, published in 1795.

Combat was joined by the greatly respected William Buckland (the discoverer of the "Red Lady of Paviland," which we discussed in the introduction to Section II), who in 1823 published his work *Reliquiae Diluvianae, or Observations on the Organic Remains contained in Caves, Fissures and Diluvial Gravel, and on Other Geological Phenomena attesting to the Action of an Universal Deluge*, in which he vigorously attacked the uniformitarian views that so directly contradicted Church dogma. Only the appearance of Sir Charles Lyell's *Principles of Geology* (1830–1833) managed finally to turn the tide of scholarly sentiment in favor of the uniformitarian view of the earth's history.

Because of the nature of their work, it was for the most part amateur and professional geologists who most frequently encountered fossilized human remains, generally embedded in strata in the floors of limestone caverns. In the roughly six decades following the 1790s, an impressive array of evidence with regard to human antiquity was found in a number of such caves in Europe and England; but the finds were dismissed or their importance unrecognized. As early as 1797, for example, John Frere (1740–1807) found chipped flint tools twelve feet deep in his excavation at Hoxne (northeast of London). These stone tools were closely associated with the remains of extinct animal species. To Frere these finds suggested a very ancient human existence, even older than the commonly accepted 6,000-year antiquity of Creation. Nobody listened. Forty years later, in 1838, Boucher de Perthes (1788–1868), a customs collector at Abbeville in the northwest of France, disclosed news of some flint "axes" he had found in gravel pit caves on the banks of the Somme River. The world laughed at his assertion that these tools were manufactured by "antediluvial man," even though they had been found in the immediate vicinity of the bones of extinct cold-adapted animals. In 1846, he published *Antiquités Celtiques et Antediluviennes*, in which he formally argued his thesis—and was attacked as a heretic by the Church.

We have already discussed William Buckland's inability in 1822 to comprehend the significance of his own find, the so-called Red Lady of Paviland. The powerful grip of Christian theology on scholars' minds blinded the intellectual establishment of the period, keeping them from seeing and appreciating the overwhelming pattern that these and numerous other finds presented. As we have emphasized repeatedly, it was the emergence of Darwinism in 1859 that freed people's vision and enabled them to face and reinterpret these materials correctly. The evolutionary perspective, then, was of critical importance for the emergence of archaeology. Without it, there was no way to interpret accurately the significance of the ancient remains that were being turned up with increasing frequency.

The excavation of rock shelters revealing human cultural remains of great antiquity was only one of several kinds of archaeological research being undertaken in the nineteenth century. The excavation and description of large prehistoric monuments and burial mounds, begun in the wake of emergent nationalism in the seventeenth century and eighteenth centuries, continued. So did the retrieval and preservation of materials accidentally brought to light by road, dam, and building excavations as the industrial revolution changed the face of the earth. By the 1800s, vast quantities of stone and metal implements had been recovered and had found their way into both private and public collections. As the volume of such artifacts mounted, museum curators were faced with the problem of how to organize and display them meaningfully.

In 1836, Christian Jurgensen Thomsen (1788–1865), curator of the Danish National Museum, published a guide to its collections in which he classified all artifacts in terms of the material from which they were made. He argued that the three classes he thus identified represented stages in cultural evolution: a *Stone Age* followed by a *Bronze Age* and then an *Iron Age*. The idea was not new—it had been proposed by Lucretius in ancient Rome—but it was new for its time. However, the *Three-Age System* fit well with the contemporary writings of early nineteenth-century social evolutionists and was of such usefulness that it quickly spread to other countries.

The Three-Age System was clearly evolutionary (and hence radical) in nature. It contained a geological perspective in that it proposed clearly defined sequences of cultural stages modeled after geological strata. It was of tremendous value in providing a conceptual framework through which archaeologists could begin systematically to study the artifacts they retrieved from the earth, and also in that it tended to support those scholars arguing for a greatly expanded vision of human antiquity.

Combined with Darwinian evolutionism, the Three-Age System became an even more powerful conceptual tool. In 1865, Sir John Lubbock (1834–1913) published his tremendously influential book *Prehistoric Times,* in which he vastly extended the Stone Age and divided it in two. He thus proposed that human prehistory be viewed in terms of the following stages: the *Paleolithic* (Old Stone Age, marked by flint tools); the *Neolithic* (New Stone Age, marked by the appearance of pottery); the *Bronze Age;* and the *Iron Age.* Although this system has continued to be refined, it still forms the basis of our understanding of world prehistory, and we continue to make use of its terminology.

At about the time Lubbock was formulating his broad outline of the stages of cultural evolution, Edouard Lartet (whom we discussed earlier) and his English colleague Henry Christy were exploring the now famous rock shelters in the Dordogne region of France. In one cave, called La Madeleine, Christy and Lartet found not only an abundance of spectacular cave art and small engravings of extinct species, such as the woolly mammoth, but also a magnificent collection of tools, including intricately carved implements of antler bone and ivory. These became the "type complex" for the identification of the Magdalenian culture, easily the most advanced and spectacular culture of Upper Paleolithic times.

Using the art work they found in the ten or so caves they explored in this region, Lartet and Christy developed a system to classify the materials they uncovered. Their approach was based on the fact that renderings of different species of animals predominated during different periods. The succession of stages they worked out for the Dordogne region was the following: (1) the Age of the Bison; (2) the Age of the Woolly Mammoth and Rhinoceros; (3) the Age of the Reindeer; and (4) the Age of the Cave Bear.

Gabriel de Mortillet (1821–1898) took the work of Lartet and Christy a step further by developing a chronology of the same region based on the tool industries found at *type sites* (sites used to represent the characteristic features of a culture). The series he ultimately settled on in the 1870s had six stages: Thenaisian, Chellean, Mousterian, Solutrean, Magdalenian, and Robenhausian. Although these materials have been reinterpreted a great deal since that time, prehistoric archaeologists still use Mortillet's approach to naming archaeological cultures and even most of the names he proposed.

The archaeologist of the late nineteenth century who most attracted public attention was probably Heinrich Schliemann (1822–1890). After intensive study of the Homerian epics, Schliemann set out to find the ancient city of Troy. He accomplished this in 1871 at a place called Hissarlik, near the western tip of Anatolia (modern Turkey). He was a romantic figure, and his quest to find the sites of Homeric legend excited public fancy and brought forth private funds to support both his own and other archaeological research. Unfortunately he was not a very skilled excavator: While digging up the highly stratified site at Hissarlik he focused his attentions on what turned out to be the wrong layer—and virtually destroyed the real Troy in the process.

As the frontiers of knowledge about human origins expanded in Europe with the emergence of increasingly specialized subdisciplines, a parallel development was taking place in the Americas. Wild speculation about the origins of Native Americans gave way to increasingly systematic research by scholars and learned amateurs. In 1784, for example, Thomas Jefferson (1743–1826) excavated an Indian burial mound in Virginia. Although his digging techniques were crude, he approached his task in a very modern manner. Rather than setting out simply to collect *artifacts*, Jefferson cut into the mound to collect *information*. His cross-section of the mound revealed ancient burial practices similiar to those of known historic groups and refuted the popularly held notion that the mound builders had buried their dead in an upright position.

By the 1840s, John Lloyd Stephens and Frederick Catherwood had established new standards for care in the recording of details in their magnificent reports about, and drawings of, the ruins of the Mayan civilization in the Yucatan peninsula, published in works such as Stephens's *Incidents of Travel in Central America: Chiapas and Yucatan* (1842).

The mounds of the southeastern United States attracted a number of excavators, most notably E. G. Squier and E. H. Davis, who described their research in an important monograph published in 1848. By the middle of the century, sufficient work had been done to justify a long synthesis of American archaeology by Samuel Haven published in 1856.

Archaeology in the New World was always very tightly connected to cultural anthropology—much more so than in Europe. This stemmed from the fact that whereas Europeans engaged in archaeological research as an extension of their researches backward from known historical times to their distant prehistoric past, Americans were investigating "foreign" societies—whether they were digging in their own backyards or engaging in ethnographic research with their displaced (and decimated) Native American neighbors. To this day this difference persists: In Europe archaeology is usually thought of as a humanity (an adjunct to history), whereas in the United States archaeology is practiced as a subdiscipline of anthropology and is viewed as a social science.

Issues in Archaeology

∙∙

In this topic we approach the study of archaeology by focusing on some of the major questions which scholars are attempting to answer today. In the first article, C. D. Darlington asks "Who Invented Agriculture?" He answers the question but, (perhaps) more importantly, also discusses the profound consequences of this development for the human species. Through agriculture, Darlington observes, "man thought himself to be consciously in control of his destiny, but he was in fact unconsciously having his destiny, his evolutionary destiny, thrust upon him. It is a situation from which we can see he has not by any means escaped."

What are some of the unintended consequences of agriculture that have become part of human destiny? For one thing, it forever changed the natural environment. Many species of wild plants and animals failed to survive the pressures farmers exerted on the environment in order to create conditions that promoted favored species. Then, agriculture also damaged the land, depleting it of nutrients and (paradoxically) creating conditions that promoted the predominance of weeds. Irrigation, the most productive form of farming, caused people to crowd together and farm more limited lands while rats bred and thrived in canals and ditches.

The concentration of farming populations into smaller land areas meant that groups of people could seize control of the land and thereby exert political control over large masses. Thus, in some regions, the State emerged as a new sociopolitical form. However, the State also arose in nonagricultural populations, as Robert L. Carneiro indicates in "How Did the State Evolve?"

A popular misconception is that agriculture was invented to relieve people from the unending drudgery and insecurities embodied in the previous, hunting and food gathering subsistence strategy. This is far from true. Recent research by Richard B. Lee, Marvin Harris, and others shows that agriculture requires more intensive and enduring labor than does hunting and food gathering. The enormous increase of agriculturally created food surpluses has never been used to reduce the amount of time or energy expended in work, but rather it has been utilized again and again to enable ever larger numbers of people to live crowded into increasingly complex social groupings.

Thus, the emergence of agriculture underlies another immensely significant, rather recent, human sociocultural invention: the city. "How Were Cities Invented?" asks J. Pfeiffer—and in doing so he also totes up the pros and cons of urban life. Most of us take cities for granted, but archaeology reveals how profoundly city dwelling has changed human existence in the last seven to eight thousand years. Thus, it can't be denied that some of the most spectacular achievements in philosophy, mathematics, the natural sciences, technical inventions, the arts, and literature were rooted in the urban way of life. In fact, most specialists refined their crafts and arts as city dwellers. But on the other side, cities also created the condition of poverty by piling on top of each other landless, unskilled, and often unemployed workers and their families. Garbage and waste disposal pose health problems in cities, and epidemic diseases in cities become extremely difficult to control. So the city, a hallmark of our civilization, is a problematic development at best—and archaeology has much to tell us of its origins, development, and possibilities.

One of the livelier debates in American archaeology is the question of when the New World first was populated. No serious scholars doubt any longer that the Americas were populated by fully evolved modern human hunting and food gathering bands—probably migrating in pursuit of big game on the Siberian plains. They crossed over the Bering Strait land bridge connecting Alaska and Siberia during the last glacial period, which marked the end of the Ice Age, and found themselves in a paradise rich in wild game and bountiful in plant life. They thrived, and their numbers grew rapidly as they expanded southward and eastward, seeking out the incredibly diverse environmental niches that met their needs and fit their fancies. Eventually, they evolved a spectacular variety of life-styles that included high civilizations in the jungles of Mesoamerica, vital communities of salmon fishers on the Northwest Coast, dazzling mound builders in the midwestern plains of North America, adobe builders in the American Southwest, and countless bands of semi-nomadic hunters and food gatherers from the Inuit (Eskimo) of Alaska to the Yahgan of Tierra del Fuego in Argentina. The question vexing archaeologists is: When did the first bands cross the Bering Straits from Siberia to Alaska?

In "The First Americans: Who Were They and When Did They Arrive?" Ben Patrusky is evenhanded in presenting the two main competing views. The older of the two, and still the one more widely held, is that this epic migration was relatively recent—say, 12,000 years ago. Many sites have been found scattered across North America (and a few in South America, too) that date from around 11,000 B.P. (before present) and that feature, in the collections of stone tools they exhibit, versions of the so-called "Clovis point" (named after a site in New Mexico): a medium-sized, leaf-shaped projectile point with a hollow groove in the base. In the view of many scholars these points were brought to the New World by Siberian migrants; and the spread of this tool kit across the continent marks the rapid expansion of the migrating groups, who encountered a fresh, virtually limitless, and unbelievably rich environment. (And, in the course of but a few centuries, the Clovis people seem to have hunted into extinction many of the great mammals who lived there, from giant sloths to horses and elephants.)

But there are dissidents who believe that human groups crossed over from Siberia much earlier—25,000 to 50,000 years ago. In the mountains of Peru, for instance, Richard MacNeish believes he has found pre-Clovis tools perhaps 25,000 years old. He and others point to tantalizing bits and pieces of evidence indicating the presence of humans in the New World thousands of years before the Clovis culture emerged. In this view, the Clovis tool horizon represents the diffusion of a new tool from one already established group to another. It may have been invented in the Americas, or it may have been brought in by a late-arriving Siberian "second wave" migration.

One of the key pieces of evidence indicating an early human presence in North America is a fossil known as Del Mar man. The bones were found several years ago, buried in a cliff overlooking the Pacific Ocean, just north of San Diego. In 1974, using a new chemical dating technique involving the rate of change in amino acids over the millenia, Jeffrey Bada, of the University of California at San Diego, estimated the fossils to be some 48,000 years old. Many anthropologists, however, questioned the validity of Bada's method, and the date has remained controversial.

In 1981, geologists James Bischoff and Robert Rosenbauer added fuel to the controversy. Using a technique based on the radioactive decay of uranium and related elements, they reexamined the Del Mar specimen and concluded it was a youngster, only some 11,000 years old. Thus, they argued, it could well be a descendant of the groups that crossed the Bering Strait about 12,000 to 13,000 years ago. The issue is not yet resolved.

Although pre-Clovis finds in general remain controversial, and the correct date for Del Mar man remains a particular bone of contention, we believe the view that the New World was first populated by human groups much earlier than 12,000 years ago, eventually will prove to be correct. But the data are here in Patrusky's article for you to evaluate and decide for yourself.

10

Who Invented Agriculture?

BY C. D. DARLINGTON

According to the notions of our forebears, early man first learned to forge and smelt iron to make his weapons and his tools. Then he tamed his beasts and tilled the earth, sowed the seeds of the plants he had collected for food, and so raised his crops. Finally, years of cultivation improved these crops to a standard that came to support agriculture. Man could now provide better fodder for his stock, and could, therefore, breed improved beasts. These developments had occurred in many parts of the world with different kinds of crops and stock on which the different civilizations were based.

This view of agriculture's origins had been reasonably supported by the European discovery of the American civilizations, and it was still generally held at the beginning of the nineteenth century. It showed man progressing almost inevitably by his own efforts, his own skill and intelligence, and in a way that commended itself well to the thought of the nineteenth century.

But in the middle of that century all these ideas were rudely shaken by a series of unforeseen discoveries. It was then that archeology began to show that agriculture had long preceded the smelting of metals. History and language began to indicate that crops had been carried far away from the places where they were first grown. And two naturalists, Darwin and De Candolle, argued that it was not cultivation in itself, but selection by the cultivator—the choice of species

and the choice of variations to sow and propagate—that had played the decisive part in improving cultivated plants.

Darwin and De Candolle thus advanced our understanding of the origins of agriculture for the first time in two thousand years. In the hundred years that have followed them, however, a far greater upheaval of ideas has occurred. It has been set off from two directions. One was the study of how plant breeding and selection actually work among primitive farmers. This we owe largely to the Russian geneticist and plant breeder Nikolai Vavilov. The other was Willard Libby's 1947 discovery of the use of radiocarbon. This led to the physical dating of prehistoric remains and settled the arguments of earlier centuries. What happened when these two fields of inquiry, so utterly remote from one another, came together?

To see how these great advances transformed the problem of the origins of agriculture, we have to look at the world as it was when agriculture began, the world of 10,000 years ago.

First, consider the people. There were about five million people in the world. They were divided into thousands of tribes, all living by various kinds of hunting or collecting, mostly by both. Like their surviving descendants, these people often had special skills for dealing with foods and fibers, drugs and poisons, weapons and boats. The tribes also included some individual

artists and craftsmen, as well as men with special knowledge of trade, especially trade in minerals—tools and ornaments, for example, made from obsidian, amber, and precious stones. But, in general, these people had a vast and accurate knowledge of what they could do with the plants, the animals, and the earth on which they depended for their living.

There was, however, one factor in their surroundings on which the main masses of mankind could not depend. This was the climate, for the climate at that time was changing unusually fast. The last Ice Age was in full retreat. The snow was melting all around what is now the temperate Northern Hemisphere. Mountain ranges were becoming passable. The oceans were rising and cutting off islands. Inland seas were drying up. In short, vast new regions were being opened or closed to human habitation.

In these circumstances it is evident that movements of people must have been taking place on a greater scale than ever before. Inevitably the greatest movements of all, and the greatest meeting and mixing of peoples, would be concentrated in those necks of land that join the three continents of the Old World and the two continents of the New. Significantly, therefore, the first evidences of settled agriculture are found close to these necks of land.

Over the last twenty years, radiocarbon dating of the organic remains in a great number of early agricultural settlements has shown

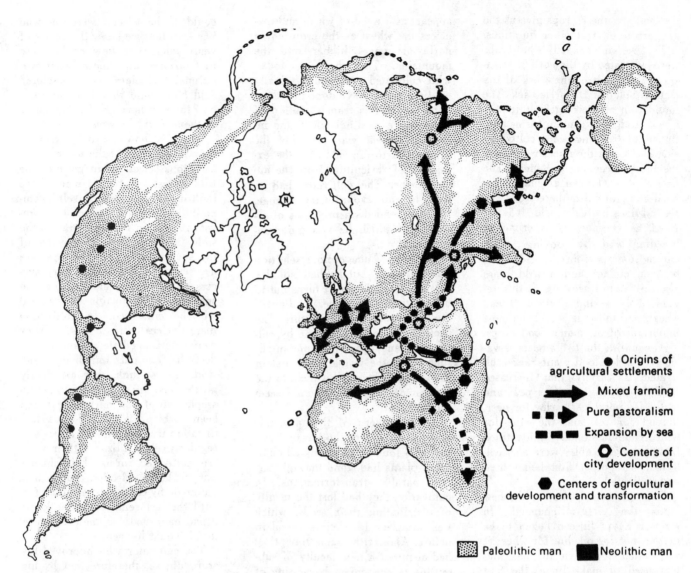

● Origins of
agricultural settlements

➡ Mixed farming

➡ Pure pastoralism

▪▪▪ Expansion by sea

◎ Centers of
city development

⬢ Centers of agricultural
development and transformation

▨ Paleolithic man   ▮ Neolithic man

beyond doubt that agriculture began at different times in different regions. And it has shown the order in which it actually began in these different regions. The use of radiocarbon has corrected many slight —and a few big—misconceptions.

First, agriculture began, not exactly in what the American Egyptologist James Breasted called the Fertile Crescent, not in the fertile valley bottoms, but rather on the hillsides and tablelands adjoining them. This nuclear zone, as it has been called, is a three-pronged area stretching from the headwaters of the Euphrates, west through Anatolia into the Balkans, south into the Jordan Valley, and east along the foot of the Zagros Mountains toward the Persian Gulf. Later

there was a fourth prong crossing Persia south of the Caspian Sea. In other words, the nuclear zone was just at the neck, or the crossroads, of the Old World.

Secondly, we find that this zone of original settlement did not expand—apart from seaside intrusions into Egypt and the Crimea— until about 4000 B.C. There are three or four silent millennia between the beginning of agriculture 10,000 years ago and the great transformation and expansion that followed it. To be sure, during this period pottery was invented. Artists and traders were attracted by the security of the permanent settlements and put their skills and goods at the service of the new, rich, settled communities. But the

great technical and biological discoveries of bronze and writing, the wheel and the horse, lay ahead.

These discoveries were made only at the end of the silent millennia, when the great geographical expansion was beginning. In the fourth millennium B.C. the tribes of grain cultivators began to move out of the nuclear zone and to settle or colonize the wild lands of the hunters and collectors, which lay around them. They moved in four main directions: into Europe, into Africa, into India, and into China. They had waited a long time to make these journeys, and they took a long time, more than a thousand years, to accomplish them. Why? The answer depends mainly on the crops they were cultivating. And, as we shall see, these crops give us the answers to several other questions.

That we know exactly what crops were cultivated by the earliest farmers is the result of the work of the Danish botanist Hans Helbaek. The foundation of their agriculture was wheat, and its two main forms continued to live and were cultivated side by side in the nuclear zone for the nine succeeding millennia. The first of these, known as emmer, existed and still exists there wild. The second does not exist wild. It is derived, as we know by experimental breeding and by looking at its chromosomes, from hybridization between emmer and a wild grass also still found growing in this region. This second grain is bread wheat, and today it is still the most important of all man's food crops.

Along with the two wheats, a variety of other food plants were cultivated, a variety that increased with the passing of time: peas and lentils for porridge, barley for beer, linseed for oil, and the vine for wine. Doubtless many unidentified fruits and vegetables were also collected, without at first being bred and cultivated.

But when men passed to the new lands the picture changed. In warmer Egypt linseed began to be grown, not for oil, but for fiber; it was retted and spun for flax and was used to make linen, the first substitute for wool. In colder Europe a new grain, oats, appeared beside the wheat. In India, cotton took the place of wool and flax. In Central Asia the native buckwheat displaced wheat and barley. On the Upper Nile, sorghum displaced the other grains. And almost everywhere various kinds of new light grains, the millets, began to take the place of the heavy-grained wheat and barley.

Some of these later displacements were no doubt due to conscious selection. But some, it seems, were quite unconscious. In 1916 a German geographer, Engelbrecht, attempted to account for these displacements. As a crop is taken into a new territory or habitat, it is apt to be invaded by new weeds. Rye

appears as a weed of wheat and displaces the wheat as the crop moves north or moves higher into the mountains. This happens today with cultivated rye, and originally wild rye would have done the same.

No doubt this transformation of crops was exceedingly slow, and indeed its speed was probably the limiting factor in allowing the expansion of agriculture from the nuclear zone. The cultivator had to wait for an evolutionary change, which depended on processes of selection of which he was quite unconscious.

The idea of unconscious selection was Darwin's, but he had no idea how far it would go. It turns out to be the key to the understanding of the development of agriculture. The decisive changes undergone by cultivated plants are not, as one might suppose, in the visible yield, but in properties of behavior which, to the layman or nonfarmer, would seem unimportant.

The discovery of this principle was the main contribution of Vavilov, who found that nearly all cultivated plants had gone through certain parallel transformations. In cultivation they had lost the faculty of distributing their seeds, which was necessary for their survival in nature. And, at the same time, they had acquired a new faculty of submitting to convenient harvesting of fruits and threshing of seed, which was necessary for their survival in the hands of the cultivator.

Take the crowning instance of Vavilov's principle. The ear of wild emmer, when it is ripe, shatters into its separate parts, each containing one grain protected by its coat, the chaff, and armed with a beard that will catch in the coat of any passing animal. When the grain falls to the ground it will dig itself in. But the ear of cultivated emmer or bread wheat does not shatter when ripe. It can be cut and carried unbroken. Only when it is threshed does it gently shed its naked grain into the farmer's bushel or bin.

This extraordinary transmutation, it might be thought, could be the result of conscious selection. It

could, if the selector were one who knew all that we know thousands of years later. But how could those first farmers have known what evolutionary changes were possible? And how could they have foreseen how the rich harvests that lay ahead of them might be won?

There is, however, an even more striking example of the scope of unconscious selection. In general, the wild ancestors of crop plants have built-in mechanisms of self-incompatibility: genetic devices that prevent the pollen from growing in the styles and fertilizing the ovules of the same plant. These devices are necessary for the evolutionary success of all wild species for they insure that a proportion of the seed will be crossbred. In cultivation these devices cease to matter. They confer no immediate advantage; indeed they can only impair the yield. And, sure enough, they are nearly always lost in cultivation. For example, wheat and barley, peas and beans, which all allowed cross-fertilization in their wild ancestors are regularly self-fertilized in their modern cultivated forms. This change was made by selection, but it was not made by conscious selection, for until the last century no one knew it had happened; no one even knew that it could happen.

The cultivator who improved his crops did so, therefore, not by his intelligent practice of plant breeding, but by his intelligent practice of cultivation. And this was a capacity for which, we cannot doubt, the cultivator himself was continually being selected.

The contrast, indeed the conflict, between the tiller of the soil and the keeper of cattle, between the peasant and the herdsman, between Cain and Abel is so ancient and obvious that we naturally think of the domestication of plants and of animals as belonging to separate and opposed problems. But this is misleading. Out of the grain farmer came the ancient civilizations.

Around the grain farmer assembled every kind of agricultural and civilized activity. Before grain farming, there was the collecting and even the cropping of roots in many parts of the world. Long before the grain farmer, there was the use of the dog for hunting, for food in time of famine, and later, for herding sheep and goats. But none of these activities led to a more complicated life, which in turn meant a more complicated, a stabler, and ultimately, a more productive society. No great development came about until the grain farmer had, during his four silent millennia, laid the foundations of the future.

The various kinds of stock and stockmen were therefore bound to have had different histories because of their different relations with the grain farmer. What these relations were are still partly obscure. The early settlements mostly contain bones of cattle, pigs, and sheep; but to what extent had these been bred and fed by the farmer and to what extent had he taken them by hunting? Did the early herdsman allow his domesticated female animals to mate with wild males or males that had gone wild? This is the practice of Nagas in India with their gaur cattle today. It is also the practice in mating dogs with wolves. The distinction between what is wild and what is domesticated is therefore harder for the archeologist to draw with stock than with crops.

Allowing for these uncertainties, we may say that sheep and pigs were probably the first to be taken under man's care, probably during the seventh millennium B.C. Later, in the sixth or fifth millennium, came the cattle. Whether their first use was for sacrifice in religious ritual will take us a long time to discover. But certainly this first introduction was quickly followed by their diversified uses for plowing, for milk, for meat, and later, in the salt-hungry regions of Africa, for blood.

When we come to the means of improving domesticated animals along their different lines, we can think of them together and we can

see them in contrast with crop plants. The herdsman, it is clear, has from the beginning understood something of the purpose and practice of selection. Indeed we may say that the first herdsmen could never have improved their lot until they understood that better animals could be raised by choosing and setting apart better parents. It is a principle that is suitably and elaborately commemorated by the story of Jacob and Laban in the Book of Genesis.

The processes of animal breeding have thus been more conscious than those of plant breeding, and this has been true at every stage. For example, when the cultivators came into India in the third millennium B.C., they allowed their cattle to hybridize with the native humped cattle. This was no doubt an unconscious and merely traditional practice. But in the Indus city of Mohenjo Daro they also deliberately domesticated new species, notably the native water buffalo. Man's dependence on conscious purpose in dealing with animals as opposed to plants is further indicated by the length of time—five thousand years after the beginning of cultivation—that it took him to acquire the initiative, skill, and audacity to domesticate the most difficult animals, the horse and the camel.

If early farmers were sometimes aware of their effects on crops and stock, it is certain that they were wholly unaware of any effects their crops and stock were having on them (that is, beyond feeding, clothing, or working for them). But those who have observed peasants and pastoralists most closely have seen that between these two great classes of men, there is a genuine and profound contrast, a contrast related to their work. The record goes back, as we saw, to the legend of Cain and Abel, which takes its root in the conflict between the desert and the sown, between the Bedouin shepherds and their peasant neighbors. But on the way, it fills a large part of our history. It is the story of the borderland struggle between the English farmers and the

Welsh drovers during the Middle Ages. It is also the story of the struggle between the farming Kikuyu and the grazing Masai in Kenya today.

How are we to describe it? In the first place it should be noted that each class is of many kinds. The nomadic pastoralist may sow crops for a quick harvest during his summer grazing, while the settled peasant may breed cattle or horses to till his land, a practice that has transferred the main labor of farming from the woman with a hoe to the man with a plow. The basic contrast remains however. It is one of character, behavior, and belief.

On the one hand, the peasant is a man who knows and loves his soil and crops. He even worships them. His life, like the lives of his ancestors for two or three hundred generations, has depended on his prudence and industry in handling the soil and crops. He is therefore deeply attached to them, and he and his women will accept serfdom rather than be separated from their land. As a consequence, they are inbred—conservative and traditional, stubborn but peaceful.

How different is the pastoralist! He is correspondingly attached to his animals, but his animals can move and usually have to move in search of pasture. He is therefore mobile, alert, and aggressive. He will steal the cattle and the women of his neighbors. Consequently, he is relatively outbred. And the most mobile of his animals, the horse and the camel, are kept by the most mobile and alert, aggressive and warlike, of herdsmen.

How, then, did this contrast arise? In part, of course, the differences were there in the ancestors, the collectors and the hunters from whom each was partly derived. But it developed during those long silent millennia because the earliest men who chose to adopt these different ways of life were themselves from the beginning dependent for survival on the crops or the stock they were raising. They were therefore dependent on their different abilities to cope with different ways of life. The croppers were in fact being unconsciously selected by their crops, and the stockmen by their stock. Each way of life was tied up together in one related and adapted system.

To put it in another way, man thought himself to be consciously in control of his destiny, but he was in fact unconsciously having his destiny, his evolutionary destiny, thrust upon him. It is a situation from which we can see he has not yet by any means escaped.

The greatest of all human experiments was man's invasion of the New World. Whether it happened fifteen or twenty thousand years ago does not much matter. What matters is that mankind had put himself into two separate boxes between which there was effectively no exchange of people or ideas, of plants or animals, or even of their diseases. That was the situation for over ten thousand years. And during that time, agriculture arose and developed independently in the two boxes. This was, as we may say, an experimental situation, for it goes a long way in showing us what matters and what does not matter for the whole process of developing agriculture.

Looking first at the similarities between the Old World and the New, it can be seen that in the New World, cultivation began around a kind of central or nuclear zone. It began about 7000 B.C., when the ice was melting at its fastest. And it began with a grain crop that the Europeans called Indian corn or maize. A variety of other crops— beans and potatoes, gourds and peppers, cotton and tobacco— slowly assembled around this early crop. But the processes of improvement and distribution show us a

number of rule-breaking novelties. Several of these concern maize.

Unlike any of the other important grains, maize has its male and female flowers, the tassels and silks, on different parts of the plant. This has meant that the ordinary evolution toward inbreeding could not occur. Maize remained, and was bound to remain, crossbred. For that reason, it ultimately became the object of the most remarkable of all crop improvements: the American hybrid corn industry of the twentieth century turned an old shortcoming into a controlled advantage.

But maize is also unique with respect to its origin. No botanists would believe that maize was derived from a slender, wild Mexican grass, teosinte. Indeed they had put the two plants into different genera, *Zea* and *Euchlaena*. Yet when the hybridization is tried, the two species are found to cross readily. Their chromosomes pair in the hybrid. And, as Dr. Paul Mangelsdorf found, the hybrid is fertile, yielding the expected recombinations of characters in the second generation.

Evidently the selection of mutations, probably conscious selection in this case, has produced the most remarkable evolutionary plant transformation known. All in the course of 9,000 years of cultivation.

There is another American crop, the sweet potato, to which we owe an equally important piece of enlightenment. This plant, coming from Mexico or Peru, was already being cultivated across the Pacific all the way to New Zealand at the time of Columbus. The Maoris had brought it there from the mid-Pacific one or two hundred years earlier, and it had since become the main crop in the North Island. They knew it as *kumara*, the same name that it had

borne in Central America. By their languages, their blood groups, their canoes, and their other crops, we know that the Maoris, like other Polynesians, came originally from Indonesia. It is the sweet potato that tells us that at some earlier time other people traveling westward from America had joined them. The two boxes of which I spoke had been almost entirely closed. But not quite.

The great difference between the Old World and the New, however, had nothing to do with these or any other crop plants. In the first place, the nuclear zone of America, instead of being a single, broad, and well-connected area, was split into two by the narrow, twisted 1,500-mile neck that runs from Tehuantepec to Panama, a track that had to be followed by everyone passing from North to South America. In the second place, stock raising was absent in America. In the previous five millennia the American Indian hunters had killed off what could have been the farmer's stock. Horses and mammoths were no longer available for domestication. All that were left were llamas and turkeys.

These two differences, together with the lesser area and resources of the New World, slowed down the development of agriculture and of civilization. The silent millennia were longer. When the two worlds were brought together in 1492, the civilizations of the New World were found to be about three millennia behind those of the Old World. Mexico and Peru proved to be not unlike the Egypt of Hatshepsut and Thutmose in 1500 B.C. The consequences of this difference in evolution, the submergence of the Amerindians, are with us now, but they are beyond our present inquiry. They show us, however, in a practical way, the overwhelming importance for us today of what happened during the distant years when men and women first began to hoe the earth and sow the seed.

11

How Did the State Evolve?

BY ROBERT L. CARNEIRO

....

For the first 2 million years of his existence, man lived in bands or villages which, as far as we can tell, were completely autonomous. Not until perhaps 5000 B.C. did villages begin to aggregate into larger political units. But, once this process of aggregation began, it continued at a progressively faster pace and led, around 4000 B.C., to the formation of the first state in history. (When I speak of a state I mean an autonomous political unit, encompassing many communities within its territory and having a centralized government with the power to collect taxes, draft men for work or war, and decree and enforce laws.)

Although it was by all odds the most far-reaching political development in human history, the origin of the state is still very imperfectly understood. Indeed, not one of the current theories of the rise of the state is entirely satisfactory. At one point or another, all of them fail. There is one theory, though, which I believe does provide a convincing explanation of how states began. It is a theory which I proposed once before (1), and which I present here more fully. Before doing so, however, it seems desirable to discuss, if only briefly, a few of the traditional theories.

Explicit theories of the origin of the state are relatively modern. Classical writers like Aristotle, unfamiliar with other forms of political organization, tended to think of the state as "natural," and therefore as not requiring an explanation. However, the age of exploration, by making Europeans aware that many peoples throughout the world lived, not in states, but in independent villages or tribes, made the state seem less natural, and thus more in need of explanation.

Of the many modern theories of state origins that have been proposed, we can consider only a few. Those with a racial basis, for example, are now so thoroughly discredited that they need not be dealt with here. We can also reject the belief that the state is an expression of the "genius" of a people (2), or that it arose through a "historical accident." Such notions make the state appear to be something metaphysical or adventitious, and thus place it beyond scientific understanding. In my opinion, the origin of the state was neither mysterious nor fortuitous. It was not the product of "genius" or the result of chance, but the outcome of a regular and determinate cultural process. Moreover, it was not a unique event but a recurring phenomenon: states arose independently in different places and at different times. Where the appropriate conditions existed, the state emerged.

Voluntaristic Theories

Serious theories of state origins are of two general types: *voluntaristic* and *coercive*. Voluntaristic theories hold that, at some point in their history, certain peoples spontaneously, rationally, and voluntarily gave up their individual sovereignties and united with other communities to form a larger political unit deserving to be called a state. Of such theories the best known is the old Social Contract theory, which was associated especially with the name of Rousseau. We now know that no such compact was ever subscribed to by human groups, and the Social Contract theory is today nothing more than a historical curiosity.

The most widely accepted of modern voluntaristic theories is the one I call the "automatic" theory. According to this theory, the invention of agriculture automatically brought into being a surplus of food, enabling some individuals to divorce themselves from food production and to become potters, weavers, smiths, masons, and so on, thus creating an extensive division of labor. Out of this occupational specialization there developed a political integration which united a number of previously independent communities into a state. This argument was set forth most frequently by the late British archeologist V. Gordon Childe (3).

The principal difficulty with this theory is that agriculture does *not* automatically create a food surplus. We know this because many agricultural peoples of the world produce no such surplus. Virtually all Amazonian Indians, for example, were agricultural, but in aboriginal times they did not produce a food surplus. That it was *technically feasible* for them to produce such a surplus is shown by the fact that, under the stimulus of European settlers' desire for food, a number of tribes did raise manioc in amounts well above their own needs, for the purpose of trading (4). Thus the technical means for generating a food surplus were there; it was the social mechanisms needed to actualize it that were lacking.

Another current voluntaristic theory of state origins is Karl Wittfogel's "hydraulic hypothesis." As I understand him, Wittfogel sees the state arising in the following way. In certain arid and semiarid areas of the world, where village farmers had to struggle to support themselves by means of small-

Reprinted by permission from *Science*, Vol. 169 (August 21, 1970), pp. 733–738, and the author. Originally published as "A Theory of the Origin of the State."

scale irrigation, a time arrived when they saw that it would be to the advantage of all concerned to set aside their individual autonomies and merge their villages into a single large political unit capable of carrying out irrigation on a broad scale. The body of officials they created to devise and administer such extensive irrigation works brought the state into being (5).

This theory has recently run into difficulties. Archeological evidence now makes it appear that in at least three of the areas that Wittfogel cites as exemplifying his "hydraulic hypothesis"— Mesopotamia, China, and Mexico— full-fledged states developed well before large-scale irrigation (6). Thus, irrigation did not play the causal role in the rise of the state that Wittfogel appears to attribute to it (7).

This and all other voluntaristic theories of the rise of the state founder on the same rock: the demonstrated inability of autonomous political units to relinquish their sovereignty in the absence of overriding external constraints. We see this inability manifested again and again by political units ranging from tiny villages to great empires. Indeed, one can scan the pages of history without finding a single genuine exception to this rule. Thus, in order to account for the origin of the state we must set aside voluntaristic theories and look elsewhere.

Coercive Theories

A close examination of history indicates that only a coercive theory can account for the rise of the state. Force, and not enlightened self-interest, is the mechanism by which political evolution has led, step by step, from autonomous villages to the state.

The view that war lies at the root of the state is by no means new. Twenty-five hundred years ago Heraclitus wrote that "war is the father of all things." The first careful study of the role of warfare in the rise of the state, however, was made less than a hundred years ago, by Herbert Spencer in his *Principles of Sociology* (8). Perhaps better known than Spencer's writings on war and the state are the conquest theories of continental writers such as Ludwig Gumplowicz (9), Gustav Ratzenhofer (10), and Franz Oppenheimer (11).

Oppenheimer, for example, argued that the state emerged when the productive capacity of settled agriculturists was combined with the energy of pastoral nomads through the conquest of the former by the latter (11, pp. 51–55). This theory, however, has two serious defects. First, it fails to account for the rise of states in aboriginal America, where pastoral nomadism was unknown. Second, it is now well established that pastoral nomadism did not arise in the Old World until after the earliest states had emerged.

Regardless of deficiencies in particular coercive theories, however, there is little question that, in one way or another, war played a decisive role in the rise of the state. Historical or archeological evidence of war is found in the early stages of state formation in Mesopotamia, Egypt, India, China, Japan, Greece, Rome, northern Europe, central Africa, Polynesia, Middle America, Peru, and Colombia, to name only the most prominent examples.

Thus, with the Germanic kingdoms of northern Europe especially in mind, Edward Jenks observed that, "historically speaking, there is not the slightest difficulty in proving that all political communities of the modern type [that is, states] owe their existence to successful warfare" (12). And in reading Jan Vansina's *Kingdoms of the Savanna* (13), a book with no theoretical ax to grind, one finds that state after state in central Africa arose in the same manner.

But is it really true that there is no exception to this rule? Might there not be, somewhere in the world, an example of a state which arose without the agency of war?

Until a few years ago, anthropologists generally believed that the Classic Maya provided such an instance. The archeological evidence then available gave no hint of warfare among the early Maya and led scholars to regard them as a peace-loving theocratic state which had arisen entirely without war (14). However, this view is no longer tenable. Recent archeological discoveries have placed the Classic Maya in a very different light. First came the discovery of the Bonampak murals, showing the early Maya at war and reveling in the torture of war captives. Then, excavations around Tikal revealed large earthworks partly surrounding that Classic Maya city, pointing clearly to a military rivalry with the neighboring city of Uaxactún (15).

Summarizing present thinking on the subject, Michael D. Coe has observed that "the ancient Maya were just as warlike as the . . . bloodthirsty states of the Post-Classic" (16).

Yet, though warfare is surely a prime mover in the origin of the state, it cannot be the only factor. After all, wars have been fought in many parts of the world where the state never emerged. Thus, while warfare may be a necessary condition for the rise of the state, it is not a sufficient one. Or, to put it another way, while we can identify war as the *mechanism* of state formation, we need also to specify the *conditions* under which it gave rise to the state.

Environmental Circumscription

How are we to determine these conditions? One promising approach is to look for those factors common to areas of the world in which states arose indigenously—areas such as the Nile, Tigris-Euphrates, and Indus valleys in the Old World and the Valley of Mexico and the mountain and coastal valleys of Peru in the New. These areas differ from one another in many ways —in altitude, temperature, rainfall, soil type, drainage pattern, and many other features. They do, however, have one thing in common: *they are all areas of circumscribed agricultural land.* Each of them is set off by mountains, seas, or deserts, and these environmental features sharply delimit the area that simple farming peoples could occupy and cultivate. In this respect these areas are very different from, say, the Amazon basin or the eastern woodlands of North America, where extensive and unbroken forests provided almost unlimited agricultural land.

But what is the significance of circumscribed agricultural land for the origin of the state? Its significance can best be understood by comparing political development in two regions of the world having contrasting ecologies —one a region with circumscribed agricultural land and the other a region where there was extensive and unlimited land. The two areas I have chosen to use in making this comparison are the coastal valleys of Peru and the Amazon basin.

Our examination begins at the stage where agricultural communities were already present but where each was still completely autonomous. Looking first at the Amazon basin, we see that agricultural villages there were numerous, but widely dispersed. Even in areas with relatively dense clustering, like the Upper Xingú basin, villages were at least 10 or 15 miles apart. Thus, the typical Amazonian community, even though it practiced a simple form of shifting cultivation which required extensive amounts of land, still had around it all the forest land needed for its gardens (*17*). For Amazonia as a whole, then, population density was low and subsistence pressure on the land was slight.

Warfare was certainly frequent in Amazonia, but it was waged for reasons of revenge, the taking of women, the gaining of personal prestige, and motives of a similar sort. There being no shortage of land, there was, by and large, no warfare over land.

The consequences of the type of warfare that did occur in Amazonia were as follows. A defeated group was not, as a rule, driven from its land. Nor did the victor make any real effort to subject the vanquished, or to exact tribute from him. This would have been difficult to accomplish in any case, since there was no effective way to prevent the losers from fleeing to a distant part of the forest. Indeed, defeated villages often chose to do just this, not so much to avoid subjugation as to avoid further attack. With settlement so sparse in Amazonia, a new area of forest could be found and occupied with relative ease, and without trespassing on the territory of another village. Moreover, since virtually any area of forest is suitable for cultivation, subsistence agriculture could be carried on in the new habitat just about as well as in the old.

It was apparently by this process of fight and flight that horticultural tribes gradually spread out until they came to cover, thinly but extensively, almost the entire Amazon basin. Thus, under the conditions of unlimited agricultural land and low population density that prevailed in Amazonia, the effect of warfare was to disperse villages over a wide area, and to keep them autonomous. With only a very few exceptions, noted below, there was no tendency in Amazonia for villages to be held in place and to combine into larger political units.

In marked contrast to the situation in Amazonia were the events that transpired in the narrow valleys of the Peruvian coast. The reconstruction of these events that I present is admittedly inferential, but I think it is consistent with the archeological evidence.

Here too our account begins at the stage of small, dispersed, and autonomous farming communities. However, instead of being scattered over a vast expanse of rain forest as they were in Amazonia, villages here were confined to some 78 short and narrow valleys (*18*). Each of these valleys, moreover, was backed by the mountains, fronted by the sea, and flanked on either side by desert as dry as any in the world. Nowhere else, perhaps, can one find agricultural valleys more sharply circumscribed than these.

As with neolithic communities generally, villages of the Peruvian coastal valleys tended to grow in size. Since autonomous villages are likely to fission as they grow, as long as land is available for the settlement of splinter communities, these villages undoubtedly split from time to time (*19*). Thus, villages tended to increase in number faster than they grew in size. This increase in the number of villages occupying a valley probably continued, without giving rise to significant changes in subsistence practices, until all the readily arable land in the valley was being farmed.

At this point two changes in agricultural techniques began to occur: the tilling of land already under cultivation was intensified, and new, previously unusable land was brought under cultivation by means of terracing and irrigation (*20*).

Yet the rate at which new arable land was created failed to keep pace with the increasing demand for it. Even before the land shortage became so acute that irrigation began to be practiced systematically, villages were undoubtedly already fighting one another over land. Prior to this time, when agricultural villages were still few in number and well supplied with land, the warfare waged in the coastal valleys of Peru had probably been of much the same type as that described above for Amazonia. With increasing pressure of human population on the land, however, the major incentive for war changed from a desire for revenge to a need to acquire land. And, as the causes of war became predominantly economic, the frequency, intensity, and importance of war increased.

Once this stage was reached, a Peruvian village that lost a war faced consequences very different from those faced by a defeated village in Amazonia. There, as we have seen, the vanquished could flee to a new locale, subsisting there about as well as they had subsisted before, and retaining their independence. In Peru, however, this alternative was no longer open to the inhabitants of defeated villages. The mountains, the desert, and the sea—to say nothing of neighboring villages—blocked escape in every direction. A village defeated in war thus faced only grim prospects. If it was allowed to remain on its own land, instead of being exterminated or expelled, this concession came only at a price. And the price was political subordination to the victor. This subordination generally entailed at least the payment of a tribute or tax in kind, which the defeated village could provide only by producing more food than it had produced before. But subordination sometimes involved a further loss of autonomy on the part of the defeated village—namely, incorporation into the political unit dominated by the victor.

Through the recurrence of warfare of this type, we see arising in coastal Peru integrated territorial units transcending the village in size and in degree of organization. Political evolution was attaining the level of the chiefdom.

As land shortages continued and became even more acute, so did warfare. Now, however, the competing units were no longer small villages but, often, large chiefdoms. From this point on, through the conquest of chiefdom by chiefdom, the size of political units increased at a progressively faster rate. Naturally, as autonomous political units increased in size, they decreased in number, with the result that an entire valley was eventually unified under the banner of its strongest chiefdom. The political unit thus formed was undoubtedly sufficiently centralized and complex to warrant being called a state.

The political evolution I have described for one valley of Peru was also taking place in other valleys, in the highlands as well as on the coast (*21*). Once valley-wide kingdoms emerged, the next step was the formation of multivalley kingdoms through the conquest of weaker valleys by stronger ones. The culmination of this process was the conquest (*22*) of all of Peru by its most powerful state, and the formation of a single great empire. Although this step may have occurred once or twice before in Andean history, it was achieved most notably, and for the last time, by the Incas (23).

Political Evolution

While the aggregation of villages into chiefdoms, and of chiefdoms into kingdoms, was occurring by external acquisition, the structure of these increasingly larger political units was being elaborated by internal evolution. These inner changes were, of course, closely related to outer events. The expansion of successful states brought within their borders conquered peoples and territory which had to be administered. And it was the individuals who had distinguished themselves in war who were generally appointed to political office and assigned the task of carrying out this administration. Besides maintaining law and order and collecting taxes, the functions of this burgeoning class of administrators included mobilizing labor for building irrigation works, roads, fortresses, palaces, and temples. Thus, their functions helped to weld an assorted collection of petty states into a single integrated and centralized political unit.

These same individuals, who owed their improved social position to their exploits in war, became, along with the ruler and his kinsmen, the nucleus of an upper class. A lower class in turn emerged from the prisoners taken in war and employed as servants and slaves by their captors. In this manner did war contribute to the rise of social classes.

I noted earlier that peoples attempt to acquire their neighbors' land before they have made the fullest possible use of their own. This implies that every autonomous village has an untapped margin of food productivity, and that this margin is squeezed out only when the village is subjugated and compelled to pay taxes in kind. The surplus food extracted from conquered villages through taxation, which in the aggregate attained very significant proportions, went largely to support the ruler, his warriors and retainers, officials, priests, and other members of the rising upper class, who thus became completely divorced from food production.

Finally, those made landless by war but not enslaved tended to gravitate to settlements which, because of their specialized administrative, commercial, or religious functions, were growing into towns and cities. Here they were able to make a living as workers and artisans, exchanging their labor or their wares for part of the economic surplus exacted from village farmers by the ruling class and spent by members of that class to raise their standard of living.

The process of political evolution which I have outlined for the coastal valleys of Peru was, in its essential features, by no means unique to this region. Areas of circumscribed agricultural land elsewhere in the world, such as the Valley of Mexico, Mesopotamia, the Nile Valley, and the Indus Valley, saw the process occur in much the same way and for essentially the same reasons. In these areas, too, autonomous neolithic villages were succeeded by chiefdoms, chiefdoms by kingdoms, and kingdoms by empires. The last stage of this development was, of course, the most impressive. The scale and magnificence attained by the early empires overshadowed everything that had gone before. But, in a sense, empires were merely the logical culmination of the process. The really fundamental step, the one that had triggered the entire train of events that led to empires, was the change from village autonomy to supravillage integration. This step was a change in kind; everything that followed was, in a way, only a change in degree.

In addition to being pivotal, the step to supracommunity aggregation was difficult, for it took 2 million years to achieve. But, once it was achieved, once village autonomy was transcended, only two or three millennia were required for the rise of great empires and the flourishing of complex civilizations.

Resource Concentration

Theories are first formulated on the basis of a limited number of facts. Eventually, though, a theory must confront all of the facts. And often new facts are stubborn and do not conform to the theory, or do not conform very well. What distinguishes a successful theory from an unsuccessful one is that it can be modified or elaborated to accommodate the entire range of facts. Let us see how well the "circumscription theory" holds up when it is brought face-to-face with certain facts that appear to be exceptions.

For the first test let us return to Amazonia. Early voyagers down the Amazon left written testimony of a culture along that river higher than the culture I have described for Amazonia generally. In the 1500's, the native population living on the banks of the Amazon was relatively dense, villages were fairly large and close together, and some degree of social stratification existed. Moreover, here and there a paramount chief held sway over many communities.

The question immediately arises: With unbroken stretches of arable land extending back from the Amazon for hundreds of miles, why were there chiefdoms here?

To answer this question we must look closely at the environmental conditions afforded by the Amazon. Along the margins of the river itself, and on islands within it, there is a type of land called várzea. The river floods this land every year, covering it with a layer of fertile silt. Because of this annual replenishment, várzea is agricultural land of first quality which can be cultivated year after year without ever having to lie fallow. Thus, among native farmers it was highly prized and greatly coveted. The waters of the Amazon were also extraordinarily bountiful, providing fish, manatees, turtles and turtle eggs, caimans, and other riverine foods in inexhaustible amounts. By virtue of this concentration of resources, the Amazon, as a habitat, was distinctly superior to its hinterlands.

Concentration of resources along the Amazon amounted almost to a kind of circumscription. While there was no sharp cleavage between productive and unproductive land, as there was in Peru, there was at least a steep ecological gradient. So much more rewarding was the Amazon River than adjacent areas, and so desirable did it become as a habitat, that peoples were drawn to it from surrounding regions. Eventually crowding occurred along many portions of the river, leading to warfare over sections of river front. And the losers in war, in order to retain access to the river, often had no choice but to submit to the victors. By this subordination of villages to a paramount chief there arose along the Amazon chiefdoms representing a higher step in political evolution than had occurred elsewhere in the basin (24).

The notion of resource concentration also helps to explain the surprising degree of political development apparently attained by peoples of the Peruvian coast while they were still depending primarily on fishing for subsistence, and only secondarily on agriculture (18). Of this seeming anomaly Lanning has written: "To the best of my knowledge, this is the only case in which so many of the characteristics of civilization have been found without a basically agricultural economic foundation" (25).

Armed with the concept of resource concentration, however, we can show that this development was not so anomalous after all. The explanation, it seems to me, runs as follows. Along the coast of Peru wild food sources occurred in considerable number and variety. However, they were restricted to a very narrow margin of land (26). Accordingly, while the *abundance* of food in this zone led to a sharp rise in population, the *restrictedness* of this food soon resulted in the almost complete occupation of exploitable areas. And when pressure on the available resources reached a critical level, competition over land ensued. The result of this competition was to set in motion the sequence of events of political evolution that I have described.

Thus, it seems that we can safely add resource concentration to environmental circumscription as a factor leading to warfare over land, and thus to political integration beyond the village level.

Social Circumscription

But there is still another factor to be considered in accounting for the rise of the state.

In dealing with the theory of environmental circumscription while discussing the Yanomamö Indians of Venezuela, Napoleon A. Chagnon (27) has introduced the concept of "social circumscription." By this he means that a high density of population in an area can produce effects on peoples living near the center of the area that are similar to effects produced by environmental circumscription. This notion seems to me to be an important addition to our theory. Let us see how, according to Chagnon, social circum-

scription has operated among the Yanomamö.

The Yanomamö, who number some 10,000, live in an extensive region of noncircumscribed rain forest, away from any large river. One might expect that Yanomamö villages would thus be more or less evenly spaced. However, Chagnon notes that, at the center of Yanomamö territory, villages are closer together than they are at the periphery. Because of this, they tend to impinge on one another more, with the result that warfare is more frequent and intense in the center than in peripheral areas. Moreover, it is more difficult for villages in the nuclear area to escape attack by moving away, since, unlike villages on the periphery, their ability to move is somewhat restricted.

The net result is that villages in the central area of Yanomamö territory are larger than villages in the other areas, since large village size is an advantage for both attack and defense. A further effect of more intense warfare in the nuclear area is that village headmen are stronger in that area. Yanomamö headmen are also the war leaders, and their influence increases in proportion to their village's participation in war. In addition, offensive and defensive alliances between villages are more common in the center of Yanomamö territory than in outlying areas. Thus, while still at the autonomous village level of political organization, those Yanomamö subject to social circumscription have clearly moved a step or two in the direction of higher political development.

Although the Yanomamö manifest social circumscription only to a modest degree, this amount of it has been enough to make a difference in their level of political organization. What the effects of social circumscription would be in areas where it was more fully expressed should, therefore, be clear. First would come a reduction in the size of the territory of each village. Then, as population pressure became more severe, warfare over land would ensue. But because adjacent land for miles around was already the property of other villages, a defeated village would have nowhere to flee. From this point on, the consequences of warfare for that village, and for political evolution in general, would be essentially as I have described them for the situation of environmental circumscription.

To return to Amazonia, it is clear that, if social circumscription is opera-

tive among the Yanomamö today, it was certainly operative among the tribes of the Amazon River 400 years ago. And its effect would undoubtedly have been to give a further spur to political evolution in that region.

We see then that, even in the absence of sharp environmental circumscription, the factors of resource concentration and social circumscription may, by intensifying war and redirecting it toward the taking of land, give a strong impetus to political development.

With these auxiliary hypotheses incorporated into it, the circumscription theory is now better able to confront the entire range of test cases that can be brought before it. For example, it can now account for the rise of the state in the Hwang Valley of northern China, and even in the Petén region of the Maya lowlands, areas not characterized by strictly circumscribed agricultural land. In the case of the Hwang Valley, there is no question that resource concentration and social circumscription were present and active forces. In the lowland Maya area, resource concentration seems not to have been a major factor, but social circumscription may well have been.

Some archeologists may object that population density in the Petén during Formative times was too low to give rise to social circumscription. But, in assessing what constitutes a population dense enough to produce this effect, we must consider not so much the total land area occupied as the amount of land needed to support the existing population. And the size of this supporting area depends not only on the size of the population but also on the mode of subsistence. The shifting cultivation presumably practiced by the ancient Maya (28) required considerably more land, per capita, than did the permanent field cultivation of say, the Valley of Mexico or the coast of Peru (29). Consequently, insofar as its effects are concerned, a relatively low population density in the Petén may have been equivalent to a much higher one in Mexico or Peru.

We have already learned from the Yanomamö example that social circumscription may begin to operate while population is still relatively sparse. And we can be sure that the Petén was far more densely peopled in Formative times than Yanomamö territory is today. Thus, population density among the lowland Maya, while giving a superficial appearance of sparseness, may actually have been high enough to provoke fighting over land, and thus provide the initial impetus for the formation of a state.

Conclusion

In summary, then, the circumscription theory in its elaborated form goes far toward accounting for the origin of the state. It explains why states arose where they did, and why they failed to arise elsewhere. It shows the state to be a predictable response to certain specific cultural, demographic, and ecological conditions. Thus, it helps to elucidate what was undoubtedly the most important single step ever taken in the political evolution of mankind.

References and Notes

1. R. L. Carneiro, in *The Evolution of Horticultural Systems in Native South America: Causes and Consequences; A Symposium*, J. Wilbert, Ed., *Antropológica (Venezuela)*, Suppl. 2 (1961), pp. 47–67, see especially pp. 59–64.
2. For example, the early American sociologist Lester F. Ward saw the state as "the result of an extraordinary exercise of the rational . . . faculty" which seemed to him so exceptional that "it must have been the emanation of a single brain or a few concerting minds. . . ." [*Dynamic Sociology* (Appleton, New York, 1883), vol. 2, p. 224].
3. See, for example, V. G. Childe, *Man Makes Himself* (Watts, London, 1936), pp. 82–83; *Town Planning Rev.* 21, 3 (1950), p. 6.
4. I have in my files recorded instances of surplus food production by such Amazonian tribes as the Tupinambá, Jevero, Mundurucú, Tucano, Desana, Cubeo, and Canela. An exhaustive search of the ethnographic literature for this region would undoubtedly reveal many more examples.
5. Wittfogel states: "These patterns [of organization and social control—that is, the state] come into being when an experimenting community of farmers or protofarmers finds large sources of moisture in a dry but potentially fertile area. . . . a number of farmers eager to conquer [agriculturally, not militarily] arid lowlands and plains are forced to invoke the organizational devices which—on the basis of premachine technology—offer the one chance of success; they must work in cooperation with their fellows and subordinate themselves to a directing authority" [*Oriental Despotism* (Yale Univ. Press, New Haven, Conn., 1957), p. 18].
6. For Mesopotamia, Robert M. Adams has concluded: "In short, there is nothing to suggest that the rise of dynastic authority in southern Mesopotamia was linked to the administrative requirements of a major canal system" [in *City Invincible*, C. H. Kraeling and R. M. Adams, Eds. (Univ. of Chicago Press, Chicago, 1960), p. 281]. For China, the prototypical area for Wittfogel's hydraulic theories, the French Sinologist Jacques Gernet has recently written: "although the

establishment of a system of regulation of water courses and irrigation, and the control of this system, may have affected the political constitution of the military states and imperial China, the fact remains that, historically, it was the pre-existing state structures and the large, well-trained labour force provided by the armies that made the great irrigation projects possible" [*Ancient China, from the Beginnings to the Empire*, R. Rudorff, Transl. (Faber and Faber, London, 1968), p. 92]. For Mexico, large-scale irrigation systems do not appear to antedate the Classic period, whereas it is clear that the first states arose in the preceding Formative or Pre-Classic period.
7. This is not to say, of course, that large-scale irrigation, where it occurred, did not contribute significantly to increasing the power and scope of the state. It unquestionably did. To the extent that Wittfogel limits himself to this contention, I have no quarrel with him whatever. However, the point at issue is not how the state increased its power but how it arose in the first place. And to this issue the hydraulic hypothesis does not appear to hold the key.
8. See *The Evolution of Society; Selections from Herbert Spencer's Principles of Sociology*, R. L. Carneiro, Ed. (Univ. of Chicago Press, Chicago, 1967), pp. 32–47, 63–96, 153–165.
9. L. Gumplowicz, *Der Rassenkampf* (Wagner, Innsbruck, 1883).
10. G. Ratzenhofer, *Wesen und Zweck der Politik* (Brockhaus, Leipsig, 1893).
11. F. Oppenheimer, *The State*, J. M. Gitterman, Transl. (Vanguard, New York, 1926).
12. E. Jenks, *A History of Politics* (Macmillan, New York, 1900), p. 73.
13. J. Vansina, *Kingdoms of the Savanna* (Univ. of Wisconsin Press, Madison, 1966).
14. For example, Julian H. Steward wrote: "It is possible, therefore, that the Maya were able to develop a high civilization only because they enjoyed an unusually long period of peace; for their settlement pattern would seem to have been too vulnerable to warfare" [*Amer. Anthropol.* 51, 1 (1949), see p. 17].
15. D. E. Puleston and D. W. Callender, *Expedition* 9 No. 3, 40 (1967), see pp. 45, 47.
16. M. D. Coe, *The Maya* (Praeger, New York, 1966), p. 147.
17. See R. L. Carneiro, in *Men and Cultures, Selected Papers of the Fifth International Congress of Anthropological and Ethnological Sciences*, A. F. C. Wallace, Ed. (Univ. of Pennsylvania Press, Philadelphia, 1960), pp. 229–234.
18. In early agricultural times (Preceramic Period VI, beginning about 2500 B.C.) human settlement seems to have been denser along the coast than in the river valleys, and subsistence appears to have been based more on fishing than on farming. Furthermore, some significant first steps in political evolution beyond autonomous villages may have been taken at this stage. However, once subsistence began to be based predominantly on agriculture, the settlement pattern changed, and communities were thenceforth concentrated more in the river valleys, where the only land of any size suitable for cultivation was located. See E. P. Lanning, *Peru Before the Incas* (Prentice-Hall, Englewood Cliffs, N.J., 1967), pp. 57–59.
19. In my files I find reported instances of village splitting among the following Amazonian tribes: Kuikuru, Amarakaeri, Cubeo, Urubú, Tuparí, Yanomamö, Tucano, Tenetehara, Canela, and Northern Cayapó. Under the conditions of easy resettlement found in Amazonia, splitting often takes place at a village population level of less than 100, and village size seldom exceeds 200. In coastal Peru, however, where land was severely restricted, villages could not fission so readily, and thus grew to population levels which, according to Lanning [*Peru Before the Incas* (Prentice-

Hall, Englewood Cliffs, N.J., 1967), p. 64], may have averaged over 300.
20. See R. L. Carneiro, *Ethnograph.-archäol. Forschungen* 4, 22 (1958).
21. Naturally, this evolution took place in the various Peruvian valleys at different rates and to different degrees. In fact it is possible that at the same time that some valleys were already unified politically, others still had not evolved beyond the stage of autonomous villages.
22. Not every step in empire building was necessarily taken through actual physical conquest, however. The threat of force sometimes had the same effect as its exercise. In this way many smaller chiefdoms and states were probably coerced into giving up their sovereignty without having to be defeated on the field of battle. Indeed, it was an explicit policy of the Incas, in expanding their empire, to try persuasion before resorting to force of arms. See Garcilaso de la Vega, *Royal Commentaries of the Incas and General History of Peru*, Part 1, H. V. Livermore, Transl. (Univ. of Texas Press, Austin, 1966), pp. 108, 111, 140, 143, 146, 264.
23. The evolution of empire in Peru was thus by no means rectilinear or irreversible. Advance alternated with decline. Integration was sometimes followed by disintegration, with states fragmenting back to chiefdoms, and perhaps even to autonomous villages. But the forces underlying political development were strong and, in the end, prevailed. Thus, despite fluctuations and reversions, the course of evolution in Peru was unmistakable: it began with many small, simple, scattered, and autonomous communities and ended with a single, vast, complex, and centralized empire.
24. Actually, a similar political development did take place in another part of Amazonia— the basin of the Mamoré River in the Mojos plain of Bolivia. Here, too, resource concentration appears to have played a key role. See W. Denevan, "The Aboriginal Cultural Geography of the Llanos de Mojos of Bolivia," *Ibero-americana No. 48* (1966), pp. 43–50, 104–105, 108–110. In native North America north of Mexico the highest cultural development attained, Middle-Mississippi, also occurred along a major river (the Mississippi), which, by providing especially fertile soil and riverine food resources, comprised a zone of resource concentration. See J. B. Griffin, *Science* 156, 175 (1967), p. 189.
25. E. P. Lanning, *Peru Before the Incas* (Prentice-Hall, Englewood Cliffs, N.J., 1967), p. 59.
26. Resource concentration, then, was here combined with environmental circumscription. And, indeed, the same thing can be said of the great desert river valleys, such as the Nile, Tigris-Euphrates, and Indus.
27. N. A. Chagnon, *Proceedings, VIIIth International Congress of Anthropological and Ethnological Sciences* (Tokyo and Kyoto, 1968), vol. 3 (*Ethnology and Archaeology*), p. 249 (especially p. 251). See also N. Fock, *Folk* 6, 47 (1964), p. 52.
28. S. G. Morley and G. W. Brainerd, *The Ancient Maya* (Stanford Univ. Press,. Stanford, Calif., ed. 3, 1956), pp. 128–129.
29. One can assume, I think, that any substantial increase in population density among the Maya was accompanied by a certain intensification of agriculture. As the population increased fields were probably weeded more thoroughly, and they may well have been cultivated a year or two longer and fallowed a few years less. Yet, given the nature of soils in the humid tropics, the absence of any evidence of fertilization, and the moderate population densities, it seems likely that Maya farming remained extensive rather than becoming intensive.

12

How Were Cities Invented?

BY JOHN PFEIFFER

The most striking mark of man's genius as a species, as the most adaptable of animals, has been his ability to live in cities. From the perspective of all we know about human evolution, nothing could be more unnatural. For over fifteen million years, from the period when members of the family of man first appeared on earth until relatively recent times, our ancestors were nomadic, small-group, wide-open-spaces creatures. They lived on the move among other moving animals in isolated little bands of a few families, roaming across wildernesses that extended like oceans to the horizon and beyond.

Considering that heritage, the wonder is not that man has trouble getting along in cities but that he can do it at all—that he can learn to live in the same place year round, enclosed in sharp-cornered and brightly-lit rectangular spaces, among noises, most of which are made by machines, within shouting distance of hundreds of other people, most of them strangers. Furthermore, such conditions arose so swiftly, practically overnight on the evolutionary time scale, that he has hardly had a chance to get used to them. The transition from a world without cities to our present situation took a mere five or six millenniums.

It is precisely because we are so close to our origins that what happened in prehistory bears directly on current problems. In fact, the expectation is that new studies of pre-cities and early cities will contribute as significantly to an understanding of today's urban complexes as studies of infancy and early childhood have to an understanding of adolescence. Cities are signs, symptoms if you will, of an accelerating and intensive phase of human evolution, a process that we are only beginning to investigate scientifically.

The first stages of the process may be traced back some fifteen thousand years to a rather less hectic era. Homo sapiens, that new breed of restless and intelligent primate, had reached a high point in his career as a hunter-gatherer subsisting predominantly on wild plants and animals. He had developed special tools, special tactics and strategies, for dealing with a wide variety of environments, from savannas and semideserts to tundras and tropical rain forests and mountain regions. Having learned to exploit practically every type of environment, he seemed at last to have found his natural place in the scheme of things—as a hunter living in balance with other species, and with all the world as his hunting ground.

But forces were already at work that would bring an end to this state of equilibrium and ultimately give rise to cities and the state of continuing instability that we are trying to cope with today. New theories, a harder look at the old theories, and an even harder look at our own tendencies to think small have radically changed our ideas about what happened and why.

We used to believe, in effect, that people abandoned hunting and gathering as soon as a reasonable alternative became available to them. It was hardly a safe or reliable way of life. Our ancestors faced sudden death and injury from predators and from prey that fought back, disease from exposure to the elements and from always being on the move, and hunger because the chances were excellent of coming back empty-handed from the hunt. Survival was a full-time struggle. Leisure came only after the invention of agriculture, which brought food surpluses, rising populations, and cities. Such was the accepted picture.

The fact of the matter, supported by studies of living hunter-gatherers as well as by the archaeological record, is that the traditional view is largely melodrama and science fiction. Our preagricultural ancestors were quite healthy, quite safe, and regularly obtained all the food they needed. And they did it with time to burn. As a rule, the job of collecting food, animal and vegetable, required no more than a three-hour day, or a twenty-one-hour week. During that time, collectors brought in enough food for the entire group, which included an appreciable proportion (perhaps 30 per cent or more) of dependents, old persons and children who did little or no work. Leisure is basically a phenomenon of hunting-gathering times, and people have been trying to recover it ever since.

Another assumption ripe for discarding is that civilization first arose in the valleys of the Tigris, Euphrates, and Nile rivers and spread from there to the rest of the world. Accumulating evidence fails to support this notion that civilization is an exclusive product of these regions. To be sure, agriculture and cities may have appeared first in the Near East, but there are powerful arguments for completely independent origins in at least two other widely separated regions, Mesoamerica and Southeast Asia.

In all cases, circumstances forced hunter-gatherers to evolve new ways of surviving. With the decline of the ancient life style, nomadism, problems began piling up. If only people had kept on moving about like sane and respectable primates, life would be a great deal simpler. Instead, they settled down in increasing numbers over wider areas, and society started changing with a vengeance. Although the causes of this settling down remain a mystery, the fact of independent origins calls for an explanation based on worldwide developments.

An important factor, emphasized recently by Lewis Binford of the University of New Mexico, may have been the melting of mile-high glaciers, which was well under way fifteen thousand years ago, and which released enough water to raise the world's oceans 250 to 500 feet, to flood previously exposed coastal plains, and to create shallow bays and estuaries and marshlands. Vast numbers of fish and wild fowl made use of the new environments, and the extra resources permitted people to obtain food without migrating seasonally. In other words, people expended less energy, and life became that much easier, in the beginning anyway.

Yet this sensible and seemingly innocent change was to get mankind into all sorts of difficulties. According to a recent theory, it triggered a chain of events that made cities possible if not inevitable. Apparently, keeping on the move had always served as a natural birth-control mechanism, in part, perhaps, by causing a relatively high incidence of miscarriages. But the population brakes were off as soon as people began settling down.

One clue to what may have happened is provided by contemporary studies of a number of primitive tribes, such as the Bushmen of Africa's Kalahari Desert. Women living in nomadic bands, bands that pick up and move half a dozen or more times a year, have an average of one baby every four years or so, as compared with one baby every two and a half years for Bushman women living in settled communities—an increase of five to eight babies per mother during a twenty-year reproductive period.

The archaeological record suggests that in some places at least, a comparable phenomenon accompanied the melting of glaciers during the last ice age. People settled down and multiplied in the Les Eyzies region of southern France, one of the richest and most-studied centers of prehistory. Great limestone cliffs dominate the countryside, and at the foot of the cliffs are natural shelters, caves and rocky overhangs where people built fires, made tools out of flint and bone and ivory, and planned the next day's hunt. On special occasions artists equipped with torches went deep into certain caves like Lascaux and covered the walls with magnificent images of the animals they hunted.

In some places the cliffs and the shelters extend for hundreds of yards; in other places there are good living sites close to one another on the opposite slopes of river valleys. People in the Les Eyzies region were living not in isolated bands but in full-fledged communities, and populations seem to have been on the rise. During the period from seven thousand to twelve thousand years ago, the total number of sites doubled, and an appreciable proportion of them probably represent year-round settlements located in small river valleys. An analysis of excavated animal remains reveals an increasing dietary reliance on migratory birds and fish (chiefly salmon).

People were also settling down at about the same time in the Near East —for example, not far from the Mediterranean shoreline of Israel and on the border between the coastal plain and the hills to the east. Ofer Bar-

Yosef, of the Institute of Archaeology of Hebrew University in Jerusalem, points out that since they were able to exploit both these areas, they did not have to wander widely in search of food. There were herds of deer and gazelle, wild boar, fish and wild fowl, wild cereals and other plants, and limestone caves and shelters like those in the Les Eyzies region. Somewhat later, however, a new land-use pattern emerged. Coastal villages continued to flourish, but in addition to them, new sites began appearing further inland— and in areas that were drier and less abundant.

Only under special pressure will men abandon a good thing, and in this case it was very likely the pressure of rising populations. The evidence suggests that the best coastal lands were supporting about all the hunter-gatherers they could support; and as living space decreased there was a "budding off," an overflow of surplus population into the second-best back country where game was scarcer. These people depended more and more on plants, particularly on wild cereals, as indicated by the larger numbers of flint sickle blades, mortars and pestles, and storage pits found at their sites (and also by an increased wear and pitting of teeth, presumably caused by chewing more coarse and gritty plant foods).

Another sign of the times was the appearance of stone buildings, often with impressively high and massive walls. The structures served a number of purposes. For one thing, they included storage bins where surplus grain could be kept in reserve for bad times, when there was a shortage of game and wild plants. They also imply danger abroad in the countryside, new kinds of violence, and a mounting need for defenses to protect stored goods from the raids of people who had not settled down.

Above all, the walls convey a feeling of increasing permanence, an increasing commitment to places. Although man was still mainly a hunter-gatherer living on wild species, some of the old options no longer existed for him. In the beginning, settling down may have involved a measure of choice, but now man was no longer quite so free to change locales when the land became less fruitful. Even in those days frontiers were vanishing. Man's problem was to develop new options, new ways of working the land more intensively so that it would provide the food that migration had always provided in more mobile times.

The all-important transition to agriculture came in small steps, establishing itself almost before anyone realized what was going on. Settlers in marginal lands took early measures to get more food out of less abundant environments—roughing up the soil a bit with scraping or digging sticks, sowing wheat and barley seeds, weeding, and generally doing their best to promote growth. To start with at least, it was simply a matter of supplementing regular diets of wild foods with some domesticated species, animals as well as plants, and people probably regarded themselves as hunter-gatherers working hard to maintain their way of life rather than as the revolutionaries they were. They were trying to preserve the old self-sufficiency, but it was a losing effort.

The wilderness way of life became more and more remote, more and more nearly irretrievable. Practically every advance in the technology of agriculture committed people to an increasing dependence on domesticated species and on the activities of other people living nearby. Kent Flannery of the University of Michigan emphasizes this point in a study of one part of Greater Mesopotamia, prehistoric Iran, during the period between twelve thousand and six thousand years ago. For the hunter-gatherer, an estimated one-third of the country's total land area was good territory, consisting of grassy plains and high mountain valleys where wild species were abundant; the rest of the land was desert and semidesert.

The coming of agriculture meant that people used a smaller proportion of the countryside. Early farming took advantage of naturally distributed water; the best terrain for that, namely terrain with a high water table and marshy areas, amounted to about a tenth of the land area. But only a tenth of that tenth was suitable for the next major development, irrigation. Meanwhile, food yields were soaring spectacularly, and so was the population of Iran, which increased more than fiftyfold; in other words, fifty times the original population was being supported by food produced on one-hundredth of the land.

A detailed picture of the steps involved in this massing of people is coming from studies of one part of southwest Iran, an 880-square-mile region between the Zagros Mountains and the Iraqi border. The Susiana Plain is mostly flat, sandy semidesert, the only notable features being man-made mounds that loom on the horizon like islands, places where people built in successively high levels on the ruins of their ancestors. During the past decade or so, hundreds of mounds have been mapped and dated (mainly through pottery styles) by Robert Adams of the University of Chicago, Jean Perrot of the French Archaeological Mission in Iran, and Henry Wright and Gregory Johnson of the University of Michigan. Their work provides a general idea of when the mounds were occupied, how they varied in size at different periods—and how a city may be born.

I magine a time-lapse motion picture of the early settling of the Susiana Plain, starting about 6500 B.C., each minute of film representing a century. At first the plain is empty, as it has been since the beginning of time. Then the pioneers arrive; half a dozen families move in and build a cluster of mud-brick homes near a river. Soon another cluster appears and another, until, after about five minutes (it is now 6000 B.C.), there are ten settlements, each covering an area of 1 to 3 hectares (1 hectare = 2.47 acres). Five minutes more (5500 B.C.) and we see the start of irrigation, on a small scale, as people dig little ditches to carry water from rivers and tributaries to lands along the banks. Crop yields increase and so do populations, and there are now thirty settlements, all about the same size as the original ten.

This is but a prelude to the main event. Things become really complicated during the next fifteen minutes or so (5500 to 4000 B.C.). Irrigation systems, constructed and maintained by family groups of varying sizes, become more complex. The number of settlements shows a modest increase, from thirty to forty, but a more significant change takes place—the appearance of a hierarchy. Instead of settlements all about the same size, there are now levels of settlements and a kind of ranking: one town (7 hectares), ten large villages (3 to 4 hectares), and twenty-nine smaller villages of less than 3 hectares. During this period large residential and ceremonial structures appear at Susa, a town on the western edge of the Susiana Plain.

Strange happenings can be observed not long after the middle of this period (about 4600 B.C.). For reasons unknown, the number of settlements decreases rapidly. It is not known whether the population of the area decreased simultaneously. Time passes, and the number of settlements increases to about the same level as before, but great changes have occurred. Three cities have appeared with monumental public buildings, elaborate residential architecture, large workshops, major storage and market facilities, and certainly with administrators and bureaucrats. The settlement hierarchy is more complex, and settlements are no longer located to take advantage solely of good agricultural opportunities. Their location is also influenced by the cities and the services and opportunities available there. By the end of our hypothetical time-lapse film, by the early part of the third millennium B.C., the largest settlement of all is the city of Susa, which covers some thirty hectares and will cover up to a square kil-

Female figurine from Tepe Yahya, Iran. A variety of sites throughout the world have yielded astonishingly ancient objects created by men who farmed and built permanent dwellings such as this stone figurine found in Tepe Yahya, Iran—a settlement that was in contact with Susa before 4000 B.C.

Hillel Burger, Peabody Museum, Harvard University

ometer (100 hectares) of territory before it collapses in historical times.

All Mesopotamia underwent major transformations during this period. Another city was taking shape 150 miles northwest of Susa in the heartland of Sumer. Within a millennium the site of Uruk near the Euphrates River grew from village dimensions to a city enclosing within its defense walls more than thirty thousand people, four hundred hectares, and at the center a temple built on top of a huge brick platform. Archaeological surveys reveal that this period also saw a massive immigration into the region from places and for reasons as yet undetermined, resulting in a tenfold increase in settlements and in the formation of several new cities.

Similar surveys, requiring months and thousands of miles of walking, are completed or under way in many parts of the world. Little more than a millennium after the establishment of Uruk and Susa, cities began making an independent appearance in northern China not far from the conflux of the Wei and Yellow rivers, in an area that also saw the beginnings of agriculture. Still later, and also independently as far as we can tell, intensive settlement and land use developed in the New World.

The valley of Oaxaca in Mexico, where Flannery and his associates are working currently, provides another example of a city in the process of being formed. Around 500 B.C., or perhaps a bit earlier, buildings were erected for the first time on the tops of hills. Some of the hills were small, no more than twenty-five or thirty feet high, and the buildings were correspondingly small; they overlooked a few terraces and a river and probably a hamlet or two. Larger structures appeared on higher hills overlooking many villages. About 400 B.C. the most elaborate settlement began to appear on the highest land, 1,500-foot Monte Albán, with a panoramic view of the valley's three arms; and within two centuries it had developed into an urban center including hundreds of terraces, an irrigation system, a great plaza, ceremonial buildings and residences, and an astronomical observatory.

At about the same time, the New World's largest city, Teotihuacán, was evolving some 225 miles to the northwest in the central highlands of Mexico. Starting as a scattering of villages and hamlets, it covered nearly eight square miles at its height (around A.D. 100 to 200) and probably contained some 125,000 people. Archaeologists are now reconstructing the life and times of this great urban center. William Sanders of Pennsylvania State University is concentrating on an analysis of settlement patterns in the area, while Rene Millon of the University of Rochester and his associates have prepared detailed section-by-section maps of the city as a step toward further extensive excavations. Set in a narrow valley among mountains and with its own man-made mountains, the Pyramid of the Sun and the Pyramid of the Moon, the city flourished on a grand scale. It housed local dignitaries and priests, delegations from other parts of Mesoamerica, and workshop neighborhoods where specialists in the manufacture of textiles, pottery, obsidian blades, and other products lived together in early-style apartments.

The biggest center in what is now the United States probably reached its peak about a millennium after Teotihuacán. But it has not been reconstructed, and archaeologists are just beginning to appreciate the scale of what happened there. Known as Cahokia and located east of the Mississippi near St. Louis, it consists of a cluster of some 125 mounds (including a central mound 100 feet high and covering 15 acres) as well as a line of mounds extending six miles to the west.

So surveys and excavations continue, furnishing the sort of data needed to disprove or prove our theories. Emerging patterns—patterns involving the specific locations of different kinds of communities and of buildings and other artifacts within communities—can yield information about the forces that shaped and are still shaping cities and the behavior of people in cities. But one trend stands out above all others: the world was becoming more and more stratified. Every development seemed to favor social distinctions, social classes and elites, and to work against the old hunter-gatherer ways.

Among hunter-gatherers all people are equal. Individuals are recognized as exceptional hunters, healers, or storytellers, and they all have the chance to shine upon appropriate occasions. But it would be unthinkable for one of them, for any one man, to take over as full-time leader. That ethic passed when the nomadic life passed. In fact, a literal explosion of differences accompanied the coming of communities where people lived close together in permanent dwellings and under conditions where moving away was not easy.

The change is reflected clearly in observed changes of settlement patterns.

Hierarchies of settlements imply hierarchies of people. Emerging social levels are indicated by the appearance of villages and towns and cities where only villages had existed before, by different levels of complexity culminating in such centers as Susa and Monte Albán and Cahokia. Circumstances practically drove people to establish class societies. In Mesopotamia, for instance, increasingly sophisticated agricultural systems and intensive concentrations of populations brought about enormous and irreversible changes within a short period. People were clamped in a demographic vise, more and more of them living and depending on less and less land—an ideal setting for the rapid rise of status differences.

Large-scale irrigation was a highly effective centralizing force, calling for new duties and new regularities and new levels of discipline. People still depended on the seasons; but in addition, canals had to be dug and maintained, and periodic cleaning was required to prevent the artificial waterways from filling up with silt and assorted litter. Workers had to be brought together, assigned tasks, and fed, which meant schedules and storehouses and rationing stations and mass-produced pottery to serve as food containers. It took time to organize such activities efficiently. There were undoubtedly many false starts, many attempts by local people to work things out among themselves and their neighbors at a community or village level. Many small centers, budding institutions, were undoubtedly formed and many collapsed, and we may yet detect traces of them in future excavations and analyses of settlement patterns.

The ultimate outcome was inevitable. Survival demanded organization on a regional rather than a local basis. It also demanded high-level administrators and managers, and most of them had to be educated people, mainly because of the need to prepare detailed records of supplies and transactions. Record-keeping has a long prehistory, perhaps dating back to certain abstract designs engraved on cave walls and bone twenty-five thousand or more years ago. But in Mesopotamia after 4000 B.C. there was a spurt in the art of inventing and utilizing special marks and symbols.

The trend is shown in the stamp and cylinder seals used by officials to place their "signatures" on clay tags and tablets, man's first documents. At first the designs on the stamp seals were uncomplicated, consisting for the most part of single animals or simple geometric motifs. Later, however, there were bigger stamp seals with more elaborate scenes depicting several objects or people or animals. Finally the cylinder seals appeared, which could be rolled to repeat a complex design. These seals indicate the existence of more and more different signatures—and more and more officials and record keepers. Similar trends are evident in potters' marks and other symbols. All these developments precede pictographic writing, which appears around 3200 B.C.

Wherever record keepers and populations were on the rise, in the Near East or Mexico or China, we can be reasonably sure that the need for a police force or the prehistoric equivalent thereof was on the increase, too. Conflict, including everything from fisticuffs to homicide, increases sharply with group size, and people have known this for a long time. The Bushmen have a strong feeling about avoiding crowds: "We like to get together, but we fear fights." They are most comfortable in bands of about twenty-five persons and when they have to assemble in larger groups—which happens for a total of only a few months a year, mainly to conduct initiations, arrange marriages, and be near the few permanent water holes during dry seasons—they form separate small groups of about twenty-five, as if they were still living on their own.

Incidentally, twenty-five has been called a "magic number," because it hints at what may be a universal law of group behavior. There have been many counts of hunter-gatherer bands, not only in the Kalahari Desert, but also in such diverse places as the forests of Thailand, the Canadian Northwest, and northern India. Although individual bands may vary from fifteen to seventy-five members, the tendency is to cluster around twenty-five, and in all cases a major reason for keeping groups small is the desire to avoid violence. In other words, the association between large groups and conflict has deep roots and very likely presented law-and-order problems during the early days of cities and pre-cities, as it has ever since.

Along with managers and record keepers and keepers of the peace, there were also specialists in trade. A number of factors besides population growth and intensive land use were involved in the origin of cities, and local and long-distance trade was among the most important. Prehistoric centers in the process of becoming urban were almost always trade centers. They typically occupied favored places, strategic points in developing trade networks, along major waterways and caravan routes or close to supplies of critical raw materials.

Archaeologists are making a renewed attempt to learn more about such developments. Wright's current work in southwest Iran, for example, includes preliminary studies to detect and measure changes in the flow of trade. One site about sixty-five miles from Susa lies close to tar pits, which in prehistoric times served as a source of natural asphalt for fastening stone blades to handles and waterproofing baskets and roofs. By saving all the waste bits of this important raw material preserved in different excavated levels, Wright was able to estimate fluctuations in its production over a period of time. In one level, for example, he found that the amounts of asphalt produced increased far beyond local requirements; in fact, a quantitative analysis indicates that asphalt exports doubled at this time. The material was probably being traded for such things as high-quality flint obtained from quarries more than one hundred miles away, since counts of material recovered at the site indicate that imports of the flint doubled during the same period.

In other words, the site was taking its place in an expanding trade network, and similar evidence from other sites can be used to indicate the extent and structure of that network. Then the problem will be to find out what other things were happening at the same time, such as significant changes in cylinder-seal designs and in agricultural and religious practices. This is the sort of evidence that may be expected to spell out just how the evolution of trade was related to the evolution of cities.

Another central problem is gaining a fresh understanding of the role of religion. Something connected with enormous concentrations of people, with population pressures and tensions of many kinds that started building up five thousand or more years ago, transformed religion from a matter of simple rituals carried out at village shrines to the great systems of temples and priesthoods invariably associated with early cities. Sacred as well as profane institutions arose to keep society from splitting apart.

Strong divisive tendencies had to be counteracted, and the reason may involve yet another magic number, another intriguing regularity that has been observed in hunter-gatherer societies in different parts of the world. The average size of a tribe, defined as a group of bands all speaking the same dialect, turns out to be about five hundred persons, a figure that depends to some extent on the limits of human memory. A tribe is a community of people who can identify closely with one another and engage in repeated face-to-face encounters and recognitions; and it happens that five hundred may represent about the number of persons a hunter-gatherer can remember well enough to approach on what would amount to a first-name basis in our society. Beyond that number the level of familiarity declines, and there is an increasing tendency to regard individuals as "they" rather than "we," which is when trouble usually starts. (Architects recommend that an elementary school should not exceed five hundred pupils if the principal is to maintain personal contact with all of them, and the headmaster of one prominent prep school recently used this argument to keep his student body at or below the five-hundred mark.)

Religion of the sort that evolved with the first cities may have helped to "beat" the magic number five hundred. Certainly there was an urgent need to establish feelings of solidarity among many thousands of persons rather than a few hundred. Creating allegiances wider than those provided by direct kinship and person-to-person ties became a most important problem, a task for full-time professionals. In this connection Paul Wheatley of the University of Chicago suggests that "specialized priests were among the first persons to be released from the daily round of subsistence labor." Their role was partly to exhort other workers concerned with the building of monuments and temples, workers who probably exerted greater efforts in the belief that they were doing it not for mere men but for the glory of individuals highborn and close to the gods.

The city evolved to meet the needs of societies under pressure. People were being swept up in a process that had been set in motion by their own activities and that they could never have predicted, for the simple reason that they had no insight into what they were doing in the first place. For example, they did not know, and had no way of knowing, that settling down could lead to population explosions.

There is nothing strange about this state of affairs, to be sure. It is the essence of the human condition and involves us just as intensely today. Then as now, people responded by the sheer instinct of survival to forces that they understood vaguely at best—and worked together as well as they could to organize themselves, to preserve order in the face of accelerating change and complexity and the threat of chaos. They could never know that they were creating what we, its beneficiaries and its victims, call civilization.

13

The First Americans:
Who Were They and When Did They Arrive?

BY BEN PATRUSKY

....

No serious archaeologist argues about the origins of the first human inhabitants of the Western Hemisphere or about how they arrived. These paleo-Indians strode—or drifted—in, from what is now Siberia across the Bering Strait, over a land bridge that joined the Old World to the New during the last great ice age. They came as big-game hunters on the trail of moving herds of giant elephants and other megafauna of the Pleistocene epoch. They were first occupants of Beringia—a continent-sized landmass linking Asia and North America—which lured them as it lured their game. Then shifting needs and opportunities propelled them farther east and south.

Not much of this is in question. But one big question remains: When did they come; how early were early humans in the New World? Since the early days of the 20th century, New World archaeologists have been debating the issue—often heatedly. Timetables abound. Robert L. Humphrey of George Washington University has dubbed the ongoing controversy "The Hollywood Complex, or my early man site is earlier than your early man site."

The heat of the debate doesn't surprise Dennis Stanford, director of paleo-Indian archaeology at the Smithsonian Institution. "People digging at the roots of America's ancestry tend to be highly messianic," he explains. "They've invested time, money, thought and often reputation. Sure they want their labors and finds to prove significant. Sometimes they're not very careful about interpreting their results."

The debate about humankind's dawning in the New World is far from settled. But in recent years highly trained archaeologists have begun to accumulate impressive bits of evidence that suggest migrations at a time much farther back than might have been accepted only a few years ago. Some human occupancy as much as 20,000 or 25,000 years ago is beginning to look, if not feasible, at

least arguable. Dates much older than that, however, while postulated, still strike more heat than light from among the disputants. At the present stage of knowledge and of dating technology, there is slim chance for the dispute over Western humankind's antiquity soon to be settled. But a critical look at the evidence and the inferences to be drawn from it can be highly suggestive.

Clovis and before

The pivotal point of the debate is on the order of 12,000 years ago—or 12,000 BP, for "before the present," in the parlance of the professionals. That represents the earliest totally accepted date for human appearance in the New World.

Evidence of human presence then is incontrovertible. It takes the form of a special kind of artifact: a man-made tool, a projectile point with a highly distinctive shape, a manufactured weapon for killing mammoths and other big game. The points are bifacially fluted; longitudinal flakes have been chipped from the base on both sides to form grooves. With fluting, the point could be attached to a wooden shaft for use as a spear or dart. These fluted points have been found at sites ranging from the Pacific coast to the Atlantic coast of North America and from Alaska to central Mexico. In the sites where carbon 14 dating is unequivocal, all the projectile points have been found to date within a very narrow window of time—11,500 to 11,000 BP.

Because the points were first found in abundance in a locale called Clovis in Blackwater Draw, New Mexico, the points have been designated Clovis points—and their manufacturers the Clovis Culture. The Clovis Culture is also often referred to by another name: the Llano Complex, for the Llano High Plains region of the Southwest. The designation embraces not just the fluted projectile points but the entire bone and

stone "tool kit" associated with them.

But were the bearers of the Clovis Culture the first inhabitants of the New World? Or were there earlier bands of migrant-hunters whose groping cultural evolution ultimately gave rise to the technologically advanced Clovis? That question is at the heart of the peopling of America debate.

That the Clovis people were the very first Americans is a position promulgated by Paul S. Martin of the University of Arizona. He has introduced the "overkill theory" to support his arguments. Martin contends that the Clovis people, already skilled big-game hunters, swept into the Americas from Alaska in a single, rapid migration about 12,000 years ago. There they encountered a hunter's paradise: a land teeming with mastodons and mammoths, sloths, giant cats, horses, camels and bison. The archaeological record shows that many of these species became extinct coincidentally with the advent of Clovis. Clovis, according to Martin, cut a rapacious swath through the hemisphere, exterminating these Ice Age mammals.

Other New World archaeologists contest the overkill hypothesis. In their view dramatic changes in climate and vegetation, in the wake of a significant glacial retreat, were the agents of extinction. More to the point, a number of these investigators are convinced that humans trod the soil of the New World far in advance of Clovis's distinctive appearance. Says Richard S. MacNeish, director of the Robert S. Peabody Foundation for Archeology: "There can be little doubt that man was here well before 12,000 years ago, as we have about 30 sites with more than 2,000 recognizable artifacts and with more than 60 radiocarbon determinations before 10,000 B.C.E. (Before the Common Era)." How much earlier than 12,000 years ago? MacNeish suggests that humans "may have first crossed the Bering Strait land bridge into the Western Hemisphere between 40,000 and 100,000 years ago."

Reprinted from MOSAIC, National Science Foundation, September/October 1980. The original title was "Pre-Clovis Man: Sampling the Evidence."

The pre-Llano vista

One of the most prominent figures in the controversy over New World habitation is anthropologist and geoscientist Vance Haynes, also of the University of Arizona. To Haynes, a self-styled "archaeological conservative" who has been stalking Clovis for more than two decades, has been delegated the *ad hoc* role of both arbiter and devil's advocate in the assessing and validating of evidence presumptive of prehistoric migrations into the New World. Haynes's judgment: "There is no one place where the evidence (for pre-Llano cultures) is so compelling that if you looked at it in a court of law you would want to be tried on the basis of that evidence."

The evidence to date for a pre-Llano presence in the New World is not yet "airtight," admits the Smithsonian's Dennis Stanford. "But some of what we do have looks really good and very compelling and can't be lightly dismissed."

Some of the key pieces of evidence of the existence of a pre-Llano people include:

• **Pikimachay Cave in Highland Peru,** where MacNeish has uncovered artifacts he insists date back as much as 21,000 to 25,000 years. "My excavations of Pikimachay Cave have proved to me that pre-10,000 B.C.E. and pre-20,000 B.C.E. remains of man do exist," he says unequivocally.

MacNeish discovered the cave in 1967. It is a huge rock shelter, 85 meters long and 25 meters deep, situated halfway up a hill stepped by ancient terraces. Meticulous excavation has revealed sequential strata of habitation, "a series of floors on which man had clearly lived," declares MacNeish. A roof-fall that occurred about 9,000 years ago securely sealed off the lower, earlier deposits from any possible intrusion or artifact contamination from strata lying above and representing a later chronology.

Beneath this rocky lid lie seven strata, showing evidence of a number of occupations by man back as far as 25,000 years. Using carbon-14 dating, University of California at Los Angeles scientists assigned BP time slots of 19,660 ± 3,000; 16,050 ± 1,200; 14,700 ± 1,400, and 14,150 ± 180 to the upper four strata, respectively, though the lowest has not been so dated. The antiquity of the earliest dated level, MacNeish reports, is confirmed by an independent analysis by Isotopes, Inc., which reported an age for that stratum of 20,200 ± 1,000.

All told, says MacNeish, almost 300 "indisputable" artifacts were unearthed in association with more than 800 bones of sloths and other extinct Ice Age mammals. Perhaps the best evidence was turned up at the upper level, dated at 14,150 BP, which was found to contain 133 artifacts, including stone projectile points and scrapers. Many of the recovered artifacts are very crude, says MacNeish, and a far cry from the sophistication of Clovis, suggesting that they were the tools of unspecialized hunters and gatherers.

• **Valsequillo Basin, Puebla, Mexico,** where in the early 1960s investigators stumbled upon a trove of extinct-animal bones as well as some crude stone artifacts along a dry river bed. Subsequent stratum-by-stratum excavation turned up an ever receding chronology of hunters slaughtering Ice Age animals. At about 30 meters down, at a level dated by carbon-14 at 22,000 years, archaeologist Cynthia Irwin Williams found evidence of a mastodon dismemberment by ancient butchers.

• **Tlapacoya, Valley of Mexico, near Valsequillo,** where Mexican investigators Jose Lorenzo and Lorena Mirambell found bones in association with a shallow depression containing charcoal that yielded a carbon-14 date of 24,000 BP (give or take 4,000 years) and presumed to be the remains of an ancient hearth. Moreover, the investigators uncovered some obsidian artifacts, including a curved blade found buried under a large tree trunk, that gave the same 24,000 BP date.

• **Del Mar in Southern California.** A group of 11 human skeletons has been found along the California coast and dated by Jeffrey Bada of the University of California at San Diego, using a technique called amino acid racemization. It is based on the assumption that amino acids in protein undergo a configurational change—from the so-called *L* or left-handed sort to the *D* or right-handed kind—as bone fossilizes, and that this switching goes on at a measurable, clocklike rate until the sample reaches half-and-half equilibrium. The oldest date determined on a skull found at Del Mar gave a racemization number of 48,000 BP. Two other samples—dated at 23,000 and 17,150 BP—have been confirmed by radiocarbon dating on bone collagen performed by the University of California at Los Angeles' Rainer Berger.

• **Santa Rosa, California,** an island 25 miles off the coast of Santa Barbara, where Berger and Phillip Orr, curator of the Santa Barbara Museum, discovered a red burn area about three meters in diameter in association with stone tools and the bones of dwarf mammoths. The supposition: that the burn area actually had served as a hearth where paleo-Indians cooked the horse-sized mammoths as far back as 40,000 years ago. Carbon-14 dates derived from bits of charcoal found in the firepit suggest the age. According to Berger, during the late Pleistocene (100,000—10,000 years ago) Santa Rosa and three other nearby islands may have formed a single landmass that was joined to the mainland via a narrow neck of land across which foraging dwarf mammoths and their human predators could readily wander.

• **Meadowcroft Rockshelter, Pennsylvania.** On a sandstone outcrop 65 kilometers southwest of Pittsburgh, James M. Adovasio of the University of Pittsburgh has unearthed an assemblage of unifacial tools associated with radiocarbon ages of 13,250, 14,850 and 15,120 years. One especially significant find was a bifacial projectile point—"like a fluted point except that it has no fluting"—that dates earlier than the Clovis point and may be ancestral to it. (A detailed discussion of

Peruvian cave. Excavations of Pikimachay Cave in Peru offer evidence that humans were in the Western Hemisphere before 20,000 B.C.E.

Richard S. MacNeish, by permission

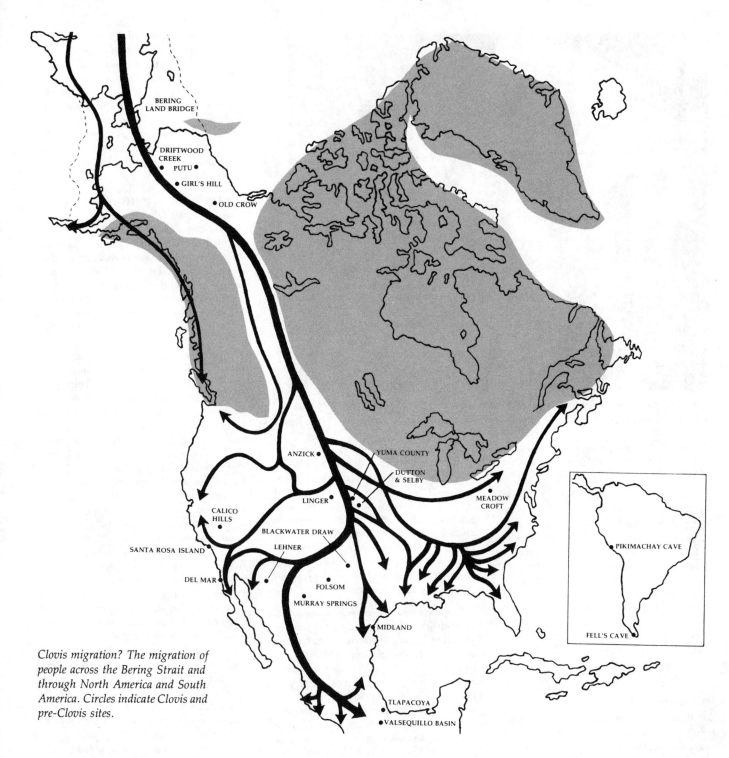

Clovis migration? The migration of people across the Bering Strait and through North America and South America. Circles indicate Clovis and pre-Clovis sites.

paleo-Indian sites in Pennsylvania and Virginia appeared in *Mosaic,* Volume 8, Number 2.)

• **The Selby and Dutton sites in eastern Colorado.** In 1975 pond-dredging crews on farms near Wray, Colorado, unearthed two Pleistocene fossil sites. Alerted to the discovery, a Smithsonian Institution archaeological team that happened to be working nearby raced to the scene. In

subsequent (and as yet far from complete) excavations, under the direction of Dennis Stanford, the team initially discovered fluted projectile points and other manifestations of Clovis. Digging deeper, they found evidence of the presence of earlier cultures that included what are called bone expediency tools. These are manufactured by producing a spiral fracture in bone and using the sharp edges for butchering or hide-working. Bone

flakes presumably the waste or debitage from tool production, and bone, apparently processed for the removal of marrow, were also found. The tools, made from the bones of Ice Age horse, bison, mammoth and camel, were found in "chronologically secure" layers extending back a possible 20,000 years. What makes the site especially exciting, according to Robert L. Humphrey, is that it "reveals the only evidence to date of an archaeological

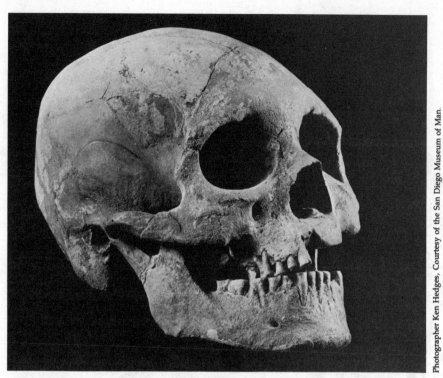

Ancestral skull? This paleo-Indian skull was dated at nearly 50,000 years old through a still-controversial amino-acid dating process developed by Jeffrey L. Bada.

Photographer Ken Hedges, Courtesy of the San Diego Museum of Man.

culture stratigraphically *in situ* below a level containing Clovis fluted points and other manifestations of the Llano Complex."

• **Old Crow Basin, Yukon Territory,** where in 1966 was discovered a caribou leg bone that had clearly been worked by human hands to produce a tool called a flesher—a back-scratcher-like implement used to scrape animal hides. William Irving of the University of Toronto and Richard Morlan of the National Museum of Man, in Ottawa, who now direct major archaeological research projects in the basin, established a carbon-14 date for the flesher of 27,000 BP. Since then, other worked-bone specimens have been found and dated as far back as 41,000 years.

Not foolproof

What says Clovis specialist Haynes to all this? "Tantalizing but not foolproof. . . .I am a skeptic. I remain a skeptic. I have yet to see *unequivocal* evidence of pre-Clovis. Each (site) has some kind of uncertainty connected with it." On his list of "uncertainties," Haynes includes:

• **Skepticism about radiocarbon dates.** Samples may become contaminated by groundwater, he says, and throw the true carbon-14 date off accordingly. Case in point: the Meadowcroft site. It is possible, he says, that rainwater could have brought in dissolved

carbon from nearby coal deposits, thus disturbing the precision of the radiocarbon date. Haynes isn't saying that is what happened. "It's just that we can't be sure it didn't happen." Haynes also expresses doubts about "one of the best pieces of evidence around for a pre-Clovis presence in the New World," the Old Crow flesher. "There's no way to say for sure that the bone was not pulled out of the ground and worked over at a much later date," he says.

• **Suspicion about amino acid racemization.** In a thorough review of this dating technique, David von Endt, a research chemist at the Smithsonian Institution, writing in a monograph on pre-Llano cultures published in 1979 by the Anthropological Society of Washington, D.C., concludes: "I view no projected amino acid date as reliable." Reason: The rate of turnover from *L*- to *D*-form amino acids depends on a mix of complicated factors that have yet to be fully reckoned into the racemization clock.

• **Uncertain primary or cultural context.** "The primary requirement," says Haynes, "is. . .an assemblage of artifacts that are clearly the work of man. Next, this evidence must lie *in situ* within undisturbed geological deposits. . . .Lastly, the minimum age of the site must be demonstrable by primary association with fossils of known age or

with material suitable for reliable isotopic dating. These requirements have now been met repeatedly for the late paleo-Indian period (Clovis) but they have not yet been met repeatedly for earlier periods." Example: the "questionable" primary context of the Santa Rosa firepit. Haynes wonders whether this so-called hearth may not actually be the product of a natural brush fire—not an uncommon phenomenon on this chaparral-dense island.

• **Artifact versus geofact, or when is a tool a tool?** Haynes talks about a "bandwagon effect, where some archaeologists see artifacts everywhere they look." In many cases, he says, the artifacts are nothing more than geofacts or ecofacts, pseudotools produced by agents other than human. "I think if we were to dig anywhere there are Pleistocene, coarse-grained sediments or bones," says Haynes, "(we) would find something that could be interpreted as artifact. In other words, there is a sort of 'background noise' in the buried record of things that can be taken as artifacts." Case in point: Calico Hills in the Mojave Desert, near Yermo, California, where in 1968 archaeologists spotted what they proposed to be crude, very ancient flint artifacts in a massive deposit of alluvial gravels of Pleistocene age. The investigators contend that some of the stone specimens show flaking marks that could have resulted only from human intervention. But Haynes, who has examined the site and specimens on six different occasions, reads the "evidence" another way. As he puts it: "Evidence for artifacts remains uncompelling. . .(and) a natural origin cannot be precluded. In fact, normal natural processes are adequate to explain the origin of all the phenomena observed. Even the best specimens could have been chipped and flaked naturally, especially in view of the fact that each 'artifact' has been selected from literally hundreds of thousands of individual pieces of chert." Similarly, two criteria seem to distinguish bone artifacts: evidence of a spiral fracture (a fundamental step in tool production or marrow processing) and of polishing (indicative of tool use). But other forces, agents other than man, can break or polish bone—e.g., trampling and gnawing by other animals.

• **Absence of stone artifacts.** Thus far Old Crow and the Selby/Dutton sites (at strata below Clovis) have yielded only bone artifacts. No stone tools are in evidence and, according to Haynes, "you can't produce flake scars by hitting bone against bone. Further, there's little to support the validity of an all-bone culture. If there were stone tools at Dutton or Old Crow, where are they?" Haynes remains skeptical about the seven tiny stone "impact flakes" suggestive of human origin turned up by Stanford's team at Dutton and described as tailings produced as a result of impact from a chopping tool.

Counterarguments

Needless to say, Haynes's arguments breed counterarguments among those convinced of a significant pre-Llano presence. Old Crow archaeologist William Irving, for example, suggests that stone tools may not be all that essential to the support of human life. In fact, he contends, bones that could have performed all the necessary tasks of hunting, piercing, butchering, skinning and perforating have been recovered from deposits at Old Crow and elsewhere. Two years ago, Dennis Stanford gave a dramatic demonstration of bone's versatility. Using only bone tools, Stanford showed how it was possible to butcher and process the remains of an elephant, operating on one that had died of natural causes at a Boston zoo.

As for the artifact versus geofact issue, Stanford readily concedes that archaeologists may be led astray by wishful thinking—"seeing what they want to see." But, he points out, with bone, for instance, there are criteria to help the investigator with a trained eye to distinguish between tool and pseudotool. For example: With tools, only the ends—the working parts—tend to become polished and worn. This discriminatory polishing doesn't often happen in nature, unless only the ends have been gnawed. But then there would generally be tooth marks to help make the distinction.

Also, bones that exhibit spiral fracture by other-than-human cause are often those broken after the bone had dried or as a result of the animal's falling or twisting its leg. In both cases these bones are not likely to exhibit impact depressions suggestive of human workmanship. Moreover, says Stanford, at the Selby and Dutton sites most of the bone-artifact specimens were broken the same way; they show single and multiple points of impact located in the same area of the bone. "These suggest a pattern that cannot be attributed to the random breakage patterns expected if the bones were either broken or polished due to natural conditions," he says.

In an effort to eliminate all doubt about bone-artifact authenticity, Stanford has been overseeing a number of experimental studies aimed at producing hard, quantifiable data on bone fracturing, modification and use. From his elephant-butchering trials, for instance, he has developed information regarding tool-wear patterns. Another study

Clovis tools. *These Clovis fluted points are from the Naco Mammoth site in Arizona, contemporary with the Clovis site.*

Courtesy of the Robert S. Peabody Foundation

has Gary Haynes, a doctoral student, feeding buffalo and horse bones to bears in the National Zoological Park in Washington, D.C., to see just how the animals break and gnaw bones. Haynes is also observing how the bones of wood bison, newly killed by wild wolves in Canada, are altered by the natural environment. In an applied offshoot, Stanford is consulting with veterinarians who are analyzing bone breaks in race horses. Are the breaks natural, or did someone break a horse's leg intentionally? The ability to discriminate has relevance for insurance companies as well as archaeologists. Stanford is hopeful that he will soon get permission to put elephant bones around a pond at the National Zoo's Conservation and Research Center near Front Royal, Virginia, to see if and how other free-to-roam animals treat the specimens.

Meanwhile, at Santa Rosa Island, museum curator Phillip Orr has built model pit barbecues to help determine whether the red-char area he and Rainer Berger discovered actually served the earliest immigrants as a hearth or whether, in fact, it was the result of a natural brush fire. His experiments produced the same kind of deep-soil burning (to a depth of about 80 centimeters) as seen in the purported pre-Llano firepit, but different from the burn pattern of a natural chaparral fire.

Whither Clovis

When Haynes, eminently known for his "insistence on methodological exactitude," drops his devil's-advocate mask, he readily professes a belief in a human presence that

may far antedate Clovis, a presence he believes will become demonstrable and unquestionable in time. In fact, he now seems near-convinced about the validity of MacNeish's Pikimachay Cave finds—specifically those from the 14,150 BP level. The Valsequillo deposits, dating from 9,000 to 21,000 years ago, also enthrall him (although the picture there remains clouded by another kind of uncertainty: unsubstantiated charges that workmen may have deliberately planted some of the would-be artifacts).

But far from quashing the debate, the strong indications of a pre-Llano presence have introduced a major new wrinkle to the controversy, having to do with the origins of the Clovis Culture. Is it, as Martin, Vance Haynes and others contend, an import by a technologically advanced people who brought their Upper Paleolithic wisdom with them from Siberia? Or is it, as MacNeish, Stanford and other pre-Llano advocates maintain, a homegrown product—an evolutionary outgrowth of already-in-place, pre-Clovis cultures? Asked another way: Is the Clovis point, that superior paleo-Indian invention that allowed Llano hunters to take full advantage of the megafauna-rich Pleistocene environment of the New World, a candidate for the first truly American patent?

In Haynes's view, even if pre-Llano hunting cultures entered the Americas more than 30,000 years ago, they did not develop into technologically skilled artisans anywhere near the caliber of Clovis. As he sees it, Clovis represents an entirely independent migratory swarm, a late-glacial sweep distinct from earlier, "inconclusive" movements into the

New World. "It now appears," says Haynes, "that the *main* peopling of the New World took place during deglaciation, when something akin to a population explosion occurred between 11,000 and 11,500 years ago by mammoth hunters entering from Alaska and finding abundant and untapped resources."

Haynes offers up this scenario: During the peak of the most recent glacial epoch—anywhere from 14,000 to 20,000 years ago, he says—a large portion of the earth's ocean water was stored in Northern Hemisphere ice sheets, causing the sea level to drop by scores of meters. What emerged was the 1,600-kilometer-wide Bering land platform, which made Alaska as much a part of the Asian continent as the North American and which allowed for easy migration from Old World to New.

The bridge, however, was not a thoroughfare from the Old world to the *whole* of the New; two great icecaps—the Cordilleran on the west, and the Laurentide on the east—covered much of Canada and much of the United States. Joining as they did at the foot of the Canadian Rockies, the giant glaciers created an ice barrier, a wall to southerly migration.

The hunters remained mired in an Alaskan cul-de-sac until about 12,000 years ago, when a period of marked glacial retreat opened a north-south corridor between the two icecaps. The progenitors of Clovis, confined until then in central Alaska, swept south in pursuit of the mammoth and other quarry. Once through, they dispersed rapidly across all of North America and into Mexico. All Clovis dates bear this out; from east to west, north to south, the Clovis artifacts fall within that 11,000-11,500 BP slot. Nor did expansion—or technological innovation—cease. For the Clovis point gave rise to an even sleeker, more advanced projectile point, dubbed the Folsom point, after Folsom, New Mexico, where a specimen was first uncovered in association with the skeletons of extinct bison. Similar fishtail stone points have been found as far as the southernmost tip of South America—Fell's Cave in Tierra del Fuego—and dated at about 10,000 BP.

Pleistocene extinctions

The transition from the use of Clovis to Folsom points approximately 11,000 years ago coincides with the extinction of Pleistocene mammoths, horses, camels and several other varieties of megafauna—which prompted Haynes's colleague, Paul Martin, to formulate the "overkill theory," ascribing extinction to the Llano influx and insisting

that they were the first inhabitants of the Americas.

Proponents of the idea of a substantial pre-Llano presence take issue with these speculations. For one, they assail the proposition that mégafauna extermination stemmed directly from an invasion of Clovis. More to blame, they say, were drastic changes in climate. With deglaciation, the desert moved north, wiping out huge areas of grassland once used for foraging. They cite the work of Russell Graham of the Illinois State Museum who, having recently completed a comprehensive examination of Pleistocene fauna, concludes: "Man's pernicious effect on the modern environment is not necessarily indicative of his impact on ancient environments. . . . Undoubtedly man's predation had an effect on the megafauna, but climatic changes are the best explanation for Pleistocene extinction." Opponents of "overkill" also wonder how it is that one of the most heavily hunted of the species, a variety of bison, is still with us, while hundreds of other animal species that Clovis and Folsom did not hunt perished. Says Dennis Stanford: "Throughout life's entire history animals have gone extinct—in most cases without any help from man."

Pre-Llano proponents also have trouble accepting the presumption of Clovis's lightning-like sweep through the hemisphere. Says Stanford: "I find it impossible to accept this idea of rapid migration. Primitive cultures tend to be conservative, hunters who explore, retreat, explore, retreat. As they move from environment to environment, they must learn to adapt, and that doesn't happen overnight." MacNeish has similar reservations: "A group of primitive people traveling into completely unknown territory would have frequently taken the wrong direction, and the group would have always been saddled with household equipment and baggage, babies, pregnant women and hobbling elders."

MacNeish proposes yet another sort of paleo-Indian-advance theory—small-group filtering or, more colloquially, the "hurry-up-and-wait" process: A band of migrants might be especially adapted for subsistence in broad ecological zones, he says, "and within these zones they would be able to move rapidly, but movement from one zone to the other would require that they build up a whole new subsistence complex; that would take considerable time. The hypothesis that Clovis and Folsom moved through dozens of radically different environmental zones from the Bering Strait to Tierra del Fuego in a thousand years thus seems unreasonable."

As such, the pre-Llano advocates suggest that Clovis, with his advanced tool kit,

developed from an indigenous population in the Americas before 11,500 years ago. "It wasn't the people that swept through America," says Stanford, "but the (technology) that diffused rapidly through already existent populations—much as the idea of tobacco use traveled from the United States through Europe to the Eskimos all in a matter of a few years."

The Siberian connection

But if paleo-Indians did indeed poke their way into the Americas long before the emergence of the Clovis Culture, who were these migrants and how did they get here, considering that a severe ice age was upon the land? Stanford: "Soviet archaeologists have found evidence that man inhabited Siberia certainly 35,000 years ago and perhaps as early as 70,000 years ago. The discovery of early occupations of Siberia greatly increases the time available for man to come across the Bering land bridge."

Moreover, he says, there is now reason to belive that the ice-free corridor from Alaska to North America was open for movement south for much longer periods than previously supposed. "In fact," says Stanford, "it may have been closed for only a short time during the whole (Ice Age) period. So it would have been possible for early hunters. . .to have entered North America long before 12,000 years ago and to have moved southward, continuing to exploit grassland environments." Further, he says, there is now even a slim possibility that an "alternative route" to the interior corridor may have been available—an ocean-side roadway that trailed down along the emerged Pacific coast.

Haynes has strong objections to this idea of a coastal route. "Even if there were such a route between the glacial ice and the ocean," he says, "it would have been an incredibly treacherous environment to negotiate. Under the prevailing circumstances it's hard to imagine people moving down the coast even in boats."

By the same token, Haynes has no problem in living with the notion of Clovis's rapid migration. As he explains: "The phenomenal dispersal of Clovis sites is more compatible with a distinct migration, related to a relatively rapid, natural event—the separation of the ice sheets to form a trans-Canadian passage—than with a sudden outgrowth from meager, indigenous cultures after 12,000 years of sluggish development for which a continuity has yet to be demonstrated."

Native technology

And how does Haynes respond to the contention that Clovis's technological know-how was born in the Americas, a product of progress in home-grown artisanship and not an import? "I do not see anything that is on a developmental sequence leading to Clovis," he says. "What you see is technology akin to Eurasia, to mammoth hunters of the Old World." He sees likenesses in the tool kits of Clovis and Old World hunters, including bifacial stone scrapers, burins (chisel-like implements), flakeknives, a bone technology of bevel-based, cylindrical points and foreshafts, shaft wrenches and the use of red ocher with burials. "The similarities are unmistakable," he says, "and to invoke independent development of all these traits in the New World from a population base for which there is only tenuous evidence does not seem reasonable as does an origin from the Siberian Paleolithic."

Conpicuously absent from the Old World tool kit, however, is the centerpiece of the Clovis Culture: the fluted projectile point. This absence is probably the key piece of evidence against those who propose an Old World origin and rapid dispersal for Clovis. Haynes, in response, explains that the development of fluted, bifacial projectile points could have taken place in Alaska or along the ice-free corridor between 14,000 and 12,000 years ago. But if so, goes the counterargument, why is there no good evidence of Clovis points in this initial New World dwelling place as is the case elsewhere in the hemisphere?

The fact is, a few fluted points *have* been found in the Far North in recent years. However, one Alaskan find, said to date from the post-Clovis period, about 9,000 years ago, is held up as evidence that Clovis developed out of an already-extant American paleo-Indian culture, and that this new technology traveled not from north to south but from south to north, representing a cultural backwash. But two other fluted points, from the Putu site in the Brooks Range, have been related to a charcoal date of 11,500 years ago. "If this date is valid," says Haynes, "it makes at least two Alaskan fluted points as old as the oldest fluted points from interior North America."

Ultimately, settlement of the controversy over the early peopling of America will likely come only with the discovery of new archaeological sites. If, for the sake of argument, a site with a Clovis point were to be found in Central America, bearing a date beyond 14,000 years ago, that would all but demolish the Clovis fast-migration theory. One the other hand, one in Alaska more than 14,000 years old would help support it. But when and where new sites will turn up remains unpredictable. "Most early man sites, probably 99 percent of them, tend to be destroyed by climate almost immediately or by subsequent geologic processes," says Stanford. "When we find one, we're usually dealing with a geological freak."

On balance then: The evidence, if not altogether conclusive, certainly strongly suggests that the New World was visited and settled by migrant hunting bands from the Old World in the shadowy recesses of time back far beyond 12,000 years ago. But it remains to be determined whether the Llano Complex developed from a local, as-yet-undiscovered, indigenous progenitor or whether it originated in the Old World and spread by way of rapid dispersal. At the moment, both positions seem equally defensible. Perhaps the wisest counsel for now is for New World archaeologists to wait and see—to postpone final judgment until new, clarifying evidence comes to light. In Haynes's words: "I think that if pre-Clovis man was really here, good evidence will be found. The important thing is not to rush into it.... What we are actually looking for is what really happened, not what we think happened."

IV
Language and Communication

○ ○

All animal species have methods of communication, by which we mean the transfer of information from one organism, or being to another. Information is defined as a stimulus that changes or affects the behavior of an organism.

Of all animal species, humankind has developed the most rich, subtle, and versatile of communication systems: language. But what is *language?* Many anthropologists think of language in terms of the thirteen design features proposed by Charles Hockett. In Hockett's terms, language is characterized by:

1. *Vocal-auditory channel.* It is produced through the nose and mouth and received through the ears.

2. *Broadcast transmission and directional fading.* A speaker can be heard in all directions; a listener can hear a speaker no matter which direction the signal is coming from.

3. *Rapid fading.* As soon as they are spoken, words dissipate and subsequently cannot be retrieved.

4. *Interchangeability.* All speakers of a language can both utter and understand the same words.

5. *Total feedback.* A speaker hears everything she or he says, can monitor it, and can correct or account for mistakes.

6. *Specialization.* Speech serves no other purpose than to communicate; as a specialized system, it can be used even when speaker and listener are engaged in other activities.

7. *Semanticity.* There are systematic connections between spoken words and standardly accepted meanings.

8. *Arbitrariness.* These connections between words and their meanings are a matter of convention; hence it is possible both to create new words with new meanings and to change the meanings of old words.

9. *Discreteness.* Human beings can produce an enormous range of sounds, but each language makes use of only a very small subset of these sounds, far from exhausting the human capacity.

10. *Displacement.* Humans can use language to communicate about things and events that are far removed from the immediate context in which they are interacting. These distant events may be separated by time, distance, or both—and may even include things that have never existed and never will (for example, mermaids).

11. *Productivity.* People regularly utter sentences that have never been said before in exactly the same manner, and they can talk about things (such as inventions or discoveries) that have never been observed.

12. *Traditional transmission.* It appears that human beings are genetically programmed to be predisposed to learn a language (or even more than one). However, the specific language that an individual eventually speaks is acquired solely through learning in a social context—it is not inherited genetically.

13. *Duality of patterning.* Language is patterned on at least two separate levels: *phonemes,* the sounds a language recognizes as significant but which by themselves have no meanings; and *morphemes,* the indivisible units of meaning of a language. The word "dog," for instance, consists of three phonemes ([d], [o], [g]) and one morpheme ([dog]).

The earliest recorded interest in language and its significance for human beings appears in the Old Testament in Genesis. First, Adam names all the creatures of the world—and through this they are placed at his disposal. Later, when through united effort in the land of Shinar humans attempted to build a tower reaching to the very heavens, God scattered them across the face of the earth and caused them to speak different tongues—thereby forever frustrating attempts at pan-human unity.

Both these themes still preoccupy modern linguists: namely, (1) the ways in which words and the categories they represent affect their speakers' experience of, and approach to, the world around them; and (2) the evolutionary tree of language, or the taxonomic relationships among languages, and the ways and rates of linguistic change.

The first recorded rigorous study of a language was accomplished in the fourth century B.C. by the Indian scholar Panini. He analyzed the structure of ancient (Vedic) Sanskrit and condensed its grammatical rules to algebra-like formulas as elegant as those of any modern grammatical analysis. In doing so, he preserved a language that might well otherwise have become extinct, and he set a standard of excellence that still inspires linguistic analysts.

Some 2,000 years later, another student of Sanskrit, Sir William Jones (1746–1794), systematized means to compare and contrast languages and thereby trace the relationships among them. He is considered by some, therefore, to be the modern "father" of comparative linguistics.

Contemporary linguistics is divided into several specialized branches and even more schools of thought. *Structural linguists* analyze individual languages, detailing their phonology (sound system), morphology (meaning representation), and syntax (the organization of language units into sequences). *Comparative (or historical) linguists* compare extant languages, trace their evolution from earlier ("proto") language forms, and attempt to reconstruct the proto-languages from which modern languages evolved. *Sociolinguists* study differences in language uses (or dialectical differences) reflecting socioeconomic groupings. And *psycholinguists* are interested in the mental apparatuses of speech perception, cognitive processes, and so on.

But human communication is not limited to language. Nonverbally, human beings communicate very important messages about many things—including their feelings about (1) themselves, (2) the person they are addressing, and (3) what they are discussing. *Kinesics* is the study of communication through gesturing, and *proxemics* is the study of the meanings of spacial patterns of people and things.

We introduce some of these and also other concerns in Topic Six, Language, Thought, and Communication.

TOPIC SIX

Language, Thought, and Communication

. . . .

There is a story, often told in introductory anthropology courses, that the Greek philosopher Plato one day posed to his students the question, "What sets human beings apart from all other creatures?"

One student came up with what seemed to be an irrefutable reply. "Humans," he said, "are featherless bipeds."

While the student was being congratulated by his peers, Plato is said to have slipped away for a while. Upon returning he announced, "Here is our scholar's human being!"—and threw into the crowd of students a freshly plucked chicken.

The question of what exactly does separate human beings as a species from all others has continued to vex philosophers and scientists. Until recently, however, there was at least one thing that most people could agree on: only human beings have language. But was that really saying something meaningful? Does the ability to speak represent fundamental properties of our species, or is it just an epiphenomenon of having the curved tongue, short jaw, and minutely controllable lips that facilitate speech? In other words, is the use of language by humans rooted in unique mental properties, or is it something much more superficial?

In "Field Report: The State of the Apes," Joyce Dudney Fleming described, in 1974, startling researches suggesting that the answer to these questions was at hand. Various scholars using plastic chips, hand-sign language, and other means to communicate with ape research subjects seemed to be concluding that, using nonlinguistic communication, apes are capable of the mental operations that underlie language use by humans. First, apes could learn an astonishingly large number of "words." Second, and more importantly, they could apply rules of grammar to the use of these "words." And third, there even appeared to be evidence that they could combine two "words" to mean something entirely new—as when the chimpanzee Washoe signed *water bird* when, for the first time, her trainer showed her a swan. Thus, it appeared that al-

though only humans speak, other animals have the mental faculties for language use in media that they are equipped to manipulate. Language no longer was the defining characteristic of our species.

This view of apes, humans, and language captured the popular imagination. And, until very recently, it went relatively unchallenged. The data, after all, were so compelling. However, a general reassessment of these researches is beginning to cast some doubt on the original findings and dampen some of the enthusiasm with which they were accepted. This trend is spearheaded by psychologist Herbert Terrace, whose research originally was intended to support the view that apes had language capacities. However, after reviewing his data, Terrace found that serious methodological problems made their interpretation problematical. And when he reviewed the methodologies of other studies (including those reported on by Fleming), he found similar flaws.

True, these apes did learn large numbers of "words." But it was questionable that they were using rules of grammar to combine them. For one thing, they may simply have learned sequences of signs just like you learn a telephone number—with no sense that the order *means* anything. Then, Terrace noted that many researchers failed to record sign productions that were out of sequence; some even "corrected" sequences that were "wrong." Further, when camera film showed the humans with whom the apes were communicating, Terrace observed that often the teachers were cueing their ape students unconsciously or leading them through sequences one sign at a time. Thus, the "grammar" of the string of signs produced by the ape was, in fact, created by the human beings interacting with the apes.

Finally, Terrace pointed out that without a full description of the context, it is impossible to assess such episodes as Washoe signing *water bird* when being shown a swan. For instance, did Washoe first sign *water* and then, when her trainer asked her to sign again, sign *bird?* In other words, did Washoe ever make a mental connection between the two "words"? The evidence does not allow us to judge.

So the "state of the apes" is much less certain than it was when this article first appeared. We do know that apes have many more skills than people originally had thought, but early optimism that their language skills approach ours now seems premature. We reprint Fleming's report here, however, to give you a flavor of the fascination that research on ape communication holds for scholars and to stimulate your imagination. What *does* set humans apart from all other creatures?

Turning from the question of whether apes have language, the next article explores what language use means for human beings. "Science and Linguistics" is part of a series of seminal articles by Benjamin Whorf, in which he proposed that the language a person speaks provides the framework for his or her organization of experiences. Put more formally, Whorf's hypothesis was that "we dissect nature along the lines laid down by our native languages." Reality, far from being objectively discernable, is in Whorf's view a culturally relative thing—constructed according to the categories each language labels, the dimensions of time and space each language incorporates, and the logical relationships expressable in each language's grammar.

This bold hypothesis both stimulated and troubled scholars. Certainly, each culture has its own "world view," fully expressable only in its own language—something that translators of literature always struggle with. But does it therefore follow that, just because the concept of time is encoded differently in English and Hopi (the language of an Indian tribe in the U.S. Southwest), the speakers of these languages *think* differently about time (as Whorf proposes)? Careful research on color perception, for instance, has shown that regardless of the categories of colors labeled by a language, speakers of different languages perceive and remember colors similarly, based on the physiology of color perception.

At present, no definitive proof or disproof of Whorf's ideas exists. His hypothesis explains some facts but not others. We think, however, that his article merits your careful attention because it poses both philosophical as well as concrete challenges. Is there an objectively discoverable Reality? Whorf's views challenge the empiricist and positivist philosophies that would answer yes. Are all languages equally well adapted for pursuing scientific research? Whorf clearly believes not—and suggests that for some kinds of scientific research, the world view of Hopi is better adapted than that of English. Whorf's article is a classic, perhaps because it raises more questions than it answers; but the questions are broad, penetrating, and important.

Of course, human beings do not communicate solely through language. A great amount of information is communicated nonverbally. In "The Sounds of Silence," Edward T. Hall and Mildred R. Hall introduce you to the world of gestures and the use of space in human communication.

We close this topic with Alan Dundes's "Seeing Is Believing." It is a light article but of interest because it illustrates one aspect of the Whorf hypothesis. Using English, Dundes shows how this language places priority on one sense over the others and, in doing so, affects how we evaluate the information we receive from the other senses.

14

Field Report:
The State of the Apes

BY JOYCE DUDNEY FLEMING

....

MAN IS NOT UNIQUE; the belief that he is has been with us forever. The foreshadowing of the death of that belief is almost as old. It may have started when ancient physicians discovered the extensive similarity between the bodies of men and other animals. It certainly was evident when Darwin's theory of evolution attained general scientific acceptance. Now the end is in sight as man is forced to concede the last significant attribute that was his and his alone—language.

The animal reaching for our holy title, only user of language, is the chimpanzee. Not one that performs like a trained seal. Not one that dutifully repeats exactly what is taught. Not one at all, but a dozen chimps, in Reno, in Santa Barbara, in Norman, Oklahoma, and in Atlanta. They have vocabularies of substantial size. They combine symbols to produce appropriate combinations that they have never before seen. They use language to manipulate their environments. They mystify their experienced teachers with unexpected abilities and insights.

The Failure of the Spoken Word. For many years we believed that chimps must be smart enough to learn a language. Yet all attempts to teach them to talk have been failures by even the most generous standards. The world's record for number of words spoken by a chimp is held by Viki, who managed to learn four words in the 1950s. Her problem was speaking. Chimpanzees cannot learn to talk, but they can learn to use a complex set of symbols to convey information. The symbols can be hand signals, pieces of plastic in different shapes and colors, geometric designs on typewriter keys; anything they can manipulate with their hands.

The record of failure turned to a record of success when Beatrice and Allen Gardner at the University of Nevada looked at communication among chimps in the wild, noticed that they used many more hand signals than vocal signals, and decided to try teaching a gestural language instead of a verbal one. They chose Washoe as their first pupil.

Washoe is a female chimpanzee who was born in the wild. She was about a year old when her language training began in June 1966. At this age her development and her needs were much like those of a human baby who is one or one and a half years old. She slept a lot, had just begun to crawl, did not have either her first canines or molars. During the first few months her daily routine was centered around diapers, bottles, and making friends with her human companions.

The Gardners chose a chimpanzee instead of one of the other higher primates because of the chimp's capacity for forming strong attachments to human beings. They believe that this high degree of sociability may be essential for the development of language. The language they chose for Washoe was American Sign Language (ASL).

ASL is a system of communication developed for deaf people and used extensively throughout North America. It is a set of hand gestures that corresponds to individual words. (The other system for the deaf, finger spelling, is not used in this research.) Many of the signs are iconic, visual representations of their meaning. For example:

drink—the thumb is extended from the fisted hand and touches the mouth,

up—the arms are extended upwards and the index finger may also point in that direction,

smell—the palm is held in front of the nose and moved slightly upward several times,

cat—the thumb and index finger come together near the corner of the mouth and are moved outward representing the cat's whiskers. This close association between sign and meaning makes it easy to learn to read some of the simple and frequently used messages.

Think Doctor. A wide range of expression is possible within this system. While learning to sign, the Gardners practiced translating songs and poems, and found that any material could be accurately signed. When technical terms and proper names present a problem they are designated by an arbitrary sign agreed upon by the community of signers. Washoe's teachers chose the signs *think doctor* and *think science* for the words psychologist and psychology.

The fact that ASL is used by human beings allows for some comparison between Washoe's signing and that seen in deaf children of deaf parents. The Gardners report that deaf parents see many similarities between Washoe's early performance, some of which was filmed, and that of deaf children learning to sign.

Washoe lived in a fully-equipped house trailer. The Gardners designed her living arrangements to exploit the possibility that she would engage in conversations— ask questions as well as answer them, describe objects as well as request them. They gave her a stimulus-rich environment, minimal restraint, constant human companionship while she was awake, and lots of games that promoted interaction between Washoe and human beings. Her teachers used no language except ASL in her presence.

Flower and Smell. The results of combining this pupil and this language in this environment are remarkable. Her teachers taught her the sign for *more* in the context of tickling, a romping, wrestling game Washoe played with them. She generalized its use to all activities and all objects. They taught her the sign for *open* using only three particular doors in her house trailer. She transferred its use to all doors, containers, drawers, the refrigerator and, finally, to water faucets. They taught her the sign for *flower*. She used it for all flowers and for a number of situations in which an odor was prominent, such as opening a tobacco pouch or entering a kitchen where food was cooking. So they gave her the sign for *smell*. She differentiated the two signs and uses each appropriately, but the error she makes in odor contexts is frequently *flower*.

When she makes mistakes, Washoe often tells her teacher more about what she knows than when she signs correctly. The Gardners started using pictures of objects to test Washoe's vocabulary after she spontaneously transferred her signs from objects to pictures of similar objects. However, if they used a photograph of a replica of the object, she made a lot of mistakes. She called them *baby*. In response to a picture of a cat she signed *cat* on almost 90 percent of the trials; to a picture of a replica of a cat she signed *cat* on 60 percent of the trials and *baby* on 40 percent. Her teachers used *baby* to refer to dolls and to human babies. To Washoe it meant something different, something like miniaturization, or replication in some artificial sense.

The First Sentence. In April 1967, less than a year after her training began, she produced her first combination of signs, a kind of sentence. Though no lessons on combinations had ever been given, her teachers had signed to her in strings. As soon as Washoe had learned eight or 10 signs she started putting them together in sets of two or three, much as small children learn to combine words. She learned some of her combinations from her teachers, but others she made up herself. For example, Washoe invented *gimme tickle* to request tickling and *open food drink* to ask that the refrigerator be opened. Her teachers had always used the signs *cold box* for this appliance.

With just 10 signs there is a large number of possible two- and three-sign combinations, but Washoe did not make sentences from random groups of signs. The ones she used were usually the ones that made sense. The signs she used in front of a locked door included *gimme key, open key, open key please*, and *open key help hurry*. The Gardners analyzed Washoe's two-sign combinations using a method like the one Roger Brown, a psycholinguist from Harvard, developed for children. They found that her earliest combinations were comparable to the earliest combinations of children in terms of the meanings expressed and of the semantic classes used. These classes express relationships such as the agent of an action (*Roger tickle*), the location of a state, action or process (*in hat*), the experiencer of a state or emotion (*Washoe sorry*).

At the end of 21 months of training, she had 34 signs that met a rigorous set of accuracy and frequency criteria. The Gardners imposed these criteria to be sure she really knew a sign before they added it to her list. Not all of Washoe's early signs referred to objects or to actions. She used *hurt, sorry* and *funny* in appropriate situations. She acquired four signs during the first seven months of training, nine during the second, and 21 during the third. Instead of becoming bogged down by all of this new material, she processed it at a faster and faster rate. After three years of training, her total vocabulary was 85 signs. After another year, it had almost doubled.

Washoe probably could have gone on this way for ever, but her human friends had other plans. Several of her teachers were leaving the project. It would be difficult for Washoe to get used to a whole new set of teachers, so the Gardners chose another plan. In October 1970, they gave up Washoe and her 160-sign vocabulary to Roger Fouts, one of their most promising graduate students, who was going to Oklahoma to continue this research.

There is a new chimpanzee in Reno now. Mojo, who came to the Gardners on the second day of her life, is just over a year old. Some of her signing partners are deaf children and adults. Gardner says, "We're going to do it right this time."

The Well-Structured Sarah. Several other researchers are starting their second generation of chimp/language research. One of these is David Premack, a professor of psychology at the University of California, Santa Barbara. His approach to studying language in chimpanzees is as neat as his wavy black hair and well-trimmed beard. He is not very interested in either language or chimpanzees. He does not care if his animals ever have the opportunity to initiate a conversation, change the subject, or use language to control their environments. He is primarily interested in the nature of intelligence. Chimps are very intelligent; language is one important way of exercising intelligence. So he uses the chimp/language research as a means to another end.

A computer would meet most of his requirements for a research subject as well as, or better than, a chimpanzee. Devising a training sequence for a chimp and writing a program for a computer have a lot in common. Either could be used to answer the question, "Can I develop a method for establishing language in this system?" But if the answer is yes, Premack wants to apply that method to human beings who have trouble learning language—autistic kids, retarded people, aphasics—and a method developed for a chimpanzee is more apt to work in these situations than one made for a computer.

In the meantime, he has learned a good deal about a chimp's linguistic abilities and admittedly is surprised by his findings. His first chimp, Sarah [see "The Education of S*A*R*A*H," PT, September 1970], was African-born and about six years old, almost an adolescent by chimpanzee standards, when the experiment began in 1968. Premack describes her as very active, highly dominant and inventive. Sarah did not live, like Washoe, in a language-rich, stimulating environment with daily invitations from human friends to play language games. She lived under standard laboratory conditions: wire cage, cement-block walls, a few toys. Her exposure to both human beings and her special language was largely limited to the one hour of language training she received five days a week.

Plastic Chips. Her symbols are a set of small pieces of plastic that vary in shape and color. Each piece stands for one word. After years of chewing and handling they are scuffed and worn like well-loved toys. A strip of metal on the back allows the pieces to be placed on a magnetized board that serves the same purpose as a blackboard in a classroom. The symbols are placed in a vertical line on the board to form sentences. Sarah often points to the symbols she is working on—thinking

PRATTLING PRIMATES. The human-chimp signing conversations go on all day in the yard, in the house, in the fields. This page shows Lucy and Bruno signing toothbrush, go there, baby, shoe *and* hat. *The opposite page illustrates a conversation about tickling and signing.*

about? translating?—while composing her answer to a difficult sentence.

There are several advantages to using a language that is physically permanent, that is written instead of gestured or spoken. You can study language without worrying about the pupil's short-term memory. When Sarah answers incorrectly you know it is not because she forgot the question that is still on the board, right in front of her. You can make her lessons easier or harder by regulating the number and kind of symbols she has to use at a given time. You can avoid the situation of a chimp pretending not to see an unpopular command delivered via ASL. But you cannot use this language anywhere, anytime. Sarah is like a mute person whose ability to communicate depends on paper and pencil.

Sarah knows about the same number of symbols as Washoe, about 130, but the ways they use their languages are as different as the ways they acquired them. Washoe gained her signs through a combination of imitation, molding and prompting. Sarah learned her symbols through standard conditioning techniques. Her teacher presented a stimulus and she responded. If her response was the correct one she received a reward. She never was punished for incorrect responses, or for anything else. If the stimulus was the teacher holding up a piece of fruit, then Sarah had to write *Ann give apple Sarah*, using the proper order and the correct names for the teacher and the fruit to get the apple.

Sarah mastered this task easily and went on to harder problems. She learned the meaning of sentences like *Sarah insert apricot red dish, grape* [and] *banana green dish*. Her accuracy on these tasks was 80 to 90 percent. She learned the difference between *red on green* and *green on red*, a difficult discrimination because she had to look at the order of the symbols to answer correctly. As with most of her language performance, her level of accuracy was 80 to 90 percent after she mastered the problem.

Sarah's Staggering List. Like Washoe, Sarah transferred her knowledge to symbols and situations outside the context of her training. For example, though she learned *on* in the context of red and green she applied it to any pair of colors. She applied *same* or *different* to any pair of objects, not just the cups and spoons used to teach her these symbols. Premack usually employed new items when testing her, to be sure that her comprehension went beyond the materials used in training.

Her language testing often required that she answer questions. Sometimes she would use the answers *yes* and *no* correctly. Sometimes she would change a question that required a negative answer to one that required a positive one, and then answer correctly. Sometimes she would steal the symbols from her teacher, form her own questions, and then answer them—correctly.

At the end of two and a half years of training, Sarah possessed a staggering list of language functions. She used words, sentences, the interrogative, class concepts, negation, pluralization, conjunction, quantifiers, the conditional, and the copula. Washoe's abilities cover only the first five on this list. There is no indication she could not learn the others; they were not taught. Unlike the Gardners, Premack deliberately set out to give Sarah many different parts of language.

However, when she has the chance, Sarah will gladly give some of them back to him. She does not like to use all the language she knows. The copula is a good example. The copula is the link between a subject and its predicate. In English it is usually the word *is* or *are*. To Sarah *apple red* seems to mean the same as *apple is red*, so she omits the copula whenever she can get away with it. The Russians agree with her. Their language has no word for this linguistic function either.

Sarah Throws a Tantrum. Premack probably has fewer problems with Sarah's language than the Gardners have with ASL, but he doesn't have any fewer problems with his chimp. About two years ago Sarah started becoming difficult to handle. She was growing up and growing stronger. The temper tantrums she threw when she made a mistake became increasingly dangerous to her teachers. Her language training stopped. Right now she is sitting in a cage in the zoology building learning no language at all. Hopefully she won't be there long.

Premack is an energetic man who acts as if he is used to getting what he wants. What he wants is a new chimp compound where the animals will have more freedom, and the opportunity to wander into a special learning center where language lessons and the attendant rewards will be available whenever the chimps are interested. In the meantime Premack is replicating Sarah's training with two more chimpanzees.

Elizabeth and Peony are five years old and each knows about 50 signs. In spite of

these similarities, and the fact that they are both female chimps, they are as different as any two five-year-olds you have ever known. Elizabeth gets involved in her lessons. She seems to enjoy the routine. Peony does not. She would rather beg for her rewards than work for them. She performs the necessary tasks in order to win the approval of her teacher, who appears to be the most important element in Peony's life. Yet under Premack's highly structured training regime, both of the chimps acquire language at about the same rate.

Little Language-Making Machines. The structure leaves its mark. Working at their language board Elizabeth and Peony look like robots, little language-making machines. If you saw only these two it would be easy to conclude that chimpanzees with language are extraordinarily well-trained circus animals that repeat a complex routine with only a vague idea about what the plastic bits they are manipulating really mean. Only their testing data, or a look at Sarah's performance, would change your mind. After hundreds of hours of training, the language is part of Sarah and she uses it with a kind of natural grace. With two years of training—one hour a day, five days a week—the younger animals still look as if they are doing someone else's work as they set out to perform their language tasks.

Chimpanzees that learn sign language do not go through this apparently mechanical stage. Because the language and the lessons are completely integrated into the daily routine, and because communication does not require equipment, their signing looks natural almost from the beginning. There are a lot of chimps signing their natural-looking language in Oklahoma. Roger Fouts has seven of them.

A Farm Full of Chimps. You remember Fouts. He completed his doctorate with the Gardners, and then took Washoe to the Institute for Primate Studies just outside of Norman, Oklahoma. The Institute, which is run by William B. Lemmon, is a little world of assorted, run-down buildings. Every building is filled with nonhuman primates except the house and the big barn that stables the cows, the peacocks, and the cats. The house is usually filled with people who divide their time between being outside talking to the primates and being inside talking about them.

The Institute seemed more like a farm to me and when I went there I asked myself why Fouts chose this place to con-

tinue his work. There must be half-a-dozen primate centers in this country that have more facilities for chimpanzees. After being on the farm only a couple of hours I could answer that question. There may be places that have more facilities, but there are few that have more chimps (the Institute has between 25 and 30), and none that treat the chimpanzees so much like human beings.

Here the chimps are partners in research, not subjects for experimentation. The treatment they receive reflects this attitude. Social needs get the same careful attention as dietary ones. The need for exposure to different kinds of stimulation is as important as the need for different kinds of medication. These features make Lemmon's Institute an excellent place to look at the problem Fouts wants to pursue, communication among chimpanzees using ASL.

To get the program started, Fouts had to get Washoe accustomed to other chimps, and other chimps used to signing. Washoe was slowly introduced to the animals on the farm. She called the ducks *water bird*, a combination she invented. Fouts gave her the sign for duck but she preferred her own nomenclature. Since her capture during the first year of her life she had seen another chimp only once, so she labeled the other chimpanzees she met *bug*. It was going to take some time before she would be comfortable with her conspecifics.

Dirty Monkey. In the meantime Fouts reinstated Washoe's language training. He taught her a new sign, *monkey*. She was happy to use it for the squirrel monkeys and for the siamangs, but she concocted a different name for a rhesus macaque who had threatened her. She called him *dirty monkey*. When Fouts asked her the sign for the squirrel monkeys again she quickly went back to just plain *monkey*. But when they returned to the macaque, it was *dirty monkey*. Before this incident Washoe has used *dirty* to describe only soiled objects or feces. Since her meeting with the aggressive macaque, she has applied this sign to various teachers when they refuse to grant her wishes.

During the early stages of her repatriation Washoe often signed to the other chimpanzees. She frequently signed *come hug* when she wished to comfort one of the younger animals who was distressed. And she signed *tickle* when she wanted to play with one of the adults. When the chimps did not respond she pursued them

until a general romping session began. She also signed *go drink*, indicating a nearby water faucet, to a chimp who was competing with her for some fruit that was being given out.

Washoe does not sign to the other chimps much anymore. After all, nobody ever answers. But that is going to change. Bruno and Booee are going to answer.

Bruno and Booee are six-year-old males. Both were born in captivity and lived in human homes for a couple of years before coming to the Institute. Eventually they will participate in an experiment with Washoe. They are learning to sign but their identical vocabularies are being carefully limited to 36 signs. Fouts hopes to induce Washoe to teach them more signs, some of the ones she knows but they do not. No one knows if she will play teacher, but Fouts's bright blue eyes twinkle at the very thought of it.

Bruno and Booee already are threatening to make linguistic history by becoming the first nonhuman animals to use an unnatural language—one not endemic to their species—to communicate with each other. They sign to each other in a number of situations Fouts devised to encourage them to do so. If they are playing and their teachers separate them, then they sign to each other. The signs are usually limited to appropriate combinations of *come, hug, hurry, Bruno* and *Booee.* The same signs appear if they are separated while one is being punished for some mischievous behavior by being made to sit in a chair. The only conversations, spontaneous two-way signing, occurred when they were required to sign *tickle* before they were allowed to romp together.

The exchanges were brief.

Bruno: *Tickle Bruno.*
Booee: *Tickle Booee.*
(Later) **Booee:** *Tickle.*
Bruno: *Booee come hurry.*
(Later) **Booee:** *Tickle Booee.*
Bruno: (Who was eating raisins): *Booee me food.*

But on the basis of such limited data neither Fouts nor any other careful researcher is going to conclude that the

LANGUAGE LESSONS. In the top two pictures Roger holds up a book and signs what this. *Ally signs* book *with his usual grandiose gestures. In the bottom two, Roger and Lucy discuss swallowing. Roger signs and Lucy repeats the sentence.*

two chimpanzees definitely were communicating. Instead he is developing a set of complex procedures for testing their ability to exchange information via signs with no human beings in the immediate area.

In the meantime, Fouts is teaching ASL to three other chimpanzees, Salomé, Ally and Lucy. All were born in captivity and placed in homes a few days after birth where they are being raised like human children.

Salomé and Her Human Sister. Salomé is two and a half years old. She has a human sister, Robin, who is two, and a set of human parents. Robin is a cherub of a child with wispy blond hair, blue eyes, and a shy but friendly smile. Salomé's face is just as friendly as Robin's, but there is little evidence of shyness. Her black eyes sparkle against her light skin as she comes out to greet me. She looks, and acts, like a bundle of innocent mischief. The two are great friends.

Salomé's motor skills are much more advanced than Robin's but the child is easily her superior when it comes to language. Robin uses about 50 words. Salomé uses about 20 signs. Both understand a lot of English. Salomé acquired her first sign, *drink,* when she was four months old. One study reports that deaf children begin to sign as early as five months. By the time she reached her first birthday, Salomé was producing sign combinations— *gimme drink, gimme food,* and *more food.*

Fouts plans to keep close tabs on the development of language in Salomé and Robin. Right now Salomé produces and comprehends some ASL, and understands a lot of English. Robin does not know ASL, but she speaks some English, and comprehends quite a bit more. She also produces and comprehends chimpanzeese. She has picked up all the natural chimpanzee vocal signals from Salomé and she uses them appropriately.

Ally has no human siblings. He is four years old and lives alone with his human mother. His ASL vocabulary contains over 70 signs. Ally is a great signer. His gestures are crisp, clear and deliberate. It is easy to imagine him lecturing a class in a large auditorium, raising his voice and articulating each word carefully for the benefit of the students in the back. After only a few hours of exposure I could read most of his well-formed signs. It took longer to reach this point with the other chimps.

What That? Like all of the Institute's home-grown chimps, Ally comprehends a large number of English words. Fouts believes that a combination of English and ASL is the best system for teaching language to chimps and he has good evidence that information can be transferred between these two systems. Fouts selected 10 objects for which Ally knew the English word, but not the ASL sign, words like spoon, nut, water and leaf. Then he tried to teach him all 10 signs by only saying the word and signing at the same time. He did not refer to the object itself at any time during the training.

A person who did not know which objects Ally had learned the signs for tested him. Without speaking, the tester held up various objects and signed *what that*. Ally successfully transferred the signs from the word to the object that the word stood for in all 10 cases. Transferring a gestural response from an auditory stimulus (word) to a visual stimulus (object), and from one language (English) to another (ASL) is an impressive feat. Neither Sarah nor Washoe could do it because each knows only one language. But Lucy might be able to.

Lucy is eight years old. Since she was two days old, she has lived with her human parents and a human brother who is 12 years older than she. Her informal training in English began as soon as she moved in and she knows a lot of it. Fouts started her ASL lessons—one or two hours per day, five days a week—a little over three years ago. With her knowledge of English and an ASL vocabulary of over 80 signs she might well be able to translate in the same way that Ally does, but she has not been tested on this kind of problem.

Instead, Fouts has been looking at the way she generalizes the application of a new sign and how the acquisition of a new sign affects the way she uses her other signs from the same class. For example, if she learns *rabbit*, does she apply it to different kinds of small animals and does it change the way she uses signs like *cat* and *dog*?

Cry Hurt Food. The signs Lucy knew for different kinds of foods were *food, drink, fruit, candy* and *banana*. Fouts tested her use of these old signs with 24 fresh fruits and vegetables, then he taught her *berry* using a cherry as an example. Obviously, a cherry is not really a berry, but it was selected because of its similarity to other foods—strawberries, cherry tomatoes, radishes, etc. In the initial testing she called most fruits *fruit* and most vegetables *food*. After learning *berry* she did the same. She used *berry* just as she uses *banana*, to name only one specific kind of fruit. She did not even use it for frozen cherries.

During this experiment she developed great names for some of the testing items. She called a radish *food* until she happened to take a bite of it, experienced its sharp taste, and signed *cry hurt food*. After this she continued to use either *cry*, or *hurt*, or both with *food* to describe radishes. Lucy started out calling a cut watermelon *drink*, then switched to *candy drink* and *fruit drink*. These names show her ability to combine her signs in unique and appropriate ways. This ability, called productivity, is an important point in the debate about whether chimps can learn a language. The same is true of her ability to understand the difference between two sets of signs which are the same except for order, the difference between *Roger tickle Lucy* and *Lucy tickle Roger*. Washoe, Sarah, Ally and Lucy all have this ability, an important part of syntax.

In five years the number of chimps with some syntactical ability probably will be 25. A popularity explosion is about to hit. The number of labs teaching artificial language to chimps doubled in 1973. Everyone who can get his hands on a young chimpanzee, gorilla, or orangutan, is trying to teach it some language based on the manual manipulation of a set of symbols. The expense of obtaining and maintaining these animals is the only thing that keeps this research from replacing the rat in the Skinner box as America's favorite learning experiment.

Lana's Yerkish Typewriter. The most interesting of the new projects is the undertaking of a team of scientists headed by Duane Rumbaugh of Georgia State University. Other members of the team are E.D. von Glasersfeld and Pier Pisani from the University of Georgia, Timothy V. Gill and Josephine V. Brown from Georgia State University, and Harold Warner and C. L. Bell from the Yerkes Primate Research Center. Their pupil is a three-year-old chimpanzee, Lana, who operates a typewriter. But Lana's typewriter is no ordinary machine. It has 50 keys with a colored background and white geometric configuration on each. The configurations represent words in a special language called Yerkish, named for Robert M. Yerkes, the great primatologist.

The keyboard is attached to a set of projectors and a PDP-8E computer. The projectors flash the configurations Lana selects on a screen in front of her. The computer makes a permanent record of all interactions with Lana, analyzes the sequences she types, and rewards her when she performs correctly. Through this system Lana asks for all of her food and drink, a look outside, music, toys, movies, and human companionship.

Rumbaugh studied cognitive abilities in primates for years and believed that it should be possible to teach Lana to read the configuration sequences projected on the screen. He never got a chance to try. Lana learned it by herself. She began pushing a few keys and checking the sequence on the screen. If her sentence was correct she finished it. If not, she pushed a key that erased it.

When Rumbaugh saw her doing this he decided to test her ability to distinguish between correct and incorrect sequences. From a second keyboard he typed part of a sentence and waited to see what Lana would do. She completed the correct segment or erased the incorrect one on about 90 percent of the trials.

After only one year of training Lana has outstripped her teachers' expectations. Already they predict conversation with her. Perhaps this system—which allows a chimpanzee to demonstrate language abilities without any possibility of cues from a human being—will be instrumental in eliminating some of the doubts expressed by scientists about the possibility of chimpanzees learning language.

The Evidence Piles Up. The scientific community is justifiably skeptical about the idea of talking chimps. All reported attempts to teach them a verbal language have been failures. But little by little the all-important evidence is piling up.

The Gardners, who pioneered with Washoe, are very conscientious about distributing information to other psychologists. In the early years of Washoe's training they periodically sent out summaries of her linguistic development. The usual response was that it was all very interesting, but that her performance would not be scientifically important until she:

1 demonstrated an extensive system of names for objects in her environment;

2 signed about objects that are not physically present;

3 used signs for concepts, not just objects, agents and actions;

4 invented semantically appropriate combinations; and

5 used proper order when it is semantically necessary.

All of these are reasonable criteria. All are demonstrated by at least one chimp, most by several. But as the type of data demanded as evidence for language becomes more complex, it is increasingly difficult to decide which criteria are reasonable.

This difficulty arises because we have no definition that allows us to recognize language outside the context of vocal human communication. This is an unusual situation.

The definition for a particular function is usually a set of principles that are common to all the systems that perform that function. Reproduction is a good ex-ample. All animals have a system of reproduction. These systems are very different from each other, but all have some principles in common. These principles allow us to recognize, and correctly label, all the different systems. But the only naturally occurring system of language belongs to human beings. What can we compare it with? How can we recognize a language that is not exactly like human language?

There is no final answer to this question, but the possibility of one becomes stronger each time Booee signs to Bruno, or Peony solves another linguistic problem. Perhaps we will get our answer if Lucy becomes pregnant from the artificial insemination planned for her, and if she bears a healthy infant, and if she teaches that infant signs. I know this is a lot of ifs, but I would like to add another one. If it happens, it will be dynamite.

15

Science and Linguistics

BY BENJAMIN LEE WHORF

....

Every normal person in the world, past infancy in years, can and does talk. By virtue of the fact, every person—civilized or uncivilized—carries through life certain naive but deeply rooted ideas about talking and its relation to thinking. Because of their firm connection with speech habits that have become unconscious and automatic, these notions tend to be rather intolerant of opposition. They are by no means entirely personal and haphazard; their basis is definitely systematic, so that we are justified in calling them a system of natural logic—a term that seems to me preferable to the term common sense, often used for the same thing.

According to natural logic, the fact that every person has talked fluently since infancy makes every man his own authority on the process by which he formulates and communicates. He has merely to consult a common substratum of logic or reason which he and everyone else are supposed to possess. Natural logic says that talking is merely an incidental process concerned strictly with communication, not with formulation of ideas. Talking, or the use of language, is supposed only to "express" what is essentially already formulated nonlinguistically. Formulation is an independent process, called thought or thinking, and is supposed to be largely indifferent to the nature of particular languages. Languages have grammars, which are assumed to be merely norms of conventional and social correctness, but the use of language is supposed to be guided not so much by them as by correct, rational, or intelligent THINKING.

Thought, in this view, does not depend on grammar but on laws of logic or reason which are supposed to be the same for all observers of the universe—to represent a rationale in the universe that can be "found" independently by all intelligent observers, whether they speak Chinese or Choctaw. In our own culture, the formulations of mathematics and of formal logic have acquired the reputation of dealing with this order of things: i.e., with the realm and laws of pure thought. Natural logic holds that different languages are essen-

tially parallel methods for expressing this one-and-the-same rationale of thought and, hence, differ really in but minor ways which may seem important only because they are seen at close range. It holds that mathematics, symbolic logic, philosophy, and so on are systems contrasted with language which deal directly with this realm of thought, not that they are themselves specialized extensions of language. The attitude of natural logic is well shown in an old quip about a German grammarian who devoted his whole life to the study of the dative case. From the point of view of natural logic, the dative case and grammar in general are an extremely minor issue. A different attitude is said to have been held by the ancient Arabians: Two princes, so the story goes, quarreled over the honor of putting on the shoes of the most learned grammarian of the realm; whereupon their father, the caliph, is said to have remarked that it was the glory of his kingdom that great grammarians were honored even above kings.

The familiar saying that the exception proves the rule contains a good deal of wisdom, though from the standpoint of formal logic it became an absurdity as soon as "prove" no longer meant "put on trial." The old saw began to be profound psychology from the time it ceased to have standing in logic. What it might well suggest to us today is that, if a rule has absolutely no exceptions, it is not recognized as a rule or as anything else; it is then part of the background of experience of which we tend to remain unconscious. Never having experienced anything in contrast to it, we cannot isolate it and formulate it as a rule until we so enlarge our experience and expand our base of reference that we encounter an interruption of its regularity. The situation is somewhat analogous to that of not missing the water till the well runs dry, or not realizing that we need air till we are choking.

For instance, if a race of people had the physiological defect of being able to see only the color blue, they would hardly be able to formulate the rule that they saw only blue. The term blue would convey no meaning to them, their language would lack color terms, and their words denoting their various sensations of blue would answer to, and translate, our words "light, dark, white, black," and so on, not our word "blue." In order to formulate the rule or norm of seeing only blue, they would need exceptional moments in which they saw other colors. The phenomenon of gravitation forms a rule without exceptions; needless to say, the untutored person is utterly unaware of any law of gravitation, for it would never enter his head to conceive of a universe in which bodies behaved otherwise than they do at the earth's surface. Like the color blue with our hypothetical race, the law of gravitation is a part of the untutored individual's background, not something he isolates from that background. The law could not be formulated until bodies that always fell were seen in terms of a wider astronomical world in which bodies moved in orbits or went this way and that.

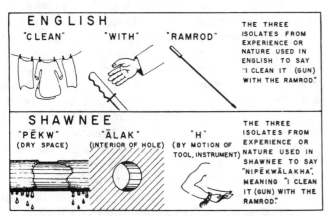

Figure 1. Languages dissect nature differently. The different isolates of meaning (thoughts) used by English and Shawnee in reporting the same experience, that of cleaning a gun by running the ramrod through it. The pronouns 'I' and 'it' are not shown by symbols, as they have the same meaning in each language. In Shawnee ni- equals 'I'; -a equals 'it.'

Similarly, whenever we turn our heads, the image of the scene passes across our retinas exactly as it would if the scene turned around us. But this effect is background, and we do not recognize it; we do not see a room turn around us but are conscious only of having turned our heads in a stationary room. If we observe critically while turning the head or eyes quickly, we shall see no motion it is true, yet a blurring of the scene between two clear views. Normally we are quite unconscious of this continual blurring but seem to be looking about in an unblurred world. Whenever we walk past a tree or house, its image on the retina changes just as if the tree or house were turning on an axis; yet we do not see trees or houses turn as we travel about at ordinary speeds. Sometimes ill-fitting glasses will reveal queer movements in the scene as we look about, but normally we do not see the relative motion of the environment

when we move; our psychic makeup is somehow adjusted to disregard whole realms of phenomena that are so all-pervasive as to be irrelevant to our daily lives and needs.

Natural logic contains two fallacies: First, it does not see that the phenomena of a language are to its own speakers largely of a background character and so are outside the critical consciousness and control of the speaker who is expounding natural logic. Hence, when anyone, as a natural logician, is talking about reason, logic, and the laws of correct thinking, he is apt to be simply marching in step with purely grammatical facts that have somewhat of a background character in his own language or family of languages but are by no means universal in all languages and in no sense a common substratum of reason. Second, natural logic confuses agreement about subject matter, attained through use of language, with knowledge of the linguistic process by which agreement is attained: that is, with the province of the despised (and to its notion superfluous) grammarian. Two fluent speakers, of English let us say, quickly reach a point of assent about the subject matter of their speech; they agree about what their language refers to. One of them, *A*, can give directions that will be carried out by the other, *B*, to *A*'s complete satisfaction. Because they thus understand each other so perfectly, *A* and *B*, as natural logicians, suppose they must of course know how it is all done. They think, for example, that it is simply a matter of choosing words to express thoughts. If you ask *A* to

Figure 2. Languages classify items of experience differently. The class corresponding to one word and one thought in language A may be regarded by language B as two or more classes corresponding to two or more words and thoughts.

explain how he got *B*'s agreement so readily, he will simply repeat to you, with more or less elaboration or abbreviation, what he said to *B*. He has no notion of the process involved. The amazingly complex system of linguistic patterns and classifications, which *A* and *B* must have in common before they can adjust to each other at all, is all background to *A* and *B*.

These background phenomena are the province of the grammarian—or of the linguist, to give him his more modern name as a scientist. The word linguist in common, and especially newspaper, parlance means something entirely different, namely, a person who can quickly attain agreement about subject matter with different people speaking a number of different languages. Such a person is better termed a polyglot or a multilingual. Scientific linguists have long understood that ability to speak a language fluently does not necessarily confer a linguistic knowledge of it, that is understanding of its background phenomena and its systematic processes and structure, any more than ability to play a good game of billiards confers or requires any knowledge of the laws of mechanics that operate upon the billiard table.

The situation here is not unlike that in any other field of science. All real scientists have their eyes primarily on background phenomena that cut very little ice, as such, in our daily lives; and yet their studies have a way of bringing out a close relation between these unsuspected realms of fact and such decidedly foreground activities as transporting goods, preparing food, treating the sick, or growing potatoes, which in time may become very much modified, simply because of pure scientific investigation in no way concerned with these brute matters themselves. Linguistics presents a quite similar case; the background phenomena with which it deals are involved in all our foreground activities of talking and of reaching agreement, in all reasoning and arguing of cases, in all law, arbitration, conciliation, contracts, treaties, public opinion, weighing of scientific theories, formulation of scientific results. Whenever agreement or assent is arrived at in human affairs, and whether or not mathematics or other specialized symbolisms are made part of the procedure, THIS AGREEMENT IS REACHED BY LINGUISTIC PROCESSES, OR ELSE IT IS NOT REACHED.

As we have seen, an overt knowledge of the linguistic processes by which agreement is attained is not necessary to reaching some sort of agreement, but it is certainly no bar thereto; the more complicated and difficult the matter, the more such knowledge is a distinct aid, till the point may be reached—I suspect the modern world has about arrived at it—when the knowledge becomes not only an aid but a necessity. The situation may be likened to that of navigation. Every boat that sails is in the lap of planetary forces; yet a boy can pilot his small craft around a harbor without benefit of geography, astronomy, mathematics, or international politics. To the captain of an ocean liner, however, some knowledge of all these subjects is essential.

When linguists became able to examine critically and scientifically a large number of languages of widely different patterns, their base of reference was expanded; they experienced an interruption of phenomena hitherto held universal, and a whole new order of significance came into their ken. It was found that the background linguistic system (in other words, the grammar) of each language is not merely a reproducing instrument for voicing ideas but rather is itself the shaper of ideas, the program and guide for the individual's mental activity, for his analysis of impressions, for his synthesis of his mental stock in trade. Formulation of ideas is not an independent process, strictly rational in the old sense, but is part of a particular grammar, and differs, from slightly to greatly, between different grammars. We dissect nature along lines laid down by our native languages. The categories and types that we isolate from the world of phenomena we do not find there because they stare every observer in the face; on the contrary, the world is presented in a kaleidoscopic flux of impressions which has to be organized by our minds—and this means largely by the linguistic systems in our minds. We cut nature up, organize it into concepts, and ascribe significances as we do, largely because we are parties to an agreement to organize it in this way—an agreement that holds throughout our speech community and is codified in the patterns of our language. The agreement is, of course, an implicit and unstated one, BUT ITS TERMS ARE ABSOLUTELY OBLIGATORY; we cannot talk at all except by subscribing to the organization and classification of data which the agreement decrees.

This fact is very significant for modern science, for it means that no individual is free to describe nature with absolute impartiality but is constrained to certain modes of interpretation even while he thinks himself most free. The person most nearly free in such respects would be a linguist familiar with very many widely different linguistic systems. As yet no linguist is in any such position. We are thus introduced to a new principle of relativity, which holds that all observers are not led by the same physical evidence to the same picture of the universe, unless their linguistic backgrounds are similar, or can in some way be calibrated.

This rather startling conclusion is not so apparent if we compare only our modern European languages, with perhaps Latin and Greek thrown in for good measure. Among these tongues there is a unanimity of major patterns which at first seems to bear out natural logic. But this unanimity exists only because these tongues are all Indo-European dialects cut to the same

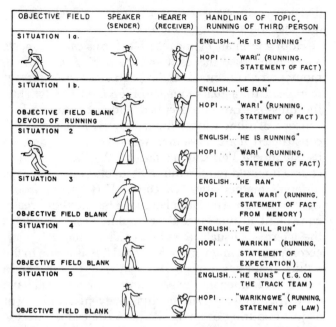

OBJECTIVE FIELD	SPEAKER (SENDER)	HEARER (RECEIVER)	HANDLING OF TOPIC, RUNNING OF THIRD PERSON
SITUATION 1a.			ENGLISH... "HE IS RUNNING" HOPI ... "WARI" (RUNNING, STATEMENT OF FACT)
SITUATION 1b. OBJECTIVE FIELD BLANK DEVOID OF RUNNING			ENGLISH... "HE RAN" HOPI ... "WARI" (RUNNING, STATEMENT OF FACT)
SITUATION 2			ENGLISH... "HE IS RUNNING" HOPI ... "WARI" (RUNNING, STATEMENT OF FACT)
SITUATION 3 OBJECTIVE FIELD BLANK			ENGLISH... "HE RAN" HOPI ... "ERA WARI" (RUNNING, STATEMENT OF FACT FROM MEMORY)
SITUATION 4 OBJECTIVE FIELD BLANK			ENGLISH... "HE WILL RUN" HOPI ... "WARIKNI" (RUNNING, STATEMENT OF EXPECTATION)
SITUATION 5 OBJECTIVE FIELD BLANK			ENGLISH... "HE RUNS" (E.G. ON THE TRACK TEAM) HOPI ... "WARIKNGWE" (RUNNING, STATEMENT OF LAW)

Figure 3. Contrast between a "temporal" language (English) and a "timeless" language (Hopi). What are to English differences of time are to Hopi differences in the kind of validity.

basic plan, being historically transmitted from what was long ago one speech community; because the modern dialects have long shared in building up a common culture; and because much of this culture, on the more intellectual side, is derived from the linguistic backgrounds of Latin and Greek. Thus this group of languages satisfies the special case of the clause beginning "unless" in the statement of the linguistic relativity principle at the end of the preceding paragraph. From this condition follows the unanimity of description of the world in the community of modern scientists. But it must be emphasized that "all modern Indo-European-speaking observers" is not the same thing as "all observers." That modern Chinese or Turkish scientists describe the world in the same terms as Western scientists means, of course, only that they have taken over bodily the entire Western system of rationalizations, not that they have corroborated that system from their native posts of observation.

When Semitic, Chinese, Tibetan, or African languages are contrasted with our own, the divergence in analysis of the world becomes more apparent; and, when we bring in the native languages of the Americas, where speech communities for many millenniums have gone their ways independently of each other and of the Old World, the fact that languages dissect nature in many different ways becomes patent. The relativity of all conceptual systems, ours included, and their dependence upon language stand revealed. That American Indians speaking only their native tongues are never called upon to act as scientific observers is in no wise to

the point. To exclude the evidence which their languages offer as to what the human mind can do is like expecting botanists to study nothing but food plants and hothouse roses and then tell us what the plant world is like!

Let us consider a few examples. In English we divide most of our words into two classes, which have different grammatical and logical properties. Class 1 we call nouns, e.g., 'house, man'; class 2, verbs, e.g., 'hit, run.' Many words of one class can act secondarily as of the other class, e.g., 'a hit, a run,' or 'to man (the boat),' but, on the primary level, the division between the classes is absolute. Our language thus gives us a bipolar division of nature. But nature herself is not thus polarized. If it be said that 'strike, turn, run,' are verbs because they denote temporary or short-lasting events, i.e., actions, why then is 'fist' a noun? It also is a temporary event. Why are 'lightning, spark, wave, eddy, pulsation, flame, storm, phase, cycle, spasm, noise, emotion' nouns? They are temporary events. If 'man' and 'house' are nouns because they are long-lasting and stable events, i.e., things, what then are 'keep, adhere, extend, project, continue, persist, grow, dwell,' and so on doing among the verbs? If it be objected that 'possess, adhere' are verbs because they are stable relationships rather than stable percepts, why then should 'equilibrium, pressure, current, peace, group, nation, society, tribe, sister,' or any kinship term be among the nouns? It will be found that an "event" to us means "what our language classes as a verb" or something analogized therefrom. And it will be found that it is not possible to define 'event, thing, object, relationship,' and so on, from nature, but that to define them always involves a circuitous return to the grammatical categories of the definer's language.

In the Hopi language, 'lightning, wave, flame, meteor, puff of smoke, pulsation' are verbs—events of necessarily brief duration cannot be anything but verbs. 'Cloud' and 'storm' are at about the lower limit of duration for nouns. Hopi, you see, actually has a classification of events (or linguistic isolates) by duration type, something strange to our modes of thought. On the other hand, in Nootka, a language of Vancouver Island, all words seem to us to be verbs, but really there are no classes 1 and 2; we have, as it were, a monistic view of nature that gives us only one class of word for all kinds of events. 'A house occurs' or 'it houses' is the way of saying 'house,' exactly like 'a flame occurs' or 'it burns.' These terms seem to us like verbs because they are inflected for durational and temporal nuances, so that the suffixes of the word for house event make it mean long-lasting house, temporary house, future house, house that used to be, what started out to be a house, and so on.

Hopi has one noun that covers every thing or being

that flies, with the exception of birds, which class is denoted by another noun. The former noun may be said to denote the class (*FC–B*)—flying class minus bird. The Hopi actually call insect, airplane, and aviator all by the same word, and feel no difficulty about it. The situation, of course, decides any possible confusion among very disparate members of a broad linguistic class, such as this class (*FC–B*). This class seems to us too large and inclusive, but so would our class 'snow' to an Eskimo. We have the same word for falling snow, snow on the ground, snow packed hard like ice, slushy snow, wind-driven flying snow—whatever the situation may be. To an Eskimo, this all-inclusive word would be almost unthinkable; he would say that falling snow, slushy snow, and so on, are sensuously and operationally different, different to contend with; he uses different words for them and for other kinds of snow. The Aztecs go even farther than we in the opposite direction, with 'cold,' 'ice,' and 'snow' all represented by the same basic word with different terminations; 'ice' is the noun form; 'cold,' the adjectival form; and for 'snow,' "ice mist."

What surprises most is to find that various grand generalizations of the Western world, such as time, velocity, and matter, are not essential to the construction of a consistent picture of the universe. The psychic experiences that we class under these headings are, of course, not destoyed; rather, categories derived from other kinds of experiences take over the rulership of the cosmology and seem to function just as well. Hopi may be called a timeless language. It recognizes psychological time, which is much like Bergson's "duration," but this "time" is quite unlike the mathematical time, *T*, used by our physicists. Among the peculiar properties of Hopi time are that it varies with each observer, does not permit of simultaneity, and has zero dimensions; i.e., it cannot be given a number greater than one. The Hopi do not say, "I stayed five days," but "I left on the fifth day." A word referring to this kind of time, like the word day, can have no plural. The puzzle picture (Fig. 3, page 107) will give mental exercise to anyone who would like to figure out how the Hopi verb gets along without tenses. Actually, the only practical use of our tenses, in one-verb sentences, is to distinguish among five typical situations, which are symbolized in the picture. The timeless Hopi verb does not distinguish between the present, past, and future of the event itself but must always indicate what type of validity the SPEAKER intends the statement to have: (a) report of an event (situations 1, 2, 3 in the picture); (b) expectation of an event (situation 4); (c) generalization or law about events (situation 5). Situation 1, where the speaker and listener are in contact with the same objective field , is divided by our language into the two conditions, 1*a* and 1*b*, which it calls present and past, respectively. This

division is unnecessary for a language which assures one that the statement is a report.

Hopi grammar, by means of its forms called aspects and modes, also makes it easy to distinguish among momentary, continued, and repeated occurrences, and to indicate the actual sequence of reported events. Thus the universe can be described without recourse to a concept of dimensional time. How would a physics constructed along these lines work, with no *T* (time) in its equations? Perfectly, as far as I can see, though of course it would require different ideology and perhaps different mathematics. Of course *V* (velocity) would have to go too. The Hopi language has no word really equivalent to our 'speed' or 'rapid.' What translates these terms is usually a word meaning intense or very, accompanying any verb of motion. Here is a clue to the nature of our new physics. We may have to introduce a new term *I*, intensity. Every thing and event will have an *I*, whether we regard the thing or event as moving or as just enduring or being. Perhaps the *I* of an electric charge will turn out to be its voltage, or potential. We shall use clocks to measure some intensities, or, rather, some RELATIVE intensities, for the absolute intensity of anything will be meaningless. Our old friend acceleration will still be there but doubtless under a new name. We shall perhaps call it *V*, meaning not velocity but variation. Perhaps all growths and accumulations will be regarded as *V*'s. We should not have the concept of rate in the temporal sense, since, like velocity, rate introduces a mathematical and linguistic time. Of course we know that all measurements are ratios, but the measurements of intensities made by comparison with the standard intensity of a clock or a planet we do not treat as ratios, any more than we so treat a distance made by comparison with a yardstick.

A scientist from another culture that used time and velocity would have great difficulty in getting us to understand these concepts. We should talk about the intensity of a chemical reaction; he would speak of its velocity or its rate, which words we should at first think were simply words for intensity in his language. Likewise, he at first would think that intensity was simply our own word for velocity. At first we should agree, later we should begin to disagree, and it might dawn upon both sides that different systems of rationalization were being used. He would find it very hard to make us understand what he really meant by velocity of a chemical reaction. We should have no words that would fit. He would try to explain it by likening it to a running horse, to the difference between a good horse and a lazy horse. We should try to show him, with a superior laugh, that his analogy also was a matter of different intensities, aside from which there was little similarity between a horse and a chemical reaction in a beaker. We should point out that a running horse is moving relative to the ground, whereas the material in the beaker is at rest.

One significant contribution to science from the linguistic point of view may be the greater development of our sense of perspective. We shall no longer be able to see a few recent dialects of the Indo-European family, and the rationalizing techniques elaborated from their patterns, as the apex of the evolution of the human mind, nor their present wide spread as due to any survival from fitness or to anything but a few events of history—events that could be called fortunate only from the parochial point of view of the favored parties. They, and our own thought processes with them, can no longer be envisioned as spanning the gamut of reason and knowledge but only as one constellation in a galactic expanse. A fair realization of the incredible degree of diversity of linguistic system that ranges over the globe leaves one with an inescapable feeling that the human spirit is inconceivably old; that the few thousand years of history covered by our written records are no more than the thickness of a pencil mark on the scale that measures our past experiences on this planet; that the events of these recent millenniums spell nothing in any evolutionary wise, that the race has taken no sudden spurt, achieved no commanding synthesis during recent millenniums, but has only played a little with a few of the linguistic formulations and views of nature bequeathed from an inexpressibly longer past. Yet neither this feeling nor the sense of precarious dependence of all we know upon linguistic tools which themselves are largely unknown need be discouraging to science but should, rather, foster that humility which accompanies the true scientific spirit, and thus forbid that arrogance of the mind which hinders real scientific curiosity and detachment.

16

The Sounds of Silence

BY EDWARD T. HALL AND MILDRED REED HALL

Bob leaves his apartment at 8:15 A.M. and stops at the corner drugstore for breakfast. Before he can speak, the counterman says, "The usual?" Bob nods yes. While he savors his Danish, a fat man pushes onto the adjoining stool and overflows into his space. Bob scowls and the man pulls himself in as much as he can. Bob has sent two messages without speaking a syllable.

Henry has an appointment to meet Arthur at 11 o'clock; he arrives at 11:30. Their conversation is friendly, but Arthur retains a lingering hostility. Henry has unconsciously communicated that he doesn't think the appointment is very important or that Arthur is a person who needs to be treated with respect.

George is talking to Charley's wife at a party. Their conversation is entirely trivial, yet Charley glares at them suspiciously. Their physical proximity and the movements of their eyes reveal that they are powerfully attracted to each other.

José Ybarra and Sir Edmund Jones are at the same party and it is important for them to establish a cordial relationship for business reasons. Each is trying to be warm and friendly, yet they will part with mutual distrust and their business transaction will probably fall through. José, in Latin fashion, moved closer and closer to Sir Edmund as they spoke, and this movement was miscommunicated as pushiness to Sir Edmund, who kept backing away from this intimacy, and this was miscommunicated to José as coldness. The silent languages of Latin and English cultures are more difficult to learn than their spoken languages.

In each of these cases, we see the subtle power of nonverbal communication. The only language used throughout most of the history of humanity (in evolutionary terms, vocal communication is relatively recent), it is the first form of communication you learn. You use this preverbal language, consciously and unconsciously, every day to tell other people how you feel about yourself and them. This language includes your posture, gestures, facial expressions, costume, the way you walk, even your treatment of time and space and material things. All people communicate on several different levels at the same time but are usually aware of only the verbal dialog and don't realize that they respond to nonverbal messages. But when a person says one thing and really believes something else, the discrepancy between the two can usually be sensed. Nonverbal-communication systems are much less subject to the conscious deception that often occurs in verbal systems. When we find ourselves thinking, "I don't know what it is about him, but he doesn't seem sincere," it's usually this lack of congruity between a person's words and his behavior that makes us anxious and uncomfortable.

Few of us realize how much we all depend on body movement in our conversation or are aware of the hidden rules that govern listening behavior. But we know instantly whether or not the person we're talking to is "tuned in" and we're very sensitive to any breach in listening etiquette. In white middle-class American culture, when someone wants to show he is listening to someone else, he looks either at the other person's face or, specifically, at his eyes, shifting his gaze from one eye to the other.

If you observe a person conversing, you'll notice that he indicates he's listening by nodding his head. He also makes little "Hmm" noises. If he agrees with what's being said, he may give a vigorous nod. To show pleasure or affirmation, he smiles; if he has some reservations, he looks skeptical by raising an eyebrow or pulling down the corners of his mouth. If a participant wants to terminate the conversation, he may start shifting his body position, stretching his legs, crossing or uncrossing them, bobbing his foot or diverting his gaze from the speaker. The more he fidgets, the more the speaker becomes aware that he has lost his audience. As a last measure, the listener may look at his watch to indicate the imminent end of the conversation.

Talking and listening are so intricately intertwined that a person cannot do one without the other. Even when one is alone and talking to oneself, there is part of the brain that speaks while another part listens. In all conversations, the listener is positively or negatively reinforcing the speaker all the time. He may even guide the conversation without knowing it, by laughing or frowning or dismissing the argument with a wave of his hand.

The language of the eyes—another age-old way of exchanging feelings—is both subtle and complex. Not only do men and women use their eyes differently but there are class, generation, regional, ethnic and national cultural differences. Americans often complain about the way foreigners stare at people or hold a glance too long. Most Americans look away from someone who is using his eyes in an unfamiliar way because it makes them self-conscious. If a man looks at another man's wife in a certain way, he's asking for trouble, as indicated earlier. But he might not be ill-mannered or seeking to challenge the husband. He might be a European in this country who hasn't learned our visual mores. Many American women visiting France or Italy are acutely embarrassed because, for the first time in their lives, men really look at them—their eyes, hair, nose, lips, breasts, hips, legs, thighs, knees, ankles, feet, clothes, hairdo, even their walk. These same women, once they have become used to being looked at, often return to the United States and are overcome with the feeling that "No one ever really looks at me anymore."

Analyzing the mass of data on the eyes, it is possible to sort out at least three ways in which the eyes are used to communicate: dominance vs. submission, involvement vs. detachment and positive vs. negative attitude. In addition, there are three levels of consciousness and control, which can be categorized as follows: (1) conscious use of the eyes to communicate, such as the flirting blink and the intimate nose-wrinkling squint; (2) the very extensive category of unconscious but learned behavior governing where the eyes are directed and when (this unwritten set of rules dictates how and under what circumstances the sexes, as well as people of all status categories, look at each other); and (3) the response of the eye itself, which is completely outside both awareness and control—changes in the cast (the sparkle) of the eye and the pupillary reflex.

The eye is unlike any other organ of the body, for it is an extension of the brain. The unconscious pupillary reflex and the cast of the eye have been known by people of Middle Eastern origin for years—although most are unaware of their knowledge. Depending on the context, Arabs and others look either directly at the eyes or deeply *into* the eyes of their interlocutor. We became aware of this in the Middle East several years ago while looking at jewelry. The merchant suddenly started to push a particular bracelet at a customer and said, "You buy this one." What interested us was that the bracelet was not the one that had been consciously selected by the purchaser. But the merchant, watching the pupils of the eyes, knew what the purchaser really wanted to buy. Whether he specifically knew *how* he knew is debatable.

A psychologist at the University of Chicago, Eckhard Hess, was the first to conduct systematic studies of the pupillary reflex. His wife remarked one evening, while watching him reading in bed, that he must be very interested in the text because his pupils were dilated. Following up on this, Hess slipped some pictures of nudes into a stack of photographs that he gave to his male assistant. Not looking at the photographs but watching his assistant's pupils, Hess was able to tell precisely when the assistant came to the nudes. In further experiments, Hess retouched the eyes in a photograph of a woman. In one print, he made the pupils small, in another, large; nothing else was changed. Subjects who were given the photographs found the woman with the dilated pupils much more attractive. Any man who has had the experience of seeing a woman look at him as her pupils widen with reflex speed knows that she's flashing him a message.

The eye-sparkle phenomenon frequently turns up in our interviews of couples in love. It's apparently one of the first reliable clues in the other person that love is genuine. To date, there is no scientific data to explain eye sparkle; no investigation of the pupil, the cornea or even the white sclera of the eye shows how the sparkle originates. Yet we all know it when we see it.

One common situation for most people involves the use of the eyes in the street and in public. Although eye behavior follows a definite set of rules, the rules vary according to the place, the needs and feelings of the people, and their ethnic background. For urban whites, once they're within definite recognition distance (16–32 feet for people with average eyesight), there is mutual avoidance of eye contact—unless they want something specific: a pickup, a handout or information of some kind. In the West and in small towns generally, however, people are much more likely to look at and greet one another, even if they're strangers.

It's permissible to look at people if they're beyond recognition distance; but once inside this sacred zone, you can only steal a glance at strangers. You *must* greet friends, however; to fail to do so is insulting. Yet, to stare too fixedly even at them is considered rude and hostile. Of course, all of these rules are variable.

A great many blacks, for example, greet each other in public even if they don't know each other. To blacks, most eye behavior of whites has the effect of giving the impression that they aren't there, but this is due to white avoidance of eye contact with *anyone* in the street.

Another very basic difference between people of different ethnic backgrounds is their sense of territoriality and how they handle space. This is the silent communication, or miscommunication, that caused friction between Mr. Ybarra and Sir Edmund Jones in our earlier example. We know from research that everyone has around himself an invisible bubble of space that contracts and expands depending on several factors: his emotional state, the activity he's performing at the time and his cultural background. This bubble is a kind of mobile territory that he will defend against intrusion. If he is accustomed to close personal distance between himself and others, his bubble will be smaller than that of someone who's accustomed to greater personal distance. People of North European heritage—English, Scandinavian, Swiss and German—tend to avoid contact. Those whose heritage is Italian, French, Spanish, Russian, Latin American or Middle Eastern like close personal contact.

People are very sensitive to any intrusion into their spatial bubble. If someone stands too close to you, your first instinct is to back up. If that's not possible, you lean away and pull yourself in, tensing your muscles. If the intruder doesn't respond to these body signals, you may then try to protect yourself, using a briefcase, umbrella or raincoat. Women—especially when traveling alone—often plant their pocketbook in such a way that no once can get very close to them. As a last resort, you may move to another spot and position yourself behind a desk or a chair that provides screening. Everyone tries to adjust the space around himself in a way that's comfortable for him; most often, he does this unconsciously.

Emotions also have a direct effect on the size of a person's territory. When you're angry or under stress, your bubble expands and you require more space. New York psychiatrist Augustus Kinzel found a difference in what he calls Body-Buffer Zones between violent and nonviolent prison inmates. Dr. Kinzel conducted experiments in which each prisoner was placed in the center of a small room and then Dr. Kinzel slowly walked toward him. Nonviolent prisoners allowed him to come quite close, while prisoners with a history of violent behavior couldn't tolerate his proximity and reacted with some vehemence.

Apparently, people under stress experience other people as looming larger and closer than they actually are. Studies of schizophrenic patients have indicated that they sometimes have a distorted perception of space, and several psychiatrists have reported patients who experience their body boundaries as filling up an entire room. For these patients, anyone who comes into the room is actually inside their body, and such an intrusion may trigger a violent outburst.

Unfortunately, there is little detailed information about normal people who live in highly congested urban areas. We do know, of course, that the noise, pollution, dirt, crowding and confusion of our cities induce feelings of stress in most of us, and stress leads to a need for greater space. The man who's packed into a subway, jostled in the street, crowded into an elevator and forced to work all day in a bull pen or in a small office without auditory or visual privacy is going to be very stressed at the end of his day. He needs places that provide relief from constant overstimulation of his nervous system. Stress from overcrowding is cumulative and people can tolerate more crowding early in the day than later; note the increased bad temper during the evening rush hour as compared with the morning melee. Certainly one factor in people's desire to commute by car is the need for privacy and relief from crowding (except, often, from other cars); it may be the only time of the day when nobody can intrude.

In crowded public places, we tense our muscles and hold ourselves stiff, and thereby communicate to others our desire not to intrude on their space and, above all, not to touch them. We also avoid eye contact, and the total effect is that of someone who has "tuned out." Walking along the street, our bubble expands slightly as we move in a stream of strangers, taking care not to bump into them. In the office, at meetings, in restaurants, our bubble keeps changing as it adjusts to the activity at hand.

Most white middle-class Americans use four main distances in their business and social relations: intimate, personal, social and public. Each of these distances has a near and a far phase and is accompanied by changes in the volume of the voice. Intimate distance varies from direct physical contact with another person to a distance of six to eighteen inches and is used for our most private activities—caressing another person or making love. At this distance, you are overwhelmed by sensory inputs from the other person—heat from the body, tactile stimulation from the skin, the fragrance of perfume, even the sound of breathing—all of which literally envelop you. Even at the far phase, you're still within easy touching distance. In general, the use of intimate distance in public between adults is frowned on. It's also much too close for strangers, except under conditions of extreme crowding.

In the second zone—personal distance—the close phase is one and a half to two and a half feet; it's at this distance that wives usually stand from their husbands in public. If another woman moves into this zone, the wife will most likely be disturbed. The far phase—two and a half to four feet—is the distance used to "keep someone at arm's length" and is the most common spacing used by people in conversation.

The third zone—social distance—is employed during business transactions or exchanges with a clerk or repairman. People who work together tend to use close social distance—four to seven feet. This is also the distance for conversation at social gatherings. To stand at this distance from someone who is seated has a dominating effect (e.g., teacher to pupil, boss to secretary). The far phase of the third zone—seven to twelve feet—is where people stand when someone says, "Stand back so I can look at you." This distance lends a formal tone to business or social discourse. In an executive office, the desk serves to keep people at this distance.

The fourth zone—public distance—is used by teachers in classrooms or speakers at public gatherings. At its farthest phase—25 feet and beyond—it is used for important public figures. Violations of this distance can lead to serious complications. During his 1970 U.S. visit, the president of France, Georges Pompidou, was harassed by pickets in Chicago, who were permitted to get within touching distance. Since pickets in France are kept behind barricades a block or more away, the president was outraged by this insult to his person, and President Nixon was obliged to communicate his concern as well as offer his personal apologies.

It is interesting to note how American pitchmen and panhandlers exploit the unwritten, unspoken conventions of eye and distance. Both take advantage of the fact that once explicit eye contact is established, it is rude to look away, because to do so means to brusquely dismiss the other person and his needs. Once having caught the eye of his mark, the panhandler then locks on, not letting go until he moves through the public zone, the social zone, the personal zone and, finally, into the intimate sphere, where people are most vulnerable.

Touch also is an important part of the constant stream of communication that takes place between people. A light touch, a firm touch, a blow, a caress are all communications. In an effort to break down barriers among people, there's been a recent upsurge in group-encounter activities, in which strangers are encouraged to touch one another. In special situations such as these, the rules for not touching are broken with group approval and people gradually lose some of their inhibitions.

Although most people don't realize it, space is perceived and distances are set not by vision alone but with all the senses. Auditory space is perceived with the ears, thermal space with the skin, kinesthetic space with the muscles of the body and olfactory space with the nose. And, once again, it's one's culture that determines how his senses are programmed—which sensory information ranks highest and lowest. The important thing to remember is that culture is very persistent. In this country, we've noted the existence of culture patterns that determine distance between people in the third and fourth generations of some families, despite their prolonged contact with people of very different cultural heritages.

Whenever there is great cultural distance between two people, there are bound to be problems arising from differences in behavior and expectations. An example is the American couple who consulted a psychiatrist about their marital problems. The husband was from New England and had been brought up by reserved parents who taught him to control his emotions and to respect the need for privacy. His wife was from an Italian family and had been brought up in close contact with all the members of her large family, who were extremely warm, volatile and demonstrative.

When the husband came home after a hard day at the office, dragging his feet and longing for peace and quiet, his wife would rush to him and smother him. Clasping his hands, rubbing his brow, crooning over his weary head, she never left him alone. But when the wife was upset or anxious about her day, the husband's response was to withdraw completely and leave her alone. No comforting, no affectionate embrace, no attention—just solitude. The woman became convinced her husband didn't love her and, in desperation, she consulted a psychiatrist. Their problem wasn't basically psychological but cultural.

Why has man developed all these different ways of communicating messages without words? One reason is that people don't like to spell out certain kinds of messages. We prefer to find other ways of showing our feelings. This is especially true in relationships as sensitive as courtship. Men don't like to be rejected and most women don't want to turn a man down bluntly. Instead, we work out subtle ways of encouraging or discouraging each other that save face and avoid confrontations.

How a person handles space in dating others is an obvious and very sensitive indicator of how he or she feels about the other person. On a first date, if a woman sits or stands so close to a man that he is acutely conscious of her physical presence—inside the intimate-distance zone—the man usually construes it to mean that she is encouraging him. However, before the man starts moving in on the woman, he should be sure what message she's really sending; otherwise, he risks bruising his ego. What is close to someone of North European background may be neutral or distant to someone of Italian heritage. Also, women sometimes use space as a way of misleading a man and there are few things that put men off more than women who communicate contradictory messages—such as women who cuddle up and then act insulted when a man takes the next step.

How does a woman communicate interest in a man? In addition to such familiar gambits as smiling at him, she may glance shyly at him, blush and then look away. Or she may give him a real come-on look and move in very close when he approaches. She may touch his arm and ask for a light. As she leans forward to light her cigarette, she may brush him lightly, enveloping him in her perfume. She'll probably continue to smile at him and she may use what ethologists call preening gestures—touching the back of her hair, thrusting her breasts forward, tilting her hips as she stands or crossing her legs if she's seated, perhaps even exposing one thigh or putting a hand on her thigh and stroking it.She may also stroke her wrists as she converses or show the palm of her hand as a way of gaining his attention. Her skin may be unusually flushed or quite pale, her eyes brighter, the pupils larger.

If a man sees a woman whom he wants to attract, he tries to present himself by his posture and stance as someone who is self-assured. He moves briskly and confidently. When he catches the eye of the woman, he may hold her glance a little longer than normal. If he gets an encouragaing smile, he'll move in close and engage her in small talk. As they converse, his glance shifts over her face and body. He, too, may make preening gestures—straightening his tie, smoothing his hair or shooting his cuffs.

How do people learn body language? The same way they learn spoken language—by observing and imitating people around them as they're growing up. Little girls imitate their mothers or an older female. Little boys imitate their fathers or a respected uncle or a character on television. In this way, they learn the gender signals appropriate for their sex. Regional, class and ethnic patterns of body behavior are also learned in childhood and persist throughout life.

Such patterns of masculine and feminine body behavior vary widely from one culture to another. In America, for example, women stand with their thighs together. Many walk with their pelvis tipped slightly forward and their upper arms close to their body. When they sit, they cross their legs at the knee or, if they are well past middle age, they may cross their ankles. American men hold their arms away from their body, often swinging them as they walk. They stand with their legs apart (an extreme example is the cowboy, with legs apart and thumbs tucked into his belt). When they sit, they put their feet on the floor with legs apart and, in some parts of the country, they cross their legs by putting one ankle on the other knee.

Leg behavior indicates sex, status and personality. It also indicates whether or not one is at ease or is showing respect or disrespect for the other person. Young Latin-American males avoid crossing their legs. In their world of *machismo* the preferred position for young males when with one another (if there is no older dominant male present to whom they must show respect) is to sit on the base of their spine with their leg muscles relaxed and their feet wide apart. Their respect position is like our military equivalent; spine straight, heels and ankles together—almost identical to that displayed by properly brought up young women in New England in the early part of this century.

American women who sit with their legs spread apart in the presence of males are *not* normally signaling a come-on—they are simply (and often unconsciously) sitting like men. Middle-class women in the presence of other women to whom they are very close may on occasion throw themselves down on a soft chair or sofa and let themselves go. This is a signal that nothing serious will be taken up. Males, on the other hand, lean back and prop their legs up on the nearest object.

The way we walk, similarly, indicates status, respect, mood and ethnic or cultural affiliation. The many variants of the female walk are too well known to go into here, except to say that a man would have to be blind not to be turned on by the way some women walk—a fact that made Mae West rich before scientists ever studied these matters. To white Americans, some French middle-class males walk in a way that is both humorous and suspect. There is a bounce and looseness to the French walk, as though the parts of the body were somehow unrelated. Jacques Tati, the French movie actor, walks this way; so does the great mime, Marcel Marceau.

Blacks and whites in America—with the exception of middle- and upper-middle-class professionals of both groups—move and walk very differently from each other. To the blacks, whites often seem incredibly stiff, almost mechanical in their movements. Black males, on the other hand, have a looseness and coordination that frequently makes whites a little uneasy; it's too different, too integrated, too alive, too male. Norman Mailer has said that squares walk from the shoulders, like bears, but blacks and hippies walk from the hips, like cats.

All over the world people walk not only in their own characteristic way but have walks that communicate the nature of their involvement with whatever it is they're doing. The purposeful walk of North Europeans is an important component of proper behavior on the job. Any male who has been in the military knows how essential it is to walk properly (which makes for a continuing source of tension between blacks and whites in the Service). The quick shuffle of servants in the Far East in the old days was a show of respect. On the island of Truk, when we last visited, the inhabitants even had a name for the respectful walk that one used when in the presence of a chief or when walking past a chief's house. The term was *sufan,* which meant to be humble and respectful.

The notion that people communicate volumes by their gestures, facial expressions, posture and walk is not new; actors, dancers, writers and psychiatrists have long been aware of it. Only in recent years, however, have scientists begun to make systematic observations of body motions. Ray L. Birdwhistell of the University of Pennsylvania is one of the pioneers in body-motion research and coined the term kinesics to describe this field. He developed an elaborate notation system to record both facial and body movements, using an approach similar to that of the linguist, who studies the basic elements of speech. Birdwhistell and other kinesicists such as Albert Sheflen, Adam Kendon and William Condon take movies of people interacting. They run the film over and over again, often at reduced speed for frame-by-frame analysis, so that they can observe even the slightest body movements not perceptible at normal interaction speeds. These movements are then recorded in notebooks for later analysis.

To appreciate the importance of nonverbal-communication systems, consider the unskilled inner-city black looking for a job. His handling of time and space alone is sufficiently different from the white middle-class pattern to create great misunderstandings on both sides. The black is told to appear for a job interview at a certain time. He arrives late. The white interviewer concludes from his tardy arrival that the black is irresponsible and not really interested in the job. What the interviewer doesn't know is that the black time system (often referred to by blacks as C.P.T.—colored people's time) isn't the same as that of whites. In the words of a black student who had been told to make an appointment to see his professor: "Man, you *must* be putting me on. I never had an appointment in my life."

The black job applicant, having arrived late for his interview, may further antagonize the white interviewer by his posture and his eye behavior. Perhaps he slouches and avoids looking at the interviewer; to him, this is playing it cool. To the interviewer, however, he may look shifty and sound uninterested. The interviewer has failed to notice the actual signs of interest and eagerness in the black's behavior, such as the subtle shift in the quality of the voice—a gentle and tentative excitement—an almost imperceptible change in the cast of the eyes and a relaxing of the jaw muscles.

Moreover, correct reading of black-white behavior is continually complicated by the fact that both groups are comprised of individuals—some of whom try to accommodate and some of whom make it a point of pride *not* to accommodate. At present, this means that many Americans, when thrown into contact with one another, are in the precarious position of not knowing which pattern applies. Once identified and analyzed, nonverbal-communications systems can be taught, like a foreign language. Without this training, we respond to nonverbal communications in terms of our own culture; we read everyone's behavior as if it were our own, and thus we often misunderstand it.

Several years ago in New York City, there was a program for sending children from predominantly black and Puerto Rican low-income neighborhoods to summer school in a white upper-class neighborhood on the East Side. One morning, a group of young black and Puerto Rican boys raced down the street, shouting and screaming and overturning garbage cans on their way to school. A doorman from an apartment building nearby chased them and cornered one of them inside a building. The boy drew a knife and attacked the doorman. This tragedy would not have occurred if the doorman had been familiar with the behavior of boys from low-income neighborhoods, where such antics are routine and socially acceptable and where pursuit would be expected to invite a violent response.

The language of behavior is extremely complex. Most of us are lucky to have under control one subcultural system—the one that reflects our sex, class, generation and geographic region within the United States. Because of its complexity, efforts to isolate bits of nonverbal communication and generalize from them are in vain; you don't become an instant expert of people's behavior by watching them at cocktail parties. Body language isn't something that's independent of the person, something that can be donned and doffed like a suit of clothes.

Our research and that of our colleagues has shown that, far from being a superficial form of communication that can be consciously manipulated, nonverbal-communication systems are interwoven into the fabric of the personality and, as sociologist Erving Goffman has demonstrated, into society itself. They are the warp and woof of daily interaction with others and they influence how one expresses oneself, how one experiences oneself as a man or a woman.

Nonverbal communications signal to members of your own group what kind of person you are, how you feel about others, how you'll fit into and work in a group, whether you're assured or anxious, the degree to which you feel comfortable with the standards of your own culture, as well as deeply significant feelings about the self, including the state of your own psyche. For most of us, it's difficult to accept the reality of another's behavioral system. And, of course, none of us will ever become fully knowledgeable of the importance of every nonverbal signal. But as long as each of us realizes the power of these signals, this society's diversity can be a source of great strength rather than a further—and subtly powerful—source of division.

17

Seeing Is Believing

BY ALAN DUNDES

Whether from early memories of playing "peek-a-boo," "showing and telling" in school, or learning the opening phrase of the national anthem—"Oh, say can you see"—the primacy of vision in American culture is affirmed again and again as infants grow to adulthood. Americans are conditioned from childhood to believe that "what you see is what you get."

There is more to such a phenomenon than immediately meets the eye. That Americans rely more on vision than on other senses doesn't mean that they are aware of it. Nor does it mean that it is a peculiarly American trait. People everywhere rely on their senses to perceive their world and order their experiences, but since my data are derived from American folk speech, I cannot speak about others. In any case, because I have been taught to mistrust hearsay, I have decided to take a look at the evidence for a visual bias and to see for myself.

In Western thought, a distinction has commonly been made between sensory perception and reasoning. The power of reason is presumably the superior of the two. According to Aristotle, there are five senses— sight, hearing, smell, taste, and touch—which provide data generally deemed less trustworthy or, at least, frequently illusory, compared to the information that is provided by the faculties of rational thought. Subjective versus objective and body versus mind are other expressions of this distinction between the sensory and the rational. If we assume, however, that reasoning cannot take place without some reference to metaphor, then it is certainly possible that much American logic and reasoning is closely tied to metaphor in general and to visual metaphor in particular.

The allegedly inferior sensory experiences seem to be ranked according to how effective or reliable a given sense is assumed to be. In American culture, the sense of sight is normally the first of the five senses to be listed. However, whether sight is actually more useful or crucial for perception than the other senses is a moot question and, in fact, does not require an answer to show that a cultural bias for the sense of sight really exists. In the present context, it is not the literal meaning of sight that is important, but the metaphorical. I believe that, metaphorically speaking, Americans tend to *see* the world around them, rather than hear, feel, smell, or taste it. It may be no accident that Americans *observe* laws and holidays.

American speech provides persuasive evidence to support the notion that "vision" is used as a metaphor for "understanding." Consider, for example, the classic punning proverb, " 'I see,' said the blind man, as he picked up his hammer and saw." The oppositional structure in this text is produced by the juxtaposition of sight and blindness. Here is a clear distinction between literal and metaphorical seeing. Literally a blind man cannot see, but figuratively he certainly can.

Americans consistently speak of "seeing" the point of an argument when, in fact, an argument is not really seen but comprehended. Intellectual positions, or "perspectives," are frequently referred to as points of *view*. When articulated, they may be introduced by such formulas as, "As I see it" or "It all depends on how you look at it."

American culture is pronouncedly concerned with empiricism, and this empiricism is explicitly visual. "Seeing is believing" and "I'm from Missouri" (which means "you've got to show me") are indications of the emphasis on seeing something for oneself and the tendency to distrust anyone else's report of a given event. "I saw it with my own (two) eyes" is a common authenticating formula, as is the invitation to "see for yourself."

Without sight, there may be disbelief or lack of faith: "I'll believe it when I see it," "That I've got to see," or "I can't picture that." Even though the reliability of vision may be questioned—"There's more to this than meets the eye"—in general, people tend to believe what they see. Thus, when something is really out of the ordinary, we say,

"I couldn't believe my eyes." Something that is incredible or unbelievable is termed "out of sight," a phrase dating from before the end of the nineteenth century.

Imagination is sometimes called "the mind's eye," but why should the mind have an eye? Probably for the same reason that patients want doctors "to see them." Telephone conversations or other purely oral–aural channels are not considered entirely satisfactory. Actually, the patient is probably relieved by *his* seeing the doctor. Seeing the doctor, in turn, is part of the widespread cultural insistence upon interviews. Literally, the word *interview* refers to A seeing B and B seeing A.

Consider the nature of American tourist philosophy—sightseeing. To "see the sights" is a common goal of tourists, a goal also reflected in the mania for snapping pictures as permanent records of what was seen. Typical travel boasting consists of inflicting an evening of slide viewing on unwary friends so that they may see what their hosts saw. This is surely a strange way of defining tourism. Visiting a foreign locale certainly involves all of the sensory apparatus. There are exotic smells and tastes, and the opportunity to savor new foods and experience the "feel" of a foreign setting is as important in understanding a country and its people as seeing them. One reason Americans frequently fail to enjoy touring as much as they might may be their almost compulsive tendency to see as many sights as possible. The seeing of many sights is, of course, consistent with a tendency to quantify living, and, specifically, with the desire to get one's money's worth.

When shopping, whether in foreign countries or at home, Americans are reluctant to buy anything "sight unseen." They prefer "to look something over," "to walk into something with their eyes open." A thorough inspection theoretically allows one to "see through" a pretense or fake. And obviously, a product can only "catch a person's eye" if he sees it.

Public "images," too, are part of

the visual pattern. But why, after all, should a person have to be depicted in a term such as image? Even though looks may be deceiving ("Never judge a book by its cover"), it seems clear that packaging that appeals to visual esthetics is equally effective whether one is hawking cigarettes or automobiles or selling political candidates.

The reduction of persons or events to purely visual terms is also evident in the use of the popular slang phrase for a detective: "private eye." By the same token, sleep is commonly referred to as "shut-eye," which obviously singles out only one aspect of the dormant state. Furthermore, this suggestion that sleep is shut-eye also implies that the waking state is marked chiefly by having one's eyes open.

As I collected examples of folk speech, I soon found that comparison of vision with the other senses reaffirmed the superiority of sight. That a "seer" can make predictions by gazing into a crystal ball, for example, suggests that vision is more effective than the other senses in fore*seeing* future events.

The same bias in favor of the visual is found in American greeting and leave-taking formulas. Examples include: "See you around," "I'll be seeing you," or "I haven't seen so-and-so in ages." Greetings may also be couched in visual terms. "It's good to see you," Americans say, rather than, "It's good to hear, smell, or feel you."

There seem to be relatively few complimentary references to hearers, smellers, talkers, and touchers. "Look, but don't touch" hints at a delight in gawking (girl-watching), and possibly at a cultural distaste for body contact. Someone who is "touchy" is not pleasant to have around. A "soft touch," which sounds as if it should have a positive connotation, is a slang term for a dupe or easy mark.

One of the most interesting pieces of evidence supporting the notion of visual superiority over the other senses is that the original version of "Seeing's believing" was presumably "Seeing's believing, but feeling's the truth." That most Americans have dropped the second portion of the proverb does not seem to be an accident. Rather, it reflects a definite penchant for the visual in contrast to the tactual. Originally, the proverb denigrated "seeing" in favor of "feeling."

Comparisons between the visual and the aural are the most common, however, with hearing considered second best. Consider "Believe nothing of what you hear and only half of what you see." Although caution is urged against believing everything one sees, seeing is surely depicted as being more reliable and trustworthy than hearing. Compare the following two statements: "I hear that X has just moved to Miami," and "I see that X has just moved to Miami." The first statement is possibly true, possibly not true: there is an element of doubt. The second, in contrast, seems to be a statement of fact.

Other instances are found in legal parlance. Although judges hear cases, there is no doubt that *hearsay*, that is, aural–oral, evidence is not in the same league as that offered by an eyewitness. Actually, the word *witness* indicates that the person was physically present during an event and saw with his own eyes the activities in question. If so, then the term *eyewitness* is redundant. Strangely enough, at *hearings* there is an insistence that *hearsay* evidence be rejected and that only *eyewitness* testimony be accepted.

On the other hand, it is interesting to recall that Justice is depicted as being blind. Justice cannot see and presumably blindness guarantees fairness. But of course, sometimes even an innocent man may be guilty "in the eyes of the law."

The eye is also more powerful than the ear insofar as it is regarded as an active rather than a passive agent. The eye looks, peers, or gazes. There is seductive power in the eye, as in "giving a girl the eye," and the malevolent power of the eye is manifested in "the evil eye." The ear, by contrast, is a passive receptacle. There is little evidence of evil ears. Remember also that "big brother is watching you," not listening to you, although bugging rooms with microphones makes listening more likely than watching. Note also that voyeurs, such as Peeping Toms, are considered to be worse than eavesdroppers. The active versus passive with respect to seeing and hearing may also be implied by the connotative differences between "spectators" and "audience."

Marshall McLuhan and his followers have suggested that the oral–aural channels of preliterate, or rather, nonliterate man may be enjoying a renaissance. According to this view, as man becomes literate, written language—which must be seen to be read—takes priority over the oral. Recently, however, radio and television have created postliterate man, whose world is once more primarily oral–aural. Many Americans learn the news of the day by hearing it on the radio rather than by reading it in newspapers. Even on television, the argument says, the news is mainly told, not shown. Then, too, telephone conversations are replacing letter writing more and more.

One can contend, however, that television has replaced radio, and thus the visual still supersedes the purely aural. Americans still prefer to get agreements in writing rather than to trust a gentleman's handshake (a tactile sign) or take someone's word or say-so (oral sign) for a contract. Once an agreement is

down in black and white, Americans watch out for, and read, the small print, with an "eye" toward avoiding an unfavorable set of conditions.

If Americans do have a deepseated penchant for the visual sense, as I have tried to suggest by examining American folk speech, the question of what it means remains to be answered. It is not just a matter of being able to see more clearly why Americans tend to look for men of vision to lead them. Much more important is the influence of folk metaphors on scientific thought. American science is not culture-free, no matter how devoutly American scientists wish that it were or think that it is.

As an anthropologist, I am struck by the fact that American anthropologists insist upon being participant observers (not voyeurs!) when they go into the field so as to gain insight into the world-views of other cultures. Why "insight"? Do all examples of problem solving by insight actually involve visual perception? And why world-view?

Anthropologists do not always agree whether man is active or passive with regard to world-view. Bronislaw Malinowski, for example, tended to consider man passive: he depicted man as being molded by the impress of a culturally patterned, cookie cutter kind of worldview, which imposed its structure upon human minds. "What interests me really in the study of the native," Malinowski said, "is his outlook on things, his *Weltanschauung*. Every human culture gives its members a definite vision of the world." In contrast, Robert Redfield, by defining world-view as "the way a people characteristically look outward upon the universe," suggested that man was a more active participant. In any case, whether man passively accepts a culturally determined world-view or actively creates a world-view system, the visual bias in the very search by anthropologists for world-view is evident.

It has been observed that for Americans the universe is essentially something they can draw a picture or diagram of. But surely a person's world is felt, smelled, tasted, and heard as well. This propensity for visual metaphorical categories may produce distortion in attempts to describe facets of American culture. It is unlikely that such distortion would even be noticed, since the distortion, like beauty, is strictly in the subjective eye of the beholder. But what happens when Americans or American scientists seek to describe features of other cultures or the features of the natural world?

It is at least possible that by looking for the world-view of other peoples, we run the risk of imposing our own rank-ordering of the senses upon data that may not be perceived in the same way by the people whose cultures are being described. If we are truly interested in understanding how other peoples perceive reality, we must recognize their cognitive categories and try to escape the confines of our own.

The history of man is full of instances of one group's conscious or unconscious attempts to impose its particular set of cognitive categories upon another group. The imposing group typically claims that its categories represent the true nature of reality (as opposed to the categories of the victimized group, which are deemed odd at best and false at

worst). Whether it is nineteenth-century American linguists searching in vain for Latin cases (for example, the dative or accusative) in American Indian languages, or a modern Western physician, imbued with the number three, trying to persuade an American Indian, who believes in the sacredness of the number four, that only three doses or inoculations are sufficient (as in a series of three polio shots), the issue is the same.

This is why it is essential for Americans (and for other peoples as well) to become aware of their dependence upon cognitive categories such as the visual metaphorical mode I have been talking about. Armed with this awareness, it is possible to appreciate more fully the aptness of the visual metaphor Ruth Benedict used to explain why so many social theorists failed to notice custom or culture: "We do not see the lens through which we look." A conscious recognition of our visual bias may help make the lens visible. We must never forget the possible relativity of our own sensory perception categories.

Inventories of the same or similar sense categories found in other cultures may help. Clifford Geertz reports, for example, that the Javanese have five senses (seeing, hearing, *talking*, smelling, and feeling), which do not coincide exactly with

our five. The delineation of such differences may teach us just how culture-bound or culture-specific our own observations of nature may be. We tend to delude ourselves into thinking we are studying the nature of nature, foolishly forgetting that we cannot observe raw or pure nature. We can perceive nature only through the mediation of culture, with its panoply of culturally relative cognitive categories.

Much of the study of "natural history" often turns out to be "cultural history" in disguise. Theories and ideas about the natural world are invariably couched in terms of a specific human language and are based upon data obtained from human observation. With human observation expressed in human language, one simply cannot avoid cultural bias. Searching for culture-free descriptions of nature may be a worthwhile goal, and perhaps man will one day succeed in achieving it. In the meantime, we must be wary of mistaking relatives for absolutes, of mistaking culture for nature. Cross-cultural comparisons of sense categories may not only reveal critical differences in the specific senses, but also whether or not the apparent priority of vision over the other senses is a human universal. For the moment, we can do little more than wait and *see*.

V Cultural Anthropology

○ ○

Cultural anthropolgy has two main areas of study. One, termed *ethnography*, is the intensive study, description, and analysis of a specific group of people and their culture. The other, *ethnology*, is the systematic comparison of materials across cultural boundaries, with the aim of detecting and specifying accurate generalizations (formerly called laws) about human behavior and culture. The concept of *culture* is central to both ethnography and ethnology.

What is *culture*? Surprisingly, although it is the central concept of anthropology, it is difficult to find exact agreement on the meaning of the term among anthropologists. Depending on their interests, some scholars emphasize the symbolic nature of culture; others, its function as a mechanism of adaptation; still others, the ways in which it structures our perception of the world; and yet others, on the ways it patterns behavior. Nevertheless, it is possible to find agreement among anthropologists with regard to some basic aspects of culture:

1. Culture is central to human existence. The biological and cultural sides of humankind evolved together, constantly affecting each other's course. The concept *human being* and the concept *culture* are thus inseparable.

2. Culture is not inherited through the genes. Each person acquires his or her culture through interaction with other members of the group(s) into which she or he is born. In other words, culture is learned.

3. Not only is culture learned, but also everything that is learned is culture. All human knowledge, all activities, all beliefs, values, mores, schemes for organizing information about the world, languages, philosophical systems, technologies, arts, and major behavioral patterns are learned and hence are aspects of culture.

4. Culture is a group phenomenon. The growing infant does not invent a culture for itself; it learns the culture of its society. Left all alone to its own devices, an infant *cannot* invent culture. Indeed, if a child is deprived of the opportunity to learn a language by the time it is five or six, it is probably unlikely ever to be able to learn one afterward.

5. Culture is patterned. All cultures of the world consist of many facets and elements. But theses are not randomly thrown together like marbles in a bag or patches on a quilt. There are systematic relationships among the elements of a culture, and change in one area is likely to cause stress or change in other areas.

6. Culture is symbolic. This means that all cultural phenomena have meanings beyond their own existence. (A cat, in American culture, is not just an animal with the label "cat." It "has nine lives," is "stealthy," and is "independent." A cat, then, as a part of our culture, represents a set of meanings; in other words, it is a symbol.) Culture, therefore, provides the backdrop of shared meanings against which all things are experienced.

As you can appreciate, the subject of cultural anthropology is vast. It embodies the study of virtually every aspect of human behavior—from how you nourish yourself to how you feel about yourself and others, from your religion (or lack of one) to how you drive a car. For convenience, we have organized the articles in this section into seven topics. Although we certainly have not come close to covering all areas of cultural anthropology. Nevertheless, we offer you interesting reading in some of the most important areas.

TOPIC SEVEN

Fieldwork

. . . .

For most anthropologists, fieldwork is one of the more significant experiences of their lives. Few anthropologists return home from the field unchanged, and for many the personal changes are quite deep and enduring. In a distant place among strangers, the fieldworker is cut off from the people and patterns that gave his or her life meaning and in terms of which she or he built a sense of self. In a very real sense, one becomes childlike: understanding little, incompetent to perform any locally valued tasks, utterly dependent on the good will of others for virtually everything. Like a child the fieldworker starts to build a social identity; to a great measure, the success of the research will depend upon how well she or he succeeds in accomplishing this task. Not the least of one's challenges is to come to terms with the world view of one's hosts and research subjects—which frequently is at significant variance with one's own.

Napoleon A. Chagnon is very candid about the emotional stress he endured in the course of "Doing Fieldwork among the Yąnomamö." One can hardly imagine a society more different from our own. However, a word of caution is in order. Without giving away the whole story, we wish to indicate that one point made by Horace Miner's "Body Ritual among the Nacirema" is that the language used by the researcher in reporting on the behavior of his or her subjects can make them seem much more foreign than they really are.

"Shakespeare in the Bush," by Laura Bohannan, and "Eating Christmas in the Kalahari," by Richard B. Lee, both deal with the problem of cross-cultural (mis)understanding. It is inevitable that the fieldworker will misunderstand—and be misunderstood by—the people she or he is studying. Good researchers, however, use instances of misunderstanding as instruments of investigation into the divergent premises of the culture of their subjects, and their own culture as well. The result can be a much deeper understanding of both.

18

Doing Fieldwork
Among the Yąnomamö
BY NAPOLEON A. CHAGNON

. . . .

The Yąnomamö[1] Indians live in southern Venezuela and the adjacent portions of northern Brazil. Some 125 widely scattered villages have populations ranging from 40 to 250 inhabitants, with 75 to 80 people the most usual number. In total numbers their population probably approaches 10,000 people, but this is merely a guess. Many of the villages have not yet been contacted by outsiders, and nobody knows for sure exactly how many uncontacted villages there are, or how many people live in them. By comparison to African or Melanesian tribes, the Yąnomamö population is small. Still, they are one of the largest unacculturated tribes left in all of South America.

But they have a significance apart from tribal size and cultural purity: the Yąnomamö are still actively conducting warfare. It is in the nature of man to fight, according to one of the myths, because the blood of "Moon" spilled on this layer of the cosmos, causing men to become fierce. I describe the Yąnomamö as "the fierce people" because that is the most accurate single phrase that describes them. That is how they conceive themselves to be, and that is how they would like others to think of them.

I spent nineteen months with the Yąnomamö,[2] during which time I acquired some proficiency in their language and, up to a point, submerged myself in their culture and way of life. The thing that impressed me most was the importance of aggression in their culture. I had the opportunity to witness a good many incidents that expressed individual vindictiveness on the one hand and collective bellicosity on the other. These ranged in seriousness from the ordinary incidents of wife beating and chest pounding to dueling and organized raiding by parties that set out with the intention of ambushing and killing men from enemy villages (Fig. 1). One of the villages discussed in the chapters that follow was raided approximately twenty-five times while I conducted the fieldwork, six times by the group I lived among.

The fact that the Yąnomamö live in a state of chronic warfare is reflected in their mythology, values, settlement pattern, political behavior and marriage practices. Accordingly, I have organized this case study in such a way that students can appreciate the effects of warfare on Yąnomamö culture in general and on their social organization and politics in particular (Fig. 1).

I collected the data under somewhat trying circumstances, some of which I will describe in order to give the student a rough idea of what is generally meant when anthropologists speak of "culture shock" and "fieldwork." It should be borne in mind, however, that each field situation is in many respects unique, so that the problems I encountered do not necessarily exhaust the range of possible problems other anthropologists have confronted in other areas. There are a few problems, however, that seem to be nearly universal among anthropological fieldworkers, particularly those having to do with eating, bathing, sleeping, lack of privacy and loneliness, or discovering that primitive man is not always as noble as you originally thought.

This is not to state that primitive man everywhere is unpleasant. By way of contrast, I have also done limited

1. The word Yąnomamö is nasalized through its entire length, indicated by the diacritical mark [ą]. When this mark appears on a word, the entire word is nasalized. The terminal vowel [-ö] represents a sound that does not occur in the English language. It corresponds to the phone [+] of linguistic orthography. In normal conversation, Yąnomamö is pronounced like "Yah-no-mama," except that it is nasalized. Finally, the words having the [-ä] vowel are pronounced at that vowel with the "uh" sound of "duck." Thus, the name Kąobawä would be pronounced "cow-ba-wuh," again nasalized.

2. I spent a total of twenty-three months in South America of which nineteen were spent among the Yąnomamö on three separate field trips. The first trip, November 1964 through February 1966, was to Venezuela. During this time I spent nineteen months in direct contact with the Yąnomamö, using my periodic trips back to Caracas to visit my family and to collate the genealogical data I had collected up to that point. On my second trip, January through March 1967, I spent two months among Brazilian Yąnomamö and one more month with Venezuelan Yąnomamö. Finally, I returned to Venezuela for three more months among the Yąnomamö, January through April 1968.

fieldwork among the Yąnomamö's northern neighbors, the Carib-speaking Makiritare Indians. This group was very pleasant and charming, all of them anxious to help me and honor bound to show any visitor the numerous courtesies of their system of etiquette. In short, they approached the image of primitive man that I had conjured up, and it was sheer pleasure to work with them. The recent work by Colin Turnbull (1966) brings out dramatically the contrast in personal characteristics of two African peoples he has studied.

Hence, what I say about some of my experiences is probably equally true of the experiences of many fieldworkers. I write about my own experiences because there is a conspicuous lack of fieldwork descriptions available to potential fieldworkers. I think I could have profited by reading about the private misfortunes of my own teachers; at least I might have been able to avoid some of the more stupid errors I made. In this regard there are a number of recent contributions by fieldworkers describing some of the discomforts and misfortunes they themselves sustained.[3] Students planning to conduct fieldwork are urged to consult them.

My first day in the field illustrated to me what my teachers meant when they spoke of "culture shock." I had traveled in a small, aluminum rowboat propelled by a large outboard motor for two and a half days. This took me from the Territorial capital, a small town on the Orinoco River, deep into Yąnomamö country. On the morning of the third day we reached a small mission settlement, the field "headquarters" of a group of Americans who were working in two Yąnomamö villages. The missionaries had come out of these villages to hold their annual conference on the progress of their mission work, and were conducting their meetings when I arrived. We picked up a passenger at the mission station, James P. Barker, the first non-Yąnomamö to make a sustained, permanent contact with the tribe (in 1950). He had just returned from a year's furlough in the United States, where I had earlier visited him before leaving for Venezuela. He agreed to accompany me to the village I had selected for my base of operations to introduce me to the Indians. This village was also his own home base, but he had not been there for over a year and did not plan to join me for another three months. Mr. Barker had been living with this particular group about five years.

We arrived at the village, Bisaasi-teri, about 2:00 P.M. and docked the boat along the muddy bank at the ter-

3. Maybury-Lewis, 1967, "Introduction," and 1965b; Turnbull 1966; L.Bohannan, 1964. Perhaps the most intimate account of the tribulations of a fieldworker is found in the posthumous diary of Bronislaw Malinowski (1967). Since the diary was not written for publication, it contains many intimate, very personal details about the writer's anxieties and hardships.

minus of the path used by the Indians to fetch their drinking water. It was hot and muggy, and my clothing was soaked with perspiration. It clung uncomfortably to my body, as it did thereafter for the remainder of the work. The small, biting gnats were out in astronomical numbers, for it was the beginning of the dry season. My face and hands were swollen from the venom of their numerous stings. In just a few moments I was to meet my first Yąnomamö, my first primitive man. What would it be like? I had visions of entering the village and seeing 125 social facts running about calling each other kinship terms and sharing food, each waiting and anxious to have me collect his genealogy. I would wear them out in turn. Would they like me? This was important to me; I wanted them to be so fond of me that they would adopt me into their kinship system and way of life, because I had heard that successful anthropologists always get adopted by their people. I had learned during my seven years of anthropological training at the University of Michigan that kinship was equivalent to society in primitive tribes and that it was a moral way of life, "moral" being something "good" and "desirable." I was determined to work my way into their moral system of kinship and become a member of their society.

My heart began to pound as we approached the village and heard the buzz of activity within the circular compound. Mr. Barker commented that he was anxious to see if any changes had taken place while he was away and wondered how many of them had died during his absence. I felt into my back pocket to make sure that my notebook was still there and felt personally more secure when I touched it. Otherwise, I would not have known what to do with my hands.

The entrance to the village was covered over with brush and dry palm leaves. We pushed them aside to expose the low opening to the village. The excitement of meeting my first Indians was almost unbearable as I duck-waddled through the low passage into the village clearing.

I looked up and gasped when I saw a dozen burly, naked, filthy, hideous men staring at us down the shafts of their drawn arrows! Immense wads of green tobacco were stuck between their lower teeth and lips making them look even more hideous, and strands of dark-green slime dripped or hung from their noses. We arrived at the village while the men were blowing a hallucinogenic drug up their noses. One of the side effects of the drug is a runny nose. The mucus is always saturated with the green powder and the Indians usually let it run freely from their nostrils. My next discovery was that there were a dozen or so vicious, underfed dogs snapping at my legs, circling me as if I were going to be their next meal. I just stood there holding my notebook, helpless and pathetic. Then the stench of the decaying vegetation and filth struck me and I almost

Fig. 1. Members of allied villages engaged in a chest-pounding duel which followed a feast.

got sick. I was horrified. What sort of a welcome was this for the person who came here to live with you and learn your way of life, to become friends with you? They put their weapons down when they recognized Barker and returned to their chanting, keeping a nervous eye on the village entrances.

We had arrived just after a serious fight. Seven women had been abducted the day before by a neighboring group, and the local men and their guests had just that morning recovered five of them in a brutal club fight that nearly ended in a shooting war. The abductors, angry because they lost five of the seven captives, vowed to raid the Bisaasi-teri. When we arrived and entered the village unexpectedly, the Indians feared that we were the raiders. On several occasions during the next two hours the men in the village jumped to their feet, armed themselves, and waited nervously for the noise outside the village to be identified. My enthusiasm for collecting ethnographic curiosities diminished in proportion to the number of

times such an alarm was raised. In fact, I was relieved when Mr. Barker suggested that we sleep across the river for the evening. It would be safer over there.

As we walked down the path to the boat, I pondered the wisdom of having decided to spend a year and a half with this tribe before I had even seen what they were like. I am not ashamed to admit, either, that had there been a diplomatic way out, I would have ended my fieldwork then and there. I did not look forward to the next day when I would be left alone with the Indians; I did not speak a word of their language, and they were decidedly different from what I had imagined them to be. The whole situation was depressing, and I wondered why I ever decided to switch from civil engineering to anthropology in the first place. I had not eaten all day, I was soaking wet from perspiration, the gnats were biting me, and I was covered with red pigment, the result of a dozen or so complete examinations I had been given by as many burly Indians. These examinations capped an otherwise grim day. The In-

Fig. 2. *One way that warfare affects other aspects of Yąnomamö social organization is in the great significance of intervillage alliances. Here members of an allied village dance excitedly in their hosts' village in anticipation of the feast and chest-pounding duel that will follow.*

dians would blow their noses into their hands, flick as much of the mucus off that would separate in a snap of the wrist, wipe the residue into their hair, and then carefully examine my face, arms, legs, hair, and the contents of my pockets. I asked Mr. Barker how to say "Your hands are dirty"; my comments were met by the Indians in the following way: They would "clean" their hands by spitting a quantity of slimy tobacco juice into them, rub them together, and then proceed with the examination.

Mr. Barker and I crossed the river and slung our hammocks. When he pulled his hammock out of a rubber bag, a heavy, disagreeable odor of mildewed cotton came with it. "Even the missionaries are filthy," I thought to myself. Within two weeks, everything I owned smelled the same way, and I lived with that odor for the remainder of the fieldwork. My own habits of personal cleanliness reached such levels that I didn't

even mind being examined by the Indians, as I was not much cleaner than they were after I had adjusted to the circumstances.

So much for my discovery that primitive man is not the picture of nobility and sanitation I had conceived him to be. I soon discovered that it was an enormously time-consuming task to maintain my own body in the manner to which it had grown accustomed in the relatively antiseptic environment of the northern United States. Either I could be relatively well fed and relatively comfortable in a fresh change of clothes and do very little fieldwork, or, I could do considerably more fieldwork and be less well fed and less comfortable.

It is appalling how complicated it can be to make oatmeal in the jungle. First, I had to make two trips to the river to haul the water. Next, I had to prime my kerosene stove with alcohol and get it burning, a tricky procedure when you are trying to mix powdered milk and fill a coffee pot at the same time: the alcohol prime always burned out before I could turn the kerosene on, and I would have to start all over. Or, I would turn the kerosene on, hoping that the element was still hot enough to vaporize the fuel, and start a small fire in my palm-thatched hut as the liquid kerosene squirted all over the table and walls and ignited. It was safer to start over with the alcohol. Then I had to boil the oatmeal and pick the bugs out of it. All my supplies, of course, were carefully stored in Indian-proof, rat-proof, moisture-proof, and insect-proof containers, not one of which ever served its purpose adequately. Just taking things out of the multiplicity of containers and repacking them afterward was a minor project in itself. By the time I had hauled the water to cook with, unpacked my food, prepared the oatmeal, milk, and coffee, heated water for the dishes, washed and dried the dishes, repacked the food in the containers, stored the containers in locked trunks and cleaned up my mess, the ceremony of preparing breakfast had brought me almost up to lunch time!

Eating three meals a day was out of the question. I solved that problem by eating a single meal that could be prepared in a single container, or, at most, in two containers, washed my dishes only when there were no clean ones left, using cold river water, and wore each change of clothing at least a week to cut down on my laundry problem, a courageous undertaking in the tropics. I was also less concerned about sharing provisions with the rats, insects, Indians, and the elements, thereby eliminating the need for my complicated storage process. I was able to last most of the day on *café con leche*, heavily sugared espresso coffee diluted about five to one with hot milk. I would prepare this in the evening and store it in a thermos. Frequently, my single meal was no more complicated than a can of sardines and a package of crackers. But at least two or three times a week I would do something sophisticated, like make oatmeal or boil rice and add a can of tuna fish or tomato paste to it. I even saved time by devising a water system that obviated the trips to the river. I had a few sheets of zinc roofing brought in and made a rain-water trap; I caught the water on the zinc surface, funneled it into an empty gasoline drum, and then ran a plastic hose from the drum to my hut. When the drum was exhausted in the dry season, I hired the Indians to fill it with water from the river.

I ate much less when I traveled with the Indians to visit other villages. Most of the time my travel diet consisted of roasted or boiled green plantains that I obtained from the Indians, but I always carried a few cans of sardines with me in case I got lost or stayed away longer than I had planned. I found peanut butter and crackers a very nourishing food, and a simple one to prepare on trips. It was nutritious and portable, and

only one tool was required to prepare the meal, a hunting knife that could be cleaned by wiping the blade on a leaf. More importantly, it was one of the few foods the Indians would let me eat in relative peace. It looked too much like animal feces to them to excite their appetites.

I once referred to the peanut butter as the dung of cattle. They found this quite repugnant. They did not know what "cattle" were, but were generally aware that I ate several canned products of such an animal. I perpetrated this myth, if for no other reason than to have some peace of mind while I ate. Fieldworkers develop strange defense mechanisms, and this was one of my own forms of adaptation. On another occasion I was eating a can of frankfurters and growing very weary of the demands of one of my guests for a share in my meal. When he asked me what I was eating, I replied: "Beef." He then asked, "What part of the animal are you eating?" to which I replied, "Guess!" He stopped asking for a share.

Meals were a problem in another way. Food sharing is important to the Yąnomamö in the context of displaying friendship. "I am hungry," is almost a form of greeting with them. I could not possibly have brought enough food with me to feed the entire village, yet they seemed not to understand this. All they could see was that I did not share my food with them at each and every meal. Nor could I enter into their system of reciprocities with respect to food; every time one of them gave me something "freely," he would dog me for months to pay him back, not with food, but with steel tools. Thus, if I accepted a plantain from someone in a different village while I was on a visit, he would most likely visit me in the future and demand a machete as payment for the time that he "fed" me. I usually reacted to these kinds of demands by giving a banana, the customary reciprocity in their culture—food for food—but this would be a disappointment for the individual who had visions of that single plantain growing into a machete over time.

Despite the fact that most of them knew I would not share my food with them at their request, some of them always showed up at my hut during mealtime. I gradually became accustomed to this and learned to ignore their persistent demands while I ate. Some of them would get angry because I failed to give in, but most of them accepted it as just a peculiarity of the subhuman foreigner. When I did give in, my hut quickly filled with Indians, each demanding a sample of food that I had given one of them. If I did not give all a share, I was that much more despicable in their eyes.

A few of them went out of their way to make my meals unpleasant, to spite me for not sharing; for example, one man arrived and watched me eat a cracker with honey on it. He immediately recognized the honey, a particularly esteemed Yąnomamö food. He knew that I would not share my tiny bottle and that it would be futile to ask. Instead, he glared at me and queried icily, "Shaki!⁴ What kind of animal semen are you eating on that cracker?" His question had the desired effect, and my meal ended.

Finally, there was the problem of being lonely and separated from your own kind, especially your family. I tried to overcome this by seeking personal friendships among the Indians. This only complicated the matter because all my friends simply used my confidence to gain privileged access to my cache of steel tools and trade goods, and looted me. I would be bitterly disappointed that my "friend" thought no more of me than to finesse our relationship exclusively with the intention of getting at my locked up possessions, and my depression would hit new lows every time I discovered this. The loss of the possession bothered me much less than the shock that I was, as far as most of them were concerned, nothing more than a source of desirable items; no holds were barred in relieving me of these, since I was considered something subhuman, a non-Yąnomamö.

The thing that bothered me most was the incessant, passioned, and aggressive demands the Indians made. It would become so unbearable that I would have to lock myself in my mud hut every once in a while just to escape from it: Privacy is one of Western culture's greatest achievements. But I did not want privacy for its own sake; rather, I simply had to get away from the begging. Day and night for the entire time I lived with the Yąnomamö I was plagued by such demands as "Give me a knife, I am poor!"; "If you don't take me with you on your next trip to Widokaiya-teri I'll chop a hole in your canoe!"; "Don't point your camera at me or I'll hit you!"; "Share your food with me!"; "Take me across the river in your canoe and be quick about it!"; "Give me a cooking pot!"; "Loan me your flashlight so I can go hunting tonight!"; "Give me medicine . . . I itch all over!"; "Take us on a week-long hunting trip with your shotgun!"; and "Give me an axe or I'll break into your hut when you are away visiting and steal one!" And so I was bombarded by such demands day after day, months on end, until I could not bear to see an Indian.

It was not as difficult to become calloused to the incessant begging as it was to ignore the sense of urgency, the impassioned tone of voice, or the intimida-

tion and aggression with which the demands were made. It was likewise difficult to adjust to the fact that the Yąnomamö refused to accept "no" for an answer until or unless it seethed with passion and intimidation—which it did after six months. Giving in to a demand always established a new threshold; the next demand would be for a bigger item or favor, and the anger of the Indians even greater if the demand was not met. I soon learned that I had to become very much like the Yąnomamö to be able to get along with them on their terms: sly, aggressive, and intimidating.

Had I failed to adjust in this fashion I would have lost six months of supplies to them in a single day or would have spent most of my time ferrying them around in my canoe or hunting for them. As it was, I did spend a considerable amount of time doing these things and did succumb to their outrageous demands for axes and machetes, at least at first. More importantly, had I failed to demonstrate that I could not be pushed around beyond a certain point, I would have been the subject of far more ridicule, theft, and practical jokes than was the actual case. In short, I had to acquire a certain proficiency in their kind of interpersonal politics and to learn how to imply subtly that certain potentially undesirable consequences might follow if they did such and such to me. They do this to each other in order to establish precisely the point at which they cannot goad an individual any further without precipitating retaliation. As soon as I caught on to this and realized that much of their aggression was stimulated by their desire to discover my flash point, I got along much better with them and regained some lost ground. It was sort of like a political game that everyone played, but one in which each individual sooner or later had to display some sign that his bluffs and implied threats could be backed up. I suspect that the frequency of wife beating is a component of this syndrome, since men can display their ferocity and show others that they are capable of violence. Beating a wife with a club is considered to be an acceptable way of displaying ferocity and one that does not expose the male to much danger. The important thing is that the man has displayed his potential for violence and the implication is that other men better treat him with respect and caution.

After six months, the level of demand was tolerable in the village I used for my headquarters. The Indians and I adjusted to each other and knew what to expect with regard to demands on their part for goods, favors, and services. Had I confined my fieldwork to just that village alone, the field experience would have been far more enjoyable. But, as I was interested in the demographic pattern and social organization of a much larger area, I made regular trips to some dozen different villages in order to collect genealogies or to recheck those I already had. Hence, the intensity of begging and in-

4. "Shaki," or, rather, "Shakiwa," is the name they gave me because they could not pronounce "Chagnon." They like to name people for some distinctive feature when possible. *Shaki* is the name of a species of noisome bee; they accumulate in large numbers around ripening bananas and make pests of themselves by eating into the fruit, showering the people below with the debris. They probably adopted this name for me because I was also a nuisance, continuously prying into their business, taking pictures of them, and, in general, being where they did not want me.

Fig. 3. Kạobawä, the wise leader, listens to identify a strange noise in the jungle.

timidation was fairly constant for the duration of the fieldwork. I had to establish my position in some sort of pecking order of ferocity at each and every village.

For the most part, my own "fierceness" took the form of shouting back at the Yạnomamö as loudly and as passionately as they shouted at me, especially at first, when I did not know much of their language. As I became more proficient in their language and learned more about their political tactics, I became more sophisticated in the art of bluffing. For example, I paid one young man a machete to cut palm trees and make boards from the wood. I used these to fashion a platform in the bottom of my dugout canoe to keep my possessions dry when I traveled by river. That afternoon I was doing informant work in the village; the

long-awaited mission supply boat arrived, and most of the Indians ran out of the village to beg goods from the crew. I continued to work in the village for another hour or so and went down to the river to say "hello" to the men on the supply boat. I was angry when I discovered that the Indians had chopped up all my palm boards and used them to paddle their own canoes[5] across the river. I knew that if I overlooked this incident I would have invited them to take greater liberties with my goods in the future. I crossed the river, docked amidst their dugouts, and shouted for the Indians to come out and see me. A few of the culprits appeared, mischievous grins on their faces. I gave a spirited lecture about

5. The canoes were obtained from missionaries, who, in turn, got them from a different tribe.

Fig. 4. Koamashima, Kąobawä's youngest wife, playing with her son, who is holding a tree frog.

how hard I had worked to put those boards in my canoe, how I had paid a machete for the wood, and how angry I was that they destroyed my work in their haste to cross the river. I then pulled out my hunting knife and, while their grins disappeared, cut each of their canoes loose, set it into the current, and let them float away. I left without further ado and without looking back.

They managed to borrow another canoe and, after some effort, recovered their dugouts. The headman of the village later told me with an approving chuckle that I had done the correct thing. Everyone in the village, except, of course, the culprits, supported and defended my action. This raised my status.

Whenever I took such action and defended my

rights, I got along much better with the Yąnomamö. A good deal of their behavior toward me was directed with the forethought of establishing the point at which I would react defensively. Many of them later reminisced about the early days of my work when I was "timid" and a little afraid of them, and they could bully me into giving goods away.

Theft was the most persistent situation that required me to take some sort of defensive action. I simply could not keep everything I owned locked in trunks, and the Indians came into my hut and left at will. I developed a very effective means for recovering almost all the stolen items. I would simply ask a child who took the item and then take the person's hammock when he was not around, giving a spirited lecture to the others as I

Fig. 5. Rerebawä during an ebene *session sitting on the sidelines in an hallucinogenic stupor.*

marched away in a faked rage with the thief's hammock. Nobody ever attempted to stop me from doing this, and almost all of them told me that my technique for recovering my possessions was admirable. By nightfall the thief would either appear with the stolen object or send it along with someone else to make an exchange. The others would heckle him for getting caught and being forced to return the item.

With respect to collecting the data I sought, there was a very frustrating problem. Primitive social organization is kinship organization, and to understand the Yąnomamö way of life I had to collect extensive genealogies. I could not have deliberately picked a more difficult group to work with in this regard: They have very stringent name taboos. They attempt to name people in such a way that when the person dies and they can no longer use his name, the loss of the word in the language is not inconvenient. Hence, they name people for specific and minute parts of things, such as "toenail of some rodent," thereby being able to retain the words "toenail" and "(specific) rodent," but not being able to refer directly to the toenail of that rodent. The taboo is

maintained even for the living: One mark of prestige is the courtesy others show you by not using your name. The sanctions behind the taboo seem to be an unusual combination of fear and respect.

I tried to use kinship terms to collect genealogies at first, but the kinship terms were so ambiguous that I ultimately had to resort to names. They were quick to grasp that I was bound to learn everybody's name and reacted, without my knowing it, by inventing false names for everybody in the village. After having spent several months collecting names and learning them, this came as a disappointment to me: I could not cross-check the genealogies with other informants from distant villages.

They enjoyed watching me learn these names. I assumed, wrongly, that I would get the truth to each question and that I would get the best information by working in public. This set the stage for converting a serious project into a farce. Each informant tried to outdo his peers by inventing a name even more ridiculous than what I had been given earlier, or by asserting that the individual about whom I inquired was married to his mother or daughter, and the like. I would have the informant whisper the name of the individual in my ear, noting that he was the father of such and such a child. Everybody would then insist that I repeat the name aloud, roaring in hysterics as I clumsily pronounced the name. I assumed that the laughter was in response to the violation of the name taboo or to my pronunciation. This was a reasonable interpretation, since the individual whose name I said aloud invariably became angry. After I learned what some of the names meant, I began to understand what the laughter was all about. A few of the more colorful examples are: "hairy vagina," "long penis," "feces of the harpy eagle," and "dirty rectum." No wonder the victims were angry.

I was forced to do my genealogy work in private because of the horseplay and nonsense. Once I did so, my informants began to agree with each other and I managed to learn a few new names, real names. I could then test any new informant by collecting a genealogy from him that I knew to be accurate. I was able to weed out the more mischievous informants this way. Little by little I extended the genealogies and learned the real names. Still, I was unable to get the names of the dead and extend the genealogies back in time, and even my best informants continued to deceive me about their own close relatives. Most of them gave me the name of a living man as the father of some individual in order to avoid mentioning that the actual father was dead.

The quality of a genealogy depends in part on the number of generations it embraces, and the name taboo prevented me from getting any substantial information about deceased ancestors. Without this information, I could not detect marriage patterns through time. I had to rely on older informants for this information, but these were the most reluctant of all. As I became more proficient in the language and more skilled at detecting lies, my informants became better at lying. One of them in particular was so cunning and persuasive that I was shocked to discover that he had been inventing his information. He specialized in making a ceremony out of telling me false names. He would look around to make sure nobody was listening outside my hut, enjoin me to never mention the name again, act very nervous and spooky, and then grab me by the head to whisper the name very softly into my ear. I was always elated after an informant session with him, because I had several generations of dead ancestors for the living people. The others refused to give me this information. To show my gratitude, I paid him quadruple the rate I had given the others. When word got around that I had increased the pay, volunteers began pouring in to give me genealogies.

I discovered that the old man was lying quite by accident. A club fight broke out in the village one day, the result of a dispute over the possession of a woman. She had been promised to Rerebawä, a particularly

agressive young man who had married into the village. Rerebawä had already been given her older sister and was enraged when the younger girl began having an affair with another man in the village, making no attempt to conceal it from him. He challenged the young man to a club fight, but was so abusive in his challenge that the opponent's father took offense and entered the village circle with his son, wielding a long club. Rerebawä swaggered out to the duel and hurled insults at both of them, trying to goad them into striking him on the head with their clubs. This would have given him the opportunity to strike them on the head. His opponents refused to hit him, and the fight ended. Rerebawä had won a moral victory because his opponents were afraid to hit him. Thereafter, he swaggered around and insulted the two men behind their backs. He was genuinely angry with them, to the point of calling the older man by the name of his dead father. I quickly seized on this as an opportunity to collect an accurate genealogy and pumped him about his adversary's ancestors. Rerebawä had been particularly nasty to me up to this point, but we became staunch allies: We were both outsiders in the local village. I then asked about other dead ancestors and got immediate replies. He was angry with the whole group and not afraid to tell me the names of the dead. When I compared his version of the genealogies to that of the old man, it was obvious that one of them was lying. I challenged his information, and he explained that everybody knew that the old man was deceiving me and bragging about it in the same village. The names the old man had given me were the dead ancestors of the members of a village so far away that he thought I would never have occasion to inquire about them. As it turned out, Rerebawä knew most of the people in that village and recognized the names.

I then went over the complete genealogical records with Rerebawä, genealogies I had presumed to be in final form. I had to revise them all because of the numerous lies and falsifications they contained. Thus, after five months of almost constant work on the genealogies of just one group, I had to begin almost from scratch!

Discouraging as it was to start over, it was still the first real turning point in my fieldwork. Thereafter, I began taking advantage of local arguments and animosities in selecting my informants, and used more extensively individuals who had married into the group. I began traveling to other villages to check the genealogies, picking villages that were on strained terms with the people about whom I wanted information. I would then return to my base camp and check with local informants the accuracy of the information. If the informants became angry when I mentioned the new names I acquired from the unfriendly group, I was almost certain that the information was accurate. For this kind of checking I had to use informants whose genealogies I knew rather well: they had to be distantly enough related to the dead person that they would not go into a rage when I mentioned the name, but not so remotely related that they would be uncertain of the accuracy of the information. Thus, I had to make a list of names I dared not use in the presence of each and every informant. Despite the precautions, I occasionally hit a name that put the informant into a rage, such as that of a dead brother or sister that other informants had not reported. This always terminated the day's work with that informant, for he would be too touchy to continue any further, and I would be reluctant to take a chance on accidentally discovering another dead kinsman so soon after the first.

These were always unpleasant experiences, and occasionally dangerous ones, depending on the temperament of the informant. On one occasion I was planning to visit a village that had been raided about a week earlier. A woman whose name I had on my list had been killed by the raiders. I planned to check each individual on the list one by one to estimate ages, and I wanted to remove her name so that I would not say it aloud in the village. I knew that I would be in considerable difficulty if I said this name aloud so soon after her death. I called on my original informant and asked him to tell me the name of the woman who had been killed. He refused, explaining that she was a close relative of his. I then asked him if he would become angry if I read off all the names on the list. This way he did not have to say her name and could merely nod when I mentioned the right one. He was a fairly good friend of mine, and I thought I could predict his reaction. He assured me that this would be a good way of doing it. We were alone in my hut so that nobody could overhear us. I read the names softly, continuing to the next when he gave a negative reply. When I finally spoke the name of the dead woman he flew out of his chair, raised his arm to strike me, and shouted: "You son-of-a-bitch! If you ever say that name again, I'll kill you!" He was shaking with rage, but left my hut quietly. I shudder to think what might have happened if I had said the name unknowingly in the woman's village. I had other, similar experiences in different villages, but luckily the dead person had been dead for some time and was not closely related to the individual into whose ear I whispered the name. I was merely cautioned to desist from saying any more names, lest I get people angry with me.

I had been working on the genealogies for nearly a year when another individual came to my aid. It was Kąobawä, the headman of Upper Bisaasi-teri, the group in which I spent most of my time. He visited me one day after the others had left the hut and volunteered to help me on the genealogies. He was poor, he explained, and needed a machete. He would work only on the condition that I did not ask him about his own parents and

other very close kinsmen who were dead. He also added that he would not lie to me as the others had done in the past. This was perhaps the most important single event in my fieldwork, for out of this meeting evolved a very warm friendship and a very profitable informant-fieldworker relationship.

Kąobawä's familiarity with his group's history and his candidness were remarkable. His knowledge of details was almost encyclopedic. More than that, he was enthusiastic and encouraged me to learn details that I might otherwise have ignored. If there were things he did not know intimately, he would advise me to wait until he could check things out with someone in the village. This he would do clandestinely, giving me a report the next day. As I was constrained by my part of the bargain to avoid discussing his close dead kinsmen, I had to rely on Rerebawä for this information. I got Rerebawä's genealogy from Kąobawä.

Once again I went over the genealogies with Kąobawä to recheck them, a considerable task by this time: they included about two thousand names, representing several generations of individuals from four different villages. Rerebawä's information was very accurate, and Kąobawä's contribution enabled me to trace the genealogies further back in time. Thus, after nearly a year of constant work on genealogies, Yąnomamö demography and social organization began to fall into a pattern. Only then could I see how kin groups formed and exchanged women with each other over time, and only then did the fissioning of larger villages into smaller ones show a distinct pattern. At this point I was able to begin formulating more intelligent questions because there was now some sort of pattern to work with. Without the help of Rerebawä and Kąobawä I could not have made very much sense of the plethora of details I had collected from dozens of other informants.

I spent a good deal of time with these two men and their families and got to know them well. They frequently gave their information in a way which related themselves to the topic under discussion. We became very close friends. I will speak of them frequently in the following chapters, using them as "typical" Yąnomamö, if, indeed, one may speak of typical anything. I will briefly comment on what these men are like and their respective statuses in the village.

Kąobawä is about 40 years old (Fig. 3). I say "about" because the Yąnomamö numeration system has only three numbers: one, two, and more-than-two. He is the headman of Upper Bisaasi-teri. He has had five or six wives so far and temporary affairs with as many more women, one of which resulted in a child. At the present time he has just two wives, Bahimi and Koamashima. He has had a daughter and a son by Bahimi, his eldest and favorite wife. Koamashima, about 20 years old, recently had her first child, a boy (Fig. 4). Kąobawä may give Koamashima to his youngest brother. Even now the brother shares in her sexual services. Kąobawä recently gave his third wife to another of his brothers because she was beshi: "horny." In fact, this girl had been married to two other men, both of whom discarded her because of her infidelity. Kąobawä had one daughter by her; she is being raised by his brother.

Kąobawä's eldest wife, Bahimi, is about thirty-five years old. She is his first cross-cousin. Bahimi was pregnant when I began my fieldwork, but she killed the new baby, a boy, at birth, explaining tearfully that it would have competed with Ariwari, her nursing son, for milk. Rather than expose Ariwari to the dangers and uncertainty of an early weaning, she killed the new child instead. By Yąnomamö standards, she and Kąobawä have a very tranquil household. He only beats her once in a while, and never very hard. She never has affairs with other men.

Kąobawä is quiet, intense, wise, and unobtrusive. He leads more by example than by threats and coercion. He can afford to be this way as he established his reputation for being fierce long ago, and other men respect him. He also has five mature brothers who support him, and he has given a number of his sisters to other men in the village, thereby putting them under some obligation to him. In short, his "natural" following (kinsmen) is large, and he does not have to constantly display his ferocity. People already respect him and take his suggestions seriously.

Rerebawä is much younger, only about twenty-two years old. (See Fig. 5.) He has just one wife by whom he has had three children. He is from Karohi-teri, one of the villages to which Kąobawä's is allied. Rerebawä left his village to seek a wife in Kąobawä's group because there were no eligible women there for him to marry.

Rerebawä is perhaps more typical than Kąobawä in the sense that he is concerned about his reputation for ferocity and goes out of his way to act tough. He is, however, much braver than the other men his age and backs up his threats with action. Moreover, he is concerned about politics and knows the details of intervillage relationships over a large area. In this respect he shows all the attributes of a headman, although he is still too young and has too many competent older brothers in his own village to expect to move easily into the position of leadership there.

He does not intend to stay in Kąobawä's group and has not made a garden. He feels that he has adequately discharged his obligations to his wife's parents by providing them with fresh game for three years. They should let him take the wife and return to his own village with her, but they refuse and try to entice him to remain permanently in Bisaasi-teri to provide them with game when they are old. They have even promised to give him their second daughter if he will stay permanently.

Although he has displayed his ferocity in many ways, one incident in particular shows what his character is like. Before he left his own village to seek a wife, he had an affair with the wife of an older brother. When he was discovered, his brother attacked him with a club. Rerebawä was infuriated so he grabbed an axe and drove his brother out of the village after soundly beating him with the flat of the blade. The brother was so afraid that he did not return to the village for several days. I recently visited his village with him. He made a point to introduce me to this brother. Rerebawä dragged him out of his hammock by the arm and told me, "This is the brother whose wife I had an affair with," a deadly insult. His brother did nothing and slunk back into his hammock, shamed, but relieved to have Rerebawä release the vise-grip on his arm.

Despite the fact that he admires Kąobawä, he has a low opinion of the others in Bisaasi-teri. He admitted confidentially that he thought Bisaasi-teri was an abominable group: "This is a terrible neighborhood! All the young men are lazy and cowards and everybody is committing incest! I'll be glad to get back home." He also admired Kąobawä's brother, the headman of Monou-teri. This man was killed by raiders while I was doing my fieldwork. Rerebawä was disgusted that the others did not chase the raiders when they discovered the shooting: "He was the only fierce one in the whole group; he was my close friend. The cowardly Monou-teri hid like women in the jungle and didn't even chase the raiders!"

Even though Rerebawä is fierce and capable of being quite nasty, he has a good side as well. He has a very biting sense of humor and can entertain the group for hours on end with jokes and witty comments. And he is one of few Yąnomamö that I feel I can trust. When I returned to Bisaasi-teri after having been away for a year, Rerebawä was in his own village visiting his kinsmen. Word reached him that I had returned, and he immediately came to see r.   He greeted me with an immense bear hug and exclaimed, "Shaki! Why did you stay away so long? Did you know that my will was so cold while you were gone that at times I could not eat for want of seeing you?" I had to admit that I missed him, too.

Of all the Yąnomamö I know, he is the most genuine and the most devoted to his culture's ways and values. I admire him for that, although I can't say that I subscribe to or endorse these same values. By contrast, Kąobawä is older and wiser. He sees his own culture in a different light and criticizes aspects of it he does not like. While many of his peers accept some of the superstitions and explanatory myths as truth and as the way things ought to be, Kąobawä questions them and privately pokes fun at some of them. Probably, more of the Yąnomamö are like Rerebawä, or at least try to be.

19

Body Ritual Among the Nacirema

BY HORACE MINER

The anthropologist has become so familiar with the diversity of ways in which different peoples behave in similar situations that he is not apt to be surprised by even the most exotic customs. In fact, if all of the logically possible combinations of behavior have not been found somewhere in the world, he is apt to suspect that they must be present in some yet undescribed tribe. This point has, in fact, been expressed with respect to clan organization by Murdock (1949:71). In this light, the magical beliefs and practices of the Nacirema present such unusual aspects that it seems desirable to describe them as an example of the extremes to which human behavior can go.

Professor Linton first brought the ritual of the Nacirema to the attention of anthropologists twenty years ago (1936:326), but the culture of this people is still very poorly understood. They are a North American group living in the territory between the Canadian Cree, the Yaqui and Tarahumare of Mexico, and the Carib and Arawak of the Antilles. Little is known of their origin, although tradition states that they came from the east. According to Nacirema mythology, their nation was originated by a culture hero, Notgnihsaw, who is otherwise known for two great feats of strength—the throwing of a piece of wampum across the river Pa-To-Mac and the chopping down of a cherry tree in which the Spirit of Truth resided.

Nacirema culture is characterized by a highly developed market economy which has evolved in a rich natural habitat. While much of the people's time is devoted to economic pursuits, a large part of the fruits of these labors and a considerable portion of the day are spent in ritual activity. The focus of this activity is the human body, the appearance and health of which loom as a dominant concern in the ethos of the people. While such a concern is certainly not unusual, its ceremonial aspects and associated philosophy are unique.

The fundamental belief underlying the whole system appears to be that the human body is ugly and that its natural tendency is to debility and disease. Incarcerated in such a body, man's only hope is to avert these characteristics through the use of the powerful influences of ritual and ceremony. Every household has one or more shrines devoted to this purpose. The more powerful individuals in the society have several shrines in their houses and, in fact, the opulence of a house is often referred to in terms of the number of such ritual centers it possesses. Most houses are of wattle and daub construction, but the shrine rooms of the more wealthy are walled with stone. Poorer families imitate the rich by applying pottery plaques to their shrine walls.

While each family has at least one such shrine, the rituals associated with it are not family ceremonies but are private and secret. The rites are normally only discussed with children, and then only during the period when they are being initiated into these mysteries. I was able, however, to establish sufficient rapport with the natives to examine these shrines and to have the rituals described to me.

The focal point of the shrine is a box or chest which is built into the wall. In this chest are kept the many charms and magical potions without which no native believes he could live. These preparations are secured from a variety of specialized practioners. The most powerful of these are the medicine men, whose assistance must be rewarded with substantial gifts. However, the medicine men do not provide the curative potions for their clients, but decide what the ingredients should be and then write them down in an ancient and secret language. This writing is understood only by the medicine men and by the herbalists who, for another gift, provide the required charm.

The charm is not disposed of after it has served its purpose, but is placed in the charm-box of the household shrine. As these magical materials are specific for certain ills, and the real or imagined maladies of the people are many, the charm-box is usually full to overflowing. The magical packets are so numerous that people forget what their purposes were and fear to use them again. While the natives are very vague on this

 Reproduced from the *American Anthropologist*, Vol. 58, 503–507, 1956, by permission of the American Anthropological Association and the author.

point, we can only assume that the idea in retaining all the old magical materials is that their presence in the charm-box, before which the body rituals are conducted, will in some way protect the worshipper.

Beneath the charm-box is a small font. Each day every member of the family, in succession, enters the shrine room, bows his head before the charm-box, mingles different sorts of holy water in the font, and proceeds with a brief rite of ablution. The holy waters are secured from the Water Temple of the community, where the priests conduct elaborate ceremonies to make the liquid ritually pure.

In the hierarchy of magical practitioners, and below the medicine men in prestige, are specialists whose designation is best translated "holy-mouth-men." The Nacirema have an almost pathological horror of and fascination with the mouth, the condition of which is believed to have a supernatural influence on all social relationships. Were it not for the rituals of the mouth, they believe that their teeth would fall out, their gums bleed, their jaws shrink, their friends desert them, and their lovers reject them. They also believe that a strong relationship exists between oral and moral characteristics. For example, there is a ritual ablution of the mouth for children which is supposed to improve their moral fiber.

The daily body ritual performed by everyone includes a mouth-rite. Despite the fact that these people are so punctilious about care of the mouth, this rite involves a practice which strikes the uninitiated stranger as revolting. It was reported to me that the ritual consists of inserting a small bundle of hog hairs into the mouth, along with cer'ain magical powders, and then moving the bundle in a highly formalized series of gestures.

In addition to the private mouth-rite, the people seek out a holy-mouth-man once or twice a year. These practitioners have an impressive set of paraphernalia, consisting of a variety of augers, awls, probes, and prods. The use of these objects in the exorcism of the evils of the mouth involves almost unbelievable ritual torture of the client. The holy-mouth-man opens the client's mouth and, using the above mentioned tools, enlarges any holes which decay may have created in the teeth. Magical materials are put into these holes. If there are no naturally occurring holes in the teeth, large sections of one or more teeth are gouged out so that the supernatural substance can be applied. In the client's view, the purpose of these ministrations is to arrest decay and to draw friends. The extremely sacred and traditional character of the rite is evident in the fact that the natives return to the holy-mouth-men year after year, despite the fact that their teeth continue to decay.

It is to be hoped that, when a thorough study of the Nacirema is made, there will be careful inquiry into the personality structure of these people. One has but to watch the gleam in the eye of a holy-mouth-man, as he jabs an awl into an exposed nerve, to suspect that a certain amount of sadism is involved. It this can be established, a very interesting pattern emerges, for most of the population shows definite masochistic tendencies. It was to these that Professor Linton referred in discussing a distinctive part of the daily body ritual which is performed only by men. This part of the rite involves scraping and lacerating the surface of the face with a sharp instrument. Special women's rites are performed only four times during each lunar month, but what they lack in frequency is made up in barbarity. As part of this ceremony, women bake their heads in small ovens for about an hour. The theoretically interesting point is that what seems to be a preponderantly masochistic people have developed sadistic specialists.

The medicine men have an imposing temple, or *latipso*, in every community of any size. The more elaborate ceremonies required to treat very sick patients can only be performed at this temple. These ceremonies involve not only the thaumaturge but a permanent group of vestal maidens who move sedately about the temple chambers in distinctive costume and headdress.

The *latipso* ceremonies are so harsh that it is phenomenal that a fair proportion of the really sick natives who enter the temple ever recover. Small children whose indoctrination is still incomplete have been known to resist attempts to take them to the temple because "that is where you go to die." Despite this fact, sick adults are not only willing but eager to undergo the protracted ritual purification, if they can afford to do so. No matter how ill the supplicant or how grave the emergency, the guardians of many temples will not admit a client if he cannot give a rich gift to the custodian. Even after one has gained admission and survived the ceremonies, the guardians will not permit the neophyte to leave until he makes still another gift.

The supplicant entering the temple is first stripped of all his or her clothes. In every-day life the Nacirema avoids exposure of his body and its natural functions. Bathing and excretory acts are performed only in the secrecy of the household shrine, where they are ritualized as part of the body-rites. Psychological shock results from the fact that body secrecy is suddenly lost upon entry into the *latipso*. A man, whose own wife has never seen him in an excretory act, suddenly finds himself naked and assisted by a vestal maiden while he performs his natural functions into a sacred vessel. This sort of ceremonial treatment is necessitated by the fact that the excreta are used by a diviner to ascertain the course and nature of the client's sickness. Female clients, on the other hand, find their naked bodies are subjected to the scrutiny, manipulation and prodding of the medicine men.

Few supplicants in the temple are well enough to do anything but lie on their hard beds. The daily ceremonies, like the rites of the holy-mouth-men, involve discomfort and torture. With ritual precision, the vestals awaken their miserable charges each dawn and roll them about on their beds of pain while performing ablutions, in the formal movements of which the maidens are highly trained. At other times they insert magic wands in the supplicant's mouth or force him to eat substances which are supposed to be healing. From time to time the medicine men come to their clients and jab magically treated needles into their flesh. The fact that these temple ceremonies may not cure, and may even kill the neophyte, in no way decreases the people's faith in the medicine men.

There remains one other kind of practitioner, known as a "listener." This witch-doctor has the power to exorcise the devils that lodge in the heads of people who have been bewitched. The Nacirema believe that parents bewitch their own children. Mothers are particularly suspected of putting a curse on children while teaching them the secret body rituals. The countermagic of the witch-doctor is unusual in its lack of ritual. The patient simply tells the "listener" all his troubles and fears, beginning with the earliest difficulties he can remember. The memory displayed by the Nacirema in these exorcism sessions is truly remarkable. It is not uncommon for the patient to bemoan the rejection he felt upon being weaned as a babe, and a few individuals even see their troubles going back to the traumatic effects of their own birth.

In conclusion, mention must be made of certain practices which have their base in native esthetics but which depend upon the pervasive aversion to the natural body and its functions. There are ritual fasts to make fat people thin and ceremonial feasts to make thin people fat. Still other rites are used to make women's breasts larger if they are small, and smaller if they are large. General dissatisfaction with breast shape is symbolized in the fact that the ideal form is virtually outside the range of human variation. A few women afflicted with almost inhuman hypermammary development are so idolized that they make a handsome living by simply going from village to village and permitting the natives to stare at them for a fee.

Reference has already been made to the fact that excretory functions are ritualized, routinized, and relegated to secrecy. Natural reproductive functions are similarly distorted. Intercourse is taboo as a topic and scheduled as an act. Efforts are made to avoid pregnancy by the use of magical materials or by limiting intercourse to certain phases of the moon. Conception is actually very infrequent. When pregnant, women dress so as to hide their condition. Parturition takes place in secret, without friends or relatives to assist, and the majority of women do not nurse their infants.

Our review of the ritual life of the Nacirema has certainly shown them to be a magic-ridden people. It is hard to understand how they have managed to exist so long under the burdens which they have imposed upon themselves. But even such exotic customs as these take on real meaning when they are viewed with the insight provided by Malinowski when he wrote (1948:70):

> Looking from far and above, from our high places of safety in the developed civilization, it is easy to see all the crudity and irrelevance of magic. But without its power and guidance early man could not have mastered his practical difficulties as he has done, nor could man have advanced to the higher stages of civilization.

References

Linton, Ralph
  1936 The Study of Man. New York, D. Appleton-Century Co.
Malinowski, Bronislaw
  1948 Magic, Science, and Religion. Glencoe, The Free Press.
Murdock, George P.
  1949 Social Structure. New York, The Macmillan Co.

20

Shakespeare in the Bush

BY LAURA BOHANNAN

....

Just before I left Oxford for the Tiv in West Africa, conversation turned to the season at Stratford. "You Americans," said a friend, "often have difficulty with Shakespeare. He was, after all, a very English poet, and one can easily misinterpret the universal by misunderstanding the particular."

I protested that human nature is pretty much the same the whole world over; at least the general plot and motivation of the greater tragedies would always be clear—everywhere—although some details of custom might have to be explained and difficulties of translation might produce other slight changes. To end an argument we could not conclude, my friend gave me a copy of *Hamlet* to study in the African bush: it would, he hoped, lift my mind above its primitive surroundings, and possibly I might, by prolonged meditation, achieve the grace of correct interpretation.

It was my second field trip to that African tribe, and I thought myself ready to live in one of its remote sections—an area difficult to cross even on foot. I eventually settled on the hillock of a very knowledgeable old man, the head of a homestead of some hundred and forty people, all of whom were either his close relatives or their wives and children. Like the other elders of the vicinity, the old man spent most of his time performing ceremonies seldom seen these days in the more accessible parts of the tribe. I was delighted. Soon there would be three months of enforced isolation and leisure, between the harvest that takes place just before the rising of the swamps and the clearing of new farms when the water goes down. Then, I thought, they would have even more time to perform ceremonies and explain them to me.

I was quite mistaken. Most of the ceremonies demanded the presence of elders from several homesteads. As the swamps rose, the old men found it too difficult to walk from one homestead to the next, and the ceremonies gradually ceased. As the swamps rose even higher, all activities but one came to an end. The women brewed beer from maize and millet. Men, women, and children sat on their hillocks and drank it.

People began to drink at dawn. By midmorning the whole homestead was singing, dancing, and drumming. When it rained, people had to sit inside their huts: there they drank and sang or they drank and told stories. In any case, by noon or before, I either had to join the party or retire to my own hut and my books. "One does not discuss serious matters when there is beer. Come, drink with us." Since I lacked their capacity for the thick native beer, I spent more and more time with *Hamlet*. Before the end of the second month, grace descended on me. I was quite sure that *Hamlet* had only one possible interpretation, and that one universally obvious.

Early every morning, in the hope of having some serious talk before the beer party, I used to call on the old man at his reception hut—a circle of posts supporting a thatched roof above a low mud wall to keep out wind and rain. One day I crawled through the low doorway and found most of the men of the homestead sitting huddled in their ragged cloths on stools, low plank beds, and reclining chairs, warming themselves against the chill of the rain around a smoky fire. In the center were three pots of beer. The party had started.

The old man greeted me cordially. "Sit down and drink." I accepted a large calabash full of beer, poured some into a small drinking gourd, and tossed it down. Then I poured some more into the same gourd for the man second in seniority to my host before I handed my calabash over to a young man for further distribution. Important people shouldn't ladle beer themselves.

"It is better like this," the old man said, looking at me approvingly and plucking at the thatch that had caught in my hair. "You should sit and drink with us more often. Your servants tell me that when you are not with us, you sit inside your hut looking at a paper."

The old man was acquainted with four kinds of "papers": tax receipts, bride price receipts, court fee receipts, and letters. The messenger who brought him letters from the chief used them mainly as a badge of office, for he always knew what was in them and told the old man. Personal letters for the few who had rela-

Reprinted with permission of the author from *Natural History* Magazine, August-September, 1966. Copyright © 1966 by Laura Bohannan.

tives in the government or mission stations were kept until someone went to a large market where there was a letter writer and reader. Since my arrival, letters were brought to me to be read. A few men also brought me bride price receipts, privately, with requests to change the figures to a higher sum. I found moral arguments were of no avail, since in-laws are fair game, and the technical hazards of forgery difficult to explain to an illiterate people. I did not wish them to think me silly enough to look at any such papers for days on end, and I hastily explained that my "paper" was one of the "things of long ago" of my country.

"Ah," said the old man. "Tell us."

I protested that I was not a storyteller. Storytelling is a skilled art among them; their standards are high, and the audiences critical—and vocal in their criticism. I protested in vain. This morning they wanted to hear a story while they drank. They threatened to tell me no more stories until I told them one of mine. Finally, the old man promised that no one would criticize my style "for we know you are struggling with our language." "But," put in one of the elders, "you must explain what we do not understand, as we do when we tell you our stories." Realizing that here was my chance to prove *Hamlet* universally intelligible, I agreed.

The old man handed me some more beer to help me on with my storytelling. Men filled their long wooden pipes and knocked coals from the fire to place in the pipe bowls; then, puffing contentedly, they sat back to listen. I began in the proper style, "Not yesterday, not yesterday, but long ago, a thing occurred. One night three men were keeping watch outside the homestead of the great chief, when suddenly they saw the former chief approach them."

"Why was he no longer their chief?"

"He was dead," I explained. "That is why they were troubled and afraid when they saw him."

"Impossible," began one of the elders, handing his pipe on to his neighbor, who interrupted, "Of course it wasn't the dead chief. It was an omen sent by a witch. Go on."

Slightly shaken, I continued. "One of these three was a man who knew things"—the closest translation for scholar, but unfortunately it also meant witch. The second elder looked triumphantly at the first. "So he spoke to the dead chief saying, 'Tell us what we must do so you may rest in your grave,' but the dead chief did not answer. He vanished, and they could see him no more. Then the man who knew things—his name was Horatio—said this event was the affair of the dead chief's son, Hamlet."

There was a general shaking of heads round the circle. "Had the dead chief no living brothers? Or was this son the chief?"

"No," I replied. "That is, he had one living brother who became the chief when the elder brother died."

The old men muttered: such omens were matters for chiefs and elders, not for youngsters; no good could come of going behind a chief's back; clearly Horatio was not a man who knew things.

"Yes, he was," I insisted, shooing a chicken away from my beer. "In our country the son is next to the father. The dead chief's younger brother had become the great chief. He had also married his elder brother's widow only about a month after the funeral."

"He did well," the old man beamed and announced to the others, "I told you that if we knew more about Europeans, we would find they really were very like us. In our country also," he added to me, "the younger brother marries the elder brother's widow and becomes the father of his children. Now, if your uncle, who married your widowed mother, is your father's full brother, then he will be a real father to you. Did Hamlet's father and uncle have one mother?"

His question barely penetrated my mind; I was too upset and thrown too far off balance by having one of the most important elements of *Hamlet* knocked straight out of the picture. Rather uncertainly I said that I thought they had the same mother, but I wasn't sure— the story didn't say. The old man told me severely that these genealogical details made all the difference and that when I got home I must ask the elders about it. He shouted out the door to one of his younger wives to bring his goatskin bag.

Determined to save what I could of the mother motif, I took a deep breath and began again. "The son Hamlet was very sad because his mother had married again so quickly. There was no need for her to do so, and it is our custom for a widow not to go to her next husband until she has mourned for two years."

"Two years is too long," objected the wife, who had appeared with the old man's battered goatskin bag. "Who will hoe your farms for you while you have no husband?"

"Hamlet," I retorted without thinking, "was old enough to hoe his mother's farms himself. There was no need for her to remarry." No one looked convinced. I gave up. "His mother and the great chief told Hamlet not to be sad, for the great chief himself would be a father to Hamlet. Furthermore, Hamlet would be the next chief: therefore he must stay to learn the things of a chief. Hamlet agreed to remain, and all the rest went off to drink beer."

While I paused, perplexed at how to render Hamlet's disgusted soliloquy to an audience convinced that Claudius and Gertrude had behaved in the best possible manner, one of the young men asked me who had married the other wives of the dead chief.

"He had no other wives," I told him.

"But a chief must have many wives! How else can he brew beer and prepare food for all his guests?"

I said firmly that in our country even chiefs had only one wife, that they had servants to do their work, and that they paid them from tax money.

It was better, they returned, for a chief to have many wives and sons who would help him hoe his farms and feed his people; then everyone loved the chief who gave much and took nothing—taxes were a bad thing.

I agreed with the last comment, but for the rest fell back on their favorite way of fobbing off my questions: "That is the way it is done, so that is how we do it."

I decided to skip the soliloquy. Even if Claudius was here thought quite right to marry his brother's widow, there remained the poison motif, and I knew they would disapprove of fratricide. More hopefully I resumed, "That night Hamlet kept watch with the three who had seen his dead father. The dead chief again appeared, and although the others were afraid, Hamlet followed his dead father off to one side. When they were alone, Hamlet's dead father spoke."

"Omens can't talk!" The old man was emphatic.

"Hamlet's dead father wasn't an omen. Seeing him might have been an omen, but he was not." My audience looked as confused as I sounded. "It *was* Hamlet's dead father. It was a thing we call a 'ghost.'" I had to use the English word, for unlike many of the neighboring tribes, these people didn't believe in the survival after death of any individuating part of the personality.

"What is a 'ghost'? An omen?"

"No, a 'ghost' is someone who is dead but who walks around and can talk, and people can hear him and see him but not touch him."

They objected. "One can touch zombis."

"No, no! It was not a dead body the witches had animated to sacrifice and eat. No one else made Hamlet's dead father walk. He did it himself."

"Dead men can't walk," protested my audience as one man.

I was quite willing to comprise. "A 'ghost' is the dead man's shadow."

But again they objected. "Dead men cast no shadows."

"They do in my country," I snapped.

The old man quelled the babble of disbelief that arose immediately and told me with that insincere, but courteous, agreement one extends to the fancies of the young, ignorant, and superstitious, "No doubt in your country the dead can also walk without being zombis." From the depths of his bag he produced a withered fragment of kola nut, bit off one end to show it wasn't poisoned, and handed me the rest as a peace offering.

"Anyhow," I resumed, "Hamlet's dead father said that his own brother, the one who became chief, had poisoned him. He wanted Hamlet to avenge him. Ham-

let believed this in his heart, for he did not like his father's brother." I took another swallow of beer. "In the country of the great chief, living in the same homestead, for it was a very large one, was an important elder who was often with the chief to advise and to help him. His name was Polonius. Hamlet was courting his daughter, but her father and her brother . . . [I cast hastily about for some tribal analogy] warned her not to let Hamlet visit her when when was alone on her farm, for he would be a great chief and so could not marry her."

"Why not!" asked the wife, who had settled down on the edge of the old man's chair. He frowned at her for asking stupid questions and growled, "They lived in the same homestead."

"That was not the reason," I informed them. "Polonius was a stranger who lived in the homestead because he helped the chief, not because he was a relative."

"Then why couldn't Hamlet marry her!"

"He could have," I explained, "but Polonius didn't think he would. After all, Hamlet was a man of great importance who ought to marry a chief's daughter, for in his country a man could have only one wife. Polonius was afraid that if Hamlet made love to his daughter, then no one else would give a high price for her."

"That might be true" remarked one of the shrewder elders, "but a chief's son would give his mistress's father enough presents and patronage to more than make up the difference. Polonius sounds like a fool to me."

"Many people think he was," I agreed. "Meanwhile Polonius sent his son Laertes off to Paris to learn the things of that country, for it was the homestead of a very great chief indeed. Because he was afraid that Laertes might waste a lot of money on beer and women and gambling, or get into trouble by fighting, he sent one of his servants to Paris secretly, to spy out what Laertes was doing. One day Hamlet came upon Polonius's daughter Ophelia. He behaved so oddly he frightened her. "Indeed,"—I was fumbling for words to express the dubious quality of Hamlet's madness—"the chief and many others had also noticed that when Hamlet talked one could understand the words but not what they meant. Many people thought that he had become mad." My audience suddenly became much more attentive. "The great chief wanted to know what was wrong with Hamlet, so he sent for two of Hamlet's age mates [school friends would have taken long explanation] to talk to Hamlet and find out what troubled his heart. Hamlet, seeing that they had been bribed by the chief to betray him, told them nothing. Polonius, however, insisted that Hamlet was mad because he had been forbidden to see Ophelia, whom he loved."

"Why," inquired a bewildered voice, "should anyone bewitch Hamlet on that account?"

"Bewitch him?"

"Yes, only witchcraft can make anyone mad, unless of course, one sees the beings that lurk in the forest."

I stopped being a storyteller, took out my notebook and demanded to be told more about these two causes of madness. Even while they spoke and I jotted notes, I tried to calculate the effect of this new factor on the plot. Hamlet had not been exposed to the beings that lurk in the forest. Only his relatives in the male line could bewitch him. Barring relatives not mentioned by Shakespeare, it had to be Claudius who was attempting to harm him. And, of course, it was.

For the moment I staved off questions by saying that the great chief also refused to believe that Hamlet was mad for the love of Ophelia and nothing else. "He was sure that something much more important was troubling Hamlet's heart."

"Now Hamlet's age mates," I continued, "had brought with them a famous storyteller. Hamlet decided to have this man tell the chief and all his homestead a story about a man who had poisoned his brother because he desired his brother's wife and wished to be chief himself. Hamlet was sure the great chief could not hear the story without making a sign if he was indeed guilty, and then he would discover whether his dead father had told him the truth."

The old man interrupted, with deep cunning, "Why should a father lie to his son?" he asked.

I hedged: "Hamlet wasn't sure that it really was his dead father." It was impossible to say anything, in that language, about devil-inspired visions.

"You mean," he said, "it actually was an omen, and he knew witches sometimes send false ones. Hamlet was a fool not to go to one skilled in reading omens and divining the truth in the first place. A man-who-sees-the-truth could have told him how his father died, if he really had been poisoned, and if there was witchcraft in it; then Hamlet could have called the elders to settle the matter."

The shrewd elder ventured to disagree. "Because his father's brother was a great chief, one-who-sees-the-truth might therefore have been afraid to tell it. I think it was for that reason that a friend of Hamlet's father—a witch and an elder—sent an omen so his friend's son would know. Was the omen true?"

"Yes," I said, abandoning ghosts and the devil; a witch-sent omen it would have to be. "It was true, for when the storyteller was telling his tale before all the homestead, the great chief rose in fear. Afraid that Hamlet knew his secret he planned to have him killed."

The stage set of the next bit presented some difficulties of translation. I began cautiously. "The great chief told Hamlet's mother fo find out from her son what he knew. But because a woman's children are always first in her heart, he had the important elder Polonius hide behind a cloth that hung against the wall of Hamlet's mother's sleeping hut. Hamlet started to scold his mother for what she had done."

There was a shocked murmur from everyone. A man should never scold his mother.

"She called out in fear, and Polonius moved behind the cloth. Shouting, 'A rat!' Hamlet took his machete and slashed through the cloth." I paused for dramatic effect. "He had killed Polonius!"

The old men looked at each other in supreme disgust. "That Polonius truly was a fool and a man who knew nothing! What child would not know enough to shout, 'It's me!'" With a pang, I remembered that these people are ardent hunters, always armed with bow, arrow, and machete; at the first rustle in the grass an arrow is aimed and ready, and the hunter shouts "Game!" If no human voice answers immediately, the arrow speeds on its way. Like a good hunter Hamlet had shouted, "A rat!"

I rushed in to save Polonius's reputation. "Polonius did speak. Hamlet heard him. But he thought it was the chief and wished to kill him to avenge his father. He had meant to kill him earlier that evening..." I broke down, unable to describe to these pagans, who had no belief in individual afterlife, the difference between dying at one's prayers and dying "unhousell'd, disappointed, unaneled."

This time I had shocked by audience seriously. "For a man to raise his hand against his father's brother and the one who has become his father—that is a terrible thing. The elders ought to let such a man be bewitched."

I nibbled at my kola nut in some perplexity, then pointed out that after all the man had killed Hamlet's father.

"No," pronounced the old man, speaking less to me than to the young men sitting behind the elders. "If your father's brother has killed your father, you must appeal to your father's age mates; *they* may avenge him. No man may use violence against his senior relatives." Another thought struck him. "But if his father's brother had indeed been wicked enough to bewitch Hamlet and make him mad that would be a good story indeed, for it would be his fault that Hamlet, being mad, no longer had any sense and thus was ready to kill his father's brother."

There was a murmur of applause. *Hamlet* was again a good story to them, but it no longer seemed quite the same story to me. As I thought over the coming complications of plot and motive, I lost courage and decided to skim over dangerous ground quickly.

"The great chief," I went on, "was not sorry that Hamlet had killed Polonius. It gave him a reason to send Hamlet away, with his two treacherous age mates, with letters to a chief of a far country, saying that Hamlet should be killed. But Hamlet changed the writing on their papers, so that the chief killed his age mates instead." I encountered a reproachful glare from one of the men whom I had told undetectable forgery was not merely immoral but beyond human skill. I looked the other way.

"Before Hamlet could return, Laertes came back for his father's funeral. The great chief told him Hamlet had killed Polonius. Laertes swore to kill Hamlet because of this, and because his sister Ophelia, hearing her father had been killed by the man she loved, went mad and drowned in the river."

"Have you already forgotten what we told you?" The old man was reproachful. "One cannot take vengeance on a madman; Hamlet killed Polonius in his madness. As for the girl, she not only went mad, she was drowned. Only witches can make people drown. Water itself can't hurt anything. It is merely something one drinks and bathes in."

I began to get cross. "If you don't like the story, I'll stop."

The old man made soothing noises and himself poured me some more beer. "You tell the story well, and we are listening. But is clear that the elders of your country have never told you what the story really means. No, don't interrupt! We believe you when you say your marriage customs are different, or your clothes and weapons. But people are the same everywhere; therefore, there are always witches and it is we, the elders, who know how witches work. We told you it was the great chief who wished to kill Hamlet, and now your own words have proved us right. Who were Ophelia's male relatives?"

"There were only her father and her brother." Hamlet was clearly out of my hands.

"There must have been many more; this also you must ask of your elders when you get back to your country. From what you tell us, since Polonius was dead, it must have been Laertes who killed Ophelia, although I do not see the reason for it."

We had emptied one pot of beer, and the old men argued the point with slightly tipsy interest. Finally one of them demanded of me, "What did the servant of Polonius say on his return?"

With difficulty I recollected Reynaldo and his mission. "I don't think he did return before Polonius was killed."

"Listen," said the elder, "and I will tell you how it was and how your story will go, then you may tell me if I am right. Polonius knew his son would get into trouble,

and so he did. He had many fines to pay for fighting, and debts from gambling. But he had only two ways of getting money quickly. One was to marry off his sister at once, but it is difficult to find a man who will marry a woman desired by the son of a chief. For if the chief's heir commits adultery with your wife, what you do? Only a fool calls a case against a man who will someday be his judge. Therefore Laertes had to take the second way: he killed his sister by witchcraft, drowning her so he could secretly sell her body to the witches."

I raised an objection. "They found her body and buried it. Indeed Laertes jumped into the grave to see his sister once more—so, you see, the body was truly there. Hamlet, who had just come back, jumped in after him."

"What did I tell you?" The elder appealed to the others. "Laertes was up to no good with his sister's body. Hamlet prevented him, because the chief's heir, like a chief, does not wish any other man to grow rich and powerful. Laertes would be angry, because he would have killed his sister without benefit to himself. In our country he would try to kill Hamlet for that reason. Is this not what happened?"

"More or less," I admitted. "When the great chief found Hamlet was still alive, he encouraged Laertes to try to kill Hamlet and arranged a fight with machetes between them. In the fight both the young men were wounded to death. Hamlet's mother drank the poisoned beer that the chief meant for Hamlet in case he won the fight. When he saw his mother die of poison, Hamlet, dying, managed to kill his father's brother with his machete."

"You see, I was right!" exclaimed the elder.

"That was a very good story," added the old man, "and you told it with very few mistakes. There was just one more error, at the very end. The poison Hamlet's mother drank was obviously meant for the survivor of the fight, whichever it was. If Laertes had won, the great chief would have poisoned him, for no one would know that he arranged Hamlet's death. Then, too, he need not fear Laertes' witchcraft; it takes a strong heart to kill one's only sister by witchcraft.

"Sometime," concluded the old man, gathering his ragged toga about him, "you must tell us some more stories of your country. We, who are elders, will instruct you in their true meaning, so that when you return to your own land your elders will see that you have not been sitting in the bush, but among those who know things and who have taught you wisdom."

21

Eating Christmas in the Kalahari

BY RICHARD BORSHAY LEE

The !Kung Bushmen's knowledge of Christmas is thirdhand. The London Missionary Society brought the holiday to the southern Tswana tribes in the early nineteenth century. Later, native catechists spread the idea far and wide among the Bantu-speaking pastoralists, even in the remotest corners of the Kalahari Desert. The Bushmen's idea of the Christmas story, stripped to its essentials, is "praise the birth of white man's god-chief"; what keeps their interest in the holiday high is the Tswana-Herero custom of slaughtering an ox for his Bushmen neighbors as an annual goodwill gesture. Since the 1930's, part of the Bushmen's annual round of activities has included a December congregation at the cattle posts for trading, marriage brokering, and several days of trance-dance feasting at which the local Tswana headman is host.

As a social anthropologist working with !Kung Bushmen, I found that the Christmas ox custom suited my purposes. I had come to the Kalahari to study the hunting and gathering subsistence economy of the !Kung, and to accomplish this it was essential not to provide them with food, share my own food, or interfere in any way with their food-gathering activities. While liberal handouts of tobacco and medical supplies were appreciated, they were scarcely adequate to erase the glaring disparity in wealth between the anthropologist, who maintained a two-month inventory of canned goods, and the Bushmen, who rarely had a day's supply of food on hand. My approach, while paying off in terms of data, left me open to frequent accusations of stinginess and hard-heartedness. By their lights, I was a miser.

The Christmas ox was to be my way of saying thank you for the cooperation of the past year; and since it was to be our last Christmas in the field, I determined to slaughter the largest, meatiest ox that money could buy, insuring that the feast and trance dance would be a success.

Through December I kept my eyes open at the wells as the cattle were brought down for watering. Several animals were offered, but none had quite the grossness that I had in mind. Then, ten days before the holiday, a Herero friend led an ox of astonishing size and mass up to our camp. It was solid black, stood five feet high at the shoulder, had a five-foot span of horns, and must have weighed 1,200 pounds on the hoof. Food consumption calculations are my specialty, and I quickly figured that bones and viscera aside, there was enough meat—at least four pounds—for every man, woman, and child of the 150 Bushmen in the vicinity of /ai/ai who were expected at the feast.

Having found the right animal at last, I paid the Herero £20 ($56) and asked him to keep the beast with his herd until Christmas day. The next morning word spread among the people that the big solid black one was the ox chosen by /ontah (my Bushman name; it means, roughly, "whitey") for the Christmas feast. That afternoon I received the first delegation. Ben!a, an outspoken sixty-year-old mother of five, came to the point slowly.

"Where were you planning to eat Christmas?"

"Right here at /ai/ai," I replied.

"Alone or with others?"

"I expect to invite all the people to eat Christmas with me."

"Eat what?"

"I have purchased Yehave's black ox, and I am going to slaughter and cook it."

"That's what we were told at the well but refused to believe it until we heard it from yourself."

"Well, it's the black one," I replied expansively, although wondering what she was driving at.

"Oh, no!" Ben!a groaned, turning to her group. "They were right." Turning back to me she asked, "Do you expect us to eat that bag of bones?"

"Bag of bones! It's the biggest ox at /ai/ai."

"Big, yes, but old. And thin.

EDITOR'S NOTE: *The !Kung and other Bushmen speak click languages. In the story, three different clicks are used:*

1. The dental click (/), as in /ai/ai, /ontah, and /gaugo. The click is sometimes written in English as tsk-tsk.

2. The alveopalatal click (!), as in Ben!a and !Kung.

3. The lateral click (//), as in //gom. Clicks function as consonants; a word may have more than one, as in /n!au.

Everybody knows there's no meat on that old ox. What did you expect us to eat off it, the horns?"

Everybody chuckled at Ben!a's one-liner as they walked away, but all I could manage was a weak grin.

That evening it was the turn of the young men. They came to sit at our evening fire. /gaugo, about my age, spoke to me man-to-man.

"/ontah, you have always been square with us," he lied. "What has happened to change your heart? That sack of guts and bones of Yehave's will hardly feed one camp, let alone all the Bushmen around /ai/ai." And he proceeded to enumerate the seven camps in the /ai/ai vicinity, family by family. "Perhaps you have forgotten that we are not few, but many. Or are you too blind to tell the difference between a proper cow and an old wreck? That ox is thin to the point of death."

"Look, you guys," I retorted, "that is a beautiful animal, and I'm sure you will eat it with pleasure at Christmas."

"Of course we will eat it; it's food. But it won't fill us up to the point where we will have enough strength to dance. We will eat and go home to bed with stomachs rumbling."

That night as we turned in, I asked my wife, Nancy: "What did you think of the black ox?"

"It looked enormous to me. Why?"

"Well, about eight different people have told me I got gypped; that the ox is nothing but bones."

"What's the angle?" Nancy asked. "Did they have a better one to sell?"

"No, they just said that it was going to be a grim Christmas because there won't be enough meat to go around. Maybe I'll get an independent judge to look at the beast in the morning."

Bright and early, Halingisi, a Tswana cattle owner, appeared at our camp. But before I could ask him to give me his opinion on Yehave's black ox, he gave me the eye signal that indicated a confidential chat. We left the camp and sat down.

"/ontah, I'm surprised at you; you've lived here for three years and still haven't learned anything about cattle."

"But what else can a person do but choose the biggest, strongest animal one can find?" I retorted.

"Look, just because an animal is big doesn't mean that it has plenty of meat on it. The black one was a beauty when it was younger, but now it is thin to the point of death."

"Well I've already bought it. What can I do at this stage?"

"Bought it already? I thought you were just considering it. Well, you'll have to kill it and serve it, I suppose. But don't expect much of a dance to follow."

My spirits dropped rapidly. I could believe that Ben!a and /gaugo just might be putting me on about the black ox, but Halingisi seemed to be an impartial critic. I went around that day feeling as though I had bought a lemon of a used car.

In the afternoon it was Tomazo's turn. Tomazo is a fine hunter, a top trance performer (*see* "The Trance Cure of the !Kung Bushmen," NATURAL HISTORY, November, 1967), and one of my most reliable informants. He approached the subject of the Christmas cow as part of my continuing Bushmen education.

"My friend, the way it is with us Bushmen," he began, "is that we love meat. And even more than that, we love fat. When we hunt we always search for the fat ones, the ones dripping with layers of white fat: fat that turns into a clear, thick oil in the cooking pot, fat that slides down your gullet, fills your stomach and gives you a roaring diarrhea," he rhapsodized.

"So, feeling as we do," he continued, "it gives us pain to be served such a scrawny thing as Yehave's black ox. It is big, yes, and no doubt its giant bones are good for soup, but fat is what we really crave and so we will eat Christmas this year with a heavy heart."

The prospect of a gloomy Christmas now had me worried, so I asked Tomazo what I could do about it.

"Look for a fat one, a young one . . . smaller, but fat. Fat enough to make us //gom ('evacuate the bowels'), then we will be happy."

My suspicions were aroused when Tomazo said that he happened to know of a young, fat, barren cow that the owner was willing to part with. Was Toma working on commission, I wondered? But I dispelled this unworthy thought when we approached the Herero owner of the cow in question and found that he had decided not to sell.

The scrawny wreck of a Christmas ox now became the talk of the /ai/ai water hole and was the first news told to the outlying groups as they began to come in from the bush for the feast. What finally convinced me that real trouble might be brewing was the visit from u!au, an old conservative with a reputation for fierceness. His nickname meant spear and referred to an incident thirty years ago in which he had speared a man to death. He had an intense manner; fixing me with his eyes, he said in clipped tones:

"I have only just heard about the black ox today, or else I would have come here earlier. /ontah, do you honestly think you can serve meat like that to people and avoid a fight?" He paused, letting the implications sink in. "I don't mean fight you, /ontah; you are a white man. I mean a fight between Bushmen. There are many fierce ones here, and with such a small quantity of meat to distribute, how can you give everybody a fair share? Someone is sure to accuse another of taking too much or hogging all the choice pieces. Then you will see what happens when some go hungry while others eat."

The possibility of at least a serious argument struck me as all too real. I had witnessed the tension that surrounds the distribution of meat from a kudu or gemsbok kill, and had documented many arguments that sprang up from a real or imagined slight in meat distribution. The owners of a kill may spend up to two hours arranging and rearranging the piles of meat under the gaze of a circle of recipients before handing them out. And I also knew that the

Christmas feast at /ai/ai would be bringing together groups that had feuded in the past.

Convinced now of the gravity of the situation, I went in earnest to search for a second cow; but all my inquiries failed to turn one up.

The Christmas feast was evidently going to be a disaster, and the incessant complaints about the meagerness of the ox had already taken the fun out of it for me. Moreover, I was getting bored with the wisecracks, and after losing my temper a few times, I resolved to serve the beast anyway. If the meat fell short, the hell with it. In the Bushmen idiom, I announced to all who would listen:

"I am a poor man and blind. If I have chosen one that is too old and too thin, we will eat it anyway and see if there is enough meat there to quiet the rumbling of our stomachs."

On hearing this speech, Ben!a offered me a rare word of comfort. "It's thin," she said philosophically, "but the bones will make a good soup."

At dawn Christmas morning, instinct told me to turn over the butchering and cooking to a friend and take off with Nancy to spend Christmas alone in the bush. But curiosity kept me from retreating. I wanted to see what such a scrawny ox looked like on butchering, and if there *was* going to be a fight, I wanted to catch every word of it. Anthropologists are incurable that way.

The great beast was driven up to our dancing ground, and a shot in the forehead dropped it in its tracks. Then, freshly cut branches were heaped around the fallen carcass to receive the meat. Ten men volunteered to help with the cutting. I asked /gaugo to make the breast bone cut. This cut, which begins the butchering process for most large game, offers easy access for removal of the viscera. But it also allows the hunter to spot-check the amount of fat on the animal. A fat game animal carries a white layer up to an inch thick on the chest, while in a thin one, the knife will quickly cut to bone. All eyes fixed on his hand as /gaugo, dwarfed by the great car-

cass, knelt to the breast. The first cut opened a pool of solid white in the black skin. The second and third cut widened and deepened the creamy white. Still no bone. It was pure fat; it must have been two inches thick.

"Hey /gau," I burst out, "that ox is loaded with fat. What's this about the ox being too thin to bother eating? Are you out of your mind?"

"Fat?" /gau shot back, "You call that fat? This wreck is thin, sick, dead!" And he broke out laughing. So did everyone else. They rolled on the ground, paralyzed with laughter. Everybody laughed except me; I was thinking.

I ran back to the tent and burst in just as Nancy was getting up. "Hey, the black ox. It's fat as hell! They were kidding about it being too thin to eat. It was a joke or something. A put-on. Everyone is really delighted with it!"

"Some joke," my wife replied. "It was so funny that you were ready to pack up and leave /ai/ai."

If it had indeed been a joke, it had been an extraordinarily convincing one, and tinged, I thought, with more than a touch of malice as many jokes are. Nevertheless, that it was a joke lifted my spirits considerably, and I returned to the butchering site where the shape of the ox was rapidly disappearing under the axes and knives of the butchers. The atmosphere had become festive. Grinning broadly, their arms covered with blood well past the elbow, men packed chunks of meat into the big cast-iron cooking pots, fifty pounds to the load, and muttered and chuckled all the while about the thinness and worthlessness of the animal and /ontah's poor judgment.

We danced and ate that ox two days and two nights; we cooked and distributed fourteen potfuls of meat and no one went home hungry and no fights broke out.

But the "joke" stayed in my mind. I had a growing feeling that something important had happened in my relationship with the Bushmen and that the clue lay in the meaning of the joke. Several days later, when most of the people had dispersed back to the bush camps, I raised the

question with Hakekgose, a Tswana man who had grown up among the !Kung, married a !Kung girl, and who probably knew their culture better than any other non-Bushman.

"With us whites," I began, "Christmas is supposed to be the day of friendship and brotherly love. What I can't figure out is why the Bushmen went to such lengths to criticize and belittle the ox I had bought for the feast. The animal was perfectly good and their jokes and wisecracks practically ruined the holiday for me."

"So it really did bother you," said Hakekgose. "Well, that's the way they always talk. When I take my rifle and go hunting with them, if I miss, they laugh at me for the rest of the day. But even if I hit and bring one down, it's no better. To them, the kill is always too small or too old or too thin; and as we sit down on the kill site to cook and eat the liver, they keep grumbling, even with their mouths full of meat. They say things like, 'Oh this is awful! What a worthless animal! Whatever made me think that this Tswana rascal could hunt!'"

"Is this the way outsiders are treated?" I asked.

"No, it is their custom; they talk that way to each other too. Go and ask them."

/gaugo had been one of the most enthusiastic in making me feel bad about the merit of the Christmas ox. I sought him out first.

"Why did you tell me the black ox was worthless, when you could see that it was loaded with fat and meat?"

"It is our way," he said smiling. "We always like to fool people about that. Say there is a Bushman who has been hunting. He must not come home and announce like a braggard, 'I have killed a big one in the bush!' He must first sit down in silence until I or someone else comes up to his fire and asks, 'What did you see today?' He replies quietly, 'Ah, I'm no good for hunting. I saw nothing at all [pause] just a little tiny one.' Then I smile to myself," /gaugo continued, "because I know he has killed something big.

"In the morning we make up a party of four or five people to cut up and carry the meat back to the camp. When we arrive at the kill we examine it and cry out, 'You mean to say you have dragged us all the way out here in order to make us cart home your pile of bones? Oh, if I had known it was this thin I wouldn't have come.' Another one pipes up, 'People, to think I gave up a nice day in the shade for this. At home we may be hungry but at least we have nice cool water to drink.' If the horns are big, someone says, 'Did you think that somehow you were going to boil down the horns for soup?'

"To all this you must respond in kind. 'I agree,' you say, 'this one is not worth the effort; let's just cook the liver for strength and leave the rest for the hyenas. It is not too late to hunt today and even a duiker or a steenbok would be better than this mess.'

"Then you set to work nevertheless; butcher the animal, carry the meat back to the camp and everyone eats," /gaugo concluded.

Things were beginning to make sense. Next, I went to Tomazo. He corroborated /gaugo's story of the obligatory insults over a kill and added a few details of his own.

"But," I asked, "why insult a man after he has gone to all that trouble to track and kill an animal and when he is going to share the meat with you so that your children will have something to eat?"

"Arrogance," was his cryptic answer.

"Arrogance?"

"Yes, when a young man kills much meat he comes to think of himself as a chief or a big man, and he thinks of the rest of us as his servants or inferiors. We can't accept this. We refuse one who boasts, for someday his pride will make him kill somebody. So we always speak of his meat as worthless. This way we cool his heart and make him gentle."

"But why didn't you tell me this before?" I asked Tomazo with some heat.

"Because you never asked me," said Tomazo, echoing the refrain that has come to haunt every field ethnographer.

The pieces now fell into place. I had known for a long time that in situations of social conflict with Bushmen I held all the cards. I was the only source of tobacco in a thousand square miles, and I was not incapable of cutting an individual off for noncooperation. Though my boycott never lasted longer than a few days, it was an indication of my strength. People resented my presence at the water hole, yet simultaneously dreaded my leaving. In short I was a perfect target for the charge of arrogance and for the Bushmen tactic of enforcing humility.

I had been taught an object lesson by the Bushmen; it had come from an unexpected corner and had hurt me in a vulnerable area. For the big black ox was to be the one totally generous, unstinting act of my year at /ai/ai, and I was quite unprepared for the reaction I received.

As I read it, their message was this: There are no totally generous acts. All "acts" have an element of calculation. One black ox slaughtered at Christmas does not wipe out a year of careful manipulation of gifts given to serve your own ends. After all, to kill an animal and share the meat with people is really no more than Bushmen do for each other every day and with far less fanfare.

In the end, I had to admire how the Bushmen had played out the farce—collectively straight-faced to the end. Curiously, the episode reminded me of the *Good Soldier Schweik* and his marvelous encounters with authority. Like Schweik, the Bushmen had retained a thoroughgoing skepticism of good intentions. Was it this independence of spirit, I wondered, that had kept them culturally viable in the face of generations of contact with more powerful societies, both black and white? The thought that the Bushmen were alive and well in the Kalahari was strangely comforting. Perhaps, armed with that independence and with their superb knowledge of their environment, they might yet survive the future.

TOPIC EIGHT

Family, Kinship, and Social Organization

. . . .

Each culture provides an accepted range of options for human activities. It thus sets limits on human behavior as well as creating its potential. Although the spectrum of accepted activities and behavior in human groups around the world is vast, there are nevertheless certain patterns that reappear in virtually every culture. These are termed *cultural universals*.

The regulation of sexual behavior is one such cultural universal. Sexual mores vary enormously from one culture to another, but all cultures apparently share one basic value—namely, that sexual intercourse between parents and their children is to be avoided. In addition, most cultures also prohibit sexual contact between brothers and sisters. The term for prohibited sex among relatives is *incest*, and because most cultures attach very strong feelings of revulsion and horror to incest, it is said to be forbidden by *taboo*.

The universal presence of the incest taboo means that individuals must seek socially acceptable sexual relationships outside their own families. All cultures provide definitions of the categories of persons who are eligible and ineligible to have sex with each other. These definitions vary greatly cross-culturally. In our society, for instance, the incest taboo covers only the nuclear family and direct linear relatives and their siblings (parents, aunts and uncles, grandparents, and so on). However, in societies organized primarily in terms of kinship ties, the categories of sexually ineligible individuals can be very large indeed, reaching out to include almost all of a person's relatives linked through either male (patrilineal) or female (matrilineal) kinship. In "The Disappearance of the Incest Taboo," Yehudi Cohen argues (1) that the roots of the taboo are in ancient patterns of alliance and trade, and (2) that in modern society the taboo may no longer serve a viable purpose.

Cultures do more than simply prohibit sex between categories of individuals. They also provide for institutionalized marriages, ritualized means for publically legitimizing sexual partnerships and designating

social positions for their offspring. The interaction of these two universals—the incest taboo and institutionalized marriage—creates a third universal: the social institution known as the family. But "Is the Family Universal?" asks Melford Spiro in a seminal article published more than a quarter century ago. Spiro uses the Israeli *kibbutz* as a means to reexamine the concept of the family. Though his article is somewhat dated now, it is considered a classic, because it forced anthropologists to rethink many of their assumptions about the forms and functions of the family. Spiro has continued his study of the same *kibbutzim* for over three decades, observing them and their members as they have grown, developed, and reacted to the vast changes that have overtaken Israeli society during that period. As his latest book, *Gender and Culture: Kibbutz Women Revisited* (1980), makes clear, Spiro himself has rethought many of his original ideas.

The remaining two articles that round out this topic share in a search for some of the less-than-obvious factors that influence the organization of social life. In "Fission in an Amazonian Tribe," Napoleon Chagnon looks at some of the consequences of a life-style that emphasizes chronic warfare, specifically with regard to patterns of marriage and the splitting apart of villages.

In "Marriage as Warfare," Charles Lindholm and Cherry Lindholm examine the impact of an enduring "marital war" on personal relationships, especially on those between spouses. Among the Pakhtun of Pakistan, the family clearly is far from being a "haven in a heartless world," as Christopher Lasch describes the family in America. Instead, it is a microcosm in which the violence of the society is mirrored and engendered and in which men dream, not of mistresses, but of unobtainable friendship. Charles Lindholm has elaborated on this study of Pakhtun society in his book *Generosity and Jealousy: Emotional Structures in a Competitive Society* (Columbia University Press, 1982). The book describes the pervasive effects of Pakhtun social structure on child rearing, politics, residence patterns, and

146

interpersonal relations. Lindholm holds that the values of generosity and hospitality, for which the Pakhtun are justly famous, can not be understood within this structure, which impels people toward relations based on enmity and jealousy. Instead, he argues, these values are expressions of underlying universal human needs for attachment—needs that the harsh Pakhtun social order reveres in its ideology and rituals, but that it does not permit in normal daily interactions.

22

The Disappearance of the Incest Taboo

BY YEHUDI COHEN

Several years ago a minor Swedish bureaucrat, apparently with nothing better to do, was leafing through birth and marriage records, matching people with their natural parents. To his amazement he found a full brother and sister who were married and had several children. The couple were arrested and brought to trial. It emerged that they had been brought up by separate sets of foster parents and never knew of each other's existence. By a coincidence reminiscent of a Greek tragedy, they met as adults, fell in love, and married, learning of their biological tie only after their arrest. The local court declared their marriage illegal and void.

The couple appealed the decision to Sweden's Supreme Court. After lengthy testimony on both sides of the issue, the court overturned the decision on the grounds that the pair had not been reared together. The marriage was declared legal and valid. In the wake of the decision, a committee appointed by Sweden's Minister of Justice to examine the question has proposed that criminal sanctions against incest be repealed. The committee's members were apparently swayed by Carl-Henry Alstrom, a professor of psychiatry. Alstrom argued that psychological deterrents to incest are stronger than legal prohibitions. The question will soon go to Sweden's Parliament, which seems prepared to follow the committee's recommendation.

Aside from illustrating the idea that the most momentous changes in human societies often occur as a result of unforeseen events, this landmark case raises questions that go far beyond Sweden's (or any other society's) borders. Some people may be tempted to dismiss the Swedish decision as an anomaly, as nothing more than a part of Sweden's unusual experiments in public welfare and sexual freedom.

But the probable Swedish decision to repeal criminal laws against incest cannot be regarded so lightly; this simple step reflects a trend in human society that has been developing for several thousand years. When we arrange human societies along a continuum from the least to the most complex, from those with the smallest number of interacting social groups to those with the highest number of groups, from those with the simplest technology to those with the most advanced technology, we observe that the incest taboo applies to fewer and fewer relatives beyond the immediate family.

Though there are exceptions, the widest extension of incest taboos beyond the nuclear family is found in the least complex societies. In a few societies, such as the Cheyenne of North America and the Kwoma of New Guinea, incest taboos extend to many remote relatives, including in-laws and the in-laws of in-laws. In modern industrial societies, incest taboos are usually confined to members of the immediate household. This contraction in the range of incest taboos is reaching the point at which they may disappear entirely.

The source of these changes in incest taboos lies in changing patterns of external trade. Trade is a society's jugular. Because every group lives in a milieu lacking some necessities that are available in other habitats, the flow of goods and resources is a society's lifeblood. But it is never sufficient merely to encourage people to form trade alliances with others in different areas. Incest taboos force people to marry outside their own group, to form alliances and to maintain trade networks. As other institutions— governments, business organizations—begin to organize trade, incest taboos become less necessary for assuring the flow of the society's lifeblood; they start to contract.

Other explanations of the incest taboo do not, under close examination, hold up. The most common assumption is that close inbreeding is biologically deleterious and will lead to the extinction of those who practice it. But there is strong evidence that inbreeding does not materially increase the rate of maladies such as albinism, total color blindness, or various forms of idiocy, which generally result when each parent carries the same recessive gene. In most cases these diseases result from chance combinations of recessive genes or from mutation.

According to Theodosius Dobzhansky, a geneticist, "The increase of the incidence of hereditary diseases in the offspring of marriages between relatives (cousins, uncle and niece or aunt and nephew, second cousins, etc.) over that in marriages between persons not known to be related is slight—so slight that geneticists hesitate to declare such marriages disgenic." Inbreeding does carry a slight risk. The progeny of relatives include more stillbirths and infant and early childhood deaths than the progeny of unrelated people. But most of these deaths are due to environmental rather than genetic factors. Genetic disadvantages are not frequent enough to justify a prohibition. Moreover, it is difficult to justify the biological explanation for incest taboos when many societies prescribe marriage to one cousin and prohibit marriage to another. Among the Lesu of Melanesia a man must avoid sexual contact with his parallel cousins, his mother's sisters' daughters and his father's brothers' daughters, but is supposed to marry his cross cousins, his mother's brothers' daughters and his father's sisters' daughters. Even though both types of cousins have the same genetic relationship to the man, only one kind is included in the incest taboo. The taboo is apparently a cultural phenomenon based on the cultural classification of people and can not be explained biologically.

Genetic inbreeding may even have some advantages in terms of natural selection. Each time a person dies of a hereditary disadvantage, his detrimental genes are lost to the population. By such a process of genetic cleansing, inbreeding may lead to the elimination, or at least to reduced frequencies, of recessive genes. The infant mortality rate

Yehudi Cohen

may increase slightly at first, but after the sheltered recessive genes are eliminated, the population may stabilize. Inbreeding may also increase the frequency of beneficial recessive genes, contributing to the population's genetic fitness. In the end, inbreeding seems to have only a slight effect on the offspring and a mixed effect, some good and some bad, on the gene pool itself. This mild consequence hardly justifies the universal taboo on incest.

Another explanation of the incest taboo is the theory of natural aversion, first propounded by Edward Westermarck in his 1891 book, *The History of Human Marriage*. According to Westermarck, children reared in the same household are naturally averse to having sexual relations with one another in adulthood. But this theory has major difficulties. First, it has a basic logical flaw: If there were a natural aversion to incest, the taboo would be unnecessary. As James Frazer pointed out in 1910, "It is not easy to see why any deep human instinct should need to be reinforced by law. There is no law commanding men to eat and drink or forbidding them to put their hands in the fire. . . . The law only forbids men to do what their instincts incline them to do; what nature itself prohibits and punishes, it would be superfluous for the law to prohibit and punish. . . . Instead of assuming, therefore, from the legal prohibition of incest that there is a natural aversion to incest, we ought rather to assume that there is a natural instinct in favour of it."

Second, the facts play havoc with the notion of natural aversion. In many societies, such as the Arapesh of New Guinea studied by Margaret Mead, and the Eskimo, young children are betrothed and raised together, usually by the boy's parents, before the marriage is consummated. Arthur Wolf, an anthropologist who studied a village in northern Taiwan, describes just such a custom: "Dressed in the traditional red wedding costume, the bride enters her future husband's home as a child. She is seldom more than three years of age and often less than a year. . . . [The] last phase in the marriage process does not take place until she is old enough to fulfill the role of wife. In the meantime, she and her parents are affinally related to the groom's parents, but she is not in fact married to the groom."

One of the examples commonly drawn up to support Westermarck's theory of aversion is the Israeli *kibbutz,* where children who have been raised together tend to avoid marrying. But this avoidance has been greatly exaggerated. There is some tendency among those who have been brought up in the same age group in a communal "children's house" to avoid marrying one another, but this arises from two regulations that separate young adults from their *kibbutz* at about the age when they might marry. The first is a regulation of the Israel Defense Forces that no married woman may serve in the armed forces. Conscription for men and women is at 18, usually coinciding with their completion of secondary school, and military service is a deeply felt responsibility for most *kibbutz*-reared Israelis. Were women to marry prior to 18, they would be denied one of their principal goals. By the time they complete their military service, many choose urban spouses whom they have met in the army. Thus the probability of marrying a person one has grown up with is greatly reduced.

The second regulation that limits intermarriage on a *kibbutz* is a policy of the federations to which almost all *kibbutzim* belong. Each of the four major federations reserves the right to transfer any member to any other settlement, especially when a new one is being established. These "seeds," as the transferred members are called, are recruited individually from different settlements and most transfers are made during a soldier's third or fourth year of military service. When these soldiers leave the army to live on a *kibbutz,* they may be separated from those they were reared with. The frequency of marriage among people from working-class backgrounds who began and completed school together in an American city or town is probably higher than for an Israeli *kibbutz;* the proclivity among American college graduates to marry outside their neighborhoods or towns is no more an example of exogamy or incest avoidance than is the tendency in Israeli *kibbutzim* to marry out.

Just as marriage within a neighborhood is accepted in the United States, so is marriage within a *kibbutz* accepted in Israel. During research I conducted in Israel between 1967 and 1969, I attended the wedding of two people in a *kibbutz* who supposedly were covered by this taboo or rule of avoidance. As my tape recordings and photographs show, it would be difficult to imagine a more joyous occasion. When I questioned members of the *kibbutz* about this, they told me with condescending smiles that they had "heard of these things the professors say."

A third, "demographic," explanation of the incest taboo was originally set forth in 1950 by Wilson Wallis and elaborated in 1959 by Mariam Slater. According to this theory, mating within the household, especially between parents and children, was unlikely in early human societies because the life span in these early groups was so short that by the time offspring were old enough to mate, their parents would probably have died. Mating between siblings would also have been unlikely because of the average of eight years between children that resulted from breast-feeding and high rates of infant mortality. But even assuming this to have been true for the first human societies, there is nothing to prevent mating among the members of a nuclear family when the life span is lengthened.

A fourth theory that is widely subscribed to focuses on the length of the human child's parental dependency, which is the longest in the animal kingdom. Given the long period required for socializing children, there must be regulation of sexual activity so that children may learn their proper roles. If the nuclear family's members are permitted to have unrestricted sexual access to one another, the members of the unit would be confused about their roles. Parental authority would be undermined, and it would be impossible to socialize children. This interpretation has much to recommend it as far as relationships between parents and children are concerned, but it does not help explain brother-sister incest taboos or the extension of incest taboos to include remote relatives.

The explanation closest to my interpretation of the changes in the taboo is the theory of alliance advocated by the French anthropologist Claude Levi-Strauss, which suggests that people are compelled to marry outside their groups in order to form unions with other groups and promote harmony among them. A key element in the theory is that men exchange their sisters and daughters in marriage with men of other groups. As originally propounded, the theory of alliance was based on the assumption that men stay put while the women change groups by marrying out, moved about by men like pieces on a chessboard. But there are many instances in which the women stay put while the men change groups by marrying out. In either case, the result is the same. Marriage forges alliances.

These alliances freed early human societies from exclusive reliance on their own limited materials and products. No society is self-sustaining or self-perpetuating; no culture is a world unto itself. Each society is compelled to trade with others and this was as true for tribal societies as it is for modern industrial nations. North America, for instance, was crisscrossed with elaborate trade networks before the Europeans arrived. Similar trade networks covered aboriginal New Guinea and Australia. In these trade networks, coastal or riverine groups gave shells and fish to hinterland people in exchange for cultivated foods, wood, and manufactured items.

American Indian standards of living were quite high before the Europeans destroyed the native trade networks, and the same seems to have been true in almost all other parts of the world. It will come as no surprise to economists that the material quality of people's lives improves to the extent that they engage in external trade.

But barter and exchange do not automatically take place when people meet. Exchange involves trust, and devices are needed to establish trust, to distinguish friend from foe, and to assure a smooth, predictable flow of trade goods. Marriage in the tribal world established permanent obligations and reciprocal rights and privileges among families living in different habitats.

For instance, when a young Cheyenne Indian man decided on a girl to marry, he told his family of his choice. If they agreed that his selection was good, they gathered a store of prized possessions — clothing, blankets, guns, bows and arrows — and carefully loaded them on a fine horse. A friend of the family, usually a respected old woman, led the horse to the tepee of the girl's elder brother. There the go-between spread the gifts for everyone to see while she pressed the suitor's case. The next step was for the girl's brother to assemble all his cousins for a conference to weigh the proposal. If they agreed to it, the cousins distributed the gifts among themselves, the brother taking the horse. Then the men returned to their tepees to find suitable gifts to give in return. Within a day or two, each returned with something roughly equal in value to what he had received. While this was happening, the bride was made beautiful. When all arrangements were completed, she mounted one horse while the return gifts were loaded on another. The old woman led both horses to the groom's camp. After the bride was received, her accompanying gifts were distributed among the groom's relatives in accordance with what each had given. The exchanges between the two families did not end with the marriage ceremony, however; they continued as a permanent part of the marriage ties. This continual exchange, which took place periodically, is why the young man's bridal choice was so important for his entire family.

Marriage was not the only integral part of external trade relationships. Another was ritualized friendship, "blood brotherhood," for example. Such bonds were generally established between members of different groups and were invariably trade partnerships. Significantly, these ritualized friendships often included taboos against marriage with the friend's sisters; sometimes the taboo applied to all their close relatives. This extension of a taboo provides an important key for understanding all incest taboos. Sexual prohibitions do not necessarily grow out of biological ties. Both marriage and ritualized friendships in primitive societies promote economic alliances and both are associated with incest taboos.

Incest taboos force people into alliances with others in as many groups as possible. They promote the greatest flow of manufactured goods and raw materials from the widest variety of groups and ecological niches and force people to spread their social nets. Looked at another way, incest taboos prevent localism and economic provincialism; they block social and economic inbreeding.

Incest taboos have their widest extensions outside the nuclear family in those societies in which technology is least well developed and in which people have to carry their own trade goods for barter or exchange with members of other groups. Often in these small societies, everyone in a community is sexually taboo to the rest of the group. When the technology surrounding trade improves and shipments of goods and materials can be concentrated (as when people learn to build and navigate ocean-going canoes or harness pack animals), fewer and fewer people have to be involved in trade. As this happens, incest taboos begin to contract, affecting fewer and fewer people outside the nuclear family.

This process has been going on for centuries. Today, in most industrial societies, the only incest taboos are those that pertain to members of the nuclear family. This contraction of the range of the taboo is inseparable from the fact that we no longer engage in personal alliances and trade agreements to get the food we eat, the clothes we wear, the tools and materials we use, the fuels on which we depend. Goods are brought to distribution points near our homes by a relatively tiny handful of truckers, shippers, merchants, entrepreneurs, and others. Most of us are only vaguely aware of the alliances, negotiations, and relationships that make this massive movement of goods possible. When we compare tribal and contemporary industrialized societies, the correspondence between the range of incest taboos and the material conditions of life cannot be dismissed as mere coincidence.

Industrialization does not operate alone in affecting the degree to which incest taboos extend beyond the nuclear family. In the history of societies, political institutions developed as technology advanced. Improvements in packaging and transportation have led not only to reductions in the number of people involved in external trade, but also to greater and greater concentrations of decision making in the hands of fewer and fewer people. Trade is no longer the responsibility of all members of a society, and the maintenance of relationships between societies has become the responsibility of a few people — a king and his bureaucracy, impersonal governmental agencies, national and multinational corporations.

To the extent that trade is conducted and negotiated by a

handful of people, it becomes unnecessary to use incest taboos to force the majority of people into alliances with other groups. Treaties, political alliances, and negotiations by the managers of a few impersonal agencies have replaced marital and other personal alliances. The history of human societies suggests that incest taboos may have outlived their original purpose.

But incest taboos still serve other purposes. For social and emotional reasons rather than economic ones, people in modern industrial societies still need to prevent localism. Psychological well-being in a diversified society depends largely on the ability to tap different ideas, points of view, life styles, and social relationships. The jugulars that must now be kept open by the majority of people may no longer be for goods and resources, but for variety and stimulation. This need for variety is what, in part, seems to underlie the preference of Israelis to marry outside the communities in which they were born and brought up. The taboo against sex within the nuclear family leads young people to explore, to seek new experiences. In a survey of a thousand cases of incest, Christopher Bagley found that incestuous families are cut off from their society's social and cultural mainstream. Whether rural or urban, he writes, "the family seems to withdraw from the general community, and initiates its own 'deviant' norms of sexual behavior, which are contained within the family circle." "Such a family," he continues, "is an isolated cultural unit, relatively untouched by external social norms." This social and cultural inbreeding is the cause of the profound malaise represented by incest.

To illustrate the correspondence between incest and social isolation, let me describe an incestuous family reported by Peter Wilson, an anthropologist. Wilson sketched a sequence of events in which a South American family became almost totally isolated from the community in which it lived, and began to practice almost every variety of incest. The decline into incest began many years before Wilson appeared on the scene to do anthropological research, when the father of five daughters and four sons made the girls (who ranged in age from 18 to 33) sexually available to some sailors for a small sum of money. As a result, the entire household was ostracized by the rest of the village. "But most important," Wilson writes, "the Brown family was immediately cut off from sexual partners. No woman would have anything to do with a Brown man; no man would touch a Brown woman."

The Browns's isolation and incest continued for several years, until the women in the family rebelled—apparently because a new road connecting their hamlet to others provided the opportunity for social contact with people outside the hamlet. At the same time the Brown men began working in new light industry in the area and spending their money in local stores. The family slowly regained some social acceptance in Green Fields, the larger village to which their hamlet belonged. Little by little they were rein-

tegrated into the hamlet and there seems to have been no recurrence of incest among them.

A second example is an upper-middle class, Jewish, urban American family that was described to me by a colleague. The Erva family (a pseudonym) consists of six people—the parents, two daughters aged 19 and 22, and two sons, aged 14 and 20. Mr. Erva is a computer analyst and his wife a dentist. Twenty-five years ago, the Ervas seemed relatively normal, but shortly after their first child was born, Mr. and Mrs. Erva took to wandering naked about their apartment, even when others were present. They also began dropping in on friends for as long as a week; their notion of reciprocity was to refuse to accept food, to eat very little of what was offered them, or to order one member of their family not to accept any food at all during a meal. Their rationale seemed to be that accepting food was receiving a favor, but occupying a bed was not. This pattern was accompanied by intense family bickering and inadvertent insults to their hosts. Not surprisingly, most of their friends wearied of their visits and the family was left almost friendless.

Reflecting Bagley's general description of incestuous families, the Ervas had withdrawn from the norms of the general community after the birth of their first child and had instituted their own "deviant" patterns of behavior. They thereby set the stage for incest.

Mr. Erva began to have intercourse with his daughters when they were 14 and 16 years old. Neither of them was self-conscious about the relationship and it was common for the father to take both girls into bed with him at the same time when they were visiting overnight. Mrs. Erva apparently did not have intercourse with her sons. The incest became a matter of gossip and added to the family's isolation.

The Erva family then moved to the Southwest to start over again. They built a home on a parcel of land that had no access to water. Claiming they could not afford a well of their own, the family began to use the bathrooms and washing facilities of their neighbors. In the end these neighbors, too, wanted nothing to do with them.

Mr. and Mrs. Erva eventually separated, he taking the daughters and she the sons. Later the younger daughter left her father to live alone, but the older daughter still shares a one bedroom apartment with her father.

Social isolation and incest appear to be related, and social maturity and a taboo on incest are also related. Within the modern nuclear family, social and emotional relationships are intense, and sexuality is the source of some of the strongest emotions in human life. When combined with the intensity of family life, sexually stimulated emotions can be overwhelming for children. Incest taboos are a way of limiting family relationships. They are assurances of a degree of emotional insularity, of detachment on which emotional maturity depends.

On balance, then, we can say that legal penalties for incest were first instituted because of the adverse economic effects of incestuous unions on society, but that today the negative consequences of incest affect only individuals. Some will say that criminal penalties should be retained if only to protect children. But legal restraints alone are unlikely to serve as deterrents. Father-daughter incest is regarded by many social workers, judges, and psychiatrists as a form of child abuse, but criminal penalties have not deterred other forms of child abuse. Moreover, incest between brothers and sisters cannot be considered child abuse. Some have even suggested that the concept of abuse may be inappropriate when applied to incest. "Many psychotherapists," claims psychologist James McCary in *Human Sexuality*, "believe that a child is less affected by actual incest than by seductive behavior on the part of a parent that never culminates in any manifest sexual activity."

Human history suggests that the incest taboo may indeed be obsolete. As in connection with changing attitudes toward homosexuality, it may be maintained that incestuous relations between consenting mature adults are their concern alone and no one else's. At the same time, however, children must be protected. But questions still remain about how they should be protected and until what age.

If a debate over the repeal of criminal laws against incest is to begin in earnest, as it surely will if the Swedish Parliament acts on the proposed reversal, one other important fact about the social history of sexual behavior must be remembered. Until about a century ago, many societies punished adultery and violations of celibacy with death. When it came time to repeal those laws, not a few people favored their retention on the grounds that extramarital sexual relationships would adversely affect the entire society. Someday people may regard incest in the same way they now regard adultery and violations of celibacy. Where the threat of punishment once seemed necessary, social and emotional dissuasion may now suffice.

For further information:

Bagley, Christopher. "Incest Behavior and Incest Taboos." *Social Problems*, Vol. 16, 1969, pp. 505-519.

Birdsell, J. B. *Human Evolution: An Introduction to the New Physical Anthropology.* Rand McNally, 1972.

Bischof, Norbert. "The Biological Foundations of the Incest Taboo." *Social Science Information*, Vol. 11, No. 6, 1972.

Fox, Robin. *Kinship and Marriage.* Penguin Books, 1968.

Slater, Mariam. "Ecological Factors in the Origin of Incest." *American Anthropologist*, Vol. 61, No. 6, 1959.

Wilson, Peter J. "Incest: A Case Study." *Social and Economic Studies*, Vol. 12, 1961, pp. 200-209.

23

Is the Family Universal?

BY MELFORD E. SPIRO

....

INTRODUCTION

The universality of the family has always been accepted as a sound hypothesis in anthropology; recently, Murdock has been able to confirm this hypothesis on the basis of his important cross-cultural study of kinship. Moreover, Murdock reports that the "nuclear" family is also universal, and that typically it has four functions: sexual, economic, reproductive, and educational. What is more important is his finding that no society "has succeeded in finding an adequate substitute for the nuclear family, to which it might transfer these functions" (1949:11). In the light of this evidence there would be little reason to question his prediction that "it is highly doubtful whether any society ever will succeed in such an attempt, utopian proposals for the abolition of the family to the contrary notwithstanding" (p. 11).

The functions served by the nuclear family are, of course, universal prerequisites for the survival of any society; and it is on this basis that Murdock accounts for its universality.

> Without provision for the first and third [sexual and reproductive], society would become extinct; for the second [economic], life itself would cease; for the fourth [educational], culture would come to an end. The immense social utility of the nuclear family and the basic reason for its universality thus begins to emerge in strong relief [p. 10].

Although sexual, economic, reproductive, and educational activities are the functional prerequisites of any society, it comes as somewhat of a surprise, nevertheless, that all four functions are served by the same social group. One would normally assume, on purely a priori grounds, that within the tremendous variability to be found among human cultures, there would be some cultures in which these four functions were distributed among more than one group. Logically, at least, it is entirely possible for these functions to be divided among various social groups within a society; and it is, indeed, difficult to believe that somewhere man's in-ventive ingenuity should not have actualized this logical possibility. As a matter of fact this possibility has been actualized in certain utopian communities—and it has succeeded within the narrow confines of these communities. The latter, however, have always constituted subgroups within a larger society, and the basic question remains as to whether such attempts could succeed when applied to the larger society.

Rather than speculate about the answer to this question, however, this paper presents a case study of a community which, like the utopian communities, constitutes a subgroup within a larger society and which, like some utopian communities, has also evolved a social structure which does not include the family. It is hoped that an examination of this community—the Israeli *kibbutz*—can shed light on this question.

MARRIAGE AND THE FAMILY IN THE *KIBBUTZ*

A *kibbutz* (plural, *kibbutzim*) is an agricultural collective in Israel, whose main features include communal living, collective ownership of all property (and, hence, the absence of "free enterprise" and the "profit motive"), and the communal rearing of children. *Kibbutz* culture is informed by its explicit, guiding principle of: "from each according to his ability, to each according to his needs." The "family," as that term is defined in *Social Structure*, does not exist in the *kibbutz*, in either its nuclear, polygamous, or extended forms. It should be emphasized, however, that the *kibbutzim* are organized into three separate national federations, and though the basic structure of *kibbutz* society is similar in all three, there are important differences among them. Hence, the term *kibbutz*, as used in this paper, refers exclusively to those *kibbutzim* that are members of the federation studied by the author.[1]

1. The field work, on which statements concerning the *kibbutz* are based, was conducted in the year 1951–1952, and was made possible by a postdoctoral fellowship awarded by the Social Science Research Council.

Reproduced by permission of the American Anthropological Association and the author from American Anthropologist, Vol. 56, 839-846, 1954. The Addendum is reprinted from *A Modern Introduction to the Family*, Norman W. Bell and Ezra F. Vogel, eds., copyright © The Free Press (The Macmillan Company) 1960.

As Murdock defines it (p. 1), the "family":

> is a social group characterized by common residence, economic cooperation, and reproduction. It includes adults of both sexes, at least two of whom maintain a socially approved sexual relationship, and one or more children, own or adopted, of the sexually cohabiting adults.

The social group in the *kibbutz* that includes adults of both sexes and their children, although characterized by reproduction, is not characterized by common residence or by economic co-operation. Before examining this entire social group, however, we shall first analyze the relationship between the two adults in the group who maintain a "socially approved sexual relationship," in order to determine whether their relationship constitutes a "marriage."

Murdock's findings reveal that marriage entails an interaction of persons of opposite sex such that a relatively permanent sexual relationship is maintained and an economic division of labor is practised. Where either of these behavior patterns is absent, there is no marriage. As Murdock puts it (p. 8):

> Sexual unions without economic cooperation are common, and there are relationships between men and women involving a division of labor without sexual gratification... but marriage exists only when the economic and the sexual are united in one relationship, and this combination occurs only in marriage.

In examining the relationship of the couple in the *kibbutz* who share a common marriage, and whose sexual union is socially sanctioned, it is discovered that only one of these two criteria—the sexual—applies. Their relationship does not entail economic co-operation. If this be so—and the facts will be examined in a moment—there is no marriage in the *kibbutz*, if by "marriage" is meant a relationship between adults of opposite sex, characterized by sexual and economic activities. Hence, the generalization that, "marriage, thus defined, exists in every known society" (p. 8), has found an exception.

A *kibbutz* couple lives in a single room, which serves as a combined bedroom-living room. Their meals are eaten in a communal dining room, and their children are reared in a communal children's dormitory. Both the man and woman work in the *kibbutz*, and either one may work in one of its agricultural branches or in one of the "service" branches. The latter include clerical work, education, work in the kitchen, laundry, etc. In actual fact, however, men preponderate in the agricultural branches, and women, in the service branches of the economy. There are no men, for example, in that part of the educational system which extends from infancy to the junior-high level. Nor do women work in those agricultural branches that require the use of heavy

machinery, such as trucks, tractors, or combines. It should be noted, however, that some women play major roles in agricultural branches, such as the vegetable garden and the fruit orchards; and some men are indispensable in service branches such as the high school. Nevertheless, it is accurate to state that a division of labor based on sex is characteristic of the *kibbutz* society as a whole. This division of labor, however, does not characterize the relationship that exists between couples. Each mate works in some branch of the *kibbutz* economy and each, as a member (*chaver*) of the *kibbutz* receives his equal share of the goods and services that the *kibbutz* distributes. Neither, however, engages in economic activities that are exclusively directed to the satisfaction of the needs of his mate. Women cook, sew, launder, etc., for the entire *kibbutz*, and not for their mates exclusively. Men produce goods, but the economic returns from their labor go to the *kibbutz*, not to their mates and themselves, although they, like all members of the *kibbutz* share in these economic returns. Hence, though there is economic co-operation between the sexes within the community as a whole, this co-operation does not take place between mates because the social structure of this society precludes the necessity for such co-operation.

What then is the nature of the relationship of the *kibbutz* couple? What are the motives for their union? What functions, other than sex, does it serve? What distinguishes such a union from an ordinary love affair?

In attempting to answer these questions it should first be noted that premarital sexual relations are not taboo. It is expected, however, that youth of high-school age refrain from sexual activity; sexual intercourse between high-school students is strongly discouraged. After graduation from high school, however, and their election to membership in the *kibbutz*, there are no sanctions against sexual relations among these young people. While still single, *kibbutz* members live in small private rooms, and their sexual activities may take place in the room of either the male or the female, or in any other convenient location. Lovers do not ask the *kibbutz* for permission to move into a (larger) common room, nor, if they did, would this permission be granted if it were assumed that their relationship was merely that of lovers. When a couple asks for permission to share a room, they do so—and the *kibbutz* assumes that they do so—not because they are lovers, but because they are in love. The request for a room, then, is the sign that they wish to become a "couple" (*zug*), the term the *kibbutz* has substituted for the traditional "marriage." This union does not require the sanction of a marriage ceremony, or of any other event. When a couple requests a room, and the *kibbutz* grants the request, their union is *ipso facto* sanctioned by society. It should be noted, however, that all *kibbutz* "couples" eventually "get married" in accordance with the marriage laws of the state—usually just before, or soon after, their first child is born—because children born out of wedlock have no legal rights according to state law.

But becoming a "couple" affects neither the status nor the responsibilities of either the male or the female in the *kibbutz*. Both continue to work in whichever branch of the economy they had worked in before their union. The legal and social status of both the male and the female remain the same. The female retains her maiden name. She not only is viewed as a member of the *kibbutz* in her own right, but her official registration card in the *kibbutz* files remains separate from that of her "friend" (*chaver*)—the term used to designate spouses.[2]

But if sexual satisfaction may be obtained outside of this union, and if the union does not entail economic co-operation, what motivates people to become "couples"? It seems that the motivation is the desire to satisfy certain needs for intimacy, using that term in both its physical and psychological meanings. In the first place, from the sexual point of view, the average *chaver* is not content to engage in a constant series of casual affairs. After a certain period of sexual experimentation, he desires to establish a relatively permanent relationship with one person. But in addition to the physical intimacy of sex, the union also provides a psychological intimacy that may be expressed by notions such as "comradeship," "security," "dependency," "succorance," etc. And it is this psychological intimacy, primarily, that distinguishes "couples" from lovers. The criterion of the "couple" relationship, then, that which distinguishes it from a relationship between adults of the same sex who enjoy psychological intimacy, or from that of adults of opposite sex who enjoy physical intimacy, is love. A "couple" comes into being when these two kinds of intimacy are united in one relationship.

Since the *kibbutz* "couple" does not constitute a marriage because it does not satisfy the economic criterion of "marriage," it follows that the "couple" and their children do not constitute a family, economic co-operation being part of the definition of the "family." Furthermore, as has already been indicated, this group of adults and children does not satisfy the criterion of "common residence." For though the children visit their parents in the latter's room every day, their residence is in one of the "children's houses" (*bet yeladim*), where they sleep, eat, and spend most of their time.

More important, however, in determining whether or not the family exists in the *kibbutz* is the fact that the

"physical care" and the "social rearing" of the children are not the responsibilities of their own parents. But these responsibilities, according to Murdock's findings, are the most important functions that the adults in the "family" have with respect to the children.

Before entering into a discussion of the *kibbutz* system of "collective education" (*chinuch meshutaf*), it should be emphasized that the *kibbutz* is a child-centered society, *par excellence*. The importance of children, characteristic of traditional Jewish culture, has been retained as one of the primary values in this avowedly antitraditional society. "The Parents Crown" is the title given to the chapter on children in an ethnography of the Eastern European Jewish village. The authors of this ethnography write (Zborowski and Herzog 1952:308):

> Aside from the scriptural and social reasons, children are welcomed for the joy they bring beyond the gratification due to the parents—the pleasure of having a child in the house. A baby is a toy, the treasure, and the pride of the house.

This description, except for the scriptural reference, applies without qualification to the *kibbutz*.

But the *kibbutz* has still another reason for cherishing its children. The *kibbutz* views itself as an attempt to revolutionize the structure of human society and its basic social relations. Its faith in its ability to achieve this end can be vindicated only if it can raise a generation that will choose to live in this communal society, and will, thus, carry on the work that was initiated by the founders of this society—their parents.

For both these reasons the child is king. Children are lavished with attention and with care to the point where many adults admit that the children are "spoiled." Adult housing may be poor, but the children live in good houses; adult food may be meager and monotonous, but the children enjoy a variety of excellent food; there may be a shortage of clothes for adults, but the children's clothing is both good and plentiful.

Despite this emphasis on children, however, it is not their own parents who provide directly for their physical care. Indeed, the latter have no responsibilities in this regard. The *kibbutz* as a whole assumes this responsibility for all its children. The latter sleep and eat in special "children's houses"; they obtain their clothes from a communal store; when ill, they are taken care of by their "nurses." This does not mean that parents are not concerned about the physical welfare of their own children. On the contrary, this is one of their primary concerns. But it does mean that the active responsibility for their care has been delegated to a community institution. Nor does it mean that parents do not work for the physical care of their children, for this is one of their strongest drives. But the fruits of their labor are not given directly to their children; they are given instead to

---

2. Other terms, "young man" (*bachur*) and "young woman" (*bachura*), are also used in place of "husband" and "wife." If more than one person in the *kibbutz* has the same proper name, and there is some question as to who is being referred to when the name is mentioned in conversation, the person is identified by adding, "the *bachur* of so-and-so," or "the *bachura* of so-and-so."

the community which, in turn, provides for all the children. A bachelor or a "couple" without children contribute as much to the children's physical care as a "couple" with children of their own.

The family's responsibility for the socialization of children, Murdock reports, is "no less important than the physical care of the children."

> The burden of education and socialization everywhere falls primarily upon the nuclear family. . . . Perhaps more than any other single factor collective responsibility for education and socialization welds the various relationships of the family firmly together [p. 10].

But the education and socialization of *kibbutz* children are the function of their "nurses" and teachers, and not of their parents. The infant is placed in the "infants' house" upon the mother's return from the hospital, where it remains in the care of nurses. Both parents see the infant there; the mother when she feeds it, the father upon return from work. The infant is not taken to its parents' room until its sixth month, after which it stays with them for an hour. As the child grows older, the amount of time he spends with his parents increases, and he may go to their room whenever he chooses during the day, though he must return to his "children's house" before lights-out. Since the children are in school most of the day, however, and since both parents work during the day, the children—even during their school vacations—are with their parents for a (approximately) two-hour period in the evening—from the time that the parents return from work until they go to eat their evening meal. The children may also be with the parents all day Saturday—the day of rest—if they desire.

As the child grows older he advances through a succession of "children's houses" with children of his own age, where he is supervised by a "nurse." The "nurse" institutes most of the disciplines, teaches the child his basic social skills, and is responsible for the "socialization of the instincts." The child also learns from his parents, to be sure, and they too are agents in the socialization process. But the bulk of his socialization is both entrusted, and deliberately delegated, to the "nurses" and teachers. There is little doubt but that a *kibbutz* child, bereft of the contributions of his parents to his socialization, would know his culture; deprived of the contributions of his "nurses" and teachers, however, he would remain an unsocialized individual.

As they enter the juvenile period, pre-adolescence, and adolescence, the children are gradually inducted into the economic life of the *kibbutz*. They work from an hour (grade-school students) to three hours (high school seniors) a day in one of the economic branches under the supervision of adults. Thus, their economic skills, like most of their early social skills, are taught

them by adults other than their parents. This generalization applies to the learning of values, as well. In the early ages, the *kibbutz* values are inculcated by "nurses," and later by teachers. When the children enter junior high, this function, which the *kibbutz* views as paramount in importance, is delegated to the "homeroom teacher," known as the "educator" (*mechanech*), and to a "leader" (*madrich*) of the inter-*kibbutz* youth movement. The parents, of course, are also influential in the teaching of values, but the formal division of labor in the *kibbutz* has delegated this responsibility to other authorities.

Although the parents do not play an outstanding role in the socialization of their children, or in providing for their physical needs, it would be erroneous to conclude that they are unimportant figures in their children's lives. Parents are of crucial importance in the *psychological* development of the child. They serve as the objects of his most important identifications, and they provide him with a certain security and love that he obtains from no one else. If anything, the attachment of the young children to their parents is greater than it is in our own society. But this is irrelevant to the main consideration of this paper. Its purpose is to call attention to the fact that those functions of parents that constitute the *conditio sine qua non* for the existence of the "family"—the physical care and socialization of children—are not the functions of the *kibbutz* parents. It can only be concluded that in the absence of the economic and educational functions of the typical family, as well as of its characteristic of common residence, that the family does not exist in the *kibbutz*.

INTERPRETATION

It is apparent from this brief description of the kibbutz that most of the functions characteristic of the typical nuclear family have become the functions of the entire *kibbutz* society. This is so much the case that the *kibbutz* as a whole can almost satisfy the criteria by which Murdock defines the "family." This observation is not meant to imply that the *kibbutz* is a nuclear family. Its structure and that of the nuclear family are dissimilar. This observation does suggest, however, that the *kibbutz* can function without the family because it functions as if it, itself, were a family; and it can so function because its members perceive each other as kin, in the psychological implications of that term. The latter statement requires some explanation.

The members of the *kibbutz* do not view each other merely as fellow citizens, or as co-residents in a village, or as co-operators of an agricultural economy. Rather do they view each other as *chaverim*, or comrades, who comprise a group in which each is intimately related to the other, and in which the welfare of the one is bound up with the welfare of the other. This is a society in which the principle, "from each according to his ability, to each according to his needs," can be practised not because its members are more altruistic than the members of other societies, but because each member views his fellow as a kinsman, psychologically speaking. And just as a father in the family does not complain because he works much harder than his children, and yet he may receive no more, or even less, of the family income than they, so the *kibbutz* member whose economic productivity is high does not complain because he receives no more, and sometimes less, than a member whose productivity is low. This "principle" is taken for granted as the normal way of doing things. Since they are all *chaverim*, "it's all in the family," psychologically speaking.

In short, the *kibbutz* constitutes a *gemeinschaft*. Its patterns of interaction are interpersonal patterns; its ties are kin ties, without the biological tie of kinship. In this one respect it is the "folk society," in almost its pure form. The following quotation from Redfield (1947) could have been written with the *kibbutz* in mind, so accurately does it describe the social-psychological basis of *kibbutz* culture.

> The members of the folk society have a strong sense of belonging together. The group... see their own resemblances and feel correspondingly united. Communicating intimately with each other, each has a strong claim on the sympathies of the others [p. 297].... the personal and intimate life of the child in the family is extended, in the folk society, into the social world of the adults.... It is not merely that relations in such a society are personal; it is also that they are familial.... the result is a group of people among whom prevail the personal and categorized relationships that characterize families as we know them, and in which the patterns of kinship tend to be extended outward from the group of genealogically connected individuals into the whole society. The kin are the type persons for all experience [p. 301].

Hence it is that the bachelor and the childless "couple" do not feel that an injustice is being done them when they contribute to the support of the children of others. The children *in* the *kibbutz* are viewed as the children *of* the *kibbutz*. Parents (who are much more attached to their own children than they are to the children of others) and bachelors, alike, refer to all the *kibbutz* children as "our children."

The social perception of one's fellows as kin, psychologically speaking, is reflected in another important aspect of *kibbutz* behavior. It is a striking and significant fact that those individuals who were born and raised in the *kibbutz* tend to practise group exogamy, although there are no rules that either compel or encourage them to do so. Indeed, in the *kibbutz* in which our field work was carried out, all such individuals

married outside their own *kibbutz*. When they are asked for an explanation of this behavior, these individuals reply that they cannot marry those persons with whom they have been raised and whom they, consequently, view as siblings. This suggests, as Murdock has pointed out, that "the *kibbutz* to its members *is* viewed psychologically as a family to the extent that it generates the same sort of unconscious incest-avoidance tendencies" (private communication).

What is suggested by this discussion is the following proposition: although the *kibbutz* constitutes an exception to the generalization concerning the universality of the family, structurally viewed, it serves to confirm this generalization, functionally and psychologically viewed. In the absence of a specific social group—the family—to whom society delegates the functions of socialization, reproduction, etc., it has become necessary for the entire society to become a large extended family. But only in a society whose members perceive each other psychologically as kin can it function as a family. And there would seem to be a population limit beyond which point individuals are no longer perceived as kin. That point is probably reached when the interaction of its members is no longer face-to-face; in short, when it ceases to be a primary group. It would seem probable, therefore, that only in a "familial" society, such as the *kibbutz*, is it possible to dispense with the family.

References
Murdock, G. P.
  1949 Social structure. New York, Macmillan.
Redfield, R.
  1947 The folk society. The American Journal of Sociology 52:293–308.
Zborowski, M. and E. Herzog
  1952 Life is with people. New York, International Universities Press.

ADDENDUM, 1958

This is, quite obviously, an essay in the interpretation, rather than in the reporting of data. After rereading the paper in 1958, I realized that the suggested interpretation follows from only one conception of the role which definitions play in science. Starting with Murdock's inductive—based on a sample of 250 societies—definitions of marriage and family, I concluded that marriage and the family do not exist in the *kibbutz*, since no single group or relationship satisfies the conditions stipulated in the definitions. If I were writing this essay today, I would wish to explore alternative interpretations, as well—interpretations which, despite Murdock's definitions, would affirm the existence of marriage and the family in the *kibbutz*. Hence, I shall here very briefly outline the direction which one alternative interpretation would take.

The *kibbutz*, it should be noted first, does not practice—nor does it sanction—sexual promiscuity. Each adult member is expected to form a more-or-less permanent bisexual union; and this union is socially sanctioned by the granting of a joint room to the couple. The resulting relationship is different from any other adult relationship in the *kibbutz* in a number of significant features. (1) It alone includes common domicile for persons of opposite sex. (2) It entails a higher rate of interaction than is to be found in any other bisexual relationship. (3) It involves a higher degree of emotional intimacy than is to be found in any other relationship. (4) It establishes (ideally) an exclusive sexual relationship. (5) It leads to the deliberate decision to have children. These characteristics which, separately and severally, apply uniquely to this relationship, not only describe its salient features but also comprise the motives for those who enter into it. The couple, in short, viewed either objectively or phenomenologically, constitutes a unique social group in the *kibbutz*.

What, then, are we to make of this group? Since economic co-operation is not one of its features, we can, using Murdock's cross-cultural indices, deny that the relationship constitutes marriage. This is the conclusion of the foregoing paper. In retrospect, however, this conclusion does not leave me entirely satisfied. First, although we deny that the relationship constitutes a marriage, it nevertheless remains, both structurally and psychologically, a unique relationship within the *kibbutz*. Moreover, it is, with the exception of the economic variable, similar to those distinctive relationships in other societies to which the term marriage is applied. Hence, if I were writing this paper today, I should want to ask, before concluding that marriage is not universal, whether Murdock's inductive definition of marriage is, in the light of the *kibbutz* data, the most fruitful, even for his large sample; and if it were agreed that it is, whether it ought not to be changed or qualified so as to accommodate the relationship between *kibbutz* "spouses." Here I can only briefly explore the implications of these questions.

If the stated characteristics of the *kibbutz* relationship are found in the analogous relationship (marriage) in other societies—and I do not know that they are—it is surely apposite to ask whether Murdock's definition could not or should not stipulate them, as well as those already stipulated. For if they are found in other societies, on what theoretical grounds do we assign a higher priority to sex or economics over emotional intimacy, for example? Hence, if this procedure were adopted (and assuming that the characteristics of the

kibbutz relationship were to be found in the marriage relationship in other societies), we would, since the *kibbutz* relationship satisfies all but one of the cross-cultural criteria, term the *kibbutz* relationship "marriage."

Alternatively, we might suggest that Murdock's definition of marriage, as well as the one suggested here, are unduly specific; that cross-cultural research is most fruitfully advanced by means of analytic, rather than substantive or enumerative, definitions. Thus, for example, we might wish to define marriage as "any socially sanctioned relationship between nonsanguineally-related cohabiting adults of opposite sex which satisfied felt needs—mutual, symmetrical, or complementary." A non-enumerative definition of this type would certainly embrace all known cases now termed "marriage" and would, at the same time, include the *kibbutz* case as well.

In the same vein, and employing similar definitional procedures, alternative conclusions can be suggested with respect to the family in the *kibbutz*. Although parents and children do not comprise a family, as Murdock defines family, they nevertheless constitute a unique group within the *kibbutz*, regardless of the term with which we may choose to designate it. (1) Children are not only desired by *kibbutz* parents, but, for the most part, they are planned. (2) These children—and no others—are called by their parents "sons" and "daughters"; conversely, they call their parents—and no other adults—"father" and "mother." (3) Parents and children comprise a social group in both an interactional and an emotional, if not in a spatial, sense. That is, though parents and children do not share a common domicile, they are identified by themselves and by others as a uniquely cohesive unit within the larger *kibbutz* society; this unit is termed a *mishpacha* (literally, "family"). (4) The nature of their interaction is different from that which obtains between the children and any other set of adults. (5) The rate of interaction between parents and children is greater than that between the children and any other set of adults of both sexes. (6) The psychological ties that bind them are more intense than those between the children and any other set of adults of both sexes.

Here, then, we are confronted with the same problem we encountered with respect to the question of *kibbutz* marriage. Because the parent-child relationship in the *kibbutz* does not entail a common domicile, physical care, and social rearing—three of the stipulated conditions in Murdock's definition of family—we concluded that the family does not exist in the *kibbutz*. But, since parents and children comprise a distinct and differentiated social group within the *kibbutz*, I am now not entirely satisfied with a conclusion which seems, at least by implication, to ignore its presence. For, surely, regardless of what else we might do with this group, we cannot simply ignore it. We can either perceive it, in cross-cultural perspective, as a unique group, and invent a new term to refer to it, or we can revise Murdock's definition of family in order to accommodate it.

Should the latter alternative be preferred, it could be effected in the following way. The stipulation of "common residence" could be qualified to refer to a reference, rather than to a membership, residence; and this is what the parental room is, for children as well as parents. When, for example, they speak of "my room" or "our room," the children almost invariably refer to the parental room, not to their room in the communal children's house. If, moreover, the educational and economic functions of the family were interpreted as responsibilities for which parents were either immediately or ultimately responsible, the *kibbutz* parent-child unit would satisfy these criteria as well. For, though parents do not provide immediately for the physical care of their children, neither do they renounce their responsibility for them. Rather, they seek to achieve this end by working jointly rather than separately for the physical welfare of all the children—including, of course, their own.

Similarly, though the parents have only a minor share in the formal socialization process, they do not simply give their children to others to be raised as the latter see fit. Rather, socialization is entrusted to specially designated representatives, nurses and teachers, who rear children, not according to their own fancy, but according to rules and procedures established by the parents. In short, though parents do not themselves socialize their children, they assume the ultimate responsibility for their socialization. Interpreted in this way, the relationship between *kibbutz* parents and children satisfies Murdock's definition of family.

To conclude, this addendum represents an alternative method of interpreting the *kibbutz* data concerning the relationship between spouses, and among parents and children. I am not suggesting that this interpretation is necessarily more fruitful than the one adopted in the paper. Certainly, however, I should want to examine it carefully before concluding, as I previously did, that marriage and the family are not universal.

24

Fission in an Amazonian Tribe

BY NAPOLEON A. CHAGNON

. . . .

FOR MILLIONS OF YEARS our ancestors passed their lives in small groups that generally ranged in size from about a dozen individuals to no more than 200. The local, day-to-day groupings of the remaining primitive societies fall within that range, and studies of our own closest relatives in the animal world, the monkeys and apes, suggest that our primate ancestors also lived in social groups whose size stayed between what one anthropologist calls the "magic numbers," i.e. from 40 or 50 individuals to about 200. At this upper extreme, both the human and animal populations fission into two or more groups.

Anthropologists who concern themselves with tribal population size and distribution generally attempt to relate population to resource availability—water, game animals, cultivable land—and try to explain the population patterns in terms of these material needs. Thus, the focus has been on general ecological relationships between man and environment, between a region's "carrying capacity" and the actual numbers of exploiters. But why should there be ten communities of 100 people rather than one community of 1,000?

Most anthropologists would tend to assume, at least for egalitarian primitive societies, that it is ecologically more efficient for the population to subdivide into ten smaller groups than remain as a single, large nucleated group. Egalitarian societies, however, are organized along principles of kinship, marriage and descent from common ancestors. It is beginning to look as if there are intrinsic limits to the size which such groups can grow to when their organization consists of only those three principles.

Recent studies have shown the great significance that kinship recognition plays in non-human primate societies. Monkeys can recognize their relatives and, just like human beings, behave in very predictable, characteristic ways towards different categories of relative. Moreover, the organization of some of the well studied monkey societies is very much a matter of kinship ties; the fissioning of monkey troops, remarkably enough, shows very striking parallels to what happens in egalitarian societies that fission. One recent study in Japan revealed that a large troop of monkeys was organized into sixteen "matrilines," each consisting of an old female, her offspring and the offspring of her daughters. The troop was heavily provisioned and had no food limitation checking its growth. As the troop got larger, internal order began breaking down and the group fissioned into two new troops, the eight highest ranking matrilines forming one troop and the eight lowest ranking matrilines forming the other.

This is essentially the same pattern of fissioning I have found in 48 months spent in the egalitarian society of the Yąnomamö Indians of southern Venezuela and adjacent portions of Brazil. The area is vast and characterized by abundant resources, and the Yąnamamö population is growing and fissioning. The data considered here is mainly genealogical; some five generations deep, it encompasses approximately 3,500 individuals (about half of whom are dead) and approximately 1,600 marriages. Additionally, I have informants' accounts of population fissioning during the past 100 years, which led to the emergence of some dozen or so villages.

Nobody knows for certain how many Yąnomamö villages there are, or how many people comprise the total population. Large areas of the tribe have never been visited or studied, so we can only make a calculated estimate of the total population. During the course of our field research, my French colleague Jacques Lizot and I visited at least 100 villages and made detailed censuses on many of them. Putting our data together and estimating the sizes of the uncontacted groups, we come up with an estimate of about 15,000 Yąnomanö in total.

The Yąnomamö can be described as a "tribe" in the

Reprinted by permission from *The Sciences*, January/February 1976. © 1976 by The New York Academy of Sciences.

following anthropological sense. Although they have no precise notion of their unity as a people, they can recognize another Yąnomamö by his or her language. Thus, the term tribe is more a linguistic notion than anything else: it does not imply any organization of a political kind that binds village to village.

The Yąnomamö language, incidentally, has not been demonstrably related to any other South American Indian language, attesting to the Yąnomamö's long separation and isolation from their neighbors. Like many primitive peoples, their word for human being is the word they use to describe themselves. Yąnomamö implies purity, if not superiority; all other people are "nabä" (foreigners, near human), potential enemies and somewhat degenerate forms of the "true" people.

The most significant social entity for the Yąnomamö is the village, a circular open structure with a cleared plaza at the center. Individual families live around the periphery of the village, under the common circular roof. There is no partitioning between households and almost everyone can hear and see almost everyone else in the village, so daily (and nightly) life is very public. Individuals know all the members of their village and are closely related to most of them. The villages range in size, as with the tribal world in general, from about 40 people to a maximum of about 250 people.

Village cohesion and social order derive mainly from the ties of kinship and the mutual obligations that stem from these ties. Daily life, economics, politics, religion and cooperation are embedded in and consequently affected by the ethical, moral and behavioral bonds inhering in kinship. There is no "economy" in a market sense: all exchanges are between kinsmen and "price" or "value" as we know it affect the transactions no more than they do within our own domestic households. Exchanges are first and foremost a component in transactions between kinsmen.

Nobody in such a community can escape the pervasive influence of the kinship system, not even the anthropologist. When I visit each village, I, too, must be incorporated into the system so that the individual residents know who I am and how to treat me. Since the headman, or leader, of the village usually has the largest number of kinsmen, I normally "relate" to him, usually by calling him "shoriwä," the Yąnomamö word that translates loosely into "brother-in-law" and "male cross-cousin."

This is a particularly affectionate relationship among the Yąnomamö. Thus, when I call the headman "shoriwä," it immediately establishes us as potential exchangers of women: I could marry the headman's sisters and he could marry mine. Furthermore, our children could marry each other, creating additional and important social bonds between us and our respective groups. As brothers-in-law we owe each other special services and must show generosity in our mutual dealings. If I have possessions the headman wants, I must give them to him—and vice-versa.

Being related to the headman of the village as brother-in-law also relates me to everyone else in the village; each person knows how he or she is related to the headman and it is a simple matter to do a little kinship arithmetic to figure out how one is related to the headman's brother-in-law. Thus, with the kin term "shoriwä" I become related to everyone in the village, and everyone knows how to behave with me. I become by extension the brother of the headman's wife, the mother's brother of his children, etc.

The villagers know that I am not really related to the headman, but the adoption of the kinship usage is the only basis for social interaction that exists. Within their own social system, villagers make very sharp and invidious distinctions. Some co-villagers are "better" than others and more trustworthy, and people in the next village over are always less trustworthy since they are less related. In this regard, the Yąnomamö operate in pretty much the same way we do when we deal with our own kin. We normally delight in a weekend visit from our parents or grandparents, but if a remote cousin and his family is passing through town and shows up for the weekend we are not likely to be so enthusiastic.

Each village may have several kinship groups of patrilineally related individuals; the oldest males in these groups will usually be politically prominent and represent the village in its dealings with other groups. The headman usually comes from the largest kinship group. It is as if a village were comprised of three or four large families—the Smiths, Joneses, Blacks and Greenes. The headman of the Smith family, "Smitty," has slightly more authority than the other heads of families.

Smitty and his family remain dependent on the others, however, especially for marriageable women; all the families are often bound together by several generations of reciprocal marriage exchanges. Smitty and his brothers (and their sons) might get wives from the Greenes and Blacks, for example, and give their sisters and daughters in return. The Yąnomamö marriage system contributes significantly to social solidarity by structuring first the kinds of kinship patterns that result from marriage and reproduction, and second the relative numbers of various types of genealogically specified marriages (such as the number of mother's brother's daughters' marriages vs. the number of father's sister's daughters').

The desire to obtain wives is very great among most of the men—the more wives the better. However, this is rather difficult. First, the Yanomamö practice infanticide and kill more girls than boys. (When I point out that what they are doing will cause a shortage of marriageable females, they optimistically assert that with all those male babies they didn't kill, the village will become powerful and they can raid their neighbors for women!) Second, if some men are successful at acquiring many wives, then other men must go without wives. Although they may resign themselves to this fate, it becomes a serious problem in village life as the unmarried men persistently attempt to seduce the other men's wives. Most of the internal village squabbles begin with arguments and disputes over women.

A fission is usually the result of gradually accumulating strife and tension within the village: as the group gets larger and its composition becomes more complex, squabbles and fights grow in frequency. Finally, the village can no longer be held together by the ties of kinship, marriage obligations and the tenuous authority of the headman. Any fight or dispute might be the spark that touches off a division of the village.

The "Browns," for example, decide to move off, taking with them their children and their children's spouses (Joneses, Blacks and Greenes). The people who leave the group will be more closely related among themselves than they are to the ones who remain behind. The two new villages might remain on relatively peaceful terms with each other, but they could enter into hostilities as their populations grow and each is better able to fend for itself in war and politics. However, if the original group had a large number of enemies before it fissioned, members of both new groups know that it would be unwise to be too independent. Otherwise, their common enemies might attack each of the groups and destroy them. In such a situation the new groups might simply build two separate villages a few hundred feet apart, pursuing increasingly independent strategies as extra-village political pressures permit.

Over time, the two villages themselves would grow and fission, and the resulting new villages would disperse even further. In this fashion a whole area—a river drainage, for example—might come to have six or eight independent villages, all descended from the same original group. Each village would have people who are related, however remotely, to the members of other villages in the same river drainage.

One cannot live among the Yanomamö for very long before realizing that if they had a choice in the matter, the villages would fission into even smaller entities—a few families—within which life would be very pleasant and happy. I have frequently heard the Yanomamö comment, "We split up into two groups because we were many and therefore always fighting among ourselves." What keeps the village from fissioning into tiny units? It appears to be the subtle pressures of the warfare system.

As is the situation with internal village fights, wars between villages usually begin in a contest over the possession of some woman. In almost every case in which I attempted to get at the cause of a particular war, the Yanomamö would look at me quizzically and hiss contemptuously: "Don't ask such stupid questions! Women! Women! Women! That's what started it! We fought over women!" The mortality rate in their wars, I might add, is staggering. In some areas as many as 30 per cent of the adult male deaths are attributable to warfare.

At the lower end of the village size scale—in the range of 40 to 60 people—warfare tactics and raiding strategies dictate that a village must contain approximately ten able-bodied men between the ages of 17 and 40. The age and sex distribution of the population require that a village must have about 40 members in order for there to be that many adult males capable of effective raiding. Therefore, a village rarely fissions until it reaches a size of about 80 inhabitants, i.e. until it reaches a size at which a fission will yield two viable villages of about 40 members.

Where warfare is particularly intense, a growing village of 80 to 100 people will probably not fission, since two smaller villages would be more vulnerable to raids than a single, larger village. Still, if a group of 150 is advantageous in the warfare system, why don't some villages grow even larger and have even more advantage? The answer to that question seems to be the limitations on organizational capacity imposed by kinship and marriage.

As most villages grow they make political alliances with other villages and exchange women with them. Young men from other villages may also move in, hoping to obtain wives. Their presence reduces the general amount of relatedness within the group. Over time, as the newcomers marry and reproduce, the composition of the village becomes more complex and the possibility for new alliance patterns increases: women can be given to create these alliances instead of to consolidate old ones. The more complex a village is, the greater the chance of sexual intrigues and, therefore, of arguments and disputes.

The conditions under which a new village is formed are crucial to its ability to grow larger. Suppose that a village is formed by twelve adults and their offspring—six men and six women who each have one spouse and several children. If the adults are not brothers and sisters, each man will be the "founder" of his own lineage; the village will have six small patrilineages at the outset, each attempting to get women from the other five. The amount and kinds of kinship and marriage interrelationships possible among their descendants will be relatively small.

Compare this to another situation in which two "families" of three brothers and three sisters each found a village. If the oldest brother of each family married all three sisters in the other family, we would have two large local descent groups whose members are very closely related to each other. Moreover, the grandchildren of the original founders would all be cousins (cross and parallel) to each other, and the cross-cousins could marry. Indeed it would be impossible to marry someone who is not a cross-cousin.

It is possible to measure the closeness of relationship between any pair of related individuals in a society by using genealogical data and a statistic known as the inbreeding coefficient. Technically the inbreeding coefficient specifies the probability that an individual will inherit, through both parents, a particular gene (allele) from some common ancestor. The statistic therefore makes it possible for anthropologists to discuss the terms "close kin" and "distant kin" objectively.

I have, with the aid of the computer, calculated these values among all 3,500 people in my sample and can characterize any village by an average amount of genealogical relationship obtaining between all possible pairs of individuals in the village. The data show that in very large villages, there is a correlation between village size and amount of relatedness in the population. The villages whose founders had a greater degree of relatedness tend to grow larger.

Since those villages that manage to grow particularly large have higher-than-usual frequencies of cross-cousin marriage, the amount of polygyny in the founding group seems to be significant in regard to village size. The effects of polygyny can be particularly dramatic in some of the Yąnomamö population blocs. In one bloc I studied, one founder had 45 children by eight wives. A number of his sons were also remarkably successful at acquiring spouses and, therefore, in producing large families: one of them had 33 children. Considering the population bloc as a whole (some six or seven villages), approximately 75 per cent of all the residents were descended from the one founder!

Given the explicitly stated desire of the Yąnomamö to live in smaller groups, it seems likely that military pressure is responsible for the fact that villages grow to 100 or 150 people, as it is for the minimum population size of 40. But whether villages grow to 200 or 250 depends on the nature of the marriage patterns and the amount of kinship relatedness that the group begins with and preserves as it grows. If there has been a modest amount of predatory or inter-group military pressure throughout the long history of human beings, then it would seem reasonable that there has been an advantage to maximizing group size. The data on the Yąnomamö suggests that there has likewise been a persistent tendency to arrange close marriages and to concentrate kinship relatedness as well. Thus, a significant amount of "inbreeding" may have been characteristic of the mating/marriage arrangement of *Homo sapiens* as a species.

25

Marriage as Warfare

BY CHARLES LINDHOLM AND CHERRY LINDHOLM

The rapid beating of the war drums reverberates along the narrow winding streets of a Pakhtun village, isolated in the remote mountain valley of Swat in northwestern Pakistan. However, it is not a battle that the drums are heralding. It is a marriage.

The Yusufzai Pakhtun of Swat are members of the great Pakhtun (or Pathan) tribe, which dominates Afghanistan and northern Pakistan. They have long been famous for their aggressive daring and bravery in warfare, their fiery pride and individualism, and their refusal to accept defeat or domination. Historically, they have always been the conquerors, never the conquered.

The nomadic Yusufzai migrated to the fertile valley of Swat from Kabul in the early sixteenth century. After defeating the local population and reducing them to landless servants, the Yusufzai settled down and became small farmers (any Yusufzai Pakhtun who lost his land joined the despised servant class and was stripped of his rights and his honor as a Pakhtun). In the nineteenth century the Swat Pakhtun won the admiration of the British for their successful resistance to colonial invasion, and they acceded to Pakistan only when assured of local autonomy. Even today, the valley of Swat is relatively free from the influence of the state, and order is maintained by personal strength and the force of custom.

Swat's climate is suitable for double cropping (wheat and clover in the spring, rice and corn in the fall), and the sparkling Swat River, which bisects the valley, provides an adequate water supply. There is an extensive irrigation system, and the hillsides are well terraced. But despite the lush appearance of the valley, overpopulation has placed a terrible strain on the resource base, and competition for control of land is fierce and sometimes deadly. Innumerable bloody battles have been waged since the Yusufzai established their rule in Swat.

Inside her house, a girl of twelve, hearing the war drums' energetic tattoo, cowers in fear on a string cot. She cries silently behind the folds of her voluminous embroidered shawl, while her relatives gather about her, their faces long and mournful. Even the bright luster of the girl's golden jewelry does little to alleviate the atmosphere of tension and distress in the household.

The girl on the cot is the new bride, and she and her family are waiting for the moment when she must leave her natal home forever and take up residence in her husband's house. The use of the war drums for a wedding is actually far from ludicrous, for marriage in Swat is very much like a prolonged combat and is recognized as such by both men and women. The relationship resembles that between two opposing countries where an ever present cold war frequently erupts into skirmishes and open conflict.

During our nine-month stay in a Swat village in 1977, we witnessed such relationships firsthand. With our twelve-year-old daughter, we lived with a Pakhtun family in three small rooms that had been constructed on the roof of their house. As friends, guests, and adopted relatives, we were accepted into the life of the village with the warmhearted generosity and hospitality for which the Pakhtun are deservedly renowned.

This remarkable hospitality, combined with an idealized notion of male friendship, is one of the three cornerstones of *Pakhtunwali*, the Pakhtun code of honor, the other two being refuge and blood revenge. This code is older than Islam and often supersedes Islamic tenets. For example, Islam allows divorce, *Pakhtunwali* does not; also, sometimes a man will swear falsely, his hand on the Holy Koran, in order to save a friend.

Although the Pakhtun are strict Sunni Muslims, they derive their identity and self-respect from the zealous observance of *Pakhtunwali*, land ownership, and tight control over women by means of a rigorous system of purdah (female seclusion). The worst insult one can offer a man is to call him *begherata*, man without honor. This pejorative has three meanings: someone who is lazy and weak, someone who has lost his land, and someone who has no control over his women. To the proud Pakhtun, loss of honor is worse than death, since it renders him unworthy of the name "Pakhtun."

The Pakhtun's liberal hospitality is generally demonstrated on the stage of the *hujera*, or men's house, where the guest is enthusiastically welcomed, made comfortable on a cot with fat cushions behind his head, served tea and the best food available, and showered with his proud host's unstinting attentions. To entertain a guest is a great honor, and the host will spare no effort to make the occasion as lavish and enjoyable as possible. Nor is this ritualized hospitality mere etiquette or a means of swelling the host's self-esteem. The warm friendliness that accompanies the ritual is genuine, deeply felt, and extremely moving. In the *hujera*, the violent Pakhtun of the battlefield, who will fight to the death for his land, for someone else's land, or to avenge any slight on his honor, becomes the epitome of cordiality, gentle dignity, and brotherly affection.

This metamorphosis is not altogether surprising. In a society where survival depends upon a man's physical and psychological toughness, there is little chance to express such emotions as affection and tenderness. The guest in the *hujera* fulfills in ritual fashion the role of the idealized friend who, according to one Pakhtun proverb,

"without invitation, will assure me of his love." This dream of the perfect friend, always a man, which has been honored in countless proverbs and poems over the centuries, is the beloved fantasy of every Pakhtun male. The friend, however, must necessarily be a stranger, for all Swat Pakhtun are, by the very nature of their harsh and competitive society, rivals and potential enemies. Naturally, given these qualifications, friendship in Swat is very rare indeed. Yet the dream persists and is acted out in the rite of hospitality whenever the opportunity arises.

In sharp contrast to the romantic image of the friend and public display of hospitality, the Pakhtun's domestic

arena, concealed behind the impenetrable walls of the purdah household, is the site of confrontations more akin to those of the battlefield.

As the drumming grows louder, the trembling bride remembers her mother's advice for a successful marriage: "You must keep power over your husband. Always speak first when he enters, even if only to cough. Sleep with your hand behind his head. Then he will miss you and never be satisfied with any other."

The girl prays that her husband will like her and that he will not humiliate her and her family by taking a second wife. That would be the worst possible catastrophe. She is of a good family and her family pride is strong.

Now the time has come for her to leave. She clutches at the cot, but her elder brother pulls her hands free and lifts her onto the palanquin that will carry her to her husband's house. The embroidered cover is dropped into place, and the girl is carried into the narrow street. Men of the husband's house are waiting to join the procession. They help with the palanquin and triumphantly bounce it about. Village boys line the route and throw stones, hoping to overturn the bride into the muddy alley. In the past, serious fights sometimes erupted because of injuries caused by this ritual stoning, but in recent years the violence has lessened.

The procession continues through the village, led by the men carrying the bride and followed by a supply of household goods from her father's house. The drums of the groom are now heard as the procession approaches his compound. Men of his family gleefully fire their rifles, and small boys toss sweets to the crowd from the low rooftops. The drumming reaches a crescendo as the party enters the groom's house. This is a tense moment. Sometimes, the groom's family tries to deny entry to the men of the bride's party, and a fight breaks out. But today everything goes smoothly, and men of both houses carry the palanquin into the inner courtyard.

Strong hands lift the bride onto a cot in the corner of the single room where she will live with her husband. The men then leave the house to begin feasting in the *hujera*. Totally enclosed in her shawl, the new bride presses

In a Swat village, a palanquin transports a bride to her new home.

Cherry Lindholm

tightly to her chest the Koran her father has given her. The women of the household surround her, talking incessantly and cajoling her to show her face. A young girl begins the drumbeat for women, and the groom's female relatives start dancing in the courtyard, celebrating the newcomer's arrival. Later, they will give her money, and in return, she will bow before them and touch their feet in token of future subservience. But, for the moment, the bride remains motionless on the cot. She will stay in this position for three days, rising only to relieve herself. On the third night her husband will creep into the house to consummate the marriage.

While the bride huddles nervously in her new home, the groom, a green-eyed man of twenty-five, is fingering his mustache in the *hujera* of a relative, a different *hujera* from the one where the feasting is taking place. He is not permitted to join in the festivities of the marriage but must hide in shame at losing his bachelor status. Twenty years ago, young grooms sometimes ran away from their home villages and had to be coaxed back to their wives. But men's shame is no longer so acute. In those days, all men slept in the *hujera* and only slipped out to visit their wives secretly at night. Women also were shyer then, and a man might not see his wife's face for a year or more. But nowadays, with the curtailment of warfare and the weakening of the village khans, or leaders, most men sleep at home with their wives.

The groom is speculating about his new wife's appearance. He has never seen her, but he has heard reports that she is light skinned and fat—an ideal beauty. His own sexual experience has been with boys his own age who played the passive role and with girls of the servant class. For him, sexual dominance is an expression of power. He hopes that the youth and innocence of his bride will render her docile and respectful. However, he fears that the marriage will be a contentious one. That is how all marriages end up. "It is because our women are no good," he muses.

For two more nights the groom stays in the *hujera*, pretending indifference to his marriage. Then, on the third night, he steals into his family's compound and opens the door of the room where his bride is waiting. He is slightly inebriated from smoking hashish. She is unveiled and afraid to look at him. Sometimes, the groom finds his bride repulsive and cannot have sex with her. Or he may have been enchanted by a male lover and rendered incapable of heterosexual intercourse. The bride has no recourse, for Pakhtun marriage is a lifetime contract. Moreover, the wife even follows her husband to heaven or hell, so that they are united for eternity.

In the room adjoining the nuptial chamber, the groom's sisters have bored a hole in the wall and are spying on the couple. The groom gives the girl a gold watch and some sweets. He begins to caress and tease her, but she is too terrified to respond, and the sexual act is rough and hasty. Thus the couple enter into married life.

The giving of a woman in marriage is a touchy business for the Swat Pakhtun. Historically, a weak lineage gave women to its stronger neighbors in order to form alliances, and victors in war expressed their triumph by taking women from the conquered. As a result, there is the suggestion that the wife givers are inferior to the wife takers—and any hint of inferiority is intolerable to a Pakhtun. Hostility toward marriage as an institution is seen in the ritual stoning of the bride's palanquin and in the fights between the bride's party and the groom's party. If divorce were allowed, no marriage would last for long.

The groom feels shame at his marriage because every Pakhtun man, not unlike the mythical American cowboy, seeks to present himself as completely self-reliant, independent, and free of obligation. But the cowboy can always reject home and family and ride away into the sunset—an option the Pakhtun man does not have. Instead, he effectively hides his wife inside the privacy of the purdah household. Her presence is known to an outsider only through the tea she prepares. The Pakhtun woman must never be seen by men who are not close family members. She must never leave the compound walls without her husband's permission. By remaining a virtual prisoner inside her husband's house, she helps to uphold his honor, for she is a part of all he possesses and her behavior is a direct reflection of his power and control.

Years ago, if a Pakhtun woman was seen by a man who was not her relative, her enraged husband would cut off her nose as a punishment and as a means of cleansing his family honor, which her carelessness had sullied. While this custom has been abandoned, severe beatings are common. And a woman found alone with a man who is not a relative has committed a killing offense, for it will be assumed that the liaison is sexual. In such a case, although the husband may not actually desire her death, the pressure of public opinion, the code of *Pakhtunwali*, which demands vengeance, and his own sense of acute shame, would all push him to take action.

Because they are able to dishonor men, women are feared. On the other hand, the woman has only physical violence to fear from her husband. Even more than the male, she is accustomed to violence from childhood. Her personal pride is far more powerful than her fear of a beating. Although she is a prisoner in her husband's house, her position is in some ways stronger than his, for she holds the weaponry for his dishonoring, whereas he holds merely a stick with which to beat her. While the wife must live with her jailer, the husband is obliged to share his house with an enemy—and an extremely tenacious and able one.

Marriage thus begins as a hostile relationship. The young bride's apprehension and the groom's shame accompany the determination of each to dominate the other. Pakhtun marriage demands a precarious balance of power, and the young partners are ready from the start to fight each other to avoid being dominated and shamed.

It is now a year after the marriage—the bride has her place within her husband's household. In her eyes, she is treated like a slave. Her mother-in-law is impossibly demanding; the girl can do nothing right. Her husband takes no notice of her beyond the servicing of his sexual needs. Recently, she has begun having fits in which she is possessed by demons. During these fits, she rolls in the dirt and must be restrained from throwing herself into the well or the fire. From her mouth, demonic voices hurl abuse at her husband

and his family. Exorcisms by a holy man, who puts sticks between her fingers and squeezes her hand painfully, are only temporarily effective. Finally, her father is asked to intervene. "If this happens again," he warns her, "I'll shoot you." The demons stop appearing.

Shortly afterward, she gives birth to a son, and her position in her husband's household improves. She is now respected, for she has contributed to perpetuating her husband's line. But her relations with her mother-in-law continue to be as unpleasant as ever.

As time goes by, the marriage proves to be as difficult as the young groom feared. Fighting goes on daily, over the wife's poorly made milk curd or over a piece of rotten meat the husband has foolishly purchased. The husband may strike out because his wife is nagging him to buy another piece of jewelry that she can show off to her neighbor; the wife may be irate because the husband, in a display of generosity, has depleted the family larder. Anything can cause a serious fight, and several times the bruised wife returns, with injured pride, to her father's house. There she is pampered by her relatives for a time, but she must go back to her husband upon his demand. She returns, and the fights continue.

Like all Pakhtun husbands, he severely beats his wife to break her of bad habits and make her submissive. The young woman nonetheless remains proud and fearless; far from becoming meek, she defends herself aggressively, clawing at her husband's face and tearing the shirt from his back. He strikes out, especially at her face, and sometimes uses a club or throws a stone at her. This is considered perfectly normal, and the wife is even somewhat proud of her battle scars. She abuses her elder sister's husband, who rarely hits his wife, as "a man with no penis." Yet her own husband fares no better, as she frequently calls curses down upon him and abuses his lineage: "Your ancestor was nothing and my ancestor was great!"

The husband, becoming wearied with the constant effort to subdue and control his defiant female adversary, dreams of defeating her once and for all by bringing in another, more tractable wife. He frequently threatens her

with this ultimate humiliation, but is unable to implement his plan because he lacks funds. Despite the proverb that "a fool can be recognized by his two wives," most men dream of a second marriage. Those few who can afford it, however, inevitably regret it, for with the arrival of a second wife, warfare begins in earnest. Each woman seeks, with magical spells and sheer contentiousness, to drive the other out. Sometimes, one wife will poison the other or, more commonly, the husband; sometimes the husband's throat is slit while he sleeps. The first wife continually badgers the husband to bring in yet a third wife, in order to humiliate the second wife as she has been humiliated. The besieged husband, who has found the second wife as irritating as the first, futilely wishes he could turn back the clock.

Although they continue to squabble, the husband and wife are actually quite fond of each other. Each admires the other's resolute pride and fighting ability. But the man cannot show his affection, for to do so would give the wife courage to dishonor him. A man who displays affection to his wife is indicating weakness, which the woman will immediately exploit in the battle for domination. She may begin leaving the house without permission, confident that the loving husband will not punish her. Then she will start having affairs with other men, thoroughly dishonoring her weakling spouse. Therefore, a man must avoid laughing with his wife or showing her any tenderness, in spite of his feelings for her. "Instead of a kiss, he gives me a bite," says the wife, baring her teeth. But if he did give her a kiss, she would begin to feel he had become emasculated.

The husband carries his feigned indifference to his wife into public life, never mentioning her to his friends. Nor do they inquire after her; to do so would be a breach of etiquette. Instead, they merely ask him, "How is your house?"

The wife is not so constrained. Confined to the compound, she spends much of her time complaining to visitors, to servants, and even to her children about the activities of her husband. Gossip about the wrongdoings of their men is the major subject of women's conversations. "All Swat

men are rotten," they say. That is the nature of men. The wife's solace is hearing the tribulations of other women and anticipating the power she will wield in her later years. By that time, her husband will be a tired old man, without the energy for fighting, her sons will be grown, and their wives will be living in her house under her rule. She will control her domestic sphere like a real matriarch, and the purdah compound, her former prison, will become her court. Indeed, the Western image of the docile purdah female is an inaccurate picture of the Pakhtun woman of Swat.

This story is representative of the marriage relations among the Yusufzai Pakhtun. Perhaps a particular couple will fight less than usual because of extraordinary meekness or compatibility. Fortunate couples may reach a sort of wary, joking understanding in old age. But, in general, the marriage relation is one of strife, violence, and struggle.

This pattern of hostility and rivalry derives from the social model of the society, which is technically termed a segmentary lineage system. This means that the Yusufzai Pakhtun trace themselves, through the male line, to a common ancestor, Yusuf, the progenitor of the entire clan. All consider themselves equal, and all have rights in the family land. Despite this ideology of equality, however, those who are strong force the weak from their land. To be a landless Pakhtun is to lose one's birthright and become a member of the servant class. Thus, each family seeks to protect itself and subordinate others.

Life in the Yusufzai village is largely a contest to determine dominance. A man's chief rival is his father's brother's son, who has a claim on the land of the common grandfather. This cousin is often one's in-law as well, since marriage with the father's brother's daughter is greatly favored in Swat. By marrying their female patrilineal cousin, the Yusufzai hope to gain control over their main political rival, but to no avail, since such marriages are notoriously hostile.

The term for the father's brother's son is *tarbur*, a word that means enemy. But the *tarbur* is also an ally, for only he can be counted upon to come to one's aid in case of an attack by a more genealogically distant adversary. Groupings occur on the basis of patrilineal kinship and only take place when there is an external threat. When the British attacked them, the Yusufzai Pakhtun forgot their internal enmities and united to expel the invader.

In this system, men constantly maneuver for power and honor. Loyalties shift easily. As one family becomes strong, others unite against it. Some families rise, but are soon torn apart by internal dissension. As the modern Pakhtun writer Ghani Khan has observed, "The Pakhtun have not become a great nation because a man would rather burn his house than see his elder brother rule it."

In such an environment, a martial air and genuine willingness to fight are absolute necessities for survival. Even hospitality, the most loving relationship found in the society, is tinged with rivalry, as hosts express their strength and dominance through lavish entertainment. The assertion of one's own pride and the denigration of other lineages is therefore the primary emotional stance of the Pakhtun. This stance is not confined to men. The women also consider all men not of their patrilineage to be of inferior quality. Every marriage is thus with an inferior, and the partners are well prepared to fight each other to uphold the honor of their respective houses.

Although the husband tries to ignore his wife, she refuses to be overlooked. Her own pride, instilled by her lineage, demands that she assert herself. The woman's place is in the house, however—patrilineal descent prevents her from inheriting land or from participating in struggles over land. Where a man's pride and identity rest in his landholdings, her honor is found in vindicating her superiority in the household. The bruises that inevitably result she regards as marks of honor. If her health is good, if she can avoid being expelled by another wife, and if she has sons, her struggle is likely to end in victory. The aging husband, beset by rivals on all sides, and even besieged by his own sons demanding their share of his land, will accept his wife's rule in exchange for relative peace in the compound.

Small wonder that the Pakhtun man dreams of the mythical friend. This dream, and the ritual of hospitality in which it finds expression, derives from the stern social order, which sets every man against every other, and which prevents any amicable relationship within the family. Deprived of any real opportunity to be affectionate and generous, the Pakhtun male releases these suppressed feelings in the rite of hospitality.

Women, on the other hand, have no great interest in hospitality, although they cook for guests for the sake of their own pride. Unlike the man, who seeks to dominate in a world of opponents, the woman strives only to dominate in the house. The man's goal is impossible, but the woman's is fairly attainable. Women are also united in a community of complaint against their husbands. They do not engage in life and death struggles over land, and in consequence, their enmities are less deep than the men's. Despite the travails and bruises of marriage, women tend to succeed in their goals, while men spend their time pursuing a chimera of friendship.

Politics and Social Control

· ·

All societies have means of molding their members' behavior to conform to group values (general orientations toward "good" and "bad," "right" and "wrong") and group norms (specific expectations of behavior depending on who the actor is and the social context in which the behavior is taking place). Anthropologists call such means the mechanisms of social control, and they distinguish between internal means and external means.

Internal means of control rely on the individual's personal acceptance—through enculturation and socialization—of his or her culture's values and norms. In other words, the individual will feel uncomfortable when the moral order of the society is violated and, therefore, will be motivated not to transgress the society's moral code or expectations. External means of control are the responses of the society or its representatives to specific actions—either to reinforce (reward) them or to diminish the likelihood of their repetition by the culprit or by others. The former, reinforcing responses, are termed *positive sanctions*. The latter, punishments, are termed *negative sanctions*. Internalized values and norms, together with positive and negative sanctions, operate in all societies. However, there is enormous cross-cultural variation in the behaviors that are reinforced or punished and in the specific forms that the means of social control take.

One of the critical issues with regard to social control is which individual or groups within a society have access to its mechanisms outside the family unit. For social control is a primary function of all political systems—that is, those social institutions organizing the application of power to the solution of public problems. (Power, after all, is the ability to compel others to do what one wants them to, and the mechanisms of social control are central to this understanding.) In "Poor Man, Rich Man, Big-Man, Chief," Marshall Sahlins compares and contrasts Melanesian and Polynesian forms of political authority and discovers that the critical factor in each is the degree to which political institutions can control the economies (production and consumption) of individual households.

In "Cannibalistic Revenge in Jalé Warfare," Klaus-Friedrich Koch examines intervillage feuding and its by-product—ritualistic cannibalism—as a means (among other things) to channel aggressive behavior into culturally acceptable patterns. Here, internalized means of social control seem quite prominent.

In "A New Weapon Stirs up Old Ghosts," W. E. Mitchell examines the interplay between internal and external means of control. The belief in ghosts promoted village harmony among the Wape of New Guinea, and quarreling was believed to result in ghostly revenge: poor hunting would plague the culprits. So long as individuals hunted for themselves and their own families with bows and arrows, such quarrels could remain private issues. But the introduction of guns in limited numbers made their new owners increasingly responsible for feeding whole villages. Private quarrels thus became public scandals, and public sanctions had to be invoked to deal with unprecedented situations. The article leaves us unsure of the outcome of this induced stress on a previously well-functioning system of social control.

26

Poor Man, Rich Man, Big-Man, Chief

BY MARSHALL D. SAHLINS

. . . .

With an eye to their own life goals, the native peoples of Pacific Islands unwittingly present to anthropologists a generous scientific gift: an extended series of experiments in cultural adaptation and evolutionary development. They have compressed their institutions within the confines of infertile coral atolls, expanded them on volcanic islands, created with the means history gave them cultures adapted to the deserts of Australia, the mountains and warm coasts of New Guinea, the rain forests of the Solomon Islands. From the Australian Aborigines, whose hunting and gathering existence duplicates in outline the cultural life of the later Paleolithic, to the great chiefdoms of Hawaii, where society approached the formative levels of the old Fertile Crescent civilizations, almost every general phase in the progress of primitive culture is exemplified.

Where culture so experiments, anthropology finds its laboratories — makes its comparisons.

In the southern and eastern Pacific two contrasting cultural provinces have long evoked anthropological interest: *Melanesia*, including New Guinea, the Bismarcks, Solomons, and island groups east to Fiji; and *Polynesia*, consisting in its main portion of the triangular constellation of lands between New Zealand, Easter Island, and the Hawaiian Islands. In and around Fiji, Melanesia and Polynesia intergrade culturally, but west and east of their intersection the two provinces pose broad contrasts in several sectors: in religion, art, kinship groupings, economics, political organization. The differences are the more notable for the underlying similarities from which they emerge. Melanesia and Polynesia are both agricultural regions in which many of the same crops—such as yams, taro, breadfruit, bananas, and coconuts—have long been cultivated by many similar techniques. Some recently presented linguistic and archaeological studies suggest that Polynesian cultures originated from an eastern Melanesian hearth during the first millennium B.C. Yet in anthropological annals the Polynesians were to become famous for elaborate forms of rank and chieftainship,

whereas most Melanesian societies broke off advance on this front at more rudimentary levels.

It is obviously imprecise, however, to make out the political contrast in broad culture-area terms. Within Polynesia, certain of the islands, such as Hawaii, the Society Islands and Tonga, developed unparalleled political momentum. And not all Melanesian polities, on the other side, were constrained and truncated in their evolution. In New Guinea and nearby areas of western Melanesia small and loosely ordered political groupings are numerous, but in eastern Melanesia, New Caledonia and Fiji for example, political approximations of the Polynesian condition become common. There is more of an upward west to east slope in political development in the southern Pacific than a step-like, quantum progression. It is quite revealing, however, to compare the extremes of this continuum, the western Melanesian underdevelopment against the greater Polynesian chiefdoms. While such comparison does not exhaust the evolutionary variations, it fairly establishes the scope of overall political achievement in this Pacific phylum of cultures.

Measurable along several dimensions, the contrast between developed Polynesian and underdeveloped Melanesian polities is immediately striking for differences in scale. H. Ian Hogbin and Camilla Wedgwood concluded from a survey of Melanesian (most western Melanesian) societies that ordered, independent political bodies in the region typically include seventy to three hundred persons; more recent work in the New Guinea Highlands suggests political groupings of up to a thousand, occasionally a few thousand, people.[1] But in Polynesia sovereignties of two thousand or three thousand are run-of-the-mill, and the most advanced chiefdoms, as in Tonga or Hawaii, might claim ten thousand, even tens of thousands. Varying step by step with such differences in size of the polity are differences in territorial extent: from a few square miles in western

1. H. Ian Hogbin and Camilla H. Wedgwood, "Local Groupings in Melanesia," *Oceania* 23 (1952–53) : 241–276; 24 (1953–54) : 58–76.

Reprinted from "Poor Man, Rich Man, Big-Man, Chief: Political Types in Melanesia and Polynesia," *Comparative Studies in Society and History*, Vol. 5, No. 3, pp. 285–303, by Marshall D. Sahlins, by permission of Cambridge University Press.

Melanesia to tens or even hundreds of square miles in Polynesia.

The Polynesian advance in political scale was supported by advance over Melanesia in political structure. Melanesia presents a great array of social-political forms: here political organization is based upon patrilineal descent groups, there on cognatic groups, or men's club-houses recruiting neighborhood memberships, on a secret ceremonial society, or perhaps on some combination of these structural principles. Yet a general plan can be discerned. The characteristic western Melanesian "tribe," that is, the ethnic-cultural entity, consists of many autonomous kinship-residential groups. Amounting on the ground to a small village or a local cluster of hamlets, each of these is a copy of the others in organization, each tends to be economically self-governing, and each is the equal of the others in political status. The tribal plan is one of politically unintegrated segments—segmental. But the political geometry in Polynesia is pyramidal. Local groups of the order of self-governing Melanesian communities appear in Polynesia as subdivisions of a more inclusive political body. Smaller units are integrated into larger through a system of intergroup ranking, and the network of representative chiefs of the subdivisions amounts to a coordinating political structure. So instead of the Melanesian scheme of small, separate, and equal political blocs, the Polynesian polity is an extensive pyramid of groups capped by the family and following of a paramount chief. (This Polynesian political upshot is often, although not always, facilitated by the development of ranked lineages. Called *conical clan* by Kirchhoff, at one time *ramage* by Firth and *status lineage* by Goldman, the Polynesian ranked lineage is the same in principle as the so-called *obok* system widely distributed in Central Asia, and it is at least analogous to the Scottish clan, the Chinese clan, certain Central African Bantu lineage systems, the house-groups of Northwest Coast Indians, perhaps even the "tribes" of the Israelites. Genealogical ranking is its distinctive feature: members of the same descent unit are ranked by genealogical distance from the common ancestor; lines of the same group become senior and cadet branches on this principle; related corporate lineages are relatively ranked, again by genealogical priority.)

Here is another criterion of Polynesian political advance: historical performance. Almost all of the native peoples of the South Pacific were brought up against intense European cultural pressure in the late eighteenth and the nineteenth centuries. Yet only the Hawaiians, Tahitians, Tongans, and to a lesser extent the Fijians, successfully defended themselves by evolving countervailing, native-controlled states. Complete with public governments and public law, monarchs and taxes, ministers and minions, these nineteenth-century states are testimony to the native Polynesian political genius, to the level and the potential of indigenous political accomplishments.

Embedded within the grand differences in political scale, structure and performance is a more personal contrast, one in quality of leadership. An historically particular type of leader-figure, the "big-man" as he is often locally styled, appears in the underdeveloped settings of Melanesia. Another type, a chief properly so-called, is associated with the Polynesian advance. Now these are distinct sociological types, that is to say, differences in the powers, privileges, rights, duties, and obligations of Melanesian big-men and Polynesian chiefs are given by the divergent societal contexts in which they operate. Yet the institutional distinctions cannot help but be manifest also in differences in bearing and character, appearance and manner—in a word, personality. It may be a good way to begin the more rigorous sociological comparison of leadership with a more impressionistic sketch of the contrast in the human dimension. Here I find it useful to apply characterizations—or is it caricature?—from our own history to big-men and chiefs, however much injustice this does to the historically incomparable backgrounds of the Melanesians and Polynesians. The Melanesian big-man seems to thoroughly bourgeois, so reminiscent of the free-enterprising rugged individual of our own heritage. He combines with an ostensible interest in the general welfare a more profound measure of self-interested cunning and economic calculation. His gaze, as Veblen might have put it, is fixed unswervingly to the main chance. His every public action is designed to make a competitive and invidious comparison with others, to show a standing above the masses that is product of his own personal manufacture. The historical caricature of the Polynesian chief, however, is feudal rather than capitalist. His appearance, his bearing is almost regal; very likely he just *is* a big man—"'Can't you see he is a chief? See how big he is?'"[2] In his every public action is a display of the refinements of breeding, in his manner always that *noblesse oblige* of true pedigree and an incontestable right of rule. With his standing not so much a personal achievement as a just social due, he can afford to be, and he is, every inch a chief.

In the several Melanesian tribes in which big-men have come under anthropological scrutiny, local cultural differences modify the expression of their personal powers. But the indicative quality of big-man authority is everywhere the same: it is *personal* power. Big-men do not come to office; they do not succeed to, nor are they installed in, existing positions of leadership over political groups. The attainment of big-man status is rather the outcome of a series of acts which elevate a person

2. Edward Winslow Gifford, *Tongan Society* (Honolulu: Bernice P. Bishop Museum Bulletin 61, 1926).

above the common herd and attract about him a coterie of loyal, lesser men. It is not accurate to speak of "big-man" as a political title, for it is but an acknowledged standing in interpersonal relations—a "prince among men" so to speak as opposed to "The Prince of Danes." In particular Melanesian tribes the phrase might be "man of importance" or "man of renown," "generous rich-man," or "center-man," as well as "big-man."

A kind of two-sidedness in authority is implied in this series of phrases, a division of the big-man's field of influence into two distinct sectors. "Center-man" particularly connotes a cluster of followers gathered about an influential pivot. It socially implies the division of the tribe into political in-groups dominated by outstanding personalities. To the in-group, the big-man presents this sort of picture:

> The place of the leader in the district group [in northern Malaita] is well summed up by his title, which might be translated as "center-man." . . . He was like a banyan, the natives explain, which, though the biggest and tallest in the forest, is still a tree like the rest. But, just because it exceeds all others, the banyan gives support to more lianas and creepers, provides more food for the birds, and gives better protection against sun and rain.[3]

But "man of renown" connotes a broader tribal field in which a man is not so much a leader as he is some sort of hero. This is the side of the big-man facing outward from his own faction, his status among some or all of the other political clusters of the tribe. The political sphere of the big-man divides itself into a small internal sector composed of his personal satellites—rarely over eighty men—and a much larger external sector, the tribal galaxy consisting of many similar constellations.

As it crosses over from the internal into the external sector, a big-man's power undergoes qualitative change. Within his faction a Melanesian leader has true command ability, outside of it only fame and indirect influence. It is not that the center-man rules his faction by physical force, but his followers do feel obliged to obey him, and he can usually get what he wants by haranguing them—public verbal suasion is indeed so often employed by center-men that they have been styled "harangue-utans." The orbits of outsiders, however, are set by their own center-men. "'Do it yourself. I'm not *your* fool,'" would be the characteristic response to an order issued by a center-man to an outsider among the Siuai.[4] This fragmentation of true authority presents special political difficulties, particularly in organizing large masses of people for the prosecution of such collective ends as warfare or ceremony. Big-men do instigate mass action, but only by establishing both extensive re-

nown and special personal relations of compulsion or reciprocity with other center-men.

Politics is in the main personal politicking in these Melanesian societies, and the size of a leader's faction as well as the extent of his renown are normally set by competition with other ambitious men. Little or no authority is given by social ascription: leadership is a creation—a creation of followership. "Followers," as it is written of the Kapauku of New Guinea, "stand in various relations to the leader. Their obedience to the headman's decisions is caused by motivations which reflect their particular relations to the leader."[5]

So a man must be prepared to demonstrate that he possesses the kinds of skills that command respect—magical powers, gardening prowess, mastery of oratorical style, perhaps bravery in war and feud. Typically decisive is the deployment of one's skills and efforts in a certain direction: towards amassing goods, most often pigs, shell monies and vegetable foods, and distributing them in ways which build a name for cavalier generosity, if not for compassion. A faction is developed by informal private assistance to people of a locale. Tribal rank and renown are developed by great public giveaways sponsored by the rising big-man, often on behalf of his faction as well as himself. In different Melanesian tribes, the renown-making public distribution may appear as one side of a delayed exchange of pigs between corporate kinship groups; a marital consideration given a bride's kinfolk; a set of feasts connected with the erection of the big-man's dwelling, or of a clubhouse for himself and his faction, or with the purchase of higher grades of rank in secret societies; the sponsorship of a religious ceremony; a payment of subsidies and blood compensations to military allies; or perhaps the giveaway in a ceremonial challenge bestowed on another leader in the attempt to outgive and thus outrank him (a potlatch).

The making of the faction, however, is the true making of the Melanesian big-man. It is essential to establish relations of loyalty and obligation on the part of a number of people such that their production can be mobilized for renown-building external distribution. The bigger the faction the greater the renown; once momentum in external distribution has been generated the opposite can also be true. Any ambitious man who can gather a following can launch a societal career. The rising big-man necessarily depends initially on a small core of followers, principally his own household and his closest relatives. Upon these people he can prevail economically: he capitalizes in the first instance on kinship dues and by finessing the relation of reciprocity appropriate among close kinsmen. Often it becomes necessary at an early phase to enlarge one's household.

3. H. Ian Hogbin, "Native Councils and Courts in the Solomon Islands," *Oceania* 14 (1943–44) : 258–283.

4. Douglas Oliver, *Solomon Islands Society* (Cambridge: Harvard University Press, 1955).

5. Leopold Pospisil, *Kapauku Papuans and Their Law* (New Haven: Yale University Press, Yale University Publications in Anthropology, no. 54, 1958).

The rising leader goes out of his way to incorporate within his family "strays" of various sorts, people without familial support themselves, such as widows and orphans. Additional wives are especially useful. The more wives a man has the more pigs he has. The relation here is functional, not identical: with more women gardening there will be more food for pigs and more swineherds. A Kiwai Papuan picturesquely put to an anthropologist in pidgin the advantages, economic and political, of polygamy:"'Another woman go garden, another woman go take firewood, another woman go catch fish, another woman cook him—husband he sing out plenty people come kaikai [i.e., come to eat].' "[6] Each new marriage, incidentally, creates for the big-man an additional set of in-laws from whom he can exact economic favors. Finally, a leader's career sustains its upward climb when he is able to link other men and their families to his faction, harnessing their production to his ambition. This is done by calculated generosities, by placing others in gratitude and obligation through helping them in some big way. A common technique is payment of bridewealth on behalf of young men seeking wives.

The great Malinowski used a phrase in analyzing primitive political economy that felicitously describes just what the big-man is doing: amassing a "fund of power." A big-man is one who can create and use social relations which give him leverage on others' production and the ability to siphon off an excess product—or sometimes he can cut down their consumption in the interest of the siphon. Now although his attention may be given primarily to short-term personal interests, from an objective standpoint the leader acts to promote long-term societal interests. The fund of power provisions activities that involve other groups of society at large. In the greater perspective of that society at large, big-men are indispensable means of creating supralocal organization: in tribes normally fragmented into small independent groups, big-men at least temporarily widen the sphere of ceremony, recreation and art, economic collaboration, of war too. Yet always this greater societal organization depends on the lesser factional organization, particularly on the ceilings on economic mobilization set by relations between center-men and followers. The limits and the weaknesses of the political order in general are the limits and weaknesses of the factional in-groups.

And the personal quality of subordination to a center-man is a serious weakness in factional structure. A personal loyalty has to be made and continually reinforced; if there is discontent it may well be severed. Merely to create a faction takes time and effort, and to hold it, still more effort. The potential rupture of per-

6. Gunnar Landtman, *The Kiwai of British New Guinea* (London: Macmillan, 1927).

sonal links in the factional chain is at the heart of two broad evolutionary shortcomings of western Melanesian political orders. First, a comparative instability. Shifting dispositions and magnetisms of ambitious men in a region may induce fluctuations in factions, perhaps some overlapping of them, and fluctuations also in the extent of different renowns. The death of a center-man can become a regional political trauma: the death undermines the personally cemented faction, the group dissolves in whole or in part, and the people re-group finally around rising pivotal big-men. Although particular tribal structures in places cushion the disorganization, the big-man political system is generally unstable over short terms: in its superstructure it is a flux of rising and falling leaders, in its substructure of enlarging and contracting factions. Secondly, the personal political bond contributes to the containment of evolutionary advance. The possibility of their desertion, it is clear, often inhibits a leader's ability to forceably push up his followers' output, thereby placing constraints on higher political organization, but there is more to it than that. If it is to generate great momentum, a big-man's quest for the summits of renown is likely to bring out a contradiction in his relations to followers, so that he finds himself encouraging defection—or worse, an egalitarian rebellion—by encouraging production.

One side of the Melanesian contradiction is the initial economic reciprocity between a center-man and his followers. For his help they give their help, and for goods going out through his hands other goods (often from outside factions) flow back to his followers by the same path. The other side is that a cumulative build-up of renown forces center-men into economic extortion of the faction. Here it is important that not merely his own status, but the standing and perhaps the military security of his people depend on the big-man's achievements in public distribution. Established at the head of a sizeable faction, a center-man comes under increasing pressure to extract goods from his followers, to delay reciprocities owing them, and to deflect incoming goods back into external circulation. Success in competition with other big-men particularly undermines internal-factional reciprocities: such success is precisely measurable by the ability to give outsiders more than they can possibly reciprocate. In well delineated big-man polities, we find leaders negating the reciprocal obligations upon which their following had been predicated. Substituting extraction for reciprocity, they must compel their people to "eat the leader's renown," as one Solomon Island group puts it, in return for productive efforts. Some center-men appear more able than others to dam the inevitable tide of discontent that mounts within their factions, perhaps because of charismatic personalities, perhaps because of the particular social organizations in which they operate. But paradoxically the ultimate defense of the center-man's position is some slackening of his drive to enlarge the funds of power. The alternative is much worse. In the anthropological record there are not merely instances of big-man chicanery and of material deprivation of the faction in the interests of renown, but some also of overloading of social relations with followers: the generation of antagonisms, defections, and in extreme cases the violent liquidation of the center-man. Developing internal contraints, the Melanesian big-man political order brakes evolutionary advance at a certain level. It sets ceilings on the intensification of political authority, on the intensification of household production by political means, and on the diversion of household outputs in support of wider political organization. But in Polynesia these constraints were breached, and although Polynesian chiefdoms also found their developmental plateau, it was not before political evolution had been carried above the Melanesian ceilings. The fundamental defects of the Melanesian plan were overcome in Polynesia. The division between small internal and larger external political sectors, upon which all big-man politics hinged, was suppressed in Polynesia by the growth of an enclaving chiefdom-at-large. A chain of command subordinating lesser chiefs and groups to greater, on the basis of inherent societal rank, made local blocs or personal followings (such as were independent in Melanesia) merely dependent parts of the larger Polynesian chiefdom. So the nexus of the Polynesian chiefdom became an extensive set of offices, a pyramid of higher and lower chiefs holding sway over larger and smaller sections of the polity. Indeed the system of ranked and subdivided lineages (conical clan system), upon which the pyramid was characteristically established, might build up through several orders of inclusion and encompass the whole of an island or group of islands. While the island or the archipelago would normally be divided into several independent chiefdoms, high-order lineage connections between them, as well as kinship ties between their paramount chiefs, provided structural avenues for at least temporary expansion of political scale, for consolidation of great into even greater chiefdoms.

The pivotal paramount chief as well as the chieftains controlling parts of a chiefdom were true office holders and title holders. They were not, like Melanesian big-men, fishers of men: they held positions of authority over permanent groups. The honorifics of Polynesian chiefs likewise did not refer to a standing in interpersonal relations, but to their leadership of political divisions—here "The Prince of Danes" *not* "the prince among men." In western Melanesia the personal superiorities and inferiorities arising in the intercourse of particular men largely defined the political bodies. In Polynesia there emerged suprapersonal structures of leadership and followership, organizations that continued independently of the particular men who occupied positions in them for brief mortal spans.

And these Polynesian chiefs did not make their positions in society—they were installed in societal positions. In several of the islands, men did struggle to office against the will and strategems of rival aspirants. But then they came *to* power. Power resided in the office; it was not made by the demonstration of personal superiority. In other islands, Tahiti was famous for it, succession to chieftainship was tightly controlled by inherent rank. The chiefly lineage ruled by virtue of its genealogical connections with divinity, the chiefs were succeeded by first sons, who carried "in the blood" the attributes of leadership. The important comparative point is this: the qualities of command that had to reside in men in Melanesia, that had to be personally demonstrated in order to attract loyal followers, were in Polynesia socially assigned to office and rank. In Polynesia, people of high rank and office *ipso facto* were leaders, and by the same token the qualities of leadership were automatically lacking—theirs was not to question why—among the underlying population. Magical powers such as a Melanesian big-man might acquire to sustain his position, a Polynesian high chief inherited by divine descent as the *mana* which sanctioned his rule and protected his person against the hands of the commonalty. The productive ability the big-man laboriously had to demonstrate was effortlessly given Polynesian chiefs as religious control over agricultural fertility, and upon the ceremonial implementation of it the rest of the people were conceived dependent. Where a Melanesian leader had to master the compelling oratorical style, Polynesian paramounts often had trained "talking chiefs" whose voice was the chiefly command.

In the Polynesian view, a chiefly personage was in the nature of things powerful. But this merely implies the objective observation that his power was of the group rather than of himself. His authority came from the organization, from an organized acquiescence in his privileges and organized means of sustaining them. A kind of paradox resides in evolutionary developments which detach the exercise of authority from the necessity to demonstrate personal superiority: organizational power actually extends the role of personal decision and conscious planning, gives it greater scope, impact, and effectiveness. The growth of a political system such as the Polynesian constitutes advance over Melanesian orders of interpersonal dominance in the human control of human affairs. Especially significant for society at large were privileges accorded Polynesian chiefs which made them greater architects of funds of power than ever was any Melanesian big-man.

Masters of their people and "owners" in a titular

sense of group resources, Polynesian chiefs had rights of call upon the labor and agricultural produce of households within their domains. Economic mobilization did not depend on, as it necessarily had for Melanesian big-men, the *de novo* creation by the leader of personal loyalties and economic obligations. A chief need not stoop to obligate this man or that man, need not by a series of individual acts of generosity induce others to support him, for economic leverage over a group was the inherent chiefly due. Consider the implications for the fund of power of the widespread chiefly privilege, related to titular "ownership" of land, of placing an interdiction, a tabu, on the harvest of some crop by way of reserving its use for a collective project. By means of the tabu the chief directs the course of production in a general way: households of his domain must turn to some other means of subsistence. He delivers a stimulus to household production: in the absence of the tabu further labors would not have been necessary. Most significantly, he has generated a politically utilizable agricultural surplus. A subsequent call on this surplus floats chieftainship as a going concern, capitalizes the fund of power. In certain islands, Polynesian chiefs controlled great storehouses which held the goods congealed by chiefly pressures on the commonalty. David Malo, one of the great native custodians of old Hawaiian lore, felicitously catches the political significance of the chiefly magazine in his well-known *Hawaiian Antiquities:*

> It was the practice for kings [i.e., paramount chiefs of individual islands] to build store-houses in which to collect food, fish, tapas [bark cloth], malos [men's loin cloths] pa-us [women's loin shirts], and all sorts of goods. These store-houses were designed by the Kalaimoku [the chief's principal executive] as a means of keeping the people contented, so they would not desert the king. They were like the baskets that were used to entrap the *hinalea* fish. The *hinalea* thought there was something good within the basket, and he hung round the outside of it. In the same way the people thought there was food in the storehouses, and they kept their eyes on the king. As the rat will not desert the pantry . . . where he thinks food is, so the people will not desert the king while they think there is food in his store-house.[7]

Redistribution of the fund of power was the supreme art of Polynesian politics. By well-planned *noblesse oblige* the large domain of a paramount chief was held together, organized at times for massive projects, protected against other chiefdoms, even further enriched. Uses of the chiefly fund included lavish hospitality and entertainments for outside chiefs and for the chief's own people, and succor of individuals or the underlying population at large in times of scarcities—bread and circuses. Chiefs subsidized craft production, promoting

in Polynesia a division of technical labor unparalleled in extent and expertise in most of the Pacific. They supported also great technical construction, as of irrigation complexes, the further returns to which swelled the chiefly fund, They initiated large-scale religious construction too, subsidized the great ceremonies, and organized logistic support for extensive military campaigns. Larger and more easily replenished than their western Melanesian counterparts, Polynesian funds of power permitted greater political regulation of a greater range of social activities on greater scale.

In the most advanced Polynesian chiefdoms, as in Hawaii and Tahiti, a significant part of the chiefly fund was deflected away from general redistribution towards the upkeep of the institution of chieftainship. The fund was siphoned for the support of a permanent administrative establishment. In some measure, goods and services contributed by the people precipitated out as the grand houses, assembly places and temple platforms of chiefly precincts. In another measure, they were appropriated for the livelihood of circles of retainers, many of them close kinsmen of the chief, who clustered about the powerful paramounts, These were not all useless hangers-on. They were political cadres: supervisors of the stores, talking chiefs, ceremonial attendants, high priests who were intimately involved in political rule, envoys to transmit directives through the chiefdom. There were men in these chiefly retinues—in Tahiti and perhaps Hawaii, specialized warrior corps—whose force could be directed internally as a buttress against fragmenting or rebellious elements of the chiefdom. A Tahitian or Hawaiian high chief had more compelling sanctions than the harangue. He controlled a ready physical force, an armed body of executioners, which gave him mastery particularly over the lesser people of the community. While it looks a lot like the big-man's faction again, the differences in functioning of the great Polynesian chief's retinue are more significant than the superficial similarities in appearance. The chief's coterie, for one thing, is economically dependent upon him rather than he upon them. And in deploying the cadres politically in various sections of the chiefdom, or against the lower orders, the great Polynesian chiefs sustained command where the Melanesian big-man, in his external sector, had at best renown.

This is not to say that the advanced Polynesian chiefdoms were free of internal defect, of potential or actual malfunctioning. The large political-military apparatus indicates something of the opposite. So does the recent work of Irving Goldman[8] on the intensity of "status rivalry" in Polynesia, especially when it is considered that much of the status rivalry in developed chiefdoms,

7. David Malo, *Hawaiian Antiquities* (Honolulu: Hawaiian Gazette Co., 1903).

8. Irving Goldman, "Status Rivalry and Cultural Evolution in Polynesia," *American Anthropologist* 57 (1957) : 680–697; "Variations in Polynesian Social Organization," *Journal of the Polynesian Society* 66 (1957) : 374–390.

as the Hawaiian, amounted to popular rebellion against chiefly despotism rather than mere contest for position within the ruling-stratum. This suggests that Polynesian chiefdoms, just as Melanesian big-man orders, generate along with evolutionary development countervailing anti-authority pressures, and that the weight of the latter may ultimately impede further development.

The Polynesian contradiction seems clear enough. On one side, chieftainship is never detached from kinship moorings and kinship economic ethics. Even the greatest Polynesian chiefs were conceived superior kinsmen to the masses, fathers of their people, and generosity was morally incumbent upon them. On the other side, the major Polynesian paramounts seemed inclined to "eat the power of the government too much," as the Tahitians put it, to divert an undue proportion of the general wealth toward the chiefly establishment. The diversion could be accomplished by lowering the customary level of general redistribution, lessening the material returns of chieftainship to the community at large—tradition attributes the great rebellion of Mangarevan commoners to such cause. Or the diversion might—and I suspect more commonly did—consist in greater and more forceful exactions from lesser chiefs and people, increasing returns to the chiefly apparatus without necessarily affecting the level of general redistribution. In either case, the well-developed chiefdom creates for itself the dampening paradox of stoking rebellion by funding its authority.

In Hawaii and other islands cycles of political centralization and decentralization may be abstracted from traditional histories. That is, larger chiefdoms periodically fragmented into smaller and then were later reconstituted. Here would be more evidence of a tendency to overtax the political structure. But how to explain the emergence of a developmental stymie, of an inability to sustain political advance beyond a certain level? To point to a chiefly propensity to consume or a Polynesian propensity to rebel is not enough: such propensities are promoted by the very advance of chiefdoms. There is reason to hazard instead that Parkinson's notable law is behind it all: that progressive expansion in political scale entailed more-than-proportionate accretion in the ruling apparatus, unbalancing the flow of wealth in favor of the apparatus. The ensuing unrest then curbs the chiefly impositions, sometimes by reducing chiefdom scale to the nadir of the periodic cycle. Comparison of the requirements of administration in small and large Polynesian chiefdoms helps make the point.

A lesser chiefdom, confined say as in the Marquesas Islands to a narrow valley, could be almost personally ruled by a headman in frequent contact with the relatively small population. Melville's partly romanticized—also for its ethnographic details, partly cribbed—account in *Typee* makes this clear enough. But the great Polynesian chiefs had to rule much larger, spatially dispersed, internally organized populations. Hawaii, an island over four thousand square miles with an aboriginal population approaching one hundred thousand, was at times a single chiefdom, at other times divided into two to six independent chiefdoms, and at all times each chiefdom was composed of large subdivisions under powerful subchiefs. Sometimes a chiefdom in the Hawaiian group extended beyond the confines of one of the islands, incorporating part of another through conquest. Now, such extensive chiefdoms would have to be coordinated; they would have to be centrally tapped for a fund of power, buttressed against internal disruption, sometimes massed for distant, perhaps overseas, military engagements. All of this to be implemented by means of communication still at the level of word-of-mouth, and means of transportation consisting of human bodies and canoes. (The extent of certain larger chieftainships, coupled with the limitations of communication and transportation, incidentally suggests another possible source of political unrest: that the burden of provisioning the governing apparatus would tend to fall disproportionately on groups within easiest access of the paramount.) A tendency for the developed chiefdom to proliferate in executive cadres, to grow top-heavy, seems in these circumstances altogether functional, even though the ensuing drain on wealth proves the chiefdom's undoing. Functional also, and likewise a material drain on the chiefdom at large, would be widening distinctions between chiefs and people in style of life. Palatial housing, ornamentation and luxury, finery and ceremony, in brief, conspicuous consumption, however much it seems mere self-interest always has a more decisive social significance. It creates those invidious distinctions between rulers and ruled so conducive to a passive—hence quite economical!—acceptance of authority. Throughout history, inherently more powerful political organizations than the Polynesian, with more assured logistics of rule, have turned to it—including in our time some ostensibly revolutionary and proletarian governments, despite every pre-revolutionary protestation of solidarity with the masses and equality for the classes.

In Polynesia then, as in Melanesia, political evolution is eventually shortcircuited by an overload on the relations between leaders and their people. The Polynesian tragedy, however, was somewhat the opposite of the Melanesian. In Polynesia, the evolutionary ceiling was set by extraction from the population at large in favor of the chiefly faction, in Melanesia by extraction from the big-man's faction in favor of distribution to the population at large. Most importantly, the Polynesian ceiling was higher. Melanesian big-men and Polynesian chiefs not only reflect different varieties and levels of political evolution, they display in different degrees the capacity to generate and to sustain political progress.

Especially emerging from their juxtaposition is the more decisive impact of Polynesian chiefs on the economy, the chief's greater leverage on the output of the several households of society. The success of any primitive political organization is decided here, in the control that can be developed over household economies. For the household is not merely the principal productive unit in primitive societies, it is often quite capable of autonomous direction of its own production, and it is oriented towards production for its own, not societal consumption. The greater potential of Polynesian chieftainship is precisely the greater pressure it could exert on household output, its capacity both to generate a surplus and to deploy it out of the household towards a broader division of labor, coopera-

tive construction, and massive ceremonial and military action. Polynesian chiefs were the more effective means of societal collaboration on economic, political, indeed all cultural fronts. Perhaps we have been too long accustomed to perceive rank and rule from the standpoint of the individuals involved, rather than from the perspective of the total society, as if the secret of the subordination of man to man lay in the personal satisfactions of power. And then the breakdowns too, or the evolutionary limits, have been searched out in men, in "weak" kings or megalomaniacal dictators—always, "who is the matter?" An excursion into the field of primitive politics suggests the more fruitful conception that the gains of political developments accrue more decisively to society than to individuals, and the failings as well are of structure not men.

27

Cannibalistic Revenge in Jalé Warfare

BY KLAUS-FRIEDRICH KOCH

. . . .

In October, 1968, two white missionaries on a long trek between two stations were killed in a remote valley in the Snow Mountains of western New Guinea, and their bodies were eaten. A few days later, warriors armed with bows and arrows gave a hostile reception to a group of armed police flown to the site by helicopter. These people, described by the newspapers as "savages living in a stone-age culture," belong to a large population of Papuans among whom I lived for nearly two years, from 1964 to 1966.

People living to the west, in the high valley of the Balim River, call them "Jalé," and this is the name that I use for them. When I read of the killing of the missionaries I was reminded of how I had first heard that the people whom I had selected for ethnographic study had anthropophagic (man-eating) predilections. After arriving at Sentani airport on the north coast, I began negotiations for transport to a mission airstrip located in the Jalémó, the country of the Jalé. "I hope the Jalé will give us permission to land," one pilot said to me. "Just a few weeks ago the airstrip was blocked because the Jalé needed the ground for a dance and a cannibalistic

Opposite page: By the time these young boys become warriors, they will be expert archers. Training begins early; boys who can hardly walk carry bows made by their fathers. Practice games perfect the proper stance.

feast to celebrate a military victory."

Our cultural heritage predisposes many people to view the eating of human meat with extreme horror. No wonder then that the literature on the subject is permeated with grossly erroneous and prejudicial ideas about the practice. Few anthropologists have been able to study cannibalism because missions and colonial governments have generally succeeded in eradicating a custom considered to epitomize, more than any other, the alleged mental primitiveness and diabolical inspirations of people with simple technologies. However, the Jalé, completely isolated from foreign influences until 1961, still practice cannibalism as an institutionalized form of revenge in warfare, which is itself an integral aspect of their life.

The Jalé live in compact villages along several valleys north and south of the Snow Mountains in east-central West New Guinea. Until the first missionaries entered the Jalémó in 1961, the Jalé were ignorant of the "outside" world. Five years later, when I left the area, many Jalé villages still had never been contacted, and culture change among the people living close to a mission station was largely limited to the acceptance of a few steel tools and to an influx of seashells imported by the foreigners.

Two weeks after I had set up camp in the village of Pasikni, a year-long truce with a neighboring village came to an end. Three days of fierce fighting ensued, during which the Pasikni warriors killed three ene-

mies (among them a small boy), raided the defeated settlement, and drove its inhabitants into exile with friends and relatives in other villages of the region. At that time I understood little of the political realities of Jalé society, where neither formal government nor forensic institutions exist for the settlement of conflicts. Later, when I had learned their language, I began to comprehend the conditions that make military actions an inevitable consequence of the absence of an effective system of political control.

From an anthropological perspective any kind of war is generally a symptom of the absence, inadequacy, or breakdown of other procedures for resolving conflicts. This view is especially applicable to Jalé military operations, which aim neither at territorial gains and the conquest of resources nor at the suppression of one political or religious ideology and its forceful replacement by another. All armed conflicts in Jalémó occur as a result of bodily injury or killing suffered in retaliation for the infliction of a wrong. Violent redress may be exacted for adultery or theft or for a breach of obligation—usually a failure to make a compensatory payment of pigs.

Jalé warfare is structured by a complex network of kin relationships. The Jalé conceptually divide their society into two parts (moieties) whose members must marry someone from the opposite side. By a principle of patrilineal descent a person always belongs to the moiety of his father. Links between kin groups created by intervillage marriages—about half the wives in a village were born elsewhere—provide the structure of trade networks and alliance politics.

Most villages contain two or more residential compounds, or wards. One hut among the group of dwellings forming a ward is considerably bigger than all the others. This is the men's house, a special domicile for men and for boys old enough to have been initiated. Women and uninitiated boys live in the smaller huts, each of which usually houses the family of one man. The residents of a men's house constitute a unified political and ritual community, and it is this community, not the village as a whole, that is the principal war-making unit.

As in all societies, there are some individuals who have more influence over the affairs of their fellows than most. In Jalémó a man gains a position of authority (which never extends much beyond the immediate kin group) through his acquisition of an esoteric knowledge of performing rituals and through the clever management of his livestock to the benefit of his relatives, for every important event demands the exchange of pigs—to solemnify or legitimate the creation of a new status or to settle a conflict. Most disputes are over women, pigs, or gardens, and any one of them may generate enough political enmity to cause a war in which many people may lose their lives and homes.

In every Jalé war one person on either side, called the "man-at-the-root-of-the-arrow," is held responsible for the outbreak of hostilities. These people are the parties to the original dispute, which ultimately escalates into armed combat. Being a man-at-the-root-of-the-arrow carries the liability of providing compensation for all injuries and deaths suffered by supporters on the battlefield as well as by all others—including women and children—victimized in clandestine revenge raids. This liability acts as a built-in force favoring an early end of hostilities.

On rare occasions blood revenge

WEST NEW GUINEA

has been prevented by delivery of wergild compensation, in the form of a pig to the kinsmen of a slain person. But only those people who, for one reason or another, cannot rally support for a revenge action and who shy away from solitary, surreptitious ambush attacks will accept such an offer if it is made at all. A negotiated peace settlement of this nature is most likely if the disputants are from the same village or if the whole settlement is at war with a common outside enemy.

When two villages are at war with each other, periods of daily combat are interrupted by short "cease-fires" during which the warriors attend to the more mundane task of garden work, but they are always prepared to counter a surprise attack launched by the enemy. After several weeks of discontinuous fighting, however, the threat of famine due to the prolonged neglect of proper cultivation induces the belligerents to maintain an informal and precarious truce. During this time small bands of kinsmen and members of the men's house of a victim whose death could not be avenged on the battlefield will venture clandestine expeditions into enemy territory, from which a successful raiding party may bring back

a pig as well. It is a revenge action of this kind that often precipitates a resumption of open warfare.

Fighting on the battlefield follows a pattern of haphazardly coordinated individual engagements, which rely on the tactic of "shoot-and-run." This technique requires a warrior to advance as far as the terrain affords him cover, discharge an arrow or two, and then run back to escape from the reach of enemy shots. When one side has been forced to retreat to its village, the fighting turns into sniping from behind huts and fences. Women and children always leave the village if an invasion is imminent and take refuge with friends and relatives in other villages. As a last resort the men retreat into the men's house, which a taboo protects from being burned. When a battle reaches this stage, the victorious warriors often plunder and burn family huts. Following a catastrophe of this extent the defeated side usually elects to abandon their village, and the warfare ceases, but the hostilities linger on until a formal peace ceremony reconciles the principal parties. Arranging the ceremony, which features the ritual slaughter and consumption of a pig, may take years of informal negotia-

Treacherous unbridged rivers are one of the obstacles the Jalé must surmount on revenge raids in distant valleys. Jalemo terrain is among the most rugged in New Guinea.

Following this ritual overture the butchers use stone adzes and bamboo knives to cut the body apart. The fleshy portions are removed from the skull, and in an established order of step-by-step incisions, the limbs are separated from the trunk, which is split open to allow removal of the gastronomically highly prized entrails. Some small, choice cuts, especially rib sections, are roasted over the fire, but the bulk of the meat is cooked with a variety of leafy vegetables.

Before and during the operation, people who are preparing the oven, tending the fire, or just standing around appraise the victim. A healthy, muscular body is praised with ravenous exclamations, but a lesser grade body is also applauded.

When the meat is done, the pit is opened and the "owners of the body," as the Jalé call the recipients of a slain enemy, distribute much of the food among the attending relatives of the person whose death the killing has avenged. It is also distributed to the allied kin groups of a person maimed or killed in the war. Eligible people from other villages who could not participate in the celebrations are later sent pieces reserved for them. If mood so moves the Jalé, they may place some of the victim's bones in a tree near the cooking site to tell travelers of their brave deed.

In the course of the dancing and singing, a poetically gifted man may introduce a new song. If the lyrics appeal to others, it becomes a standard piece in the repertoire. The songs commemorate fortunate and tragic events from past wars, and a typical verse goes like this:

Ngingi, your mother
bakes only tiny potatoes for you.
Isel, your mother too
bakes only the ends of potatoes
for you.
We shall bake big potatoes for you
On the day of Kingkaen's return.

tions between people who have relatives on both sides. Afterward, dances in both villages and pig exchanges on a large scale consolidate the termination of the conflict.

"People whose face is known must not be eaten," say the Jalé. Consequently, cannibalism is normally not tolerated in wars between neighboring villages, and the few incidents that did occur during the lifetime of the oldest Pasikni men are remembered as acts of tragic perversion. In wars between villages separated by a major topographic boundary such as a mountain ridge, however, cannibalistic revenge is an integral part of the conflict.

While territorially confined hostilities usually end within a few years, interregional wars may last for more than a generation. During this long period revenge parties from either side venture sporadic expeditions into hostile areas, keenly avoiding any confrontation in battle and seeking instead to surprise lone hunters or small groups of women working in distant gardens. The geography of interregional wars favors long-lasting military alliances that have a stability quite unlike the temporary and shifting allegiances that personal kin connections and trading partnerships create in local conflicts.

If an enemy is killed during a foray into hostile territory, the raiders will make every effort to bring the body home. If tactical exigencies demand that the revenge party retreat without the victim, an attempt is made to retrieve at least a limb. The avengers always present the body to an allied kin group that has lost a member in the war. In return they receive pigs and are feted at a victory dance, during which the victim's body is steam-cooked in an earth oven dug near the village. Before the butchering begins, the head is specially treated by ritual experts: eyelids and lips are clamped with the wing bones of a bat to prevent the victim's ghost from seeing through these apertures. Thus blinded, it will be unable to guide a revenge expedition against its enemies.

After the head has been severed, it is wrapped in leaves. To insure more revenge killings in the future, some men shoot reed arrows into the head while it is dragged on the ground by a piece of vine. Then the head is unwrapped and swung through the fire to burn off the hair. This is accompanied by loud incantations meant to lure the victim's kinsmen into sharing his fate.

Several hundred loops of split liana vine are worn by Jalé men day and night. As an expression of masculinity, younger men wear more loops than their elders. Penis sheaths, cut from gourds, are tied around the body.

Three-day battle culminates in plunder of an enemy village and burning of selected huts, as victorious warriors watch from a nearby ridge. After such a drastic defeat, a village is usually abandoned and open hostilities cease.

Killed from ambush as he returned from battle, the victim, below, is carried to his funeral by members of his own village. The body will be cremated.

Ngingi and Isel are the names of two men from a hostile village, the home of a young woman named Kingkaen who was killed in an ambush attack in September, 1964. The lines make fun of the men who, because of Kingkaen's death, have to eat poor food prepared by the inept hands of senile women.

When the festival of revenge is over, the members of the men's house group of the owners of the body arrange for the ritual removal of the victim's ghost from their village. Rhythmically voicing efficacious formulas and whistling sounds, a ceremonial procession of men carries a special arrow into the forest, as far into enemy territory as is possible without risk. A small lump of pig's fat is affixed to the arrow by an expert in esoteric lore. (Pig's fat used for ritual purposes becomes a sacred substance that is applied in many different contexts.) The arrow is finally shot toward the enemy village. This, the Jalé believe, will make the ghost stay away from their own village, but as a further precaution they block the path with branches and plants over which spells are said.

Protective rites of this kind, and the vengeance ritual described above, are the only aspects of Jalé cannibalism that may be viewed as "religious." The actual consumption of human meat and organs does not constitute an act with intrinsic "supernatural" effects. Instead, as my Jalé friends repeatedly assured me, their reason for eating an enemy's body is that man tastes as good as pork, if not better. And they added that the bad enemies in the other valley had eaten some of their people.

These descriptions of Jalé rituals and beliefs do not sufficiently explain the practice of cannibalism. To do so would necessitate the compilation of all available information about this custom from every part of the world. On the basis of these data an extensive study would have to be made of the ecological and cultural variables found to be associated with institutionalized cannibalism. Perhaps it would then be possible to recognize specific ecological and sociological features that appear to be correlated with the consumption of human meat, but the task of interpreting the custom as a sociopsychological phenomenon would still remain.

It is obvious that the enigmatic nature of cannibalism has invited many writers to speculate about its origin and its biopsychic basis. Aristotle attributed anthropophagy among tribes around the Black Sea to their feral bestiality and morbid lust. In 1688 a treatise was published in Holland entitled *De natura et moribus anthropophagorum* ("On the Nature and Customs of Anthropophagi"), and some ethnographers writing in the nineteenth century still regarded the rejection of cannibalism as the "first step into civilization." Certainly, the consumption by man of a member of his own species is as much a problem for evolutionary bioanthropology as it is for ethnology and psychology. I have made an extensive survey of the various theories proposed by earnest scholars to elucidate the phenomenon, and I have found that, at best, a few hypotheses appear plausible for the interpretation of certain aspects of some cannibalistic practices.

In Jalémó the eating of a slain enemy, in addition to its dietary value, certainly indicates a symbolic expression of spite incorporated into an act of supreme vengeance. Violent retaliation, in turn, must be seen as a consequence of certain sociopsychological conditions that determine the degree of aggressive behavior expected and tolerated in their culture. Cross-cultural studies by anthropologists have supported theories that are applicable to Jalé society. An accepted model of personality development demonstrates that societies in which boys grow up in intimate association with their mothers, who dominate a household situation in which the boy's male elders, especially their fathers, do not take part, are characterized by a high level of physical violence. Sociological models developed from large-scale comparative research predict that in societies in which small kin groups operate as relatively independent political units, warfare within the society is a common means of resolving conflict.

Both models squarely apply to Jalé society. First, young boys, separated from the community of the men's house until their initiation, are socialized in a female environment. Second, the wards of a village are not integrated by a centralized system of headmanship, and no political cooperation exists between them until they are threatened by, or faced with, actual hostility from other villages. These are the critical variables that partially determine the bellicosity and violence I have observed.

No specific hypothesis can be given to explain the cannibalism that the Jalé incorporate in their vengeance. It is certain, however, that no understanding can be achieved by applying precepts of Western thought. In a missionary's travelogue published seventy years ago, the author, speaking of an African tribe, recounted:

Once, when told by a European that the practice of eating human flesh was a most degraded habit, the cannibal answered, "Why degraded? You people eat sheep and cows and fowls, which are all animals of a far lower order, and we eat man, who is great and above all; it is you who are degraded!"

Jalé warriors celebrate a battlefield triumph with a victory dance. Brilliant bird of paradise feathers punctuate the scene.

28

A New Weapon Stirs Up Old Ghosts

BY WILLIAM E. MITCHELL

....

When, in 1947, the Franciscan friars went to live among the nearly 10,000 Wape people of New Guinea, the principal native weapons were bone daggers and the bow and arrow. Even then, game was scarce in the heavily populated mountains where the Wape live, and the killing of a wild pig or a cassowary, New Guinea's major game animals, was an important village event. The Wape live in the western part of the Sepik River Basin. Their small villages lie along the narrow ridges of the Torricelli Mountains, above the sago palm swamps where women process palm pith, the Wape staff of life.

Today the Wape hunter's principal weapon is still the bow and arrow and game is even scarcer. This is partially the result of a new addition to the hunter's armory—the prosaic shotgun—which has had a profound moral impact on Wape village life.

The first guns were brought into this area in the late 1940s and early 1950s by missionaries, traders, and Australian government officials. Although natives were not permitted to own guns, they could use them if employed by a white man to shoot game for his table. This was a very prestigious job.

In 1960, government regulations were changed to permit natives to purchase single-shot shotguns. At first only a few Wape men, living in villages close to the government station and helpful to government officials, were granted gun permits. Eventually more permits were is-

sued, but today, in hopes of preserving the remaining game, one permit is issued for every 100 people.

Within ten years of the granting of the first gun permits, a belief and behavioral system had evolved around the shotgun. It was based on traditional Wape hunting lore but had distinctive elaborations stemming from native perceptions of the teachings of government officials and missionaries. For descriptive purposes I call this system of formalized beliefs and ritual the "Wape shotgun cult." It is one of several Wape ceremonial cults, but the only one originating after contact with Europeans. Although the specific practices of the shotgun cult vary from village to village, the underlying beliefs are the same.

In creating the shotgun cult the Wape faced the challenge of adapting an introduced implement to their culture. Unlike steel axes and knives, which replaced stone adzes and bamboo knives, the shotgun has never replaced the bow and arrow. The shotgun is a scarce and expensive machine. This, together with the European sanctions imposed upon its introduction, places it in a unique position, both symbolically and behaviorally, among the Wape.

The cult is a conservative institution. It breaks no new cognitive ground by challenging established Wape concepts. Instead it merges traditional hunting concepts with European moral teachings to create a coherent system. The cult upholds

traditional beliefs, accepts European authority, and most important, provides an explanation for unsuccessful hunting.

In 1970, my family and I arrived in Lumi, a small mountain settlement, which is the government's subdistrict headquarters in the middle of Wapeland. For the next year and a half, we lived in the village of Taute, near Lumi. There my wife and I studied Wape culture.

Taute, which has a population of 220, is reached by narrow foot trails, root strewn and muddy, passing through the dense, damp forest. The low houses—made of sago palm stems and roofed with sago thatch—are scattered about in the sandy plaza and among the coconut palms and breadfruit trees along the ridge. Towering poinsettias, red and pink hibiscus, and multicolored shrubs contrast with the encircling forest's greens and browns. A few small latrines perch on the steep slopes, concessions to Western concepts of hygiene. In the morning, flocks of screeching cockatoos glide below the ridge through the rising mists. When the breadfruit trees are bearing, giant fruit bats flop across the sky at dusk.

Since the mid-1950s the Franciscan friars have maintained, off and on, a religious school in Taute. There, Wape boys are instructed by a native catechist in Catholicism,

Mani, represented by a high conical mask, is a spirit who can insure good hunting. As he prances about the village, his joyful mien amuses the children.

simple arithmetic, and Melanesian Pidgin. A priest from Lumi visits the village several times a year, and the villagers, Catholic and heathen alike, are proud of their affiliation with the Franciscans and staunchly loyal to them. But their Catholicism is nominal and superficial—a scant and brittle frosting that does not mask their own religious beliefs, which dominate everyday life.

The ethos of Wape society is oriented around sacred curing rituals. Whereas some Sepik cultures aggressively center their ceremonial life around headhunting and the raising of sturdy and brave children, the Wape defensively center theirs in the ritual appeasement of malevolent ghosts and forest demons, who they believe cause sickness. Most men belong to one of the demon-curing cults where, once initiated as priests, they are responsible for producing the often elaborate curing ceremonies for exorcising the demon from the afflicted.

The little money that exists among the Wape is earned primarily by the men, who work as two-year contract laborers on the coastal and island copra plantations. Because of the lack of money to buy canned meats, the scarcity of game, and the paucity of fish in the mountain streams, the protein intake of the Wape is exceedingly low. The most common meal is sago dumplings and boiled leaves. Malnutrition is common among youngsters, and physical development is generally retarded. According to studies by Dr. Lyn Wark, a medical missionary who has worked widely among the Wape, the average birth weight of the Wape baby is the lowest recorded in the world. Correspondingly, secondary sex characteristics are delayed. For example, the mean age for the onset of menses is over eighteen years.

Before contact with Westerners, Wape men were naked and the women wore short string skirts. Today most men wear shorts and the women wear skirts purchased from Lumi's four small stores. To appear

in a semblance of European dress, however meager or worn, is a matter of pride and modesty to both sexes. "Savages" do not wear clothes, but white men and those who have been enlightened by white men do. In this sense, the Wape's Western-style dress represents an identification with the politically and materially powerful white man. The identification is with power; it is an ego-enhancing maneuver that permits the Wape to live with dignity, even though they are subservient to Western rule and influence. The tendency of the Wape to identify with, and incorporate, the alien when it serves to preserve their culture will help us to understand how they have woven diverse cultural strands into the creation of the shotgun cult.

From the first day I arrived in Taute, the men repeatedly made two urgent requests of me. One was to open a store in the village, saving them the difficult walk into Lumi; the other was to buy a shotgun to help them kill game. This was the

least, they seemed to indicate, a fair-minded and, in Wape terms, obviously rich neighbor should do. One of the hardest things the anthropologist in the field must learn is to say "no" to deserving people. To be stingy is almost to be un-American, but we had come half-way around the world to learn about the Wape way of life, not to introduce stores and shotguns that would alter the established trading and hunting patterns.

After several months the people of the major Taute hamlets, Kafiere, where we lived, and Mifu, a ten-minute walk away, each decided to buy a group-owned shotgun. The investment was a sizable forty-two Australian dollars; forty dollars for the gun and two dollars for the gun permit. Each hamlet made a volunteer collection from its members and I, as a fellow villager,

Left, men carry a wild pig into a hunting camp. There it will be ritually butchered and distributed to other villagers by the owner of the cartridge, which the gunman, below used to kill the animal.

contributed to both guns. A week later the villagers purchased the guns from one of the Lumi stores, and I began to learn about the shotgun's ritual and moral importance to the Wape. The villagers were already familiar with the significance of the shotgun for they had purchased one several years before. The cult ended, however, when the gun broke.

The shotgun, like Melanesian Pidgin, is associated by the Wape with Europeans and modernity. Not surprisingly, Pidgin is favored for shotgun parlance. The licensed gunman is not only called *sutboi* ("shootboy") but also *laman* ("law man"), the latter a term that connotes his official tie to European law and government as perceived by the villagers.

When a candidate for a gun permit appears before the government official in Lumi, he is examined orally on the use of firearms, then given an unloaded shotgun and tested on his handling knowledge. Under the direct and questioning gaze of the examining official, candidates sometimes become flustered. One inadvertently aimed the gun first toward the wife of the assistant district commissioner and then toward a group of observers. His examination ended ignominiously on the spot.

If the candidate passes the test and the examining official approves of his character, he is then lectured on the use of the gun: only the candidate can fire it, he must willingly shoot game for his fellow villagers, and the gun must be used exclusively for hunting. He is strongly warned that if any of these rules are broken or if there is trouble in the village, he will lose the gun and the permit and will be imprisoned.

The candidate's friends and the inevitable audience are present for the lecture. Here, as in many spheres of native life, the official's power is absolute, and the Wape know this from long experience. Guns have been confiscated or destroyed without reimbursement, and gunmen have been jailed.

The official's charge to the candidate is willingly accepted. Henceforth, he will never leave the village without carrying his gun. He is now a *laman*, and he has the gun and permit, printed entirely in English, to prove it.

The government official's strong sanctions against village quarrels are motivated by his fear that the gun might be used in a dispute among villagers. The sanctions are further upheld by the missionaries' and catechists' sermons against quarreling and wrongdoing as they attempt to teach the Christian doctrine of brotherly love. The message the villagers receive is this: To keep the white man's gun, they must follow the white man's rules. This the Wape do, not in servile submission, but with some pride because the presence of the gun and the public focus on morality mark the village as progressive and modern. The licensed gunman, therefore, is not only the guardian of the gun but of village morality as well.

Rain or shine, he is expected to go into the forest without compensation to hunt for his fellow villagers, who give him cartridges with some personal identifying mark upon them. After a gunman makes a kill, the owner of the cartridge receives the game and distributes it according to his economic obligations to others. But the gunman, like the bow and arrow hunter, is forbidden to eat from the kill; to do so would jeopardize further successful hunting.

In the hamlet of Kafiere, the clan that had contributed the most money toward the gun and on whose lands the most game was to be found appointed Auwe as gunman. But Auwe's wife, Naiasu, was initially against his selection. Her previous husband, Semer, now dead several years, had been Kafiere's first *sutboi* and she argued that the heavy hunting responsibilities of a *sutboi* took too much time, forcing him to neglect his own gardening and hunting obligations.

When Auwe first requested a gun permit he was turned away. The vil-

lagers believed that the ghost of Naiasu's dead husband, Semer, had followed Auwe to Lumi and influenced the examining official against him. Semer's ghost was acting to fulfill Naiasu's wish that her young son, now Auwe's stepson, would have a stepfather who was always available. This was the first of many stories I was to hear about the relationship between ghosts and the gun. When Auwe returned to Lumi for a second try, he passed the examination and was given the official permit.

The hamlet now had its own gun and hunting could begin in earnest. The first step was an annunciation feast called, in Pidgin, a *kapti* ("cup of tea"). Its purpose was to inform the villagers' dead ancestors about the new gun. This was important because ancestral ghosts roam the forest land of their lineage, protecting it from intruders and driving game to their hunting descendants. The hunter's most important hunting aide is his dead male relatives, to whom he prays for game upon entering his hunting lands. The dead remain active in the affairs of the living by protecting them from harm, providing them with meat, and punishing those who have wronged them.

The small sacrificial feast was held in front of Auwe's house. Placing the upright gun on a makeshift table in the midst of the food, Auwe rubbed it with sacred ginger. One of Auwe's elderly clansmen, standing and facing his land, called out to his ancestors by name and told them about the new gun. He implored them to send wild pigs and cassowaries to Auwe.

Several men spoke of the new morality that was to accompany hunting with a gun. The villagers should not argue or quarrel among themselves; problems must be settled quietly and without bitterness; malicious gossip and stealing were forbidden. If these rules were not obeyed, Auwe would not find game.

In traditional Wape culture there is no feast analogous to the *kapti*. Indeed, there are no general com-

munity-wide feasts. The *kapti* is apparently modeled on a European social gathering.

For the remainder of my stay in Taute, I followed closely the fortunes of the Taute guns and of guns in nearby villages as well. All seemed to be faced with the same two problems: game was rarely seen; and when seen, was rarely killed. Considering that a cartridge belongs to a villager, not the gunman, how was this economic loss handled? This presented a most intriguing and novel problem for there were no analogs to this type of predicament within the traditional culture. By Wape standards, the pecuniary implications of such a loss, although but a few Australian shillings, could not graciously be ignored by the loser. At the very least the loss had to be explained even if the money for the cartridges could not be retrieved.

Now I understood the concern about the ancestral ghosts. If the hunter shot and missed, the owner of the fired shells was being punished by being denied meat. Either he or a close family member had quarreled or wronged another person whose ghost-relative was securing revenge by causing the hunter to miss. This, then, was the functional meaning of the proscription against quarreling. By avoiding disputes, the villagers were trying to prevent the intervention of ancestral ghosts in human affairs. In a peaceful village without quarrels, the gunman could hunt undisturbed by vengeful ghosts chasing away game or misrouting costly shells.

Although a number of factors in European culture have influenced the shotgun cult, the cult's basic premise of a positive correlation between quarreling and bad hunting is derived directly from traditional Wape culture. In bow and arrow hunting, an individual who feels he was not given his fair share of a hunter's kill may punish the hunter by gossiping about him or quarreling openly with him. The aggrieved person's ancestral ghosts revenge the slight by chasing the game away from the offending hunter or misdirecting his arrows. But this is a private affair between the hunter and the angered person; their quarrel has no influence upon the hunting of others. And it is rare for an issue other than distribution of game to cause a ghost to hinder a bowman's success. The hunter's prowess is restored only when the angered person performs a brief supplication rite over the hunter.

This, then, is the conceptual basis for the tie between quarreling and bad hunting. Originally relevant only to bow and arrow hunting, it was then broadened to accommodate the government's pronouncements about the shotgun and keeping the village peace. And it applies perfectly to the special circumstances of shotgun hunting. Because the shotgun is community owned and many villagers buy cartridges for it, the villagers are identified with both the gun and the gunman. As a proxy hunter for the villagers, the gunman is potentially subject to the ghostly sanctions resulting from their collective wrongs. Thus gun hunting, unlike bow and arrow hunting, is a community affair and the community-wide taboo against quarrels and personal transgressions is the only effective way to prevent spiteful ghosts from wrecking the hunt.

No village, however, even if populated by people as disciplined and well behaved as the Wape, can constantly live in the state of pious peace considered necessary for continuous good gun hunting. When the hunting is poor, the gunman must discover the quarrels and wrongs within the village. After having identified the individuals whose ancestral ghosts are sabotaging the hunting, the gunman must also see to it that they implore the ghosts to stop. Embarrassed by the public disclosure, they will quickly comply.

The common method for detecting points of friction within the village is to bring the villagers together for a special meeting. The gunman will then document in detail his misfortunes and call on the villagers to find out what is ruining the hunting. If confessions of wrongdoing are not forthcoming, questioning accusations result. The meeting, beginning in Pidgin, moves into Wape as the discussion becomes more complex and voluble. It may last up to three hours; but even if there is no resolution, it always ends amiably—at least on the surface. For it is important to create no new antagonisms.

The other technique for locating the source of the hunting problem is to call in a professional clairvoyant. As the villagers must pay for his services, he is usually consulted only after a series of unsuccessful meetings. Clairvoyants have replaced the shamans, who were outlawed by the government and the mission because they practiced sorcery and ritual murders. The Wape do not consider a clairvoyant a sorcerer; he is a man with second sight who is experienced in discovering and treating the hidden causes of intractable problems. As such, shotguns are among his best patients.

Mewau, a clairvoyant from a neighboring village, held a "shotgun clinic" in Taute to examine the Mifu and Kafiere guns. For about an hour he examined the two guns and questioned the villagers. Then he declared the reasons for their misfortune.

Kapul, a dead Mifu shaman, was preventing the Mifu gun from killing game because a close relative of the gunman had allegedly stolen valuables from Kapul's daughter. Because of the family ties between the gunman and the thief, Kapul's ghost was punishing the gunman.

The Kafiere gun, Mewau declared, was not able to find game because a widow in the village felt that her dead husband's clan had not previously distributed game to her in a fair way. By interfering with the Kafiere gun, her husband's ghost was punishing his clan for the neglect of his family.

Once the source of trouble is named, there are several possible types of remedial ritual depending upon the seriousness of the situation. For example, the circumstances surrounding the naming of the husband's ghost were considered serious, and a *kapti* was held to placate him. Another, simpler ritual involves the preparation of taro soup, which the gunman consumes. But the simplest, commonest remedial rite is the supplication ritual without sacrificial food offerings, a ritual in which I became involved.

Mifu's gunman had shot a pig with one of his own cartridges but did not give me the small portion due me as a part owner of the gun. Partly as a test to see if my ancestors counted for anything in Taute and partly because I did not want to let this calculated slight go unchallenged, I, in typical Wape fashion, said nothing to the gunman but gossiped discreetly about his selfishness. The gunman continued to hunt but had no further success. When his bad luck persisted, a meeting was called to find out the reason. The gunman asked me if I was angry because I had not been given my portion of the pig. When I acknowledged my anger, he handed the shotgun to me and I dutifully spoke out to my ancestors to stop turning the game away from the gun.

But the gunman still had no success in the hunt, and the villagers decided there were other wrongs as well. The search for the offending ghosts continued. Eventually the villagers became so discouraged with the Mifu gun that they stopped giving cartridges to the gunman. The consensus was that a major undetected wrong existed in the hamlet, and until it was uncovered and the guilty ghost called off, hunting with the gun was senseless and extravagant. Thus the propriety of a remedial rite is established if there is success on the next hunt. The system is completely empirical; if no game is seen or if seen, is not killed, then the search for the wrong must continue.

Wape people are generally even tempered, and their villages, in contrast to many in New Guinea, strike the newcomer as almost serene. But the social impact of the guns at this time was pervasive, and life in Taute literally revolved around the guns and their hunting fortunes. Whereas the villagers previously had kept to their own affairs, they now became embroiled in meeting after meeting, seeking out transgressions, quarrels, and wrongdoing. As the gunman continued to have bad luck, his efforts to discover the cause became more zealous. A certain amount of polarization resulted: the gunman accused the villagers, the men accused the women, and the adults accused the young people of hiding their wrongs. And a few who had lost many cartridges wondered if the *sutboi* was keeping the game for himself. But no one ever suggested that he was an inexperienced shotgun hunter. The gunman was generally considered to be blameless; in fact, the more game he missed, the more self-righteous he became and the more miscreant the villagers.

Six months of poor hunting had gone by; the villagers felt that the only recourse left to them was to bring a bush demon named *mani* into the village from the jungle for a festival. The *mani*'s small stone heart is kept enshrined in a rustic altar in a corner of Kafiere's ceremonial house and after a kill the animal's blood is smeared upon it. The *mani* will reward the village with further kills only if he is fed with blood. *Mani* is the only spirit,

other than ghosts, who can cause both good and bad hunting depending upon the way he is treated. Soon after the shotgun arrived in Taute, the gunman and some other men left their homes to sleep in the men's ceremonial house to keep *mani*'s stone heart warm. They thought *mani*, in appreciation, would send game to the gunman.

When little game was killed, the villagers decided on the hunting festival. In a special house outside of the village, men constructed the great conical mask that depicts *mani*. For several weeks they worked to cover the mask's frame with the spathes of sago palm fronds painted with designs traditional to *mani*. Finally, a priest of the *mani* cult, wearing a 20-foot-high mask festooned with feathers and leaves, pranced into the village to the thunderous beat of wooden drums.

For the next week and a half men from other villages who wished us well came and joined in the all-night singing of the *mani* song cycle. In the morning, if the weather was clear, *mani* led the bow and arrow hunters and the gunman to the edge of the village and sent them on their way to hunting success. But in spite of the careful attentions the villagers directed toward *mani*, he rewarded them with only one wild pig. The villagers became openly discouraged, then annoyed. Finally the hunters, disgusted and weary from numerous

long futile hunts, and other men, their shoulders sore and bloody from constantly carrying the heavy mask around the plaza, decided that *mani* was simply taking advantage of them; all of their hard work was for nothing. Disgusted, they decided to send *mani* back to his home in the forest.

One late afternoon the *mani* appeared in the plaza but he did not prance. He walked slowly around the plaza, stopping at each house to throw ashes over himself with his single bark cloth arm. The villagers said he was in mourning because he had to leave by dusk and would miss the company of men. Silently the people watched the once gay and graceful *mani* lumber out of the village. The men and boys followed him into the forest. Then the gunman split open the mask, to insure the spirit's exit and eventual return to his forest home, and hurled it over the edge of the cliff into the bush below.

A few months after the *mani* hunting festival, the shotgun cult as I had known it in Taute ceased to function. All but one of the able young men of the hamlet of Kafiere went off to work on a coastal plantation for two years. With no young men, the ceremonial activities of the hunting and curing cults were suspended and the fault-finding meetings halted until their return. The drama and excitement of the previous months had vanished with the men.

TOPIC TEN

Economy and Society

· ·

All societies have institutionalized the production, distribution, and consumption of material goods and services—that is, they have an *economic system*. The form of a society's economy will have a profound impact on many other social institutions—a point well made in Marshall Sahlin's study of the political economies of Melanesia and Polynesia, which we included in the previous topic ("Poor Man, Rich Man, Big-Man, Chief"). In "Subsistence Strategies and the Organization of Social Life," David E. K. Hunter reviews data from archaeology and ethnology to indicate ways in which economies influence other aspects of social life. In doing so, he begins with the simplest hunting and food-gathering societies and ends with a sketch of modern industrial society. As you will see, one of the critical factors is not so much the specific subsistence strategy employed by a society, but whether or not the economy is organized around the production and distribution of surpluses.

Allen Johnson, in his article "In Search of the Affluent Society," focuses on consumption rather than on production. He argues that the narrow economist's view is inadequate for assessing economic systems—that a critical variable is the quality of life an economic system permits its participants. In comparing a "simple" Amazonian society to French society, Johnson shows that, contrary to what you might believe, the "simple" society provides its members with more time for visiting, play, conversation, and rest than does French society. And he shares with us some of the personal questions this raises for him.

29

Subsistence Strategies and the Organization of Social Life

BY DAVID E. K. HUNTER

....

The sun beats down on the parched grasses, and its heat radiates from the rocky soil of the Kalahari Desert in southern Africa. Across the bleached landscape three men move slowly, in single file, keeping a line of thorny bushes between them and the herd of grazing giraffes. They have prayed and they have prepared their hunting arrows with poison freshly made from beetle paste. Now, with luck, one of them will wound a giraffe and they will follow it—for days, if necessary—until the poison works itself throughout the giant creature's bloodstream and slowly numbs and paralyzes it. Carefully avoiding its desperate last kicks, the men will use their clubs and spears to kill the animal. They will butcher it wherever it has fallen, cutting the meat into strips to dry in the sun. Then, finally, the men will return to their families camped in brush-and-hide windbreaks around a waterhole. The bones, the hide, and the meat will be passed from hand to hand, divided according to ancient customs, distributed along lines of family and kinship.

The people described here belong to the !Kung San (formerly known as the Bushmen); about 45,000 still live a semi-nomadic hunting and food-gathering existence in the Kalahari Desert. Their camps are small, numbering ten to thirty members, and they are communal and egalitarian. The sharing of food is fundamental to their way of life, and when, for whatever reasons, food sharing breaks down, the camp ceases to be a meaningful social unit: people pack their few belongings and move elsewhere, to camps of their relatives.

ECONOMY, SOCIETY, AND THE COMPARATIVE METHOD

In its most general sense, *economy* refers to the organized ways in which a society produces (or otherwise secures), distributes, and consumes its material goods (raw materials, products, and so on) and its services (that is, the patterns of behavior that supply individuals with their needs). Economic institutions are interlaced with the other social institutions of a society—indeed,

so much so, that separating them out for study is quite difficult. In order to do so here, and to indicate some of the ways in which economy and society are interwoven, this article focuses on strategies of subsistence and the ways in which such strategies affect and are affected by the organization of social groupings.

In order to keep this discussion reasonably brief and to the point, subsistence strategies will be considered under five main categories: hunting and food gathering, horticulture, pastoralism, agriculture, and industrialism. Inevitably, this classification has meant doing some violence to the actual facts—overlooking the ways in which the different strategies actually blend into or overlap with each other and stereotyping various social groups in terms of predominant features while downplaying (or even overlooking) other facets of their economic lives. This is the price one pays for using the comparative method; it is justified, however, if the main patterns it highlights nevertheless have something important to teach.

Anthropologists, in attempting to study and compare societies (both past and present) around the world, must take into account the tremendous impact of European imperialism and colonialism on the societies of Africa, Asia, and the Americas. Those societies that managed to survive into modern times often are distorted versions of their ancestral forms. Their populations were decimated by European diseases, their diversified subsistence systems were subordinated to the single cash-crop demands of European markets, their social life and political systems were torn apart by a tremendous increase in organized warfare (Sahlins 1972). However, while keeping these facts in mind, anthropologists have been able to note certain recurring patternings of social life that seem to be tightly tied to basic subsistence strategies.

Hunting and Food-Gathering Societies

The earliest human societies subsisted by foraging for vegetable foods and small game, fishing, collecting shellfish, and hunting larger animals. In modern times, the world's simplest and most marginal societies still subsist using these methods. They depend to a large degree on tools made of stone, wood, and bone.

Similarities among Hunting and Food-Gathering Societies. Although there are significant cultural differences among such groups, and in spite of the fact that they occupy environments varying from deserts to frozen wastelands, nevertheless there are certain recurring features of economic and social organizations that hunters and food-gatherers share—features that set them off from other kinds of societies. Contrary to both popular and scholarly preconceptions, hunting and food-gathering peoples do not work very hard. In fact, more time is spent socializing than in procuring food, which occupies perhaps some five hours per day (Sahlins 1972:1–39). Their communities are mobile and small. On the whole, social relationships among individuals tend to be quite egalitarian, at least in part because there is little private property. There is no social class differentiation, nor even institutionalized positions of prestige that are limited to favored subgroups.

In general, men are primarily responsible for hunting and for protecting the group. The women often hunt smaller game and forage for food (both animal and vegetable), typically providing some 60 to 70 percent of the total calories consumed by the group (Lee 1969). Women also take primary responsibility for raising the children. Marriage, in one or another form, in universally present, with monogamy the dominant form. Most social life is organized in terms of people's kinship relations. That is, the ways in which people are related to each other determines whether or not they may marry, what kinds of food or material goods they will exchange with each other, whether they observe the same taboos, and so on.

Differences among Hunting and Food-Gathering Societies. In spite of all these similarities, significant differences in societal organization do exist among contemporary hunting and food-gathering societies (Martin 1974). For one thing, political organization takes several forms, including male-centered kinship groups, female-centered kinship groups, and groups organized along kinship lines irrespective of gender. Those groups living in harsh climates and with a correspondingly low productivity are quite small, often numbering less than a few hundred individuals. But where nature is bountiful or affords special means of accumulating food surpluses (as on the Northwest Coast of North America, where annual salmon runs provided abundant food that could be stored for year-round consumption), hunting and food-gathering societies grew large, numbering into the thousands. Similarly, whereas most such groups are semi-nomadic because of their

need to search for food, those who inhabit rich environments have developed sedentary village settlements. And with surplus food production and a sedentary life-style, social inequality is institutionalized among hunting and food-gathering groups just as it is in more technologically advanced societies (Martin and Voorhies 1975).

Horticultural Societies

Some 12,000 to 15,000 years ago, coinciding with the retreat of the last glaciers, a drying trend occurred in what previously had been rich, subtropical climates. The giant deserts of Africa, Asia, and the Middle East took shape. Even beyond their constantly expanding borders, new arid conditions made the age-old hunting and food-gathering way of life precarious. Some groups continued to eke out an existence using the old subsistence techniques. Others crowded together in the more abundant regions, harvesting wild grains until population pressures drove them out into less favorable environments. There they attempted to recreate the rich environments they had left. And in doing so, they created a whole new way of subsisting: the domestication of plants and animals (Flannery 1965, 1968). This process seems to have repeated itself at least three times in three different places: in the Far East in Thailand some 11,000 years ago; in the Middle East, about 10,000 years ago; and in Mesoamerica, some 6,000 to 9,000 years ago. From these three centers of origin, the domestication of plants and animals spread outward, until it became the most widespread means of subsistence and the economic base upon which all civilizations were built.

Recent research, reported in 1980 and 1981, indicates that people living in widely scattered areas of the world may well have domesticated some plant and animal species as early as 19,000 years ago. Wheat and barley, for example, apparently were being grown along the Nile fully 8,000 years before these grains were domesticated in Mesopotamia. And Charles Nelson, an anthropologist at the University of Massachusetts at Boston, reports evidence of early domestication of cattle in Kenya, southern Europe, and southwestern Egypt. But these societies did not develop civilizations on their own. Nelson theorizes that for civilization to arise, several elements must combine in a fertile environment. First, plants and animals must be domesticated, and the technology for harvesting and storing crops must be developed. Then, a society must come into contact with other societies, diversifying its domesticated plant and animal species and opening itself both to trade and to the new ideas that inevitably come with commerce. When this happens, food becomes more abundant and overpopulation ensues. The result, Nelson argues, is the birth of civilization. Apparently, though plants and animals were domesticated in many places, the *combination* of elements leading to the birth of civilization occurred in only three places: the Far East, the Middle East, and Mesoamerica.

You should not imagine that the domestication of plants and animals brought an easier work load or more leisure time to its inventors. Whereas hunting and food-foraging peoples work perhaps three to four days (averaging five hours per day) out of every week to secure their food, food *producers* (domesticators) must work every day—and long hours at that! Marvin Harris (1975:233–255), after comparing research on the energy spent and calories produced by five societies, concludes that the advantage of food production over hunting and food gathering lies in the ability of food producers to sustain settlements, rather than in any labor-saving improvements in productivity or in increased leisure time.

Horticulture is a technical term referring to the planting of gardens and fields using only human muscle power and the mechanical advantage of handheld tools (such as digging sticks and hoes), whereas *agriculture* refers to the use of an animal-drawn plow. There are two distinct approaches to horticulture: subsistence farming (producing only enough to feed the group) and surplus farming. The differences between the two are quite profound.

Subsistence Farming. Subsistence farmers live in environments that are unfavorable to cultivation. They are most often found in tropical or subtropical jungles where the forest constantly must be cleared away and always threatens to overgrow the fields. Every few years subsistence farmers must move their settlements when new fields have to be cleared. Their settlements are small, and competition among neighboring villages typically is high. In fact, ongoing feuding, raiding, and even prescheduled battles between the forces of nearby villages are not uncommon. Political organization rarely extends beyond the village, and usually it is based on positions that are inherited by males through the kinship system.

Where the environment is less difficult, competition and fighting among villages drop remarkably, and the political system frequently is organized around kinship-related women rather than men (Otterbein and Otterbein 1965). In this context, few differences in power and prestige exist between men and women. In fact, relationships between the sexes approach the egalitarian qualities generally found in hunting and food-gathering societies.

Although, in the richer environments, the production of surplus food is technologically possible, surplus production simply is not a culturally valued norm. Hence role specialization is relatively undeveloped—

not very much greater than among hunting and food-gathering groups. It seems, therefore, that with an abundant environment and little by way of tradable surpluses, social stratification and the institutionalization of prestige ranking are minimal.

Surplus Farming. Surplus farmers live in densely populated, permanent settlements. They have highly elaborated political institutions that tend to be male-dominated and structured by kinship relations. There is occupational specialization with the institutionalization of prestige differences, and social stratification is well established. Because the production of surpluses is a culturally valued norm, such societies often are expansionistic, with differentiated military force. Expansion means more land and more (captured) labor, which in turn allows the centralized accumulation of greater surpluses that can be used to pay for political support, specialized craftspeople, and conspicuous consumption.

As in hunting and food-gathering societies, women in horticultural societies perform most of the productive work associated with securing food. Although the men will do the heaviest work, such as clearing the fields, it is usually the women who prepare the fields, plant the crops, tend and harvest them, and share the food with their husbands and extended families (D'Andrade 1966, Murdock 1937).

Pastoralist Societies

Pastoralism is an approach to food production that relies on herding and animal husbandry to satisfy the bulk of a group's needs. Animal herds provide milk, dung (for fuel), skin, sheared fur, and even blood (which is drunk as a major source of protein in East Africa).

Pastoralist societies have flourished in many regions that are not suitable for plant domestication, such as semi-arid desert regions and the northern tundra plains of Europe and Asia. They are also found in less severe climates, including East African savannas and mountain grasslands. However, pastoralism almost never occurs in forest or jungle regions. It is an interesting fact, which scholars have not been able to explain, that no true pastoralist societies ever emerged in the Americas prior to the arrival of the Europeans.

Although many pastoralist groups rely partly on horticulture to subsist, most are nomads (or semi-nomads) who follow their herds in a never-ending quest for pasture lands and water. Hence, such societies typically consist of relatively small, mobile communities. When needed resources are predictable, pastoralist societies typically are composed of stable groups united under strong political figures. When resources are not predictable, they are quick to split apart and compete with each other. Hence, centralized political leadership does not appear (Salzman 1967). To the extent that political organization does exist, pastoralist societies generally are organized around male-centered kinship groups.

Pastoralism rests on three strategic resources: animal herds, pasture lands, and water. Animals usually are more or less equally available to all families in pastoralist groups. But access to the latter two resources often varies widely among families in such societies. Hence, although there are great differences of wealth in some pastoralist groups, rarely is there institutionalized stratification. When social classes and centralized political organization do develop, they appear to be responses to expansionist pressures from neighboring state-level societies.

When, through bonds of kinship, pastoralist societies have organized into those enormous sociopolitical entities called hordes, their extreme mobility, fierceness, and kinship-based fanatic loyalty have made them into extraordinary military powers. As such, nomadic pastoralists have influenced the course of civilization far more than their numbers alone would suggest. It was to keep out Central Asian hordes that the emperors of the Chou dynasty in China built the Great Wall in the third and fourth centuries B.C. And it was nomadic pastoralist armies who, in the fourth and fifth centuries A.D., drove the final nails into the coffin of the Roman Empire in the West. In fact, many of the states of ancient Asia, the Middle East, and Eastern Europe arose partly in protective response to pastoralist raids. But in fairness it must be said that pastoralists influenced civilizations not only through their destructiveness. In what is now Hungary, for example, the nomads themselves first established some of the oldest politically centralized societies in Europe (Cohen 1974).

Agricultural Societies

Agriculture, as we noted before, is plant cultivation that makes use of the plow. Agriculture is more efficient than horticulture. Plowing makes use of the far greater muscle power of draft animals, and it also turns the topsoil much deeper than does hoeing, allowing for better airing and fertilizing of the ground and thus improving the yield. Nevertheless, early agriculture probably did not yield much more than food gatherers in bountiful environments were able to harvest. However, by around 5500 B.C., farmers in the Middle East not only were using the plow, but *irrigation* as well. With irrigation, farming became capable of producing vast surpluses—enough to feed large numbers of people who did not produce food themselves.

Reliance on irrigated agriculture had several drastic and interrelated consequences for society. It pulled ever-growing populations together into those areas where irrigation could be practiced—into broad river valleys like those of the Nile in Egypt, the Tigris and Euphrates in the Middle East, the Huangho (Yellow River) in China, and the Danube and Rhine in Europe. This rapidly rising and geographically compressed population density gave rise to cities and to new social forms. For the first time, society was *not* organized principally in terms of kinship. Rather, occupational diversity and institutional specialization (including differentiated political, economic, and religious institutions) predominated.

Dependence on irrigation had additional, even more far-reaching, consequences. Irrigation projects are large and complicated. They consist of dams, canals and elaborate systems of ditches whose use must be carefully coordinated. The planning and building of such projects takes experts with the time and authority to direct the efforts of hundreds and even thousands of specialized laborers and farmers. This can be accomplished only by a society with centralized political organization. And it is clear that at least in the case of Chinese civilization, the organizational demands of irrigation farming led to the emergence of the centralized state (Wittfogel 1957).

Irrigated agriculture also made land that was suitable for farming into a scarce resource. Those who controlled access to arable land and its use soon were rich and powerful. They could command the payment of taxes and political support. By taxing the bulk of agricultural surpluses, political leaders could employ bureaucracies to implement their plans and armies to protect their privileges—both from external enemies and internal rebels. Thus social classes became entrenched, and the State evolved. Not surprisingly, the State is the most warlike of all sociopolitical forms (Otterbein 1970). For agricultural (and industrial) societies, conquest makes economic sense because it brings new farmlands and food producers under the State's control, increasing the surpluses at its disposal and thereby making possible ever more ambitious undertakings.

Industrial Society

The industrial revolution was a European and American phenomenon. Industrialism consists of the use of mechanical means (machines and chemical processes) for the production of goods. Contrary to its name the industrial "revolution" at first developed slowly. It had begun primarily in England early in the eighteenth century and gained momentum by the turn of the nineteenth century (Eli Whitney built a factory for the mass production of guns near New Haven, Connecticut in 1798). By the mid-1800s, it had swung into high gear with the invention of the steam locomotive and Henry Bessemer's development of large-scale production techniques at his steel works in England in 1858. It is called a "revolution" because of the enormous changes industrialism brought about in society.

Industrial society is characterized by more than just the use of mechanical means for production. It is an entirely new form of society that requires an immense, mobile, diversely specialized, highly skilled, and well-coordinated labor force. Among other things, this means that the labor force must be educated. Imagine the difficulties facing even the least skilled factory worker who cannot read. Hence an educational system open to all is a hallmark of industrial society—something that was not necessary in pre-industrial times. Industrialism also requires the creation of highly organized systems of exchange between the suppliers of raw materials and industrial manufacturers on the one hand, and between the manufacturers and consumers on the other.

Like agricultural societies, industrial societies inevitably are stratified. The nature of the stratification varies, depending on whether the society allows private ownership of capital (capitalism) or puts all capital in the hands of the State (socialism). However, all industrial societies may be said to have at least two social classes: (1) a large labor force that produces goods and services but has no say in what is done with them; and (2) a much smaller class that determines what shall be produced and how it shall be distributed.

Industrialism brought about a tremendous shift of populations. Over the past century and a half, vast numbers of rural peasants and farmers have migrated from the countryside to the cities, transforming themselves into what is called an urban proletariate. Kinship, which still played an important role in the organization of preindustrial agricultural society, now plays a much smaller role in patterning public affairs. (Some newly emergent industrial societies, such as those Arab states like Saudi Arabia that grew into existence from a nomadic pastoralist base, still are organized sociopolitically in terms of kinship relations.) Similarly, religious institutions, which in preindustrial society were very closely tied to political institutions, no longer dominate the scene—industrial society is highly secularized. (An exception to this generalization is the existence of so-called civil religions, such as Marxist-Leninism in socialist countries; another is the recent creation of a new Islamic state in Iran by followers of the Ayatollah Khomeini.) In general, the predominant form of social and political organization in industrial society is the bureaucracy—that least personal of all formal organizations, itself having been inspired by the model of the efficiently functioning machine the symbol of industrial production and of industrial society as a way of life.

SOCIETY AND ECONOMY

This article attempts to indicate some of the ways in which the economy and other social institutions are interwoven to make up the fabric of society. To accomplish this, it has focused on one aspect of economy—namely, the major strategies of subsistence that societies around the world employ. This is not meant to suggest that all social institutions are created only in response to—or caused by—subsistence strategies (or other aspects of the economy). That kind of a simplistic, one-way causal view, called economic determinism, enjoyed a vogue around the turn of this century before it was thoroughly refuted by careful research. Even those anthropologists who study cultural ecology—that is, the ways in which peoples' cultures adapt them to their environments—do not propose that environments or even subsistence strategies directly cause specific sociocultural forms to emerge. Rather, anthropologists recognize that human groups exist in dynamic relationships with the environment, that they both respond to and act upon the environment, and that the ways in which they interact with the environment have consequences for their social lives individually and as social groups.

Within this set of interdependent relationships, each society picks its way making use of culturally inherited patterns and also newly acquired, invented, or discovered techniques of production and distribution. Hence, in every generation, each society recreates and also modifies (to whatever degree) its design for living, its particular solutions to the problems of existence. Using the comparative method, anthropologists are able to point to some of the patterned commonalities and differences among societies. Here, I have highlighted these by organizing them in terms of the five major approaches to, or strategies for, subsistence.

References

Cohen, Yehudi A.
   1974 "Pastoralism," in Yehudi A. Cohen (ed.), *Man in Adaptation: The Cultural Present* (2nd ed.), Chicago: Aldine.

D'Andrade, Roy
   1966 "Sex differences and cultural institutions," in Eleanor Maccoby (ed.), *The Development of Sex Differences*, Stanford: Stanford University Press.

Flannery, Kent V.
   1965 "The ecology of early food production in Mesoamerica," *Science*, vol. 147:1247–1256.
   1968 "Archaeological systems theory and early Mesopotamia," in Betty J. Meggars (ed.), *Anthropological Archaeology in the Americas*, Washington, D.C.: The Anthropological Society of Washington.

Harris, Marvin
   1975 *Culture, People, Nature*, New York: Thomas Y. Crowell.

Martin, M. Kay, and Barbara Voorhies
   1975 *The Female of the Species*, New York: Columbia University Press.

Murdock, George Peter
   1937 "Comparative data on the division of labor by sex," *Social Forces*, vol. 16:551–553.

Otterbein, Keith
   1970 *The Evolution of War*, New Haven, Conn.: Human Relations Area Files.

Otterbein, Keith, and Charlotte Swanson Otterbein
   1965 "An eye for an eye, a tooth for a tooth: a cross-cultural study of feuding, "*American Anthropologist*, vol. 67:1470–1482.

Sahlins, Marshall
   1972 *Stone Age Economics*, Chicago: Aldine

Salzman, Philip C.
   1967 "Political organization among nomadic peoples," *Proceedings of the American Philosophical Society*, vol. 3:115–131.

Wittfogel, Karl
   1957 *Oriental Despotism,* New Haven, Conn.: Yale University Press.

30

In Search of the Affluent Society

BY ALLEN JOHNSON

One of the paradoxes of modern life is the persistence of suffering and deep dissatisfaction among people who enjoy an unparalleled abundance of material goods. The paradox is at least as old as our modern age. Ever since the benefits and costs of industrial technology became apparent, opinion has been divided over whether we are progressing or declining.

The debate grows particularly heated when we compare our civilization with the cultures of "primitive" or "simpler" peoples. At the optimistic extreme, we are seen as the beneficiaries of an upward development that has brought us from an era in which life was said to be "nasty, brutish, and short," into one of ease, affluence, and marvelous prospects for the future. At the other extreme, primitives are seen as enjoying idyllic lives of simplicity and serenity, from which we have descended dangerously through an excess of greed. The truth is a complex mix of these two positions, but it is striking how difficult it is to take a balanced view. We are attracted irresistibly to either the optimistic or the pessimistic position.

The issue is of more than academic interest. The modern world is trying to come to grips with the idea of "limits to growth" and the need to redistribute wealth. Pressures are mounting from the environment on which we depend and from the people with whom we share it. Scientists, planners, and policy makers are now talking about "alternative futures," trying to marshal limited resources for the greater good of

humanity. In this context it is useful to know whether people living in much simpler economies than our own really do enjoy advantages we have lost.

In his book *The Affluent Society*, economist John Kenneth Galbraith accepts the optimistic view, with some reservations. According to him, the modern trend has been toward an increase in the efficiency of production; working time has decreased while the standard of living has risen through a growth in purchasing power. One of Galbraith's reservations is that he does not see this growth as an unmitigated good. He sees our emphasis on acquiring goods as left over from times when the experience of poverty was still real and thinks we are ready to acknowledge our wealth and reduce our rates of consumption. The trend over the last 100 years toward a shorter work week, he argues, demonstrates that we are relinquishing some of our purchasing power in exchange for greater leisure.

Galbraith's view that modern affluence both brings us greater leisure and fills our basic needs better than any previous economic system is widespread. Yet the first part of this view is almost certainly wrong, and the second is debatable. Anthropologist Marshall Sahlins has shown that hunting-and-gathering economies, such as those found among the Australian aborigines and the San of southern Africa, require little work (three to four hours per adult each day) to provide ample and varied diets. Although they lack our abundance of goods, material needs are satisfied in a

leisurely way, and in their own view, people are quite well off.

Sahlins points out that there are two roads to affluence: our own, which is to produce more, and what he calls the Buddhist path, which is to be satisfied with less. Posing the problem of affluence in this way makes it clear that affluence depends not only on material wealth but also on subjective satisfaction. There is apparently plenty of room for choice in designing a life of affluence.

Recent studies of how people in different societies spend their time allow us to make a fairly objective comparison of primitive and modern societies. In one analysis, Alexander Szalai studied middle-class French couples residing in six cities in France—Arras, Besançon, Chalon-sur-Saône, Dunkerque, Épinal, and Metz. Orna Johnson and I, both of us anthropologists, collected similar data when we lived among the Machiguenga Indians of Peru for some 18 months, which were spread over one long and two shorter visits.

The Machiguenga live in extended family groups scattered throughout the Amazon rain forest. They spend approximately equal amounts of time growing food in gardens carved out of the surrounding forest and in hunting, fishing, and collecting wild foods. They are self-sufficient; almost everything they consume is produced by their own labors using materials that are found close at hand. Despite some similarities in how the French and the Machiguenga spend their time (for instance, in the way work is apportioned between the sexes), the differences between the societies are applicable to our purposes.

For reasons that will become clear, we divide ways of spending time into three categories: production time, consumption time, and free time. Production time refers to what we normally think of as work, in which goods and services are produced either for further production (capital goods) or for direct consumption (consumption goods). Consumption time refers to time spent using consumption goods. Eating, and what we think of as leisure time—watching television, visiting amusement parks, playing tennis—is spent this way. Free time is spent in neither production nor consumption; it includes sheer idleness, rest, sleep, and chatting.

Of course, these three categories of time are arbitrary. We could eliminate the difference between consumption time and free time, for example, by pointing out that the French consume beds and the Machiguenga consume mats during sleep. But we want to distinguish time spent at the movies or driving a car from time spent doing nothing—sitting idly by the door or casually visiting neighbors. This supports a main contention of our research: that little agreement now exists on exactly how to measure the differences between dissimilar societies.

For comparative purposes, we broke down our data into five categories of people, two for the Machiguenga and three for the French. For the relatively simple Machiguenga society, a division by gender was sufficient for studying patterns in time use. But for the more complex French society, a male-female breakdown was insufficient because such a division does not allow for working women. We divided the French data into three categories: men, working women, and housewives.

In production time French workers, both men and women, spend more time working outside the home than the Machiguenga do. French men work one and a half hours more per day away from home than do Machiguenga men;

employed French women work four hours more per day than do Machiguenga women. French housewives work less outside the home than Machiguenga women do, but they make up for this difference by exceeding their Machiguenga counterparts in work inside the home. French men spend more time working inside the home than do Machiguenga men. All told, French men spend more time engaged in production than do Machiguenga men, and French women (both working and housewives) spend more time in production activities than do Machiguenga women.

The French score equal to or higher than the Machiguenga on all measures of consumption. French men spend more

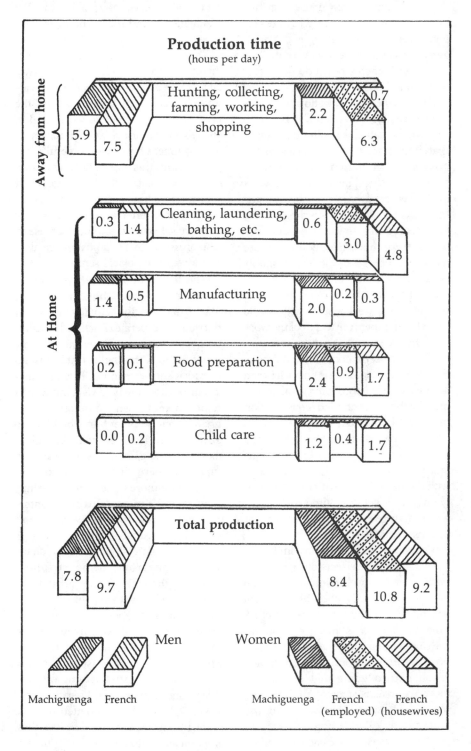

than three times as many hours in consumption as do Machiguenga men; French women consume goods at four or five times the rate of Machiguenga women, depending on whether they are employed or are housewives.

It is in the category of free time that the Machiguenga clearly surpass the French. Machiguenga men spend more than 14 hours per day engaged in free time, compared with nearly 10 hours for their French counterparts, and Machiguenga women have much more free time than French women do—whether or not the French women work.

The immediate question concerns differences in the overall pattern. It seems undeniable, as Sahlins has argued, that modern technological progress has not resulted in more free time for most people. The shrinking of the work week in the last century is probably nothing more than a short-term wrinkle in the historical trend toward longer work weeks. If our modern economy provides us with more goods, it is not simply because technical efficiency has increased. Indeed, the trend toward a shorter work week ended with World War II; since then, the length of the work week has remained about the same.

The increase of consumption time at the expense of free time is both a loss and a gain. Here we encounter a subtle, complex problem. Increased consumption may add excitement and pleasure to what would otherwise be considered boring time. On the other hand, this increase has the effect of crowding time with consumption activities so that people begin to feel that "time is short"—which may detract from the enjoyment of consumption.

Economist Staffan Burenstam Linder has looked at the effects of higher production and consumption of goods on our sense of time. To follow his argument we must move from the level of clock time to that of subjective time, as measured by our inner sense of the tempo of our lives. According to Linder, as a result of producing and consuming more, we are experiencing an increasing scarcity of time. This works in the following way. Increasing efficiency in production means that each individual

must produce more goods per hour; increased productivity means, though it is not often mentioned in this context, that to keep the system going we must consume more goods. Free time gets converted into consumption time because time spent neither producing nor consuming comes increasingly to be viewed as wasted. Linder's theory may account for the differences between the ways the Machiguenga and the French use their time.

The increase in the value of time (its increasing scarcity) is felt subjectively as an increase in tempo or pace. We are always in danger of being slow on the production line or late to work; and in our leisure we are always in danger of wasting time. I have been forcefully impressed with this aspect of time during several field visits to the Machiguenga. It happens each time I return to their communities that, after a period of two or three days, I sense a definite decrease in time pressure; this is a physiological as well as a psychological sensation.

This feeling of a leisurely pace of life reflects the fact that among the Machiguenga daily activities are never hurried or desperate. Each task is allotted its full measure of time, and free time is not felt to be boring or lost but is accepted as entirely natural. These feelings last throughout the field visit, but when I return home I am conscious of the pressure and sense of hurry building up to its former level. Something similar, though fleeting, happens on vacation trips—but here the pressure to consume, to see more sights while traveling, or to get one's money's worth in entertainment constantly asserts itself, and the tempo is usually kept up.

Linder sees a kind of evolutionary progression from "time surplus" societies through "time affluence" societies, ending with the "time famine" society of developed countries. The famine is expressed not only in a hectic pace, but also in a decline of activities in which goods are not consumed rapidly enough, such as spending time with the elderly and providing other social services. As Galbraith has pointed out, we neglect basic social needs because they are seen as economically unproductive.

Not only do we use our time for almost frantic consumption, but more of our time is also devoted to caring for the increasing number of goods we possess. The Machiguenga devote three to four times more of their production time at home to manufacturing (cloth and baskets, for example) than they do to maintenance activities, such as cleaning and doing the laundry; the French pattern is the reverse. This may help account for the failure of modern housewives to acquire more leisure time from their appliances, a situation that has prompted anthropologist Marvin Harris to refer to appliances as "labor-saving devices that don't save work."

On both objective and subjective grounds, then, it appears that economic growth has not given us more leisure time. If anything, the increasingly hectic pace of leisure activities detracts from our enjoyment of play, even when the increased stimulation they bring is taken into account. When we consider the abundance of goods, however, the situation is obviously different. The superiority of modern industrial technology in producing material goods is clear. The Machiguenga, and other people at a similar technological level, have no doubts on this score either. Despite their caution, which outsiders are apt to label "traditionalism," they really do undertake far-reaching changes in their ways of life in order to obtain even small quantities of industrial output.

One area in which the Machiguenga clearly need (and warmly welcome) Western goods is medicine. Despite hopeful speculations in popular writings that Amazon Indians have secret herbal remedies that are effective against infections, cancer, and other conditions, the curative powers of Machiguenga medicine are circumscribed. Antibiotics, even the lowly sulfa pill, are highly effective and much in demand for skin sores, eye infections, and other painful endemic health problems. Medicines to control such parasites as amoebae and intestinal worms bring immediate relief to a community, although people are eventually reinfected. In terms of human well-being, then, even the most romantic defender of the simple life must grant that modern medicines improve the lives of primitive people.

I am much less certain about what other Western goods to offer as evidence of the comparative lack of affluence among the Machiguenga. They have a great abundance of food, for example; they produce at least twice as many calories of food energy as they consume. (The excess production is not surplus so much as a security margin in case someone should fall ill or relatives unexpectedly come to stay for a time.) The Machiguenga diet is highly varied and at times very tasty. The people are attractive and healthy, with no apparent signs of malnutrition. Although they are somewhat underweight by modern standards, these standards may reflect average weights of modern populations that the Machiguenga would regard as overweight.

The highly productive food economy of the Machiguenga depends on metal tools obtained from Peruvian traders. Without an outside source of axes, the Machiguenga would have to give up their semisedentary existence and roam the forest as nomads. Should this happen, they could support fewer people in the same territory—but, if other hunter-collector groups can be used as evidence, nomadic life would result in even shorter workdays. Once again, in quantities of food as well as in quantities of time, the Machiguenga fit Sahlin's model of primitive affluence.

Our affluence exceeds Machiguenga affluence, but as in the case of time, there is the quality of life to take into account. My personal experiences in the field illustrate this aspect of the contrast. In preparing to leave for our first year-long visit to the Machiguenga, Orna and I decided to limit ourselves to the clothing and supplies that would fit into two trunks. This decision led to much agonizing over what to take and what to leave behind. Although we had both been in the field before, we had never gone anywhere quite so remote and we could not imagine how we would get along with so few goods.

The truth, however, was that we were absurdly oversupplied. As our field work progressed we used less and less of our store of goods. It even became a burden to us, since our possessions had to be dried in the sun periodically to prevent rot. As we grew close to the people we were living among, we began to be embarrassed by having so many things we did not really need.

Once, after a long rainy period, I laid my various footgear side by side in the sun to dry. There were a pair of hiking boots, a pair of canvas-topped jungle boots, and two pairs of sneakers. Some men came to visit and began inspecting the shoes, fingering the materials, commenting on the cleats, and trying them on for size. Then the discussion turned to how numerous my shoes were, and one man remarked that I had still another pair. There were protests of disbelief and I was asked if that was true. I said, "No, that's all I have." The man then said,

"Wait," and went inside the house, returning with an "extra pair" of sneakers that I had left forgotten and unused in a corner of the room for months. This was not the only occasion on which I could not keep track of my possessions, a deficiency unknown to the Machiguenga.

My feelings about this incident were compounded when I discovered that, no matter which pair of shoes I wore, I could never keep up with these men, whose bare feet seemed magically to grip the slipperiest rocks or to find toe holds in the muddy trails. At about this time I was reading Alfred Russel Wallace's narrative of his years in the Amazon, in which he relates that his boots soon wore out and he spent his remaining time there barefoot—an achievement that continues to fill me with awe. My origi-

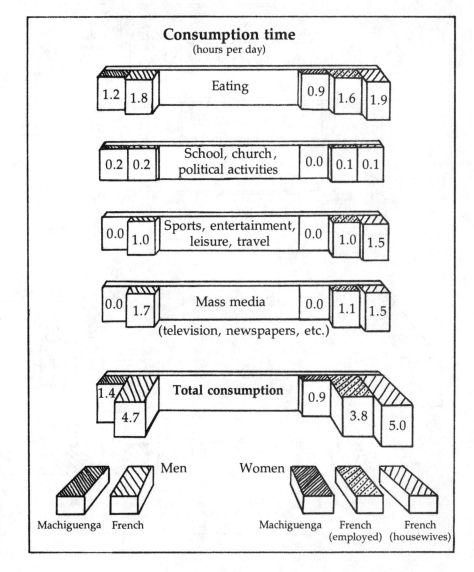

Consumption time
(hours per day)

Eating — Machiguenga: Men 1.2, Women 1.8; French: Women 0.9, employed 1.6, housewives 1.9

School, church, political activities — 0.2, 0.2 / 0.0, 0.1, 0.1

Sports, entertainment, leisure, travel — 0.0, 1.0 / 0.0, 1.0, 1.5

Mass media (television, newspapers, etc.) — 0.0, 1.7 / 0.0, 1.1, 1.5

Total consumption — 1.4, 4.7 / 0.9, 3.8, 5.0

Men — Machiguenga, French
Women — Machiguenga, French (employed), French (housewives)

---

nal pride in being well shod was diminished to something closely resembling embarrassment.

This experience brings up the question of whether goods are needed in themselves or because demand for them has been created by the producers. Galbraith stresses that we cannot simply assume that goods are produced to meet people's real needs. The billions of dollars spent each year on advertising indicate that not all consumer wants arise from basic needs of the individual, but that some are created in consumers by the producers themselves. This turns things around. Instead of arguing, as economists usually do, that our economic system serves us well, we are forced to consider that it may be we who serve the system by somehow agreeing to want the things it seems bent on producing, like dozens of kinds of shoes.

To most economists there is no justification for criticizing the purchasing habits of modern consumers. Purchases simply reflect personal preference, and it smacks of arrogance and authoritarianism to judge the individual decisions of free men and women. Economist Kenneth Boulding has referred sarcastically to such attempts as "theonomics." Economists assume that if there were more satisfying pathways of consumption, people would choose them. But the role of advertising in creating wants leaves open the question of the relationship between the consumption of goods and the fulfillment of needs.

When the task is to consume more, there are three ways of complying. One is to increase the amount of time spent consuming; this is one way the French differ from the Machiguenga. Another way is to increase the total number of goods we possess and to devote less time to each one individually. In a sense, this is what I was doing with the five pairs of shoes. The third way is to increase the elaborateness (and hence the cost of production) of the items we consume. The following instance, which took place at a Machiguenga beer feast, demonstrates that even those manufactured items we consider most practical are both elaborate and costly.

At Machiguenga beer feasts, which last for two or three days until the beer is gone, men often make recreational items like drums and toys. At one beer feast that had been going on for a day and a half, I watched a drum being made. The monkey-skin drumheads were being readied, and I noticed that the man next to me was about to make holes in the edge of the skin for the gut that would be used to tighten the drumhead. I had in my pocket an elaborate knife of fine steel, which had among its dozen separate functions (scissors, file, tweezers, etc.) a leather punch. By the time I had pulled the knife out and opened the punch, my neighbor had already made a

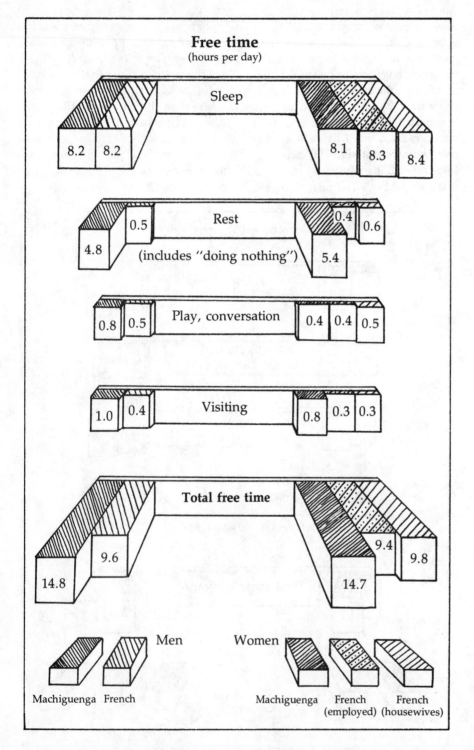

Free time
(hours per day)

Sleep

8.2 8.2   8.1 8.3 8.4

Rest
(includes "doing nothing")

0.5   0.4 0.6
4.8   5.4

Play, conversation

0.8 0.5   0.4 0.4 0.5

Visiting

1.0 0.4   0.8 0.3 0.3

Total free time

9.6   9.4 9.8
14.8   14.7

Men   Women

Machiguenga French   Machiguenga French   French
                                    (employed) (housewives)

perfect hole with a scrap of broken kitchen knife he had kept close at hand.

Then he noticed my knife and wanted to see it. He noted its fine workmanship and passed it around to others, who tested its sharpness and opened all its parts, asking me to explain each one. They wanted to know how much it cost and how they could obtain one.

I interpret this experience in two ways. First, the knife was overelaborate. The Machiguenga met all their own needs for clothing, shelter, and containers with much simpler tools. Second, the elaborateness of the knife was itself an attraction, and its remarkable design and quality of materials could not help but draw the men's attention. They wanted the knife—not craving it, but willing to make serious efforts to get it or something similar if the opportunity arose. It is characteristic of a developed culture's contact with small, isolated societies that the developed culture is not met as a whole, but rather in highly selective ways that emphasize manufactured goods and the aura of the great, mysterious power that made them.

Our examples do not prove that the Machiguenga enjoy a higher quality of life than people who live in an industrial society, but they are not intended to. They do show that the quantitative abundance of consumption goods does not automatically guarantee an advantage to the consumer. And although our experiences among the Machiguenga make it easy to argue for the high quality of their lives— as reflected in their warm family ties, peaceable manners, good humor, intimacy with nature, and impressive integrity—it is also true that we would have regarded a permanent life there as a great personal sacrifice. Orna and I came home partly because it is home, where our lives have meaning, and partly because we did not want to go without some creature comforts that we, for better or worse, regard as highly desirable.

It seems likely, however, that an increasing supply of creature comforts and stimulation will bring us into a dangerous relationship with our environment. Such a confrontation might lead us to think about the costs involved in producing and consuming less. In traditional terms this is almost unthinkable, because the relative affluence of communities has been restricted to quantitative measures such as per capita income or gross national product, which can only increase (good), stay the same (bad), or decline (worse). But these numerical measures, which always discover the highest standard of living in the developed nations of the West, do not necessarily touch on all the factors that contribute to a good quality of life. The concept of quality of life suggests something more complex: a balancing-out of diverse satisfactions and dissatisfactions, not all of which are bought and sold in the marketplace.

Social scientists are trying to develop a broad range of indexes, such as those called "social indicators," that attempt to measure the quality of individual well-being. It has not been the theoreticians but the planners directly involved in applying economic thought to directed social changes, like urban renewal and rural development, who have insisted on such measures. Instead of relying on a single measure, like per capita income, they have added unemployment rates, housing, mental health, cultural and educational resources, air quality, government efficiency, and social participation. Communities, or nations, may rank low on one measure but high on another, and this makes comparisons both fairer and more realistic.

Even here problems remain. For one thing, the social indicators themselves sometimes sacrifice understanding of quality for measures of quantity. For example, the measure of "mental health" has been the suicide rate per 100,000 population—surely a restricted interpretation of the concept. Despite its obvious shortcomings, the measure has the advantage of specifying exactly what we mean by the term "mental health." In comparing communities or cultures we need standard measures, even though quality and quantity are ultimately incompatible.

When we discuss non-Western societies, the existing social indicators do not work very well. Unemployment, housing, and mental health all become hard to define. Economists, for example, often label free time in other cultures as "hidden unemployment"; by clever use of this negative term, they have transformed what might be a good thing into something that sounds definitely bad. In our case, Machiguenga housing, made of palm fronds, palm wood, and various tropical hardwoods, would never qualify as good housing in terms of a housing code, but it is cool, well ventilated, comfortable, and secure. Thus we are still far from developing criteria that allow us to compare the quality of life, or affluence, in diverse societies.

The economy of the United States is changing rapidly. Yet when we try to construct models of the alternative futures open to us, we falter because we lack the means to evaluate them. To turn this process over to the marketplace is not the same as turning it over to the "people" in some absolute democratic sense. People's behavior in the marketplace is strongly influenced, often by subterfuge, by producers who try to convince them that their interests coincide.

To accept the influence of the producers of goods without criticism, while labeling all other efforts to influence consumer patterns as "interference" or "theonomics," amounts to simple bias. Certainly a degree of open-mindedness about what a good quality of life is, and more efforts at learning about the quality of life in other communities, are invaluable as we chart our uncertain future.

For further information:

Andrews, Frank M. and Stephen B. Withey. *Social Indicators of Well-Being: Americans' Perception of Life Quality.* Plenum, 1976.

Galbraith, John Kenneth. *The Affluent Society.* Houghton Mifflin, 1958.

Linder, Staffan Burenstam. *The Harried Leisure Class.* Columbia University Press, 1970.

Sahlins, Marshall. *Stone Age Economics.* Aldine-Atherton, 1972.

TOPIC ELEVEN

Cultural Ecology

. . . .

Cultural ecology is rather a new subfield of anthropology, although it was anticipated by environmental determinism, which flourished around the turn of the century and later was discredited. Cultural ecologists study the ways in which cultural patterns act to adapt people to the stressful conditions imposed on them by their environment. They avoid a deterministic stance by acknowledging that there are many alternative patterns of behavior that can adapt a group to a given environment. Thus, when cultural ecologists explain a pattern of behavior in terms of its adaptive significance, they do not claim to be able to say *why* a particular pattern is adopted in preference to others. Instead, they contend that, given the facts of the environment, it is possible to make sense of a pattern of behavior that seems at first glance to be curious, or even "foolish" or damaging.

Marvin Harris, perhaps the best known exponent of cultural ecology, tackles the question of the taboo among Jews and Muslims against eating pork in "The Riddle of the Pig." He goes beneath the surface of religious prohibition and finds the logic of this proscription in the environment of the Middle East—and in the tastiness of pork. Similarly Michael Harner provides a new way of understanding "The Enigma of Aztec Sacrifice" by pointing to the severe protein shortage in Mexico and Mesoamerica at the time of the rise of their high civilizations. Harner's theory (and even his acceptance of the assumption of a protein shortage) has generated considerable debate among anthropologists. It is explained in greater detail in his more technical article,

"The Ecological Basis for Aztec Sacrifice" (*American Ethnologist,* February 1977).

Harner's critics question his data on the frequency of famine in Aztec Mexico and point out that the Spanish chronicles on which Harner relies were, at least to some degree, self-serving in justifying the Spanish conquest and, therefore, would be likely to embellish on Aztec atrocities. Several of his critics have further noted that many of the human sacrifices came at harvest time—precisely when the Aztecs did not need additional protein. Finally, Barbara Price argues that Harner's method of analysis is simplistic. She believes it is important to analyze cannibalism in Aztec society in terms of the interaction of all major Aztec social institutions, the political system in particular. In her view, human flesh was consumed mostly by the noble families and represented a perquisite of power in Aztec society, not a staple protein commodity.

John B. Calhoun's "Plight of the Ik and Kaiadilt Is Seen as a Chilling Possible End for Man" takes the horrifying testimony produced by the research of Colin Turnbull among the Ik of Uganda and Geoffrey Bianchi among the Kaiadilt in Australia, and shows that the decay of virtually all sustaining aspects of a society is predictable in certain contexts. Calhoun has investigated these contexts experimentally among populations of mice and sees alarming parallels there to the fate of the two peoples discussed in this essay. One cannot read this article without becoming deeply concerned over the directions taken by our own society.

31

Riddle of the Pig

BY MARVIN HARRIS

When the God of the ancient Hebrews told them not to eat pork, He must have realized that generations of scholars were going to try to figure out why. From my ecological perspective, I would like to offer an explanation that relates Jewish and Muslim attitudes toward the pig to the cultural and natural ecosystems of the Middle East.

Naturalistic explanations for the taboo on pork go back to Maimonides, who lived in the twelfth century. Maimonides said that God had intended the ban on pork as a public health measure since swine's flesh "had a bad and damaging effect upon the body." This explanation gained favor in the mid-nineteenth century when it was discovered that there was a parasite present in undercooked pork that caused trichinosis.

Impressed by this rational answer to the ancient riddle, American Jews who belonged to the reformed congregations proceeded forthwith to revoke the scriptural taboo on the grounds that if properly cooked, pork no longer menaced the community's health. But Maimonides's explanation has a big hole in it: the flesh of all undercooked domestic animals can serve as a vector for human diseases. Cattle, sheep, and goats, for example, transmit brucellosis and anthrax, both of which have fatality rates as high as that of trichinosis.

Although Maimonides's explanation must be rejected, I think he was closer to the truth than modern anthropologists, including Sir James Frazer, renowned author of *The Golden Bough*. Frazer declared that pigs, like "all so-called unclean animals were originally sacred; the reason for not eating them was that many were originally divine." This doesn't help us very much since the sheep, goat, and cow were also once worshiped in the Middle East, and yet their meat is much enjoyed by all ethnic and religious groups in the area.

Other scholars have suggested that pigs, along with the rest of the foods prohibited in the Bible, were the original totem animals of the Hebrew clans. But why interdict the consumption of a valuable food resource? After all, eagles, ravens, spiders, and other animals that are of only limited significance as a source of human food are also used as clan totems.

Maimonides at least tried to place the taboo in a natural context in which definite, intelligible forces were at work. His mistake was that he conceived of public health much too narrowly. What he lacked was an understanding of the threat that the pig posed to the integrity of the broad cultural and natural ecosystem of the ancient Hebrew habitat.

I think we have to take into account that the protohistoric Hebrews—the children of Abraham— were adapted to life in the rugged, sparsely inhabited arid lands between Mesopotamia and Egypt. Until their conquest of the Jordan Valley in Palestine, which began in the thirteenth century B.C., they were primarily nomadic pastoralists, living almost entirely on their sheep, goats, and cattle. But like all pastoral peoples they maintained close relationships with sedentary agriculturalists who held the oasis and fertile river valley.

From time to time certain Hebrew lineages adopted a more sedentary, agriculturally oriented mode of existence, as appears to have been the case with the Abrahamites in Mesopotamia, the Josephites in Egypt, and the Isaacites in the western Negev. But even during the climax of urban and village life under David and Solomon, the herding of sheep, goats, and cattle continued to play a vital, if not predominant, economic role everywhere except in the irrigated portions of the Jordan Valley.

Within the over-all pattern of this mixed farming and pastoral complex, the divine prohibition against pork constituted a sound ecological strategy. During periods of maximum nomadism, it was impossible for the Israelites to raise pigs, while during the semi-sedentary and even fully village farming phases, pigs were more of a threat than an asset. The basic reason for this is that the world zones of pastoral nomadism correspond to unforested plains and hills that are too arid for rainfall agriculture and that cannot easily be irrigated. The domestic animals best adapted to these zones are the ruminants— cattle, sheep, and goats. Because ruminants have sacks anterior to their stomachs, they are able to digest grass, leaves, and other foods consisting mainly of cellulose more efficiently than any other mammals.

The pig, however, is primarily a creature of forests and shaded river banks. Although it is omnivorous, its best weight gain is from food low in cellulose—nuts, fruits, tubers, and especially grains, making it a direct competitor of man. It cannot subsist on grass alone and nowhere in the world do fully nomadic pastoralists raise significant numbers of pigs. The pig has the further disadvantage of not being a practical source of milk and of being difficult to herd over long distances.

Above all, the pig is ill-adapted to the heat of the Negev, the Jordan Valley, and the other biblical lands. Compared to cattle, goats, and sheep, the pig is markedly incapable of maintaining a constant body temperature when the temperature rises.

In spite of the expression "to sweat like a pig," it has now become clear that pigs can't sweat through their relatively hairless skins. Human beings, the sweatiest of all mammals, cool themselves by evaporating as much as three ounces of body liquid per hour from each square foot of body surface. The best a pig can manage is one-tenth ounce per square foot, and none of this is sweat. Even sheep evaporate twice as much body liquid through their skins as pigs. And sheep have the advantage of thick white wool, which both reflects the sun's rays and provides insulation when the ambient temperature rises above body temperature. According to L. E. Mount of the Agricultural Research Council Institute of Animal Physiology in Cambridge, England, adult pigs will die if exposed to direct sunlight and air temperatures over 97 degrees F. In the Jordan Valley, air temperatures of 110 degrees occur almost every summer and there is intense sunshine throughout the year.

To compensate for its lack of protective hair and its inability to sweat, the pig must dampen its skin with external moisture. It usually does this by wallowing in fresh, clean mud, but if nothing else is available, it will cover its skin with its own urine and feces. Mount reports that below 84 degrees F. pigs kept in pens deposit their excreta away from their sleeping and feeding areas, while above 84 degrees they excrete throughout the pen.

Sheep and goats were the first animals to be domesticated in the Middle East, possibly as early as 9000 B.C. Pigs were domesticated in the same general region about 2,000 years later. Bone counts conducted by archeologists at early prehistoric village farming sites show that sheep and goats were in the majority while the domesticated pig was almost always a relatively minor part—about 5 percent—of the village fauna. This is what one would expect of a creature that ate the same food as man, couldn't be milked, and had to be provided with shade and mudholes. Domesticated pigs were from the beginning an economical and ecological luxury, especially since goats, sheep, and cattle provided milk, cheese, meat, hides, dung, fiber, and traction for plowing. But the pig, with its rich, fatty meat, was a delectable temptation—the kind, like incest and adultery, that mankind finds difficult to resist. And so God was heard to say that swine were unclean, not only as food, but to the touch as well. This message was repeated by Mohammed for the same reason: it was ecologically more adaptive for the people of the Middle East to cater to their goats, sheep, and cattle. Pigs tasted good but they ate you out of house and home and, if you gave them a chance, used up your water as well. Well, that's my answer to the riddle of why God told the Jews and the Muslims not to eat pork. Anyone have a better idea?

32

The Enigma of Aztec Sacrifice

BY MICHAEL HARNER

On the morning of November 8, 1519, a small band of bearded, dirty, exhausted Spanish adventurers stood at the edge of a great inland lake in central Mexico, staring in disbelief at the sight before them. Rising from the center of the lake was a magnificent island city, shining chalk white in the early sun. Stretching over the lake were long causeways teeming with travelers to and from the metropolis, Tenochtitlán, the capital of the Aztec empire, now known as Mexico City.

The Spaniards, under the command of Hernán Cortés, were fresh from the wars of the Mediterranean and the conquest of the Caribbean. Tough and ruthless men, numbering fewer than four hundred, they had fought their way up from the eastern tropical coast of Mexico. Many had been wounded or killed in battles with hostile Indians on the long march. Possibly all would have died but for their minuscule cavalry of fifteen horses—which terrified the Indians, who thought the animals were gods—and the aid of a small army of Indian allies, enemies of the Aztecs.

The panorama of the Aztec citadel across the water seemed to promise the Spaniards the riches that had eluded them all their lives. One of them, Bernal Díaz del Castillo, later wrote: "To many of us it appeared doubtful whether we were asleep or awake . . . never yet did man see, hear, or dream of anything equal to our eyes this day." For the Spaniards, it was a vision of heaven.

Slightly more than a year and half later, in the early summer of 1521, it was a glimpse of hell. Again the Spaniards found themselves on the lakeshore, looking toward the great capital. But this time they had just been driven back from the city by the Aztec army. Sixty-two of their companions had been captured, and Cortés and the other survivors helplessly watched a pageant being enacted a mile away across the water on one of the major temple-pyramids of the city. As Bernal Díaz later described it,

The dismal drum of Huichilobos sounded again, accompanied by conches, horns, and trumpetlike instruments. It was a terrifying sound, and when we looked at the tall *cue* [temple-pyramid] from which it came we saw our comrades who had been captured in Cortés' defeat being dragged up the steps to be sacrificed. When they had hauled them up to a small platform in front of the shrine where they kept their accursed idols we saw them put plumes on the heads of many of them; and then they made them dance with a sort of fan in front of Huichilobos. Then after they had danced the *papas* [Aztec priests] laid them down on their backs on some narrow stones of sacrifice and, cutting open their chests, drew out their palpitating hearts which they offered to the idols before them.

Cortés and his men were the only Europeans to see the human sacrifices of the Aztecs, for the practice ended shortly after the successful Spanish conquest of the Aztec empire. But the extremity of Aztec sacrifice has long persisted in puzzling scholars. No human society known to history

A temple-pyramid at the Maya site of Tikal, Guatemala. The steep steps of Mesoamerican pyramids may have facilitated tumbling down the bodies of victims after sacrifice.

Reprinted with permission from *Natural History* Magazine, April 1977. Copyright © 1977 by The American Museum of Natural History. Revisions by the author, 1978. Photography by Phillip Whitten.

approached that of the Aztecs in the qualitities of people offered as religious sacrifices: 20,000 a year is a common estimate.

A typical anthropological explanation is that the religion of the Aztecs required human sacrifices; that their gods demanded these extravagant, frequent offerings. This explanation fails to suggest why that particular form of religion should have evolved when and where it did. I suggest that the Aztec sacrifices, and the cultural patterns surrounding them, were a natural result of distinctive ecological circumstances.

Some of the Aztecs' ecological circumstances were common to ancient civilizations in general. Recent theoretical work in anthropology indicates that the rise of early civilizations was a consequence of the pressures that growing populations brought to bear on natural resources. As human populations slowly multiplied, even before the development of plant and animal domestication, they gradually reduced the wild flora and fauna available for food and disrupted the ecological equilibriums of their environments. The earliest strong evidence of humans causing environmental damage was the extinction of many big game species in Europe by about 10,000 B.C., and in America north of Mexico by about 9,000 B.C. Simultaneously, human populations in broad regions of the Old and New Worlds had to shift increasingly to marine food resources and small-game hunting. Finally, declining quantities of wild game and food plants made domestication of plants and animals essential in most regions of the planet.

Two sixteenth-century drawings from the Florentine Codex *of Bernardino de Sahagun. On the preceding page, the victim's heart is offered to the sun. At right, priests sacrifice a youth who had been chosen to personify the Aztec deity Tezcatlipoca for a year. Accompanied by a retinue, the future victim often strolled as a god on earth, playing one of his clay flutes. When he finally ascended to the temple-pyramid platform, he broke his flutes, one by one, on the steps. The vast majority of victims did not enjoy such presacrificial status.*

In the Old World, domestication of herbivorous mammals, such as cattle, sheep, and pigs, proceeded apace with that of food plants. By about 7,200 B.C. in the New World, however, ancient hunters had completely eliminated herbivores suitable for domestication from the area anthropologists call Mesoamerica, the region of the future high civilizations of Mexico and Guatemala. Only in the Andean region and southern South America did some camel-related species, especially the llama and the alpaca, manage to survive hunters' onslaughts, and thus could be domesticated later, along with another important local herbivore, the guinea pig. In Mesoamerica, the guinea pig was not available, and the Camelidae species became extinct several thousand years before domesticated food production had to be seriously undertaken. Dogs, such as the Mexican hairless, and wildfowl, such as the turkey, had to be bred for protein. The dog, however, was a far from satisfactory solution because, as a

carnivore, it competed with its breeders for animal protein.

The need for intensified domesticated food production was felt early, as anthropologist Robert Carneiro has pointed out, by growing populations in fertile localities circumscribed by terrain poorly suited to farming. In such cases, plants always became domesticated, climate and environment permitting, but herbivorous mammals apparently could not, unless appropriate species existed. In Mesoamerica, the Valley of Mexico, with its fertile and well-watered bottomlands surrounded by mountains, fits well Carneiro's environmental model. In this confined area, population was increasing up to the time of the Spanish conquest, and the supply of wild game was declining. Deer were nearly gone from the Valley by the Aztec period.

The Aztecs responded to their increasing problems of food supply by intensifying agricultural production with a variety of ingenious techniques, including the reclamation of

soil from marsh and lake bottoms in the chinampa, or floating garden, method. Unfortunately, their ingenuity could not correct their lack of a suitable domesticable herbivore that could provide animal protein and fats. Hence, the ecological situation of the Aztecs and their Mesoamerican neighbors was unique among the world's major civilizations. I have recently proposed the theory that large-scale cannibalism, disguised as sacrifice, was the natural consequence of these ecological circumstances.

The contrast between Mesoamerica and the Andes, in terms of the existence of domesticated herbivores, was also reflected in the numbers of human victims sacrificed in the two areas. In the huge Andean Inca empire, the other major political entity in the New World at the time of the conquest, annual human sacrifices apparently amounted to a few hundred at most. Among the Aztecs, the numbers were incomparably greater. The commonly mentioned figure of 20,000, however, is unreliable. For example, one sixteenth-century account states that 20,000 were sacrificed yearly in the capital city alone, another reports this as 20,000 infants, and a third claims the same number as being slaughtered throughout the Aztec empire on a single particular day. The most famous specific sacrifice took place in 1487 at the dedication of the main pyramid in Tenochtitlán. Here, too, figures vary: one source states 20,000, another 72,344, and several give 80,400.

In 1946 Sherburne Cook, a demographer specializing in American Indian populations, estimated an overall annual mean of 15,000 victims in a central Mexican population reckoned at two million. Later, however, he and his colleague Woodrow Borah revised his estimate of the total central Mexican population upward to 25 million. Recently, Borah, possibly the leading authority on the demography of Mexico at the time of the conquest, has also revised the estimated number of persons sacrificed in central Mexico in the fifteenth century to 250,000 per year, equivalent to one percent of the total population. According to Borah, this figure is consistent with the sacrifice of an esti-

mated 1,000 to 3,000 persons yearly at the largest of the thousands of temples scattered throughout the Aztec Triple Alliance. The numbers, of course, were fewer at the lesser temples, and may have shaded down to zero at the smallest.

These enormous numbers call for consideration of what the Aztecs did with the bodies after the sacrifices. Evidence of Aztec cannibalism has been largely ignored or consciously or unconsciously covered up. For example, the major twentieth-century books on the Aztecs barely mention it; others bypass the subject completely. Probably some modern Mexicans and anthropologists have been embarrassed by the topic: the former partly for nationalistic reasons; the latter partly out of a desire to portray native peoples in the best possible light. Ironically, both these attitudes may represent European ethnocentrism regarding cannibalism—a viewpoint to be expected from a culture that has had relatively abundant livestock for meat and milk.

A search of the sixteenth-century literature, however, leaves no doubt as to the prevalence of cannibalism among the central Mexicans. The Spanish conquistadores wrote amply about it, as did several Spanish priests who engaged in ethnological research on Aztec culture shortly after the conquest. Among the latter, Bernardino de Sahagún is of particular interest because his informants were former Aztec nobles, who supplied dictated or written information in the Aztec language, Nahuatl.

According to these early accounts, some sacrificial victims were not eaten, such as children offered by drowning to the rain god, Tlaloc, or persons suffering skin diseases. But the overwhelming majority of the sacrificed captives apparently were consumed. A principal—and sometimes only—objective of Aztec war expeditions was to capture prisoners for sacrifice. While some might be sacrificed and eaten on the field of battle, most were taken to home communities or to the capital, where they were kept in wooden cages to be fattened until sacrificed by the priests at the temple-pyramids. Most of the sacrifices involved tearing out the

heart, offering it to the sun and, with some blood, also to the idols. The corpse was then tumbled down the steps of the pyramid and carried off to be butchered. The head went on the local skull rack, displayed in central plazas alongside the temple-pyramids. At least three of the limbs were the property of the captor if he had seized the prisoner without assistance in battle. Later, at a feast given at the captor's quarters, the central dish was a stew of tomatoes, peppers, and the limbs of his victim. The remaining torso, in Tenochtitlán at least, went to the royal zoo where it was used to feed carnivorous mammals, birds, and snakes.

Recent archeological research lends support to conquistadores' and informants' vivid and detailed accounts of Aztec cannibalism. Mexican archeologists excavating at an Aztec sacrificial site in the Tlatelolco section of Mexico City between 1960 and 1969 uncovered headless human rib cages completely lacking the limb bones. Associated with these remains were some razorlike obsidian blades, which the archeologists believe were used in the butchering. Nearby they also discovered piles of human skulls, which apparently had been broken open to obtain the brains, possibly a choice delicacy reserved for the priesthood, and to mount the skulls on a ceremonial rack.

Through cannibalism, the Aztecs appear to have been attempting to reduce very particular nutritional deficiencies. Under the conditions of high population pressure and class stratification that characterized the Aztec state, commoners or lower-class persons rarely had the opportunity to eat any game, even the domesticated turkey, except on great occasions. They often had to content themselves with such creatures as worms and snakes and an edible lake-surface scum called "stone dung," which may have been algae fostered by pollution from Tenochtitlán. Preliminary research seems to indicate that although fish and waterfowl were taken from the lakes, most of the Aztec poor did not have significant access to this protein source and were forced to be near-vegetarians, subsisting mainly on domesticated plant

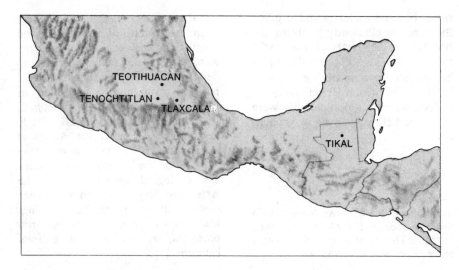

foods such as maize and beans.

The commoners theoretically could get the eight essential amino acids necessary for building body tissues from maize and beans. (A combination of the two foods complement each other in their essential amino acid components.) However, recent nutritional research indicates that in order to assure that their bodies would use the eight essential amino acids to rebuild body tissues, and not simply siphon off the dietary protein as energy, the Aztec commoners would have had to consume large quantities of maize and beans simultaneously or nearly simultaneously year-round. But crop failures and famines were common. According to Durán, a sixteenth-century chronicler, poor people often could not obtain maize and beans in the same season, and hence could not rely upon these plants as a source of the essential amino acids. How did the Aztecs know they needed the essential amino acids? Like other organisms perfected under natural selection, the human body is a homeostatic system that, under conditions of nutritional stress, tends to seek out the dietary elements in which it is deficient. Without this innate capacity, living organisms could not survive.

Another Aztec dietary problem was the paucity of fats, which were so scarce in central Mexico that the Spaniards resorted to boiling down the bodies of Indians killed in battle in order to obtain fat for dressing wounds and tallow for caulking boats. While the exact amount of

fatty acids required by the human body remains a subject of uncertainty among nutritionists, they agree that fats, due to their slower rate of metabolism, provide a longer-lasting energy source than carbohydrates. Fatty meat, by providing not only fat, which the body will use as energy, but also essential proteins, assures the utilization of the essential amino acids for tissue building. Interestingly, prisoners confined by the Aztecs in wooden cages prior to sacrifice could be fed purely on carbohydrates to build up fat.

In contrast to the commoners, the Aztec elite normally had a diet enriched by wild game imported from the far reaches of the empire where species had not been so depleted. But even nobles could suffer from famines and sometimes had to sell their children into slavery in order to survive. Not surprisingly, the Aztec elite apparently reserved for themselves the right to eat human flesh, and conveniently, times of famine meant that the gods demanded appeasement through many human sacrifices.

At first glance, this prohibition against commoners eating human flesh casts doubt on cannibalism's potential to mobilize the masses of Aztec society to engage in wars for prisoners. Actually, the prohibition was, if anything, a goad to the lower class to participate in these wars since those who single-handedly took captives several times gained the right to eat human flesh. Successful warriors became members of the Aztec elite and their descendants shared their

privileges. Through the reward of flesh-eating rights to the group most in need of them, the Aztec rulers assured themselves an aggressive war machine and were able to motivate the bulk of the population, the poor, to contribute to state and upper-class maintenance through active participation in offensive military operations. Underlying the war machine's victories, and the resultant sacrifices, were the ecological extremities of the Valley of Mexico.

With an understanding of the importance of cannibalism in Aztec culture, and of the ecological reasons for its existence, some of the Aztecs' more distinctive institutions begin to make anthropological sense. For example, the old question of whether the Aztecs' political structure was or was not an "empire" can be reexamined. One part of this problem is that the Aztecs frequently withdrew from conquered territory without establishing administrative centers or garrisons. This "failure" to consolidate conquest in the Old World fashion puzzled Cortés, who asked Moctezuma to explain why he allowed the surrounded Tlaxcalans to maintain their independence. Moctezuma reportedly replied that his people could thus obtain captives for sacrifice. Since the Aztecs did not normally eat people of their own polity, which would have been socially and politically disruptive, they needed nearby "enemy" populations on whom they could prey for captives. This behavior makes sense in terms of Aztec cannibalism: from the Aztec point of view, the Tlaxcalan state was preserved as a stockyard. The Aztecs were unique among the world's states in having a cannibal empire. Understandably, they did not conform to Old World concepts of empire, based on economies with domesticated herbivores providing meat or milk.

The ecological situation of the Aztecs was probably an extreme case of problems general to the high population pressure societies of Mesoamerica. Cannibalism encouraged the definition of the gods as eaters of human flesh and led almost inevitably to emphasis on fierce, ravenous, and carnivorous deities, such as the jaguar and the serpent, which are characteristic of Mesoamerican pantheons. Pre-Columbian populations could, in turn, rationalize the more grisly aspects of large-scale cannibalism as consequences of the gods' demands. Mesoamerican cannibalism, disguised as propitiation of the gods, bequeathed to the world some of its most distinctive art and architecture. The temple-pyramids of the Maya and the Toltecs, and of the pre-Aztec site at Teotihuacán in the valley of Mexico, resemble those of the Aztecs in appearance and probably had similar uses. Even small touches, such as the steepness of the steps on pyramids in Aztec and other Mesoamerican

ruins, become understandable given the need for efficiently tumbling the bodies from the sacrificial altars to the multitudes below. Perhaps those prehistoric scenes were not too dissimilar from that which Bernal Díaz described when his companions were sacrificed before his eyes in Tenochtitlán:

Then they kicked the bodies down the steps, and the Indian butchers who were waiting below cut off their arms and legs and flayed their faces, which they afterwards prepared like glove leather, with their beards on, and kept for their drunken festivals. Then they ate their flesh with a sauce of peppers and tomatoes.

Gruesome as these practices may seem, an ecological perspective and population pressure theory render the Aztec emphasis on human sacrifice understandable as a natural and rational response to the material conditions of their existence. In *Tristes Tropiques,* the French anthropologist Claude Levi-Strauss described the Aztecs as suffering from "a maniacal obsession with blood and torture." A materialist ecological approach reveals the Aztecs to be neither irrational nor mentally ill, but merely human beings who, faced with unusual survival problems, responded with unusual behavior.

33

Plight of the Ik and Kaiadilt Is Seen as a Chilling Possible End for Man

BY JOHN B. CALHOUN

. . . .

The Mountain—how pervasive in the history of man. A still small voice on Horeb, mount of God, guided Elijah. There, earlier, Moses standing before God received the Word. And Zion: "I am the Lord your God dwelling in Zion, my holy mountain."

Then there was Atum, mountain, God and first man, one and all together. The mountain rose out of a primordial sea of nothingness—Nun. Atum, the spirit of life, existed within Nun. In creating himself, Atum became the evolving ancestor of the human race. So goes the Egyptian mythology of creation, in which the Judaic Adam has his roots.

And there is a last Atum, united in his youth with another mountain of God, Mt. Morungole in northeasternmost Uganda. His people are the Ik, pronounced eek. They are the subject of an important new book, *The Mountain People,* by Colin M. Turnbull (Simon and Schuster, $6.95). They still speak Middle-Kingdom Egyptian, a language thought to be dead. But perhaps their persistence is not so strange. Egyptian mythology held that the waters of the life-giving Nile had their origin in Nun. Could this Nun have been the much more extensive Lake Victoria of 40 to 50 millennia ago when, near its borders, man groped upward to cloak his biological self with culture?

Well might the Ik have preserved the essence of this ancient tradition that affirms human beginnings. Isolated as they have been in their jagged mountain fastness, near the upper tributaries of the White Nile, the Ik have been protected from cultural evolution.

What a Shangri-la, this land of the Ik. In its center, the Kidepo valley, 35 miles across, home of abundant game; to the south, mist-topped Mt. Morungole; to the west the Niangea range; to the north, bordering the Sudan, the Didinga range; to the east on the Kenya border, a sheer drop of 2,000 feet into the Turkanaland of cattle herdsmen. Through ages of dawning history few people must have been interested in encroaching on this rugged land. Until 1964 anthropologists knew little of the Ik's existence. Their very name, much less their language, remained a mystery until, quite by chance, anthropologist Colin M. Turnbull found himself among them. What an opportunity to study pristine man! Here one should encounter the basic qualities of humanity unmarred by war, technology, pollution, over-population.

Turnbull rested in his bright red Land Rover at an 8,000-foot-high pass. A bit beyond this only "navigable" pass into the Kidepo Valley, lay Pirre, a police outpost watching over a cluster of Ik villages. There to welcome him came Atum of the warm, open smile and gentle voice. Gray-haired at 40, appearing 65, he was the senior elder of the Ik, senior in authority if not quite so in age. Nattily attired in shorts and woolen sweater—in contrast to his mostly naked colleagues—Atum bounced forward with his ebony walking stick, greeted Turnbull in Swahili, and from that moment on took command as best he could of Turnbull's life. At Atum's village a plaintive woman's voice called out. Atum remarked that that was his wife—sick, too weak to work in the fields. Turnbull offered to bring her food and medicine. Atum suggested he handle Turnbull's gifts. As the weeks wore on Atum picked up the parcels that Turnbull was supplying for Atum's wife.

One day Atum's brother-in-law, Lomongin, laughingly asked Turnbull if he didn't know that Atum's wife had been dead for weeks. She had received no food or medicine. Atum had sold it. So she just died. All of this was revealed with no embarrassment. Atum joined the laughter over the joke played on Turnbull.

Another time Atum and Lojieri were guiding Turnbull over the mountains, and at one point induced him to push ahead through high grass until he broke through into a clearing. The clearing was a sheer 1,500-foot drop. The two Iks rolled on the ground, nearly bursting with laughter because Turnbull just managed to catch himself. What a lovable cherub this Atum! His laughter never ended.

New meaning of laughter

Laughter, hallmark of mankind, not shared with any other animal, not even primates, was an outstanding trait of the Ik. A whole village rushed to the edge of a low cliff and joined in communal laughter at blind old Lo'ono who lay thrashing on her back, near death after stumbling over. One evening Iks around a fire watched a child as it crawled toward the flames, then writhed back screaming after it grasped a gleaming coal. Laughter erupted. Quiet came to the child as its mother cuddled it in a kind of respect for the merriment it had caused. Then there was the laughter of innocent childhood as boys and girls gathered around a grandfather, too weak to walk, and drummed upon his head with sticks or pelted him with stones until he cried. There was the laughter that binds families together: Kimat, shrieking for joy as she dashed off with the mug of tea she had snatched from her dying brother Lomeja's hand an instant after Turnbull had given it to him as a last token of their friendship.

Laughter there had always been. A few old people remembered times, 25 to 30 years ago, when laughter mirrored love and joy and fullness of life, times when beliefs and rituals and traditions kept a bond with the "millions of years" ago when time began for the Ik. That was when their god, Didigwari, let the Ik down from heaven on a vine, one at a time. He gave them the digging stick with the instruction that they could not kill one another. He let down other people. To the Dodos and Turkana he gave cattle and spears to kill with. But the Ik remained true to their instruction and did not kill one another or neighboring tribesmen.

For them the bow, the net and the pitfall were for capturing game. For them the greatest sin was to overhunt. Mobility and cooperation ever were part of them. Often the netting of game required the collaboration of a whole band of 100 or more, some to hold the net and some to drive game into it. Between the big hunts, bands broke up into smaller groups to spread over their domain, then to gather again. The several bands would each settle for the best part of the year along the edge of the Kidepo Valley in the foothills of Mt. Morungole. There they were once again fully one with the mountain. "The Ik, without their mountains, would no longer be the Ik and similarly, they say, the mountains without the Ik would no longer be the same mountains, if indeed they continued to exist at all."

In this unity of people and place, rituals, traditions, beliefs and values molded and preserved a continuity of life. All rites of passage were marked by ceremony. Of these, the rituals surrounding death gave greatest meaning to life. Folded in a fetal position, the body was buried with favorite possessions, facing the rising sun to mark celestial rebirth. All accompanying rituals of fasting and feasting, of libations of beer sprinkled over the grave, of seeds of favorite foods planted on the grave to draw life from the dust of the dead, showed that death is merely another form of life, and reminded the living of the good things of life and of the good way to live. In so honoring the dead by creating goodness the Ik helped speed the soul, content, on its journey.

Such were the Ik until wildlife conservation intruded into their homeland. Uganda decided to make a national park out of the Kidepo Valley, the main hunting ground of the Ik. What then happened stands as an indictment of the myopia that science can generate. No one looked to the Ik to note that their hunter-gatherer way of life marked the epitome of conservation, that the continuance of their way of life would have added to the success of the park. Instead they were forbidden to hunt any longer in the Kidepo Valley. They were herded to the periphery of the park and encouraged to become farmers on dry mountain slopes so steep as to test the poise of a goat. As an example to the more remote villages, a number of villages were brought together in a tight little cluster below the southwest pass into the valley. Here the police post, which formed this settlement of Pirre, could watch over the Ik to see that they didn't revert to hunting.

These events contained two of the three strikes that knocked out the spirit of the Ik. *Strike No. 1:* The shift from a mobile hunter-gatherer way of life to a sedentary farming way of life made irrelevant the Ik's entire repertoire of beliefs, habits and traditions. Their guidelines for life were inappropriate to farming. They seemed to adapt, but at heart they remained hunters and gatherers. Their cultural templates fitted them for that one way of life.

Strike No. 2: They were suddenly crowded together at a density, intimacy and frequency of contact far greater than they had ever before been required to experience. Throughout their long past each band of 100 or so individuals only temporarily coalesced into a whole. The intervening breaking up into smaller groups permitted realignment of relationships that tempered conflicts from earlier associations. But at the resettlement, more than 450 individuals were forced to form a permanent cluster of villages within shouting distance of each other. Suppose the seven million or so inhabitants of Los Angeles County were forced to move and join the more than one million inhabitants of the more arid San Diego County. Then after they arrived all water, land and air communication to the rest of the world was cut off abruptly and completely. These eight million people would then have to seek survival completely on local resources without any communication with others. It would be a test of the ability of human beings to remain human.

Such a test is what Dr. Turnbull's book on the Mountain People is all about. The Ik failed to remain human. I have put mice to the same test and they failed to remain mice. Those of you who have been following SMITHSONIAN may recall from the April 1970 and the January 1971 issues something about the projected demise of a mouse population experiencing the same two strikes against it as did the Ik.

Fate of a mouse population

Last summer I spoke in London behind the lectern where Charles Darwin and Alfred Wallace had presented their papers on evolution—which during the next century caused a complete revision of our insight into what life is all about and what man is and may become. In summing up that session of 1858 the president remarked that nothing of importance had been presented before the Linnean Society at that year's meeting! I spoke behind this same lectern to a session of the Royal Society of Medicine during its symposium on "Man in His Place." At the end of my paper, "Death Squared: The Explosive Growth and Demise of a Mouse Population," the chairman admonished me to stick to my mice; the insights I had presented could have no implication for man. Wonderful if the chairman could be correct—but now I have read about the Mountain People, and I have a hollow feeling that perhaps we, too, are close to losing our "mountain."

Turnbull lived for 18 months as a member of the Ik tribe. His identity transfer became so strong that he acquired the Ik laughter. He laughed at seeing Atum suffer as they were completing an extremely arduous journey on foot back across the mountains and the Kidepo Valley from the Sudan. He felt pleasure at seeing Lokwam, local "Lord of the Flies," cry in agony from the beating given him by his two beautiful sisters.

Well, for five years I have identified with my mice, as they lived in their own "Kidepo Valley"—their contrived Utopia where resources are always abundant and all mortality factors except aging eliminated. I watched their population grow rapidly from the first few colonizers. I watched them fill their metal "universe" with organized social groups. I watched them bring up a host of young with loving maternal care and paternal territorial protection—all of these young well educated for mouse society. But then there were too many of these young mice, ready to become in-

Unwanted by Ik society, an old man, who remembered times of human caring, lies among the rocks of the mountain, quietly awaiting a lonely death.

volved in all that mice can become, with nowhere to go, no physical escape from their closed environment, no opportunity to gain a niche where they could play a meaningful role. They tried, but being younger and less experienced they were nearly always rejected.

Rejecting so many of these probing youngsters overtaxed the territorial males. So defense then fell to lactating females. They became aggressive. They turned against their own young and ejected them before normal weaning and before adequate social bonds between mother and young had developed. During this time of social tension, rate of growth of the population was only one third of that during the earlier, more favorable phase.

Strike No. 1 against these mice: They lost the opportunity to express the capacities developed by older mice born during the rapid population growth. After a while they became so rejected that they were treated as so many sticks and stones by their still relatively well-adjusted elders. These rejected mice withdrew, physically and psychologically, to live packed tightly together in large pools. Amongst themselves they became vicious, lashing out and biting each other now and then with hardly any provocation.

Strike No. 2 against the mice: They reached great numbers despite reduced conceptions and increased deaths of newborn young resulting from the dissolution of maternal care. Many had early been rejected by their mothers and knew little about social bonds.

Often their later attempts at interaction were interrupted by some other mouse intervening unintentionally as it passed between two potential actors.

I came to call such mice the "Beautiful Ones." They never learned such effective social interactions as courtship, mating and aggressive defense of territory. Never copulating, never fighting, they were unstressed and essentially unaware of their associates. They spent their time grooming themselves, eating and sleeping, totally individualistic, totally isolated socially except for a peculiar acquired need for simple proximity to others. This produced what I have called the "behavioral sink," the continual accentuation of aggregations to the point that much available space was unused despite a population increase to nearly 15 times the optimum.

All true "mousity" was lost. Though physically they still appeared to be mice, they had no essential capacities for survival and continuation of mouse society. Suddenly, population growth ceased. In what seemed an instant they passed over a threshold beyond which there was no likelihood of their ever recouping the capacity to become real mice again. No more young were born. From a peak population of 2,200 mice nearly three years ago, aging has gradually taken its toll until now there are only 46 sluggish near-cadavers comparable to people more than 100 years old.

It was just such a fading universe Colin Turnbull found in 1964. Just before he arrived, *Strike No. 3* had set in: starvation. Any such crisis could have added the coup de grace after the other two strikes. Normally the Ik could count on only making three crops every four years. At this time a two-year drought set in and destroyed almost all crops. Neighboring tribes survived with their cultures intact. Turkana herdsmen, facing starvation and death, kept their societies in contact with each other and continued to sing songs of praise to God for the goodness of life.

By the beginning of the long drought, "goodness" to the Ik simply meant to have food—to have food for one's self alone. Collaborative hunts were a thing of the past, long since stopped by the police and probably no longer possible as a social effort, anyway. Solitary hunting, now designated as poaching, became a necessity for sheer survival. But the solitary hunter took every precaution not to let others know of his success. He would gorge himself far off in the bush and bring the surplus back to sell to the police, who were not above profiting from this traffic. Withholding food from wife, children and aging parents became an accomplishment to brag and laugh about. It became a way of life, continuing after the government began providing famine relief. Those strong enough to go to

Rains temporarily turned the Ik's mountain green just before Turnbull returned for a visit.

the police station to get rations for themselves and their families would stop halfway home and gorge all the food, even though it caused them to vomit.

Village of mutual hatred

The village reflected this reversal of humanity. Instead of open courtyards around each group of huts within the large compound, there was a maze of walls and tunnels booby trapped with spears to ward off intrusion by neighbors.

In Atum's village a whole band of more than 100 individuals was crowded together in mutual hostility and aloneness. They would gather at their sitting place and sit for hours in a kind of suspended animation, not looking directly at each other, yet scanning slowly all others who might be engaged in some solitary task, watching for someone to make a mistake that would elicit the symbolic violence of laughter and derision.

They resembled my pools of rejected withdrawn mice. Homemaking deteriorated, feces littered doorsteps and courtyard. Universal adultery and incest replaced the old taboo. The beaded virgins' aprons of eight-to-twelve-year-old girls became symbols that these were proficient whores accustomed to selling their wares to passing herdsmen.

One ray of humanity left in this cesspool was 12-year-old, retarded Adupa. Because she believed that food was for sharing and savoring, her playmates beat her. She still believed that parents were for loving and to be loved by. They cured her madness by locking her in her hut until she died and decayed.

The six other villages were smaller and their people could retain a few glimmers of the goodness and fullness of life. There was Kuaur, devoted to Turnbull, hiking four days to deliver mail, taunted for bringing food home to share with his wife and child. There was Losiké, the potter, regarded as a witch. She offered

water to visitors and made pots for others. When the famine got so bad that there was no need for pots to cook in, her husband left her. She was no longer bringing in any income. And then there was old Nangoli, still capable of mourning when her husband died. She went with her family and village across Kidepo and into the Sudan where their village life turned for a while back to normality. But it was not normal enough to keep them. Back to Pirre, to death, they returned.

All goodness was gone from the Ik, leaving merely emptiness, valuelessness, nothingness, the chaos of Nun. They reentered the womb of beginning time from which there is no return. Urination beside the partial graves of the dead marked the death of God, the final fading of Mount Morungole.

My poor words give only a shadowy image of the cold coffin of Ik humanity that Turnbull describes. His two years with the Ik left him in a slough of despondency from which he only extricated himself with difficulty, never wanting to see them again. Time and distance brought him comfort. He did return for a brief visit some months later. Rain had come in abundance. Gardens had sprung up untended from hidden seeds in the earth. Each Ik gleaned only for his immediate needs. Granaries stood empty, not refilled for inevitable scarcities ahead. The future had ceased to exist. Individual and social decay continued on its downward spiral. Sadly Turnbull departed again from this land of lost hope and faith.

Last summer in London I knew nothing about the Ik when I was so publicly and thoroughly chastised for having the temerity to suspect that the behavioral and spiritual death my mice had exhibited might also befall man. But a psychiatrist in the audience arose in defense of my suspicion. Dr. Geoffrey N. Bianchi remarked that an isolated tribe of Australian Aborigines mirrored the changes and kinds of pathology I had seen among mice. I did not know that Dr. Bianchi was a member of the team that had studied these people, the Kaiadilt, and that a book about them was in preparation, *Cruel, Poor and Brutal Nations* by John Cawte (The University Press of Hawaii). In galley proof I have read about the Kaiadilt and find it so shattering to my faith in humanity that I now sometimes wish I had never heard of it. Yet there is some glimmer of hope that the Kaiadilt may recover—not what they were but possibly some new life.

A frail, tenacious people, the Kaiadilt never numbered more than 150 souls where they lived on Bentinck Island in the Gulf of Carpentaria. So isolated were they that not even their nearest Aboriginal neighbors, 20 miles away, had any knowledge of their existence until in this century; so isolated were the Kaiadilt from their nearest neighbors that they differ from them in such heredity markers as blood type and fingerprints. Not until the early years of this century did an occasional visitor from the Queensland Government even note their existence.

For all practical purposes the first real contact the Kaiadilt had with Western "culture" came in 1916 when a man by the name of McKenzie came to Bentinck with a group of male mainland Aborigines to try to establish a lime kiln. McKenzie's favorite sport was to ride about shooting Kaiadilt. His helpers' sport was to commandeer as many women as they could, and take them to their headquarters on a neighboring island. In 1948 a tidal wave poisoned most of the freshwater sources. Small groups of Kaiadilt were rounded up and transported to larger Mornington Island where they were placed under the supervision of a Presbyterian mission. They were crowded into a dense cluster settlement just as the Ik had been at Pirre.

Here they still existed when the psychiatric field team came into their midst 15 years later. They were much like the Ik: dissolution of family life, total valuelessness, apathy. I could find no mention of laughter, normal or pathological. Perhaps the Kaiadilt didn't laugh. They had essentially ceased the singing that had been so much a part of their traditional way.

The spiritual decay of the Kaiadilt was marked by withdrawal, depression, suicide and tendency to engage in such self-mutilation as ripping out one's testes or chopping off one's nose. In their passiveness some of the anxiety ridden children are accepting the new mold of life forced upon them by a benevolent culture they do not understand. Survival with a new mold totally obliterating all past seems their only hope.

So the lesson comes clear, and Colin Turnbull sums it up in the final paragraph of his book: "The Ik teach us that our much vaunted human values are not inherent in humanity at all, but are associated only with a particular form of survival called society, and that all, even society itself, are luxuries that can be dispensed with. That does not make them any the less wonderful or desirable, and if man has any greatness it is surely in his ability to maintain these values, clinging to them to an often very bitter end, even shortening an already pitifully short life rather than sacrifice his humanity. But that too involves choice, and the Ik teach us that man can lose the will to make it."

Sex Roles

· ·

In the first part of this century, social events (including the Russian Revolution and the rise of socialism) and academic schools of thought (such as behaviorism in psychology) underlined the view that human beings are extraordinarily malleable and that social, historical, and cultural factors are preeminent over biological causes in shaping human behavior. Thus, the noted anthropologist Franz Boas and his students led the intellectual movement that, among other things, attacked the viability of the concept of "race" and took an activist stance in combatting racism.

In this context, the subject of differences between the human sexes became critical. One feature of the organization of social life that is present in all known societies is the cultural attribution of significance to differences between males and females. Notions of "maleness" and "femaleness" vary enormously across cultures, but the distinction between the sexes is made universally, and sex-role attributions and expectations are important organizers of social existence everywhere. Do innate biological differences between the sexes account for these distinctions?

In the early 1930s, Margaret Mead studied and lived with three societies in New Guinea. As she reported in her book *Sex and Temperament* (which we have excerpted as the first article of this topic), she found that in these societies the attribution of qualities of character to the two sexes differed remarkably—both among the societies and in contrast to ours. In her book, which quickly achieved notoriety, Mead argued for the point of view that human nature is "not rigid and unyielding" and that "cultural rhythms are stronger and more compelling than the physiological rhythms which they overlay and distort."

The public was more enthusiastic over *Sex and Temp-erament* than were anthropologists, who noted that her research was limited to a matter of months, that she relied on data provided by only one or two informants, that data and hypotheses were poorly separated, and that a subjective bias in the interpretation of the data was all too evident. Even Mead's husband, Reo Fortune, who had collaborated with her in this research, rejected her view that the Arapesh did not distinguish between male and female temperaments.

With the reemergence of feminism in America during the late 1960s and 1970s, *Sex and Temperament* was enshrined as a "classic," and its obvious shortcomings were overlooked, because its contents could be used to validate feminist critiques of contemporary social life. Mead herself participated in the feminist movement, but at the same time she expressed unease about the overinterpretation of her New Guinea materials by the writers of feminist tracts. We offer you "Sex and Temperament" here because it has had such a pervasive impact on the American scholarly and sociopolitical scene, and because—despite its shortcomings—it remains a stimulating and provocative presentation of ethnographic materials.

In "Society and Sex Roles," Ernestine Friedl asks this question: Why do men have power over women in most societies? Her study of societies at differing levels of complexity shows a broad range to such dominance—from the extreme dominance of Inuit (Eskimo) men to the Hadza men and women (of Tanzania) who are relatively equal in terms of social status. Friedl finds a positive correlation between the degree to which men control the production of food and the sexual stratification of social life. She ends her article with some extrapolations to sex-role changes we might expect in modern industrial society.

34

Sex and Temperament

BY MARGARET MEAD

. . . .

WE HAVE now considered in detail the approved personalities of each sex among three primitive peoples. We found the Arapesh—both men and women—displaying a personality that, out of our historically limited preoccupations, we would call maternal in its parental aspects, and feminine in its sexual aspects. We found men, as well as women, trained to be co-operative, unaggressive, responsive to the needs and demands of others. We found no idea that sex was a powerful driving force either for men or for women. In marked contrast to these attitudes, we found among the Mundugumor that both men and women developed as ruthless, aggressive, positively sexed individuals, with the maternal cherishing aspects of personality at a minimum. Both men and women approximated to a personality type that we in our culture would find only in an undisciplined and very violent male. Neither the Arapesh nor the Mundugumor profit by a contrast between the sexes; the Arapesh ideal is the mild, responsive man married to the mild, responsive woman; the Mundugumor ideal is the violent aggressive man married to the violent aggressive woman. In the third tribe, the Tchambuli, we found a genuine reversal of the sex-attitudes of our own culture, with the woman the dominant, impersonal, managing partner, the man the less responsible and the emotionally dependent person. These three situations suggest, then, a very definite conclusion. If those temperamental attitudes which we have traditionally regarded as feminine—such as passivity, responsiveness, and a willingness to cherish children—can so easily be set up as the masculine pattern in one tribe, and in another be outlawed for the majority of women as well as for the majority of men, we no longer have any basis for regarding such aspects of behaviour as sex-linked. And this conclusion becomes even stronger when we consider the actual reversal in Tchambuli of the position of dominance of the two sexes, in spite of the existence of formal patrilineal institutions.

The material suggests that we may say that many, if not all, of the personality traits which we have called masculine or feminine are as lightly linked to sex as are the clothing, the manners, and the form of head-dress that a society at a given period assigns to either sex. When we consider the behaviour of the typical Arapesh man or woman as contrasted with the behaviour of the typical Mundugumor man or woman, the evidence is overwhelmingly in favour of the strength of social conditioning. In no other way can we account for the almost complete uniformity with which Arapesh children develop into contented, passive, secure persons, while Mundugumor children develop as characteristically into violent, aggressive, insecure persons. Only to the impact of the whole of the integrated culture upon the growing child can we lay the formation of the contrasting types. There is no other explanation of race, or diet, or selection that can be adduced to explain them. We are forced to conclude that human nature is almost unbelievably malleable, responding accurately and contrastingly to contrasting cultural conditions. The differences between individuals who are members of different cultures, like the differences between individuals within a culture, are almost entirely to be laid to differences in conditioning, especially during early childhood, and the form of this conditioning is culturally determined. Standardized personality differences between the sexes are of this order, cultural creations to which each generation, male and female, is trained to conform. There remains, however, the problem of the origin of these socially standardized differences.

While the basic importance of social conditioning is still imperfectly recognized—not only in lay thought, but even by the scientist specifically concerned with such matters—to go beyond it and consider the possible influence of variations in hereditary equipment is a hazardous matter. The following pages will read very differently to one who has made a part of his thinking a recognition of the whole amazing mechanism of cultural conditioning—who has really accepted the fact that the same infant could be developed into a full participant in any one of these three cultures—than they will read to one who still believes that the minutiae of cultural behaviour are carried in the individual germ-plasm. If it is said, therefore, that when we have grasped the full significance of the malleability of the human organism and the preponderant importance of cultural conditioning, there are still further problems to solve, it must be remembered that these problems come *after* such a comprehension of the force of conditioning; they cannot precede it. The forces that make children born among the Arapesh grow up into typical Arapesh personalities are entirely social, and any discussion of the variations which do occur must be looked at against this social background.

With this warning firmly in mind, we can ask a further question. Granting the malleability of human nature, whence arise the differences between the standardized personalities that different cultures decree for all of their members, or which one culture decrees for the members of one sex as contrasted with the members of the opposite sex? If such differences are culturally created, as this material would most strongly suggest that they are, if the new-born child can be shaped with equal ease into an unaggressive Arapesh or an aggressive Mundugumor, why do these striking contrasts occur at all? If the clues to the different personalities decreed for men and women in Tchambuli do not lie in the physical constitution of the two sexes—an assumption that we must reject both for the Tchambuli and for our own society—where can we find the clues upon which the Tchambuli, the Arapesh, the Mundugumor, have built? Cultures are man-made, they are built of human materials; they are diverse but comparable structures within which human beings can attain full human stature. Upon what have they built their diversities?

We recognize that a homogeneous culture committed in all of its gravest institutions and slightest usages to a co-operative, unaggressive course can bend every child to that emphasis, some to a perfect accord with it, the majority to an easy acceptance, while only a few deviants fail to receive the cultural imprint. To consider such traits as aggressiveness or passivity to be sex-linked is not possible in the light of the facts. Have such traits, then, as aggressiveness or passivity, pride or humility, objectivity or a preoccupation with personal relationships, an easy response to the needs of the young and the weak or a hostility to the young and the weak, a tendency to initiate sex-relations or merely to respond to the dictates of a situation or another person's advances—have these traits any basis in temperament at all? Are they potentialities of all human temperaments that can be developed by different kinds of social conditioning and which will not appear if the necessary conditioning is absent?

When we ask this question we shift our emphasis. If we ask why an Arapesh man or an Arapesh woman shows the kind of personality that we have considered in the first section of this book, the answer is: Because of the Arapesh culture, because of the intricate, elaborate, and unfailing fashion in which a culture is able to shape each new-born child to the cultural image. And if we ask the same question about a Mundugumor man or woman, or about a Tchambuli man as compared with a Tchambuli woman, the answer is of the same kind. They display the personalities that are peculiar to the cultures in which they were born and educated. Our attention has been on the differences between Arapesh men and women as a group and Mundugumor men and women as a group. It is as if we had represented the Arapesh personality by a soft yellow, the Mundugumor by a deep red, while the Tchambuli female personality was deep orange, and that of the Tchambuli male, pale green. But if we now ask whence came the original direction in each culture, so that one now shows yellow, another red, the third orange and green by sex, then we must peer more closely. And leaning closer to the picture, it is as if behind the bright consistent yellow of the Arapesh, and the deep equally consistent red of the Mundugumor, behind the orange and green that are Tchambuli, we found in each case the delicate, just discernible outlines of the whole spectrum, differently overlaid in each case by the monotone which covers it. This spectrum is the range of individual differences which lie back of the so much more conspicuous cultural emphases, and it is to this that we must turn to find the explanation of cultural inspiration, of the source from which each culture has drawn.

There appears to be about the same range of basic temperamental variation among the Arapesh and among the Mundugumor, although the violent man is a misfit in the first society and a leader in the second. If human nature were completely homogeneous raw material, lacking specific drives and characterized by no important constitutional differences between individuals, then individuals who display personality traits so antithetical to the social pressure should not reappear in societies of such differing emphases. If the variations between individuals were to be set down to accidents in the genetic process, the same accidents should not be repeated with similar frequency in strikingly different cultures, with strongly contrasting methods of education.

But because this same relative distribution of individual differences does appear in culture after culture, in spite of the divergence between the cultures, it seems pertinent to offer a hypothesis to explain upon what basis the personalities of men and women have been differently standardized so often in the history of the human race. This hypothesis is an extension of that advanced by Ruth Benedict in her *Patterns of Culture*. Let us assume that there are definite temperamental differences between human beings which if not entirely hereditary at least are established on a hereditary base very soon after birth. (Further than this we cannot at present narrow the matter.) These differences finally embodied in the character structure of adults, then, are the clues from which culture works, selecting one temperament, or a combination of related and congruent types, as desirable, and embodying this choice in every thread of the social fabric—in the care of the young child, the games the children play, the songs the people sing, the structure of political organization, the religious observance, the art and the philosophy.

Some primitive societies have had the time and the robustness to revamp all of their institutions to fit one extreme type, and to develop educational techniques which will ensure that the majority of each generation will show a personality congruent with this extreme emphasis. Other societies have pursued a less definitive course, selecting their models not from the most extreme, most highly differentiated individuals, but from the less marked types. In such societies the approved personality is less pronounced, and the culture often contains the types of inconsistencies that many human being display also; one institution may be adjusted to the uses of pride, another to a casual humility that is congruent neither with pride nor with inverted pride. Such societies, which have taken the more usual and less sharply defined types as models, often show also a less definitely patterned social structure. The culture of such societies may be likened to a house the decoration of which has been informed by no definite and precise taste, no exclusive emphasis upon dignity or comfort or pretentiousness or beauty, but in which a little of each effect has been included.

Alternatively, a culture may take its clues not from one temperament, but from several temperaments. But instead of mixing together into an inconsistent hotchpotch the choices and emphases of different temperaments, or blending them together into a smooth but not particularly distinguished whole, it may isolate each type by making it the basis for the approved social personality for an age-group, a sex-group, a caste-group, or an occupational group. In this way society becomes not a monotone with a few discrepant patches of an intrusive colour, but a mosaic, with different groups displaying different personality traits. Such specializations as these may be based upon any facet of human endowment—different intellectual abilities, different artistic abilities, different emotional traits. So the Samoans decree that all young people must show the personality trait of unaggressiveness and punish with opprobrium the aggressive child who displays traits regarded as appropriate only in titled middle-aged men. In societies based upon elaborate ideas of rank, members of the aristocracy will be permitted, even compelled, to display a pride, a sensitivity to insult, that would be deprecated as inappropriate in members of the plebeian class. So also in professional groups or in religious sects some temperamental traits are selected and institutionalized, and taught to each new member who enters the profession or sect. Thus the physician learns the bed-side manner, which is the natural behaviour of some temperaments and the standard behaviour of the general practitioner in the medical profession; the Quaker learns at least the outward behaviour and the rudiments of meditation, the capacity for which is not necessarily an innate characteristic of many of the members of the Society of Friends.

So it is with the social personalities of the two sexes. The traits that occur in some members of each sex are specially assigned to one sex, and disallowed in the other. The history of the social definition of sex-differences is filled with such arbitrary arrangements in the intellectual and artistic field, but because of the assumed congruence between physiological sex and emotional endowment we have been less able to recognize that a similar arbitrary slection is being made among emotional traits also. We have assumed that because it is convenient for a mother to wish to care for her child, this is a trait with which women have been more generously endowed by a carefully teleological process of evolution. We have assumed that because men have hunted, an activity requiring enterprise, bravery, and initiative, they have been endowed with these useful attitudes as part of their sex-temperament.

Societies have made these assumptions both overtly and implicitly. If a society insists that warfare is the major occupation for the male sex, it is therefore insisting that all male children display bravery and pugnacity. Even if the insistence upon the differential bravery of men and women is not made articulate, the difference in occupation makes this point implicitly. When, however, a society goes further and defines men as brave and women as timorous, when men are forbidden to show fear and women are indulged in the most flagrant display of fear, a more explicit element enters in. Bravery, hatred of any weakness, of flinching before pain or danger—this attitude which is so strong a component of *some human* temperaments has been selected as the key to masculine behaviour. The easy unashamed display of fear or suffering that is congenial to a different temperament has been made the key to feminine behaviour.

Originally two variations of human temperament, a hatred of fear or willingness to display fear, they have been socially translated into inalienable aspects of the personalities of the two sexes. And to that defined sex-personality every child will be educated, if a boy, to suppress fear, if a girl, to show it. If there has been no social selection in regard to this trait, the proud temperament that is repelled by any betrayal of feeling will display itself, regardless of sex, by keeping a stiff upper lip. Without an express prohibition of such behaviour the expressive unashamed man or woman will weep, or comment upon fear or suffering. Such attitudes, strongly marked in certain temperaments, may by social selection be standardized for everyone, or outlawed for everyone, or ignored by society, or made the exclusive and approved behaviour of one sex only.

Neither the Arapesh nor the Mundugumor have made any attitude specific for one sex. All of the energies of the culture have gone towards the creation of a single human type, regardless of class, age, or sex. There is no division into age-classes for which different motives or different moral attitudes are regarded as suitable. There is no class of seers or mediums who stand apart drawing inspiration from psychological sources not available to the majority of the people. The Mundugumor have, it is true, made one arbitrary selection, in that they recognize artistic ability only among individuals born with the cord about their necks, and firmly deny the happy exercise of artistic ability to those less unusually born. The Arapesh boy with a tinea infection has been socially selected to be a disgruntled, antisocial individual, and the society forces upon sunny co-operative children cursed with this affliction a final approximation to the behaviour appropriate to a pariah. With these two exceptions no emotional rôle is forced upon an individual because of birth or accident. As there is no idea of rank which declares that some are of high estate and some of low, so there is no idea of sex-difference which declares that one sex must feel differently from the other. One possible imaginative social construct, the attribution of different personalities to different members of the community classified into sex-, age-, or caste-groups, is lacking.

When we turn however to the Tchambuli, we find a situation that while bizarre in one respect, seems nevertheless more intelligible in another. The Tchambuli have at least made the point of sex-difference; they have used the obvious fact of sex as an organizing point for the formation of social personality, even though they seem to us to have reversed the normal picture. While there is reason to believe that not every Tchambuli woman is born with a dominating, organizing, administrative temperament, actively sexed and willing to initiate sex-relations, possessive, definite, robust, practical and impersonal in outlook, still most Tchambuli girls grow up to display these traits. And while there is definite evidence to show that all Tchambuli men are not, by native endowment, the delicate responsive actors of a play staged for the women's benefit, still most Tchambuli boys manifest this coquettish play-acting personality most of the time. Because the Tchambuli formulation of sex-attitudes contradicts our usual premises, we can see clearly that Tchambuli culture has arbitrarily permitted certain human traits to women, and allotted others, equally arbitarily, to men.

If we then accept this evidence drawn from these simple societies which through centuries of isolation from the main stream of human history have been able to develop more extreme, more striking cultures than is possible under historical conditions of great intercommunication between peoples and the resulting heterogeneity, what are the implications of these results? What conclusions can we draw from a study of the way in which a culture can select a few traits from the wide gamut of human endowment and specialize these traits, either for one sex or for the entire community? What relevance have these results to social thinking?

35

Society and Sex Roles

BY ERNESTINE FRIEDL

. . . .

"Women must respond quickly to the demands of their husbands," says anthropologist Napoleon Chagnon describing the horticultural Yanomamo Indians of Venezuela. When a man returns from a hunting trip, "the woman, no matter what she is doing, hurries home and quietly but rapidly prepares a meal for her husband. Should the wife be slow in doing this, the husband is within his rights to beat her. Most reprimands . . . take the form of blows with the hand or with a piece of firewood. . . . Some of them chop their wives with the sharp edge of a machete or axe, or shoot them with a barbed arrow in some nonvital area, such as the buttocks or leg."

Among the Semai agriculturalists of central Malaya, when one person refuses the request of another, the offended party suffers *punan*, a mixture of emotional pain and frustration. "Enduring *punan* is commonest when a girl has refused the victim her sexual favors," reports Robert Dentan. "The jilted man's 'heart becomes sad.' He loses his energy and his appetite. Much of the time he sleeps, dreaming of his lost love. In this state he is in fact very likely to injure himself 'accidentally.'" The Semai are afraid of violence; a man would never strike a woman.

The social relationship between men and women has emerged as one of the principal disputes occupying the attention of scholars and the public in recent years. Although the discord is sharpest in the United States, the controversy has spread throughout the world. Numerous national and international conferences, including one in Mexico sponsored by the United Nations, have drawn together delegates from all walks of life to discuss such questions as the social and political rights of each sex, and even the basic nature of males and females.

Whatever their position, partisans often invoke examples from other cultures to support their ideas about the proper role of each sex. Because women are clearly subservient to men in many societies, like the Yanomamo, some experts conclude that the natural pattern is for men to dominate. But among the Semai no one has the right to command others, and in West Africa women are often chiefs. The place of women in these societies supports the argument of those who believe that sex roles are not fixed, that if there is a natural order, it allows for many different arrangements.

The argument will never be settled as long as the opposing sides toss examples from the world's cultures at each other like intellectual stones. But the effect of biological differences on male and female behavior can be clarified by looking at known examples of the earliest forms of human society and examining the relationship between technology, social organization, environment, and sex roles. The problem is to determine the conditions in which different degrees of male dominance are found, to try to discover the social and cultural arrangements that give rise to equality or inequality between the sexes, and to attempt to apply this knowledge to our understanding of the changes taking place in modern industrial society.

As Western history and the anthropological record have told us, equality between the sexes is rare; in most known societies females are subordinate. Male dominance is so widespread that it is virtually a human universal; societies in which women are consistently dominant do not exist and have never existed.

Evidence of a society in which women control all strategic resources like food and water, and in which women's activities are the most prestigious has never been found. The Iroquois of North America and the Lovedu of Africa came closest. Among the Iroquois, women raised food, controlled its distribution, and helped to choose male political leaders. Lovedu women ruled as queens, exchanged valuable cattle, led ceremonies, and controlled their own sex lives. But among both the Iroquois and the Lovedu, men owned the land and held other positions of power and prestige. Women were equal to men; they did not have ultimate authority over them. Neither culture was a true matriarchy.

Patriarchies are prevalent, and they appear to be strongest in societies in which men control significant goods that are exchanged with people outside the family. Regardless of who produces food, the person who gives it to others creates the obligations and alliances that are at the center of all political relations. The greater the male monopoly on the distribution of scarce items, the stronger their control of women seems to be. This is most obvious in relatively simple hunter-gatherer societies.

Hunter-gatherers, or foragers, subsist on wild plants, small land animals, and small river or sea creatures gathered by hand; large land animals and sea mammals hunted with spears, bows and arrows, and blow guns; and fish caught with hooks and nets. The 300,000 hunter-gatherers alive in the world today include the Eskimos, the Australian aborigines, and the Pygmies of Central Africa.

Foraging has endured for two million years and was replaced by farming and animal husbandry only 10,000 years ago; it covers more than 99 percent of human history. Our foraging ancestry is not far behind us and provides a clue to our understanding of the human condition.

Hunter-gatherers are people whose ways of life are technologically simple and socially and politically egalitarian. They live in small groups of 50 to 200 and have neither kings, nor priests, nor social classes. These conditions permit anthropologists to observe the essential bases for inequalities between the sexes without the distortions induced by the complexities of contemporary industrial society.

The source of male power among hunter-gatherers lies in their control of a scarce, hard to acquire, but necessary nutrient—animal protein. When men in a hunter-gatherer society return to camp with game, they divide the meat in some customary way. Among the !Kung San of Africa, certain parts of the animal are given to the owner of the arrow that killed the beast, to the first hunter to sight the game, to the one who threw the first spear, and to all men in the hunting party. After the meat has been divided, each hunter distributes his share to his blood relatives and his in-laws, who in turn share it with others. If an animal is large enough, every member of the band will receive some meat.

Vegetable foods, in contrast, are not distributed beyond the immediate household. Women give food to their children, to their husbands, to other members of the household, and rarely, to the occasional visitor. No one outside the family regularly eats any of the wild fruits and vegetables that are gathered by the women.

The meat distributed by the men is a public gift. Its source is widely known, and the donor expects a reciprocal gift when other men return from a successful hunt. He gains honor as a supplier of a scarce item and simultaneously obligates others to him.

These obligations constitute a form of power or control over others, both men and women. The opinions of hunters play an important part in decisions to move the village; good hunters attract the most desirable women; people in other groups join camps with good hunters; and hunters, because they already participate in an internal system of exchange, control exchange with other groups for flint, salt, and steel axes. The male monopoly on hunting unites men in a system of exchange and gives them power; gathering vegetable food does not give women equal power even among foragers who live in the tropics, where the food collected by women provides more than half the hunter-gatherer diet.

If dominance arises from a monopoly on big-game hunting, why has the male monopoly remained unchallenged? Some women are strong enough to participate in the hunt and their endurance is certainly equal to that of men. Dobe San women of the Kalahari Desert in Africa walk an average of 10 miles a day carrying from 15 to 33 pounds of food plus a baby.

Women do not hunt, I believe, because of four interrelated factors: variability in the supply of game; the different skills required for hunting and gathering; the incompatibility between carrying burdens and hunting; and the small size of seminomadic foraging populations.

Because the meat supply is unstable, foragers must make frequent expeditions to provide the band with gathered food. Environmental factors such as seasonal and annual variation in rainful often affect the size of the wildlife population. Hunters cannot always find game, and when they do encounter animals, they are not always successful in killing their prey. In northern latitudes, where meat is the primary food, periods of starvation are known in every generation. The irregularity of the game supply leads hunter-gatherers in areas where plant foods are available to depend on these predictable foods a good part of the time. Someone must gather the fruits, nuts, and roots and carry them back to camp to feed unsuccessful hunters, children, the elderly, and anyone who might not have gone foraging that day.

Foraging falls to the women because hunting and gathering cannot be combined on the same expedition. Although gatherers sometimes notice signs of game as they work, the skills required to track game are not the same as those required to find edible roots or plants. Hunters scan the horizon and the land for traces of large game; gatherers keep their eyes to the ground, studying the distribution of plants and the texture of the soil for hidden roots and animal holes. Even if a woman who was collecting plants came across the track of an antelope, she could not follow it; it is impossible to carry a load and hunt at the same time. Running with a heavy load is difficult, and should the animal be sighted, the hunter would be off balance and could neither shoot an arrow nor throw a spear accurately.

Pregnancy and child care would also present difficulties for a hunter. An unborn child affects a woman's body balance, as does a child in her arms, on her back, or slung at her side. Until they are two years old, many hunter-gatherer children are carried at all times, and until they are four, they are carried some of the time.

An observer might wonder why young women do not hunt until they become pregnant, or why mature women and men do not hunt and gather on alternate days, with some women staying in camp to act as wet nurses for the young. Apart from the effects hunting might have on a mother's milk production, there are two reasons. First, young girls begin to bear children as soon as they are physically mature and strong enough to hunt, and second, hunter-gatherer bands are so small that there are unlikely to be enough lactating women to serve as wet nurses. No hunter-gatherer group could afford to maintain a specialized female hunting force.

Because game is not always available, because hunting and gathering are specialized skills, because women carrying heavy loads cannot hunt, and because women in hunter-gatherer societies are usually either pregnant or caring for young children, for most of the last two million years of human history men have hunted and women have gathered.

If male dominance depends on controlling the supply of meat, then the degree of male dominance in a society should vary with the amount of meat available and the amount supplied by the men. Some regions, like the East African grasslands and the North American woodlands, abounded with species of large mammals; other zones, like tropical forests and semideserts, are thinly populated with prey. Many elements affect the supply of game, but theoretically, the less meat provided exclusively by the men, the more egalitarian the society.

All known hunter-gatherer societies fit into four basic types: those in which men and women work together in communal hunts and as teams gathering edible plants, as did the Washo Indians of North America; those in which men and women each collect their own plant foods although the men supply some meat to the group, as do the Hadza of Tanzania; those in which male hunters and female gatherers work apart but return to camp each evening to share their acquisitions, as do the Tiwi of North Australia; and those in which the men provide all the food by hunting large game, as do the Eskimo. In each case the extent of male dominance increases directly with the proportion of meat sup-

plied by individual men and small hunting parties.

Among the most egalitarian of hunter-gatherer societies are the Washo Indians, who inhabited the valleys of the Sierra Nevada in what is now southern California and Nevada. In the spring they moved north to Lake Tahoe for the large fish runs of sucker and native trout. Everyone—men, women, and children—participated in the fishing. Women spent the summer gathering edible berries and seeds while the men continued to fish. In the fall some men hunted deer but the most important source of animal protein was the jack rabbit, which was captured in communal hunts. Men and women together drove the rabbits into nets tied end to end. To provide food for the winter, husbands and wives worked as teams in the late fall to collect pine nuts.

Since everyone participated in most food-gathering activities, there were no individual distributors of food and relatively little difference in male and female rights. Men and women were not segregated from each other in daily activities; both were free to take lovers after marriage; both had the right to separate whenever they chose; menstruating women were not isolated from the rest of the group; and one of the two major Washo rituals celebrated hunting while the other celebrated gathering. Men were accorded more prestige if they had killed a deer, and men directed decisions about the seasonal movement of the group. But if no male leader stepped forward, women were permitted to lead. The distinctive feature of groups such as the Washo is the relative equality of the sexes.

The sexes are also relatively equal among the Hadza of Tanzania but this near-equality arises because men and women tend to work alone to feed themselves. They exchange little food. The Hadza lead a leisurely life in the seemingly barren environment of the East African Rift Gorge that is, in fact, rich in edible berries, roots, and small game. As a result of this abundance, from the time they are 10 years old,

Hadza men and women gather much of their own food. Women take their young children with them into the bush, eating as they forage, and collect only enough food for a light family meal in the evening. The men eat berries and roots as they hunt for small game, and should they bring down a rabbit or a hyrax, they eat the meat on the spot. Meat is carried back to the camp and shared with the rest of the group only on those rare occasions when a poisoned arrow brings down a large animal—an impala, a zebra, an eland, or a giraffe.

Because Hadza men distribute little meat, their status is only slightly higher than that of the women. People flock to the camp of a good hunter and the camp might take on his name because of his popularity, but he is in no sense a leader of the group. A Hadza man and a woman have an equal right to divorce and each can repudiate a marriage simply by living apart for a few weeks. Couples tend to live in the same camp as the wife's mother but they sometimes make long visits to the camp of the husband's mother. Although a man may take more than one wife, most Hadza males cannot afford to indulge in this luxury. In order to maintain a marriage, a man must supply both his wife and his mother-in-law with some meat and trade goods, such as beads and cloth, and the Hadza economy gives few men the wealth to provide for more than one wife and mother-in-law. Washo equality is based on cooperation; Hadza equality is based on independence.

In contrast to both these groups, among the Tiwi of Melville and Bathurst Islands off the northern coast of Australia, male hunters dominate female gatherers. The Tiwi are representative of the most common form of foraging society, in which the men supply large quantities of meat, although less than half the food consumed by the group. Each morning Tiwi women, most with babies on their backs, scatter in different directions in search of vegetables, grubs, worms, and small game such as bandicoots, lizards, and opossums. To track the game, they use hunting dogs. On most days women return to camp with some meat and with baskets full of *korka*, the nut of a native palm, which is soaked and mashed to make a porridge-like dish. The Tiwi men do not hunt small game and do not hunt every day, but when they do they often return with kangaroo, large lizards, fish, and game birds.

The porridge is cooked separately by each household and rarely shared outside the family, but the meat is prepared by a volunteer cook, who can be male or female. After the cook takes one of the parts of the animal traditionally reserved for him or her, the animal's "boss," the one who caught it, distributes the rest to all near kin and then to all others residing with the band. Although the small game supplied by the women is distributed in the same way as the big game supplied by the men, Tiwi men are dominant because the game they kill provides most of the meat.

The power of Tiwi men is clearest in their betrothal practices. Among the Tiwi, a woman must always be married. To ensure this, female infants are betrothed at birth and widows are remarried at the gravesides of their late husbands. Men form alliances by exchanging daughters, sisters, and mothers in marriage and some collect as many as 25 wives. Tiwi men value the quantity and quality of the food many wives can collect and the many children they can produce.

The dominance of the men is offset somewhat by the influence of adult women in selecting their next husbands. Many women are active strategists in the political careers of their male relatives, but to the exasperation of some sons attempting to promote their own futures, widowed mothers sometimes insist on selecting their own partners. Women also influence the marriages of their daughters and granddaughters, especially when the selected husband dies before the bestowed child moves to his camp.

Among the Eskimo, representative of the rarest type of forager society, inequality between the sexes is matched by inequality in supplying the group with food. Inland Eskimo men hunt caribou throughout the year to provision the entire society, and maritime Eskimo men depend on whaling, fishing, and some hunting to feed their extended families. The women process the carcasses, cut and sew skins to make clothing, cook, and care for the young; but they collect no food of their own and depend on the men to supply all the raw materials for their work. Since men provide all the meat, they also control the trade in hides, whale oil, seal oil, and other items that move between the maritime and inland Eskimos.

Eskimo women are treated almost exclusively as objects to be used, abused, and traded by men. After puberty all Eskimo girls are fair game for any interested male. A man shows his intentions by grabbing the belt of a woman and if she protests, he cuts off her trousers and forces himself upon her. These encounters are considered unimportant by the rest of the group. Men offer their wives' sexual services to establish alliances with trading partners and members of hunting and whaling parties.

Despite the consistent pattern of some degree of male dominance among foragers, most of these societies are egalitarian compared with agricultural and industrial societies. No forager has any significant opportunity for political leadership. Foragers, as a rule, do not like to give or take orders, and assume leadership only with reluctance. Shamans (those who are thought to be possessed by spirits) may be either male or female. Public rituals conducted by women in order to celebrate the first menstruation of girls are common, and the symbolism in these rituals is similar to that in the ceremonies that follow a boy's first kill.

In any society, status goes to those who control the distribution of valued goods and services outside the family. Equality arises when both sexes work side by side in food production, as do the Washo, and the products are simply distributed among the workers. In such circumstances, no person or sex has greater access to valued items than do others. But when women make no contribution to the food supply, as in the case of the Eskimo, they are completely subordinate.

When we attempt to apply these generalizations to contemporary industrial society, we can predict that as long as women spend their discretionary income from jobs on domestic needs, they will gain little social recognition and power. To be an effective source of power, money must be exchanged in ways that require returns and create obligations. In other words, it must be invested.

Jobs that do not give women control over valued resources will do little to advance their general status. Only as managers, executives, and professionals are women in a position to trade goods and services, to do others favors, and therefore to obligate others to them. Only as controllers of valued resources can women achieve prestige, power, and equality.

Within the household, women who bring in income from jobs are able to function on a more nearly equal basis with their husbands. Women who contribute services to their husbands and children without pay, as do some middle-class Western housewives, are especially vulnerable to dominance. Like Eskimo women, as long as their services are limited to domestic distribution they have little power relative to their husbands and none with respect to the outside world.

As for the limits imposed on women by their procreative functions in hunter-gatherer societies, childbearing and child care are organized around work as much as work is organized around reproduction. Some foraging groups space their children three to four years apart and have an average of only four to six children, far fewer than many women in other cultures. Hunter-gatherers nurse their infants for extended periods, sometimes for as long as four years. This custom suppresses ovulation and limits the size of their families. Sometimes, although rarely, they practice infanticide. By limiting reproduction, a woman who is gathering food has only one child to carry.

Different societies can and do adjust the frequency of birth and the care of children to accommodate whatever productive activities women customarily engage in. In horticultural societies, where women work long hours in gardens that may be far from home, infants get food to supplement their mothers' milk, older children take care of younger children, and pregnancies are widely spaced. Throughout the world, if a society requires a woman's labor, it finds ways to care for her children.

In the United States, as in some other industrial societies, the accelerated entry of women with preschool children into the labor force has resulted in the development of a variety of child-care arrangements. Individual women have called on friends, relatives, and neighbors. Public and private child-care centers are growing. We should realize that the declining birth rate, the increasing acceptance of childless or single-child families, and a de-emphasis on motherhood are adaptations to a sexual division of labor reminiscent of the system of production found in hunter-gatherer societies.

In many countries where women no longer devote most of their productive years to childbearing, they are beginning to demand a change in the social relationship of the sexes. As women gain access to positions that control the exchange of resources, male dominance may become archaic, and industrial societies may one day become as egalitarian as the Washo.

For further information:

Friedl, Ernestine. *Women and Men: An Anthropologist's View.* Holt, Rinehart and Winston, 1975.

Martin, M. Kay, and Barbara Voorhies, eds. *Female of the Species.* Columbia University Press, 1977.

Murphy, Yolanda, and Robert Murphy. *Women of the Forest.* Columbia University Press, 1974.

Reiter, Rayna, ed. *Toward an Anthropology of Women.* Monthly Review Press, 1975.

Rosaldo, M. Z., and Louise Lamphere, eds. *Women, Culture, and Society.* Stanford University Press, 1974.

Schlegel, Alice, ed. *Sexual Stratification: A Cross-Cultural View.* Columbia University Press, 1977.

Strathern, Marilyn. *Women In Between: Female Roles in a Male World.* Academic Press, 1972.

Cherry Lindholm

36

Life Behind the Veil

BY CHERRY LINDHOLM AND CHARLES LINDHOLM

The bazaar teems with activity. Pedestrians throng the narrow streets, wending past donkey carts, cyclists and overloaded vehicles. Vendors haggle in the dark doorways of their shops. Pitiful beggars shuffle among the crowds, while bearded religious mendicants wander about, their eyes fixed on a distant world.

Drifting among the mobs of men are, here and there, anonymous figures hidden beneath voluminous folds of material, who float along like ships in full sail, graceful, mysterious, faceless, instilling in the observer a sense both of awe and of curiosity. These are the Moslem women of the Middle East. Their dress is the customary *chador*, which they wear when obliged to leave the privacy of their homes. The *chador* is but one means by which women maintain their *purdah*, the institution of female seclusion, which requires that women should remain unseen by men who are not close relatives and strikes Westerners as so totally foreign and incomprehensible.

Sometimes the alien aspect is tempered with a touch of Western familiarity. A pair of plastic sunglasses may gleam from behind the lace that covers the eyes, or a platform shoe might peep forth from beneath the hem of the flowing *chador*. Nevertheless, the overall presence remains one of inscrutability and is perhaps the most striking image of Middle Eastern societies.

We spent nine months in one of the most strict of all the *purdah* societies, the Yusufzai Pakhtun of the Swat Valley in the North-West Frontier Province of Pakistan. ("Pakhtun" is the designation preferred by the tribesmen, who were generally called Pathans in the days of the British *raj*.)

We had come to the Swat Valley after a hair-raising ride on a rickety bus from Peshawar over the 10,280-foot Malakand Pass. Winston Churchill came this way as a young war correspondent attached to the Malakand Field Force in 1897. As we came into the valley, about half the size of Connecticut, we passed a sign that said WELCOME TO SWAT. We were fortunate to have entrée into the community through a Swati friend we had made eight years before. In Swat, women are secluded inside the domestic compound except for family rituals, such as marriage, circumcision and funerals, or visits to saints' tombs. A woman must always be in the protective company of other women and is never allowed out alone. It tells a great deal about the community that the word for husband in Pakhto, the language of the Pakhtun, is *khawund*, which also means God.

However, as everywhere, rules are sometimes broken or, more frequently, cleverly manipulated. Our Pakhtun host's stepmother, Bibi, an intelligent and forceful woman, was renowned for her tactics. Once, when all the females of the household had been forbidden to leave the compound to receive cholera inoculations at the temporary clinic next door, Bibi respectfully bowed her head and assured the men they could visit the mosque with easy minds. Once the men had gone, she promptly climbed the ladder to the flat roof and summoned the doctor to the door of her compound. One by one, the women extended their bare arms through the doorway and received their shots. Later, Bibi could honestly swear that no woman had set foot outside the compound walls.

Despite such circumventions, *purdah* is of paramount importance in Swat. As one Pakhtun proverb succinctly states: "The woman's place is in the home or the grave." Years ago in Swat, if a woman broke her *purdah*, her husband might kill her or cut off her nose as punishment and as a means of cleansing his honor. If a woman is caught alone with a unrelated man, it will always be assumed that the liaison is sexual, and public opinion will oblige her husband to shoot her, even if he does not desire her death; to go unavenged is to be known henceforth as *begherata*, or man without honor. As such, he would no longer have the right to call himself Pakhtun.

A shameless woman is a threat to the whole society. Our host remembered witnessing, 30 years ago when he was a child, the entire village stoning an adulteress. This punishment is prescribed by Islamic law, though the law requires there be four witnesses to the sexual act itself to establish guilt. Nowadays, punishments for wifely misdemeanors have become less harsh, though adulterous wives are still killed.

SEDUCTION

In the rural areas, poorer families generally cannot maintain *purdah* as rigorously as their wealthier neighbors, for often the wife must help her husband in the fields or become a servant. Nevertheless, she is required to keep her hair covered at all times and to interact with men to a minimum. Here again, the rules are sometimes flouted, and a poor woman might entice a man with her eyes or even, according to village men who claimed personal experiences, become more aggressive in her seductive attempts and actually seize a man in a deserted alleyway and lure him into her house. Often, the man is persuaded. Such a woman will accept money from her lover, who is usually a man from a wealthy family. Her husband is then a *begherata*, but some men acquiesce to the situation because of the money the wife is earning or because of fear of the wife's socially superior and more powerful lover. But most poor men,

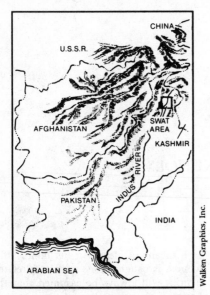

Swat is reached by a 10,280-foot deep pass in the mountains of the Hindu Kush.

and certainly all of the elite, keep their women under strict control.

In the Islamic Middle East, women are viewed as powerful and dangerous beings, highly sexual and lacking in personal discipline and discrimination. In Middle Eastern thought, sexual intercourse itself, though polluting, lacks the same negative connotations it has in the West. It has always been believed that women have sexual climaxes, and there is no notion of female frigidity. Male impotence, however, is well-documented, and some middle-aged and even young men admitted to us that they had lost their interest in women. Sometimes, though rarely, a young bridegroom will find himself incapable of consummating his marriage, either because he finds his bride unattractive or because he has been previously enchanted by a male lover and has become impotent in a heterosexual relationship. Homosexuality has never been seen as aberrant in the Middle East. As a famous Afghan saying humorously declares: "A woman is for bearing children, a boy is for pleasure, but ecstasy is a ripe watermelon!" However, with Western influence, homosexuality in the Middle East is now less overt. But even when it was common and open, the man was still expected to marry and produce children.

Men must marry, though women are regarded as a chaotic and anarchic force. They are believed to possess many times the sexual desire of men and constitute a potential threat to the family and the family's honor, which is based in large measure on the possession and control of women and their excessive and dangerous sexuality.

Among the Pakhtun of Swat, where the male-female relation is one of the most hostile in the Middle East, the man avoids showing affection to his wife, for fear she will become too self-confident and will begin to assert herself in ways that insult his position and honor. She may start by leaving the compound without his permission and, if unchecked, may end by bringing outside men into the house for sexual encounters, secure in the knowledge that her husband, weakened by his affection for her, will not take action. This course of events is considered inevitable by men and women alike and was illustrated by a few actual cases in the village where we lived.

Women are therefore much feared, despite the pronouncements of male supremacy. They must be controlled, in order to prevent their alarming basic natures from coming to the fore and causing dishonor to their own lineages. Purdah is generally described as a system that serves to protect the woman, but implicitly it protects the men and society in general from the potentially disruptive actions of the powerful female sex.

Changes are occurring, however, particularly in the modern urban centers. The educated urban woman often dispenses with the chador, replacing it with a simple length of veiling draped over the head or across the shoulders; she may even decide to adopt modest Western dress. The extent of this transformation will depend partly upon the attitude of the community in which she lives.

In the urban centers of the stricter purdah regions the public display of purdah is scrupulous, sometimes even more striking than that of the tribal village. Behind the scenes, though, the city-dwelling woman does have more freedom than she would have in the village. She will be able to visit not only relatives but friends without specific permission from her husband, who is out at work all day. She may, suitably veiled, go shopping in the bazaar, a chore her husband would have undertaken in the village. On the whole, the city woman will have a great deal more independence, and city men sometimes lament this weakening of traditional male domination.

The urbanized male may speak of the custom-bound tribesmen (such as the Swat Pakhtun, the Bedouin nomads of Saudi Arabia or the Qashqai herdsmen of Iran) as country bumpkins, yet he still considers their central values, their sense of personal pride, honor and autonomy, as cultural ideals and views the tribesmen, in a very real way, as exemplars of the proper mode of life. Elite families in the cities proudly emphasize their tribal heritage and sometimes send their sons to live for a year or so with distant tribal cousins, in order to expose them to the tribesman's integrity and moral code. The tribesman, on the other hand, views his urbanized relatives as weak and womanly, especially with reference to the slackening of purdah in the cities. Though the purdah female, both in the cities and in the tribal areas, rarely personifies the ideal virtues of silence, submission and obedience, the concept of purdah and male supremacy remains central to the male identity and to the ideology of the culture as a whole.

The dynamic beneath the notion of male supremacy, the institution of purdah and the ideology of women's sexual power becomes apparent when one takes an overall view of the social structure. The family in the Middle East, particularly in the tribal regions, is not an isolated element; kinship and marriage are the underlying principles that structure action and thought. Individuals interact not so much according to personal preference as according to kinship.

The Middle Eastern kinship system is known to anthropologists as a segmentary-lineage organization; the basic idea is that kinship is traced through one line only. In the Middle East, the system is patrilineal, which means that the male line is followed, and all the links through women are ignored. An individual can therefore trace his relationship to any other individual in the society and know the exact genealogical distance between them; i.e., the distance that must be traced to reach a common male ancestor. The system obliges men to defend their patrilineal relatives if they are attacked, but if there is no external force threatening the lineage, then men struggle against one another according to the principle of genealogical distance. This principle is nicely stated in a famous Middle Eastern proverb: "I against my brothers; my brothers and I against my cousins; my cousins, my brothers and I against the world." The cousins in question are of course patrilineal.

PROMISCUITY PHOBIA

Within this system, women appear to have no role, though they are the units of reproduction, the mothers of the sons who will carry on the patriline. Strange as it may seem, this is the core contradiction of the society: The "pure" patriline itself is actually descended from a woman. This helps explain the exaggerated fear of women's promiscuity and supposedly voracious sexuality. In order to protect the patriline, women must be isolated and guarded. Their sexuality, which threatens the integrity of the patriline, must be made the exclusive property of their husbands. Women, while being absolutely necessary for the perpetuation of the social order, are simultaneously the greatest threat to it.

The persistent denigration of women is explained by this core contradiction. Moslem society considers women naturally inferior in intelligence and ability—childlike, incapable of discernment, incompetent to testify in court, prey to whims and fancies. In tribal areas, women are prohibited from inheritance, despite a Koranic injunction, and in marriage they are purchased from their fathers like a commodity. Were women not feared, these denials of her personhood would be unnecessary.

Another unique element of Middle Eastern culture is the prevalence of marriage with the father's brother's daughter. In many areas, in fact, this marriage is so favored that a boy must give explicit permission to allow his patrilineal female cousin to marry elsewhere. This peculiar marriage form, which is found nowhere else in the world, also serves to negate the woman by merging her lineage with that of her husband, since both are members of the same patriline (indeed, are the offspring of brothers). No new blood enters, and the sanctity of the patriline is steadily maintained.

However, this ploy gives rise to other problems: Cousin marriage often divides the brothers rather than uniting them. Although the bride-price is usually reduced in such marriages, it is always demanded, thus turning the brothers into opponents in a business negotiation. Furthermore, giving a woman in Swat carries an implication of inferiority; historically, victors in war took women from the vanquished. Cousin marriage thùs renders the brothers' equality questionable. Finally, the young couple's fights will further alienate the brothers, especially since such marriages are notoriously contentious. This is because patrilineal male cousins are rivals for the common grandfather's inheritance (in fact, the Swati term for father's brother's son is *tarbur*, which also means enemy), and a man who marries his patrilineal cousin is mar-

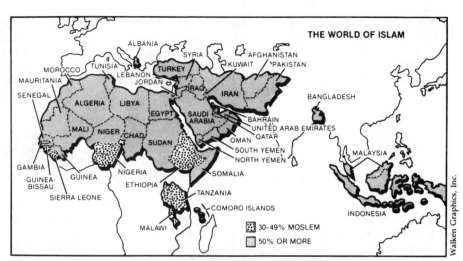

The world of Islam began when Mohammed preached in Saudi Arabia in the seventh century. It fanned out, carrying purdah with it, into Asia and into Africa south of the Sahara.

rying the sister of his lifelong opponent. Her loyalty is with her brother, and this is bound to cause frequent disputes.

Though the girl is treated like goods, she does not see herself as such. The fundamental premise of tribal life is the equality of the various landed families. There are very few hierarchies in these societies, and even the leaders are often no more than first among equals. Within this system, which has been described as a nearly perfect democracy, each *khan* (which means landowner and literally translates as king) family sees itself as superior to all others. The girls of the household feel the same pride in their lineage as their brothers and cannot help but regard their husbands' families through jaundiced eyes. The new bride is prepared to defend the honor of her family, even though they have partially repudiated her by negotiating the marriage. Her identity, like that of a man, rests on her lineage pride, which she will fight to uphold. The husband, meanwhile, is determined to demonstrate his domination and mastery, since control of women is the nexus of a man's sense of self-respect.

Hostility is thus built into marriage by the very structure of the society, which pits every lineage against every other in a never-ending contest to maintain an equilibrium of power within this markedly egalitarian culture. The hostility of the marriage bond is evident from its beginnings. The reluctant bride is torn from her cot in her family's house and ensconced on a palanquin that strongly resembles a bier. The war drums that announce the marriage procession indicate the nature of the tie, as does the stoning of the palanquin by the small boys of the

village as it is carried through the dusty streets. When the bride arrives at her new husband's house, his family triumphantly fires their rifles into the air. They have taken a woman! The young wife cowers in her veils as she is prodded and poked curiously by the females of the husband's house who try to persuade her to show her face. The groom himself is nowhere to be seen, having retreated to the men's house in shame. In three days, he will creep to her room and consummate the marriage. Taking the virginity of the bride is a highly charged symbolic act, and in some areas of the Middle East the display of the bloody nuptial sheet to the public is a vital part of the wedding rite. Breaking the hymen demonstrates the husband's possession of his wife's sexuality. She then becomes the most junior adult in the household, subordinate to everyone, but, most especially, under the heavy thumb of her mother-in-law.

The household the bride enters will be that of her husband's father, since the system, as well as being patrilineal, is also patrilocal. She will be surrounded by his relatives and will be alone with her husband only at night. During the day he will pay no attention to her, for it is considered shameful for a man to take note of his wife in front of others, particularly his father and mother. Within the compound walls, which shield the household from the rest of the world, she is at the mercy of her new family.

DOMESTIC BATTLES
Life within the compound is hardly peaceful. Wives squabble among themselves, and wives who have built a power base by having sons even quarrel with the

old matriarch, their mother-in law. This is usually a prelude to a couple moving out of the house into their own compound, and husbands always blame their wives for the breakup of the extended family, even though they, too, will be glad to become the masters of their own homes and households.

But the worst fights among women are the fights between women married to the same man. Islam permits polygamous marriage, and legally a man may have four wives. Not all men are financially able to take more than one wife, but most men dream of marrying again, despite the Swati proverb that says, "I may be a fool, but not so much of a fool as the man with two wives." Men who can afford it often do take a second wife. The reason is not sexual desire, for wives do not mind if their husbands have liaisons with prostitutes or promiscuous poor women. Rather, the second wife is brought in to humiliate an overly assertive first wife. Bringing in a second wife is a terrible insult; it is an expression of contempt for the first wife and her entire lineage. The insult is especially cutting in Swat, where divorce is prohibited (though it is permitted in the Koran) and where a disliked wife must either endure her lot or retreat to her family's house and a life of celibacy. Small wonder then that households with two wives are pits of intrigue, vituperation and magical incantation, as each wife seeks to expel the other. The Koran says a man should only practice polygamy if he is sure he can treat each wife equally; the only man we met who was able to approximate this ideal was a man who never went home. He spent his time in the men's house, talking with his cronies and having his meals sent to him.

The men's house is the best-built structure in any village, along with the mosque, which is also prohibited to women. It is a meeting place for the clan, the center for hospitality and refuge and the arena for political manipulation. This is where the visitor will be received, surrounded by men who gossip, doze or clean their rifles. Here, the guest might well imagine that women do not even exist. Only the tea and food that is sent over from the compound nearby tell him of the women working behind the walls.

Formerly, in Swat, most men slept in the men's house, visiting their wives secretly late at night and returning before daybreak. But now only a few elders and some ne'er-do-well youths live permanently in the elegant, aging buildings.

Sometimes, however, a man may be obliged to move to the men's house for a few days if his wife makes his home too uncomfortable, for women too have their own weapons in the household battles. Arguments may flare up over almost anything: the husband buying a rotten piece of meat or forgetting to bring home a length of material, the wife ruining some curd or gossiping too much with a neighbor. The wife may then angrily refuse to cook, obliging the husband to retreat to the men's house for food. The man's weapon in fights is violence, while the woman can withdraw domestic services at will.

In the early days of a marriage, when the bride is new to the household and surrounded by her husband's people, she may be fairly meek. But when her status has improved as a result of producing sons, she will become more aggressive. Her lacerating tongue is renowned, and she will also begin to fight back physically as well as verbally. Finally, her exasperated husband may silence her with a blow from a heavy stick he keeps for that purpose. No shame is attached to beating one's wife, and men laugh about beatings they have administered. The women themselves, though they decry their men's brutality, proudly display their scars and bruises, characterizing a neighbor who is relatively gentle to his wife as "a man with no penis."

The older a woman gets, the more powerful and fearless she becomes. She is aided by her sons who, though respecting their father, regard him as an obstacle to their gaining rights in land. The old man, who gains his stature from his landholding, is always reluctant to allot shares to his grown sons. Furthermore, the sons' ties of affection are much stronger with the mother. The elderly father, who is generally 10 or 15 years older than his wife, is thus surrounded by animosity in his own house. The situation of the earlier years has reversed itself, and the wife, who began alone and friendless, gains allies in her old age, while the husband becomes isolated. Ghani Khan, a modern Pakhtun writer, has described the situation well: "The Pakhtun thinks he is as good as anyone else and his father rolled into one and is fool enough to try this even with his wife. She pays for it in her youth, and he in his old age."

But many women do not live to see their triumph. In northern Swat, for every 100 women over the age of 60 there are 149 men, compared to the more equal

100 to 108 ratio below 60. The women are worn out by continual childbearing, breast-feeding and a lack of protein. Though fertile in places, the Swat valley is heavily overpopulated with an estimated one million people, and survival is always difficult. The diet consists chiefly of bread, rice, seasonal vegetables and some dairy products. Meat is a rarity and goes to the men and boys as a matter of course. They perpetuate the patrilineal clan and must survive, while women can always be replaced. The lives of men are hard, but the lives of women are harder, as witnessed by their early deaths.

In this environment, people must learn to be tough, just as they must learn to fit the structure of the patrilineal system. Child-rearing serves both functions.

The birth of a boy in Swat is greeted by rejoicing, while the birth of a girl is an occasion for gloom. But the first few years for both sexes are virtually identical. Like most Middle Easterners, the Swatis practice swaddling, binding the baby tightly so that it is immobilized. Ostensibly, this is to help the baby sleep and prevent it from blinding itself with its flailing hands, but anthropologists have hypothesized that swaddling actually serves to develop a certain character type: a type which can withstand great restraint but which also tends to uncontrolled bursts of temper. This hypothesis fits Swat, where privation and the exigencies of the social structure demand stoicism, but where violent temper is also useful. We often saw Swati children of all ages lose themselves in tantrums to coerce their parents, and such coercion was usually successful. Grown men and women as well are prone to fits of temper, and this dangerous aspect makes their enemies leery of pressing them too hard.

Both sexes are indoctrinated in the virtues of their family and its lineage. In marital fights this training is obvious, as both partners heatedly assert, "Your ancestor was nothing, and mine was great!" At a man's death his sister, not his wife, is his chief mourner. And if a woman is killed it is her brother, not her husband, who avenges her.

Child training in Swat produces strong characters. When they give affection, they give it wholeheartedly, and when they hate, they hate bitterly. The conditions under which they live are cruel and cramped, and they respond with cruelty and rigidity in order to survive. But at the same time, the people are able to bear their hard lives with pride and dignity.

TOPIC THIRTEEN

Belief and Ritual

. . . .

"As members of society, most of us see only what we expect to see, and what we expect to see is what we are conditioned to see when we have learned the definitions and classifications of our culture," anthropologist Victor Turner has observed. But the statement is incomplete; it omits any mention of *beliefs*—bodies of assumptions about the nature of things bolstered by selected facts—which are embedded in every culture and, along with the categories Turner mentions, powerfully organize our experiences of the world around us and our attempts to deal with the world thus conceived.

Belief systems deal with everything human beings can imagine. Instrumental or rational-technical belief systems are concerned primarily with concrete phenomena and tasks: What kind of person makes a good spouse? Which stocks are likely to yield bushels of money to investors? What training methods and dietary regimens should marathon runners undergo? Instrumental beliefs provide answers to these and countless other questions concerning day-to-day existence.

Other beliefs take us beyond daily concerns and address more profound questions such as the purpose of human existence, the phenomenon of death, and the existence of entities that inherently cannot be verified by the human senses. Such transcendental beliefs always invoke the "larger picture" when the believers use them to address concrete tasks or specific issues, such as in the case of the Bolivian tin miners described by June Nash in "Devils, Witches, and Sudden Death." Without their instrumental and transcendental beliefs, these miners could hardly be expected to cope with the extreme stresses of their extraordinarily dangerous work.

Rituals are repeated and stereotyped activities, handed down from generation to generation, that express certain transcendental and instrumental beliefs. Often, rituals mark important social transitions, such as birth, puberty, marriage, and death. In "Cargo Cults," Peter Worsley narrates the emergence of a complex of beliefs and rituals in the South Pacific, as the indigenous cultures were subjected to severe stresses following contact with the industrial world. The cargo cults incorporated symbolic representations of industrial technology to bolster traditional belief systems, which were increasingly difficult to sustain in the context of invading armies. A paradox indeed—but rituals seem uniquely suited to the resolution, on an entirely different level, of those inevitable contradictions that people everywhere must cope with in their daily lives.

37

Devils, Witches, and Sudden Death

BY JUNE NASH

....

Tin miners in the high Andean plateau of Bolivia earn less than a dollar a day when, to use their phrase, they "bury themselves alive in the bowels of the earth." The mine shafts—as much as two miles long and half a mile deep—penetrate hills that have been exploited for more than 450 years. The miners descend to the work areas in open hauls; some stand on the roof and cling to the swaying cable as the winch lowers them deep into the mine.

Once they reach their working level, there is always the fear of rockslides as they drill the face of the mine, of landslides when they set off the dynamite, of gas when they enter unfrequented areas. And added to their fear of the accidents that have killed or maimed so many of their workmates is their economic insecurity. Like Wall Street brokers they watch international price quotations on tin, because a difference of a few cents can mean layoffs, loss of bonuses, a cut in contract prices—even a change of government.

Working in the narrow chimneys and corridors of the mine, breathing the dust- and silicate-filled air, their bodies numbed by the vibration of the drilling machines and the din of dynamite blasts, the tin miners have found an ally in the devil, or Tio (uncle), as he is affectionately known. Myths relate the devil to his pre-Christian counterpart Huari, the powerful ogre who owns the treasures of the hills. In Oruro, a 13,800-foot-high mining

center in the western Andes of Bolivia, all the miners know the legend of Huari, who persuaded the simple farmers of the Uru Uru tribe to leave their work in the fields and enter the caves to find the riches he had in store. The farmers, supported by their ill-gained wealth from the mines, turned from a virtuous life of tilling the soil and praying to the sun god Inti to a life of drinking and midnight revels. The community would have died, the legend relates, if an Inca maiden, Nusta, had not descended from the sky and taught the people to live in harmony and industry.

Despite four centuries of proselyting, Catholic priests have failed to wipe out belief in the legend, but the principal characters have merged with Catholic deities. Nusta is identified with the Virgin of the Mineshaft, and is represented as the vision that appeared miraculously to an unemployed miner.

The miners believe that Huari lives on in the hills where the mines are located, and they venerate him in the form of the devil, or Tio. They believe he controls the rich veins of ore, revealing them only to those who give him offerings. If they offend the Tio or slight him by failing to give him offerings, he will withhold the rich veins or cause an accident.

Miners make images of the Tio and set them up in the main corridors of each mine level, in niches cut into the walls for the workers to rest. The image of the Tio varies in appearance according to the fancy

of the miner who makes him, but his body is always shaped from ore. The hands, face, horns, and legs are sculptured with clay from the mine. Bright pieces of metal or burned-out bulbs from the miners' electric torches are stuck in the eye sockets. Teeth are made of glass or crystal sharpened "like nails," and the mouth is open, gluttonous and ready to receive offerings. Sometimes the plaster of Paris masks worn by the devil dancers at Carnival are used for the head. Some Tios wear embroidered vests, flamboyant capes, and miners' boots. The figure of a bull, which helps miners in contract with the devil by digging out the ore with its horns, occasionally accompanies the image, or there may be *chinas*, female temptresses who are the devil's consorts.

The Tio is a figure of power: he has what everyone wants, in excess. Coca remains lie in his greedy mouth. His hands are stretched out, grasping the bottles of alcohol he is offered. His nose is burned black by the cigarettes he smokes down to the nub. If a Tio is knocked out of his niche by an extra charge of dynamite and survives, the miners consider him to be more powerful than others.

Another spirit present in the mines but rarely represented in images is the Awiche, or old woman. Although some miners deny she is the Pachamama, the earth goddess worshiped by farmers, they relate to her in the same way. Many of the miners greet her when they enter the mine, saying, "Good-day, old woman. Don't let anything happen to me today!" They ask her to intercede with the Tio when they feel in danger; when they leave the mine safely, they thank her for their life.

Quite the opposite kind of feminine image, the Viuda, or widow, appears to miners who have been drinking *chicha*, a fermented corn liquor. Miners who have seen the Viuda describe her as a young and beautiful *chola*, or urbanized Indian, who makes men lose their minds—and sometimes their paychecks. She, too, is a consort of the devil and recruits men to make contracts with him, deluding them with promises of wealth.

When I started working in Oruro during the summer of 1969, the men told me about the *ch'alla*, a ceremonial offering of cigarettes, coca, and alcohol to the Tio. One man described it as follows:

"We make the *ch'alla* in the working areas within the mine. My partner and I do it together every Friday, but on the first Friday of the month we do it with the other workers on our level. We bring in banners, confetti, and paper streamers. First we put a cigarette in the mouth of the Tio and light it. After this we scatter alcohol on the ground for the Pachamama, then give some to the Tio. Next we take out our coca and begin to chew, and we also smoke. We serve liquor from the bottles each of us brings in. We light the Tio's cigarette, saying 'Tio, help us in our work. Don't let any accidents happen.' We do not kneel before him as we would before a saint, because that would be sacrilegious.

"Then everyone begins to get drunk. We begin to talk about our work, about the sacrifices that we make. When this is finished, we wind the streamers around the neck of the Tio. We prepare our *mesas* [tables of offerings that include sugar cakes, llama embryos, colored wool, rice, and candy balls].

"After some time we say, 'Let's go.' Some have to carry out those who are drunk. We go to where we change our clothes, and when we

A model of the Tio, shaped by the workers, sits in a mine alcove. If the image survives an explosion, it is considered very powerful.

June Nash

come out we again make the offering of liquor, banners, and we wrap the streamers around each others' necks. From there on, each one does what he pleases."

I thought I would never be able to participate in a *ch'alla* because the mine managers told me the men didn't like to have women inside the mine, let alone join them in their most sacred rites. Finally a friend high in the governmental bureaucracy gave me permission to go into the mine. Once down on the lowest level of San José mine, 340 meters below the ground, I asked my guide if I could stay with one of the work crews rather than tour the galleries as most visitors did. He was relieved to leave me and get back to work. The men let me try their machines so that I could get a sense of what it was like to hold a 160-pound machine vibrating in a yard-wide tunnel, or to use a mechanical shovel in a gallery where the temperature was 100° F.

They told me of some of their frustrations—not getting enough air pumped in to make the machines work at more than 20 percent efficiency and constant breakdowns of machinery, which slowed them up on their contract.

At noon I refused the superintendent's invitation to eat lunch at level O. Each of the men gave me a bit of his soup or some "seconds," solid food consisting of noodles, potatoes, rice, and spicy meat, which their wives prepare and send down in the elevators.

At the end of the shift all the men in the work group gathered at the Tio's niche in the large corridor. It was the first Friday of the month and the gang leader, Lino Pino, pulled out a bottle of fruit juice and liquor, which his wife had prepared, and each of the men brought out his plastic bag with coca. Lino led the men in offering a cigarette to the Tio, lighting it, and then shaking the liquor on the ground and calling for life, "Hallalla! Hallalla!"

We sat on lumps of ore along the rail lines and Lino's helper served us, in order of seating, from a little tin cup. I was not given any priority, nor was I forgotten in the rounds. One of the men gave me coca from his supply and I received it with two hands, as I had been taught in the rituals aboveground. I chewed enough to make my cheek feel numb, as though I had had an injection of novocaine for dental work. The men told me that coca was their gift from the Pachamama, who took pity on them in their work.

As Lino offered liquor to the Tio, he asked him to "produce" more mineral and make it "ripen," as though it were a crop. These rituals are a continuation of agricultural ceremonies still practiced by the farmers in the area. The miners themselves are the sons or grandsons of the landless farmers who were recruited when the gold and silver mines were reopened for tin production after the turn of the century.

A month after I visited level 340, three miners died in an explosion there when a charge of dynamite fell down a shoot to their work site and exploded. Two of the men died in the mine; the third died a few days later in the hospital. When the accident occurred, all the men rushed to the elevators to help or to stare in fascinated horror as the dead and injured were brought up to level O. They carried the bodies of their dead comrades to the social center where they washed the charred faces, trying to lessen the horror for the women who were coming. When the women came into the social center where the bodies were laid out, they screamed and stamped their feet, the horror of seeing their husbands or neighbors sweeping through their bodies.

The entire community came to sit in at the wake, eating and drinking in the feasting that took place before the coffins of their dead comrades. The meal seemed to confirm the need to go on living as well as the right to live.

Although the accident had not occurred in the same corridor I had been in, it was at the same level. Shortly after that, when a student who worked with me requested permission to visit the mine, the manager told her that the men were hinting that the accident had happened because the gringa (any foreign-born, fair-haired person, in this case myself) had been inside. She was refused permission. I was disturbed by what might happen to my relations with the people of the community, but even more concerned that I had added to their sense of living in a hostile world where anything new was a threat.

The miners were in a state of uneasiness and tension the rest of that month, July. They said the Tio was "eating them" because he hadn't had an offering of food. The dead men were all young, and the Tio prefers the juicy flesh and blood of the young, not the tired blood of the sick older workers. He wanted a k'araku, a ceremonial banquet of sacrificed animals.

There had not been any scheduled k'arakus since the army put the mines under military control in 1965. During the first half of the century, when the "tin barons"— Patiño, Hochschild, and Arayamao—owned the mines, the administrators and even some of the owners, especially Patiño, who had risen from the ranks, would join with the men in sacrificing animals to the Tio and in the drinking and dancing that followed. After nationalization of the mines in 1952, the rituals continued. In fact, some of the miners complained that they were done in excess of the Tio's needs. One said that going into the mine after the revolution was like walking into a saloon.

Following military control, however, the miners had held the ritual only once in San José, after two men had died while working their shift. Now the Tio had again shown he was hungry by eating the three miners who had died in the accident. The miners were determined to offer him food in a k'araku.

At 10:30 P.M. on the eve of the devil's month, I went to the mine with Doris Widerkehr, a student, and Eduardo Ibañez, a Bolivian artist. I was somewhat concerned about how we would be received after what the manager of the mine had said, but all the men seemed glad we had come. As we sat at the entry to the main shaft waiting for the yatiris, shamans who had been contracted for the ceremony, the miners offered us chicha and cocktails of fruit juice and alcohol.

When I asked one of the men why they had prepared the ritual and what it meant, his answer was:

"We are having the k'araku because a man can't die just like that.

We invited the administrators, but none of them have come. This is because only the workers feel the death of their comrades.

"We invite the Pachamama, the Tio, and God to eat the llamas that we will sacrifice. With faith we give coca and alcohol to the Tio. We are more believers in God here than in Germany or the United States because there the workers have lost their soul. We do not have earthquakes because of our faith before God. We hold the crucifix to our breast. We have more confidence before God."

Most miners reject the claim that belief in the Tio is pagan sacrilege. They feel that no contradiction exists, since time and place for offerings to the devil are clearly defined and separated from Christian ritual.

At 11:00 P.M. two white llamas contributed by the administration were brought into level 0 in a company truck. The miners had already adorned the pair, a male and a female, with colored paper streamers and the bright wool earrings with which farmers decorate their flocks.

The four *yatiris* contracted for did not appear, but two others who happened to be staying at the house of a miner were brought in to perform the ceremony. As soon as they arrived, the miners took the llamas into the elevator. The male was on the right and the female to his left, "just the same as a marriage ceremony," one miner commented. Looking at the couple adorned with bright streamers and confetti, there was the feeling of a wedding.

Two men entered the elevator with the llamas and eight more climbed on top to go down to level 340. They were commissioned to take charge of the ritual. All the workers of 340 entered to participate in the ceremony below and about 50 men gathered at level 0 to drink.

At level 340 the workers guided the *yatiris* to the spot where the accident had occurred. There they cast liquor from a bottle and called upon the Tio, the Awiche, and God to protect the men from further ac-

cidents—naming all the levels in the mine, the various work sites, the different veins of ore, the elevator shaft, and the winch, repeating each name three times and asking the Tio not to eat any more workers and to give them more veins to work. The miners removed their helmets during this ritual. It ended with the plea for life, "Hallalla, hallalla, hallalla." Two bottles of liquor were sprinkled on the face of the rock and in the various work places.

The *yatiris* then instructed the men to approach the llamas with their arms behind their backs so that the animals would not know who held the knife that would kill them. They were also told to beg pardon for the sacrifice and to kiss the llamas farewell. One miner, noting what appeared to be a tear falling from the female's eye, cried and tried to comfort her. As the men moved around the llamas in a circle, the *yatiris* called on the Malkus (eagle gods), the Awiche, the Pachamama, and finally the Tiyulas (Tios of the mines), asking for their care.

The female llama was the first to be sacrificed. She struggled and had to be held down by two men as they cut her jugular vein. When they disemboweled her, the men discovered that she was pregnant, to which they attributed the strength of her resistance. Her blood was caught in a white basin.

When the heart of the dying llama had pumped out its blood, the *yatiri* made an incision and removed it, using both his hands, a sign of respect when receiving an offering. He put the still palpitating heart in the basin with the blood and covered it with a white cloth on which the miners placed *k'oa*—an offering made up of herbs, coca, wool, and sweets—and small bottles of alcohol and wine.

The man in charge of the ceremony went with five aides to the site of the principal Tio in the main corridor. There they removed a piece of ore from the image's left side, creating a hole into which they

put the heart, the blood, and the other offerings. They stood in a circle, their heads bent, and asked for safety and that there be no more accidents. In low voices, they prayed in Quechua.

When this commission returned, the *yatiris* proceeded to sacrifice the male llama. Again they asked the Tio for life and good ore in all the levels of the mine, and that there be no accidents. They took the heart, blood, *k'oa*, and bottles of alcohol and wine to another isolated gallery and buried it for the Tio in a place that would not be disturbed. There they prayed, "filled with faith," as one commented; then returned to the place of the sacrifice. The *yatiris* sprinkled the remaining blood on the veins of ore.

By their absorption and fervid murmuring of prayers, both young and old miners revealed the same faith and devotion. Many of them wept, thinking of the accident and their dead companions. During the ritual drinking was forbidden.

On the following day those men charged with responsibility for the ritual came to prepare the meat. They brought the two carcasses to the baker, who seasoned them and cooked them in large ovens. The men returned at about 1:15 P.M. to distribute the meat. With the meat, they served *chicha*. Some sprinkled *chicha* on the ground for the Pachamama, saying "Hallalla," before drinking.

The bones were burned to ashes, which were then offered to the Tio. The mine entrance was locked shut and left undisturbed for 24 hours. Some remarked that it should be closed for three days, but the company did not want to lose that much time.

During the *k'araku* the miners recognize the Tio as the true owner of the mine. "All the mineral that comes out from the interior of the mine is the 'crop' of the devil and whether one likes it or not, we have to invite the Tio to drink and eat so that the flow of metal will continue," said a young miner who studied evenings at the University of Oruro.

All the workers felt that the failure of the administrators to come to the *k'araku* indicated not only their lack of concern with the lives of the men but also their disregard of the need to raise productivity in the mine.

When the Tio appears uninvited, the miners fear that they have only a short time to live. Miners who have seen apparitions say the Tio looks like a gringo—tall, red-faced, with fair hair and beard, and wearing a cowboy hat. This description, hardly resembles the images sculptured by the miners, but it does fit the foreign technicians and administrators who administered the mines in the time of the tin barons. To the Indian workers, drawn from the highland and Cochabamba farming areas, the Tio is a strange and exotic figure, ruthless, gluttonous, powerful, and arbitrary in his use of that power, but nonetheless attractive, someone to get close to in order to share that power. I was beginning to wonder if the reason I was accepted with such good humor by the miners, despite their rule against women in the mines, was because they thought I shared some of these characteristics and was a match for the devil.

Sickness or death in the family can force a man in desperation to make a contract with the devil. If his companions become aware of it, the contract is destroyed and with it his life.

The miners feel that they need the protection of a group when they confront the Tio. In the *ch'alla* and the *k'araku* they convert the power of the Tio into socially useful production. In effect, the rituals are ways of getting the genie back into the bottle after he has done his miracles. Security of the group then depends upon respect toward the sacrificial offering, as shown by the following incident told me by the head of a work gang after the *k'araku*:

"I know of a man who had a vein of ore near where the bones of the sacrificial llama were buried. Without advising me, he made a hole with his drill and put the dynamite in. He knew very well that the bones were there. On the following day, it cost him his life. While he was drilling, a stone fell and cut his head off.

"We had to change the bones with a ceremony. We brought in a good shaman who charged us B$500 [about $40], we hired the best orchestra, and we sang and danced in the new location where we laid the bones. We did not work in that corridor for three days, and we spent all the time in the *ch'alla*."

Often the miners are frightened nearly to death in the mine. A rock falls on the spot they have just left, a man falls in a shaft and is saved by hitting soft clay at the bottom, a tunnel caves in the moment after a man leaves it—these are incidents in a day's work that I have heard men say can start a *haperk'a*, or fear, that can take their lives.

A shaman may have to be called in to bring back the spirit that the Tio has seized. In one curing, a frightened miner was told to wear the clothing he had on when the Tio seized his spirit and to enter and give a service to the Tio at the same spot where he was frightened. The shaman himself asked the Tio to cure his patient, flattering him, "Now you have shown your power, give back his spirit."

The fear may result in sexual impotency. At one of the mines, Siglo XX, when there is full production, a dynamite blast goes off every five minutes in a section called Block Haven. The air is filled with smoke and the miners describe it as an inferno. Working under such tension, a shattering blast may unnerve them. Some react with an erection, followed by sexual debilitation. Mad with rage and fear, some miners have been known to seize a knife, the same knife they use to cut the dynamite leads, and castrate themselves. When I visited Block Haven, I noticed that the Tio on this level had a huge erection, about a foot long on a man-sized figure.

The workers said that when they find themselves in a state of impotency they go to the Tio for help. By exemplifying what they want in the Tio, they seek to repair the psychic damage caused by fear.

After feasting on the meat of the llamas and listening to stories of the Tio, I left the mine. The men thanked me for coming. I could not express the gratitude I felt for restoring my confidence in continuing the study.

Shortly thereafter I met Lino Pino returning from a fiesta for a miraculous saint in a nearby village. He asked me if I would be *madrina* at his daughter's forthcoming confirmation, and when I agreed, his wife offered me a tin cup with the delicious cocktail she always prepares for her husband on the days of the *ch'alla*, and we all had a round of drinks.

Later, when I knelt at the altar rail with Lino and his daughter as we received the wafer and the wine, flesh and blood of another sacrifice victim, I sensed the unity in the miners' beliefs. The miraculous Virgin looked down on us from her marbelized, neon-lit niche, her jewelled finger held out in benediction. She was adequate for that scene, but in the mine they needed someone who could respond to their needs on the job.

In the rituals of the *ch'alla* and the *k'araku* the power of the Tio to destroy is transformed into the socially useful functions of increasing mineral yield and giving peace of mind to the workers. Confronted alone, the Tio, like Banquo's ghost, makes a man unable to produce or even to go on living. Properly controlled by the group, the Tio promises fertility, potency, and productivity to the miners. Robbed of this faith, they often lose the faith to continue drilling after repeated failure to find a vein, or to continue living when the rewards of work are so meager. Knowing that the devil is on your side makes it possible to continue working in the hell that is the mines.

38

Cargo Cults

BY PETER M. WORSLEY

....

Patrols of the Australian Government venturing into the "uncontrolled" central highlands of New Guinea in 1946 found the primitive people there swept up in a wave of religious excitement. Prophecy was being fulfilled: The arrival of the Whites was the sign that the end of the world was at hand. The natives proceeded to butcher all of their pigs—animals that were not only a principal source of subsistence but also symbols of social status and ritual preeminence in their culture. They killed these valued animals in expression of the belief that after three days of darkness "Great Pigs" would appear from the sky. Food, firewood and other necessities had to be stock-piled to see the people through to the arrival of the Great Pigs. Mock wireless antennae of bamboo and rope had been erected to receive in advance the news of the millennium. Many believed that with the great event they would exchange their black skins for white ones.

This bizarre episode is by no means the single event of its kind in the murky history of the collision of European civilization with the indigenous cultures of the southwest Pacific. For more than 100 years traders and missionaries have been reporting similar disturbances among the peoples of Melanesia, the group of Negro-inhabited islands (including New Guinea, Fiji, the Solomons and the New Hebrides) lying between Australia and the open Pacific Ocean. Though their technologies were based largely upon stone and wood, these peoples had highly developed cultures, as measured by the standards of maritime and agricultural ingenuity, the complexity of their varied social organizations and the elaboration of religious belief and ritual. They were nonetheless ill prepared for

the shock of the encounter with the Whites, a people so radically different from themselves and so infinitely more powerful. The sudden transition from the society of the ceremonial stone ax to the society of sailing ships and now of airplanes has not been easy to make.

After four centuries of Western expansion, the densely populated central highlands of New Guinea remain one of the few regions where the people still carry on their primitive existence in complete independence of the world outside. Yet as the agents of the Australian Government penetrate into ever more remote mountain valleys, they find these backwaters of antiquity already deeply disturbed by contact with the ideas and artifacts of European civilization. For "cargo"—Pidgin English for trade goods—has long flowed along the indigenous channels of communication from the seacoast into the wilderness. With it has traveled the frightening knowledge of the white man's magical power. No small element in the white man's magic is the hopeful message sent abroad by his missionaries: the news that a Messiah will come and that the present order of Creation will end.

The people of the central highlands of New Guinea are only the latest to be gripped in the recurrent religious frenzy of the "cargo cults." However variously embellished with details from native myth and Christian belief, these cults all advance the same central theme: the world is about to end in a terrible cataclysm. Thereafter God, the ancestors or some local culture hero will appear and inaugurate a blissful paradise on earth. Death, old age, illness and evil will be unknown. The riches of the white man will accrue to the Melanesians.

Although the news of such a movement in one area has doubtless often inspired similar movements in other areas, the evidence indicates that these cults have arisen independently in many places as parallel responses to the same enormous social stress and strain. Among the movements best known to students of Melanesia are the "Taro Cult" of New Guinea, the "Vailala Madness" of Papua, the "Naked Cult" of Espiritu Santo, the "John Frum Movement" of the New Hebrides and the "Tuka Cult" of the Fiji Islands.

At times the cults have been so well organized and fanatically persistent that they have brought the work of government to a standstill. The outbreaks have often taken the authorities completely by surprise and have confronted them with mass opposition of an alarming kind. In the 1930s, for example, villagers in the vicinity of Wewak, New Guinea, were stirred by a succession of "Black King" movements. The prophets announced that the Europeans would soon leave the island, abandoning their property to the natives, and urged their followers to cease paying taxes, since the government station was about to disappear into the sea in a great earthquake. To the tiny community of Whites in charge of the region, such talk was dangerous. The authorities jailed four of the prophets and exiled three others. In yet another movement, that sprang up in declared opposition to the local Christian mission, the cult leader took Satan as his god.

Troops on both sides in World War II found their arrival in Melanesia heralded as a sign of the Apocalypse. The G.I.'s who landed in the New Hebrides, moving up for the bloody fighting on Guadalcanal, found the natives furiously at work preparing airfields, roads and docks for the magic ships and planes that they believed were coming from "Rusefel" (Roosevelt), the friendly king of America.

The Japanese also encountered millenarian visionaries during their southward march to Guadalcanal. Indeed, one of the strangest minor military actions of World War II occurred in Dutch New Guinea, when Japanese forces had to be turned against the local Papuan inhabitants of the Geelvink Bay region. The Japanese had at first been received with great joy, not because their "Greater East Asia Co-Prosperity Sphere" propaganda had made any great impact upon the Papuans, but because the natives regarded them as harbingers of the

new world that was dawning, the flight of the Dutch having already given the first sign. Mansren, creator of the islands and their peoples, would now return, bringing with him the ancestral dead. All this had been known, the cult leaders declared, to the crafty Dutch, who had torn out the first page of the Bible where these truths were inscribed. When Mansren returned, the existing world order would be entirely overturned. White men would turn black like Papuans, Papuans would become Whites; root crops would grow in trees, and coconuts and fruits would grow like tubers. Some of the islanders now began to draw together into large "towns"; others took Biblical names such as "Jericho" and "Galilee" for their villages.

Soon they adopted military uniforms and began drilling. The Japanese, by now highly unpopular, tried to disarm and disperse the Papuans; resistance inevitably developed. The climax of this tragedy came when several canoe-loads of fanatics sailed out to attack Japanese warships, believing themselves to be invulnerable by virtue of the holy water with which they had sprinkled themselves. But the bullets of the Japanese did not turn to water, and the attackers were mowed down by machine-gun fire.

Behind this incident lay a long history. As long ago as 1857 missionaries in the Geelvink Bay region had made note of the story of Mansren. It is typical of many Melanesian myths that became

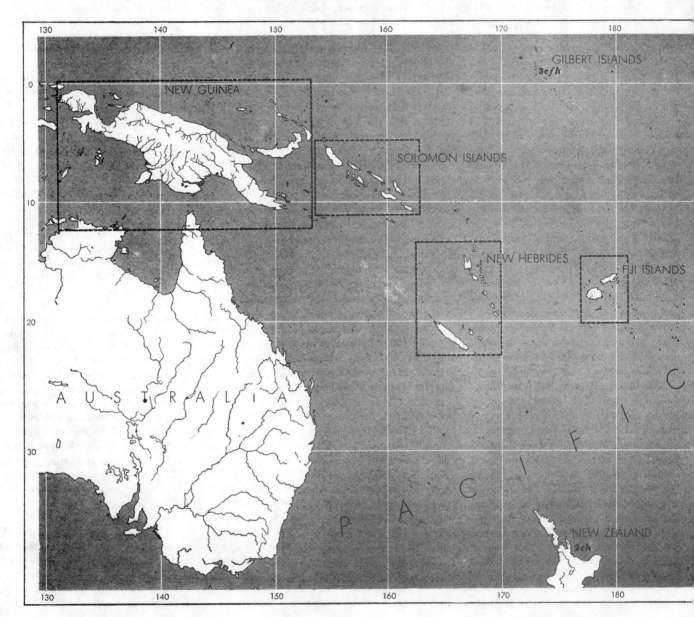

confounded with Christian doctrine to form the ideological basis of the movements. The legend tells how long ago there lived an old man named Manamakeri ("he who itches"), whose body was covered with sores. Manamakeri was extremely fond of palm wine, and used to climb a huge tree every day to tap the liquid from the flowers. He soon found that someone was getting there before him and removing the liquid. Eventually he trapped the thief, who turned out to be none other than the Morning Star. In return for his freedom, the Star gave the old man a wand that would produce as much fish as he liked, a magic tree and a magic staff. If he drew in the sand and stamped his foot, the drawing would become real.

Manamakeri, aged as he was, now magically impregnated a young maiden; the child of this union was a miracle-child who spoke as soon as he was born. But the maiden's parents were horrified, and banished her, the child and the old man. The trio sailed off in a canoe created by Mansren ("The Lord"), as the old man now became known. On this journey Mansren rejuvenated himself by stepping into a fire and flaking off his scaly skin, which changed into valuables. He then sailed around Geelvink Bay, creating islands where he stopped, and peopling them with the ancestors of the present-day Papuans.

The Mansren myth is plainly a creation myth full of symbolic ideas relating to fertility and rebirth. Comparative

SOUTH PACIFIC, scene of the religious disturbances known as cargo cults, is shown in this map. Most cargo cults have been in Melanesia, shown here as four regions enclosed in broken rectangles. Each of these regions is shown in a detailed map in the following pages. Also shown on this map are three outlying cargo cults, two of them Polynesian and the third Micronesian. Numbers on these maps indicate individual cults. Letters refer to typical features of cults (see number and letter keys accompanying each map).

1 MAMAIA MOVEMENT TAHITI 1930-1944
2 HAU-HAU MOVEMENT NEW ZEALAND
                                        1860-1871
3 ONOTOA TROUBLES GILBERT ISLANDS
                                        1932

a MYTH OF THE RETURN OF THE DEAD
b REVIVAL OR MODIFICATION OF
       PAGANISM
c INTRODUCTION OF CHRISTIAN
       ELEMENTS
d CARGO MYTH
e BELIEF THAT NEGROES WILL
       BECOME WHITE MEN AND
       VICE VERSA
f BELIEF IN A COMING MESSIAH
g ATTEMPTS TO RESTORE NATIVE
       POLITICAL AND ECONOMIC
       CONTROL
h THREATS AND VIOLENCE AGAINST
       WHITE MEN
i UNION OF TRADITIONALLY
       SEPARATE AND UNFRIENDLY
       GROUPS

evidence—especially the shedding of his scaly skin—confirms the suspicion that the old man is, in fact, the Snake in another guise. Psychoanalytic writers argue that the snake occupies such a prominent part in mythology the world over because it stands for the penis, another fertility symbol. This may be so, but its symbolic significance is surely more complex than this. It is the "rebirth" of the hero, whether Mansren or the Snake, that exercises such universal fascination over men's minds.

The 19th-century missionaries thought that the Mansren story would make the introduction of Christianity easier, since the concept of "resurrection," not to mention that of the "virgin birth" and the "second coming," was already there. By 1867, however, the first cult organized around the Mansren legend was reported.

Though such myths were widespread in Melanesia, and may have sparked occasional movements even in the pre-White era, they took on a new significance in the late 19th century, once the European powers had finished parceling out the Melanesian region among themselves. In many coastal areas the long history of "blackbirding"—the seizure of islanders for work on the plantations of Australia and Fiji—had built up a reservoir of hostility to Europeans. In other areas, however, the arrival of the Whites was accepted, even welcomed, for it meant access to bully beef and cigarettes, shirts and paraffin lamps, whisky and bicycles. It also meant access to the knowledge behind these material goods, for the Europeans brought missions and schools as well as cargo.

Practically the only teaching the natives received about European life came from the missions, which emphasized the central significance of religion in European society. The Melanesians already believed that man's activities—whether gardening, sailing canoes or bearing children—needed magical assistance. Ritual without human effort was not enough. But neither was human effort on its own. This outlook was reinforced by mission teaching.

The initial enthusiasm for European rule, however, was speedily dispelled. The rapid growth of the plantation economy removed the bulk of the able-bodied men from the villages, leaving women, children and old men to carry on as best they could. The splendid

NEW GUINEA has been a prolific breeder of cargo cults, resulting from the impact of Dutch, German, British and Japanese rule on its Stone Age cultures. At present the western portion is held by the Netherlands but claimed by Indonesia. The southeast (Papua) and northeast (U.N. Trust Territory of New Guinea) are governed by Australia.

a	MYTH OF THE RETURN OF THE DEAD	**f**	BELIEF IN A COMING MESSIAH
b	REVIVAL OR MODIFICATION OF PAGANISM	**g**	ATTEMPTS TO RESTORE NATIVE POLITICAL AND ECONOMIC CONTROL
c	INTRODUCTION OF CHRISTIAN ELEMENTS	**h**	THREATS AND VIOLENCE AGAINST WHITE MEN
d	CARGO MYTH	**i**	UNION OF TRADITIONALLY SEPARATE AND UNFRIENDLY GROUPS
e	BELIEF THAT NEGROES WILL BECOME WHITE MEN AND VICE VERSA		

4 KORERI MOVEMENT NUMFOR, DUTCH NEW GUINEA 1911
5 KORERI MOVEMENT BIAK, DUTCH NEW GUINEA 1939
6 KORERI MOVEMENT BIAK, DUTCH NEW GUINEA 1886
7 KORERI MOVEMENT BIAK, GEELVINK BAY, DUTCH NEW GUINEA 1942-1947
8 SIMSON INCIDENT HOLLANDIA, DUTCH NEW GUINEA 1940- ?
9 PAMAI MOVEMENT LAKE SENTANI, DUTCH NEW GUINEA 1928
10 NIMBORAN MOVEMENT LAKE SENTANI, DUTCH NEW GUINEA 1945
11 NINIGO ISLANDS MOVEMENT NINIGO ISLANDS, NEW GUINEA 1945- ?
12 BLACK KINGS MOVEMENT AITAPE, WEWAK, NEW GUINEA 1930
13 GREAT PIGS WEST-CENTRAL NEW GUINEA 1946
14 HINE MOVEMENT WABAG, CENTRAL NEW GUINEA 1945
15 BLACK KINGS MOVEMENT MOUNT HAGEN, NEW GUINEA 1940
16 NATIVE KING KERAM RIVER, CENTRAL NEW GUINEA 1943-1945
17 GHOST WIND KAINANTU, CENTRAL NEW GUINEA 1940-1947
18 TOMMY KABU COOPERATIVE MOVEMENT PURARI DELTA, PAPUA 1945-1947
19 BATAWI INCIDENT WESTERN PAPUA
20 GERMAN WISLIN SAIBAI, TORRES STRAIT 1913-1915
21 VAILALA MADNESS PAPUA 1919-1931
22 FILO INCIDENT MEKEO, PAPUA 1940-1941
23 GOILALA AND GOGODARA CULT PAPUA 1945
24 PIG KILLING KAIRUKU, PAPUA 1937
25 THREE BLACK KINGS WEWAK, NEW GUINEA 1948-1949
26 MAMBU MOVEMENT MADANG, NEW GUINEA 1937-1940
27 TIFU INCIDENT RAMU, MADANG, NEW GUINEA 1951
28 BLACK KING MOVEMENT MADANG, NEW GUINEA 1935
29 KUKUAIK MOVEMENT KARKAR ISLAND, NEW GUINEA 1940- ?
30 CARGO CULT MADANG, NEW GUINEA 1940
31 CARGO CULT MADANG, NEW GUINEA 1934
32 YALI INCIDENT MADANG, NEW GUINEA 1945-1955
33 GARIA MOVEMENT MADANG, NEW GUINEA 1940- ?
34 SECOND COMING OF CHRIST RAI COAST, NEW GUINEA 1936
35 LETUB MOVEMENT MADANG, NEW GUINEA 1939-1940
36 EEMASANG MOVEMENT HUON PENINSULA, NEW GUINEA 1927- ?
37 COMING OF JESUS EASTERN HIGHLANDS, CENTRAL NEW GUINEA 1943-1945
38 TIMO INCIDENT HUON PENINSULA, NEW GUINEA 1922
39 THREE BLACK KINGS FINSCHHAFEN, NEW GUINEA 1945- ?
40 LAZARUS MOVEMENT HUON PENINSULA, NEW GUINEA 1933
41 SOSOM INCIDENT MOUNT GOLDBERG, NEW GUINEA 1936
42 MOROBE MOVEMENT MOROFE, NEW GUINEA 1933-1936
43 MARKHAM VALLEY MOVEMENT MARKHAM VALLEY, NEW GUINEA 1932-1934
44 YERUMOT INCIDENT TOEPFER RIVER, NEW GUINEA 1930- ?
45 SCHWAERMEREI RAWLINSON RANGE, NEW GUINEA 1933
46 MARKHAM VALLEY MOVEMENT MARKHAM VALLEY, NEW GUINEA 1932-1934
47 BAIGONA MOVEMENT MASSIM, NEW GUINEA 1912-1919
48 TARO CULT NORTHEAST NEW GUINEA 1914-1928
49 PIG KILLING NORTH PAPUA 1930
50 PIG KILLING NORTHEAST PAPUA 1930
51 ASSISI CULT NORTHEAST PAPUA 1930-1944
52 MILNE BAY MOVEMENT MASSIM, NEW GUINEA 1893- ?
53 PALIAU MOVEMENT MANUS AND BALUAN, ADMIRALTY ISLANDS 1946-1954
54 THE NOISE RAMBUDJON, ADMIRALTY ISLANDS 1946-1948 (?)
55 BATARI MOVEMENT GALILO, NEW BRITAIN 1940-1946
56 BAINING TROUBLES NEW BRITAIN 1955
57 BAINING MOVEMENT NEW BRITAIN 1929-1930
58 KOKOPO MOVEMENT NEW BRITAIN 1930 (?)
59 NAMATANAI MOVEMENT NEW IRELAND 1939

vision of the equality of all Christians began to seem a pious deception in face of the realities of the color bar, the multiplicity of rival Christian missions and the open irreligion of many Whites.

For a long time the natives accepted the European mission as the means by which the "cargo" would eventually be made available to them. But they found that acceptance of Christianity did not bring the cargo any nearer. They grew disillusioned. The story now began to be put about that it was not the Whites who made the cargo, but the dead ancestors. To people completely ignorant of factory production, this made good sense. White men did not work; they merely wrote secret signs on scraps of paper, for which they were given shiploads of goods. On

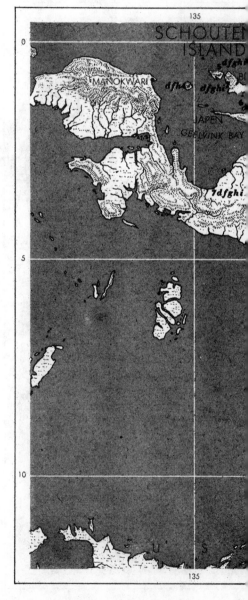

the other hand, the Melanesians labored week after week for pitiful wages. Plainly the goods must be made for Melanesians somewhere, perhaps in the Land of the Dead. The Whites, who possessed the secret of the cargo, were intercepting it and keeping it from the hands of the islanders, to whom it was really consigned. In the Madang district of New Guinea, after some 40 years' experience of the missions, the natives went in a body one day with a petition demanding that the cargo secret should now be revealed to them, for they had been very patient.

So strong is this belief in the existence of a "secret" that the cargo cults generally contain some ritual in imitation of the mysterious European customs which are held to be the clue to the white man's extraordinary power over goods and men. The believers sit around tables with bottles of flowers in front of them, dressed in European clothes, waiting for the cargo ship or airplane to materialize; other cultists feature magic pieces of paper and cabalistic writing. Many of them deliberately turn their backs on the past by destroying secret ritual objects, or exposing them to the gaze of uninitiated youths and women, for whom formerly even a glimpse of the sacred objects would have meant the severest penalties, even death. The belief that they were the chosen people is further reinforced by their reading of the Bible, for the lives and customs of the people in the Old Testament resemble their own lives rather than those of the Europeans. In the New Testament they find the Apocalypse, with its prophecies of destruction and resurrection, particularly attractive.

Missions that stress the imminence of the Second Coming, like those of the Seventh Day Adventists, are often accused of stimulating millenarian cults among the islanders. In reality, however, the Melanesians themselves rework the doctrines the missionaries teach them, selecting from the Bible what they themselves find particularly congenial in it. Such movements have occurred in areas where missions of quite different types have been dominant, from Roman Catholic to Seventh Day Adventist. The reasons for the emergence of these cults, of

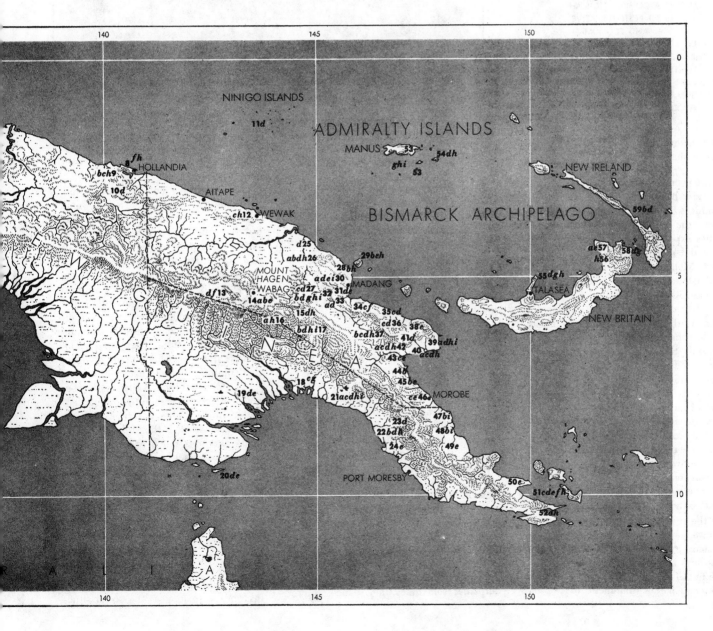

SOLOMON ISLANDS, administered by Australia and Great Britain, are another center of cargo cults, some caused by the cataclysmic impact of World War II. The data contained in these maps and tables, prepared by the author and Jean Guiart of the Ecole des Hautes Etudes in Paris, are not a complete list of cargo cults. Many dates are only approximate.

a MYTH OF THE RETURN OF THE DEAD
b REVIVAL OR MODIFICATION OF PAGANISM
c INTRODUCTION OF CHRISTIAN ELEMENTS
d CARGO MYTH
e BELIEF THAT NEGROES WILL BECOME WHITE MEN AND VICE VERSA
f BELIEF IN A COMING MESSIAH
g ATTEMPTS TO RESTORE NATIVE POLITICAL AND ECONOMIC CONTROL
h THREATS AND VIOLENCE AGAINST WHITE MEN
i UNION OF TRADITIONALLY SEPARATE AND UNFRIENDLY GROUPS

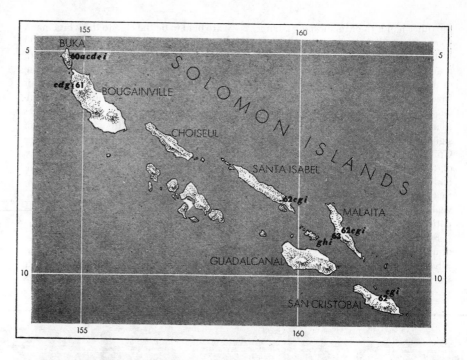

60 BUKA MOVEMENTS　NORTHERN SOLOMON ISLANDS　1913-1935
61 BOUGAINVILLE MOVEMENT　NORTHERN SOLOMON ISLANDS　1935-1939
62 MAASINA (MARCHING) RULE　MALAITA, SOLOMON ISLANDS　1945-1958
63 CHAIR AND RULE CULT　MALAITA, SOLOMON ISLANDS　1935

course, lie far deeper in the life-experience of the people.

The economy of most of the islands is very backward. Native agriculture produces little for the world market, and even the European plantations and mines export only a few primary products and raw materials: copra, rubber, gold. Melanesians are quite unable to understand why copra, for example, fetches 30 pounds sterling per ton one month and but 5 pounds a few months later. With no notion of the workings of world-commodity markets, the natives see only the sudden closing of plantations, reduced wages and unemployment, and are inclined to attribute their insecurity to the whim or evil in the nature of individual planters.

Such shocks have not been confined to the economic order. Governments, too, have come and gone, especially during the two world wars: German, Dutch, British and French administrations melted overnight. Then came the Japanese, only to be ousted in turn largely by the previously unknown Americans. And among these Americans the Melanesians saw Negroes like themselves, living lives of luxury on equal terms with white G.I.'s. The sight of these Negroes seemed like a fulfillment of the old

prophecies to many cargo cult leaders. Nor must we forget the sheer scale of this invasion. Around a million U. S. troops passed through the Admiralty Islands, completely swamping the inhabitants. It was a world of meaningless and chaotic changes, in which anything was possible. New ideas were imported and given local twists. Thus in the Loyalty Islands people expected the French Communist Party to bring the millennium. There is no real evidence, however, of any Communist influence in these movements, despite the rather hysterical belief among Solomon Island planters that the name of the local "Masinga Rule" movement was derived from the word "Marxian"! In reality the name comes from a Solomon Island tongue, and means "brotherhood."

Europeans who have witnessed outbreaks inspired by the cargo cults are usually at a loss to understand what they behold. The islanders throw away their money, break their most sacred taboos, abandon their gardens and destroy their precious livestock; they indulge in sexual license or, alternatively, rigidly separate men from women in huge communal establishments. Sometimes they spend days sitting gazing at the horizon for a glimpse of the long-awaited ship or airplane; sometimes they dance, pray

and sing in mass congregations, becoming possessed and "speaking with tongues."

Observers have not hesitated to use such words as "madness," "mania," and "irrationality" to characterize the cults. But the cults reflect quite logical and rational attempts to make sense out of a social order that appears senseless and chaotic. Given the ignorance of the Melanesians about the wider European society, its economic organization and its highly developed technology, their reactions form a consistent and understandable pattern. They wrap up all their yearning and hope in an amalgam that combines the best counsel they can find in Christianity and their native belief. If the world is soon to end, gardening or fishing is unnecessary; everything will be provided. If the Melanesians are to be part of a much wider order, the taboos that prescribe their social conduct must now be lifted or broken in a newly prescribed way.

Of course the cargo never comes. The cults nonetheless live on. If the millennium does not arrive on schedule, then perhaps there is some failure in the magic, some error in the ritual. New breakaway groups organize around "purer" faith and ritual. The cult rarely disappears, so long as the social situa-

NEW HEBRIDES AND NEW CALEDONIA are, respectively, Anglo-French and French possessions. One New Caledonian cult placed Messianic hopes in the Communist Party.

FIJI ISLANDS are a British colony. Although generally Christianized, they have spawned several semi-Christian cargo cults.

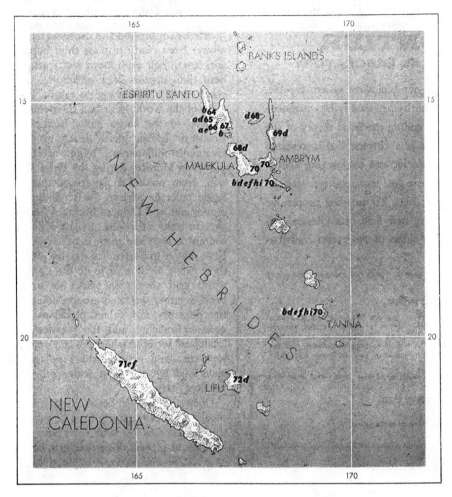

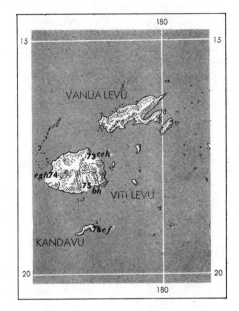

64 MAMARA MOVEMENT (NAKED CULT) WEST-CENTRAL ESPIRITU SANTO,
    NEW HEBRIDES 1945-1951
65 ATORI INCIDENT SOUTH ESPIRITU SANTO, NEW HEBRIDES 1945
66 RONGOFURO AFFAIR SOUTH ESPIRITU SANTO, NEW HEBRIDES 1914-1923
67 AVA-AVU INCIDENT SOUTH-CENTRAL ESPIRITU SANTO, NEW HEBRIDES 1937
68 MALEKULA NATIVE COMPANY CENTRAL NEW HEBRIDES 1950
69 BULE INCIDENT MELSISI, PENTECOST, NEW HEBRIDES 1947
70 JOHN FRUM MOVEMENT TANNA, NEW HEBRIDES 1938-1958
71 PWAGAC INCIDENT NORTHERN NEW CALEDONIA 1941
72 "COMMUNIST PARTY" LIFU, NEW CALEDONIA 1947

a MYTH OF THE RETURN OF THE DEAD
b REVIVAL OR MODIFICATION OF
    PAGANISM
c INTRODUCTION OF CHRISTIAN
    ELEMENTS
d CARGO MYTH
e BELIEF THAT NEGROES WILL
    BECOME WHITE MEN AND
    VICE VERSA
f BELIEF IN A COMING MESSIAH
g ATTEMPTS TO RESTORE NATIVE
    POLITICAL AND ECONOMIC
    CONTROL
h THREATS AND VIOLENCE AGAINST
    WHITE MEN
i UNION OF TRADITIONALLY
    SEPARATE AND UNFRIENDLY
    GROUPS

73 TUKA MOVEMENT CENTRAL VITI LEVU,
    FIJI 1873-1920
74 APOLOSI MOVEMENT WEST VITI LEVU,
    FIJI 1914-1940
75 LUVE-NI-WAI CENTRAL VITI LEVU,
    FIJI 1880- ?
76 KELEVI SECT KADAVU, FIJI 1945-1947

a MYTH OF THE RETURN OF THE DEAD
b REVIVAL OR MODIFICATION OF
    PAGANISM
c INTRODUCTION OF CHRISTIAN
    ELEMENTS
d CARGO MYTH
e BELIEF THAT NEGROES WILL
    BECOME WHITE MEN AND
    VICE VERSA
f BELIEF IN A COMING MESSIAH
g ATTEMPTS TO RESTORE NATIVE
    POLITICAL AND ECONOMIC
    CONTROL
h THREATS AND VIOLENCE AGAINST
    WHITE MEN
i UNION OF TRADITIONALLY
    SEPARATE AND UNFRIENDLY
    GROUPS

tion which brings it into being persists.

At this point it should be observed that cults of this general kind are not peculiar to Melanesia. Men who feel themselves oppressed and deceived have always been ready to pour their hopes and fears, their aspirations and frustrations, into dreams of a millennium to come or of a golden age to return. All parts of the world have had their counterparts of the cargo cults, from the American Indian ghost dance to the communist-millenarist "reign of the saints" in Münster during the Reformation, from medieval European apocalyptic cults to African "witch-finding" movements and Chinese Buddhist heresies. In some situations men have been content to wait and pray; in others they have sought to hasten the day by using their strong right arms to do the Lord's work. And always the cults serve to bring together scattered groups, notably the peasants and urban plebeians of agrarian societies and the peoples of "stateless" societies where the cult unites separate (and often hostile) villages, clans and tribes into a wider religio-political unity.

Once the people begin to develop secular political organizations, however, the sects tend to lose their importance as vehicles of protest. They begin to relegate the Second Coming to the distant future or to the next world. In Melanesia ordinary political bodies, trade unions and native councils are becoming the normal media through which the islanders express their aspirations. In recent years continued economic prosperity and political stability have taken some of the edge off their despair. It now seems unlikely that any major movement along cargo-cult lines will recur in areas where the transition to secular politics has been made, even if the insecurity of prewar times returned. I would predict that the embryonic nationalism represented by cargo cults is likely in future to take forms familiar in the history of other countries that have moved from subsistence agriculture to participation in the world economy.

VI
Modernization and Culture Change

○ ○

Modernization refers to the global transformation of society, a transformation that has its roots in the emergence of the industrial revolution. Although its particular manifestations vary widely due to local social, historical, cultural, political, and economic conditions (and also environmental riches and limitations), students of modernization have noted that certain elements characterize this phenomenon everywhere. As summarized by anthropologist Helen Henderson, these include the following:

1. Subsistence farming gives way to cultivation of agricultural products for the market, and new jobs are created in trade, manufacturing, and administration.

2. New sources of energy are exploited, and individual wage earners operate machines within the industrial system.

3. Specialized educational institutions are created to bring literacy to the masses and impart new skills and knowledge.

4. Urban areas develop rapidly as rural immigrants flow into cities in search of economic opportunities. Urbanites cut their ties with their extended kin, are freed from many traditional restraints, and step into new social roles.

5. The functions of the family change (and the form may as well). It is no longer a unit of production but specializes in the socialization of offspring and the organization of consumption.

6. Some scholars would add that modernization also introduces new forms of alienation into the lives of industrial workers, who lose control over the product of their labor and whose work tends to be repetitive and dull.

Modernization, therefore, means far more than a series of adjustments in indigenous economic systems. Rather, it refers to qualitative changes in the organization of society, in culture, and even in individual personalities.

TOPIC FOURTEEN

The Social Costs of Modernization

. . . .

Modernization is a European invention. It was exported from Europe (and America, its descendant) to the so-called Third World through the politics of colonialism and the sociopolitical economy of imperialism. Although its benefits to indigenous societies have been tabulated in terms of increased life spans, better health conditions, rising literacy, and broadened opportunities, the social costs of modernization have been high.

The imperialist nations systematically destroyed the indigenous societies' subsistence economies, converting them to specialized cash-crop (rubber, tobacco) or mineral (metal ores, diamonds) economies. Whereas before modernization the native populations easily could provide for their own subsistence needs, they suddenly were forced to participate in an economic system that was controlled from afar, that kept down the prices of what they had to offer, that made them dependent on imported goods priced high, and that kept their wages low. Thus modernization created poverty in many areas of the world whereas, before, the concept simply had no meaning.

In "Requiem for a Lost People," William W. Howells documents the horrifying story of the complete annihilation of the aboriginal population of Tasmania (an island south of Australia) by land-hungry European settlers in the nineteeth century. In "Societies on the Brink," David Maybury-Lewis lays out current rationales for the continuing destruction of small, semi-isolated societies and also presents anthropologically based arguments against this ongoing trend. He advocates social pluralism and suggests that the alternatives are grim.

The final article in this topic describes "The Irish Tinkers," nomadic groups similar to gypsies who are mostly descendants of peasants and artisans forced to leave their lands by war, poverty, and famine. George and Sharon B. Gmelch describe the Tinkers' marginal existence as tinsmiths and repairers of household goods and the changes in their group and family life that are coming about as Ireland's economy increasingly encroaches on their occupational niche. Gradually, they are being assimilated into Irish industrial society—but on its lowest socioeconomic rung, as "itinerant" welfare-dependents.

39

Requiem for a Lost People

BY WILLIAM W. HOWELLS

No segment of humankind can have been rushed into oblivion as speedily as the aboriginals of Tasmania. Dark-skinned and woolly-haired, superficially they looked like Africans, though this is only skin-deep. Anthropologists regret their rapid passing; there is a great deal they would have liked to ask the Tasmanians, but in the early nineteenth century anthropology was a science unborn. There are other things to regret.

Tasmania is the shield-shaped island lying south of Australia's southeast corner. Its towns today give off a staid provincial air, and its countryside is rich in apples and flowers, but a hundred and fifty years ago the keynotes were kangaroos and violence. The island is a little like New England—north for south of course, since it lies in the other hemisphere. Its northern coast, nearest Australia, has the same latitude in the south as has New York in the north, and its southern end, with the city of Hobart, has about the latitude of Portland, Maine. But Tasmania lacks New England's antic weather. Deep snow may fall in the high interior, which is colder than the coast, and there are glaciers in the mountains. Still, while there was some risk from exposure if they were separated from companions and fire, the native Tasmanians essentially wore no clothes. On the shore, winters are mild and summers are cool. Over the year, the average temperature for the day changes only about eighteen degrees, from 46° to 64° Fahrenheit, compared with a swing of well over forty degrees in coastal New England. In fact, the thermometer may go up and down more during a single Tasmanian day than does the day's average during the whole year. Tell that in Boston.

During the late ice age it was colder, with larger glaciers in the center. Almost 25,000 years ago, while it was still a peninsula of Australia, aboriginal hunters are known to have entered Tasmania, to be marooned about twelve thousand years later, when the world's major ice sheets melted and the seas rose.

They were a culturally simple people, like their surviving cousins in Australia, and as time went on they became simpler still, their recent equipment being the most modest on record. When seen by Europeans, they lacked boomerangs, dogs, and hafted stone tools, all of which were invented or acquired in Australia after the original Tasmanians had left. And for some mysterious reason they gave up the catching of fish, although they continued to appreciate shellfish. Evidently the land was good to them, with kangaroos and other marsupials to hunt, and the climate temperate enough so that an occasional cape of animal skin was all they ever wore. Two centuries ago about four thousand natives lived all over the island, except in the rugged mountains. Then, in thirty years, settlers from Australia and England wiped them out.

In the last crisis two men tried to stave off the extermination but only facilitated it, each in his own way. They were Governor George Arthur, with his printed proclamations and "picture boards," and G. A. Robinson, who went out to talk to the natives directly, in their own language. The Tasmanians themselves were neither ferocious nor hostile at first, as much testimony made clear too late. They were dangerous enough when provoked, and they fought to a limited extent among themselves over such things as trespass on hunting grounds or abduction of women, two offenses that the whites at once carried to intolerable excess. As for the "settlers," there could hardly have been a better team to carry out the annihilation. They were convicts, mostly hard cases from Australia. The first lot was accompanied by a handful of freemen given very small land grants to work with convict labor. Since a person might in those days be transported for what now pass as minor crimes (like stealing cars in Massachusetts?), some convicts were fairly decent men, but many, along with the soldiers sent to guard them, were capable of vicious brutality and in fact took pleasure in it. For a hundred years now, the fate of the Tasmanians has been a source of shame and lamentation, in today's high-minded Hobart as in the world at large. But in that time and place, it seems clear now, no other outcome was likely, as the repellent tragedy ran its course.

It started early, with the Risdon Massacre. The first arrivals from Sydney set up camp in 1803 along the mouth of the Derwent River in the vicinity of Hobart, founded a little later. They had already been officially enjoined to treat the natives with kindness, and threatened with punishment for violence to them. But there seems to have been little contact with Tasmanians as the first small farms were set up. Then, on a day in May 1804, about three hundred aboriginals—men, women, and children—appeared out of the woods forming a half-circle to surround kangaroos driven ahead of them. They had no spears, only clubs, and the fact that women and children joined in shows that they were not a war party. But a farmer a short distance away appears to have been frightened, and the semicircle seemed to be surrounding the camp. The officer in command of the soldiers (drunk, by accounts) was persuaded by the camp surgeon to fire on them with cannon loaded with grapeshot, killing a number. How many was not known, since the natives carried off some badly wounded members. The surgeon entertained the chaplain with a dissection of one corpse, and sent some pickled bones to Australia. Children were captured as well.

A few days later, the aboriginals retaliated with an attack on sailors gathering oysters, though no one was killed. In the next couple of years inexpert farming (the settlers were largely townspeople originally) and inept government supply led to a serious food shortage in the colony, which the governor met by setting a good price on kangaroo meat and encouraging hunting. Off into the bush went all who could be given a gun—not homesteaders, but their convict bond servants. Many of these saw at once how much better a free bush life was than harsh treatment and forced labor in the colony. Bushrangers increased in number as time went on, becoming dangerous men skilled in bushcraft, desperadoes of the worst sort who preyed on and murdered settlers, costing successive governors much effort in capturing and hanging them.

They also figured prominently in the long erosion of the native Tasmanians. But hostilities grew up gradually, and developed into the Black War only twenty years later. In spite of the Risdon Massacre, the local natives seemed not to be vindictive, only careful, and of course for some years aboriginals elsewhere in the large island knew little about the whites. Witnesses say they were friendly and helpful at the very start. Later, even when most settlers considered the Tasmanians enemies, other settlers could wander safely in the bush, and their young people joined aboriginal groups in hunting.

Nevertheless, new colonists were pressing up the whole fertile eastern side of the island, and from about 1818 people with more money and importance were taking out large grants of land. Beyond them roamed the bushrangers, capturing native women and often killing off a husband in the process—Tasmanian

men were very jealous of their wives. Wifeless settlers often did the same; Robinson, for example, was told of cases in which "stockkeepers had chained the females to their huts with bullock chains for the purpose of fornication." Partners in all this were seal hunters along the north coast, who had established themselves even before the colony in the south, and who remained effectively out of its control. They were American, British, New Zealander, or Polynesian, and as free of restraint or scruple as the bushrangers. Such a man usually supplied himself with two to five aboriginal women for sex and slavery, to help in sealing, hunting kangaroos, and skinning birds, and to be shot out of hand if they failed to get the work done or tried to escape. This glib description covers many specific accounts of atrocities, which we will do without. The point is that, whether or not a Tasmanian husband was actually dispatched for every woman taken, the women were removed as aboriginal mothers, with devastating effects on the next generation. When they gave birth to half-caste children, the women regarded them as despicable and usually killed them.

Bear in mind that the testimony, nauseating as it is, comes from our side, the European. If all the things Tasmanians saw and suffered could be known, the effect would be even more appalling. Settlers were outraged at

The Conciliation, *oil painting by Benjamin Duterrau, 1840. George Augustus Robinson, protector of aboriginals, is shown with native Tasmanians on Bruny Island. The woman beside him is thought to be Truganini. Reproduced courtesy of the Tasmanian Museum and Art Gallery.*

interference with their land-clearing, and the occasional spearing of cattle by natives: it did not occur to them that Tasmanians, not using the land for farming, might likewise have a sense of outrage—apart from their feelings at being shot up by any white man who took it into his mind. Of course, the Tasmanians were not passive, although reprisal on their part was long in becoming common. Their weapons were simple: carefully chosen stones, and long wooden javelins with fire-hardened points, both thrown with extraordinary marksmanship even at a distance. In later years they used ruses to draw a farmer away from his house, spearing the family in his absence. They were always skilled stalkers and ambushers. They developed the trick of walking while dragging a javelin, between the big toe and the next, through the grass where it could not be seen. Stark naked, such a man seemed to be unarmed—certainly with nothing up his sleeve—until he could approach a settler within easy spearing distance. (Tit for tat, one farmer taught himself to do the same thing with a shotgun.) Some such

Truganini, the last full-blooded Tasmanian aboriginal to live in Tasmania, died May 8, 1876, and was buried near Hobart. She reportedly had feared a fate similar to the last aboriginal male, William Lanne, who had died seven years before. On the eve of his funeral, a surgeon acting for a scientific society allegedly removed Lanne's skull and substituted another, and competitors made off with his hands and feet. The night after the burial, what remained of the corpse was removed from the grave and was never recovered.

Two years after Truganini's burial, she was exhumed and her skeleton put on display in the Tasmanian Museum and Art Gallery. There it remained for nearly a hundred years. Last April, in response to pressure from people of Tasmanian-aboriginal descent, Truganini's skeleton was cremated and the ashes scattered in Tasmania's D'Entrecasteaux Channel.

This photograph of Truganini was taken in 1866 by Charles A. Wooley and is reproduced courtesy of the Tasmanian Museum and Art Gallery.

things they invented on their own, and others they picked up from white bushrangers. They even made up bushranging groups themselves in a few instances. An Australian aboriginal convict named Mosquito was sent to Hobart to be a police scout. Bored, he ended by forming a gang of shantytown Tasmanians and taking to the bush, where he enjoyed a long outburst of crime before he was apprehended and suspended.

Back at the center, officialdom tried to control things, with ever smaller success, until at last its hand was forced against the natives willy-nilly, as a result of the cumulative acts of its own unruly subjects. Governor after governor tried in good conscience to carry out the early admonition not to harm the aboriginals, at least as far as words would serve. David Collins in 1810 ordered that violence against the natives be dealt with in the same manner as violence against a "civilized person." Thomas Davey in 1814 proclaimed that recent hostility of the natives was traceable to ill-treatment, especially the kidnapping of children. William Sorrell in 1817-1819 said the same, at great length, sternly forbidding such abductions. Governor Arthur arrived in 1824 and promptly issued a proclamation that he would punish ill-treatment of natives. And he did so, handing out 25 lashes to some colonists who had brutalized native women. (Such brutalities, which usually escaped punishment, were chaining a woman to a log, burning another with firebrands, and making another wear the head of her fresh-killed husband around her neck, and do not include outright murders by shooting, pushing onto a fire, and so on.)

In 1828, Arthur posted another proclamation, again admitting the depredations of the whites, but now trying to calm things by ordering the Tasmanians to stay out of the settled areas unless they procured official passports to gather shellfish on the coast. Of course the natives could not read this document even if they should see it; and the governor had no hot line to the interior—in fact one problem all along was that chiefs who one would expect could be negotiated with did not exist. So in early 1830, Arthur made one more try at proclaiming even-handed treatment for the natives, in a way they might grasp, with his famous picture boards.

They were the 1830 equivalent of propaganda leaflets dropped behind enemy lines. The message is clear enough, to us; its intentional simplicity read something like this: "Natives and whites can mingle in amity; natives should come meet Governor (recognize him by cocked hat); black spear white, black hang; white shoot black, white hang." Citizens who saw them thought them hilarious. But the idea was ingenious, and at least better than printed officialese in its promise of getting across. (It seems to have been suggested by a colonist who had seen a charcoal drawing on a tree done by aboriginals, which showed a settler cart train they had been watching from hiding.) The boards were hung in trees where it was thought aboriginals would see them.

The picture boards had no effect. And the message was false, as earlier proclamations had been. Blacks had indeed been hanged in plenty, some for killing settlers and some who were falsely accused of murders committed by whites. But in the whole story no white was ever hanged for killing a black, in spite of cases of solid testimony to the killing. And little other punishment was handed out for all the murders, kidnappings, maimings, and other crimes against the blacks. This was not, however, squeamishness about using the gallows; on one occasion a single sitting of judges sentenced 37 whites to hang for offenses against whites.

The picture boards were a watershed—the last attempt at asserting native rights to justice. Actually, the wind had been blowing the other way ever more strongly, and the end came rather quickly. Although the governors wanted to protect the Tasmanians, or said they did, nobody else cared; and anyhow, a governor's constituency was the colonists, not the Tasmanians. Nor was a sense of moral responsibility the same as moral conviction. The government, whether local or back home in Britain, was nonplussed by the seemingly homeless, wandering naked savages, and compassion for these uncivilized folk did not extend to letting them interfere with the civilized spreading of farms and towns in a supposedly new and open land. As to spreading the gospel, for once the clergy sat on its hands and did nothing worth mentioning in behalf of the aboriginals. And the ordinary colonist's sense of humanity is epitomized by one of them. This jolly specimen amused a perfectly friendly black by holding an empty pistol to his own head and clicking the trigger. Then he suggested it was the native's turn at the same silly game, handed him a loaded pistol, and watched with satisfaction as the poor man blew his own brains out.

In any case, there was no road back. From about 1825 the Black War was on in earnest. After a generation of their special education by the whites, the

Tasmanians were waging total war, with their own cruelties and killings of personally innocent (not always, of course) settlers and their families. The Tasmanians were so successful, in spite of their primitive weapons and their dwindling numbers, that they were actually driving homesteaders back into the towns. The settlers demanded protection, and the government decided that the only solution to the aboriginal problem was extermination (certainly the settlers' choice) or holing them up somewhere out of the way. Governor Arthur's attempt to apply the second expedient was his most bizarre scheme of all, the Black Line.

This came in 1830, just after the picture boards, which were a last despairing cry and far too late. The Line was supposed to operate like a vast kangaroo surround, as used by the natives, starting at the perimeter of the whole settled southeastern third of the island and driving the Tasmanians before it into a cul-de-sac in the Tasman Peninsula at the island's corner. Such a drive had actually been used on the Australian mainland, with a degree of success. But the plains of Victoria were not the rugged and forested terrain of Tasmania. And the Black Line was not black, or thin red, but white, being composed partly of soldiers and partly of convicts but mostly of civilians, taking leave from whatever they were doing in farm or town to become instant woodsmen. It was a major effort for the still modest colony, although it was like executing the Schlieffen Plan with something over three thousand men having little or no training. The government doubtless had no idea how far aboriginal numbers had already ebbed, but there were still significant tribes in the area.

Governor Arthur organized the whole thing on paper in detail. D-day was October 7 and the Line, 120 miles long, started off with a man supposedly at every sixty yards. The story of the operation is a novel in itself. It would be superhuman, in that country, to maintain such a line in order. There were a few actual encounters with natives, and a few fancied ones. Some of these "Down Under Deerslayers" were wounded by their own comrades. One Tasmanian man was caught, as well as a boy about fifteen. Two more were shot dead. After seven weeks, the Line arrived at the neck of the Tasman Peninsula in great excitement and anticipation of the bag of aboriginals hemmed in there by the

human net. The peninsula was scoured; it was empty. Newspapers poured scorn on the campaign for having spent £30,000 of His Majesty's money to catch one black man. But the £30,000 had, after all, gone into colonial pockets, and the participants agreed they had had a very good time.

The operation was perhaps the least harmful thing that was ever visited on the Tasmanians, who must have been amazed as they slipped through the Line or watched it pass them by. More effective measures against them were already afoot. One was "roving parties."

With the Black War heating up and with settlers and natives shooting on sight, Governor Arthur in 1826 had proclaimed the need to capture certain natives who had become adept in directing attacks (by learning from the whites), and the next year he divided the country into military districts and then proclaimed martial law—all this, remember, before the picture boards and the Black Line. In 1829 Arthur authorized six parties, staffed by convicts but headed by relatively responsible men, to hunt for natives, and in 1830—but still before the ambitious Line—he offered rewards of £5 a head (£2 for a child) for natives taken alive. This is just the system that has brought the orang-utan to the verge of extinction because, as a newspaper predicted correctly at the time, several would be killed for one captured. The methods of such parties, official or informal, varied from attempts to capture with limited loss of life to outright search-and-destroy missions. In 1827 an informal posse to avenge the death of a settler reported killing or wounding about sixty Tasmanians; and in another case, a party of police that had come under a stone-throwing attack caught the attackers in a defile and killed seventy of them, dashing the brains of the children. The formal roving parties had by the end of 1832 captured 236 aboriginals, obviously at great cost to tribal life.

The other arm of the pincers was George Augustus Robinson, who earned the title of Conciliator. He was raised in the building trades in London, had come to Tasmania to improve himself, and would retire at last to England, living in affluence and mingling with the gentry in Bath, where he died. He was good-hearted though jealous of his prerogatives. He was a devout Wesleyan; he missionized and preached to the Tasmanians as opportunity afforded, but did not let it interfere with his main

object of communication. He had great fortitude, self-possession, and persistence. He became convinced by everything he heard, and by his own contacts, that the aboriginals were essentially mild and inoffensive, that their rights had been trampled on, and that they could be conciliated by decent treatment, if it were honest and official. His method was to go out among them everywhere; he had a few helpers, black and white, all unarmed, but he put himself at the head of his party and usually kept the other whites out of sight.

He had arrived in Tasmania in 1824, the same year as Governor Arthur. He soon formed his opinions but had no way of acting on them. Then in March 1829, the governor, in one of his deeds of good intention, published an advertisement in The Hobart Town Gazette seeking a man of good character who would try to effect friendly connections with the Tasmanians by taking charge of those on Bruny Island, across the bay from Hobart. The island was already partly settled by whites of the bad sort, and the surviving blacks needed protection and provisions, having little of either.

Robinson at once applied for and got the job, insisting on the salary being raised from £50 to £100 a year. He started his work in a week and carried it on for some months, but it does not seem to have been much of a success in helping the natives, who were a little too close to white civilization. However, it was an experience for Robinson. He observed a surprising mortality rate among the natives, from afflictions of unclear nature. In less than two months he had accumulated a vocabulary of 115 words of the local language and was also preaching in it to the aboriginals. With little formal education and no training he went on recording names and some words on his travels, noting where the languages were different; in spite of his crude renderings this has been an important source of information on these lost tongues. Finally, on Bruny he had met Truganini, an extraordinary girl of sixteen or seventeen, small of build, obviously intelligent, lively, resourceful, brave, and attractive. During his stay she was married (rather against her will) to Wooraddy, who had been mooning after her as the story opened. These two, and a few more Tasmanians from Bruny Island and elsewhere, were to accompany Robinson in all his travels, with Truganini as a constant source of intelligence he could not otherwise get, even when she did not know the language of an area.

At the beginning of 1830, Robinson started on his mission to conciliate outlying natives, a mission that would last some five years. He set out from Hobart westward along the coast, with his aboriginals and a few whites, including convicts. He was supported by a whaleboat and a schooner, but he himself went on foot—a trek sometimes extremely arduous—all around the shore, with inland excursions, until he reached Launceston in the northeast, just as the Black Line was kicking off to the south. He spent the next twelve months ranging through the northern interior and visiting the sealers, actually getting many of them to part with their Tasmanian women by threatening government action. The governor was impressed with the apparent success of Robinson in conciliating and bringing in natives, and promised him full support, giving him as his next objective the rounding up of the feared Big River tribe. On the last day of 1831, Robinson made friendly contact with two "sanguinary tribes," the Big River and Oyster Bay, and found that they came to a total of 26 persons: sixteen men, nine women, and one child, who put themselves under his protection. These figures alone reveal a people without a future.

Robinson made three more expeditions between 1832 and 1834, to remnant peoples in the still-wild west. In September 1832, a group of blacks he met in the northwest decided to spear him and his own natives, and he barely escaped by crossing a river on pieces of floating wood—he could not swim—pushed by Truganini. This was his closest call, as recorded in his long, immensely detailed journal. It is full of action, showing that his mission was no triumphal parade, but a long tussle of making contact in unmapped places through unknown languages, persuading aboriginals of his good intentions, and seeing many of those he persuaded change their minds and run off again. It contains his enumeration and naming of natives as he tried to learn facts; and it is larded with stories, some quite fresh, of horrors perpetrated by blacks and whites—though mostly by the latter and sometimes more sickening than any already mentioned. All this time he was bringing in parties of submitted aboriginals. The presumed last lot of Tasmanians was found at the

Tasmanian aboriginals at Oyster Cove. Taken in 1858 by Francis Russell (Bishop) Nixon, the photograph shows nearly all of the members of the race then living.

end of 1834 (by Robinson's sons after he had gone back to Hobart in August): it was made up of four women, one man, and three boys, who had wanted to turn themselves in but had been shot at by every white who saw them. One family or small group, however, is known to have remained at large until 1842.

The Conciliator had succeeded: he had rounded up Tasmania's aboriginals in a way everyone—official, humanitarian, or extirpationist—could approve. He was given public praise and reward, though he felt it was not prompt enough nor in a measure he was entitled to (he was recompensed for his captures at a kind of wholesale rate, less than the £5 a head previously offered). At his request he was made commandant of the new aboriginal settlement on Flinders Island, off the northeast corner of Tasmania, where all the natives were placed, after some smaller and less hospitable islands had been tried out.

In this windy place, now wearing clothing, which was probably often damp, the captives declined rapidly. There were not many, anyhow. Robinson's listing of natives he met is less than 300, showing how the population beyond the settlement zone had already shrunk, and he brought in less than 200—the roving parties rather more. Many Tasmanians never reached the settlement: of the tribe that had tried to kill him in September 1832, he and his people obtained the submission of eleven in July 1833; nine of these died inside three

weeks. When he took up residence on Flinders in 1835, there were only 106 on the island, not counting some he brought with him. Tuberculosis, influenza, and pneumonia continued the execution: in 1837 alone there were 29 deaths. There were a few births, but all infants died in a matter of weeks. Robinson left Tasmania in 1839, to become Protector of the Aborigines in Victoria, Australia. It is possible he took a few Tasmanians with him.

So aboriginal life was extinguished in Tasmania thirty years after the Risdon Massacre. Aboriginal bodies, it is true, went on breathing a while longer, like the mythical dead snake wriggling until sundown. Forty-four survivors (including some half-castes) were taken off Flinders in 1847 and brought down to Oyster Cove near Hobart. By 1854 sixteen were left. By 1870 there was one: hardy little Truganini herself.

She died in 1876, and so they ended. Actually, Robinson had been forced, some time earlier, to return a dozen or so aboriginal women to their sealer consorts on Cape Barren Island, and for all we know one or more of these may have outlived her. At any rate, from such unions there has grown up a present-day population of perhaps two thousand part-aboriginals. But with Truganini's death there went out the last known spark of native speech and ideas and memories. After twenty thousand years.

40

Societies on the Brink

BY DAVID MAYBURY-LEWIS

Small societies around the world are currently threatened with extinction. The threat, either implicit or explicit, that they must die so that we may live is something we normally conceal from ourselves under comfortable phrases like "the social costs of development," or "the price of progress." The assumptions behind this sort of thinking need to be examined.

We need first to try to develop some perspective on a problem that is often debated with considerable passion. If we consider the whole span of human history, then it is clear that the majority of the peoples of the world lived until quite recent times in relatively small and relatively isolated societies. The emergence of powerful tribes, nations, or empires threatened the physical existence and certainly the cultural continuity of smaller, weaker peoples. This is a process that is as old as humankind itself. What has rendered it more dramatic in recent centuries is the development of what we are pleased to call "Western technology." This placed the nations of Western Europe and, later, North America at an enormous advantage and hastened the process of physical and cultural extinction of weaker peoples. Even China, an ancient and powerful civilization which hardly qualifies as a small-scale society, was shaken to its very foundations by the impact of the West. It was able to recover because of its vast reserves, demographic and otherwise. Small societies cannot recover. Instead, they face destruction, either by physical extinction or by absorption into the larger ones that press in on them.

The process has long been recognized; scholars have tried to grapple with its implications since the earliest days of the European expansion. For a while it was a matter for serious debate whether humanoid creatures encountered in other lands were really humans at all. The people in the other lands were equally puzzled. A British party was at first kept in cages by the Singhalese, who tried to determine whether or not they were actually human. We have similar reports from other parts of the world. In fact, even when the conventional attributes of humanity were granted to alien peoples, debate still raged as to whether they were fully human and therefore entitled to fully human treatment (whatever that might be by the standards of the time and place). Thus it became a matter of grave consequence whether they were or were not considered to be endowed with souls. Similarly, arguments raged as to whether peoples who apparently possessed the basic physical and mental equipment of human beings could nevertheless put themselves beyond the pale by practicing "inhuman" customs.

Cannibalism was usually regarded as one such practice. One can imagine with what *frisson* the Europeans of the sixteenth century read Hans Staden's *True History and Description of the Land of the Savage, Naked and Ugly Maneating Peoples of the New World of America* (1557). The Tupinamba Indians, who once held Staden captive, regularly and ritually killed and ate their prisoners. It was considered a heroic death. A captive warrior, who in some cases might have been living with his captors for years and might even have raised a family there, was led out and clubbed to death in a ceremonial duel, after which the entire community ate him to partake of his heroic essence. Staden also pointed out that the same Tupinamba were horrified by the cruelty of the Europeans with whom they came in contact. They considered the Europeans to be in some sense beyond the pale because of their inhuman customs, such as the routine use of torture in trials and punishments, and the practice of slavery.

The relativistic implications of the Tupinamba view were not, unfortunately, taken seriously by European scholars. The debates concerning the essential humanity of alien peoples and the rights to which they were entitled were conducted in strictly European terms. Even when the arguments were genuine—as in the case of the famous series of debates before the Spanish crown between Las Casas and Sepúlveda—the results were self-serving. When the debate went against the Indians, the local authorities considered that they had learned opinion on their side. When it came out favorably to the Indians, the local authorities refused to abide by its outcome. In the last analysis, the principal argument was power. The stronger tended to find justifications for using the weaker, or at the very least for making the weaker over in the image of the conqueror.

I have referred to these centuries-old arguments because modern versions of them still persist in our own thinking, both in our conventional wisdom and in the assumptions made by our theorists. On the one hand we have what may be called the liberal, neo-Darwinian view that small, weak societies are fated for extinction and that there is not much that can be done about it. Perhaps indeed, according to this view, there is not much that should be done about it, for why expend energy and resources in trying to interfere with irreversible processes that are part of the order of things? On the other hand, there is an orthodox Marxist position that holds that such societies are backward and out of step historically. They must therefore be assisted in getting in phase with history as rapidly as possible or they will be crushed by the relentless and irreversible force of historical process. But the results in practical terms of these two views are monotonously similar. Small societies are extinguished, culturally, or physically, or both.

These arguments are unsatisfactory. There is no natural or historical law that militates against small societies. There are only political choices. In fact the rhetoric of both the United States and the Soviet Union, to take the two strongest powers in the world today, stresses cultural pluralism as a goal for their own

In the northern Kalahari of Botswana, a San boy squeezes water from a grass sponge into his sister's mouth. The scene reflects the traditional San hunting-and-gathering way of life; the water comes from a depression in the trunk of a monongo tree, whose protein-rich nuts are a vital food source. In the years since this picture was taken, however, cultural change among the San has increased dramatically as a neighboring cattle-keeping people, the Herero, have encroached on their territories.

societies and indeed for the world at large. The fact that this rhetoric is not often put into practice is not a matter of natural or historical necessity but of political convenience.

A small society is of course a relative concept. Many nations are small compared with the superpowers but overwhelmingly large compared with some peoples in remote jungle regions who have just come into contact with the outside world. It is the societies at the lower end of this continuum with which I am primarily concerned, although the fact that it is a continuum and that the problem transcends the fate of isolated, tribal populations has certain implications, which I shall also discuss.

Anthropologists have often come to the defense of these tiny, tribal peoples. When they do, these anthropologists are

normally attacked with a battery of arguments that need to be explicitly stated and examined.

First it is contended that anthropologists want tribal peoples left alone simply to preserve a traditional way of life. They therefore want to halt the push to explore and exploit the resources of the earth. They are sentimentalists who stand up for the right of a few to live their own lives in backwardness and ignorance as against the right of the many to use the resources available. Anthropologists are therefore the enemies of development.

This is a serious misrepresentation, which makes the defenders of the rights of small-scale societies seem like the nineteenth-century Luddites, who went around smashing machines in a futile effort to halt the Industrial Revolution. Whether isolated, tribal societies would be better off if the world left them alone is an academic matter. They are not going to be permitted to live in isolation. The people who speak up for them do not argue that they should be left alone or that all exploration and development should be halted. On the contrary, we assume that isolated societies will not be left alone and are therefore concerned with how to soften the impact of inevitable contact so that it will not destroy them in the name of progress. To return to the Luddite analogy for a moment, we do not try to stem the Industrial Revolution by breaking the machines. We accept its inevitability but question the necessity of chaining children to the machines (as was done in nineteenth-century England) as a means of capital formation.

A second argument is a malicious variation on the first one. According to that, it is claimed that anthropologists would like to keep tribal peoples isolated in what amount to human zoos for their own research purposes.

Again this is a misrepresentation. Anthropologists and others who take an interest in such small societies argue that these peoples' contacts with the outside world should be regulated if they are not to prove destructive. A small society must therefore have a guaranteed territory that it can call its own. This should not be a reservation in the sense that its inhabitants are confined to and imprisoned on it, but rather a home base, which the members of the society can use as a springboard in their efforts to come to terms with the outside world.

Another variation on these arguments stresses the immorality of preventing "backward" peoples from enjoying the benefits of civilization. Who, it is asked, has the right to insist that a relatively isolated society be left alone, to manage without modern medicine and modern consumer goods? Some ardent proponents of this theme wax so eloquent that they make the anxious anthropologist seem like a puritan who is determined to deny color TV to the natives. But the argument, once again, is a distortion of a position that gets little hearing.

Those people who are concerned about the effects of contact are merely urging caution, based on an understanding of the possible harmful effects of such contact. One would have thought that the grim historical record of death, disease, and despair that also accompany the arrival of civilization in remote areas would be sufficient grounds for advocating a cautious approach. We now know a good deal about the diseases that are introduced and we know too that they tend to be unremitting, while the provision of modern medicine is often fitful or inadequate. At a later stage in the process, we know too that the introduction of new industries in remote and not-so-remote areas can lead to cultural breakdown and personal despair within the local population *as well as* providing jobs, increasing income, and so on. This is a familiar dilemma even in advanced societies, which is why people are so anxious to have a say in what happens to their own communities. There is an uneasy suspicion that the arrival of, say, an oil refinery may on balance produce costs for the people of the community where it is located and benefits for people elsewhere. We understand this element of trade-off keenly enough in advanced societies and yet we often seek to impose oil refineries or their equivalents on societies much less able to cope with them. When the results are not cottages and TV sets but disruption and even death, we tend to shrug our shoulders and reassure ourselves that such costs are unavoidable. I am arguing here that this is not so, and that such costs can be minimized even if not avoided altogether.

But the most insidious argument used against those who speak up for small societies is insidious precisely because it seems so reasonable. Why, it is asked, should such societies be protected anyway? What are the advantages of protecting their way of life? There are in fact many that have been claimed. We can learn from their life styles, since we are clearly so desperately unhappy with our own. We can learn from their views of the world, particularly as concerns the general interrelatedness of things on earth. Many Americans are, for example, discovering a harmony in American Indian views of the world which they find conducive not only to inner peace but also to a more effective use of the environment. There are other arguments that are frequently advanced as reasons for protecting the life style of small societies in different parts of the world. We need to do so in order to further our understanding of human cultural variation. We know too little about how societies work and about how they can be made to work *for* people rather than against them. Besides, it is claimed, the members of the small society will be more useful citizens in the larger one if they come into it with something of their own heritage intact. Then again, there may be genetic advantages in seeing that such groups are not physically extinguished, and so on.

But these are the wrong questions. Supposing we decided that we had nothing more to learn from small societies; that there was no particular genetic advantage in seeing them survive physically and no particular social or philosophical advantage in seeing them survive culturally. Would that then give us the right to eliminate these cultures? Would we be willing to apply a similar reasoning to the sick, the weak, or the aged in our own culture? The question, put that way, is horrifying, which is precisely why I called the original question insidious. If we accept it as a legitimate question, then we find ourselves debating the question of whether it is *useful* to permit another culture to survive. But useful to whom? Presumably the usefulness of their physical and social existence is not in doubt for the members of that culture. What we are in fact debating is whether their existence is useful to *us*. Such thinking can lead to the gas chambers and has done so in our own time. That is why the original question is the wrong one. The fundamental reason why we must help other cultures to survive is because in all conscience we have no alternative. It is a moral imperative of the sort that insists that the strong ought not to trample on the rights of the weak.

Some writers have referred to the process by which a powerful society extinguishes a weaker culture as *ethnocide*, and have argued that this is (and should be recognized as) a crime analogous to genocide. I understand and sympathize with the passion that informs this view, but I find the formulation of it unhelpful. Homicide is hard enough to define and the arguments concerning the circumstances under which it may or may not be justified are complex. Genocide is even more difficult and its use as a term of opprobrium all too often depends on the point of view of the user. I find the concept of ethnocide more difficult still, and much too vague to be helpful. The moment of a culture's death, even more so than that of a person, is difficult to perceive. The manner of its passing, save in the most obvious cases, is hard to evaluate.

Take some hypothetical cases. A society may occupy the territory of another so that the members of the latter are deprived of their livelihood. Or it may send missionaries into a territory, who then seek to undermine the culture they find. Alternatively, a timber company may move into an area and pay the local people for cutting down the forests off which they have traditionally lived. Again, a new industry may move into an area and effect profound changes in its way of life. Now, all of these changes have some disruptive effect on the local culture. At the same time all of them, save presumably the first instance, bring some benefits. How is one to decide on the precise ratio of costs to benefits that constitutes ethnocide? Indeed, how does one deal with the paradox of a society that may collaborate in its own ethnocide, permitting its culture to be extinguished in exchange for the benefits obtained from another society? In my view, the concept of *ethnocide* is too much of an either/or, life-or-death concept, and does little to help us understand situations where often it is not clear how to knock the gun out of the murderer's hand, or even who the murderer is or which is the gun.

I would insist instead that we are dealing with processes of contact and rapidly induced change that have in the past been known to have serious and even fatal consequences. The problem then is how to soften the contact and how to regulate the change so that its consequences for the small societies are minimally harmful. We are seeking to minimize the costs and to maximize the benefits for the people contacted.

This is not easy to do, however, since the benefits usually accrue to the wider society while the costs are borne largely by the contacted culture. We are thus dealing with a problem as old as humankind itself, namely that of protecting the weak against the strong. It is a problem that is unlikely to disappear and for which there are no easy solutions. Yet there are some things that can be done.

In the first place it is important to insist, as I have done here, on the right of other societies to their own ways of life. Such an insistence is not banal. This right is neither generally accepted nor generally understood. That is why it must be established that small-scale societies are not condemned to disappear by the workings of some abstract historical process. On the contrary, small societies may be shattered and their members annihilated, but this happens as a result of political choices made by the societies that impinge upon them, and for which the powerful must take responsibility. It is not, in any case, inevitable. The smaller societies can be assisted to deal with the impact of the outside world at comparatively little cost to those who bear down upon them. We have now come to recognize the principle that it is reasonable to set aside some part of the profits from the extraction of resources from the earth to be used to offset the ecological damage that may have been done in the process of extracting them. A similar understanding of the human costs of development and a willingness to deal with them is all that is necessary.

Such understanding and willingness cannot be taken for granted. It has to be cultivated and the attempt to cultivate it will not always be successful. It is unlikely, for example, that anybody, however eloquent or theoretically brilliant, could have convinced Hitler of the right of German Jews to their own cultural integrity. In such cases there may be no redress other than warfare or revolution. In many instances, however, the ways of persuasion have hardly been tried, and it is largely out of ignorance that planners make decisions that have such fatal costs for the small societies caught up in their plans. It is therefore vital that anthropologists and others concerned about the problem make people aware of its dimensions and point out that the cost of assisting small societies to become successful ethnic minorities is a comparatively small one, which may well be offset in the long run by the benefits the wider society will reap as a result.

Of course, attempts to protect threatened small-scale societies will not always be successful. The politics of some situations indicate that the minorities are doomed, if not physically, then at least as distinct cultures or subcultures. Yet this is no reason to abandon the effort in despair, any more than we abandon the efforts to avoid war or to construct just societies because these efforts are so often frustrated. I consider the effort to protect the cultural integrity of small-scale societies an issue of equal importance. We are talking not merely about the fate of tiny enclaves of people, buried in the last jungle refuges of this earth. What we are really talking about is the ability of human beings to discover ways to live together in plural societies. It seems to me that this is the critical issue of our times. Our success or failure in this endeavor may well decide whether people anywhere will be able to live in societies based on a minimum of mutual tolerance and respect. The alternatives are unpleasant to contemplate.

41

The Irish Tinkers

BY GEORGE GMELCH AND SHARON BOHN GMELCH

In Holland they are called the Woon-wagonbewoners, in Norway the Taters, in Sweden the Tattare, and in Ireland the Tinkers or Travellers. Many of them are descendants of tradesmen and peasants who were forced from their land by famine, war, or poverty. They pursue a nomadic life similar to that of the Romany Gypsies, and the two groups have often intermarried. Among the Irish Tinkers, however, intermarriage with Gypsies has been limited because the latter never came to Ireland in large numbers or remained very long.

Tinkers have long occupied the bottom rung of Ireland's socioeconomic ladder. In recent decades the shift to settled urban life has brought them improved living conditions and opportunities. Yet our field research among the Tinkers from July 1971 to September 1972 and again for four months during 1975 reveals that their social position remains fundamentally unchanged. While some have been integrated into settled Irish society, many Tinkers are dispirited and demoralized by what outsiders see as a positive step toward modernization. The move to the city has been accompanied by a collapse of their traditional way of life.

Today, as in the past, the Tinkers are a deprived minority with the classic stigmata of dispossessed peoples: poverty, illiteracy, low self-esteem, high infant mortality, and minimal participation in national institutions. Yet the Tinkers provide us with a case in which the most common bases for discrimination are absent.

Like the majority of the sedentary population, the Irish Tinkers are white, English speaking, Roman Catholic, and native to Ireland. Nevertheless, they form a distinct ethnic group. They marry almost exclusively within their group, their cultural patterns differ from those of the wider society, and they identify themselves and are identified by others as being separate.

In the past, nomadism was primarily responsible for creating social boundaries between the Tinkers and the settled Irish. The trades and services performed by the Tinkers were in limited demand in any one area. The result was a life in which many families were on the move every week or two, pursuing new markets for their goods and skills.

Tinsmithing is the oldest and best known of their trades, and it is from this occupation that the name Tinker originates. Fashioning the goods by hand, itinerant tinsmiths supplied country people with a variety of useful articles including pots and pans, mugs, kettles, milk pails, lanterns, even parts for stills for the production of bootleg whiskey.

Repair work also kept them busy. In an age when consumer goods were meant to last a lifetime, they tightened loose handles, replaced worn-out and rusty bottoms, and plugged leaks with solder aided by a "Tinker's dam"—a ring of dough placed around the hole to keep the molten solder from running off. They also mended umbrellas and even stitched broken china back together with wire.

Many Tinkers traded or sold animals to farmers: heavy workhorses for plowing, and donkeys for pulling milk carts to the creamery. Tinker families in their colorful barrel-top wagons with small herds of pinto or piebald horses in tow were once a common sight at Irish county fairs.

The Tinkers' economic activities followed the agricultural cycle of the rural population. In the early summer months when the bogs began to dry, Tinker men could earn a day's wages or meals by cutting turf, or peat—the country people's primary source of fuel. During the harvest season they helped the farmers bring in hay, pulled beets, and lifted potatoes. Around Christmas and again at Easter many of the men swept chimneys, their pay determined by the number of cans of soot they were able to collect. The Tinkers were itinerant jacks-of-all-trades who performed a variety of tasks depending on the needs of the farmers they approached.

Traveller women sold small household wares such as scrubbing brushes, boot polish, needles, and thread. If the farm wife she approached refused to buy her goods, the peddler begged, usually for fresh farm products. When her pleas failed, the Tinker responded with a curse: "May you get an angry cancer" or "May the curse of God melt you." Imprecations of this sort were so common they became a byword for the useless: "It isn't worth a Tinker's damn."

Some of the women also practiced fortunetelling. A favorite method was "tossing cups," divining the future from the shapes made by the tea leaves that adhered to the sides and bottom of an emptied cup.

Although they were welcomed for the many useful services they provided, the Tinkers remained apart from the settled Irish community. They camped on the roadside in wagons and simple tents constructed of oil-soaked burlap sacks stretched over hooped willow branches. Their campsites were usually located along *boreens*, or side roads, on the outskirts of towns and villages.

As nomads, the Tinkers were often regarded with suspicion and distrust. Although settled folk might be fond of individual Tinkers who frequently passed through their area, they treated itinerants in general as outcasts. If the Travellers were slow to leave a particular site, or if they were suspected of trespassing or pilfering, the *garda* (police) would force them to move on.

Over the last two decades, the Tinkers' rural way of life has been dramatically altered by the effects of modernization. New consumer goods and machinery have made most of their traditional occupations obsolete. Inexpensive mass-produced tinware and plastic containers have eliminated the demand for handmade goods. Even repair jobs have disappeared, for it is cheaper to replace plastic and enamelware vessels than to repair them.

As more of Ireland's farmers have acquired tractors and trucks, the demand for workhorses and donkeys has declined sharply. Mechanized potato and beet diggers have taken the place of itinerant farm labor. Other labor-saving devices, such as milking machines, have become commonplace with the introduction of electricity into rural areas. And expanded rural bus service and increased ownership of private automobiles have brought provincial towns and shops within reach of most farm wives.

Even a change in the natural environment helped undermine the Travellers' economy. The Tinkers have long supplemented their daily diet with wild rabbits caught in wire snares. But in the mid-1950s many owners of large farms deliberately released rabbits infected with myxomatosis—the disease used to exterminate marauding rabbits in Europe and Australia. Within a few years rabbits were so scarce that most men ceased hunting them.

In search of a new livelihood, the Tinkers have left the countryside for Ireland's towns and cities. Their migration occurred in two stages. During the early 1950s many families abandoned their regular travel routes and moved to the outskirts of provincial towns where government unemployment offices were located and new economic opportunities could be found.

A second wave of migration, which began in the mid-1960s and still continues, brought many families to the capital city of Dublin. In 1952 fewer than 25 families were camped in Dublin; by 1976 their numbers had grown to a total of 359 families, or approximately 2,500 individuals—over one fifth of the country's Tinker population.

One factor that drew many Travellers to Dublin was the tremendous outpouring of charity that resulted when a government commission, established to investigate the problems itinerants created in the city (women begging in the streets, litter and squalor in roadside camps, damage caused by wandering horses), went further than anyone had anticipated. Its 1963 report documented the deplorable state of Ireland's Tinker population—the widespread poverty, unemployment, illiteracy, and an infant mortality rate nearly four times the national average.

The media focused national attention on the commission's findings and the "itinerant problem" became a national disgrace. Charities that had formerly ignored the Travellers' plight now opened their doors to them. In 1965 the Dublin Itinerant Settlement Committee, which later expanded into a nationwide movement, was formed to aid the Tinkers and help settle them.

Many of the settled Irish expressed their sympathy by giving alms. Begging soon became a highly lucrative occupation for the Tinker women. Simply by donning soiled and tattered clothing and carrying a baby, or a bundle of clothes wrapped in a shawl to resemble one, a woman could collect several pounds a day on the city streets. Others, appealing door to door in residential areas, were able to gather enough food and clothing to maintain their families.

Among urban Traveller families the changed economy has led to a shift in sex roles. The women have increased independence, and the men have lost much of their traditional authority. Money once controlled exclusively by men is now divided. Most urban Tinker women no longer turn over their earnings to their husbands; some have even opened postal savings accounts in their own names. Women now have a say in selecting mates for their teen-age children, and in deciding when to move and with whom to camp.

Following a dispute with another family, Marty MacDonagh decided to move to a new camp. Ignoring the objections of his wife, he loaded their wagon, hitched up the horse, and started to leave. But when it became apparent that his wife would not follow, he turned back and unpacked.

A change in the role of family provider—the one who contributes the greatest share toward the family's support—usually results in a shift in power. And there is no doubt that the Traveller women are gaining power. As one Tinker woman said, "Today the Travellin' women is gettin' very bold and what makes them so bold is that they're under no compliment to the men now that they're doin' most of the work beggin'."

The economic role of the men is now almost completely limited to collecting the large quantities of scrap metal that are available in the city. Private homes, slum clearance projects, construction sites, factories, and dumps provide a ready supply. Each day Tinker men go from place to place in search of discarded machinery, abandoned automobiles, worn-out home appliances, and any junk with metal content. They also collect second-hand furniture and clothing that can be used or resold. The scrap is piled on horse-drawn carts or trucks and taken back to the camps for sorting and cleaning.

As the number of Tinkers who have migrated to the cities has increased, however, competition for scrap has become intense and profits have declined. Also, many businesses have realized the value of scrap metal and have begun to charge for it. Even the supply of scrap has declined in the last few years because many items once made of metal are now made of plastic. As a result the urban men's earnings have dwindled as those of the women have risen.

The role of men in the family has diminished in a number of other ways as well. In the past one of the primary responsibilities of Tinker men was caring for the family's means of transportation—maintaining the wagon or cart and looking after the animals—a role of importance in a nomadic society. As the Tinkers have settled near towns and switched from horses to trucks and cars, these responsibilities have become obsolete. In a few Dublin families the men do little more than gather wood and keep the campfire going.

The move to the city has also resulted in changes in the marriage patterns of the group. Urban Tinkers now marry two to three years earlier than rural Travellers of the previous generation. In Dublin it is not uncommon for 14- and 15-year-old girls to be "matched" by their parents.

One reason for this change is the loss of parental control. Tinkers traditionally place a high value on premarital chastity. In the country, teen-age girls were closely supervised and not allowed to mix with boys. Today, however, it has become difficult for parents to keep a close watch on their teen-age children. Large campsites and easy access to the city provide numerous opportunities for secret meetings between the sexes.

Some parents attempt to cope with the problem by shifting to a new camp, but this is rarely more than a temporary solution. More often parents try to protect the chastity of their daughters and the family's reputation by making early matches for their children.

There has also been a marked increase in the number of marriages between first and second cousins. Of the 37 marriages recorded during our field research in Dublin, 16 were of this type. This increase reflects the uncertain and ambivalent relations among Tinker kin groups whose members have become strangers to one another.

In the past, the Travellers drew their mates from other lineages that traveled the same territory. Since the advent of Tinker urbanization, however, groups that traditionally intermarried have tended to lose contact. In an already uncertain environment, families are reluctant to marry their children into groups unrelated to them or about which they know little. Therefore they seek suitable mates for their children among the offspring of their own brothers and sisters. In the words of one woman: "Travellin' People believe that cousins will have more nature for one another, and they won't use no violence on each other. If they aren't happy together, they may stick on just for the sake of bein' so near a relation, bein' of the same blood."

Many lament the change from their former way of life. Although it often meant drafty shelters, wet clothes, and empty stomachs, it gave them an autonomy and economic independence they have lost. As one elderly Tinker woman said: "The Travellin' People are goin' pure savage over all these handouts. The men don't know what to do with themselves. It has more of them gone pure stupid with drink. Years ago Travellers never had much money to spare for drink, now they're livin' in the pubs. Travellin' People today have no respect in themselves. Too many people is doin' too much for 'em. If they really want to do good, they'll give the men work and stop payin' 'em for doin' nothin'."

These changes have eroded the romantic stereotype of the Tinkers as carefree, adventuresome vagabonds. The Tinkers are now viewed, at best, as objects of charity and sympathy; at worst, they are regarded as parasites, a noxious social problem.

Few Irish realize or are willing to concede that by collecting scrap metal, secondhand clothing and rags, the Tinkers are serving an important economic and ecological function: the recycling of resources that would otherwise be wasted. Moreover, by such foraging they resist the possibility of becoming totally dependent on charity.

One response to the negative attitudes and stereotypes of settled society has been a desire among Tinkers to shed their identity. In rural areas assimilation into settled society is difficult, if not impossible. Their way of life makes them highly visible and keeps them separate from the wider society. Even the more conventional trailers and houses many Tinkers now inhabit stand out. Most housed families live at special itinerant sites that are often surrounded by chain-link fencing. The small houses are easily identifiable as government-financed prefabricated dwellings known as tigins.

Individually, Tinkers can be identified by their appearance. Their poor grooming and ill-fitting, unfashionable, secondhand clothing distinguish them from the settled Irish. Women, especially in rural areas, wear long plaid skirts and shawls similar to those of the peasantry of a century ago.

Some settled Irish claim they can recognize Tinkers by their distinctive "sweet" smell—from campfire smoke, perspiration, and dried urine. Others say they have a characteristic walk, described as a "swinging gait" or "jauntiness." City dwellers claim they can spot Tinkers by their generalized country accent and their deep, husky voices, a product of lifelong exposure to the drafty, wet Irish climate.

Odd pronunciation of words, such as "childer" for children, and archaic pronunciation, such as "dreepin" for dripping, are common in Tinker speech, as are antiquated words and expressions, such as "vexed" or "tormented" for angry and "vessels" for dishes:

Nevertheless, in urban areas, where the large population affords some anonymity, Tinkers have the opportunity to "pass" and thus avoid the discrimination directed against them.

Tinkers sometimes hide their identity by using symbols or signs that are incongruous with their mode of life. Some Travellers, particularly sensitive about their illiteracy, carry newspapers when in public. One man manipulated several symbols of Tinker identity in order to obtain automobile insurance. Rather than list his name on the application as John Connors and indicate that he lived at an itinerant site named Walcot, he referred to himself as Mr. John O'Connor, the form common among settled Irish, of "Walcot House." He listed his occupation as that of a self-employed landscape gardener, which would explain his ownership of a truck and would be difficult for the company to disprove.

Outward appearance alone is not sufficient to disguise a Tinker; patterns of behavior must also be altered. By the standards of the settled Irish community, Tinkers often behave inappropriately in public places. When tired of standing or walking, Traveller women may simply sit down on the nearest sidewalk or curb, no matter how crowded or dirty it is. While not all Tinkers are well versed in the behavior of the settled Irish, most are aware of the conduct they must avoid.

Before entering a Dublin pub one afternoon, a mother instructed her 20-year-old daughter, admonishing her, "Don't talk loud," "Don't curse," "Don't use Gammon" (an argot spoken by Tinkers), "Go with manners," and "Be friendly." Once outside the pub the daughter resumed her typical behavior and begged from a passerby.

A few Tinkers are proficient as "cultural commuters"; they maintain a close affiliation with the Tinker population while regularly passing as settled Irish. One woman, for example, passes as an ordinary member of the settled working class during the day when employed as a domestic in several Irish homes. At night she returns to the Tinker camp, consistently declining her employers' offers to drive her home and refusing to give them her address. Despite her success, settled Irish are so attuned to the symbols of Tinker identity that it is very difficult for individuals to conceal them all.

Occasionally Travellers renounce membership in their own group and attempt to become permanent members of settled society. Moving in with a settled community, however, does not automatically lead to social acceptance. In some small Irish towns, clusters of families that have lived among the villagers for three or four generations are still known as "Tinkers." Only when individual families settle in urban areas are there real chances of passing, for only there can they find the anonymity that is the stigmatized person's key to assimilation. But for a gregarious people who value close personal relationships, this anonymity often proves to be bought at too high a price.

In order to effectively conceal their itinerant background, it is necessary for housed families to prevent other Travellers from coming to visit them. "Loneliness" is the most common reason Tinkers give for returning to life on the road.

In the minds of some, the advantages of life on the road are more than equal to the benefits of assimilation. Tinker men, for example, value their autonomy and freedom from the regimentation and fixed work schedules of the urban working classes. "I'm me own boss" is a common boast. They also deride the congested, cluttered, drab slums of central Dublin. By comparison, the lush spring and summer vegetation that surrounds most of the Traveller campsites, even those on the urban fringe, is a delight.

The head of one family that had tried to adjust to the settled life and found it wanting commented: "The wife and me both had jobs. Five days a week up at half seven each morning and for what? Just to pay the bills and rent. After seven years we still had nothin', and me nerves were nearly gone." This family now lives in a covered wagon in a field on the outskirts of Dublin.

The Tinkers have adapted to recent changes in their economic and social environment by modifying or intensifying many of their traditional behavior patterns. As their rural trades gradually became obsolete, for example, they modified the traditional pattern of door-to-door solicitation of work and alms, and began intensively begging and scavenging instead of seeking new occupations. They have coped with their own uncertainty, with mistrust, and with the social problems of large urban camps by intensifying social devices found in their traditional culture, such as secretiveness, withdrawal from interaction with nonkin, close-kin marriages, and shifting camps.

Although the Tinkers have so far been able to cope with the urban environment by making minimal adjustments, not all these changes have been desirable. Responses that satisfy immediate subsistence or social needs may have long-range negative consequences. While scavenging, begging, and welfarism have increased the real income of many families, they have also promoted dependency, loss of pride, and changes in family relations.

The Travellers' adaptation is understandable, both on an individual and on a cultural basis. When human beings attempt to cope with new situations, their responses are aimed primarily at lessening immediate anxiety and psychic pain. The excessive consumption of alcohol by Tinker men and a family's shift from camp to camp to avoid conflict or boredom are obvious examples of this kind of response.

When cultures are confronted with a new environment, they are likely to turn first to familiar patterns and culturally sanctioned alternatives. Most cultures are conservative; people change only enough to meet the immediate demands of a given situation. Truly innovative change occurs when preferred and familiar methods no longer work. The Tinkers currently lack the resources to develop more innovative, and in the long run more satisfactory, responses to their situation. Employment is a case in point. Though most Travellers value economic independence, prejudice on the part of the settled community and lack of requisite skills, notably literacy, prevent them from obtaining conventional jobs. If they could hold regular employment, many problems that confront families that wish to settle would diminish. But because the Travellers are unable to correct basic social inequities, they must cope with existing circumstances as best they can.

While few Tinkers have been successfully integrated into settled Irish society, settlement does seem to be the path of the future. Should such an adaptation become widespread, we can only speculate as to whether a distinct Tinker society will continue to exist. As long as some Tinkers preserve their itinerant lifestyle, they will provide a source of identification for their settled fellows. Yet the total cleavage with Tinker society that passing requires might lead to a complete breakdown of ties between settled and nomadic Travellers.

Dependence on welfare and begging could be the gravest threat to Tinker culture. As one Traveller said about Dubliners, "The people in the houses don't even call us Travellers or Tinkers no more, but just plain 'itinerants.' Some calls us the 'itinerant problem.' Half the Travellin' People don't know what itinerant means." When a society loses its economic independence and its name, little else endures. Unless the Tinkers can regain their autonomy and self-respect, they may be incorporated into settled Irish society.

For further information:

Adams, Barbara, et al. *Gypsies and Government Policy in England*. Heinemann Educational Books, 1975.

Commission on Itinerancy. *Report of the Commission on Itinerancy*. Dublin: The Stationery Office, 1963.

Gmelch, George. *The Irish Tinkers: The Urbanization of an Itinerant People*. Cummings Publishing Co., 1977.

Gmelch, Sharon Bohn. *Tinkers and Travellers*. McGill-Queens University Press, 1976.

MacMahon, Bryan. "A Portrait of Tinkers." *Natural History*, Vol. 80, No. 10, 1971.

TOPIC FIFTEEN

Applied Anthropology

....

The application of anthropological research to the solution of problems raises many serious questions. For example, who should decide what problems need addressing? Who should control the programs that are built to address them? Who should have the last word in the design of such programs?

These questions are particularly troublesome where applied anthropology projects are intended to help economically marginal and politically oppressed groups—be these Peruvian peasants, Indian tribes in the United States, or inner-city self-help associations. During the Viet Nam war, anthropologists were recruited by the U.S. armed forces to design propaganda programs and to seek ways of improving the military's anti-guerrilla tactics. (This caused a storm of debate within the American Anthropological Association, which responded by developing a code of ethics for professional anthropologists emphasizing the research subjects' rights to know both the nature of a project and the intended use of its findings.)

But there is another side to the coin: Anthropology can, in its study of "foreign" ways, discover traditional definitions of, and approaches to, problems that challenge our own society. Such study may lead to worthwhile modifications in the way our society does things. Arthur Kleinman, in "The Failure of Western Medicine," argues that the technologizing of medical practice has led to a loss of vision: namely, we do not see that the *whole* person must be treated (people are more than the sum of their organs). Non-Western approaches to curing address people's *experiences* of their illnesses, as well as their diseases; in doing so, they have a lot to teach our neighborhood doctors.

42

The Failure of Western Medicine

BY ARTHUR KLEINMAN

Increasing numbers of patients are turning from professional health care to alternative forms of treatment—from orthopedic surgeons to chiropractors, from ophthalmologists to optometrists, from physicians to native healers. This lack of confidence in Western medicine springs, I believe, from the physician's disregard for the patient apart from his or her disease. This was not always so.

Several decades ago, before their ability to control disease began to increase dramatically, Western physicians were interested in treating both disease *and* illness—the way the patient perceives and experiences his disorder, in the context of family and society. Today, however, most physicians limit their care to the cure of disease—the biological disorder. If, for instance, a person has cancer, the physician uses surgery, radiation, and chemotherapy to treat the malignant tumor. But the modern physician's training leaves him unequipped to treat the illness: how the cancer is experienced by the patient, what meaning it holds for him, his family, friends, and fellow workers.

In one interview I witnessed, an anxious 20-year-old patient with kidney disease asked his doctor, "When will I be able to return to school?" The physician replied, "We'll see. I'm sorry I have to go now. I can't answer any more questions. Why don't you speak to the nurse?" When I asked the doctor why he failed to answer the patient's questions on this and five other occasions, he said, "The patient's questions don't matter. Nothing is gained from talking to him, except get-

ting him to take the medicine properly and to follow the right diet. It is much more important to study the laboratory findings. They show what is really going on inside his kidneys."

In this frank expression of the "veterinary" tendency in modern medicine, the physician failed to recognize that the experience of a biological disorder is distinct from the disorder itself. Sickness begins with a person's awareness of a change in his bodily feelings that is labeled either by the sufferer or his family as being "ill." The person does not experience the presence of bacteria or organ malfunction; he senses pain, disorientation, and distress. Others do not see the patient's disease. They respond to his behavior, to his illness. But instead of treating the patient's experiences, the modern physician restricts himself to attacking the bacteria or restoring the organ's function; there is no regular relationship between the disease and the illness. Patients with the same disease—a heart ailment, for instance—may experience different illnesses: One person may be debilitated and another not. The web of personal significance surrounding each illness represents some special combination of threat, loss, and gain. In addition, illness may, and often does, occur without disease. Fifty percent of patients' visits to doctors are for complaints without any clear biological basis.

Because the illness exists apart from the disease, but each is affected by the other, physicians may diagnose a disease properly but fail to cure it. Patients who do not understand the treatment or

who disagree with the physician's explanation often fail to follow the prescribed treatment. In one case, a professor insisted that he did not have coronary artery disease and resisted treatment, believing that to admit the disease would make him an invalid. It was not until a psychiatrist intervened that the cardiologist discussed the disease frankly with the patient and described the limited changes in his way of life that the treatment would entail.

This lack of concern with illness has contributed to the increasing tendency of patients to disregard doctors' instructions, the dissatisfaction with the quality of medical care, the explosive growth in malpractice suits, and to the trend in many industrial countries toward self-care. As a result, many scholars are reevaluating the effectiveness of Western medicine; others are recording native-healing practices in various countries and comparing them with the methods of Western physicians.

Unlike physicians, native healers focus on the patient's illness. They concentrate on the social and cultural aspects of treatment, dealing with sickness as a human problem that affects family functions and tears at the web of meaning that integrates day to day life, not as just an isolated event in the life of the patient. Native healers primarily use symbolic, religious, and ritualistic treatments. Their definition of illness as a social and cultural experience is a crucial part of the healing process.

Although studies of native healers have provided a rich record of medical practices in other cultures, they have not provided solid information about the success of folk healing. Too often researchers have taken the patient's word immediately after the therapeutic rite as the measure of the healer's success: "I feel better"; "The pain is gone"; "I can walk." Almost no one has studied patients over time after their healing experience to determine whether the treatment succeeded or failed—and why.

As a physician and an anthropologist, I am in a unique position to study folk medicine, working from a perspective that is both cultural and medical. On my three field trips to Taiwan, I have observed more than 500 patients being treated by Taiwanese shamans, or *tang-ki*, (literally, "divining youth"), as well as 25 *tang-kis* going through their healing rituals. I have studied several *tang-kis* and their patients extensively over months and even years. During my study of one *tang-ki*, I visited his shrine on seven consecutive nights and observed his new patients, whose complaints ranged from sickness to business problems to "bad fate." In order to determine the effectiveness of the *tang-ki's* treatment, for two months I followed a group of patients who were seen by the *tang-ki* on three consecutive evenings.

Tang-kis vary in their methods. Some spend more time talking to patients; some emphasize rituals; some specialize in prescribing medicines; and some are famous for treating certain kinds of problems and sicknesses. Despite these differences, they generally spend more time with their patients and explain more to them than either Western or traditional Chinese doctors do.

In Taiwan, encounters with Western-style doctors average just under five minutes, while those with Chinese-style physicians average seven and a half minutes. Encounters with the *tang-ki* last up to several hours in the shrine, but only five to 10 minutes are spent in formal consultation with the entranced *tang-ki*; most communication is between the patient and the *tang-ki's* assistants or other individuals at the shrine, who act as go-betweens. However, virtually all the time of the shaman-patient relationship is spent in explaining the disease and treatment, whereas Chinese-style doctors offer explanations to their patients for one and a half minutes and Western-style doctors for 40 seconds.

Since the *tang-ki's* advice is offered during a trance, it is usually either unintelligible or couched in special terms. Assistants, therefore, form a vital link between the healer and the patient. They interpret the *tang-ki's* instructions regarding rituals, medicine, changes in life style, and the solution of practical problems. They offer patients psychological support, calm them, and listen sympathetically to their complaints. Their function is similar to that of hospital social-service workers, paraprofessionals, and nurses.

Most patients report being satisfied with the care provided by *tang-kis* and believe this care to be at least partially successful. Despite this feeling, most patients who approach a *tang-ki* hedge their bets. Believing that full healing requires the cooperation of both god and man, they also go to a professional physician. Although *tang-kis* do not object to this dual treatment, they do not encourage it. Many claim they can cure all disorders, even cancer. At times, a *tang-ki's* claims keep his patients from seeking medical treatment for serious illnesses. In the case of a young woman suffering from acute hepatitis, a reliance on the powers of the *tang-ki* brought her close to death. But such effects are unusual in my experience.

One *tang-ki* I concentrated on lives and practices in Taipei. His explanations of sickness and healing contain a mixture of supernatural, classical Chinese medical, popular medical, and Western medical ideas.

During the seven nights I watched this *tang-ki* at work in his shrine, I counted 122 new patients. Fifty-four came seeking treatment for sickness; 33 came to have their fate foretold or their bad fortune treated; 24 came because of business or financial problems; and 11 came about personal or family problems. Most of the new patients were lower class, two thirds were female, and all were Taiwanese. At least one quarter were young children or infants.

The patients complained of a wide range of sicknesses: acute infections of the nose and throat, intestinal disorders (such as diarrhea), chronic disorders such as low back pain, arthritis, asthma, and emphysema. Other frequent complaints were chronic, vague symptoms that were the physiological manifestations of such psychological problems as anxiety, depression, and hysteria. Many children suffered from irritability, sleeplessness, and crying fits that were diagnosed as colic by local pediatricians, but treated by the shamans and the families of the children as "fright," a folk syndrome in Chinese culture.

Healing sessions occur every night at the shrine. The process begins after dinner and lasts until early the next morning. It can be divided into two separate parts: first, the time when the *tang-ki* is in his trance and consults with new patients (approximately one hour); and second, the rest of the evening, when the patients socialize with the members of the *tang-ki's* cult, praying, falling into trances, dancing, speaking in tongues, and engaging in activities with strong sexual overtones. Men and women massage each other, women rub the insides of their thighs, and men thrust their pelvises forward and back in imitation of the sex act. This ecstatic behavior, which is encouraged—and even expected—in the *tang-ki's* shrine, is unusual in Chinese culture and unsanctioned in any other public place.

After registering with one of the *tang-ki's* assistants, new patients burn incense and pray, asking the *tang-ki's* god about their problem. The patient throws divination blocks (half-moon-shaped pieces of wood) onto the floor and reads the god's reply to his prayer in their pattern; after the blocks indicate the god's consent, the patient waits for the *tang-ki* to go into a trance. An assistant then calls the patient, who consults with the entranced *tang-ki* about his problem. Occasionally the *tang-ki* asks a few questions, but more often he simply speaks to the patient in the name of the god believed to possess him. The *tang-ki* then prescribes various routine therapies for the patient's illness (ashes to drink, charms to eat or wear, brief therapeutic rituals, herbal medicines to drink, or certain foods to eat). He also gives advice to help the patient resolve practical problems and cope with personal and family distress. Then he pronounces the patient cured. The patient is instructed to return to the shrine regularly so that he will become possessed by the *tang-ki's* god; this possession will cast off sickness, which is frequently attributed to an attempted possession by another god. On returning to the shrine the patient is encouraged to become a regular member of the *tang-ki's* cult.

With each patient, the *tang-ki* performs two short rituals. In one he writes a charm in the air over the patient in order to transfer the god's power to him. In the other he moves his hands rapidly in front of the patient and makes a motion as if he were throwing something to the ground. This ritual cleanses the patient of bad spirits and evil influences. In the case of middle-aged or elderly people, he may massage the patients. Because of the sexual connotations, he avoids this ritual with younger patients.

After spending five minutes with the *tang-ki* the patient returns to his seat. He does not consult again with the entranced *tang-ki* but remains in the shrine for several hours, sitting quietly, meditating, praying, or resting. He talks with other patients who regularly attend the shrine and with the *tang-ki's* assistants, and he may engage in such ritual activities as burning spirit money to please an angry god or spirit, or buying special foods (which are later eaten by the patient and his family) to offer as sacrifices to the gods. If he obeys the *tang-ki's* directions, he will attend the shrine regularly, enter trances, and become a cult member in the hope of avoiding a relapse.

To ascertain the effectiveness of the *tang-ki's* treatment, I interviewed 12 of his patients in their homes two months after their first visit to the shrine. I had intended to interview 19 consecutive patients, but two gave the *tang-ki's* assistants wrong addresses and could not be located; three refused to be interviewed;

and two had moved out of the city.

I asked each patient to evaluate the treatment and to explain why it had succeeded or failed. I asked if either their symptoms or their behavior had changed and if they thought any improvement could have resulted from the natural course of their sickness. I also asked whether they had had other health care for the problem along with the *tang-ki's* treatment. I gathered a brief history of each patient's sickness and assessed his or her physiological and psychological status. Because I was unable to perform standard medical tests (such as physical examinations, x-rays, blood tests, or psychological exams), my judgment of a patient's condition was limited to personal observation.

At first the *tang-ki's* treatment seemed outstanding; of the 12 patients, 10 claimed that the treatment was at least partially effective, and only two patients claimed that it was a failure. Six of the patients claimed to be fully healed. But all 10 patients who claimed some degree of healing suffered from one of three kinds of problems: chronic but not dangerous illnesses in which I observed symptoms that persisted after treatment; self-limiting diseases that would have cured themselves without treatment; and psychological problems with physical manifestations. In all of these disorders, managing the personal, social, and cultural problems of illness is more important than treating the medical problems of disease.

The two cases that were not cured were the only ones involving severe disorders, one physiological and the other psychological. The first was a six-year-old girl with acute kidney disease whose condition worsened while her parents were taking her to the *tang-ki*; she subsequently spent a month undergoing modern medical treatment. The second was a 22-year-old girl with suicidal tendencies and a serious behavioral disorder, who was taken to the shrine against her will by her mother. She reported no improvement, but psychiatric care did not help either. Her mother felt that the *tang-ki* would have been effective had the girl tried him longer.

The patients who claimed improvement after the *tang-ki's* treatment defined healing in various ways. For some, changes in symptoms were most important; a lessening or departure of pain overshadowed other aspects of the treatment. In other cases changes in general attitude were deemed most important. If a patient felt better psychologically after attending the shrine, if he came away with a better outlook on life, he considered the *tang-ki* to have been effective. Social changes were also important, especially for women; they were able to derive benefits from getting out of the house and away from family stresses, socializing with friends, and enjoying the exciting atmosphere of the shrine. For some, the evaluation of the therapy was based on cultural belief. The very fact that the appropriate ritual was performed and the supernatural cause of the illness confirmed, provided evidence of healing.

Five of the 10 patients who claimed that the *tang-ki* helped them reported positive changes in both their symptoms and their attitudes (they felt happier); two reported improvements in symptoms but no attitude change; one reported no change in symptoms but a positive change in attitude; one even reported a worsening in symptoms but an improvement in attitude; and one, a 10-year-old boy with disciplinary problems, was reported to have had an improvement in his behavior. (There were no changes in his symptoms, since there were no symptoms to begin with.)

Clearly the patients evaluated their care in different ways. These differences frequently carried over into particular settings outside the patients' homes. Several patients told me that they would never give a negative evaluation of the *tang-ki's* treatment in his shrine, since to do so might prejudice the gods against them and make their conditions worse. Others could not bring themselves to dispute the *tang-ki*, his assistants, and the regular shrine attenders who constantly told them that they were being healed, even if they felt no improvement. Occasionally patients credited the *tang-ki* with curing them even when they had taken medication prescribed by a Western-style doctor (and known to be effective) during their healing.

More important than the differences among the patients in their evaluations of treatment are the differences between the *tang-ki* and modern Western-style physicians in their definitions of healing. Although the *tang-ki* agreed with the 10 patients who said they were healed, and reinforced these feelings by encouraging the patients to think of themselves as healed, my evaluations of their conditions, based on Western medical standards, differed. Only a few of the 10 cases seemed to provide evidence that supported the effectiveness of the *tang-ki*, and in these natural remission and the placebo effect could not be ruled out.

When it comes to curing acute, severe, medically defined diseases, the *tang-kis* are ineffective. However, the *tang-ki's* shrine, which forms part of the patient's social network, supports him through his sickness. The "clinical reality" of the shrine reflects the culture and society of Taiwan and has more in common with popular cultural beliefs and behavior than the clinical realities of Western-style and Chinese-style doctors' offices, where patients sit quietly and perhaps apprehensively awaiting their turn with the physician and where crucial personal and social problems relating to their sicknesses generally go untreated. The shrine puts the patient at ease; it provides what Jerome Frank has called "expectant faith," an expectation of cure that prepares the patient for successful treatment—even in the case of incurable diseases. Most important, its clinical reality routinely assures treatment of illness-related problems and through their resolution may alleviate some diseases as well.

Most primary medical care is directed toward treating people with disorders similar to those the native healer treats. Both physicians and native healers treat people with minimal chronic and psychosomatic complaints. But the modern physician is likely to fail with patients because he is trained to ignore the illness and to deal only with the disease. This pattern, which is built into the training of Western doctors, fails when applied to the healing of illness, a much more common complaint. Apparently aware of the distinction, the Taiwanese go to physicians for cures of life-threatening diseases, but to native healers for illnesses.

The solution to the problem of health care may not lie with the native healer, even in developing countries. My observation of them indicates that shamans and other religious healers are too tightly bound by social and cultural constraints to be able to diagnose and treat disease systematically and effectively. Secular native healers, like Chinese-style doctors in the People's Republic of China, on the other hand, may be in a good position to integrate biomedical practices with their healing activities—although some are probably no better than Western physicians at treating illness. A more fundamental approach to health in the Third World would be to train people who already have experience in treating illnesses to recognize and manage routine diseases. The "barefoot doctors" of the People's Republic of China may already have accomplished this.

But Western physicians could broaden their own skills and knowledge, allowing them to treat both disease and illness. I am recommending not that Western physicians learn to go into trances or ask patients to burn spirit money, but that they learn to treat sickness in the context of the patient's psychology and culture. Physicians need, for example, to question patients about what they think caused their problems; how they think their illnesses should be treated; what threats, losses, and gains their sickness represents; and what conflicts they perceive between their values and the doctor's professional values.

Doctors need to be as precise in defining the life problems created by an illness as in investigating its biological basis. They should be as competent in prescribing behavioral and social management strategies for treating the illness as in prescribing technological interventions for the disease. This takes time, effort, and training. But only when physicians again treat the patient's illness, as well as his disease, and treat it with a systematic approach based on the findings of clinical social science, not with a folksy parody of shamans or old-time general practitioners, will the persistent dissatisfaction with modern medicine begin to fade. Following the example of the native healer, though not his specific methods, may be the best way to introduce humanistic medicine into the developed world.

For further information:

Eisenberg, Leon. "Disease and Illness." *Culture, Medicine and Psychiatry*, Volume 1, 1977, pp. 9-24.

Kleinman, Arthur. *Patients and Healers in the Context of Culture*. University of California Press, forthcoming.

Kleinman, Arthur, and L. H. Sung. "Why Do Indigenous Practitioners Successfully Heal?" *Social Science and Medicine*, in press.

Kleinman, Arthur, et al., eds. *Culture and Healing in Asian Societies*. Schenkman Publishing Company, 1978.

Glossary

Abbevillean (or Chellean) culture The earlier of two stages in the hand ax (bifacial core tool) tradition, lasting approximately 1,000,000 to 400,000 B.P.; found across southerly and medium latitudes of the Old World, radiating out from Africa to southwest Europe and as far east as India; associated with *Homo erectus*.

absolute dating Physical-chemical dating methods that tie archaeologically retrieved artifacts into clearly specified time ranges calculated in terms of an abstract standard, such as the calendar.

acclimatization The process by which an organism's sweat glands, metabolism, and associated mechanisms adjust to a new and different climate.

acculturation Those adaptive cultural changes that come about in a minority culture when its adherents come under the influence of a more dominant society and take up many of the dominant culture's traits.

Acheulian culture The second stage of the hand ax bifacial core tool tradition; associated primarily with *Homo erectus*; found in southern and middle latitudes all across the Old World from India to Africa and West Europe; lasting in toto from about 400,000 to 60,000 B.P.

adaptation The processes by which groups become fitted, physically and culturally, to particular environments over several generations. This comes about through natural selection on the biological level and the modification and selective passing on of cultural traits and practices on the cultural level.

adaptational approach A theoretical approach to cultural change with the underlying assumption that, in order to survive, human beings must organize themselves into social, economic, and political groups that somehow fit in with the resources and challenges of a particular environment.

adultery Sexual intercourse by a married person with a person other than the legal spouse.

Aegyptopithecus An especially important Oligocene ape form, dated to 28 million years ago, and found in the Fayum area of Egypt. It represents a probable evolutionary link between the prosimian primates of the Paleocene and Eocene, and the apes of the Miocene and Pliocene. *Aegyptopithecus* probably was ancestral to *Dryopithecus*, and thus possibly to modern apes and humans.

affinal kin A kin relationship involving one marriage link (for example, a husband is related by affinity to his wife and her consanguineals).

age grades Specialized hierarchical associations based on age that cut across entire societies.

agnatic kin Kin related to one through males.

agonistic interactions A term used mostly to refer to animal behavior that is aggressive or unfriendly, including the behavior of both the initiator and the recipient of aggression.

agriculture Domesticated food production involving minimally the cultivation of plants but usually also the raising of domesticated animals; more narrowly, plant domestication making use of the plow (versus horticulture).

alleles Alternative forms of a single gene.

alliance theory A theoretical approach to the study of descent that emphasizes reciprocal exchanges among descent groups as the basic mechanism of social integration.

allomorph In language, one of the different-sounding versions of the same morpheme (unit of meaning).

allophone In language, one of the different sounds (phones) that represent a single phoneme.

alveolar ridge Thickened portions of the upper and lower interior jaws in which the teeth are set.

ambilineal descent The reckoning of descent group membership by an individual through either the mother's or the father's line—at the individual's option. See also *cognatic descent*.

androgens The hormones, present in relatively large quantities in the testes, that are responsible for the development of the male secondary sex characteristics.

angular gyrus An area of the brain crucial to human linguistic ability that serves as a link between the parts of the brain that receive stimuli from the sense organs of sight, hearing, and touch.

animatism The attribution of life to inanimate objects.

animism The belief that objects (including people) in the concretely perceivable world have a nonconcrete, spiritual element. For human beings, this element is the soul.

anomie The state of normlessness, usually found in societies undergoing crises, that renders social control over individual behavior ineffective.

Anthropoidea Suborder of the order of Primates that includes monkeys, apes, and humans.

anthropology The systematic study of the nature of human beings and their works, past and present.

anthropometry A subdivision of physical anthropology concerned with measuring and statistically analyzing the dimensions of the human body.

anthropomorphism The ascription of human characteristics to objects not human—often deities or animals.

antigens Proteins with specific molecular properties located on the surface of red blood cells.

ape A large, tailless, semi-erect primate of the family *Pongidae*. Living species include the orangutan, gorilla, chimpanzee, gibbon, and siamang.

applied anthropology The use of anthropological concepts, methods, theories, and findings to achieve a desired social goal.

archaeological site See *site*.

archaeology The systematic retrieval, identification, and study of the physical and cultural remains that human beings and their ancestors have left behind them deposited in the earth.

aristocracy The privileged, usually land-owning, class of a society (for example, the ruling nobility of prerevolutionary France).

articulatory features Speech events described in terms of the speech organs employed in their utterance rather than from the nature of the sounds themselves.

artifact Any object manufactured, modified, or used by human beings to achieve a culturally defined goal.

ascribed status The social position a person comes to occupy on the basis of such uncontrollable characteristics as sex, age, or circumstances of birth.

assemblage The artifacts of one component of a site.

assimilation The disappearance of a minority group through the loss of particular identifying physical or sociocultural characteristics.

associated regions Broad regions surrounding the three geographical centers where agriculture was invented. Here different plants and animals were domesticated, and then spread individually throughout the whole area.

Aurignacian culture Upper Paleolithic culture that some scholars claim may represent a separate Middle Eastern migration into Europe; flourished in western Europe from 33,000 to 25,000 B.P. The Aurignacians began the European tradition of bone carving. The skeletal remains associated with this culture are the famous Cro-Magnon fossils.

australopithecine An extinct grade in hominid evolution found principally in early to mid-Pleistocene in eastern and southern Africa, usually accorded subfamily status (*Australopithecinae*, within *Hominidae*).

Austrolopithecus afarensis Early austrolopithecine form, dating to over 3.5 million years ago, found in the Afar region of Ethiopia. Current debate centers on whether or not this form was directly ancestral to human beings.

Australopithecus africanus The original type specimen of australopithecines discovered in 1924 at Taung, South Africa, and dating from approximately 3.5 million years ago to approximately 1.6 million years ago. Belongs to the gracile line of the australopithecines.

Australopithecus boisei One of two species of robust australopithecines, appearing approximately 1.6 million years ago in sub-Saharan Africa.

Australopithecus habilis See *Homo habilis*.

Australopithecus robustus One of two species of robust australopithecines, found in both eastern and southern Africa, first appearing about 3.5 million years ago.

avunculocal residence The practice by which a newlywed couple establishes residence with, or in the locale of, the groom's maternal uncle. A feature of some matrilineal societies that facilitates the men's maintaining their political power.

Aztec civilization Final Postclassic Mesoamerican civilization, dated from about A.D. 1300 to 1521, when Cortes conquered and destroyed the empire. The Aztec capital at Tenochtitlán (now Mexico City) housed some 300,000 people. Aztec society was highly stratified, dominated by a military elite.

balanced reciprocity The straightforward exchange of goods or services that both parties regard as equivalent at the time of the exchange.

baboon Large, terrestrial Old World monkey. Baboons have long, doglike muzzles, short tails, and are highly organized into troops.

band The simplest level of social organization; marked by very little political organization and consisting of small groups (50 to 300 persons) of families.

bartering The exchange of goods whose equivalent value is established by negotiation, usually in a market setting.

bifaces Stone artifacts that have been flaked on two opposite sides, most typically the hand axes produced by *Homo erectus*.

bifurcation Contrast among kin types based on the distinction between the mother's and father's kinfolk.

bilateral descent The reckoning of descent through both male and female lines. Typically found in Europe, the United States, and Southeast Asia.

bilateral kin A kin relationship in which an individual is linked equally to relatives of both sexes on both sides of the family.

bilocal residence The practice by which a newlywed couple has a choice of residence, but must establish residence with, or in the locale of, one or the other set of parents.

bipedalism The predominant use of the hind (two) legs for locomotion.

blade tool A long and narrow flake tool that has been knocked off a specially prepared core.

bound morpheme In language, a unit of meaning (represented by a sound sequence) that can only occur when linked to another morpheme (for example, suffixes and prefixes).

B.P. An abbreviation used in archaeology, meaning before the present.

brachiation A method of locomotion, characteristic of the pongids, in which the animal swings hand over hand through the trees, while its body is suspended by the arms.

breeding population In population genetics, all individuals in a given population who potentially, or actually, mate with one another.

brideprice A gift from the groom and his family to the bride and her family prior to their marriage. The custom legitimizes children born to the wife as members of her husband's descent group.

Broca's area An area of the brain located toward the front of the dominant side of the brain that activates, among other things, the muscles of the lips, jaw, tongue, and larynx. A crucial biological substratum of speech.

brow ridge A continuous ridge of bone in the skull, curving over the eyes and connected across the bridge of the nose.

burins Chisel-like Upper Paleolithic stone tools produced by knocking small chips off the end(s) of a blade, and used for carving wood, bone, and antlers to fashion spear and harpoon points. Unlike end scrapers, burins were used for fine engraving and delicate carving.

call systems Systems of communication of nonhuman primates, consisting of a limited number of specific sounds (calls) conveying specific meanings to members of the group, largely restricted to emotional or motivational states.

capitalism Economic system featuring private ownership of the means of production and distribution.

cargo cults Revitalization movements (also designated as revivalist, nativistic, or millenarian) that received their name from movements in Melanesia early in the twentieth century. Characterized by the belief that the millenium will be ushered in by the arrival of great ships or planes loaded with European trade goods (cargo).

carotene A yellowish pigment in the skin.

caste A hereditary, endogamous group of people bearing a common name and often having the same traditional occupation.

caste system A stratification system within which the social strata are hereditary and endogamous. The entire system is sanctioned by the mores, laws, and usually the religion of the society in question.

Catarrhini Old World anthropoids; one of two infraorders of the suborder of *Anthropoidea*, order of Primates. Includes Old World monkeys, apes, and humans.

catastrophism A school of thought, popular in the late eighteenth and early nineteenth centuries, proposing that old life forms became extinct through natural catastrophes, of which Noah's flood was the latest.

cephalic index A formula for computing long-headedness and narrow-headedness:

$$\frac{\text{head breadth}}{\text{head length}} \times 100$$

A low cephalic index indicates a narrow head.

Cercopithecoidea One of two superfamilies of the infraorder *Catarrhini*, consisting of the Old World monkeys.

cerebral cortex The "grey matter" of the brain, associated primarily with thinking and language use. The expansion of the cortex is the most recent evolutionary development of the brain.

ceremonial center Large permanent site that reveals no evidence of occupation on a day-to-day basis. Ceremonial centers are composed almost exclusively of structures used for religious purposes.

Chavin culture Highland Peruvian culture dating from about 1000 to 200 B.C. It was the dominant culture in the central Andes for some 700 years.

Chellean handax A bifacial core tool from which much (but not all) of the surface has been chipped away, characteristic of the Abbevillean (or Chellean) culture. Produced by *Homo erectus*.

chiefdom Estate, place, or dominion of a chief. Currently the term is used also to refer to a society at a level of social integration a stage above that of tribal society, characterized by a redistributive economy and centralized political authority.

chimpanzee (*Pan troglodytes***)** Along with the gorilla and the orangutan, one of the great apes; found exclusively in Africa; one of *Homo sapiens'* closest relatives.

choppers Unifacial core tools, sometimes called pebble tools, found associated with *Homo habilis* in Olduvai sequence, and also with *Homo erectus* in East Asia.

chromosomal sex The sex identity of a person determined by the coded message in the sex chromosome contributed by each parent.

chromosome Helical strands of complex protein molecules found in the nuclei of all animal cells, along which the genes are located. Normal human somatic cells have forty-six chromosomes.

circumcision The removal of the foreskin of a male or the clitoral sheath of a female.

circumscription theory Theory of the origins of the state advanced by Robert Carneiro and others that emphasizes natural and social barriers to population expansion as major factors in producing the state.

civilization Consists of all those life-styles incorporating at least four of the following five elements: (1) agriculture; (2) urban living; (3) a high degree of occupational specialization and differentiation; (4) social stratification; and (5) literacy.

clan An exogamous unilineal kin group consisting of two or more lineages tracing descent from an unknown, perhaps legendary, founder.

class A stratum in a hierarchically organized social system; unlike a caste, endogamy is not a requirement (though it is often favored), and individuals do have the possibility (though not the probability) of moving to a neighboring stratum.

class consciousness An awareness by members of a social stratum of their common interests.

Classical archaeology A field within archaeology that concerns itself with the reconstruction of the classical civilizations, such as Greece, Rome, and Egypt.

Classic period Spectacular and sophisticated Mesoamerican cultural period dated from A.D. 300 to 900; marked by the rise of great civilizations and the building of huge religious complexes and cities. By A.D. 500, the Classical city of Teotihuacán housed some 120,000 people.

class system A stratification system in which the individual's position is usually determined by the economic status of the family head, but the individual may potentially rise or fall from one class to another through his or her own efforts or failings.

cognatic descent A form of descent by which the individual may choose to affiliate with either the mother's or father's kinship group. See also *ambilineal descent*.

cognatic kin Those relatives of all generations on both sides of the family, out to some culturally defined limit.

collateral kin Those nonlineal relatives in one's own generation on both sides of the family, out to some culturally defined limit.

colonialism The process by which a foreign power holds

political, economic, and social control over another people and establishes outposts of its own citizens among that people.

comparative linguistics (historical linguistics) A field of linguistics that attempts to describe formally the basic elements of languages and the rules by which they are ordered into intelligible speech.

communication The exchange of information between two or more organisms.

communist society A society marked by public or state ownership of the means of production and distribution.

composite family The situation in which multiple marriages are practiced or in which the residence rule requires a couple to reside with parents. See also *extended family; polygamy.*

consanguineal kin A kin relationship based on biological connections only.

continental drift Hypothesis introduced by Alfred Wegener, in the early twentieth century, of the breakup of a super-continent, Pangaea, beginning around 225 million years ago and resulting in the present positions of the continents.

core tool A rough, unfinished stone tool shaped by knocking off flakes, used to crush the heads of small game, to skin them, and to dissect the carcasses.

couvade The custom, in many societies, for fathers to participate in the period of recuperation, after their wives give birth, by remaining inactive for a long period of time—often much longer than the women.

cranial index Anatomical measure computed on skeletal material, otherwise similar to the cephalic index.

cranium The skull, excluding the jaw.

creation myth A religiously validated tale, unique to each culture, in which ancestors become separated from the rest of the animal kingdom, accounting for the society's biological and social development.

Cro-Magnon A term broadly referring to the first modern humans, from 40,000 to 10,000 B.P. Specifically refers to humans living in southwestern France during the same period.

cross-cousins Cousins related through ascending generation linking kin (often parental siblings) of the opposite sex (for example, mother's brother's children or father's sister's children).

cultural anthropology The study of the cultural diversity of contemporary societies. It can be divided into two aspects: ethnography and ethnology.

cultural area A part of the world in which the inhabitants share many of the elements of culture, such as related languages, similar economic systems, social systems, and ideological systems; an outmoded concept that is seldom used.

cultural assemblage See *assemblage.*

cultural components (of a site) All the different divisions that can be found in a site.

cultural ecology (of a group) The ways in which a group copes with and exploits the potentials of its environment.

cultural evolution The process of invention, diffusion, and elaboration of the behavior that is learned and taught in groups and is transmitted from generation to generation; often used to refer to the development of social complexity.

cultural relativism A methodological orientation in an-thropology, the basis of which is the idea that every culture is unique and therefore each cultural item must be understood in its own terms.

culture The patterned behavior and mental constructs that individuals learn, are taught, and share within the context of the groups to which they belong.

cuneiform Wedged-shaped writing developed by the Sumerian civilization.

cytoplasm The living matter in a cell, except the nucleus.

Darwinism The theoretical approach to biological evolution first presented by Charles Darwin and Alfred Russel Wallace in 1858. The central concept of the theory is natural selection, referring to the greater probability of survival and reproduction of those individuals of a species having adaptive characteristics for a given environment.

demographic study Population study, primarily concerned with such aspects of population as analyses of fertility, mortality, and migration.

dental formula The number of incisors, canines, premolars, and molars found in one upper and one lower quadrant of a jaw. The human formula, which we share with the apes and Old World monkeys, is shown below:

I	C	P	M
2	1	2	3
2	1	2	3

deoxyribonucleic acid (DNA) The hereditary material of the cell, capable of self-replication and of coding the production of proteins carrying on metabolic functions.

descent The practice of bestowing a specific social identity on a person as a consequence of his or her being born to a specific mother and/or father.

descent group A corporate entity whose membership is acquired automatically as a consequence of the genealogical connections between members and their offspring.

descent rule The principle used to trace lineal kin links from generation to generation. A child is filiated to both of its parents, but the descent rule stresses one parent's line and sex as links with others, over the other parent's line and sex.

descriptive kinship terminology The classification of kinspeople in ego's (the individual's) own generation, with a separate kin term for each kin type.

descriptive linguistics The careful recording, description of, and structural analysis of existing languages.

diachronics The comparative study of culture and society as they change through time in a specified geographical area.

differential fertility A major emphasis in the modern (or synthetic) theory of evolution, which stresses the importance of an organism actually reproducing and transmitting its genes to the next generation.

diffusion The spread of cultural traits from one people to another.

diffusionism The belief held by some European cultural anthropologists of the nineteenth and early twentieth century that all culture began in one or a few areas of the world and then spread outward.

diluvialism A school of thought, popular in the late eighteenth and early nineteenth centuries, claiming that Noah's flood accounted for the existence of extinct fossil forms.

diploid number The number of chromosomes normally found in the nucleus of somatic cells. In humans, the number is forty-six.

displacement The process by which sexual, aggressive, or other energies are diverted into other outlets. When these outlets are socially approved, the process is called sublimation.

divination The use of magic to predict the behavior of another person or persons, or even the course of natural events.

division of labor The universally practiced allotment of different work tasks to subgroupings of a society. Even the least complex societies allot different tasks to the two sexes and also distinguish different age groups for work purposes.

DNA See *deoxyribonucleic acid*.

domesticants Domesticated plants and/or animals.

dominance hierarchy The social ranking order supposed to be present in most or all primate species.

dominant allele The version of a gene that masks out other versions' ability to affect the phenotype of an organism when both alleles co-occur heterozygotically.

double descent A form of descent by which an individual belongs both to a patriline and a separate matriline, but usually exercises the rights of membership in each group separately and situationally.

dowry The wealth bestowed on a bride or a new couple by her parents.

Dryopithecus The most common Miocene ape genus, known from Africa, Europe, and Asia, and dated from 20 to 10 million years ago. A forest-dwelling ape with about six or seven species, *Dryopithecus* was most probably ancestral to modern apes and may have been ancestral to humans.

duality of patterning A feature of human language, it consists of sequences of sounds that are themselves meaningless (phonemes) and also of units of meaning (morphemes).

ecological niche Features of the environment(s) that an organism inhabits, that pose problems and create opportunities for the organism's survival.

ecology The science of the interrelationships between living organisms and their natural environments.

ecosystem A system containing both the physical environment and the organisms that inhabit it.

egalitarian society A society that makes all achieved statuses equally accessible to all its adult members.

emics The culturally organized cognitive constructs of a people being investigated (the "folk perspective"). See *etics*.

enculturation The lifelong process of learning one's culture and its values and learning how to act within the acceptable limits of behavior in culturally defined contexts.

endogamy The custom by which members of a group marry exclusively within the group.

environment All aspects of the surroundings in which an individual or group finds itself, from the geology, topography, and climate of the area to its vegetational cover and insect, bird, and animal life.

estrogens The hormones, produced in relatively large quantities by the ovaries, that are responsible for the development of female secondary sex characteristics.

estrous cycle The approximately four-week reproductive cycle of female mammals.

estrus The phase of the approximately four-week cycle in female mammals during which the female is receptive to males and encourages copulation.

ethnic group A group of people within a larger social and cultural unit who identify themselves as a culturally and historically distinct entity, separate from the rest of that society.

ethnicity The characteristic cultural, linguistic, and religious traditions that a given group of people use to establish their distinct social identity—usually within a larger social unit.

ethnocentrism The tendency of all human groups to consider their own way of life superior to all others and to judge the life-styles of other groups (usually negatively) in terms of their own value system.

enthnographic analogy A method of archaeological interpretation in which the behavior of the ancient inhabitants of an archaeological site is inferred from the similarity of their artifacts to those used by living peoples.

ethnography The intensive description of individual societies, usually small, isolated, and relatively homogeneous.

ethnology The systematic comparison and analysis of ethnographic materials, usually with the specification of evolutionary stages of development of legal, political, economic, technological, kinship, religious, and other systems.

etics The perspective of Western social science in general and anthropology in particular, as applied to the study of different cultures. See *emics*.

evolution The progress of life forms and social forms from the simple to the complex. In Herbert Spencer's terms, evolution is "change from an indefinite, incoherent homogeneity to a definite, coherent heterogeneity; through continuous differentiations and integrations." In narrow biological terms, evolution is the change in gene and allele frequencies within a breeding population over generations.

evolutionary progress The process by which a social or biological form can respond to the demands of the environment by becoming more adaptable and flexible. In order to achieve this, the form must develop to a new stage of organization that makes it more versatile in coping with problems of survival posed by the environment.

excessive fertility The notion that organisms tend to reproduce more offspring than actually survive; one of the principal points in Darwin's theory of organic evolution.

exchange marriage Usually describes the situation in which two men marry each other's sister. The term is sometimes used for more complicated patterns in which groups exchange women to provide wives for the men.

exogamy The custom by which members of a group regularly marry outside the group.

extended family A linking together of two or more nuclear families: horizontally, through a sibling link; or vertically, through the parent-child link.

family A married couple or other group of adult kinsfolk and their immature offspring, all or most of whom share a common dwelling and who cooperate economically.

family of orientation (family of origin) Nuclear or elementary family (consisting of husband, wife, and offspring) into which an individual is born and is reared and in which he or she is considered a child in relation to the parents.

family of procreation Nuclear or elementary family (consisting of husband, wife, and offspring) formed by the marriage of an individual, in which he or she is a parent.

feudalism The sociopolitical system characterizing medieval Europe, in which all land was owned by a ruling aristocracy that extracted money, goods, and labor (often forced) from the peasant class in return for letting the peasants till the soil.

fictive kin Extensions of the affect and social behavior usually shown toward genealogically related kin to particular persons with whom one has special relationships— godparents, blood brothers, and so on.

field study The principal methods by which anthropologists gather information, using either the participant-observation technique to investigate social behavior, excavation techniques to retrieve archaeological data, or recording techniques to study languages.

flake tool A tool made by preparing a flint core, then striking it to knock off a flake, which then can be worked further to produce the particular tool needed.

folklore Refers to a series of genres or types of culturally standardized stories transmitted from person to person (usually orally or by example).

folk taxonomy The cognitive categories and their hierarchical relations characteristic of a particular culture by which a specific group classifies all the objects of the universe it recognizes.

foraging society A society with an economy based solely on the collection of wild plant foods, the hunting of animals, and/or fishing.

Foramen magnum The "large opening" in the cranium of vertebrates through which the spinal cord passes.

formal negative sanction Deliberately organized, social response to individuals' behavior that usually takes the form of legal punishment.

formal positive sanction Deliberately organized, social response to individuals' behavior that takes the form of a ceremony sponsored by a central authority conveying social approval.

formal sanction Socially organized (positive or negative) response to individuals' behavior that is applied in a very visible, patterned manner under the direct or indirect leadership of authority figures.

fossils Remains of plant and animal forms that lived in the past and that have been preserved through a process by which they either leave impressions in stone or become stonelike themselves.

free morpheme In language, a unit of meaning (represented by a sound sequence) that can stand alone.

functionalism A mode of analysis, used particularly in the social sciences, that attempts to explain social and cultural phenomena in terms of the contributions they make to the maintenance of sociocultural systems.

functionalist anthropology A perspective of anthropology associated with Bronislaw Malinowski and A. R. Radcliffe-Brown. The former emphasized the meeting of biological and psychological "needs," the latter social "needs."

gametes The sex cells that, as sperm in males and eggs in females, combine to form a new human being as a fetus in a mother's womb.

gender identity The attachment of significance to a self-identification as a member of a sexually defined group and the adopting of behavior culturally appropriate to that group.

gender roles Socially learned behaviors that are typically manifested by persons of one sex and rarely by persons of the opposite sex in a particular culture.

gene The unit of biological heredity; a segment of DNA that codes for the synthesis of a single protein.

gene flow (admixture) The movement of genes from one population into another as a result of interbreeding in cases where previous intergroup contact had been impossible or avoided because of geographical, social, cultural, or political barriers.

gene frequency The relative presence of one allele in relation to another in a population's gene pool.

gene pool The sum total of all individuals' genotypes included within a given breeding population.

generalized exchange (reciprocity) The giving of gifts without expecting a direct return but in expectation of an "evening out" of gifts in the long run.

generative grammar (transformational grammar) A theory about a specific language that accounts in a formal manner for all the possible (permitted) strings of elements of that language and also for the structural relationships among the elements constituting such strings.

genetic drift The shift of gene frequencies as a consequence of genetic sampling errors that come from the migration of small subpopulations away from the parent group, or natural disasters that wipe out a large part of a population.

genetic load The number of deleterious or maladaptive genes that exist in the gene pool of a population or entire species.

genetic plasticity A characteristic of the human species that allows humans to develop a variety of limited physiological and anatomical responses or adjustments to a given environment.

genotype The genetic component that each individual inherits from his or her parents.

geographic center One of three regions in the world—the Middle East, East Asia, and the Americas—in which agriculture probably was invented independently.

gift exchange The giving of a gift from one group or individual to another with the expectation that the gift will be returned in similar form and quantity at the time or at a later date.

glottochronology A mathematical technique for dating language change.

gonadal sex Refers to the form, structure, and position of the hormone-producing gonads (ovaries, located within the pelvic cavity in females, and testes, located in the scrotum in males).

gorilla (*Gorilla gorilla*) The largest of the anthropoid (Great) apes and of the living primates; found exclusively in Africa.

government The administrative apparatus of the political organization in a society.

gracile australopithecines One of the two lines of australopithecine development, first appearing about 3.5 million years ago; usually refers to the fossil forms *Australopithecus africanus* and *Australopithecus afarensis*.

grammar According to Leonard Bloomfield, "the meaningful arrangements of forms in a language."

grid system A method of retrieving and recording the positions of remains from an archaeological dig.

Habilis. See *Homo habilis.*

habitation site A place where whole groups of people spent some time engaged in the generalized activities of day-to-day living.

hand ax An unspecialized flint bifacial core tool, primarily characteristic of the Lower and Middle Paleolithic, made by chipping flakes off a flint nodule and using the remaining core as the tool; produced by *Homo erectus*, later by *Homo sapiens neanderthalensis*.

hand ax tradition A technological tradition developed out of the pebble tool tradition, occuring from about 600,000 to about 60,000 years ago during the Lower and Middle Paleolithic; primarily associated with *Homo erectus*.

haploid number The number of chromosomes normally occurring in the nucleus of a gamete (sex cell). For humans, the number is twenty-three (one-half the diploid number).

Harappan civilization Civilization in the northwest corner of the Indian subcontinent (roughly, in present-day Pakistan), which reached its peak about 2000 B.C. Its major cities were Mohenjo-Daro and Harappa.

Hardy-Weinberg law The principle that in large breeding populations, under conditions of random mating and where natural selection is not operating, the frequencies of genes or alleles will remain constant from one generation to the next.

hemoglobin Complex protein molecule that carries oxygen through the bloodstream, giving blood its red color.

heredity (genetics) The innate capacity of an individual to develop characteristics possessed by its parents and other lineal ancestors.

heritability The proportion of the measurable variation in a given trait in a specified population estimated to result from hereditary rather than environmental factors.

heterozygote The new cell formed when the sperm and egg contain different alleles of the same gene.

heterozygous A condition in which two different alleles occur at a given locus (place) on a pair of homologous (matched pair of) chromosomes.

historical archaeology The investigation of all literate societies through archaeological means.

historical linguistics The study of the evolutionary tree of language. Historical linguistics reconstructs extinct "proto" forms by systematically comparing surviving language branches.

holism The viewing of the whole context of human behavior—a fundamental theme of anthropology.

Holocene The most recent geologic epoch; it began about 10,000 years ago.

homeostasis The process by which a system maintains its equilibrium using feedback mechanisms to accommodate inputs from its environment.

home range (of a primate group) An area through which a primate group habitually moves in the course of its daily activities.

hominid The common name for those primates referred to in the taxonomic family *Hominidae* (modern humans and their nearest evolutionary predecessors).

Hominidae Human beings, one of *Hominoidea*. See also *hominid*.

Hominoidea One of two superfamilies of *Catarrhini*, consisting of apes and human beings.

Homo erectus Middle Pleistocene hominid form that is the direct ancestor of *Homo sapiens*. It appeared about 1.9 million years ago, flourished until about 200,000 to 250,000 years ago. *H. erectus* was about five feet tall, with a body and limbs that were within the range of variation of modern humans, and had a cranial capacity ranging from 900 to 1200 cubic centimeters.

Homo habilis ("handy man") A fossil form, dating from more than 2 million years ago, whose evolutionary status is disputed. Some physical anthropologists regard it as early *Homo*—the first members of our own genus. Others regard it as an advanced form of gracile australopithecine. This is the earliest hominid with which stone tools have been found in unambiguous relationship.

Homo sapiens neanderthalensis The first subspecies of *Homo sapiens*, appearing some 300,000 years ago and becoming extinct about 35,000 B.P. Commonly known as Neanderthal man.

Homo sapiens sapiens The second subspecies of *Homo sapiens*, including all contemporary humans, appearing about 60,000 years ago. The first human subspecies was the now extinct *Homo sapiens neanderthalensis*.

homologous A matched pair; usually refers to chromosomes, one from each parent, having the same genes in the same order.

homozygote The new cell formed when the sperm and egg contain the same allele of a particular gene.

homozygous A condition in which identical genes occur at a certain locus on homologous (matched pair) chromosomes.

horizontal extended family A household and cooperating unit of two siblings and their respective spouses and children.

hormonal sex The type of hormone mix (estrogens or androgens) produced by the gonads.

horticulture The preparation of land for planting and the tending of crops using only the hoe or digging stick; characterized especially by the absence of use of the plow.

hunting and gathering society A society that subsists on the collection of plants and animals existing in the natural environment. See *foraging society*.

hybrid vigor The phenomenon that occurs when a new generation, whose parent groups were from previously separated breeding populations, is generally healthier and larger than either of the parent populations.

hydraulic theory A theory of the origins of the state advanced by Karl Wittfogel that traces the rise of the state to the organization, construction, and maintenance of vast dam and irrigation projects.

hypothesis A tentative assumption, which must be tested, about the relationship(s) between specific events or phenomena.

ideology A belief system linked to and legitimating the political and economic interests of the group that subscribes to it.

imperialism The expansionist policy of nation-states by

which one state assumes political and economic control over another.

Inca Empire Empire of the Late Horizon period of Peruvian prehistory, dated about A.D. 1438 to 1540. The ninth and tenth Incas (kings) seized control of a 3,000-mile-long empire stretching from Quito to central Chile. The Incas had a highly sophisticated political organization.

incest Usually refers to sexual relations between father and daughter, mother and son, or brother and sister. In some societies the definition is extended to include larger numbers of consanguineal relatives, especially if the society is organized along the principle of lineages and clans.

incest taboo The nearly universal prohibition against sexual intercourse between family members, with the limits of incest varying from culture to culture on the basis of the society's kinship system and forms of social organization.

independent invention The process whereby two or more cultures develop similar elements without the benefit of cultural exchange or even contact.

independent assortment See *Law of Independent Assortment.*

Indus Valley civilization See *Harappan civilization.*

industrialism The form of production characterizing post-agricultural societies, in which goods are produced by mechanical means using machines and labor organized into narrowly defined task groups that engage in repetitive, physically simplified, and highly segmented work.

industrialization The process involving the growth of manufacturing industries in hitherto predominantly agrarian, pastoral, or foraging societies.

industrial society A society with a high degree of economic development that largely utilizes mechanization and highly segmented labor specialization for the production of its goods and services.

infanticide The killing of a baby soon after birth.

informal sanction A social response to an individual's behavior that is enacted individually by group members, with minimal organization by social authority.

informant A member of a society who establishes a working relationship with a fieldworker, providing him or her with information regarding that society.

instrumental belief system An organized set of ideas about phenomena necessary for survival and for performing day-to-day (functional) tasks.

integration, cultural The condition of harmonious pattern maintenance potentially characterizing cultural systems.

interglacial Refers to periods during which glaciers retreat and a general warming trend occurs in the climate.

internalized controls An individual's beliefs and values that mirror the beliefs and values of the group culture and that induce the individual to behave in ways appropriate to that culture.

invention The development of new ideas, techniques, resources, aptitudes, or applications that are adopted by a society and become part of its cultural repertoire.

involution Evolution through which a biological or social form adapts to its environment by becoming more and more specialized and efficient in exploiting the resources of that environment. Sometimes called specific evolution.

irrigation The artificial use of water for agriculture by means of human technology when naturally available water (rainfall or seasonal flooding) is insufficient or potentially too destructive to sustain desired crop production.

ischial callosities Bare, calloused areas of skin on the hindquarters, frequently found in terrestrial or semiterrestrial Old World monkeys.

kill site A place where prehistoric people killed and butchered animals.

kibbutz A collective settlement in Israel with strong emphasis on communal life and values; one of the forms of cooperative agricultural villages in Israel that is collective (to a greater or less degree) in the organization of work, ownership of all resources, child rearing, and living arrangements.

kin category A terminologically distinguished aggregate of persons with whom one might or might not have frequent interaction, but who are conceived to stand in a clearly understood genealogical relationship to the user of the term.

kindred The network of relatives linked genealogically to a person in a culturally specified manner. Each such network is different for each person, with the exception of siblings.

kinesics The study of body movement as a mode of communication.

kin group A terminologically distinguished aggregate of persons with whom one stands in specified genealogical relationships and with whom one interacts frequently in terms of these relationships.

kinship The social phenomenon whereby people establish connections with each other on the basis of genealogical linkages in culturally specified ways.

kinship terminology The set of contrasting terms that designate the culturally significant genealogical linkages between people and the social networks these perceived relationships generate.

knuckle walking The characteristic mode of terrestrial locomotion of orangutans, chimpanzees, and gorillas. These apes walk with a partially erect body posture, with the forward weight of the body supported by the arms and the hands touching the ground, fingers curled into the palm so that the back of the fingers bear the weight.

language The characteristic mode of communication practiced by all human beings, consisting of sounds (phonemes) that are strung together into a virtually limitless number of meaningful sequences.

Law of Independent Assortment Gregor Mendel's second principle. It refers to the fact that the particular assortment of alleles found in a given gamete is independently determined.

Law of Segregation Gregor Mendel's first principle. It states that, in reproduction, a set of paired alleles separate (segregate) in a process called meiosis into different sex cells (gametes); thus, either allele can be passed on to offspring.

legal sanction A formal, socially enacted negative response to an individual's or group's noncompliance with the law, or a legal decision meant to compel that compliance.

lemur A diurnal, semiterrestrial prosimian having stereoscopic vision. Lemurs are found only on the island of Madagascar.

levirate The practice by which a man is expected to marry the wife or wives of a deceased brother.

lineage A unilineal, consanguineal kin group tracing descent from a known ancestor and found in two forms: pa-trilineage, in which the relationship is traced through males; and matrilineage, in which the relationship is traced through females.

linguistic anthropology A subfield of anthropology entailing the study of language forms across space and time and their relation to culture and social behavior.

linguistics The study of language, consisting of two large subcategories: (1) historical linguistics, which is concerned with the evolution of languages and language groups through time, and with reconstructing extinct proto-languages from which historically known languages differentiate; and (2) descriptive linguistics, which focuses on recording, transcribing, and analyzing the structures of languages distributed across the world today.

little tradition The localized cultures of rural villagers living in the broader cultural and social contexts of mass indus-trial society, with its "great tradition." Currently the term is rarely used because it is very ethnocentric.

locus The position of a gene on a chromosome.

"Lucy" See *Australopithecus afarensis.*

Magdalenian culture The most advanced of the Upper Paleolithic cultures, dating from 17,000 to 10,000 B.P. Con-fined to France and northern Spain, the Magdalenian cul-ture marks the climax of the Upper Paleolithic in Europe. The Magdalenians produced a highly diversified tool kit but are most famous for their spectacular cave art.

magic The usually ritualized behavior that is intended to con-trol, or at least to influence significantly, the basic proces-ses of the universe without recourse to perceptibly instru-mental acts.

mana A diffuse force or energy-like entity that suffuses through various objects, places, and even people; recog-nized in various parts of the world but especially well known in Polynesia and Melanesia.

market economy A system in which goods and services are exchanged, and their relative values established, in mar-ketplaces, generally via the use of money as a standard of value.

market exchange The process of distributing goods and ser-vices and establishing their relative value (frequently in terms of money) at centers of trade known as markets.

marriage A difficult term to define, given enormous cross-cultural variety. However, all societies recognize (publicly) connections between two or more persons that confer so-cial legitimacy to their children—which is the basic minimum of marriage.

matriarchy A form of family organization characterized by the domination of domestic life or society as a whole by women.

matricentric family A family that is headed by a woman, often serially married to a number of men.

matrifocal family A family form in which the mother, some-times assisted by other women of the household, is the most influential socializing agent and is central in terms of cultural values, family finances, patterns of decision-making, and affective ties.

matrilateral prescriptive cross-cousin marriage The rule by which a man must choose his spouse from among his mother's brother's daughters or their social equivalents.

matrilineage A kinship group made up of people all of whom trace relationships to one another through female links and are descended from a known female ancestor.

matrilineal descent The principle by which lineal kin links are traced exclusively through females—that is, a child is de-scended from his or her mother, mother's mother, and so on.

matrilocal residence The practice by which a newlywed couple moves into residence with, or in the locale of, the bride's mother's kin group.

Maya civilization The best-known Classic Mesoamerican civilization, located on the Yucatan peninsula and dated from before A.D. 300 to 900. Less intensely urban than Teotihuacán, it is marked by the building of huge ceremo-nial centers, such as Tikal in Guatemala.

melanin The brown, granular sustance found in the skin, hair, and some internal organs that gives a brownish tint or color to the areas in which it is found.

Mesolithic (Middle Stone Age) A term of convenience used by archaeologists to designate immediately preagricultural societies in the Old World, 13,000 to 6,000 B.C. A frequently used diagnostic characteristic is the presence of microliths, small blades often set into bone or wood handles to make sickles for the harvesting of wild grains. In Europe, this period also featured the invention of the bow and arrow as a response to the emergence of forests with the shift from Pleistocene to Holocene climate.

messianic movement A revitalization movement based on the belief that a person or god will arrive to cure the evils of the world.

metallurgy The techniques of separating metals from their ores and working them into finished products.

microlith A small stone tool made from bladettes, or frag-ments of blades, associated with the Mesolithic period, approximately 13,000 to 6,000 B.C.

migration A permanent or semipermanent change of resi-dence by a group, usually involving movement over large distances.

millenarianism A revivalistic movement reacting to the per-ceived disparity between ideal and real social conditions, with the belief that this gap is about to close, usually with disastrous consequences for nonbelievers.

minority A group that is distinguished from the larger society of which it is a part by particular traits, such as language, national origin, religion, values, or customs. The term may also be used to refer to groups that, though a plurality in numbers, are nevertheless discriminated against socially, politically, and/or economically by the society's dominant patterns (for example, women in the United States).

modernization The process whereby traditional social units (such as tribes or villages) are integrated into larger, over-arching units (such as nation-states), while at the same time being split into units of production (such as factories) and consumption (such as nuclear families) that are charac-teristic of industrial societies.

moiety The name used to refer to a group that is one of two units of a larger group (for example, each clan of a society composed of two clans is a moiety). Both groups are usu-ally, but not always, based on unilineal descent and are exogamous.

money A medium of exchange characteristic of market economies that is easily replaceable and/or exchangeable for another of like kind, portable, divisible into combinable units, and accepted by all participants in the market system in which it is used.

monkey A small or medium-sized quadrupedal primate. There are two groups of monkeys: Old World and New World. Only New World monkeys have prehensile tails. Most monkeys are arboreal, have long tails, and are vegetarians.

monogamy The marriage rule that permits both the man and the woman only one spouse at a time.

monogenesis The theory that the human species had only one origin.

mores The important norms of a society. They have compelling social and emotional commitment and are rationalized by the society's belief system.

morpheme The smallest unit of meaning in a language.

morphological sex The physical appearance of a person's genitals and secondary sex characteristics.

multilinear evolution The study of cultural evolution recognizing regional variation and divergent evolutionary sequences.

mutation A rapid and permanent change in genetic material.

myths Sacred tales or narratives that usually deal with the issue of origins (of nature, society, humans) and/or transformations.

nasal index The ratio calculated from the width and height measurements of the nose; it was used by early physical anthropoligists to classify human "races."

national character Personality characteristics shared by the inhabitants of a nation—no longer a scientifically valued concept.

nativism A revitalization movement initiated by members of a society to eliminate foreign persons, customs, and objects in order to improve their own way of life.

natural selection The process through which certain environmentally adaptive biological features are perpetuated at the expense of less adaptive features.

Neanderthal man (*Homo sapiens neanderthalensis*) A subspecies of *Homo sapiens* living from approximately 300,000 years ago to about 35,000 years ago and thought to have been descended from *Homo erectus*. See also *Homo sapiens neanderthalensis*.

negative reciprocity A form of gift exchange in which the giver attempts to get the better of the exchange.

negative sanction A punitive social response to an individual's behavior that does not meet with group approval.

neoclassicism A new school of geneticists who propose that most of the molecular variations in natural populations are selectively neutral.

Neolithic (New Stone Age) A stage in cultural evolution marked by the appearance of ground stone tools and frequently by the domestication of plants and animals, starting some 10,000 years ago.

neolocal residence The practice by which a newlywed couple is expected to establish its own independent residence, living with neither the husband's nor the wife's parents or relatives.

neontology A division of physical anthropology that deals with the comparative study of living primates, with special emphasis on the biological features of human beings.

network study An analysis of interpersonal relations, usually focused on a particular individual (ego), that examines the character of interactions between ego and other individuals.

New Archaeology Primarily an American development, the New Archaeology attempts to develop archaeological theory by using rigorous, statistical analysis of archaeological data within a deductive, logical framework.

nomadism A characteristic trait associated with a number of ecologically adaptive systems, in which continuing residential mobility is necessary for the subsistence of the group, with a resulting lack of permanent abode.

nonverbal communication The transmission of communication between organisms without the use of speech. Modes of communication include gesturing (with voice and body) and manipulating space between the communicating organisms.

norm A standard shared by members of a social group to which members are expected to conform.

nuclear family A small social unit consisting of a husband and wife and their children, typical of a monogamous marriage with neolocal residence; also forms a functioning subunit of extended and otherwise composite families.

oasis hypothesis A theory of plant and animal domestication advanced by V. Gordon Childe, in which he suggests that in the arid Pleistocene environment, humans and animals congregated around water resources, where they developed patterns of mutual dependence.

Oldowan culture The oldest recognized Lower Paleolithic assemblage, whose type site is Olduvai Gorge (Tanzania), dating from about 2.2 to 1 million years ago and comprising unifacial core (pebble) tools and crude flakes

Olmec culture The first civilization in Mesoamerica and the base from which all subsequent Mesoamerican civilizations evolved. Located in the Yucatan peninsula, it is dated from 1500 to 400 B.C., Olmec art first appeared in 1250 B.C., and the civilization flourished at its height from 1150 to 900 B.C.

order A taxonomic rank. *Homo sapiens* belongs to the order of Primates.

orangutan (*Pongo pygmaeus*) A tree-dwelling great ape found only in Borneo and Sumatra. It has four prehensile limbs capable of seizing and grasping, and very long arms. The orangutan is almost completely arboreal.

ovaries The female gonads, located within the pelvic cavity.

Paleolithic (Old Stone Age) A stage in cultural evolution, dated from about 2.5 million to 10,000 years ago, during which chipped stone tools, but not ground stone tools, were made.

paleontology, human A subdivision of physical anthropology that deals with the study of human and hominid fossil remains.

paradigm, scientific A concept introduced by Thomas Kuhn (1962): the orthodox doctrine of a science, its training exercises, and a set of beliefs with which new scientists are enculturated.

paralinguistics The study of the nonphonemic phonetic overlays onto the phonological system used to convey special (connotative) meanings.

parallel cousins Cousins linked by ascending generation relatives (often parental siblings) of the same generation and sex (for example, mother's sister's or father's brother's children).

participant observation A major anthropological field research method formally conceptualized by Bronislaw Malinowski, in which the ethnographer is immersed in the day-to-day activities of the community being studied.

pastoralism A type of ecological adaptation found in geographically marginal areas of Europe, Asia, and Africa where natural resources cannot support agriculture, and hence the people are partially or entirely devoted to the care and herding of animals.

patriarchy A form of family organization in which power and authority are vested in the males and in which descent is usually in the male line, with the children being members of the father's lineage, clan, or tribe.

patrilateral parallel cousin marriage A marriage between brothers' children.

patrilineage An exogamous descent group based on genealogical links between males that are traceable back to a known male ancestor.

patrilineal descent The principle by which lineal kin links are traced through males (that is, a child is descended from his or her father, father's father, and so forth).

patrilocal residence A postmarital residence rule by which a newlywed couple takes up permanent residence with or near the groom's father's extended kin group.

peasants Rural, agricultural members of civilizations who maintain a very traditional life-style (often rejecting urban values) while tied into the wider economic system of the whole society through markets, where they sell their produce and purchase goods.

pebble tool The first manufactured stone tools consisting of somewhat larger than fist-sized pieces of flint that have had some six or seven flakes knocked off them; unifacial core tools; associated with *Homo habilis* in Africa and also *Homo erectus* in East Asia.

persistence hunting A unique hunting ability of humans in which prey is hunted over vast distances, often for days at a time.

pharynx The throat above the larynx.

phenotype The visible expression of a gene or pair of genes.

phoneme In language, the basic unit of recognized but meaningless sound.

phylogeny The tracing of the history of the evolutionary development of a life form.

phonetic laws Patterns of change in the sounds used by languages as they evolved, expressed as rules or principles of change.

phonological system The articulatory phonetics and the phonemic system of a language.

phonology The combined study of phonetics and phonemics.

phratry A unilineal descent group composed of at least two clans claiming to be related by kinship. When there are only two such clans, each is called a moiety.

physical anthropology The study of human beings as biological organisms across space and time. Physical anthropology is divided into two areas: (1) paleontology, which is the study of the fossil evidence of primate evolution, and (2)

neontology, which is the comparative biology of living primates.

pigmentation Skin color.

Piltdown man A human skull and ape jaw "discovered" in England in 1911 and thought by some to be a "missing link" in human evolution. It was exposed as a fraud in 1953.

Pithecanthropus erectus See *Homo erectus*.

plate tectonics The branch of geology that studies the movement of the continental plates over time; popularly known as "continental drift."

Platyrrhini One of two infraorders of the primate suborder *Anthropoidea*, consisting of all the New World monkeys; characterized by vertical nostrils and, often, prehensile tails.

plow An agricultural tool generally requiring animal power, used to loosen, aerate, and invert the soil so as to cover weeds, expose a large area of soil to weathering, and prepare a seed bed. Its presence differentiates agriculture from horticulture (limited to the use of digging sticks and hoes).

pluralism A characteristic of many complex societies, marked by the presence of several or numerous subgroups that coexist within a common political and economic system.

political anthropology The field of cultural anthropology that deals with that aspect of social behavior known as political organization and that concerns itself specifically with the organization and management of the public affairs of a society, especially pertaining to the sources and uses of power.

political economy The interpretation of the economy and the system of power and authority in a society, most frequently studied from a conflict theory perspective.

political organization That subsystem of social organization that specifically relates to the individuals or groups who are responsible for managing affairs of public policy or who control the appointment or action of those individuals or groups.

polyandrous family A family in which a woman has more than one husband at the same time.

polyandry A relatively rare form of multiple marriage in which a woman has more than one husband at the same time.

polygamy Any form of marriage in which more than two persons are married to one another.

polygenesis The theory that the human species had more than one origin.

polygynous family A family in which a man has more than one wife at the same time.

polygyny The most common form of multiple marriage, allowing a man to have more than one wife at the same time.

pongid A common term for the members of the *Pongidae* family, including the five modern apes: the orangutan, gorilla, chimpanzee, gibbon, and siamang.

positive sanctions A social response to an individual's behavior that takes the form of a reward.

positivism An approach to knowledge embodying empiricism and the scientific method, with its built-in tests for truth.

possession A trance state based on the culturally supported belief that curative or malevolent spirits may displace people's personalities and use their bodies as vehicles for temporary residence.

potassium-argon (KAr) dating An absolute dating technique that uses the rate of decay of radioactive potassium (K^{40}) into argon (Ar^{40}) as its basis. The half-life of K^{40} is 1.3 billion ± 40 million years.

potlatch Ceremonial feasting accompanied by the giving of gifts to guests according to rank; practiced by the Indians of the Northwest Coast of the United States and Canada; a form of economic redistribution.

power, political The ability of leaders to compel compliance with their orders.

prehistoric archaeology The use of archaeology to reconstruct prehistoric times.

Primates The order of mammals that includes humans, the apes, Old and New World monkeys, and prosimians.

primatologist One who studies primates.

profane All that which is ordinary, or not sacred.

prosimii (prosimian) The most primitive suborder of Primates, including lemurs, lorises, tarsiers, and similar creatures.

Protestant ethic A set of values, originally associated with the rise and spread of Protestantism in Europe, that celebrates the virtues of self-discipline, hard work, initiative, acquisitiveness, and thrift.

proxemics The study of the manipulation and meaning of space.

psychological sex The self-image that a person holds about his or her own sexual identity.

quadrupedalism Locomotion by the use of four feet.

quarry site In archaeology, a place where prehistoric people dug for flint, tin, copper, and other materials.

race A folk category of the English language that refers to discrete groups of human beings who are uniformly separated from one another on the basis of arbitrarily selected phenotypic traits.

racial minorities Groups that are categorically separated from the majority members of the larger society on the basis of arbitrarily selected phenotypic traits.

radiocarbon (C^{14}) dating An absolute physical-chemical dating technique that uses the rate of decay of radioactive carbon (C^{14}) which is present in all plants, to stable carbon (C^{12}) as its basis. The half-life of C^{14} is 5568 ± 30 years. The technique is useful for dating remains from 5000 to 50,000 years old, although a new technique may extend its range to about 100,000 years while reducing the margin of error.

Ramapithecus A late Miocene hominoid, found in India, Kenya, and Europe, who lived in open woodland areas from 14 to 9 million years ago. *Ramapithecus* is accepted by some scholars as the first true hominid, though recent discoveries have cast doubt on this position.

random (genetic) drift A shift in gene and allele frequencies in a population due to sampling "error." When a small breeding population splits off from a larger one, its collection of genes may not adequately represent the allele frequencies of the larger population. These differences compound over succeeding generations, until the two populations are quite distinct. Along with mutation, gene flow, and natural selection, random drift is one of the mechanisms of organic evolution.

range (of a primate) See *home range*.

rank society A society in which there is equal access to land and other economic resources but unequal access to positions of prestige.

recessive allele A version of a gene that is not able to influence an organism's phenotype when it is homologous with another version of the gene. See also *dominant allele*.

reciprocity The giving and receiving of gifts, usually consisting of material items, favors, or specific forms of labor.

redistribution The enforced giving of surplus goods to a centralized authority, who then distributes them back to members of the society according to social conventions and his own predilections.

reference group The aggregate of people that an individual uses for comparison when assessing or evaluating his or her own and others' behavior.

reformulation The modification of a new cultural trait, or cluster of traits, by a group to fit its own traditions and circumstances; part of the process of culture trait diffusion.

relative dating In archaeology, the determination of the sequence of events; a relative date specifies that one thing is older or younger than another.

religious beliefs The sets of convictions held by members of a society with regard to the supernatural, transcendental, and fundamental issues, such as life's meaning.

revitalization movements Religious movements of a reformative nature that arise among exploited or disorganized groups (often after socioeconomic or political traumas) and that attempt to reinject culturally salient meaning into people's lives—often through a radical assault on existing conditions and/or institutions.

revivalistic movement A revitalization movement espousing the reintroduction of previous religious (or political) forms.

ribonucleic acid (RNA) Any of the nucleic acids containing ribose. One type—messenger RNA—carries the information encoded in the DNA to the site of protein synthesis located outside the nucleus.

rifting The sliding of the continental masses against one another's edges.

rites of passage Rituals marking changes in status or social position undergone as a person passes through the culturally recognized life phases of his or her society.

rites of solidarity Various rituals, usually but not necessarily religious, which in addition to their intended purposes also develop and maintain feelings of group cohesiveness among participants.

rituals Culturally prescribed, consistently repeated, patterned sequences of (group) behavior.

RNA See *Ribonucleic acid*.

robust australopithecines One of two lines of australopithecines, appearing some 3.5 million years ago and surviving until approximately 1 million years ago or even later; thought to have embodied two successive species, *Australopithecus robustus* and *Australopithecus boisei*.

role conflict The emotional stress experienced by a person whose socially expected behaviors are irreconcilable. This happens when a person occupies diverse social positions (statuses) yet in a given situation must act in terms of two or more of them (for instance, a U.S. senator who is also a stockholder asked to vote on legislation that would affect the corporation in which he or she owns shares).

roles The expected (normative) behaviors that every society associates with each of its statuses.

Rosetta stone A tablet containing three parallel texts written in Egyptian hieroglyphics, demotic script, and Greek. In 1822, Jean François Champollion used the stone to decode the hieroglyphics.

sacred A category of things, actions, and so on set apart as holy and entitled to reverence.

salvage archaeology The attempt to preserve archaeological remains from destruction by large-scale projects of industrial society (such as a dam or highway construction).

sanctions, social The responses a social group makes as a consequence of an individual's behavior.

savanna Tropical or subtropical grasslands.

scapulimancy The use of charred cracks in the burned scapula (shoulder bone) of an animal to divine the future.

scientific racism Research strategies based on the assumption that groups' biological features underlie significant social and cultural differences. Not surprisingly, this kind of research always manages to find "significant" differences between "races."

scraper An Upper Paleolithic stone tool made from blades with a retouched end; used for carving wood, bone, and antlers to make spear points.

secondary sex characteristics Physiological changes developing at and after puberty, such as body hair, breasts, and voice changes.

Segregation, Law of See *Law of Segregation.*

self-concept A person's perceptions and evaluative feelings about his or her continuity, boundaries, and qualities.

semantics The relationship between signs and what they represent; the study of semantics is essentially the study of meaning.

semiotic The study of signs and sign-using behavior in general.

serial marriage The process by which a man or woman marries and divorces a series of partners in succession.

seriation A technique of relative dating in which the relative dates of artifacts may be reconstructed by arranging them so that variations in form or style can be inferred to represent a developmental sequence and, hence, chronological order.

sexual dimorphism A difference between the males and females of a species that is not related directly to reproductive functions.

sexual identity The expectations about male and female behavior that affect the individual's learning ability, choice of work, and feelings about herself or himself.

shamanism The process by which certain gifted persons establish (usually with the aid of a trance or an ecstatic state of excitement) direct communication with the supernatural for the benefit of their social group.

sickle cell A red blood cell that has lost its normal circular shape and has collapsed into a half-moon shape.

sickle-cell anemia An often fatal disease caused by a chemical mutation that changes one of the amino acids in normal hemoglobin. The mutant sickle-cell gene occurs in unusually high frequency in parts of Africa and the Arabian peninsula. Individuals heterozygotic for the sickle-cell gene have a special resistance to malaria; homozygots suffer the severe anemia.

sign An object, gesture, or sound that represents something else.

silent trade A form of exchange with no face-to-face interaction between the parties involved, often practiced where potential for conflict between groups exists. Traded items are simply left at agreed-upon places by both parties.

site A concentration of the remains of (human) activities, or artifacts.

slash-and-burn agriculture A shifting form of cultivation with recurrent, alternate clearing and burning of vegetation and planting in the burnt fields; also called swidden (or shifting) cultivation.

slavery An extreme form of coerced work organization wherein the rights to people and their labor are owned by others, and in which both subordinate and superordinate positions are inherited.

social class A stratum in a social hierarchy based on differential group access to means of production and control over distribution; usually but not necessarily endogamous, with little—but some—openness.

social control Practices that induce members of a society to conform to the expected behavior patterns of their culture; also, mechanisms through which a society's rulers ensure the masses' conformity with the rules of the social order.

Social Darwinism The doctrine that makes use, or misuse, of Charles Darwin's biological evolutionary principles to explain or justify existing forms of social organization. The theory was actually formulated by Herbert Spencer.

social identity The socially recognized characteristics of a person that indicate his or her social position(s).

socialism A socioeconomic form characterized by public ownership of all strategic resources and major distribution mechanisms. It features centralized economic and social planning, and it is conceived by some Marxists to be a transitional stage to communism, in which centralized bureaucracies will "wither away."

social mobility The upward or downward movement of individuals or groups of individuals in a society consisting of social hierarchies and unequal distribution of such social resources as occupations, education, power, and wealth.

social organization The ordering of social relations within social groups whereby individuals' choices and decisions are visibly patterned.

social stratification An arrangement of statuses or groups within a society into a pattern of socially superior and inferior ranks (or groups) that are open to a greater or lesser degree.

social structure The total pattern of eco-centered relationships (such as kinship systems and friendship networks) that occur within a society.

societal structure The total aggregate of discrete, bounded subgroups that compose a society.

society A socially bounded, spacially contiguous aggregation of people who participate in a number of overarching institutions and share to some degree an identifiable culture, and that contains within its boundaries some means of production and units of consumption—with relative stability across generations.

sociobiology The systematic study of the biological basis of social behavior.

sociogram The full description, in the form of a catalog, of all the social behaviors of a species.

sociolinguistics The study of the societal correlates to variations in the patterning of linguistic behavior.

somatic cells The cells that make up all the bodily parts and that are constantly dying and being replaced; does not include central nervous system cells or sex cells.

sorcery A negatively connotative term to refer to magic—the use of supernatural agencies—to further the practitioner's goals.

sororal polygyny A marriage involving two or more sisters as wives of the same man at one time.

sororate The practice by which women are expected to marry the husband of a deceased sister.

spacing mechanisms The behaviors between neighboring groups of animals that help to maintain them at some distance from each other.

speciation The process of gradual separation of one interbreeding population into two or more separate, noninterbreeding populations.

species The largest naturally occurring population that interbreeds (or is capable of interbreeding) and produces fully fertile offspring.

speech community An aggregate of persons who share a set of conventions about how verbal communication is to take place.

state A set of institutions in a stratified society that operates to maintain the status quo by: (1) organizing the provision of needed services; (2) planning the production and use of needed resources; (3) quelling internal discontent by buying off or subduing rebellious minorities or subordinate classes; and (4) organizing, administering, and financing the protection of the society against hostile external forces.

statuses The interrelated positions in a society, with each position carrying certain expectations of behavior (roles) with respect to those persons occupying the same and/or interrelated positions.

stereoscopic vision Overlapping fields of vision resulting when the eyes are located toward the front of the skull, improving depth perception.

stereotype The attribution of certain presumed, invariable personality or behavioral characteristics to all members of a particular group, most notably those groups defined by religion, sex, nationality, or ethnicity.

stimulus diffusion The transfer of a basic idea from one culture to another, in which the idea is reinterpreted and modified to the extent that it becomes unique to the receiving group.

strategic resources The category of resources vital to a group's survival.

stratified society A society in which there is a structured inequality of access among groups not only to power and prestige, but also to the strategic resources that sustain life.

stratigraphy The arrangement of archaeological deposits in superimposed layers, or strata.

structural-functionalism An anthropological school of thought emphasizing the mutual interdependence of all parts and subgroups of a society, interpreting relationships between such groupings as contributing to the ongoing pattern maintenance of the society.

structuralism An analytical approach based on the assumption that observed phenomena are specific instances of the underlying, generalized principles of relationship or structure.

structural linguistics The study of the internal structures of the world's languages.

subculture The culture of a subgroup of a society that shares its fundamental values, but that also has its own distinctive folkways, mores, values, and world view.

subsistence strategies Technological skills, tools, and behaviors that a society uses to meet its subsistence needs.

substantivists A group of economic anthroplogists who deny that economic models derived from developed market economies can be applied universally to all economic systems.

supernatural Refers to all things that are believed to exist but are beyond verifiability through the human senses.

supernatural beliefs Organized systems of thoughts, ideas, and concerns regarding entities whose existence is not verifiable through the human senses.

superposition In archaeology, the perception that, under normal circumstances, a stratum found lying under another stratum is relatively older than the stratum under which it is lying.

supraorbital ridge The torus, or bony bar, surmounting orbital (eyeball) cavities; it is large and continuous in apes and quite small and divided in *Homo sapiens*.

swidden farming Shifting cultivation, with recurrent, alternate clearing and burning of vegetation and planting in the burnt fields. Fallow periods for each plot last many times longer than the periods of cultivation. See also *slash-and-burn agriculture*.

symbol A sign that represents some other (complex) thing with which it has no intrinsic connection.

synchronics The comparison of biological, linguistic, archaeological, and ethnographic data across a wide geographical area at one arbitrarily selected point in time.

syntax The relationships between signs. The study of syntax is the study of the rules of sequence and combination of signs.

synthetic theory (of evolution) A modern theory of evolution based on the Darwinian theory but emphasizing differential fertility (as opposed to differential mortality).

systematics The study of the kinds and diversity of objects and of the types of relationships existing among them.

taboo (tabu) The belief in negative supernatural consequences that attach to the performance of certain acts or the violation of certain objects or places.

tabula rasa The concept proposed by John Locke (1690) that people are born with blank minds and that they learn everything they come to know through their life experiences, socialization, and enculturation into groups.

taxonomy The science of constructing classifications of organisms.

technology A society's use of knowledge, skills, implements, and sources of power in order (1) to exploit and partially control the natural environment and (2) to engage in production and reproduction of its goods and services.

tell A stratified mound created entirely through long periods of successive occupation by a series of groups.

tenancy A form of forced agricultural labor under which farmers plant their crops in the land owner's fields but owe the land owner a certain proportion of the crops they harvest.

territoriality Defense by an animal of a geographically delimited area.

testes The male gonads, suspended outside the body cavity in the scrotum.

test pit In archaeology, a pit that is dug at carefully selected positions in a site to reveal information about buried artifacts and stratigraphy.

thalassemia Like sickle-cell anemia, a blood anemia carried by populations that are or have been in malaria-infested areas of the world—especially around the Mediterranean, Asia Minor, and southern Asia. Like sickle-cell anemia, it also represents an example of balanced polymorphism.

Third World Originally referred to non-Western peoples of the colonized societies of Asia, Africa, and Latin America. More recently, the term has also been associated with national minorities within the United States and Canada, such as Chicanos, blacks, Native Americans, Puerto Ricans, and Asian-Americans.

Three-Age System The concept delineated by Christian Thomsen (1836) in which he identified three successive stages in cultural evolution: the Stone Age, the Bronze Age, and the Iron Age.

Toltec civilization Postclassic Mesoamerican civilization, dated from A.D. 900 to about 1300. The Toltecs perpetuated many of the themes of Classic culture. Their capital of Tula was sacked around 1160, and they were eventually replaced by the Aztecs.

totemism The symbolic association of plants, animals, and objects with groups of people, especially the association of exogamous clans with animal species as their emblems and/or mythological ancestors.

trade The exchange of goods between people.

traditionalizm The organizing of behavior in terms of standards derived from the past.

tradition (archaeological) The similarity in cultural elements and forms over a considerable span of time at a given site or group of sites in a geographically delimited area.

transcendental belief system A belief system providing people with organized ideas regarding states of existence inherently beyond the capacities of their senses to register and about things that are impossible for them to learn from their personal experience.

transhumance The seasonal migration of domesticated livestock and their herders for the purpose of grazing different pastures at different times of the year; usually rotation between highlands and lowlands.

tribalism The orientation toward tribal membership—rather than toward citizenship in nation-states—as the criterion of political allegiance and behavior.

tribe A relatively small group of people (small society) who share a culture, speak a common language or dialect, and share a perception of their common history and uniqueness. Often refers to unstratified social groups with a minimum of (or no) centralized political authority at all, organized around kinship lines.

type site In archaeology, a site used to represent the characteristic features of a culture.

typology A method of classifying objects according to hierarchically arranged sets of diagnostic criteris.

underdevelopment The condition of state-level societies that have been exploited by the industrialization of the European, American, and Japanese nations and that have themselves failed to benefit from industrialization.

underwater archaeology The retrieval and study of ships, dwellings, and other human remains that have been covered over by waters in the course of time.

undifferentiated (social) system A social system in which the ascriptive qualities of sex, age, or kinship determine social relations in most domains of society.

Uniformitarianism The theory, developed by Charles Lyell, that the geological processes shaping the earth are uniform and continuous in character.

unilineal descent The reckoning of kinship connections through either exclusively female (matrilineal descent) or male (patrilineal descent) links.

unilineal evolution The theory that all human societies evolve through specific stages that are usually defined in terms of the occurrence of increasingly complex social and cultural elements.

unit of deposition All the contents of each stratum in an archaeological site that are conceived to have been deposited at the same point in time (as measured by archaeologists).

unit of excavation Subdivision of an archaeological site made by an archaeologist to record the context in which each remain is found.

Upper Paleolithic culture The culture produced by modern *Homo sapiens sapiens*, beginning about 35,000 years ago. It is characterized by pervasive blade tool production, an "explosion" of artistic endeavors (cave painting), highly organized large-game hunting, and the efficient exploitation of previously uninhabited ecological niches—including the population of the New World, perhaps beginning as early as 40,000 years ago.

urban anthropology The application of anthropological research techniques and methods of analysis to the study of people living in cities.

urbanism An ill-defined term designating those qualities of life that presumably characterize all city life-styles.

urbanization The worldwide process of the growth of cities at the expense of rural populations.

uterine kin Kin related to one through female links.

uxorilocal residence The practice by which a newlywed couple takes up residence near the bride's mother's family but does not become a subordinate group contained within a larger extended family.

Valdivian culture A coastal Ecuadorian culture, dated from 3200 B.C., in which the earliest pottery found in the Americas has been unearthed. Some archaeologists believe the pottery was introduced to the New World by Japanese visitors from the Jomon culture—a view hotly disputed by others.

values The ideals of a culture that are concerned with appropriate goals and behavior.

verbal communication The uniquely human use of language to communicate.

vertical extended family A family in which parents, their married children, and their grandchildren share a residence and constitute a functioning social unit.

virilocal residence The practice by which a newlywed couple moves near the residence of the groom's father but does not become a subordinate group contained within a larger extended family.

voluntary association A group of persons who join together for a common objective or on the basis of a mutual interest.

Wernicke's area The brain site where verbal comprehension takes place, located in the temporal lobe of the dominant hemisphere.

Westernization The transplanting of industrial European-American institutions to developing countries.

witchcraft The use of magic to control the behavior of another person or persons.

world view *(Weltanschauïng)* The corpus of beliefs about the world shared by members of a society, and represented in their myths, lore, ceremonies, social conduct, general values, and so on.

yeomanry In feudal societies, those who were granted special privileges in land and produce in exchange for military service in the militia of the lord.

Zinjanthropus A 1.75-million-year-old australopithecine fossil found in Kenya by Mary Leakey and thought to be a form of *Australopithecus robustus*.